THE COLLECTED WORKS OF

KEN WILBER

VOLUME FOUR

INTEGRAL PSYCHOLOGY

TRANSFORMATIONS OF CONSCIOUSNESS

SELECTED ESSAYS

SHAMBHALA
Boston & London
1999

Shambhala Publications, Inc.
Horticultural Hall
300 Massachusetts Avenue
Boston, Massachusetts 02115
www.shambhala.com

See page 719 for a continuation of the copyright page.

9 8 7 6 5 4 3 2 1

First Edition
Printed in the United States of America
∞This edition is printed on acid-free paper that meets the American National Standards Institute Z39.48 Standard.
Distributed in the United States by Random House, Inc., and in Canada by Random House of Canada Ltd

Library of Congress Cataloging-in-Publication Data
Wilber, Ken.
[Works. 1998]
The collected works of Ken Wilber.—1st ed.
p. cm.
Includes bibliographical references and indexes.
Contents: v. 1. The spectrum of consciousness ; No boundary.—
v. 2. The Atman Project; Up from Eden—
v. 3. A sociable god; Eye to eye.
—ISBN 1-57062-501-8 (v. 1: cloth: alk. paper).
—ISBN 1-57062-502-6 (v. 2: cloth: alk. paper).
—ISBN 1-57062-503-4 (v. 3: cloth: alk. paper)
—ISBN 1-57062-504-2 (v. 4: cloth: alk. paper)
1. Consciousness. 2. Subconsciousness. 3. Self-perception.
4. Psychology—Philosophy. 5. East and West. I. Title.
BF311.W576 1999 97-45928
191—DC21 CIP

CONTENTS

A NOTE TO THE READER

CONTAINED HEREIN is the book *Integral Psychology,* which was written specifically for this volume and is published here for the first time. *Integral Psychology* is a condensed version of an as-yet unpublished two-volume text of psychology, spirituality, and consciousness studies. As such, *Integral Psychology* is at this time the definitive statement of my general psychological model, and my other writings in the field should be coordinated with its views. Those who are reading this volume for ideas on psychology/spirituality might therefore wish to read *Integral Psychology* first, and then use the other texts in this volume (and my other works) to fill in the details of the overview offered in *Integral Psychology.*

INTRODUCTION TO VOLUME FOUR

THE WORKS IN THIS VOLUME all explore the implications of an evolutionary view of the Kosmos, from matter to mind to spirit. What would psychology, sociology, cultural studies, philosophy, and spirituality look like if we adopted an evolutionary or developmental approach? What fundamental insights might we gain? What recalcitrant dilemmas might be softened? What intractable problems might begin to yield? I hasten to add that evolution or development by no means covers the whole story of the Kosmos; it is simply a very important part of the whole story, a part that, when the following works were originally written, was alarmingly being ignored.

Interestingly, psychologists have recently conducted significant research on the development of the idea of development itself. That is, using extensive tests of how individuals picture the world around them (their "worldviews"), psychologists have been able to determine the general stages through which worldviews develop (including in different cultures and subcultures). As we will see later in this volume, there is a remarkable uniformity to the general findings. To give one example now, the work of Deirdre Kramer suggests that the worldviews of men and women progress through these stages:

Preformism—This is a simple lack of differentiation.

Formism/mechanism—Features are differentiated but not integrated; static forms therefore predominate and are related by gross mechanistic generalizations.

Static relativism/contextualism—This involves a rejection of static forms and the beginning of relativity and contextualism. When this view matures, full *systems* come into view, and the next stage emerges:

Static systems—At this stage, reports Kramer, the individual "constructs systems of self, other, and interpersonal relationships that subsume apparent contradictions into more integrated, coherent structures [which include] the integration of consistencies and inconsistencies into systems."[1] But these structures and systems are still *static:* "While the concepts may feature holism, they are generally static—they do not stress the dynamic, changing, actively constructed nature of such systems." When the *dynamic* nature of systems is grasped, the next stage emerges:

Dynamic relativism/contextualism—This stage is marked by "an awareness that social-cognitive systems are culturally and historically bound." In other words, this is a contextual/constructivist stance, with *relativism* and *pluralism* defining all frames of reference. These frames are all dynamic and constantly subject to change. "In a contextual/relativistic worldview, random change is basic to all reality, and knowledge is embedded in its broader context, whether the context is the cultural/historical one, the cognitive framework, or the immediate physical and psychological context." Likewise, "The broader social, historical, moral, and physical context influences how one will approach and act in a situation. What aspect of a situation one focuses on will influence his or her interpretation or understanding of the situation. Every person, society, group and situation is unique (because every situation is unique and change is random)."

But precisely because there is as yet no way to interrelate these pluralistic contexts—since each remains "incommensurate" with the others (or put still another way: since there is no "meta-narrative" that mutually interrelates all the different contexts)—this worldview is ultimately fragmented and chaotic: "Prediction is impossible, as all people and events are unique and continually change in unsystematic ways. Consequently, contradiction runs rampant. There is no order to such a universe; any order is imposed externally or via one's cognitive framework." That is, all order is thought to be imposed by structures of power or ideology (patriarchy, logocentrism, anthropocentrism, androcentrism, speciesism, phallocentrism, etc.). Because multiple contexts are grasped, but because *the rich networks of interconnections between multiple contexts are not grasped,* this worldview remains disjointed and fragmented. However, when the relationships between multiple contexts are discovered, the next worldview begins to emerge.

Dynamic dialecticism—Here all multiple contexts are seen to be mutually interactive over both space and time, constituting an organic order that emerges from the nonpredictable play of its parts. Each whole is a part of other wholes indefinitely, related by tension, resolution, and recurrence. "In an organicist/dialectical worldview, all phenomena are in continual movement or activity, characterized by the ongoing tension between events, their [limitation], and the resolution of that [limitation] into momentary structures that soon begin to create new tensions, initiating the cycle again. The dialectical whole (i.e., the momentary structures) is characterized by emergence (i.e., the whole redefines and transcends its constitutive elements) and reciprocity (i.e., a change in any one element in a system influences and in turn is influenced by a change in other parts of the system). Thus, in a dialectical system, all elements are interrelated and reflections of the same underlying, essential unity."

What particularly separates this worldview (dynamic/developmental dialecticism) from its predecessor (dynamic relativism/contextualism) is its *increased capacity to hold multiple contexts in mind,* across both space and time: "In a dialectical system there is a relationship among such contexts. In a contextualist system there is no such relationship. . . . A contextual perspective would contend that the opposing value systems of two cultures or two generations are unrelated"—because they are supposedly incommensurable and purely relativistic. But a further growth of consciousness allows the recognition of deeper and wider connections, which discloses, among other things, a *directionality* to the changes that were thought to be random at the preceding level of development: "At the dynamic dialectical level, perfect prediction is also impossible, because of the emergent quality of evolving structures. However, there is nevertheless a direction to such change, and a relationship among contrasting [pluralistic and contextual] systems." This directionality and relationship is dynamic, dialectical, developmental, and evolutionary. "Change occurs through evolution, where conflicts are resolved and redefined by newer, more encompassing solutions which yield new conflicts, and so on. People, groups and society naturally evolve through different phases. The whole of the organization transcends and gives meaning to parts."

(This directionality is exemplified in the theories of Hegel, Aurobindo, Whitehead, Teilhard de Chardin, Ilya Prigogine, Jürgen Habermas, Jean Gebser, Michael Murphy, among others, and includes such notions as increasing relative autonomy, increasing complexity, increasing differentiation-and-integration, and increasing dialectical inclusiveness: transcend and include, or negate and preserve).[2]

Kramer notes that at the previous stage of dynamic relativism, "systems are differentiated into meta-systems of culturally and historically relative, dynamic systems that cannot be explained apart from their immediate cultural or historical contexts. Finally, at the dynamic dialectical level, these contexts are reintegrated into a more encompassing structure where such contexts are seen as arising in relation to one another and evolving in a systematic fashion."

Thus, as Kramer summarizes the situation, the next-to-highest stage of worldview development involves "the differentiation of dynamic systems into culturally and historically defined contexts"; while the next stage goes one step further and integrates those differentiations, resulting in "the dialectical integration of cultural and historical systems into evolving social structures." Thus, this highest stage of development is a stage that is conscious of development. Or, as Julian Huxley used to say, evolution becomes conscious of itself.

Now, I do not myself believe that "dynamic dialectical systems" is *the* very highest level of worldview development possible. As is the case with such studies—and precisely because evolution produces greater depth, less span (i.e., there are fewer representatives of the higher levels)—exactly what constitutes "the" highest level is open to further research. In my own system, for example, the stage of dynamic dialecticism—which is generated by what I call *vision-logic*—is simply the opening to even higher stages of transrational, transpersonal development. That is, dynamic dialecticism (or mature vision-logic) might be thought of as the highest of the *mental* realms, or the highest philosophy capable of being grasped by the ordinary mind, beyond which lie *transmental* or *supramental* developments altogether (psychic, subtle, causal, and nondual).

Nonetheless, this mature vision-logic, with its dynamic/dialectical/developmental worldview, is the level *through which* most of the great modern philosopher-sages (such as Hegel, Whitehead, Gebser, and Aurobindo) have written and continue to write, even though they are often expressing insights seen at the even higher, transpersonal, transmental levels—and for the simple reason that, in order to mentally communicate at all, the mental realms must be used. These great philosopher-sages speak through the highest of the mental realms—the vision-logic mind—even as they are trying to communicate even higher transmental truths and realities.

Vision-logic is certainly the level through which I have attempted to write most of my works, although how well I have succeeded remains to be seen. But in trying to write from a "late" or "high" vision-logic, my major nemesis has almost always been the worldview of "early" or "low" vision-logic, namely, the worldview of dynamic relativism and extreme pluralism, also known as *deconstructive postmodernism.*[3]

I have always viewed vision-logic (which Gebser called the *integral-aperspectival* mind) as itself developing in two or three major substages. What most defines vision-logic *at any stage* is simply its capacity for systems thinking, and, at the very least, systems must first be differentiated, and then integrated. Early or low vision-logic (along with late formal operational thought) *recognizes* and *differentiates* systems, and then—as Kramer's studies suggest—late or high vision-logic *integrates* these disparate systems, contexts, and cultures into dynamic/dialectic/developmental structures of an underlying unity or mutuality.[4]

As I would later suggest (in *Sex, Ecology, Spirituality* and *The Marriage of Sense and Soul*), the Western Enlightenment (or modernity), using its late formal operational and early vision-logic capacities, managed to *differentiate* the major cultural value spheres of science, art, and morals, but failed to integrate them. Postmodernity, whose task *was to take up this integration and complete it,* began most promisingly by even more clearly differentiating the many pluralistic cultural spheres—and then promptly aborted its own development at that delicate point, leaving the world with no way to relate the many different contexts that postmodernism had unearthed. Leaving the world, that is to say, in a completely fragmented, chaotic, fractured state, often while loudly claiming that its postmodern deconstructions were the only way to heal the planet, heal America, heal the world, and so forth. Under the ostensibly noble guise of pluralism, relativism, incommensurate paradigms, and cultural diversity, postmodernism opened up the world to a richness of multiple voices, but then stood back to watch the multiple voices degenerate into a Tower of Babel, each voice claiming to be its own validity, yet few of them actually honoring the values of the others. Each was free to go its own way, whereupon everybody went in vigorously different ways. "Consequently, contradictions run rampant. There is no order to such a universe. . . ." This did not ultimately liberate the many pluralistic voices, but merely sent them scurrying off, isolated and alienated, to the far corners of a fragmented world, there to suckle themselves in solitude.

For this reason, I have always defined myself as a *constructive* postmodernist, in contrast to a merely deconstructive postmodernist.[5] In *The Marriage of Sense and Soul* I would identify three especially important ideas that tend to define most forms of postmodernism: contextualism, constructivism, and pluralism. All three of those are earmarks of early vision-logic or the dynamic relativism worldview, which means all three are *very important*—but very limited—aspects of a post-Enlightenment, postmodern worldview. For they are completed and fulfilled *only* as they themselves are mutually interrelated with their own wider contexts, producing not merely aperspectivism (multiple contexts) but *integral-aperspectivism,* or the multiple contexts brought together in integrated and dynamic dialecticism (of a mature vision-logic). Thus, *constructive postmodernism* (as I use the term) takes up the multiple contexts freed by dynamic relativism, and then integrates them into mutually interrelated networks (of dynamic dialecticism), as opposed to deconstructive and extreme postmodernism, which simply remains arrested at a lower-order worldview, fragmented and stuck in a morass of unrelated differentiations and mutually suspicious contexts, each choking in its own isolated world.

None of these particulars was fully clear to me as I wrote the works in this volume (except *Integral Psychology,* a recent addition). All that I was really aware of was that the dynamic dialectical worldview was everywhere under attack by the dynamic relativism worldview, and that the promises of a constructive postmodernism were quickly hardening into extreme, recalcitrant, deconstructive postmodernism. Cultural relativism, like a corrosive acid eating into steel, was rapidly destroying many hard-gained, cross-culturally valid truths; and in their place, an important acknowledgment of many cultural relativities, but all left lying in a rubble of narcissism and nihilism.

Sociocultural Evolution, included in this volume, is perhaps noteworthy because it was the first of my many defenses of dynamic dialecticism against dynamic relativism, although I did not use those specific terms, nor did I particularly think of this argument itself in developmental ways. What I did think was how pernicious extreme postmodernism had become. This short book was written right after *A Sociable God,* and in the same terse, abstract style. I had just met Treya at the time, and personal events soon crowded out professional writing—so much so that I actually forgot I had written this book; I just rediscovered it while looking over earlier writings for the *Collected Works.* It is published here for the first time. What is so astonishing about this piece is how perfectly it reflects the struggle between dynamic relativism and dynamic dialecticism. It would be almost two decades before an evolutionary/developmental/dialectical worldview would again start to come to the forefront in cultural studies. In the meantime, all of the pieces in this volume were written against the surging currents of extreme postmodernism, anti-evolutionism, contextualism, and relativism.

The volume opens with "A Unified Theory of Development," which was originally published in the *Journal of Humanistic Psychology* as "Two Patterns of Transcendence." It was perhaps the clearest statement up to that time of my "phase-3" model of development and evolution (which, in the context of the four quadrants, is the model I still hold);[6] namely, the idea of relatively universal basic structures (levels or waves of development) through which numerous different developmental lines or streams proceed in a largely independent fashion. The basic waves themselves are simply a sophisticated version of the Great Nest of Being, matter to body to mind to soul to spirit, with each senior nest transcending and including its predecessor(s). Through the levels (or nests or waves) of this Great Holarchy, at least a dozen different developmental lines (such as cognition, affects, morals, self-identity, and needs) proceed relatively independently, so that a person can be at a very high level of development in some lines, a medium level in other lines, and a low level in still others—all at the same time. *Overall development, then, follows no set pattern or linear sequence whatsoever,* even though many of the individual lines do.

This phase-3 model was first presented in "Ontogenetic Development: Two Fundamental Patterns," in the *Journal of Transpersonal Psychology* 13, no. 1, 1981 (which was included in volume three of the *Collected Works*). That was followed by a two-part series in the same journal, "The Developmental Spectrum and Psychopathology: Part 1, Stages and Types of Pathology; Part 2, Treatment Modalities," which were then included in *Transformation of Consciousness: Conventional and Contemplative Perspectives on Development* (included in this volume), which I coedited with Harvard psychologists Jack Engler and Daniel P. Brown (with contributions by Mark Epstein, Jonathan Lieff, and John Chirban). Both Engler and Brown had done pioneering—and still unsurpassed—research into the cross-cultural stages of the meditative path. What they found—using, I might add, a perspective of dynamic dialecticism—was the following: "The major [spiritual] traditions we have studied in their original languages present an unfolding of meditation experiences in terms of a *stage model:* for example, the Mahamudra from the Tibetan Mahayana Buddhist tradition; the Visuddhimagga from the Pali Theravada Buddhist tradition; and the Yoga Sutras from the Sanskrit Hindu tradition [these were subsequently checked against Chinese and Christian sources]. The models are sufficiently similar to suggest an underlying common invariant sequences of stages, despite vast cultural and linguistic differences as well as styles of practice. . . . The results strongly suggest that the stages of meditation are in fact of cross-cultural and universal applicability (at a deep, not surface, analysis)." In the same volume we included an in-depth study by Harvard theologian John Chirban of the stages of spiritual development evidenced by saints in Eastern Orthodox Christianity. Chirban's conclusion: "Although each saint describes his own experience (often in his own unique way), basic parallels emerge as one compares the stages of the saints with one another. This sameness confirms the catholicity of their experience . . ."—and the catholicity (or universal applicability) of the basic waves of consciousness themselves, which are similarly reflected in these numerous cross-cultural sources.

Two of the papers in this volume—"Death, Rebirth, and Meditation" and "Stages of Meditation"—explore the highest waves of the Great Nest according to anuttaratantrayoga, or "Highest Yoga Tantra," which, next to Dzogchen, is said to be the highest of the Buddha's teachings. This yoga possesses an unsurpassed grasp of the extraordinary interrelation between conscious states and bodily energies. According to this teaching, in order to master the mind, one must concomitantly master the body's subtle energies—chi, prana, rLung, ki—and this yoga is an exquisite system of harnessing these subtle energies at every stage of development, right up to and including the enlightened state of Clear Light Emptiness.

Those who maintain that, when it comes to consciousness, Buddhism eschews the Great Chain and only recognizes the five skandhas—form, sensation, perception, impulse/image, and conceptual consciousness—might examine the Highest Yoga teachings, which maintain that those five levels of consciousness apply only to "gross consciousness," beyond which lie several levels of what is referred to as "subtle consciousness," and beyond those, several levels of "very subtle [or causal] consciousness"—in other words, the entire Great Nest, which is also in full accord with the general Mahayana Buddhist doctrine of the nine levels/waves of consciousness—five senses, sense-mind, higher mind, collective mind, and pure nondual buddha-mind. These Highest Yoga teachings are carefully outlined in these two papers, and their relevance to a full spectrum view of human growth and development is obvious, I believe.

Another important item becomes quite clear as one studies (and practices) these texts of higher development. Several critics have, over the years, scolded me for implying that there are strong similarities between, for example, the Buddhist Dharmakaya (and Emptiness) and the Vedanta causal body (and nirguna Brahman).

And yet, according to Highest Yoga tantra, one type of the Dharmakaya is experienced in *deep dreamless sleep* (formless consciousness); the Sambhogakaya, in the *dream state;* and the Nirmanakaya, in the *waking state.* But notice: according to Vedanta, the causal body is experienced in deep dreamless sleep, the subtle body is experienced in the dream state, and the gross body in the waking state. Therefore, if you believe that there are similarities in deep dreamless sleep between individuals, it follows that there are some profound similarities between the Buddhist Dharmakaya and the Hindu causal body. (And likewise, similarities between the Buddhist Sambhogakaya and Hindu subtle body, and the Nirmanakaya and gross body.)

Of course there are many important differences between these Buddhist and Hindu notions, and those need to be rigorously honored. And yet—simultaneously—there seem to be important and profound similarities. In all of my writings I have tried to emphasize both—certain similarities in deep features, important differences in surface features—and thus I am always a little chagrined when accused of championing only one or the other.

Pulling together all of these strands of development—conventional and contemplative, orthodox and meditative, Western and Eastern—suggested that there is indeed a universally available *spectrum of consciousness* (in deep, not surface, features), through which individuals develop at their own pace and in their own way. That is what *Transformations of Consciousness* accomplished, I believe. Comparing and contrasting numerous maps of development from around the world—and using some of them to fill in gaps in the others—resulted in a "master template" of overall consciousness development, a master template that was, in fact, a sophisticated and modernized version of the Great Nest of Being.

At the time, of course, the Great Nest was under brutal attack by the dynamic relativists (from deconstructionists to feminists to deep ecologists). The Great Nest was said to be *inherently* (and here follows a list of dirty words) hierarchical, patriarchal, elitist, logocentric, eurocentric, phallocentric, phallologocentric, anti-ecological, repressive, and marginalizing. None of those is true. The Great Nest, as I have often pointed out, is not a hierarchy in the sense of a rigid one-way ranking, with the senior dimensions rejecting and repressing the lower (which is how it is always pictured by its critics), but rather is a holarchy, where each senior dimension transcends and includes its predecessor(s), as in the holarchy atoms, molecules, cells, organisms.[7] Cells don't repress molecules, they embrace them. Likewise with the Great Nest: each senior dimension enfolds, envelopes, and embraces all the preceding dimensions: spirit transcends and includes soul, which transcends and includes mind, which transcends and includes body, which transcends and includes matter—a series of concentric spheres of loving embrace, with spirit transcending all and embracing all. That some types of hierarchies can be misused to repress or oppress condemns the misuse, not all hierarchies per se.

Likewise with the other condemnations hurled at the Great Nest by the politically correct. In a footnote written at the time, I was already trying to blunt the attacks: "The 'politically correct' (PC) claim is that all of modern civilization is now dominated by thinking that is Eurocentric, logocentric, and sexist, and that the only politically adequate or correct view is therefore one that is, by contrast, radically egalitarian and pluralistic [dynamic relativism/contextualism], and denies that any worldview can be 'better' than another. The problem with this view is that, while it claims to be admirably liberal—in that nothing can be said to be 'better' or 'higher'—it ends up absolutely reactionary: if nothing is better, then there is and can be no liberal agenda, there can be no impetus to improve a present state of affairs according to a blueprint of a 'better' state of affairs. It utterly lacks a coherent and integrative vision of possibilities [as Kramer would discover for all dynamic relativism]. Moreover, radical pluralism is itself a Eurocentric, logocentric notion.

"The perennial philosophy [and Great Nest], on the other hand, first arose in the matriarchy, and thus cannot be charged with inherent sexism; it arose in illiterate peoples, and thus is not logocentric; and it first flourished in what are now Second and Third World countries—it is hardly Eurocentric. Furthermore, it offers what PC thought cannot: an integrative vision that, while allowing each expression its own free space, points to a 'better' state of affairs: namely, the supreme identity. It thus has inherent in it a genuine liberal agenda: increasing freedom on both an individual and societal level."[8]

I have always felt, from the time of my first book to today, that starting one's studies with the perennial philosophy is a sane, generous, and wise idea, if for no other reason than that the Great Nest is not a metaphysical postulate or abstruse philosophy, but rather represents some five thousand years of codifications of *direct phenomenological experiences* of the higher dimensions of human consciousness disclosed by consensually validated means. Put simply, the Great Nest is primarily *a summary of direct meditative experiences,* it is not an abstract metaphysics or ungrounded philosophy, and if we are looking for clues to unlocking the human potential, it would be most unwise to ignore the perennial philosophy, the world's first great psychotechnology for entering higher states of consciousness. But, of course, some would say that with extreme postmodernism, unwisdom was on the rampage, and the perennial philosophy was one of the first great casualties.

Having said that, I should also point out that, in addition to being one of the perennial philosophy's staunchest defenders, I have been one of its harshest critics. Notice that in the previous paragraph I said the perennial philosophy is a good place to *start*—but it is not a good place to stop. The fact is, as accurate as the Great Nest theorists were in mapping much of higher individual development, they did not grasp the intricacies of cultural context; they did not understand that the Great Nest itself evolves over time; they did not understand the correlations of states of consciousness with brain neurophysiology; they did not understand the interdependence of modes of production and worldviews. In short, they did not generally differentiate the Great Nest into the four quadrants (see *Integral Psychology* in this volume). Even though the more sophisticated Great Nest theorists (Plotinus, Asanga, Vasubandhu, Fatsang, Tsongkhapa, etc.) had access to higher forms of vision-logic (they were clearly operating with meta-systematic thought, even though they were also transcending it in contemplation), nonetheless they simply lacked the data, the empirical evidence, that would *fill the content* of their vision-logic with information about different cultures, radically different social contexts, the nature of brain physiology, and the anthropological records showing evidence of phylogenetic evolution—and *therefore* their dynamic dialectical worldview was largely confined to the unfolding of systems across time in individuals only (meditation was conceived by all of them in a developmental stage model, a micro-evolutionary dialecticism). But their overall view of the Great Nest was thus, by default, closer to the nature of Kramer's "static systems" view, which is exactly why, in just recent times, the traditional Great Nest was open to devastating criticism (correct as far as it went) from the dynamic relativists—a criticism I definitely share. As I strenuously argued in *The Marriage of Sense and Soul* and *Integral Psychology*, the Great Nest desperately needs to be modernized and postmodernized: it needs to recognize the importance of cultural context, relativistic surface features, correlations with modern scientific discoveries, sensitivity to minorities that the mythic-agrarian structure marginalized, the important of pluralistic voices, and so on.

Rather, what I have objected to in the torrent of attacks by the dynamic relativists is that, instead of trying to understand the enduring contributions of the perennial philosophy and the Great Nest theorists, and then weeding out their inadequacies, partialities, falsehoods, and limitations—so as to integrate their enduring truths with the newly emerging truths of modernity and postmodernity—the dynamic relativists have simply trashed the entire show, thrown one huge and precious baby out with a ton of bathwater, and sat back smugly congratulating themselves on having deconstructed what was, in fact, the collective wisdom of several millennia of the greatest men and women this planet has ever seen.

My approach to the perennial philosophy has been, instead, to try to take up and preserve those abiding truths that are as significant today as when they were first discovered, and then integrate them with the newly emerging truths of modernity and postmodernity. The idea is take the *static systems* view of the Great Nest, process it through the *differentiations* offered by *dynamic relativism* (e.g., the differentiation of the four quadrants, or simply the Big Three contexts of art, morals, and science), and then expose those multiple contexts to the *integration* offered by *dynamic dialecticism* (or developmental/integral embrace). This in effect integrates the best of premodernity (the Great Nest), modernity (differentiation of the Big Three), and postmodernity (integration of the Big Three via mature vision-logic, which was supposed to be the actual aim of postmodernism before it derailed into accentuating the previous differentiations while celebrating its incapacity to integrate them). All of these themes, as we will see, form the starting point of *Integral Psychology*.

So I have always been most ambivalent when a critic has identified me as a "perennial philosopher," when that is clearly a half-truth at best. In fact, just as I have spent much time trying to salvage the essentials of the Great Nest from the pluralistic relativists, I have also spent much time trying to move the Great Nest into the modern and postmodern world—*against the wishes* of the traditional perennial philosophers, such as Frithjof Schuon, René Guénon, Seyyed Nasr, and Ananda Coomaraswamy. For all of those theorists generally embrace a *static system* view of the Great Nest; they imagine that its truths are embedded in the mind of God in an unchanging and unchangeable fashion (as if God were incapable of thinking up a new idea); they actively deny versions of the Great Nest that are updated via dynamic relativism and dynamic dialecticism; their "archetypes" are not patterns of unfolding and evolving habits, but everlasting concrete imprints hammered into the world by a vigorously unimaginative God.

When that static-system conception is taken to the next level of worldview development, all of those permanent, unyielding, static forms are deconstructed (and rightly so) by dynamic relativism—*on the way to* their reintegration by dynamic dialecticism into evolving systems of inter-contextual embrace (all-level, all-quadrant). The traditional perennial philosophers simply refuse, on point of honor, to see their systems *mutually interacting* with the modern and the postmodern world, but rather see in the latter variations on the theme of the Great Satan: the modern world rejects the Great Chain, so it must be deeply confused, whereas many of the traditional items modernity rejects stand in dire need of rejection. But the perennialists have pulled themselves out of this mutual dialogue, and instead have taken to nagging the world to get back to that good ole time religion. But Spirit-in-action, in one of its forms as the unfolding world, has simply moved on, it seems.[9]

Transformations of Consciousness took as a reference point an enduring truth of the Great Nest of Being: the unfolding of ever-richer realms of consciousness, from matter to body to mind to soul to spirit. My chapters focused on outlining a full-spectrum model of consciousness, which consisted of three major components: (1) the *basic structures* or levels or waves of consciousness—*matter,* vital *body* (sensation, perception, impulse), *mind* (image, symbol, concept, rule/role, formal-reflexive, vision-logic), *soul* (psychic, subtle), and *spirit* (causal, nondual); (2) the numerous different *developmental lines or streams* (such as self-identity, self-needs, and morals) that proceed through those major waves; and (3) the *self* (or self-system), which has to integrate all of the various waves and streams.

Focusing on the self and its journey through the basic waves of the Great Nest, I examined *the major milestones in the self's development.* Each milestone of self-development I called a *fulcrum,* which is a 1-2-3 process of fusion/embeddedness, differentiation/transcendence, and inclusion/integration. That is, the growth of the self involves a progressive identification with a particular wave in the Great Nest, followed by a differentiation from (and transcendence of) that wave, which is then included and integrated from the next higher wave in the Great Holarchy.[10] The self's evolution is thus transcend-and-include, as deeper and higher waves of the Great Nest of Being unfold in its own case, from matter to body to mind to soul to spirit.

Of course, development is not nearly as sequential as that sounds; and, given the fact that there are actually numerous different developmental lines all moving relatively independently through the Great Nest, the self's *overall development* is very uneven and nonlinear—it can make progress in cognitive, emotional, psychological, spiritual, and other lines *in a very uneven way,* nor must any of those lines be completed before the others can begin. There is nothing sequential or stage-like about overall development.

Although I stated that position quite often, beginning in 1981, the most common criticism of my work has been that it is a rigidly linear, stage-by-stage model—a so-called "ladder" view of development. Of course, it didn't help that I often drew the spectrum of consciousness in a ladder-like way (as in fig. 11 on page 149). But that "ladder" simply represents the various waves through which the numerous different developmental streams can progress independently, at their own rate, in their own way, so that, as I said, overall development follows no linear sequence at all.

The critics who misrepresented my position took that "ladder" as the total story of development as I conceived it, which not only ignored the many independent streams, all cascading over each other in a richly nonlinear way, but also ignored the important role played by *altered states.* As I had made clear, beginning with *A Sociable God* (1983), a person at virtually any stage of development can have various types of *peak experiences* and other altered states, including spiritual peak experiences of the transpersonal realms, and these follow no set sequence, either. (All of these topics are discussed at length in *Integral Psychology.*)

What seemed to confuse a few critics is that, even though overall development is not linear or sequential, a great deal of empirical evidence continues to demonstrate that many of the *individual developmental lines* themselves (such as cognitive, ego, and moral) do in fact unfold in a relatively invariant, holarchical sequence (they unfold through the universal waves of the Great Nest of Being—preconventional to conventional to postconventional to post-postconventional.

This evidence is discussed at length in *Integral Psychology,* and summarized in figs. 2 and 3 in that book, which we will discuss in a moment).

The preponderance of evidence strongly suggests that this sequentiality is also true for the developmental line of *self-identity,* or what Jane Loevinger has investigated as "ego development." I call this immediate sense of self-identity the "proximate self" because it is intimately expressed as an "I" (in distinction to the distal self or "me"). And, as I started to say, each time the *proximate self* moves through a basic wave of the Great Nest, it goes through a *fulcrum* of its own development: it first identifies with a new wave, then disidentifies with and transcends that wave, then includes and integrates that wave from the next higher, wider wave. I summarized the Great Nest as possessing nine basic waves of consciousness (sensorimotor, phantasmic-emotional, rep-mind, rule/role mind, formal-reflexive, vision-logic, psychic, subtle, and causal/nondual), and therefore I outlined the *nine correlative fulcrums* that the self goes through in a complete evolution or development through the entire Great Nest.

Each time the self steps up to a new and higher sphere in the Great Nest of Being, it can do so in a relatively healthy fashion—which means it smoothly differentiates and integrates the elements of that level—or in a relatively pathological fashion—which means it either *fails to differentiate* (and thus remains in fusion/fixation/arrest) or it *fails to integrate* (which results in repression, alienation, fragmentation). Each wave of the Great Nest has a qualitatively different architecture, and thus each fulcrum (and pathology) likewise has a qualitatively different structure. I therefore outlined *nine levels of pathology* (psychosis, borderline, neurosis, script, identity, existential, psychic, subtle, causal), and suggested the correlative *treatment modalities* that seem to best address these different waves of pathology (pacification, structure building, uncovering, cognitive, introspection, existential, the path of yogis, saints, and sages). All of these—the nine basic waves, the correlative self-fulcrums, the types of self pathology that can be generated if something goes wrong at each fulcrum, and the treatment modalities that seem bested suited to each—are listed in figure 11 (page 149).[11]

Needless to say, these were meant only as the most general of generalizations, useful insofar as they alert us to the very different contours of the various waves in the Great Nest of Being, and the correlatively different fulcrums of the self's journey through those waves. All too often, one particular psychotherapeutic approach (psychoanalysis, Gestalt, neurolinguistic programming, holotropic breathwork, transactional analysis, biological psychiatry, etc.) is used for *all* types of psychopathologies, often with unfortunate results. Rather, the one thing we learn from the existence of the multiple waves of the spectrum of consciousness is just how many different dimensions of existence there are, and how a sensitivity to these multiple dimensions demands a multiplicity of treatment modalities.

The nine general levels of therapy that I outlined are meant to be suggestive only; they are broad guidelines as to what we can expect, based on a careful reading of the evidence compiled by numerous different schools of development psychology and contemplative spirituality (an overview of this evidence is given in *Integral Psychology*). There is, needless to say, a great deal of overlap between these therapies. For example, I list "script pathology" and "cognitive therapy" as being especially relevant to fulcrum-4, which is where the self identifies, for the first time, with the rule/role mind. That is, the self can begin to take the *role* of others and learn the *rules* of its society. If something goes wrong during this general development period (which typically covers ages 6 to 12), the result is a "script pathology," a series of distorted, untrue, unfair ideas and scripts about one's self and others. Cognitive therapy has excelled in rooting out these maladaptive scripts and replacing them with more accurate, benign, and therefore healthy ideas and self-concepts. But to say cognitive therapy focuses on this wave of consciousness development is *not* to say it has no benefit at other waves, for clearly it does. The idea, rather, is that the farther away we get from this wave, the less relevant (but never completely useless) cognitive therapy becomes. Developments in fulcrums 1 and 2 are mostly preverbal and preconceptual, so conceptual reprogramming does not directly address these levels; and developments beyond fulcrum-6 are mostly transmental and transrational, so mental reprogramming, in and of itself, is limited in its effectiveness. So it is not that a given therapy applies to one narrow wave of development, but that, in focusing on one or two waves, most forms of therapy increasingly lose their effectiveness when applied to more distant realms.

Also, it is generally true, as I first suggested in *The Spectrum of Consciousness,* that the therapies of one level will acknowledge and often use the therapies from lower levels, but they are reluctant to recognize any level higher than their own. Thus, classical psychoanalysis will recognize the importance of instinctual and emotional drives, but downplay the importance of cognitive scripts themselves. Cognitive therapists emphasize the importance of those scripts but downplay or ignore the importance of the total psychophysical organism (or centaur), which humanistic and existential therapists emphasize. And existential therapists often vehemently deny the importance or even existence of the transpersonal and transrational levels. By assigning each therapy a general level of the overall spectrum of consciousness, I was also taking those particular facts into account—the therapy at one level will usually acknowledge and even use all of the therapies from lower levels, rarely from any higher (whose existence, in fact, they usually pathologize).

Transformations of Consciousness focused almost exclusively on interior developments in individuals—focused, that is, on what I would later call the Upper Left quadrant. Its conclusions are still quite sound for that quadrant, I believe, but a more balanced view would also include insights from all four quadrants, even when trying to understand individual development and pathology. The subjective events in individual consciousness are *always* intimately interrelated with objective events (such as brain physiology), intersubjective events (such as cultural background and context), and interobjective events (such as social institutions and the techno-economic base). As *Sex, Ecology, Spirituality* and *A Brief History of Everything* explained at length, all four of those quadrants mutually interact (they are embedded in each other), and thus all of them are required to understand any of them. The conclusions of *Transformations of Consciousness* are still valid; they simply need to be inserted into a four-quadrant view, which would include an understanding of the role of neurophysiology on consciousness development and neuropharmacology on psychopathology (Upper Right), as well as the role of multiple cultural contexts (Lower Left) and modes of social production (Lower Right)—all of which, as we will see, are emphasized in *Integral Psychology.* Ironically, now that biological psychiatry and cognitive science have attempted to reduce all interior consciousness to objective "its"—reduce Upper Left to Upper Right—the conclusions of *Transformations of Consciousness* need all the more seriously to be included in an integral view of consciousness.

The great sages, we might suppose, have traversed all, or certainly most, of the waves in the Great Nest of Being; but since that is relatively rare, few therapists would ever see all nine fulcrums of self development. Many therapists told me, after reading *Transformations of Consciousness,* that what they saw in therapy did not look like that nine-level map! I quite agree. In fact, most forms of typical psychotherapy deal only with a few levels: mostly fulcrum-3 (which involves uncovering and integrating repressed feelings and shadow elements), fulcrum-4 (which involves belongingness needs and cognitive reprogramming of harsh scripts), and fulcrums 5 and 6 (which involve self-esteem and self-actualization). In terms of "contacting feelings" and "uncovering the shadow," most therapeutic work occurs at fulcrum-3, which is the point where the conceptual mind first emerges and differentiates-and-integrates the body (typically during the Oedipal/Electra period, ages 3 to 6). Therapies that have focused on this important fulcrum include, of course, psychoanalysis and two of its more popular and effective offshoots, Gestalt Therapy and Transactional Analysis (both of which also focus on cognitive scripts, which thicken at fulcrum-4, but both of which aim to dig deeper, into fulcrum-3, and expose the psychodynamics and repressed feelings that often underlie script pathology). I have therefore included "A Working Synthesis of Transactional Analysis and Gestalt Therapy," which was published in *Psychotherapy: Theory, Research, and Practice* (and was actually written in phase-1, with an awkward style, but it is still quite generally valid, in my opinion). It more accurately gives the flavor of one type of actual therapy (focused on fulcrum-3) than does my abstract overview in *Transformations of Consciousness.*[12]

"Paradigm Wars" was a simplified overview of the waves of development, their correlative worldviews, and the pathologies that could occur at each. As a simplified overview, it did not specifically distinguish between basic structures, the correlative worldviews, the self and its fulcrums, and the related pathologies, but simply discussed them all together as a single unfolding through the Great Nest. Its simple point was that each level of development has a different view of the world—a different worldview, a different paradigm—and that consequently, each of us has, in simply growing up, *already gone through at least a half-dozen paradigm revolutions,* from archaic to magic to mythic to rational to integrative (on the way to transmental levels altogether).

"Two Humanistic Psychologies?" was in part a response to Rollo May, who, along with Albert Ellis and Kirk Schneider, had at the time begun a concerted attack on the general transpersonal orientation (made wonderfully unforgettable by Albert Ellis's serious claim that the transpersonalists were the people most likely to start a nuclear holocaust). I answered all three of them in various publications, of which "Two Humanistic Psychologies?" covers all the relevant points. I had just moved to San Francisco from Cambridge and was living with Frances Vaughan and Roger Walsh. Rollo and I had struck up a friendship and began holding seminars together at his exquisite house in Tiburon. We were good friends, I believe, but Rollo became increasingly exasperated at the many flaky trends in the transpersonal movement—as had I and most serious transpersonalists. He lashed out at the entire movement, perhaps understandably, and I responded (as I likewise did with Schneider and Ellis). This paper still stands, in my opinion, as a succinct statement of the crucial differences between the humanistic-existential worldviews and those of a more spiritual and transpersonal nature—as well as pinpointing exactly what can go so very wrong with all of them. Rollo spotted the catastrophes, missed the truths.

Right before I moved to San Francisco (in 1983) I was living in Cambridge, Massachusetts, where I had gone to try to help salvage *ReVision Journal,* which Jack Crittenden and I had cofounded when I was still in Lincoln, Nebraska. (Jack—along with the journal—was in Cambridge, which is why I moved there). At the time, *ReVision's* stated philosophy was one of dynamic dialecticism plugged into the entire Great Nest of Spirit (it has since become a bastion of dynamic relativism, which is why Jack and I are no longer associated with it). I drew together many of the articles we had published into a book, *The Holographic Paradigm,* which I published right before I left for San Francisco. Its introduction is included in this volume. (I was in the awkward position, as editor, of being virtually the only contributor who did not believe the holographic paradigm was based on good science or good mysticism, for reasons I explained in *Eye to Eye,* and for reasons that can be found in the introduction to *Quantum Questions,* included in this volume. Naturally, the book became an international bestseller.)

I happily arrived in San Francisco and settled down in Frances's beautiful house, where a downstairs room was graciously made available to me. My move was financed by a generous grant from the Foundation for Inner Peace and Judith Skutch, publisher of a *Course in Miracles.* I myself was not a devoted follower of the *Course,* but I did find it profound and moving in many ways, and was glad to add my expertise to elucidating its meaning in any way I could. The *Course* community—most of whom lived in Tiburon—included Judith Skutch and her husband, Whit Whitson; Bill Thetford, the co-scribe of the *Course* (Helen, the main scribe, had recently died), one of the most gentle, beautiful, wise, and dear men I have even known (he, too, has deceased); his friend Pat Hopkins; Bob Skutch, a founding member of the Foundation; and Frances and Roger, who saw in the *Course* a version of the perennial philosophy that spoke in terms most modern men and women could hear. When I published *Eye to Eye* (included in volume three), I dedicated it to all of those people "for providing a place and means to write, and for simply being the gifts that they are."

Right after I had assembled *Eye to Eye, A Sociable God* hit the bookstores, and its dynamic dialecticism was aggressively attacked by the waves of dynamic relativists who were in the process of drenching academia. "Sociocultural Evolution" was written in response. But by then I had met Terry Killam and proposed to her ten days later, and our wedding was scheduled four months thence. We were renting San Keen's rustic old house in Muir Beach, madly in love, oblivious to the world—which didn't stop me from completing two more books in those four months: *Quantum Questions: Mystical Writings of the World's Great Physicists* and then *Transformations of Consciousness.*

Throughout *Transformations of Consciousness* (and throughout several of the works included in this volume), there is frequent reference to a work-in-progress called *System, Self, and Structure,* which I have been working on (and mostly not working on) for fifteen years. Meant to be a comprehensive textbook of integral psychology, its writing has been repeatedly interrupted by dramatic life events, so much so that I have always wondered if I seriously wanted to write it (I have, after all, managed to write everything I really wanted to). A central part of this two-volume text is a detailed discussion of almost two hundred different theorists, from developmental psychologists to cultural anthropologists to contemplative sages. Included in the book are dozens of charts, outlining around one hundred of the developmentalists that I discuss.

For this volume of the *Collected Works,* I decided that I would include these charts, which are rather striking—and then decided that the only way to do so would be with extensive commentary, whereupon I decided to simply write a condensed version of *System, Self, and Structure* and include that as well. It is published in this volume for the first time, under the title *Integral Psychology,* along with many of the charts.

These charts are especially important in giving the more accurate correlations of my system with others'. For example, in books from *Transformations of Consciounsess* to *A Brief History of Everything,* I have as a simplification correlated concrete operational thinking with conventional morality, and formal operational with postconventional. More accurate correlations recognize that conventional levels of morality are also constructed by formal operational thinking, and that some postconventional levels are constructed by postformal thinking. These more accurate correlations are given in the charts, which should be used for my actual correlations as of this writing.

At the same time, I should say that I take, and have always taken, a rather loose approach to exact correlations among different systems. I do not believe that there is one correct picture of human development, of which these various researchers are giving partial glimpses. Development is more like the Mississippi River, with literally thousands of real and different currents all scurrying toward the ocean of One Taste, and different types of research tools (from Kohlberg's moral tests to Loevinger's sentence completion test to Selman's tests of role taking to the Profiles of Meditative Experience test) all plug into the Mississippi at a different point and give us different readings. There are as many different developmental levels and lines as there are different tests plopped into the River. There is no reason to suppose that these many different tests—there are hundreds of them from around the world—will simply line up perfectly next to each other so we can all see that they are identical. Rather, they are all measuring fairly different currents in this great Stream of samsara; some of the currents are quite close to each other (moral development and ideas of the good life, for example); some of them are far removed (cognitive development and psychosexual development). But all of them are anchored in the very real currents of a very real River. Moreover—and here is the general dynamic dialecticism claim—the River itself has a series of major waves that are fairly universal, through which all these independent streams run. And therefore we can—to some degree—line up these various streams or developmental lines according to which general waves they are moving through at any given time. The basic waves (or basic structures) are listed in each of the diagrams, and then the various developmental lines and streams are listed next to them. Most of these correlations are accurate, I believe, to about plus-or-minus 1.5 stages, and many of the specific correlations were given by the theorists themselves. At the very least, one is indeed struck with the *general similarity* in these hundreds of streams as they rush through the same basic waves of the great River of life.

Integral Psychology is at this time the definitive statement of my psychological model, and my other writings in the field should be coordinated with its views. In fact, as suggested in the prefatory Note, it might be a good idea to read *Integral Psychology* first and then use the other texts in this volume (and my other works) to fill in the details of the overview offered in *Integral Psychology*.

I completed *Transformations of Consciousness* about a month before Treya and I were married. Ten days after the wedding ceremony, she was diagnosed with a very aggressive form of breast cancer. The next volume

(Grace and Grit) tells that story. *Transformations of Consciousness* was the last theoretical book I would write for ten years. Treya changed my life dramatically, for the good in every way, and it would take that long for me to grow into the grace that was so freely offered. We would spend the next five years fighting a losing battle with the disease, though in the process we both won our souls.

Notes

1. All Kramer quotes are from "Development of an Awareness of Contradiction Across the Life Span and the Question of Postformal Operations," in Michael L. Commons et al, *Adult Development, Volume 1, Comparison and Applications of Developmental Models,* Westport, Connecticut: Praeger, 1989.
2. See *Sex, Ecology, Spirituality,* chap. 2, section "Twenty Tenets."
3. See David Ray Griffin's SUNY series on postmodernism.
4. In short, the move from formop to early vision-logic to late vision-logic is a move from *universal formalism* to *pluralistic relativism* to *universal integralism.* (See *Boomeritis* for a full discussion of these phases.)

   More technically, transitional vision-logic (along with late formal operational thought) *recognizes* systems (static formal systems), early vision-logic differentiates systems (relativism/pluralism) and begins to relate them (meta-systematically but relativistically), middle and late vision-logic *integrates* these systems paradigmatically and cross-paradigmatically (dynamic dialecticism). See the discussion and charts in *Integral Psychology* at the end of this volume.

   As that discussion makes clear, there is general agreement as to the higher stages of these types of differentiations-and-integrations, resulting in relativistic systems (low), systems of systems (middle), and systems of systems of systems (high). But there is still a great deal of disagreement as to how much of these integrations can be accomplished by formal operational thought, and how much is due to a qualitatively higher cognitive activity of postformal (vision-logic) thought. For this reason, when I sometimes vacillate on how to divide these capacities between formop and vision-logic, it is not a vacillation as to the actual stages themselves, but simply as to what to call them. Some researchers feel that formal operational thought itself is capable of handling all systematic, relativistic, meta-systematic, and dialectical thinking, but most researchers feel that at least some of those capacities require postformal (vision-logic) operations. I obviously agree with the latter, but exactly where to draw the line between formal and postformal remains highly disputed. But none of this should obscure the actual stages of increasing differentiation-and-integration that everybody agrees are occurring.

   As rough *generalizations,* I refer to *modernity* and Enlightenment thinking as being under the province of late formop and early vision-logic—which recognizes and differentiates systems (especially the cultural value spheres of art, science, and morals); and I refer to *postmodernity* (in its best sense) as being middle-to-late vision-logic, with its mandate to integrate those differentiations. This includes those thinkers who, no matter when they lived, spoke essentially through a mature vision-logic—e.g., Hegel, Whitehead, Aurobindo, Schelling, Plotinus, Habermas, Longchenpa, Gebser, Murphy.

Another factor uniting most of the theories of higher (postformal) stages of adult development is the discovery that, just as we find a move from relativistic/contextual to dialectical/integrative, so we find a move from *relativism* (where no one perspective can be said to be better) to *commitment* (as in Perry's well-known research), where, even though various perspectives are relative, nonetheless deeper contexts can be found that allow and even demand a commitment—that is, there are ways to anchor the good, the true, and the beautiful, even in the midst of relativism. Or, put another way, relativism is again superceded by the recognition of deeper and wider patterns relating various contexts. Once again development is found to proceed from a rigid universal formalism (where all judgments are felt to be certain) to a pluralistic, relativistic contextualism (where no judgments are possible) to a genuine commitment (where judgments are again possible, but tempered and enriched by multiple contexts unified in a global perspectivism). The historical parallels are again obvious: from a modernity grounded in uniformitarianism and certain of its (allegedly) universal laws (many of which are simply the laws of wealthy bourgeois white males); to an early postmodernism swamped in unending relativities and pluralistic contexts, paralyzed by an inability to judge anything; to a constructive postmodernism (slowly emerging), which sets all contexts in a universal-global perspective and can therefore unify and integrate the pluralities, and thus make consistent judgments about relative worth and relative development—and therefore ground an authentic commitment. See *Boomeritis* for a further discussion this topic.

5. See David Ray Griffin's SUNY press series on postmodern philosophy; see also *Sex, Ecology, Spirituality* and particularly *Boomeritis*.
6. I have, for convenience, divided my overall work into four general phases. Phase-1 was Romantic (a "recaptured-goodness" model), which posited a spectrum of consciousness ranging from subconscious to self-conscious to superconscious (or id to ego to God), with the higher stages viewed as a return to, and recapture of, original but lost potentials. Phase-2 was more specifically evolutionary or developmental (a "growth-to-goodness" model), with the spectrum of consciousness unfolding in developmental stages or levels. Phase-3 added developmental lines to those developmental levels—that is, numerous different developmental lines (such as cognitive, conative, affective, moral, psychological, spiritual, etc.) proceeding in a relatively independent manner through the basic levels of the overall spectrum of consciousness. Phase-4 added the idea of the four quadrants—the subjective (intentional), objective (behavioral), intersubjective (cultural), and interobjective (social) dimensions—of each of those levels and lines, with the result being—or at least attempting to be—a comprehensive or integral philosophy. *The Atman Project* is a phase-2 work, *Transformations of Consciousness* is phase-3, and *Integral Psychology* is phase-4.

7. See *The Eye of Spirit,* chap. 1.
8. This was published in *Grace and Grit* (p. 88n) but was written around 1984.
9. My numerous criticisms of the perennial philosophy have been published in several places. "The Neo-Perennial Philosophy"—a criticism of the static systems view in favor of a dynamic dialecticism—was written at the same time as most of the works in this volume; it was published in *Quest* magazine (and included in *The Eye of Spirit*). Strong criticisms of the perennial philosophy can be found throughout *The Eye of Spirit; Sex, Ecology, Spirituality;* and *Integral Psychology,* as well as the introductions to volumes 2 and 3 in the Collected Works. Many of these criticisms are summarized in *One Taste.*
10. The word "holon" makes its first major appearance in *Transformations of Consciousness,* although the concept itself has been present since my first book: in *Spectrum of Consciousness,* each level was described as a whole that is part of the whole of next level, a concept for which Koestler's wonderful term "holon" was made to order. In editing *Transformations* I occasionally added the word "holarchy" to be consistent.
11. In the original version of the two JTP papers that were included in *Transformations of Consciousness,* I included a discussion of the prenatal and perinatal phases of development, which I referred to as fulcrum-0. For various editorial reasons, fulcrum-0 was not included in the final version of the JTP papers, nor therefore in *Transformations of Consciousness.* In *A Brief History of Everything* I used the original version of the diagram of the fulcrums, which included fulcrum-0, with its pathology and treatment modalities, and I have put that original version back into *Transformations of Consciousness* in this volume (see fig. 11, page 149). There is, however, no discussion of that fulcrum in the text; readers are referred to *Sex, Ecology, Spirituality* and *The Eye of Spirit* for a full discussion of the perinatal fulcrum.
12. Since most of the books I have published are in fact abstract overviews and summaries, I am always looking for opportunities to publish more detailed pieces. The paper on Gestalt and Transactional Analysis concluded that it was legitimate to characterize the general ego structure as a tripartite structure: the P-A-C ego, consisting of (at least) Parent, Adult, and Child ego states. All of that research was condensed into a paragraph or two in *The Atman Project,* with no indication of the extensive documenting evidence. In fact, it wasn't until *Sex, Ecology, Spirituality* that I had the luxury of including endnotes that began to elucidate the types of reasoning and research that went into the abstract summaries and overviews in the body of the text.

A UNIFIED THEORY OF DEVELOPMENT

ABSTRACT: *This article is a response to Michael Washburn's "Two Patterns of Transcendence," in which he maintains that there are two dominant but incompatible paradigms in transpersonal psychology: Jung's Analytic Psychology and Wilber's Spectrum Psychology. The conclusion of this article is that the two psychological paradigms are not incompatible, and that the Jungian model can, in essential respects, be incorporated into the spectrum model.*

MICHAEL WASHBURN (1988; 1990) has given a very clear and concise summary of what he sees as the two dominant paradigms in transpersonal psychology, namely, Jung's Analytic Psychology and my own Spectrum Psychology. Washburn characterizes Jung's view as "spiral-to-integration" or "U-turn toward origins," and my view he somewhat unflatteringly (and, as we shall see, incorrectly) terms "ladder-to-oneness" or "straight ascent." Washburn then argues that both these views are logically consistent and theoretically acceptable, and that, therefore, one model cannot displace or incorporate the other, and consequently a unified theory of transcendence is highly unlikely.

In the course of Washburn's presentation, it thus becomes necessary for him to attempt to show that the "straight ascent" model does not and cannot incorporate the types of psychological and theoretical concerns addressed by the "U-turn toward origins" model, and thus the "straight ascent" model might have some profound errors or at least inadequacies in it. Washburn then proceeds to compare and contrast the two models according to "five critical issues on which the paradigms disagree." The point is that if the disagreements hold, and both models can be shown to be plausible, and they are both mutually incompatible, then it follows that no integration or synthesis of them is possible.

The crux of Washburn's argument is that the "straight-ascent" model has no comprehension of a return to source or a "U-turn toward origins." I can state my response to that very simply: I believe that Washburn, as careful and articulate as he is, has nonetheless fundamentally misunderstood and misrepresented my own position in a way that artificially makes it look as if the two paradigms cannot be brought together in some sort of major accord. I will thus try to show that the so-called straight ascent model actually incorporates the essence of the "U-turn toward origins," but does so in a fashion both metaphysically and scientifically sounder than the Jungian/Washburn attempt.

I have always had a great deal of respect and appreciation for Washburn's work. He is a very gifted writer, and he always brings enormous clarity and insight to any topic he tackles. The present case is no exception. Even though I believe Washburn has made some major errors, his presentation has again greatly helped to clarify the issues involved. In this case, alas, I believe that Washburn has done for the Jungian model what Hume did for empiricism: by making it consistent, he made it unbelievable.

Let me begin by saying that I used to be a firm believer in the Jungian model. I still use much of Jung's terminology, and I consider him a pioneering genius of the first order. In particular, I found these concepts profoundly important: archetypes, personal and collective unconscious, individuation, persona, shadow, ego, and Self. I have now come to find many of those concepts slightly to highly problematic, at least as conceived by Jungians.

I am now preparing a book-length treatment of what I feel are the limitations and distortions of the Jungian model (as well as an appreciation of those aspects of Jungian theory that seem to have withstood modern scholarship), so at this point let me say only that I am not alone in being a mystically oriented theorist who is basically an ex-Jungian. It used to be that if one were spiritually oriented, Jung was the only psychology game in town. But now, from both Eastern and Western spiritual teachers, there is a growing rejection of major Jungian tenents, and a strong criticism of what are perceived to be some of his fundamental distortions of the spiritual process.

There are several examples of these critics. Augustine Leonard stated that "In comparison and because his method is so strict, Freud is less dangerous [from the spiritual point of view]. That which Jung calls religion, that which he honestly believes to be religion, is not religion at all; not even from the empirical point of view. It appears to be only a very incidental manifestation" (quoted in McNamara, 1981). Or, as William McNamara (1981), OCD, put it in *Christian Mysticism: The Art of the Inner Way:* "If I had to choose between Jung and Freud as a spiritual guide, I would choose Freud." His point is that Freud simply dismissed religion, whereas Jung distorted it. And, coming from the East, John Reynolds (1989), under the auspices of Namkhai Norbu (holder of the Dzogchen lineage, the highest teachings in Buddhism), has pointed out that almost all of Jung's knowledge of Tibetan Buddhism (and hence Eastern transcendence) came from the very misleading translations of Evans-Wentz. It is my own belief that the monolithic structure of Jungian (and neo-Jungian) thought is starting to crumble, and its monopoly on spiritual psychology is irrevocably deteriorating. And though much of Jungian thought is worth salvaging, much more needs to be jettisoned. I believe Washburn's article highlights cogently the insuperable difficulties of the Jungian paradigm.

During the time that I was a Jungian, or at least a quasi-Jungian, I was most impressed with Jung's developmental scheme (which was particularly well-explained by Edinger [1972] and summarized in Washburn's article). In this scheme, the ego starts out unconsciously one with or immersed in the Self or Ground. Then, through a process of alienation and separation from Self, the ego emerges as an individual and isolated entity. The emergence and consolidation of the independent ego occupies roughly the first half of life. In the second half of life, the ego *returns* to the Self, but this time in a conscious fashion. The sense of identity shifts from ego to Self (although the ego remains as a conventionally functioning entity). Thus the Jungians postulate what I have elsewhere (Wilber, 1982) technically termed a "U-turn"—and they place this U-turn right in the middle of development (this is the "U-turn" to which Washburn constantly refers, though he fails to mention where he got that specific term).

Notice that I am not arguing with these three overall stages of development (namely, pre-egoic to egoic to trans-egoic)—I have written on them extensively (Wilber, 1983). Rather, I am strongly disagreeing with the characterization of the pre-egoic state (the actual womb and neonatal state) as a state of unconscious unity with Self, the *same* unity recaptured by the trans-egoic states in mystical awareness. This is a romantic notion that was popular during the time of Schelling, from whom Jung appropriated the idea; but it is a rather outmoded notion, not supported by modern research nor, in fact, by the vast majority of the perennial traditions.

At any rate, I used to believe this Jungian version of the U-turn, and in fact, I began writing two books that were to prove this Jungian schema. The first book, *The Atman Project,* was to examine ontogenetic development and demonstrate that the infant starts out one with the Self in a type of unconscious mystical union (one with the breast, the mother, and the world). This primary ground and primal union is eventually abandoned or actually repressed (what I called the primary repression) in order to produce an isolated and alienated ego. This first leg I called the Outward Arc (OA). Then, on the second leg, or the Inward Arc (IA), the ego returns (the U-turn) to its primal Ground or Self, only this time in a conscious fashion, thus resurrecting its primordial identity with Self and Source (the whole trans-egoic phase). I actually used the following diagram, which can still be found in *The Atman Project,* to depict overall development and growth (see fig. 1).*

This is essentially the model Washburn is presenting. His stages are more or less identical to mine, and he often uses my terminology (both of which he freely acknowledges), although Washburn, of course, treats them in his own original and highly insightful way.

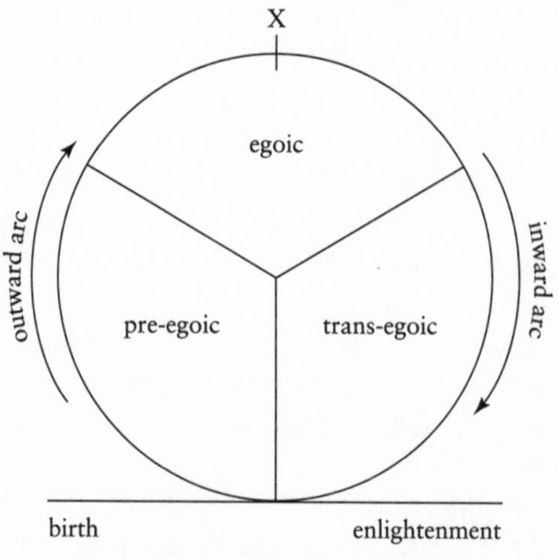

Figure 1

*[This is the wilber-1 model.]

But already there was a problem. By the time I was halfway through the original version of *The Atman Project,* I realized that no matter how I turned and twisted it, the Jungian model would not work. A massive amount of evidence had piled up against it. Virtually the entire pantheon of the perennial philosophy, all of modern psychology and psychiatry (except the Jungians and the Norman O. Brown types), and the entire weight of developmental psychology and evolutionary theory—*all* of it stood in sharp disagreement with the Romantic/Jungian model. This was extremely disconcerting to me.

In a type of mental anguish, I set aside *The Atman Project* and decided to look at the phylogenetic evidence, hoping I could still prop up the Jungian U-turn model with help from anthropology. And here it all seemed very promising. Didn't the world's great myths all speak of a Golden Age, an Eden of Paradise that was lost to produce the modern fallen age, but could be regained to usher in Heaven on Earth? Bolstered by the massive works of Campbell and other like-minded interpreters, I tried to assemble the phylogenetic case.

To my horror, the overall evidence just did not support the Jungian view. One had only to look at the torturous romantic re-interpretations of anthropological data that Campbell, for example, would give to virtually any primitive act in order to prove it was transcendental. Human sacrifice—that is, deliberate homicide—Campbell said, with a straight face, was a form of transcending ego. You know, "Well, there goes that ego!"

To make a long story short, I was forced to abandon the Jungian model (although salvaging what I think are some of its accurate points). I rewrote *The Atman Project* and *Up from Eden,* using the spectrum model I developed instead (the so-called "ladder-to-oneness"), which had its inspiration not in Jung, but in the perennial philosophy in general and the Great Chain of Being in particular.* This model very easily incorporates not only most of the great wisdom traditions (including, contra Washburn, Taoism and Tantra), but also, and just as importantly, the essential features of modern developmental psychology, as well as dynamic system theories (chaos theories) and evolutionary theory in general. And yes, this evolutionary conception is what might be described as an "ascending spiral" development (it is not a "straight ascent" as Washburn claims; he even acknowledges that this model has all sorts of ups and downs and dialectical spirals). But indeed, the overall

*[This is the wilber-2 model.]

thrust of the evolutionary spiral has an ascendent aspect to it, and might be represented simplistically as in figure 2. Even more schematically, we can represent it as in figure 3. That was the evolutionary, developmental, spirally ascending spectrum model that I presented in *Atman Project* and *Eden,* where, on the whole, evolution or development was seen as moving from matter to body to mind to soul to spirit.

Let me give one technical point here (and I will again use diagrams to try to simplify the issue). Although Washburn refers to my model as a "ladder," it is actually much closer to a bar graph (as in fig. 4). Beginning

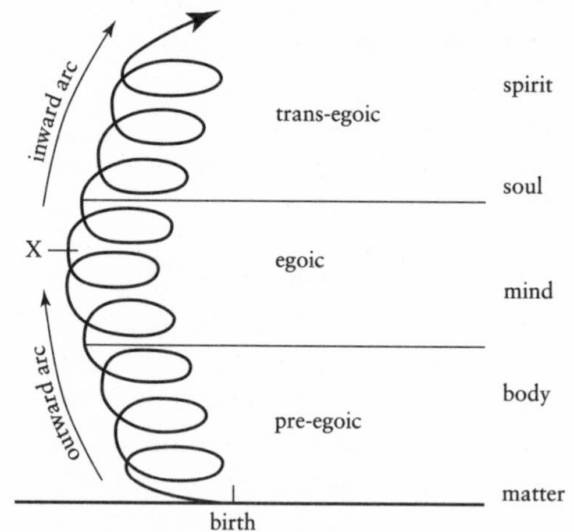

FIGURE 2

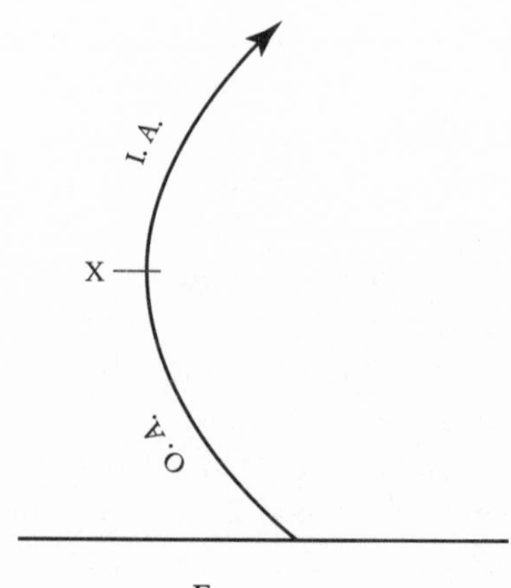

FIGURE 3

with (or, more actually, shortly after) *The Atman Project,* I have consistently maintained that bio-psycho-spiritual development could best be represented by numerous strands or *developmental lines* (following Anna Freud), and these lines each run a *spectrum* from least to most developed levels. I have equated that overall spectrum with consciousness itself (going from subconscious to self-conscious to superconscious, or prepersonal to personal to transpersonal). Thus, each *level* of consciousness has numerous different developmental *lines.** In a series of publications, I have suggested that there are *separate* developmental lines for cognitive capacity, sense of time, sense of space, motivation, moral sense, self-sense, natural epistemology, conative capacity, affect, object relations, and interpersonal capacity—to name the most prominent. These various developmental lines apparently can evolve in a somewhat independent manner, although some developmental lines seem to be prerequisites for others. For example, cognitive development is necessary, but not sufficient, for interpersonal competence, which is necessary, but not sufficient for, moral development (Kohlberg, 1981; Loevinger, 1976; Selman, 1971).

A person's overall growth, then, could be plotted on a bar graph (as in fig. 4), with the growth of some lines necessary, but not sufficient for, the growth of others. In the spectrum model,† the dynamic process that holds all the various developmental lines together in something of a co-

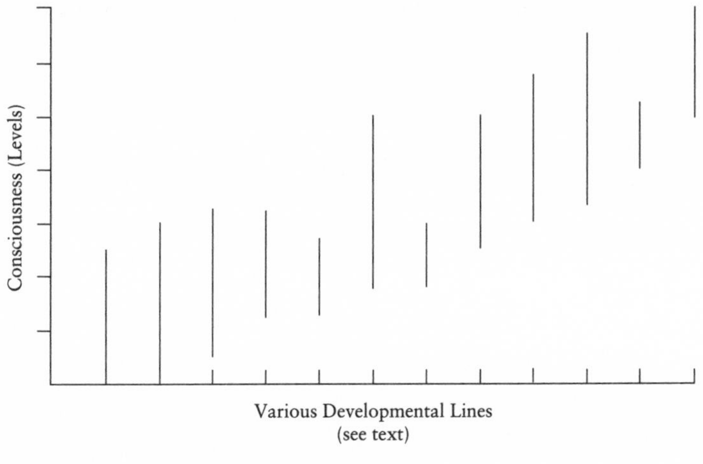

FIGURE 4

*[This is the wilber-3 model.]

†[I.e., wilber-3.]

herent whole is called the "self-system" (see Wilber, Engler & Brown, 1986). As for the consciousness scale (the *y*-axis), I often just number the levels, but sometimes I will affix names to each level that approximate the type of activity most characteristic of that level of consciousness (e.g., sensoriphysical, emotional-sexual, mental-egoic, existential, psychic, subtle, causal, and so on).

Finally, I usually condense figure 4 into something like figure 5, where the *y*-axis on figure 4 is now represented as a ladder-like symbol, and the various branches schematically indicate just a few of the developmental levels, through which the various lines run. This is the diagram that causes the term "ladder-like" to be used with my model, but I hope that it is now clear that an actual and simple ladder-like structure is not what I have in mind. Among other things, a simple ladder-like model overlooks regressions and spiraling or dialectical movements; it overlooks the fact that the higher does not "sit on" the lower but enfolds, envelops, and embraces the lower (as a cell embraces molecules and molecules embrace atoms); it overlooks involution; and, most important, it overlooks the quasi-independent nature of the various developmental lines.

Interestingly, I still used the circular diagram (similar to fig. 1) in both *Atman Project* and *Eden,* though I also added ascending spiral diagrams and tables. But I kept the circular (or U-turn) diagram because I still realized that there was indeed a U-turn in overall metaphysical develop-

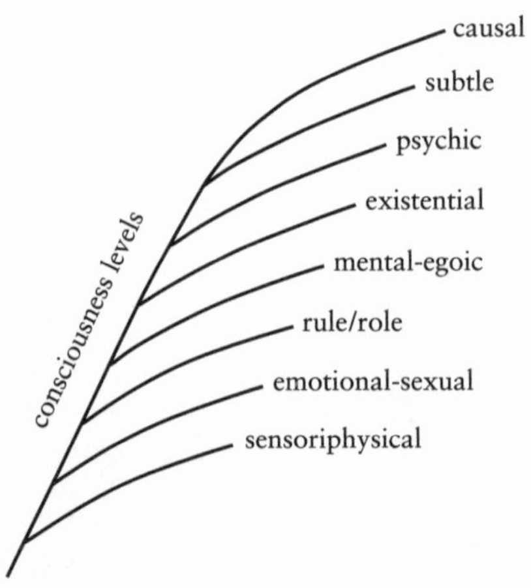

Figure 5

ment, but it did not occur where the Jungians imagined. And this was the key to the whole problem.

The idea itself is simple, but the semantics are somewhat confusing, so I will try to be as clear as I can. First, notice that I had gone from the model depicted in figure 1 to the model depicted in figures 2 and 3 (as well as figs. 4 and 5, but to make this presentation simpler, I will just use figs. 2 and 3). In figure 1, the U-turn model, the Outward Arc is marked by the emergence of the ego from the primal Ground. A U-turn then abruptly occurs right in the middle of development (at the top of the circle, marked *X*), and the self then eventually returns (or may return) to the primal Ground. A subtle version of this model is what Washburn presents. (Notice that in the ascending or evolutionary spectrum model, there is still an outward arc—the creation of an outwardly oriented ego—and an inward arc—the transcending of that ego. These are marked on figs. 2 and 3.)

Now, with reference to the evolutionary spectrum model (figs. 2 and 3): According to such representatives of the perennial philosophy as Aurobindo (n.d.), Coomaraswamy (1957), and Huston Smith (1976), prior to any evolution at all there must be a *prior* movement of *involution*. That is, before the higher stages can unfold from (or rather through) the lower, they must first be enfolded or "lost" in the lower. Before there can be ascent, there must be descent. This prior movement of the higher descending into the lower is termed "involution," and once involution has occurred, then the reverse process, that of evolution, can occur.

This can be depicted as in figure 6, where I have represented involution (or the enfolding of the higher in the lower) by the descending arc on the right side. This, incidentally, is virtually identical with the diagram I used to summarize the final spectrum model in *The Atman Project* (p. 187; CW2, p. 251). In figure 6, I have also added five of the most common levels of the Great Chain of Being taken from the perennial philosophy (matter, body, mind, soul, and spirit). The point is that in involution, the self moves from spirit to soul to mind to body to matter, where it appears, at birth, as basically just a body in a material world (although it comes, as Wordsworth said, "trailing clouds of glory"). The self is then ready to begin its return journey from material body to mind to soul to spirit (the evolutionary or developmental spiral).

This model, then, also has a U-turn, but it is not where the Washburn/

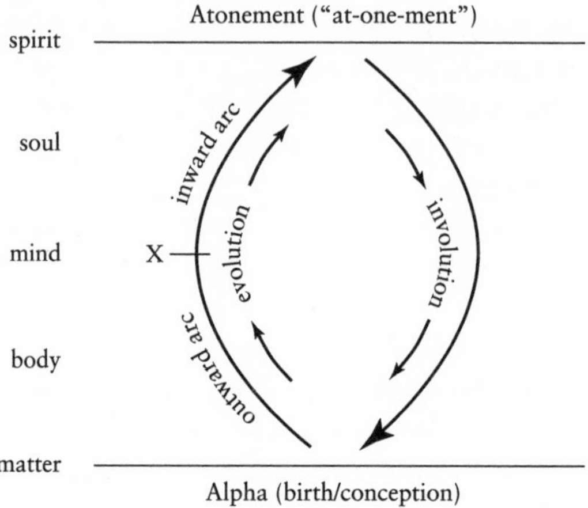

Figure 6

Jungian model imagines it. But before we go into that, it would help to look more carefully at the notion of involution itself.

Involution

In the perennial philosophy in general, involution has four distinct but closely related meanings. One is cosmological: Involution is the descent of spirit into matter, a process which creates the universe (during, say, the Big Bang), and from which evolution may then proceed. In this sense, involution simply means manifestation. It is not that matter (or manifestation in general) is separate from Spirit or even set against Spirit. Rather, matter is simply the densest form of Spirit, Spirit in its "otherness," or alienated Spirit (Hegel), an alienation or "sinful" state that evolution (or return to Spirit *as* Spirit) can reverse.

Two, involution can also mean the various stages of the afterlife state or Bardo, where the soul, having been immersed directly in Spirit, then begins to flee Spirit and descend into lower and denser realms, eventuating in isolated and alienated rebirth in a physical body, thus to be "born in sin." Again, it is not that matter or body is sinful; it is that matter and body perceived apart from Spirit is sinful, meaning fallen or alienated or not-realizing-Source. Incidentally, the involutionary steps from Spirit to mind to material body are exactly the three stages of the after-death Bardo described in *The Tibetan Book of the Dead* (Fremantle & Trungpa, 1975).

Three, involution means most directly the moment-to-moment creation of separation and isolation where there is in fact only radical union with Spirit. As I put it in *The Atman Project:* "In this moment and this moment and this, an individual *is* Buddha, is Atman, is the Dharmakaya—*but,* in this moment and this moment and this, he ends up as John Doe, as a separate self, as an isolated body apparently bounded by other isolated bodies. At the beginning of *this* and every moment, each individual *is* God as the Clear Light; but by the *end* of this same moment—in a flash, in the twinkling of an eye—he winds up as an isolated ego. This moment-to-moment phenomenon we call the microgenetic involution of the spectrum of consciousness" (p. 175).

Thus, involution is not something that merely or even especially occurred prior to birth or in some distant cosmological past. Involution is actually said to be occurring right now, in this moment, as we separate or alienate ourselves from Ground and Source. For moment to moment, we move away from Spirit, we involve, we descend; and thus we must *return* to Source and Self—we must grow and evolve to reverse this Fall. Thus, in Buddhism, the eight vijnanas (or levels of consciousness) involve out of the amala (Spirit), and simultaneously evolve back to the amala. The technique for "speeding up" this evolution, or the return to amala (Source), is simply meditation, which is said to proceed, of course, in a stage or hierarchical-developmental (or ascending spiral) sequence—since involution was a descending spiral (Brown, 1977; Brown & Engler, 1980).

Fourth and finally, involution has a simple tantric, yogic, or bodily meaning. When you inhale, it is said that you are literally breathing in Spirit (cosmic prana), from the crown of the head (and throat) to the lower abdomen and genital area. This is said to be a descent of Light (or spirit) into Life (or matter and body). This is involution. When you then exhale, the Life-energy (also known as kundalini) is said to flow up the back of the spine to the crown of the head and back to infinity. This is Life returned to Light, or the ascent of spirit from its slumbering state in matter and body (at the base of the spine) to its prior abode as pure spirit itself (beyond the crown). This ascent, of course, is evolution.

Three points about that. One, involution and evolution are connected very concretely to the body and its breathing. With every inhalation you are said to breathe spirit into your bodily being, where you feel separation and isolation; that is, with every in-breath you incarnate as a separate body, as a separate-self sense. But with every exhalation you release the separate-self sense back to infinity. This is an actual practice in many yogic and tantric texts, and it serves to remind us of the very concrete mechanics of separate existence, of involution and evolution.

Two, it serves to remind us that involution is not merely or even especially a "bad thing." Involution as in-breath is the way we bring Spirit into life, and animate it, and incarnate it in a joyful and expressive way. Descent (or involution) is "bad" only when it is disconnected from evolution (or ascent). In fact, when involution and evolution are cut off from each other, both are distorted. Ascent without descent is repression, or arid asceticism—earth-denying, sex-denying, life-denying. It tends to be patriarchal, sexist, and nature-destructive. Descent without ascent, on the other hand, is body-bound, orgiastic, impulsive; it is heaven-denying, and glorifies the earth and underworld with no connection to a Radiance beyond. It tends to be matriarchal, static, and anti-evolutionary. The point is that both of these movements are needed to balance the inadequacies and disharmonies of the other. Both ascent and descent have profound roles to play, when they are joined in harmonious union.

Three—and not surprisingly—descent is traditionally associated with the female Goddess, who brings Light down into Life and into the earth and into the body; and ascent is associated with the male God, who lifts Life up into Light and release and return. The in-breath is Goddess descending; the out-breath is God ascending. The whole point of Tantra is to unify God and Goddess in an unbroken circle of continuity and communion (*tantra* means "continuity"); ascent and descent in a divine marriage.

As a side point, let me say that those of my critics who have charged my "hierarchical-developmentalism" with patriarchal-sexism do so only by concentrating on the ascent side of the model and ignoring the descent side. This is understandable, since most Western psychological schools deal with developmental ascent, and since I am trying to integrate many of those schools, I have concentrated on the ascent. But that is only half of the overall model as I see it.

Comparison of the Two Models

Now compare the two models. Is one linear? Absolutely not. Both have U-turns. Washburn's major point is that the spectrum model cannot accommodate the U-turn, and therefore is flawed. All his "five crucial issues" hang on this one. But the spectrum model most definitely has the

U-turn, cosmologically, ontogenetically, and microgenetically (Washburn deals only with ontogeny).

I have marked a point *X* on both my model and Washburn/Jung's (see figs. 1 and 6). For Washburn, *X* is the U-turn, the point where he believes that development and evolution necessarily begin to regress back to lower levels. In my opinion, Washburn correctly understands that there must be some sort of U-turn (because we have indeed fallen from union with Spirit and must reverse that Fall). However, because Washburn seems to have no understanding of involution, he is forced to put the U-turn (point *X*) smack in the middle of the evolutionary arc, smack in the middle of ongoing development (instead of at its correct point, labeled "alpha" in figure 6). Nothing like what Washburn postulates—development abruptly reversing its stages in midcourse—even remotely happens to any other known evolutionary or developmental sequences. Indeed, according to modern dynamical theories of evolution, each growth stage is irreversible. It either continues to higher stages, remains as is, or totally breaks down. It does not start going backwards.

The actual reasons that I eventually found it impossible to place the U-turn at point *X* (and placed it instead at point alpha) are carefully outlined in an article published previously in the *Journal of Humanistic Psychology* (Wilber, 1982; the discussion of this particular topic alone occupied nine full pages) and in an essay entitled "The Pre/Trans Fallacy" (in Wilber, 1983). I shall not repeat those extensive arguments here.

Instead, let me just say that one of the main reasons that Washburn, the Romantics, and the Jungians place the U-turn at point *X* is that at point *X* the *feeling* of alienation is indeed the greatest. At pre-*X* (or pre-egoic) stages there is no *sense* of alienation, and at trans-*X* (or trans-egoic) stages there is no sense of alienation. On this both systems agree. But according to Washburn/Jung, there is no *actual* alienation at pre-*X* because the nascent ego is slumbering blissfully in the Ground, one with Self but in an unconscious fashion. For them, point *X* is the height of actual alienation as well as the height of sensing or actually feeling that alienation.

According to the spectrum view, there is actual alienation in the pre-*X* stages, but one is simply unaware of it. In fact, the pre-*X* stages, not the *X* stages, are the height of alienation from Spirit (or Spirit slumbering). As development occurs into the *X* or egoic stages, the person goes from subconscious to self-conscious, and thus the person awakens to his or her own alienation, an alienation that was ontologically present from birth. But *X* itself is not the height of *actual* alienation—point alpha is. *X* is simply the height of *being aware* of fundamental alienation (plus whatever existential angst stage X may contribute itself). *X* is not the height of the disease; it is in fact halfway through the cure (or the evolutionary spiral back to Spirit).

If my hand gets a severe case of frostbite, I cannot feel anything in it; only as my hand starts to thaw out does it begin to hurt. This pain does not occur at the height of the actual frostbite; rather, it occurs about halfway through the cure or "warming up." Or again: if my leg falls asleep, I feel nothing; but as it starts to wake up, it hurts like hell. Just so for the slumbering soul, the nascent soul that is asleep from birth and must "wake up." Point *X* is the point of starting to wake up (or "warm up"); it is not actual Hell, it just feels like it. But the Jungian/Washburn position confuses "hurts the most" with "is the worst"; that is, confuses the painful awareness of alienation (which occurs at point *X*) with fundamental or ontological alienation itself (which goes all the way back to point alpha).

In short, for Washburn, *X* is the height of actual alienation from Self and Ground; for me, it is halfway back toward Self and Ground (and, for the first time, painfully aware of its predicament). And this return is certainly not purchased by regression and retreat, but by continued growth and development (or "waking up").

This is not to say that regression cannot occur. It often does, and can be very valuable for growth. But it is not *mandatory* as a mechanism of growth. Regression is something that may happen to one degree or another at various times in development, but it is not the dynamic of development itself. Rather, to give only one example, according to modern evolutionary theory, the dynamic is that of self-regulation leading to higher-order holistic integrations—"self-development through self-transcendence" (Jantsch), not self-development through wholesale and mandatory reversal and regression.

Some Fine Points

That summarizes my major objection to the Jung/Washburn model. I would like now briefly to address several of Washburn's technical points. I will simply take them randomly.

1. Washburn states that the majority of the perennial traditions support the spectrum model, but that at least two major traditions—the

biblical and the hero's odyssey—support his model. According to the hero myths, the hero must first descend into the underworld, or confront his own "hell," before he can ascend (transformed) to the upperworld (or heaven). Washburn takes this "descent" as an example of his version of the U-turn, namely, a regression to origins before transformed ascent.

But here, I believe, Washburn misses the central point: The hero is not *regressing* to the underworld, because the hero *has never before been to the underworld.* You simply cannot return to that which you are now contacting for the first time; you cannot regress or return to a place you have never been before. When the hero encounters hell, he is doing so for the first time; he is therefore simply taking a step forward in his own development; he's not regressing (a regressed hero could not possibly handle hell).

Rather, the hero's odyssey is simply a mythic metaphor for the coming to terms with our own unrealized potentials, some of which are archaic and "lower," some of which are evolved and "higher." This encounter may involve a regression to aspects of the self that were repressed in early development, but regression is neither theoretically mandatory (since the dynamic of actual growth is irreversible structuralization) nor pragmatically always the case (most stages of growth—moral, cognitive, self—are *never* involved in wholesale regression to earlier states).

I am certainly not denying that the hero's odyssey—anyperson's odyssey—will face at times horrendous crises and literal hells. In fact, I have postulated that life/death crises occur (in varying degrees) at virtually *every* stage of growth and development, as the self dies to that stage and is reborn to the next. These crises can and do occur into even the highest stages of spiritual growth.

But Washburn talks as if there is just this one nice big "go-through-hell" U-turn, after which growth is sweetness and light. According to Washburn, Heaven cannot be reached until and unless Hell is gone through. Once Hell is negotiated, Heaven may be found ahead. For me, it is much more complex: *Each* stage of growth toward Heaven has its own potential Hell—and some of the higher or Heavenly battles are much more horrendous than the battles with the lower and relatively simple underworld. (I have chronicled, for example, nine major stages of growth, and pointed out very specifically the numerous pathologies or "hells" of each stage; see Wilber et al. [1986]).

2. As for the alleged biblical support of Washburn's model, I believe Washburn again misses the central point; according to all versions of

biblical (and subsequent theological) doctrine, the infant is *born* in sin. It is not, as Washburn believes, that the infant is born embedded in paradise (albeit unconscious) and *then* sins by separating from the primal Ground (at around 2 years of age). Washburn, again, wants to place the U-turn at some point in the middle of growth and evolution (point *X*), rather than at its beginning (point alpha) where it belongs, as all biblical doctrine clearly realizes.

In short, even these two traditions do not support Washburn's model of ontogenetic development, but are in fact consonant with my own version of growth and the placement of the U-turn.

Now I believe that Washburn wants to put the U-turn at point *X* instead of point alpha for a simple reason: To put the U-turn at point alpha (or conception) clearly implies that something came *before* point alpha and the U-turn. Implies, that is, *some* theory of consciousness (or the soul's) existence prior to birth. It implies metaphysics, not mere psychology or a merely psychologized spirituality. Notice, for Washburn, that life begins at birth and ends at death. He seems to want to confine the whole of spiritual consciousness to what transpires on the material plane, with this birth, in this life, and not face the issue of life after death, or, more generally, consciousness transcendent to (but inclusive of) matter. His version of spirituality, in other words, seems to me to be a very reductionistic, materialistic, empiricistic worldview; it wants to confine events to this gross dimension and to the simple curve of evolution, thus ignoring the entire issue of prior involution (or the genuinely subtler and causal dimensions of existence itself). And therefore, in my opinion, Washburn *must* put the U-turn somewhere in the course of events *during* evolution (since he has nowhere else to place it). Everything is thus confined to the events between bodily life and death. Consciousness and spirit prior to this manifest world (but not other to this manifest world) is thus entirely ignored by Washburn. In my opinion, then, Washburn's whole thrust is not, as he describes it, "a transpersonal theory of human development," but rather a humanistic reduction of transpersonal development.

3. Washburn (1990) states strongly that:

> Wilber's indictment of [Washburn's version of] the U-turn is based on an unproved and questionable assumption, namely, that pre-egoic and trans-egoic correlates are similar only in appearance. This assumption, after all, is precisely the point in dis-

> pute, and it is just this assumption that the spiral view rejects. The spiral view denies that pre-egoic and trans-egoic correlates have only illusory affinities . . . and advances the contrary position that these correlates are intimately related, indeed that they reflect the very same potentials at two different levels of expression.

But if this is so—if pre and trans are the same thing at two different levels (a strange notion itself)—it is true in no other area of development that we know. For example, preconventional and postconventional moral stages have virtually nothing in common; they are poles apart; they are most definitely *not* "the very same potentials at two different levels of expression." This would be like saying a Hell's Angel and Mahatma Gandhi are really doing the same thing from a different angle. Likewise, preoperational and postoperational (or formal operational) cognitions share virtually no potentials at all, any more than, say, preschool and graduate school are the same thing seen differently. And similarly in the development of object relations, motivation, ego development, and interpersonal relations, the pre stages and the trans (or post) stages have very little in common. The evidence for this is almost overwhelming, so it is rather hard for me see how Washburn states that this view is "unproved and questionable."

What is questionable, in my opinion, is Washburn's lumping the pre-egoic with the transegoic, calling that lump the "non-egoic ground," and then putting the ego at the height of alienation from this lump. This is the classic "pre/trans fallacy," which Washburn is otherwise so careful to avoid.

4. I believe that that particular pre/trans confusion rests in part on what seems to me to be Washburn's somewhat naive and romantic view of the actual state of the neonatal and infant self (or, generally, the self from birth to 18 months). For Washburn, the infant self is actually one with the Ground (or Self) and thus exists, according to Washburn (1988), in "a seamless and omni-inclusive whole." He describes this early infantile and pre-egoic state in amazingly glowing terms: "The power of the Ground pulsates through the infant's body in rising and expanding waves of bliss. This power continuously wells up and through the neonate's being, buoying it, lulling it, and rendering it felicitously content. The affective tone . . . is one of superabundant well-being." Washburn concludes by stating that "original embedment is a condition of unqualified unity and bliss . . . a state of at-one-ment."

That is clearly a highly romantic reading of the first few months of life. A more balanced view, and one much more consistent with modern research on child development, is that the neonatal self might occasionally feel ecstatic or blissful feelings, but it is also a highly fragmented, disjointed, and nonintegrated system, experiencing rage, fear, and pain as often as "superabundant well-being." The neonatal self is not a unified whole; the most we can deduce is that it is a fragmented system of rudimentary ego nuclei, ruled by reflex, physiological discharge, rudimentary affect and irritability (Chess & Thomas, 1985; Kagan, 1984; Stern, 1985; White, 1985).

I believe Washburn is forced to eulogize and elevate the status of this disjointed pre-egoic state for two simple reasons: (a) The transegoic state is, more or less, a unified whole which is often accompanied by feelings of bliss, fullness, and superabundance; and (b) Washburn believes that the transegoic state is a resurrection of a condition that was foreshadowed in the pre-egoic state. And *therefore* the pre-egoic state must be imbued with characteristics that are precusors to the transegoic state—hence his simple pre/trans fallacy, and hence his incredibly romantic reading of the newborn.

5. Washburn (1990) states: "The spiral paradigm agrees with the ladder paradigm in holding that full self-realization is a condition of higher unity. However, the spiral paradigm differs from the ladder paradigm in holding that this higher unity is one within which the individual self or ego remains present." This is a semantic squabble; it depends entirely upon how you define self or ego. If ego is defined as an exclusive identity with the individual bodymind, then a "higher unity" is not possible until that ego (or exclusive identity) is broken. This is why Washburn himself refers to the higher stages as transegoic. *That* ego must be dissolved. But if by ego you mean the functional and conventional personality that relates to conventional reality, then of course that ego remains in existence even as higher unitites are discovered. I have maintained that position consistently since my first book (Wilber, 1977), where I quoted Benoit in support: "It is not the ego but the exclusive identity with the ego that is the problem."

6. During my neo-Jungian days, I wrote a long essay (Wilber, 1979) that outlined the development of infantile sexuality and its relation to spirituality. Washburn has apparently studied it, as he referenced the anthology in which it appeared. Its main conclusion was that "God-consciousness is not sublimated sexuality; sexuality is repressed God-consciousness."

Now that view makes perfect sense if you place the U-turn at point *X* instead of at point alpha, which of course I did at the time. Since Washburn endorses what I believe is that same error, it is no surprise to find, ten years later, in Washburn's (1988) book: "Contrary to the Freudian position, then, according to which spirit is sublimated libido, the position that I am advancing is that libido is repressed spirit."

The problem with that view is that it unmistakably means that enlightened beings can have no libido or no sex, which is silly. Some, indeed, are ascetic in relation to the gross plane in general: they restrain their use of money, food, and sex in their desire for disciplined awareness. But that hardly means that they could not genitally function, period. In my opinion, this is yet another example of the pre/trans fallacy—in this case, the lumping of pregenital with transgenital and then confusing the two. Contra Washburn (and my own earlier model), libido is not repressed spirit; libido is simply the lowest *expression* of spirit, but an expression nonetheless (which is precisely why Tantra uses sexuality to climb back to spirituality, which it could never do if the one were merely the repression of the other). In other words, sexuality and spirituality are not mutually exclusive or even incompatible, which they would have to be if one were simply the repression of the other.

Conclusion

Washburn's original point was that there are two incompatible but coherent models of psychospiritual development, and that since they are in fact incompatible, then no truly unified theory of transcendence is possible. Central to Washburn's thesis is that the so-called "ladder model" contains no U-turn toward origins, whereas the Jungian/Washburn model does. Based on this central point, Washburn lists a half-dozen or so issues on which the two models disagree, but all these issues, both he and I agree, depend on the existence and placement of the U-turn.

I have pointed out that the "ladder model" most definitely has a U-turn toward origins, and has had one, in one form or another, from the very beginning. But I increasingly came to believe that the Jungian version of the U-turn (which Washburn represents) is profoundly incorrect, at odds not only with the perennial philosophy but also with the bulk of modern research on psychological development (and evolutionary and dynamic systems theory in general). I subsequently rejected that "regressive" view of evolution and replaced it with an involutionary/evolutionary paradigm, of descent and ascent, with the U-turn appearing, correctly I believe, between them (and not in the middle of evolution itself).

Be that as it may, the "ladder model" does indeed possess a very real U-turn, at which point Washburn's central objection collapses, along with the essentials of his corollary points. It is my belief that the involutionary/evolutionary paradigm thus encompasses the essential truths of the Jungian/Washburn paradigm, but rejects what I believe are various errors and misinterpretations and pre/trans fallacies. And, as Washburn admits, the involutionary/evolutionary paradigm has the added advantage of being supported in most essential respects by both the majority of the perennial traditions and the bulk of modern psychological developmental theory.

And finally, since I believe the Jungian/Washburn model is wrong in certain central points (such as the placement of the U-turn), there is no need to try to incorporate or integrate those apparent errors into a unified theory of transcendence; rather, we simply reject them (just as the Ptolemaic system is not integrated in modern astronomy, but jettisoned). If we reject the Jungian/Washburn errors while incorporating the accurate and important points of that model, I believe a unified theory of psychospiritual growth and transcendence is indeed possible, and that the involutionary/evolutionary model—which does attempt to incorporate the accurate elements of Jungian theory—is a step in that right direction.

References

Aurobindo, Sri (n.d.). *The life divine.* Pondicherry, India: Centenary Library.

Brown, D. (1977). A model for the levels of concentrative meditation. *International Journal of Clinical and Experimental Hypnosis, 25,* 236–73.

Brown, D. P., and Engler, J. (1980). The stages of mindfulness meditation: A validation study. *Journal of Transpersonal Psychology* 12: 143–92.

Chess, S., & Thomas, A. (eds.). (1985). *Annual progress in child psychiatry and child development 1984.* New York: Brunner/Mazel.

Coomaraswamy, A. K. (1957). *The dance of Shiva.* New York: Noonday.

Edinger, E. F. (1972). *Ego and archetype.* Baltimore: Penguin.

Fremantle, F., and Trungpa, C. (1975). *The Tibetan book of the dead.* Berkeley, Calif.: Shambhala Publications.

Freud, A. (1963). The concept of developmental lines. *Psychoanalytic Study of the Child* 8: 245–65.

Kagan, J. (1984). *The nature of the child.* New York: Basic Books.
Kohlberg, L. (1981). *Essays on moral development,* vol. 1. San Francisco: Harper & Row.
Loevinger, J. (1976). *Ego development.* San Francisco: Jossey-Bass.
McNamara, W. (1981). *Christian mysticism.* Warwick, N.Y.: Amity House.
Reynolds, J. (1989). *Self-liberation through seeing with naked awareness.* Barrytown, N.Y.: Station Hill.
Samuels, A. (1985). *Jung and the post-Jungians.* London: Routledge & Kegan Paul.
Selman, R. (1971). The relation of role-taking to the development of moral judgment in children. *Child Development* 42: 79–92.
Smith, H. (1976). *Forgotten truth.* New York: Harper.
Stern, D. N. (1985). *The interpersonal world of the infant.* New York: Basic Books.
Washburn, M. (1988). *The ego and the dynamic ground.* Albany: SUNY Press.
———. (1990). Two patterns of transcendence. *Journal of Humanistic Psychology* 30 (3).
White, B. L. (1985). *The first three years of life.* New York: Prentice-Hall.
Wilber, K. (1979). Are the chakras real? In J. White (ed.), *Kundalini, evolution and enlightenment.* New York: Doubleday Anchor. Also in *The Collected Works of Ken Wilber* (CW), vol. 1.
———. (1980). *The Atman project.* Wheaton, Ill.: Quest Books. CW2.
———. (1981). *Up from Eden.* New York: Doubleday Anchor. CW2.
———. (1982). Odyssey: A personal inquiry into humanistic and trans-personal psychology. *Journal of Humanistic Psychology,* 22 (1): 57–90. CW2.
———. (1983). *Eye to eye.* New York: Doubleday Anchor. CW3.
Wilber, K., Engler, J., and Brown, D. P. (1986). *Transformations of consciousness.* Boston: Shambhala Publications.

from

TRANSFORMATIONS OF CONSCIOUSNESS

Introduction

KEN WILBER, JACK ENGLER,
AND DANIEL P. BROWN

THE CENTRAL THEME of *Transformations of Consciousness* is that the time is now ripe for what Engler and Wilber have called a "full-spectrum model" of human growth and development, a model that includes the psychodynamic, object-relational, and cognitive lines studied by conventional psychology and psychiatry, but also takes into serious account the "higher" or "subtler" lines and stages embodied in the world's great contemplative and meditative disciplines.

Taken together, these various approaches—conventional and contemplative—seem to point to a general, universal, and cross-cultural spectrum of human development, consisting of various developmental lines and stages that, however otherwise different their specific cultural or surface features might appear, nevertheless share certain recognizable similarities or deep features. Further, the different stages of this developmental spectrum are apparently vulnerable to qualitatively distinct psychopathologies, which in turn yield to qualitatively different treatment modalities (or therapies in general).

Those three topics—the various stages of development (conventional and contemplative), the corresponding levels of possible pathology or dis-ease, and the correlative or appropriate therapeutic interventions—are the central concerns of this volume. Jack Engler is speaking for all of the authors when he states: "My hope is that as Buddhist, Western, and other ethnopsychiatric systems of clinical practice confront one another in our culture, often for the first time, a more integrated, full-spectrum model of human development, its vulnerabilities and the therapeutic interventions necessary to repair them, may result."

Conventional and Contemplative Schools of Development

The *stage model* is one of the most widely used tools in Western psychology. Although different theorists define it in slightly different ways, most would agree with the following summary by Thomas McCarthy (1978):

> [The stage model specifies] an invariant sequence of discrete and increasingly complex developmental stages, whereby no stage can be passed over and each higher stage implies or presupposes the previous stages. This does not exclude regressions, overlaps, arrested developments, and the like. Stages are constructed wholes that differ qualitatively from one another; phase-specific schematic can be ordered in an invariant and hierarchically structured sequence; no later phase can be [stably] attained before earlier ones have been passed through, and elements of earlier phases are preserved, transformed, and reintegrated in the later. In short, the developmental-logical approach requires the specification of a hierarchy of structural wholes in which the later, more complex, and more encompassing developmental stages presuppose and build upon the earlier.

This type of developmental-stage approach has been fruitfully applied to psychosexual, cognitive, ego, moral, affective, object-relational, kinesthetic, and linguistic lines of development—in short, virtually the entire gamut of development studied by conventional psychology and psychiatry (all of which, for convenience, we will call "typical" or "conventional" development).

Further, most of these conventional stage-models have claimed to be largely invariant, cross-cultural, and "quasi-universal" (Habermas, 1976). Thus, for example, in psychosexual development, no culture has been found where phallic development precedes oral; in cognitive development, images universally precede symbols, which precede concepts, which precede rules; and in moral development, preconventional orientations always appear to precede conventional and then postconventional modes. However much the fine points of these various models might be argued (the specific issues are far from settled), it is generally acknowledged that most of the stage-models presented by conventional psychology and psychiatry claim to be invariant and cross-cultural (in a general fashion); and, within broad limits, most of them have adduced enough evidence to make their claims plausible. As we will see below, to claim that a particular *sequence* of stages is genuinely invariant *is* to claim that it is cross-cultural: despite the vast differences in the surface features of the stages, the deep features are essentially similar—this is the claim of most conventional developmental-stage models.

What is not often realized, however, is that the same type of developmental-stage approach is exemplified in the world's great contemplative and meditative disciplines. As Brown and Engler carefully point out, "The major [contemplative] traditions we have studied in their original languages present an unfolding of meditation experiences in terms of a *stage model:* for example, the *Mahamudra* from the Tibetan Mahayana Buddhist tradition; the *Visuddhimaggi* from the Pali Theravada Buddhist tradition; and the *Yoga Sutras* from the Sanskrit Hindu tradition. *The models are sufficiently similar to suggest an underlying common invariant sequence of stages, despite vast cultural and linguistic differences as well as styles of practice.*"

We seem to be faced, then, with two broad ranges or classes of development, which we have loosely called "conventional" and "contemplative"; both contain various strands or lines that are, in part, amenable to a stage conception; and both claim a general, universal, and cross-cultural validity. The question then remains, how are these two classes related, if at all? Are they different descriptions of similar developmental sequences? Do they describe parallel lines of development? Do they refer to different lines, or even levels, of development altogether? Are they related along a general continuum? If so, where does typical development stop and contemplative development begin? Indeed, can the contemplative stages be considered real in any objective-empirical sense, or are they merely idiosyncratic and subjective belief-systems? In short, how are these classes related, if at all?

One of the ways of approaching this difficult topic is to search among the texts of the contemplative schools for any that, in addition to describing the strictly contemplative stages of development, also attempt to situate these stages vis-à-vis normal or typical (or noncontemplative) development. This would give us a broad scale of reference that might indicate how the two ranges—conventional and contemplative—might be related.

Take, for example, the works of Aurobindo, perhaps India's greatest modern philosopher-sage. Aurobindo has described the overall life cycle as including the following major stages (brief explanations appear in parentheses):

1. Sensorimotor (physical, sensory; and locomotive aspects)
2. Vital-emotional-sexual ("prana"; roughly, libido or bioenergy)
3. Will-mind (simple representational and intentional thought)
4. Sense-mind (thought operations performed on sensory or concrete objects)
5. Reasoning mind (thought operations performed on abstract objects)
6. Higher mind (synthetic-integrative thought operations, "seeing truth as a whole")
7. Illumined mind (transcends thought and "sees truth at a glance"; psychic or inner illumination and vision)
8. Intuitive mind (transcendental-archetypal awareness; "subtle cognition and perception")
9. Overmind (unobstructed, unbounded spiritual awareness)
10. Supermind (absolute identity with and as spirit; this is not really a separate level, but the "ground" of all levels)

Notice that Aurobindo's first six stages clearly seem similar to some of the stages investigated by conventional psychology and psychiatry. In particular, if one examines Aurobindo's meticulous descriptions of these first six stages, one finds that they bear striking and detailed resemblances to aspects of the works of Piaget, Loevinger, and Kohlberg (see "The Spectrum of Development," pages 80–116 of this volume, for a brief summary of these comparisons). Almost all conventional stage-models, however, stop somewhere around Aurobindo's stage 6; not many give accounts of developmental stages beyond that point (though few deny their possible existence).

On the other hand, the stages described in contemplative texts are demonstrably similar to Aurobindo's higher stages, 7 through 10. Moreover, Aurobindo's version of overall development gives a smooth account of the transitions between all the stages; there is no feeling of an abrupt rupture between the typical or normal stages (1–6) and the contemplative or transpersonal stages (7–10). Rather, one gets the impression that development, if not fixated or arrested, can proceed rather naturally into the higher or contemplative stages, each of which is marked by a refinement and enhancement of cognitive, volitional, and perceptual capacities. The point is that because Aurobindo has attempted to describe both the "lower-intermediate" stages of development (typically investigated in greater detail by conventional psychology) and the "higher" stages (of meditative development), such a scheme may be used to help tentatively situate the various developmental stages described by conventional and contemplative schools.

Although this is by no means the only way to "fit together" the conventional and contemplative schools, it does seem to be one of the simplest and most appealing. As Engler and Wilber have both pointed out, the contemplative stages of development are probably not parallel (or alternative) to the normal, typical, or conventional stages of development, but rather refer to different and higher stages of development altogether (although this by no means precludes very complex interactions between the two; a rigidly linear and unidirectional model is not at all what we have in mind). This interpretation, at any rate, is corroborated by such "overview models" as Aurobindo's.

Other such general overview models can be found in Kabbalah, Da Free John, Gurdjieff, Sufism, certain Christian contemplative schools, and aspects of Vajrayana and Vedanta. It should be emphasized, however, that these models give us little more than rather crude skeletal outlines. In particular, when these models describe the lower stages of development, they are almost totally lacking in a knowledge of object-relations, self-development, and psychodynamics, which so decisively define these stages and have been so intensively studied by conventional psychology and psychiatry.

One of the aims of *Transformations of Consciousness* is to begin to flesh out this skeleton by bringing together, for the first time, both of these major schools of development—conventional and contemplative. For if it is true that the conventional schools have much to learn from the contemplative schools (especially about possibly higher development), it is equally true—and, we believe, as urgent—that the contemplative schools surrender their isolation and apparent self-sufficiency and open themselves to the vital and important lessons of contemporary psychology and psychiatry.

The Nature and Meaning of "Stages," Higher and Lower

It might be appropriate, at this point, to briefly discuss the meaning of the word "stage," as used by both conventional and contemplative schools. One of the most obvious features of the various stage-models in both traditions is that, even when they purport to describe the same developmental line, they often report different numbers of stages in that line. For example, the level of general development that Aurobindo simply calls "the intuitive mind" actually contains, according to some traditions, anywhere from three to seven discrete levels. Are these levels actually discrete? That is, do they actually exist as quasi-universal deep structures, or are they merely tradition-bound, idiosyncratic, or culturally-generated surface structures? Just how many levels of contemplative development are there?

Brown and Engler have begun to answer this question by generating a "master template" culled from various contemplative traditions (Theravada, Mahayana, Hindu, Christian, and Chinese). In chapter 8 [of *Transformations*] Brown summarizes this template, which contains six major stages, each divided into three substages, for a total of eighteen. As of this writing, [1986] it appears that most of these are in fact quasi-universal deep structures, not merely idiosyncratic surface structures. But at this point we do not have enough information to decide in *all* cases, and thus the decisions on these types of issues (how to divide or subdivide stages) are somewhat arbitrary, although that does not render them the less useful: the stage-model claim is simply that, in any developmental sequence, certain classes of behavior stably emerge only after certain other classes; and if some of those classes are eventually found to contain other discrete classes, then we have simply enriched our understanding of the sequence, not denied it.

Thus, for example, Jane Loevinger initially postulated four stages of ego development. Refined research subsequently led her to conclude that there are at least ten stages. Likewise, if someone discovered a basic cognitive stage between symbols and concepts, it still would not alter the fact that symbols emerge before concepts, and concepts emerge only after symbols—and it is that relative "before" and "after" that constitutes one of the central claims of developmental theories (i.e., if the before and after relation of class r and class z can be demonstrated to be cross-culturally invariant, then we are justified in suspecting that, at some level of analysis, there are quasi-universal deep structures involved, regardless of how many classes may or may not subsequently be found in between them). Conversely, subsequent research might indicate that what we had previously thought to be two discrete stages are actually variations on one stage, with a broader deep structure, that alone stands up to cross-cultural scrutiny. But it is exactly these kinds of concerns that introduce a modicum of arbitrariness into any stage-model. The models presented in this volume are no exception.

Traditionally, developmentalists have used several criteria for establishing that a particular behavioral array has, at its base, a quasi-universal deep structure. The most common is that "Stages may be viewed as existing in some objective sense to the extent that the behaviors associated with them emerge in an order that cannot be altered by environmental factors" (Brainerd, 1978). That various classes of phenomena emerge in an order that cannot be altered by environmental factors *is* to say that those classes possess an invariant (quasi-universal) structure, or else their sequence *could* be altered by contingent factors; that is, invariant sequence means quasi-universal class structures are involved at some level, or the sequence would not and could not be invariant. Wobble in the structure would mean wobble in the sequence (which is precisely a definition of surface structure).

On the other hand, virtually all developmentalists acknowledge that "decisions about how to slice up the stream of behavioral change are based on external criteria such as economy and elegance. Hence, there might be *several different models that could be posited, all of which would be equally valid descriptions of change in the organism*" (Brainerd, 1978). (Again, the models in this volume are no exception.) However, this does not negate the possible quasi-universal nature of the different stage-models; it simply says that, if you slice the stream from this particular angle, you will always see the same basic phenomena, in the same order, wherever the stream appears. Likewise, researchers usually agree that there are no precise demarcation lines between stages. The situation appears more like a rainbow, with each color shading into the others, which nevertheless does not prevent us from recognizing that orange is different from blue.

Finally, most developmentalists acknowledge that the task of stage definition is a process whereby "We select certain instants in the course of dynamic change, take 'snapshots' of the system at those instants, and use those snapshots as descriptions of the system at a particular stage of development" (Simon, 1962). Different series of snapshots are obviously possible, and each series usually yields significant information; but if the shots effectively "catch" a deep structure, the order between the phenomena in those shots will be invariant, and vice versa: we have a "stage."

The Plan of the Book

All of the authors of the chapters in *Transformations of Consciousness* present various stage conceptions, some of contemplative development

(Brown; Brown and Engler; Chirban), some of conventional as well as contemplative development (Engler; Epstein and Lieff; Wilber). It would be useful, then, if we could introduce some very general terminology that would help situate the various authors in relation to each other. Since we have already introduced Aurobindo's simple "overview" model, we can use that, and attach our general terminology to it, as shown in table 1. Here we have introduced three broad ranges of overall development (prepersonal, personal, and transpersonal), each divided, for convenience, into three stages. With this rough map, we can now explain the outline and basic themes of this volume. While individual authors may differ on specific points (most of which will become obvious upon reading their particular chapters), all share a general consensus.

One of the central themes of this book is that different stages of development are vulnerable to qualitatively distinct psychopathologies. Even using Aurobindo's crude map ("crude" because it does not take into account the different lines of development among the various stages), we might expect to find, correlative with nine general stages of development, nine general levels of possible pathology (Aurobindo himself suggested such). In chapter 1, Jack Engler opens this discussion by keying on the three general levels of prepersonal object-relations development and their corresponding levels of psychopathology: psychotic, borderline, and psychoneurotic. These levels are all loosely referred to as "pre-

Table 1
Comparison of General Terminology of Developmental Stages

Aurobindo's Overview	*General Terminology*	
1. Sensorimotor		prepersonal
2. Vital-emotional		stages
3. Will-mind	typical or	
	conventional	
4. Sense-mind	development	personal
5. Reasoning-mind		stages
6. Higher-mind		
7. Illumined-mind	contemplative	transpersonal
8. Intuitive-mind	development	stages
9. Overmind		

personal" because this range of development involves the stages leading up to the emergence of a rational-individuated-personal selfhood. Summarizing the relevant data from conventional psychiatric research, Engler points out that because these are developmentally distinct levels of psychopathology, they typically respond to different types of therapeutic intervention (psychotic and borderline: structure-building techniques; psychoneurotic: uncovering techniques). Engler then carefully distinguishes these psychopathologies from another qualitatively and developmentally distinct class, those we have called contemplative or transpersonal, pointing out that what conventional approaches consider normalcy (a fully differentiated-integrated ego structure) is actually, from this broader view, a case of developmental arrest (if development proceeds no further).

Engler's central message is significant and timely: meditative disciplines effect a transcendence of the normal separate-self sense, but the developmental prerequisite for this is a strong, mature, well-differentiated psyche and a well-integrated self-structure with a sense of cohesiveness, continuity, and identity. Engler points out some of the severe psychiatric complications that can occur when individuals with significant prepersonal developmental arrests engage in transpersonal or contemplative practices. In fact, Engler notes, such individuals may actually be drawn to contemplative practices as a way to rationalize their inner sense of emptiness, poorly differentiated self and object representations, and lack of self-cohesion.

In chapter 2, Mark Epstein and Jonathan Lieff continue this developmental line of analysis by examining the three broad stages of contemplative or transpersonal development and pointing out that each of these stages may evidence its own particular type of psychopathology. As they put it, "Meditation may be conceptualized as a developmental process that may produce side effects anywhere along the continuum. Some of these side effects may be pathological in nature while some may be temporary distractions or hindrances." The three broad classes or levels of pathology that they report involve vulnerabilities at (1) the stage of preliminary practices; (2) access stage; and (3) advanced stage (samadhi and insight). This cartography is simple and concise, and offers an immediately useful, if general, classification.

Wilber's presentation occupies chapters 3–5 and serves, in a sense, as a bridge between Engler's and Epstein and Lieff's. He discusses the three general levels of prepersonal pathology noted by Engler (psychotic, borderline, and psychoneurotic), the three general levels of transpersonal pathology noted by Epstein and Lieff (which Wilber calls psychic, subtle, and causal), and then suggests three general classes of pathology intermediate between them (which he calls cognitive-script, identity, and existential). This results in nine general levels (not lines) of overall development, with nine corresponding levels of potential psychopathology. Wilber then provides a preliminary discussion of the types of therapeutic interventions that seem most appropriate for each of these levels of pathology. He prefaces all of this with a chapter summarizing his own spectrum model and the relevant research in conventional psychology and psychiatry.

In the remaining chapters, contemplative development moves to the foreground. In chapters 6 and 7, Brown and Engler present a validation study on the stages of meditation using the Rorschach. The results have significant and far-reaching implications: "In each of the criterion groups," they report, "there are unique qualitative features in the Rorschachs which are distinctly different from those of the other groups. This finding in itself suggests that there are indeed different stages of meditation practice. Even more interesting is the fact that the specific qualitative features of the Rorschachs for each group are consistent with the classical descriptions of the psychological changes most characteristic of that stage of practice. Such convergence of the Rorschach qualitative features on the one hand, and the classical descriptions on the other, may be an important step toward establishing the cross-cultural validation of the psychological changes at each major stage of the practice." Further, Brown and Engler point out, "These Rorschachs illustrate that the classical subjective reports of meditation stages are more than religious belief systems; they are valid accounts of the cognitive-perceptual and affective changes that occur with intensive meditation. . . ."

In chapter 8, Brown zeroes in on the meditative stages themselves, and gives perhaps the most complete, detailed, and sophisticated cartography of contemplative development yet to appear. This cartography was culled from an intensive study of Theravada, Mahayana, and Yogic texts (and later checked against other contemplative traditions, Christian, Chinese, etc.). Although Brown's contemplative cartography is essentially similar to models such as Wilber's (e.g., in *System, Self, and Structure,* Wilber, like Brown, gives six major contemplative stages, each with three substages), Brown's model has manifold advantages: it is based on the canonical languages, direct study and translation of the central texts, and extensive interviews with teachers and practitioners.

As such, this cartography easily establishes itself as a standard in the field.

With the exception of Wilber's presentation, most of the chapters in this volume deal with Eastern—and usually Buddhist—contemplative disciplines. We have every reason to believe, however, that the major contemplative stages (and their corresponding vulnerabilities) are of cross-cultural and quasi-universal applicability. Indeed, Brown and Wilber have elsewhere written extensively on this topic (see, for example, Wilber, 1981b). In chapter 9, therefore, Harvard clinical psychologist and theologian John Chirban turns his attention to the stages of contemplative development as evidenced and described by some of the outstanding saints of Christianity. His conclusion: "Although each saint described his own experience (often in his own unique way), basic parallels emerge as one compares the stages of the saints with one another. This sameness confirms the catholicity of their experience. . . . Five stages can be identified which are basically consistent amongst all ten saints." These stages are quite similar to those of Brown and Wilber, giving added credence to the catholicity of contemplative development. We placed this chapter last as an invitation to *all* meditative traditions—as well as the different psychological and psychiatric disciplines—to join us in this mutually enriching dialogue between conventional and contemplative schools, aimed at the creation of a more integrated, full-spectrum model of human growth and development.

Chapter Introductions and Tables

Chapter 1, "Therapeutic Aims in Psychotherapy and Meditation: Developmental Stages in the Representation of Self," by Jack Engler

In the Introduction, we suggested three broad ranges of development—prepersonal, personal, and transpersonal—each divided, for convenience, into three stages. In this chapter, Jack Engler focuses on the three general stages of object-relations development in the prepersonal realm, and the corresponding types of psychopathology—psychotic, borderline, and psychoneurotic—that may result due to developmental arrests or failures at a particular stage. He then carefully distinguishes this entire range of development from the contemplative or transpersonal stages. He sees two great arcs of human development: one leading up to a personal, substantially individuated self-sense, and one leading beyond it. His conclusion is simple but profound: You have to be somebody before you can be nobody.

Chapter 2, "Psychiatric Complications of Meditation Practice," by Mark D. Epstein and Jonathan D. Lieff

In this chapter, our simple division of the transpersonal realm into three broad stages is fleshed out and refined by Mark Epstein and Jonathan Lieff. They point out that the three general stages of transpersonal or contemplative development—preliminary, intermediate, and advanced—may each be vulnerable to particular types of psychiatric complications. Their classification is simple and concise, and is of immediate help in beginning to sort out the difficult issues that are raised once one starts examining the full spectrum of human development.

Chapter 3, "The Spectrum of Development," by Ken Wilber (renumbered as chapter 1 for this volume; see pages 80–116).

Chapter 4, "The Spectrum of Psychopathology," by Ken Wilber (renumbered here as chapter 2; see pages 117–133)

Chapter 5, "Treatment Modalities," by Ken Wilber (renumbered here as chapter 3; see pages 134–160)

Chapter 6, "The Stages of Mindfulness Meditation: A Validation Study" (Part 1: Study and Results) by Daniel P. Brown and Jack Engler

The traditional accounts of the stages of meditation have often presented a problem with regard to their status as "objective" realities. Do these stages have a general cross-cultural validity, or are they merely subjective belief systems or expectation results? The task of the research reported in this chapter is, as Brown and Engler put it, "to determine just what sort of validity these textual accounts have."

In this chapter, Brown and Engler present the study itself and its results, a study that included intensive interviews with practitioners and teachers, a quantitative measure they developed and titled "A Profile of Meditative Experience" (POME), and the Rorschach. Although the Rorschach was originally used as a personality measure, Brown and Engler found that "practitioners at different levels of the practice gave records that looked very distinct. In fact, the Rorschach records seemed to correlate with particular stages of meditation. Common features were more outstanding than individual differences at each level of practice." Using the Rorschach as a measure of cognitive and perceptual change, Brown and Engler found that "the specific qualitative features of the Rorschachs for each group are consistent with the classical descriptions of the psychological changes most characteristic of that stage of practice. Such convergence of the Rorschach qualitative features on the one hand, and the classical descriptions [of the stages of meditation] on the other, may be an important step toward establishing the cross-cultural validation of the psychological changes at each major stage of the practice." In chapter 6, Brown and Engler present a detailed discussion of the meanings of these results.

Chapter 7, "The Stages of Mindfulness Meditation: A Validation Study" (Part 2: Discussion), by Daniel P. Brown and Jack Engler

In the previous chapter, Brown and Engler presented the results of a Rorschach validation study of the stages of mindfulness meditation. In this chapter they discuss the meanings and implications of those results.

Their conclusion: "These Rorschachs illustrate that the classical subjective reports of meditation stages are more than religious belief systems; they are valid accounts of the perceptual changes that occur with intensive meditation. . . ." Brown and Engler conclude the study with some reflection on the relationship between meditation and therapeutic change.

Chapter 8, "The Stages of Meditation in Cross-Cultural Perspective," by Daniel P. Brown

Controversy over "the stages of meditation" has usually centered on two questions: (1) whether these stages may be said to exist in any objective fashion (i.e., possess external validity); and (2), if these stages do possess external validity, to what extent are they cross-cultural or quasi-universal?

In chapters 6 and 7, Brown and Engler presented substantial evidence that the stages of meditation are in fact "real"—that is, they seem to represent demonstrable cognitive, perceptual, and affective changes that follow a developmental-stage model.

In chapter 8, Daniel Brown addresses the second question by presenting an in-depth cartography of meditative stages drawn from three different traditions—the Tibetan Mahamudra, the Hindu Yoga Sutras, and the Theravada Vipassana (this cartography was subsequently cross-checked with other contemplative texts, Christian, Chinese, etc.). The results strongly suggest that the stages of meditation are in fact of cross-cultural and universal applicability (at a deep, not surface, analysis).

Not only does this cartography tend to support the more literary claims of a "transcendent unity of religions," it goes a long way toward helping to resolve some of the central conflicts between "theistic" and "nontheistic" approaches to contemplation (e.g., Hindu versus Buddhist). By cutting his analysis at a sufficiently deep level, Brown is able to demonstrate "how a Hindu and Buddhist meditator progress through the same eighteen stages of meditation and yet have different experiences along the stages because of the different perspectives which are taken. Since perspectivism is unavoidable in meditation, as in any other mode of inquiry, each of the descriptions of meditation experience in the respective traditions is valid, though different." The perspective, however, has an influence on the outcome of the progression of experiences: while the path of meditation stages is similar across cultures, the experience of the outcome, enlightenment, is not. In this sense, Brown's conclusion is the opposite of stereotypical notions of mystical experience that perennial philosophers have usually meant by the "transcendent unity of religions": there are many paths to the same end. Brown's in-depth analysis of meditation experiences suggests the opposite: there is one path which leads to different ends, different enlightenment experiences.

[See the tables on pages 64–75 for Brown's summary of the meditative stages in three major contemplative traditions.]

STAGE I. PRELIMINARY ETHICAL PRACTICES

Underlying Structure	*Mahāmudrā*	*Visuddhimagga*	*Yogasūtras*	*Psychology*
Faith	Causing Faith to Arise (*dad pa'i 'don pa*) Awakening Recognition			self-efficacy
I.A. Attitude Change	ORDINARY PRELIMINARIES Opportunity Impermanence/Death Cause/Effect Sufferings of Saṃsāra			attitude change reactance perceived control
I.B. Intrapsychic Change Turning Inward	EXTRAORDINARY PRELIMINARIES Refuge Vow		OBSERVANCES (*niyama*) Going into Onself (*svādhyāyāḥ*, 2:32)	
Fostering Outcome Expectations	Enlightened Attitude which Desires		Establishing a Connection (*samprayogaḥ*)	expectation effects
Study/Reflection	Enlightened Attitude which Perseveres		Practice (*abhyāsa*)	
Transformation of the Stream of Consciousness	Mental Factors		Removing Doubt (*vitarkābandhane*)	objective self-awareness of:

Eradication of Negative States	Confession/rDorje Sems 'pa Meditation		Cleansing (*shaucha*)	negative affective states
Cultivation of Positive States	Offerings/Mandala Offering		Contentment (*saṃtoṣa*)	positive affective states
Transformation of Cognitions in Stream	Guru Yoga		Identification with Ishvara (*Ishvarapranidhanani*)	cognitions
I.C. Behavioral Change	ADVANCED PRELIMINARIES		RESTRAINTS (*yamas*)	behavioral therapy
Regulation of Life-Style and Social Behavior	Virtue-Practice	PRECEPTS (*śīla*) 13 Ascetic Practices (*dhutanganiddesa*)	Five Restraints	
Restriction of Sensory Input	Binding-Senses		Subjugation of Body/Mind (*tapas*)	environmental/milieu therapy
Awareness Training	Recollection/Total Awareness			absorption/flow

Stage II. Preliminary Body and Mind Training

Underlying Structure	*Mahāmudrā*	*Visuddhimagga*	*Yogasūtras*	*Psychology*
	THREE ISOLATIONS			
II.A. Body Awareness Training	ISOLATION OF THE BODY (*lus dben*)		POSTURES (*āsana,* 2:46–53)	regulation of muscle output
II.B. Calming the Breath and Thinking	ISOLATION OF SPEECH (*ngag dben*)		BREATH-CONTROL (*prāṇāyāma,* 2:49–53)	voluntary control of breathing rhythm; reduction of thinking
II.C. Rearrangement of the Stream of Consciousness	ISOLATION OF THE MIND (*sems dben*)		SENSE-WITHDRAWAL (*pratyahāra,* 2:54–55)	increased reality-distance
Deconstruction of Thinking				deautomatization of thinking

Stage III. Concentration With Support

Underlying Structure	*Mahāmudrā*	*Visuddhimagga*	*Yogasūtras*	*Psychology*
III.A.1. Effortful Concentration on external object	CONCENTRATION IN FRONT (*mngon du*)	BEGINNER'S SIGN (*parikammanimitta* 4:22)	CONCENTRATION (external) (*dhāraṇā traṭākam*) (3:1)	categorizing

III.A.2. Maintaining Effortless Concentration on internal object	CONCENTRATION INSIDE (*nang du*) visualization of the Body of the Tathāgatā	EIDETIC SIGN (*uggahanimitta* 4:30)	CONCENTRATION (internal) (*dhāraṇā cakra*) (3:1) visualization of the deity, Hari	object constancy
III.B. Relaxed Recognition of changing internal events of the seed	SKILL (*rtsal*) Recognition (*ngo shes*) of the various (*sna tshogs*) discontinuous events of the emanating seed (*'char ba'i thig le*)	LIKENESS SIGN (*paṭibhāganimitta* 4:31)	CONTEMPLATION (*dhyāna*) (3:2) Recognition (*pratyāya*) of continuous transformation (*vṛtti*) of same continuum (*ekātanatā*) of seed (*biṇdu*)	pattern recognition
III.C. Stopping Gross Perception	BEING DONE WITH (*zad pa*)	SAFEGUARDING THE SIGN (4:34)	DWINDLING FLUCTUATIONS [OF MIND-STUFF] (*kshīnavritti*, 1:41)	preattentive perceptual synthesis
	Breath-Holding (*bum ba can*) Space-Yoga		Breath-Holding (*kumbhaka*)	
Awareness of the Flow of Light	STOPPING THE MIND (*sems med*)		SEED SAMĀDHI, GROSS OBJECTS (*sthūla*) (3:3)	

STAGE IV. CONCENTRATION WITHOUT SUPPORT

Underlying Structure	*Mahāmudrā*	*Visuddhimagga*	*Yogasūtras*	*Psychology*
IV.A. Tuning in Subtle Perception	HOLDING FAST (*sgrim ba*)	TEN SKILLS OF ACCESS (*upachāra*) exertion (4:51–56)	SEED SAMADHI, SUBTLE OBJECT (*súkṣma*) (1:44) *nirvitarkāsamādhi*	change in self-system
loss of self-representation	loss of "I" (*nga*)		loss of sense-interpreter (*manas*)	loss of self-representation
discovering flow of light without gross constructions	subtle cognition (*'phra rtog*)		shining forth only of light (*arthamatranirbhāsa*) devoid of its own form (*svarupashūnya*, 1:43)	
IV.B. Recognizing the Subtle Flow	LETTING GO (*lhod pa*)	relaxing (4:57–62)	*savicārasamādhi*	
loss of self-agency	loss of "acting" (*byas ba*)		loss of "I-acting" (*ahaṃkara*)	loss of self-agency
flow of light as a stream	recognition (*ngo shes*) of flow of light		Recognition (*pratyaya*) of flow of light	

IV.C. Collapse of Ordinary Observer; Restructuring Perspective	BALANCING (*btang snyoms*)	SKILLFUL DEVELOPMENT (4:50)	*nirvicārasamādhi*	
new perspective of awareness	concomitant awareness (*lhan ne; sgo nas*)	mentality/materiality (*nāmarūpa*)	reflecting awareness (*buddhi*)	freeing awareness from self-structures
discontinuous/continuous stream	discrete discontinuous flashes (*val le*)		continuously vibrating energy field (*tanmātra*) (1:47)	temporal information-processing holonomic perception
Branch Paths	GREAT SEED (simultaneous) PSYCHIC POWERS	ABSORPTIONS (successsive)	[PSYCHIC POWERS]	

STAGE V. INSIGHT MEDITATION

Underlying Structure	*Mahāmudrā*	*Visuddhimagga*	*Yogasūtras*	*Psychology*
V.A. High-Speed Search of Subtle Flow	THE VIEW	PURIFICATION OF VIEW (18:1–36)	SAMĀDHI WITHOUT SUPPORT	high-speed controlled search
Arising factors Nature of flow	propensities (*bag chags*) discontinuous (*so sor rtog pa*)		impressions (*saṃskāras*) continuous (*parināma*)	
Establishing the Category of Insight Category of insight	Examination-Meditation (*dpyad sgom*) non-entityness (*ngo bo nyid med*)	Chapters 14–17 on the aggregate, etc. dependent origination	Chapter I sameness (*tulya*) in change (*parināma*)	
Underlying category in meditation on Flow	Samādhi-Meditation (*'jog sgom*)	KNOWLEDGE OF BODY AND MIND	TRANSFORMATION INTO CESSATION (*nirodhaparināma*, 3:9)	
	Emptiness of Person — Emptiness of Phenomena	Nāma — Rūpa	Recognition of Means — Recognition of Matter	
Setting Up Serial Exhaustive Search Recognition of Flow	Putting-in-Order Bringing Forth Insight Rearrangement		*nirodhaparināma* (3:9) calm flow (*prashāntavahīta*, 3:10)	
B. High-Speed Search of Gross Mental Contents	SKILL; REVERSE SAMĀDHI	OVERCOMING DOUBT (19:1–27) REVERSE ORDER	TRANSFORMATION INTO SAMĀDHI (*samādhiparināma*)	high-speed automatic search

Search of Gross Events	whatever arises (gangshar)	CONDITIONALITY	multiplicity of things (*sarvārthata*, 3:11)	
Divided Attention	immediately, arising arise, stay, cease (the unit) arise/pass away	PATH/NOT PATH (20:1–130) CLEAR COMPREHENSION (20:13–92)	TRANSFORMATION INTO ONE-POINTEDNESS (*ekagratāparināma*, 3:12); "that rising up and ceased as similar"	
V.C. High-Speed Search of Temporal Interactions	YOGA OF UNSPREADING	ARISING/PASSING AWAY SAMĀDHI (20:93–104; 21:3–9)		high-speed search of temporal interactions
Category	arising/passing away of discontinuous flashes	arising/passing away of discontinuous flashes	sameness of change of one/many manifestations of continuous field	
Analysis	Nāgārjuna's dialectic	focus on passing away	change of dharma vs. unchanging substrate (*dharmin*) (3:14)	
Result: interconnectedness	Non-Dissolution (*ma'gag pa*)	Dissolution (21:10–28)	Unity (3:53–55); "Wisdom is That which pertains to the entire universe, everything outside of time"	
Branch Path	Ten Corruptions	Ten Corruptions	Psychic Powers	

STAGE VI. EXTRAORDINARY MIND AND ENLIGHTENMENT

Underlying Structure	*Mahāmudrā*	*Visuddhimagga*	*Yogasūtras*	*Psychology*
VI.A. Relationship of Interconnected and Ordinary Time/Space Minds	YOGA OF ONE TASTE	KNOWLEDGE & VISION	ANALYSIS OF *VASANAS*	
Keeping the View	Pointing Out	cessation		
Category	non-entityness	MISERY (21:29–42)	sameness in change	
Coupling	SIMULTANEOUSNESS OF MIND (*zung 'jug*)		remove interval (*ānantarya*, 4:9)	
Non-Reactivity	self-occurring (*rang' byung*)	DISPASSION (21:43–44)	eternal desire (4:10)	
Chain of Karmic Activity across Levels of Mind	dawning wisdom	DESIRE FOR DELIVERANCE (21:45–46)	possible non-existence of *vāsanās* (4:11)	
Recognition of Subtle Karmic Interactions	SIMULTANEOUSNESS OF COGNITION & PERCEPTION	REOBSERVATION (21:47–60)	diverse mindstuff/same entity (*vastu*, 4:14–17)	
Resultant Spontaneous Interactions of Extraordinary Mind	KNOWLEDGE OF THE ORDINARY	EQUANIMITY (21:61–78)	Thatness of an Entity (4:14)	

VI.B. Relationship of Interconnected and Enlightened Minds	YOGA OF NON-MEDITATION	INSIGHT LEADING TO EMERGENCE (21.83–110)	relation of *prākṛti* & *puruṣa* (4:18–23)	
awareness turned on itself	RECOGNIZING WISDOM IN THE CONTINUUM	" "	" "	
establishing the primordial state of mental interactions	MEANS TO SET UP	CONFORMITY (21:128–136)	[mind] for the sake of Other (*parārtham*, 4:24)	
ENLIGHTENMENT	Basis	Change of Lineage (22:3–9)	Cessation (*vinivṛtti*, 4:25–26)	quantum shifts
	Path	Path	Other Recognitions (*pratyayātarani*, 4:27)	
	Fruition (Three Buddha Bodies)	Fruition (Supreme-Silence, 22:15–18)	Raincloud Samādhi (*dharmameghasamādhi*, 4:29)	
VI.C. Relationship of Enlightened and Ordinary Minds	REVIEW	REVIEW (22:19)	review (4:33–38)	
		Second, Third & Fourth Enlightenment (22:22–30)		

Summary

	THE STAGES OF MEDITATION	PERSPECTIVE	
		Buddhism	Yoga
Attitude, Affect Behavior	I. PRELIMINARY ETHICAL PRACTICES A. Generation of Faith; Attitude Change B. Formal Study; Intrapsychic Transformation C. Sensory/Behavioral Regulation Uninterrupted Awareness Training	(photon-like)	mind-as-light (wave-like)
Thinking	II. PRELIMINARY MIND/BODY TRAINING A. Body Awareness Training B. Calming Breathing and Thinking C. Re-arrangement of the Stream of Consciousness	discontinuous momentariness	continuous transformation of same thing
Perception	III. CONCENTRATION WITH SUPPORT A.1. Concentration Training; Decategorizing A.2. Internalization; Rearrangement of Image B. Recognition of Various Patterns of all Sense Modalities from the Seed C. Stopping the Mind, i.e., Gross Perception	discontinuously emanating seed	continuously transforming seed
Self	IV. CONCENTRATION WITHOUT SUPPORT A. Tuning in Subtle Perception B. Recognizing the Subtle Flow C. Collapse of Ordinary Observer; Restructuring of Perspective	discontinuous immediate events Concomitant Perspective (Access)	continuous vibration of *tanmātras* Reflection of *puruṣa* (*buddhi*)

Time/Space	V. INSIGHT PRACTICE A. High-Speed Search of Subtle Flow; Eradication of Self; Derealization	emptiness non-entityness (*ngo bo nyid med*)	cessation of sense-impressions
	B. High-Speed Search of Gross Mental Events; Shifts in Perceived Duration & Frequency of Events of Subtle Flow; Arising Only; Full Event in Slow Motion; Quick Flashing Psychic Powers; Raptures; White Light	discrete flashes	sameness (*tulya*) transformation of one substratum (*dharmin*)
	C. Analysis of Mind-Moments and Their Succession; The Problem of Perceived Time-Space	Non-dissolution	Unity
	Interconnectedness of all potential events	Co-dependent Origination of All Realms and Times	Unity of Manifest Cosmos (*prākrti*)
Cosmos	VI. ADVANCED INSIGHT A. Equanimity of Interrelated Events; Interaction of Specific Events B. Stopping all Mental Activity/Reactivity		
	Enlightenment Moments: Basis: Cessation of Mental Content; Vast Awareness	Non-dissolution	All Interactions of Manifest Cosmos
	Path: Return of Mental Content from Changed Locus of Awareness		Raincloud Samādhi

Chapter 9, "Developmental Stages in Eastern Orthodox Christianity" by John T. Chirban

In previous chapters, both Wilber and Brown have argued for the cross-cultural or quasi-universal nature of the deep structures of the stages of contemplation (although, in Wilber's opinion, different contemplative traditions reach different heights of that development). In this chapter, John Chirban examines the lives of some of the great saints of the Eastern Orthodox Church, a church that, within the Christian tradition, has particularly kept alive the contemplative path. "Although each saint described his own experience (often in his own unique way)," reports Chirban, "basic parallels emerge as one compares the stages of the saints with one another. This sameness confirms the catholicity of their experience. . . ." Chirban concludes that "five stages can be identified which are basically consistent amongst all ten saints and theologians." These stages are: (1) Image, (2) Metanoia (conversion), (3) Apatheia (purification or transformation), (4) Light (illumination), and (5) Theosis (union).

For comparison, we may note the similarities with Wilber's model. The stage of Image is the "natural state of the person," i.e., the state before contemplative development begins (the personal realm). Metanoia is a conscious decision to begin the life of contemplation; this is similar to the "preliminary practices" described by Wilber, Brown, Epstein, et al. Apatheia is the stage of "purification" and the beginning transcendence of exclusively worldly pursuits, i.e., the psychic stage of initial contemplative immersion. Light is the stage of illumination, i.e., the subtle realm of audible illumination and archetypal luminosity. Theosis is the stage of God-union, which, when described by the saints as "unknowing," "invisible," "darkness," "mystery," "glorious nothingness," clearly refers to the unmanifest or causal realm. Similar correlations can be drawn with Brown's model, providing added evidence for the catholicity of contemplative development."

[See the tables on pages 77–79 for Chirban's summary of the meditative stages according to the great saints of the Eastern Orthodox Christian Church.]

Schematic Drawing of Spiritual Development

APOPHATIC APPROACHES

STAGES	*St. Isaac the Syrian*	*St. Seraphim of Sarov*	*St. Gregory Palamas*	*St. John Climacos*	*St. Maximos*	*St. Dionysios*
V THEOSIS	(3) Perfection	Acquisition of the Holy Spirit	(3) Theosis	Step 30 Likening	(3) ’Aεί Eἶναι Eternal Being	(3) Unification Prayer of Union
		Kingdom Righteousness Peace		Steps 29		(Prayer of Quiet)
IV LIGHT		Illumination	(2) Divine Light Pure Hesychasm	Steps 28, 27 Hesychasm		(2) Illumination
						(Prayer of Recollection)

STAGES	*St. Isaac the Syrian*	*St. Seraphim of Sarov*	*St. Gregory Palamas*	*St. John Climacos*	*St. Maximos*	*St. Dionysios*
III APATHEIA	(2) Purification					(1) Purification
				Spiritual Development		(Prayer of Mind)
II METANOIA	(1) Repentance		(1) Prayer Labor	(1) Steps 1–26	(2) Εὐ Εἶναι (Well-Being)	
		Prayer Fasting Almsgiving				(Prayer of Simplicity)
I IMAGE					(1) Εἶναι (being)	

	APOPHATIC APPROACHES			CATAPHATIC APPROACHES	
	St. Gregory of Nyssa	*St. Basil*	*St. Macarios*	*Evagrios*	*Origen*
V	(3) Knowledge of God	(3) θέωσις	‘Απομάλυψις		‘Ομοίωσις
	(2) Cloud (Darkness)	Luminous		(3) Προσευχή	(3) Πνευματικός Γάμος Θεολογία
IV	(Light)	(Illumination)	φωτισμός	(2) θεωρία (Γνωσις)	(2) Φυσική θεωρία
III	’Απάθεια Παρρησία (God Confidence)	(2) Καθαρότης Καρδίας		(1) Πράξις (Πνευματική)	Πρακτικός
II	’Επίκτασις (Tension)	(1) Σοφία	(Baptism)		
	(Darkness of Sin)	(Intellectual Knowledge)			
		(Journey of Knowledge)	Υλυκήτις		
I		(Image of God)			(Εἴκών) Intellectual States

1

The Spectrum of Development

In this and the following two chapters [renumbered as 1, 2, and 3], Ken Wilber presents a summary of his particular version of a full-spectrum model of human growth and development. This model has been developed in over a half-dozen books on the topic, and represents one of the more ambitious if speculative attempts to bridge conventional and contemplative schools of thought.

Wilber's model contains, in addition to the various lines of human development (affective, cognitive, moral, ego, object-relations, etc.), two dozen or so levels or stages of development, through which each of the various lines may progress. Consonant with the "overview" model presented in the Introduction, Wilber has limited his presentation to nine of the most basic and central levels (three each in the prepersonal, personal, and transpersonal realms).

In this chapter, Wilber briefly discusses each of these nine levels or stages, along with the self (or self-system) that is developing through these stages. In the next chapter, he discusses the particular pathologies that may arise at any of these levels; and in the following chapter, he suggests the types of treatment modalities or therapeutic interventions that seem most appropriate for each of these classes of pathology.

In a sense, Wilber's presentation serves as a bridge between Engler's and Epstein/Lieff's. Wilber discusses the three levels of "pre-personal" pathology noted by Engler (psychotic, borderline, and neurotic), the three levels of "transpersonal" pa-

thology noted by Epstein and Lieff (beginning, access, and advanced), and then, based on recent research in cognitive and existential psychology, suggests three classes of pathology in the intermediate or "personal" realm.

This chapter is divided into two parts. In Part I, Wilber offers a brief overview of his spectrum model. In Part II, he presents a concise summary of the recent developments in psychoanalytic developmental psychology (including the work of Mahler, Kernberg, Blanck and Blanck, and Kohut). In the closing section, he attempts to point out just how closely these two models can be integrated, to mutual advantage, and this integration serves as the platform for the central discussions of chapter [2] and chapter [3].

I HAVE, IN A SERIES of publications (Wilber, 1977; 1979; 1980a; 1981a; 1981b; 1983), attempted to develop an overall or spectrum model of psychology, one that is developmental, structural, holarchical, and systems-oriented, and that draws equally on Eastern and Western schools. Vis-à-vis psychopathology the conclusion I reached was that the spectrum of consciousness is also a spectrum of (possible) pathology. If consciousness develops through a series of stages, then a developmental "lesion" at a particular stage would manifest itself as a particular type of psychopathology, and an understanding of the developmental nature of consciousness—its structures, stages, and dynamics—would prove indispensable to both diagnosis and treatment.

This presentation, therefore, offers an outline summary of both my prior work in this area and a present work-in-progress *(System, Self, and Structure)*. This is a somewhat hazardous undertaking because large amounts of material must be condensed into rather generalized and occasionally overly-simplified statements. Within these limitations, however, the following is a brief overview of this research and theory. Readers interested in more detailed presentations may wish to consult my other works.

This presentation reflects my growing conviction that developmental theory can benefit from the contribution of both conventional and transpersonal approaches. Connections between such apparently divergent orientations may now be productive, given recent work in both areas. In fact, an adequate grasp of the full range of human capacities, from lowest to highest, may require a combined and integrated conception—one not less comprehensive than the model outlined here.

Part I: The Spectrum of Consciousness

In the model of psychological development that I have proposed, the structures or formations of the psyche are divided into two general types: the basic structures and the transition structures (each of which contains numerous different developmental lines). The *basic structures* are those structures that, once they emerge in development, tend to remain in existence as relatively autonomous units or sub-units in the course of subsequent development (similar to Koestler's "holons").* *Transition structures,* on the other hand, are phase-specific and phase-temporary structures that tend to be more or less entirely replaced by subsequent phases of development. That is, where particular basic structures tend to be subsumed, included, or subordinated in subsequent development, particular transition structures tend to be negated, dissolved, or replaced by subsequent development (I will give several examples below). Negotiating these structural developments is the self (or self-system), which is the locus of identification, volition, defense, organization, and "metabolism" ("digestion" of experience at each level of structural growth and development).

These three components—(1) the basic structures, (2) the transition stages, and (3) the self-system—are central to the spectrum model of development and pathology, and so I will present a brief discussion of each.

The Basic Structures

The most notable feature about a basic structure or level of consciousness is that, once it emerges in human development, it tends to *remain in existence* in the life of the individual during subsequent development. Even though it is eventually transcended, subsumed, and subordinated by the self's movement to higher basic structures, it nevertheless retains a relative autonomy and functional independence.

The basic structures of consciousness are, in effect, similar to what is known as the Great Chain of Being (Smith, 1976). Some versions of the Great Chain give only two levels (matter and spirit); others give three (matter, mind, and spirit); still others give four or five (matter, body, mind, soul, and spirit). Some are very sophisticated, giving literally dozens of the basic structures of the overall spectrum of consciousness.

---

*Thus, in this presentation, "hierarchy" always means "holarchy."

In *System, Self, and Structure* (and to a less precise degree in *The Atman Project* and *Eye to Eye*), I present two dozen or so basic structures that seem, at this time, to be genuinely cross-cultural and universal. These were arrived at by a careful comparison and analysis of most of the major schools of psychology and religion, both East and West. The structural models of Freud, Jung, Piaget, Arieti, Werner, and others were compared and contrasted with the structural models presented in the psychological systems of the world's contemplative traditions (Mahayana, Vedanta, Sufism, Kabbalah, Christian mysticism, Platonism, Aurobindo, Free John, etc.). From these structural comparisons, a master template was constructed, with each tradition (East and West) filling in any "gaps" apparently left by the others.

This master template contains, as I said, around two dozen basic structures, which span both conventional and contemplative development. For this presentation, I have selected what seem to be the nine most central and functionally dominant structures. These are depicted in figure 1. In table 1,* I have presented a few correlations (with Aurobindo, Yoga psychology, Mahayana, and Kabbalah) to give a rough idea of the apparent universality of these major basic structures *(The Atman Project* gives similar correlations among more than two dozen systems, East and West, and these are greatly refined in *System, Self, and Structure).*

The basic structures of consciousness development shown in figure 1 may be very briefly (and somewhat simplistically) outlined as follows (proceeding up the holarchy):

1. *Sensoriphysical*—the realms of matter, sensation, and perception (the first three Buddhist skandhas); Piaget's sensorimotor level, Aurobindo's physical-sensory, etc.

2. *Phantasmic-emotional*—the emotional-sexual level (the sheath of bioenergy, élan vital, libidio, or prana; the fourth Buddhist skandha, the pranamayakosha in Vedanta, etc.) and the phantasmic level (Arieti's [1967] term for the lower or *image* mind, the simplest form of mental "picturing" using only images).

3. *Rep-mind*—an abbreviation for "representational mind," or Piaget's preoperational thinking ("preop"). The rep-mind develops in two stages—that of *symbols* (2–4 yrs), and that of *concepts* (4–7 yrs) [Arieti, 1967; Piaget, 1977]. A symbol goes beyond a simple image (the phan-

*[This table is numbered 2 in *Transformations of Consciousness;* some tables and figures have been renumbered for this publication.]

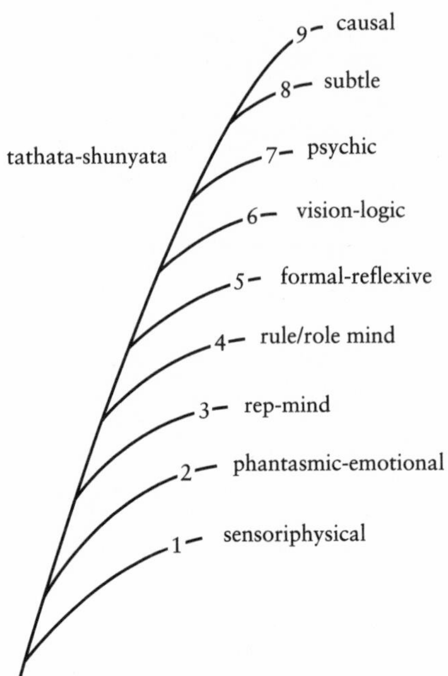

Figure 1. The Basic Structures of Consciousness

tasmic mind) in this essential respect: an image represents an object pictorially, while a symbol can represent it nonpictorially or verbally. Thus, for example, the mental image of a tree looks more or less like a real tree, whereas the word-symbol "t-r-e-e" does not look like a tree at all; symbolic representation is a higher, more difficult, and more sophisticated cognitive operation. A *concept* is a symbol that represents, not just one object or act, but a *class* of objects or acts—an even more difficult cognitive task. A symbol denotes; a concept connotes. But no matter how advanced the rep-mind is over its phantasmic predecessor, one of its most striking features is that it *cannot easily take the role of other.* It is, as Piaget would say, still very egocentric. This is very similar to Aurobindo's "will-mind," the third chakra in Yoga psychology, etc.

4. *Rule/role mind*—This is similar, for example, to Piaget's concrete operational thinking ("conop"). Conop, unlike its rep-mind predecessor, can begin to take the *role* of others. It is also the first structure that can clearly perform *rule* operations, such as multiplication, division, class inclusion, hierarchization, etc. (Flavell, 1970; Piaget, 1977). Aurobindo describes this structure as the mind that operates on sensory or concrete objects—very similar to Piaget.

Table 1
Correlation of Basic Structures of Consciousness in Four Systems

Basic Structures	*Aurobindo*	*Mahayana*	*Yogic Chakras*	*Kabbalah*
Sensoriphysical	Physical subconscient		1. Physical world and instincts; hunger/thirst	Malkhut
Phantasmic-emotional	Vital-emotional	5 vijnanas (the 5 senses)	2. Emotional-sexual level	Yesod
Rep-mind	Will-mind (lower concepts; cf. "preop")		3. Intentional mind; power	
Rule/role mind	Sense-mind (a concrete-based mind; cf. "conop")	Manovijnana (the gross or concrete reflecting mind; coordinates senses)	4. Community-mind; love	Hod/Netzach
Formal-reflexive	Reasoning mind (not concrete-based; cf. "formop")		5. Rational-verbal mind; communication	
Vision-logic	Higher-mind (Mass-network Ideation/vision)	Manas (the higher mind; conveyor between individual mind and alayavijnana or collective mind)		Tiferet
Psychic	Illumined mind		6. Ajna; "third eye"; psychic cognitions	
Subtle	Intuitive mind	Tainted-alayavijnana (collective-archetypal mind; vasanas-seeds)	7. Sahasrara; crown; beginning of higher "chakras" beyond and within the sahasrara	Gevurah/ Chesed
Causal	Overmind			Binah/Chokhmah
Ultimate	Supermind/Satchitananda	Pure Alaya	Shiva/Paramatman/Purusha	Keter Ein Sof

5. *Formal-reflexive mind*—This is similar to Piaget's formal operational thinking ("formop"). It is the first structure that can not only think about the world but think about thinking; hence, it is the first structure that is clearly self-reflexive and introspective (although this begins in rudimentary form with the rule/role mind). It is also the first structure capable of hypothetico-deductive or propositional reasoning ("if *a*, then *b*"), which, among other things, allows it to take genuinely pluralistic and more universal views (Flavell, 1970; Piaget, 1977; Wilber, 1982). Aurobindo calls this level the "reasoning mind," a mind that is not bound to sensory or concrete objects, but instead apprehends and operates on *relationships* (which are not "things").

6. *Vision-logic*—Numerous psychologists (e.g., Bruner, Flavell, Arieti) have pointed out that there is much evidence for a cognitive structure beyond or higher than Piaget's "formal operational." It has been called "dialectical," "integrative," "creative synthetic," "integral-aperspectival," and so forth. I prefer the term "vision-logic." In any case, it appears that whereas the formal mind establishes relationships, vision-logic establishes *networks* of those relationships (i.e., just as formop "operates on" conop, so vision-logic "operates on" formop). Such vision or panoramic logic apprehends a mass network of ideas, how they influence each other and interrelate. It is thus the beginning of truly higher-order synthesizing capacity, of making connections, relating truths, coordinating ideas, integrating concepts. Interestingly, this is almost exactly what Aurobindo called "the higher mind," which "can freely express itself in single ideas, but its most characteristic movement is a mass ideation, a system or totality of truth-seeing at a single view; the relations of idea with idea, of truth with truth, self-seen in the integral whole." This, obviously, is a highly *integrative* structure; indeed, in my opinion it is the highest integrative structure in the *personal* realm; beyond it lie transpersonal developments.

7. *Psychic*—The psychic level may be thought of as the culmination of vision-logic and visionary insight; it is perhaps best epitomized by the sixth chakra, the "third eye," which is said to mark the beginning or opening of transcendental, transpersonal, or contemplative developments: the individual's cognitive and perceptual capacities apparently become so pluralistic and universal that they begin to "reach beyond" any narrowly personal or individual perspectives and concerns. According to most contemplative traditions, at this level an individual *begins* to learn to very subtly inspect the mind's cognitive and perceptual capac-

ities, and thus to that extent begins to *transcend* them. This might also lead to temporary experiences of oneness with the world (panenhenic or nature mysticism). This is Aurobindo's "illumined mind," the "preliminary stages" of meditation in Hinduism and Buddhism, etc. According to Aurobindo,

> The perceptual power of the inner [psychic] sight is greater and more direct than the perceptual power of thought. As the higher mind [i.e., vision-logic] brings a greater consciousness into the being than the idea and its power of truth [formop], so the illumined mind [psychic level] brings a still greater consciousness through a Truth sight and Truth Light and its seeing and seizing power; it illumines the thought-mind with a direct inner vision and inspiration; it can embody a finer and bolder revealing outline and a larger comprehension and power of totality than thought-conception can manage.

8. *Subtle*—The subtle level is said to be the seat of actual archetypes, of Platonic Forms, of subtle sounds and audible illuminations *(nada, shabd),* of transcendent insight and absorption (Aurobindo; Da Free John, 1977; Evans-Wentz, 1971; Guénon, 1945; Rieker, 1971). Some traditions, such as Hinduism and Gnosticism, claim that, according to direct phenomenological apprehension, this level is the home of personal deity-form (ishtadeva in Hinduism, yidam in Mahayana, demiurge in Gnosticism, etc.), cognized in a state known as savikalpa samadhi in Hinduism (Blofeld, 1970; Hixon, 1978; Jonas, 1958). In Theravada Buddhism, this is the realm of the jhanas, or the stages of concentrative meditation into archetypal "planes of illumination" or "Brahma realms." In vipassana meditation, this is the stage-realm of pseudonirvana, the realm of illumination and rapture and initial transcendental insight (Goleman, 1977; Nyanamoli, 1976). It is Aurobindo's "intuitive mind"; Gevurah and Chesed in Kabbalah, and so on. (My reasons for concluding that all of these phenomena share the same *deep structure* of subtle-level consciousness are given in *Eye to Eye* [Wilber, 1983].)

9. *Causal*—The causal level is said to be the unmanifest source or transcendental ground of all the lesser structures; the Abyss (Gnosticism), Emptiness (Mahayana), the Formless (Vedanta) (Chang, 1974; Deutsche, 1969; Jonas, 1958; Luk, 1962). It is realized in a state of consciousness known variously as nirvikalpa samadhi (Hinduism),

jnana samadhi (Vedanta), the eighth of the ten ox-herding pictures (Zen); the stage of effortless insight culminating in nirvana (vipassana); Aurobindo's "Overmind" (Da Free John, 1977; Goleman, 1977; Guénon, 1945; Kapleau, 1965; Taimni, 1975). Alternatively, this stage is described as a universal and formless Self (Atman), common in and to all beings (Hume, 1974; Schuon, 1975). Aurobindo: "When the Overmind [causal] descends, the predominance of the centralizing ego-sense is entirely subordinated, lost in largeness of being and finally abolished; a wide cosmic perception and feeling of boundless universal self replaces it . . . an unlimited consciousness of unity which pervades everywhere . . . a being who is in essence one with the Supreme Self."

10. *Ultimate or Nondual*—Passing fully through the state of cessation or unmanifest causal absorption, consciousness is said finally to reawaken to its prior and eternal abode as nondual Spirit, radiant and all-pervading, one and many, only and all—the complete integration and identity of manifest Form with the unmanifest Formless. This is classical sahaj and bhava samadhi; the state of turiya (and turiyatita), absolute and unqualifiable Consciousness as Such, Aurobindo's "Supermind," Zen's "One Mind," Brahman-Atman, the Svabhavikakaya (Chang, 1974; Da Free John, 1978; Hixon, 1978; Kapleau, 1965; Mukerjee, 1971). Strictly speaking, the ultimate is not one level among others, but the reality, condition, or suchness of all levels. By analogy, the paper on which figure 1 is drawn represents this fundamental ground of empty-suchness.

Allow me to make a few additional remarks on those levels, particularly the higher or transpersonal stages (7 through 10). In *System, Self, and Structure,* I present seven transpersonal stages (low and high psychic, low and high subtle, low and high causal, and ultimate), each divided into three substages (beginning or preliminary, access or practicing, and culmination or mastery). I do believe, however, that the nine or ten major levels presented in figure 1 are *functionally dominant in development,* and that an adequate and fairly accurate account of development can be presented with just these nine general levels—their selection, in other words, is not entirely arbitrary (there is considerable support in the *philosophia perennis* for such "functional condensation"; Vedanta, for instance, maintains that the literally dozens of stages of overall development are functionally and structurally dominated by only five major levels, and these in turn are condensed and manifested in only three major states—gross, subtle, and causal. It is a slightly expanded version of this view that I am here representing).

More arbitrary, however, is my particular wording and description of the major stages themselves, particularly the higher or transpersonal ones. More precise descriptions and explanations of these stages can be found in *System, Self, and Structure*. The reader may also consult chapter 8 [of *Transformations of Consciousness*], where Daniel Brown gives a detailed explanation of some eighteen stages in transpersonal development. I should only like to point out that my contemplative cartography and Brown's are in broad and substantial agreement, reflecting the growing research and conclusion that "upon close inspection of the classical texts, the sequence of experiences reported within the concentration meditation traditions and the changes reported within the mindfulness approaches do *not* vary greatly from one meditation system to the next. Although there were noticeable differences in the progression of meditation experiences, the phenomenological reports themselves exhibited a highly similar underlying psychological organization when analyzed longitudinally (i.e., along the progression of experiences taking place from the beginning through the end of a meditative path)" (Maliszewski et al., 1981). These similarities—what I call "deep structures" as opposed to "surface structures"—are here condensed and represented as four major transpersonal stages—psychic, subtle, causal, and nondual.

The Transition Stages (or Self-Stages)

The transition structures are ones that are not included and subsumed in subsequent development but tend instead to be negated, dissolved, or *replaced* by subsequent development. Take, for example, the works of Piaget and Kohlberg. Piaget's cognitive structures are, for the most part, *basic* structures (sensorimotor is level 1–2, preoperational is 3, concrete operational is 4, and formal operational is 5). Once these levels come into existence, they remain in existence during subsequent development; in fact, each level becomes, in Piaget's system, the operand or "object" of the next higher level. Thus a person at, say, basic level 5 has *simultaneous* access to, and use of, levels 1 through 4; they are all still present, and all still performing their necessary and appropriate tasks and functions.

Kohlberg's moral stages, however, are phase-specific *transition* structures: someone at, say, moral stage 3 does not simultaneously act equally from stage 1. Stage 3 *replaced* stage 2, which replaced stage 1, and so on. Although the moral transition structures depend on or "rest on" the basic cognitive structures (as both Piaget and Kohlberg have pointed out), the two otherwise refer to different types of structures (i.e., basic and transitional).

A simple metaphor may be useful to explain this distinction. The basic structures themselves are like a ladder, each rung of which is a level in the Great Chain of Being. The self (or the self-system) is the climber of the ladder. At each rung of that climb, the self has a different view or perspective on reality, a different sense of identity, a different type of morality, a different set of self-needs, and so on. These changes in the sense of self and its reality, which shift from level to level, are referred to as transition structures, or, more often, as the *self-stages* (since these transitions intimately involve the self and its sense of reality).

Thus, as the self climbs from say, rung 4 to rung 5, its limited perspective at rung 4 is *replaced* by a new perspective at rung 5. Rung 4 itself *remains in existence,* but the limitations of its perspective do not. That is why the basic structures of consciousness are more or less *enduring* structures, but the self-stages are transitional, temporary, or phase-specific.

Each basic structure, then, *supports* various phase-specific transitional structures or self-stages, such as different self-needs (investigated by Maslow), different self-identities (investigated by Loevinger), and different sets of moral responses (investigated by Kohlberg). In table 2, I have for convenience included the basic structures of consciousness with some of their correlative (and transitional) self-needs, self-identities, and self-moralities, based on the work of Maslow, Loevinger, and Kohlberg. Thus, for example, when the self is *identified* with the rule/role level, its self-need is for belongingness, its self-sense is conformist, and its moral sense is conventional; when (and if) it subsequently *identifies* with the formal-reflexive level, its need is for self-esteem, its self-sense is individualistic, its moral sense is postconventional, and so on. (*System, Self, and Structure* presents similar correlations with the works of Fowler; Erikson; Broughton; Selman; Graves; Peck; and others. For this presentation I have selected Maslow, Loevinger, and Kohlberg as examples, simply because their work is probably best known. [For the possible relation of these different aspects of the self-stages to each other, see Loevinger, 1976.] Notice that the scales of Kohlberg and Loevinger "run out" around level 5 or 6, reflecting the neglect of most conventional researchers for the transpersonal stages of self-development).

Table 2
Correlation of Basic Structures of Consciousness with Three Aspects of the Self-Stages

Basic Structure	*Maslow (Self-Needs)*	*Loevinger (Self-Sense)*	*Kohlberg (Moral Sense)*	
Sensoriphysical		Autistic		
	(Physiological)	Symbiotic	(Premoral)	
Phantasmic-emotional		Beginning impulsive		0. Magic wish
Rep-mind	Safety	Impulsive	I. Preconventional	1. Punishment/obedience
		Self-protective		2. Naive hedonism
Rule/role mind	Belongingness	Conformist	II. Conventional	3. Approval of others
		Conscientious-conformist		4. Law and order
Formal-reflexive	Self-esteem	Conscientious	III. Postconventional	5. Individual rights
		Individualistic		6. Individual principles of conscience
Vision-logic	Self-actualization	Autonomous		
		Integrated		
Psychic	Self-transcendence			Kohlberg has recently suggested a higher, seventh stage:
Subtle	Self-transcendence			7. Universal-spiritual
Causal	Self-transcendence			

The Self-System

So far, we have briefly examined the basic rungs or levels in the overall ladder of development, and the transition stages (or self-stages) that occur as the self "climbs" or progresses through those rungs in the course of its own growth. We turn now to the climber itself: the self (or self-system or self-structure). Drawing on the research of numerous and varied theorists and clinicians, I have postulated that the self-system possesses the following basic characteristics:

1. *Identification*—The self is the locus of identification, the locus of what the self will call the "I/me" versus the "not-I/me." I sometimes divide the overall or total self-system (what Freud called the "Gesamt-Ich") into the *central* or *proximate self* (which is experienced as "I") and the *distal self* (which is experienced as "me"); the former is the subjective self, the latter, the objective self, though both are phenomenologically felt as the Gesamt-Ich.

2. *Organization*—As in scholastic philosophy, the self is that which gives (or attempts to give) unity to the mind; this is almost identical to the modern psychoanalytic concept of the self as "the process of organizing": "The self is not merely a synthesis of the underlying psychic parts or substructures, but an *independent organizing* principle, a 'frame of reference' against which to measure the activities or states of these substructures" (Brandt, 1980).

3. *Will*—The self is the locus of free choice, but free only within the limits set by the basic structures of its present level of adaptation (e.g., the self at rung 3, or preop, is not free to form hypotheses, which occur at rung 5 or formop).

4. *Defense*—The self is the locus of the defense mechanisms (which develop and change hierarchically from level to level of the basic structures); defense mechanisms in general are considered normal, necessary, and phase-appropriate functions; however, if over- or underemployed, they become morbid or pathological.

5. *Metabolism*—One of the central tasks of the self is to "digest" or "metabolize" the experiences presented to it at each rung of development. "The basic assumption of developmental theory is that experience must become 'metabolized' to form structure." Object relations theo-

rists, such as Guntrip (1971), speak of pathology as "failed metabolism"—the self fails to digest and assimilate significant past experiences, and these remain lodged, like a bit of undigested meat, in the self-system, generating psychological indigestion (pathology). The basic structures of consciousness, in fact, can be conceived as *levels of food*—physical food, emotional food, mental food, spiritual food (cf. *A Sociable God*). These levels of food, as we will see, are really levels of object relations, and how the self handles these "food-objects" ("self-objects") is a central factor in psychopathology.

6. *Navigation*—At any rung on the developmental ladder (except the two end points), the self is faced with several different "directional pulls." On the one hand, it can (within limits) choose to remain on its present level of development, or it can choose to release its present level of development in favor of another. If it releases its present level, it can move up the holarchy of basic structures or it can move down. *On* a given level, then, the self is faced with preservation vs. negation, holding on vs. letting go, living that level vs. dying to that level, identifying with it vs. disidentifying with it. *Between* levels the self is faced with ascent vs. descent, progression vs. regression, moving up the hierarchy to levels of increasing structuralization, increasing differentiation-and-integration, or moving down to less organized, less differentiated and less integrated structures. These four "drives" are represented in figure 2.

Summary of Overall Development

We can now summarize the form of overall development as follows: As the basic structures or rungs begin chronologically to emerge and develop, the self can *identify* with them (becoming, in turn, a physical self,

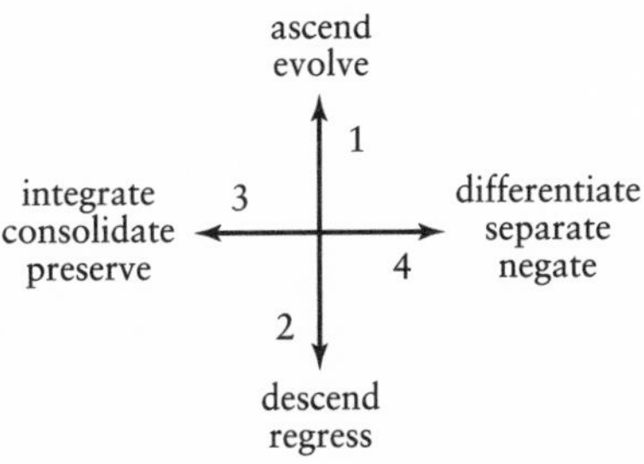

FIGURE 2. Four "Drives" Affecting the Self-Stages

an emotional-body self, a mental self, and so on). Once centrally identified with a particular basic structure, the self, or the self's preservation drive, will seek to consolidate, integrate, and organize the resultant overall complex. This initial identification with a particular basic structure is normal, necessary, and phase-appropriate, and it gives rise to the particular self-stage (impulsive, conformist, individualistic, etc.) associated with or supported by that basic structure (see table 2 for correlations).

If, however, the central self is to ascend the holarchy of basic structural development—to grow—then eventually it must release or negate its *exclusive* identification with its present basic rung in order to identify with the next higher rung in the developmental ladder. It must accept the "death," negation, or release of the lower level—it must disidentify with or detach from an exclusive involvement with that level—in order to ascend to the greater unity, differentiation, and integration of the next higher basic level.

Once identified with the new and higher basic structure, a new and phase-specific self-stage swings into existence: a new self-sense, with new self-needs, new moral sensibilities, new object relations, new forms of life, new forms of death, new forms of "food" to be metabolized, and so forth. The lower self-stage is (barring fixation) released and negated, but the lower basic structure remains in existence as a necessary rung in the ladder of consciousness, and must therefore be *integrated* in the overall newly configured individual. Once on the new and higher level, the self then seeks to consolidate, fortify, and preserve *that* level, until it is once again strong enough to die to that level, *transcend* that level (release or negate it), and so ascend to the next developmental rung. Thus, both preservation and negation (or life and death) apparently have important phase-specific tasks to accomplish.

It is fascinating to note that modern psychoanalytic ego psychology has come to an almost identical view. The dual-instinct theory, in fact, has evolved into a theory of *eros* as an integrating, consolidating, pulling-together, or preserving force, and aggression *(thanatos)* as a differentiating, separating, dissolving, or negating force—both of which are phase-specifically appropriate for overall development. This view began with Freud's 1940 reformulation:

> The aim of the first of these basic instincts [preservation] is to establish ever greater unities and to preserve them thus—in short, to bind together; the aim of the second [negation] is, on the contrary, to undo connections [dissolve or negate them].

Heinz Hartmann (1958) took the next step:

> Differentiation [separation-negation] must be recognized, along with synthesis [integration-preservation] as an important function of the ego. Since we somehow connect the synthetic function of the ego with the libido, it is plausible to assume an analogous relationship between differentiation and destruction, particularly since Freud's recent inferences about the role of free aggression in mental life.

Blanck and Blanck (1974) summarize the most recent view: "Libido will seek connection while aggression will seek and maintain separation and individuation." Aggression or negation, in other words, need no longer be viewed as merely or even predominantly hostile or destructive. Erikson proposed the term "aggressivity" to connote "those aspects of the aggressive drive which are growth promoting and self-assertive rather than hostile and destructive" (in Blanck & Blanck, 1974). In other words, there is "healthy aggression" as well as "morbid aggression," just as there is "healthy preservation" as well as "morbid preservation."

Accordingly, it may be concluded that preservation and negation both serve important phase-specific tasks, and that *pathology seems to develop if either (or both) of these tasks is misnavigated.* "Healthy" or "normal" preservation occurs when the identifications and object relations of a particular level are being built, consolidated, and integrated ("neutralized libido builds object relations" [Blanck & Blanck, 1974]). Morbid preservation, on the other hand, occurs when the once-appropriate identifications and object relations of a particular level are not released to allow room for newer and higher ones. Morbid preservation, in other words, is nothing but *fixation.*

Healthy or normal negation serves several important functions. *Horizontally,* it helps differentiate self and object representations ("neutralized aggression powers the developmental thrust toward separation-individuation" [Blanck & Blanck, 1974]); *vertically,* it helps the disidentification, differentiation, separation, or transcendence of a lower level in favor of a higher. Morbid negation, on the other hand, is a differentiation or disidentification from a component before it has been properly integrated, digested, and assimilated. The component is merely split off from the personality. Morbid negation, in other words, is simply *repression* (or dissociation, splitting, etc., depending upon the level of structural organization of the defense itself).

Such is a brief background summary of the spectrum model—its basic structures, the self-system, the self-stages, and repression/fixation. We can now turn our attention to a similar background summary for the recent developments in psychoanalytic ego psychology.

Part II: The Conventional Background

In this section I will present a short overview of some of the newer developments in conventional psychology and psychiatry, particularly those schools known as object-relations theory, self psychology, and psychoanalytic ego psychology. For these schools, too, have increasingly adopted a *developmental* perspective, and I will briefly summarize the various stages of self-development as they conceive them. Since these schools are *particularly interested in psychopathology and its treatment,* we will also begin to focus more intently on pathology and its genesis.

Toward the end of this section, I will begin to point out how these conventional stages fit in the overall spectrum of development outlined in Part I. But perhaps we can say this much in advance: These conventional schools are in general agreement that there are three broad levels or stages of self-development in the prepersonal realm (that is, leading up to and including the oedipal phase, at around age 5–7 yrs). I will try to show that these three general stages occur as the self negotiates the first three basic rungs of development (as shown in fig. 1). Conventional psychology and psychiatry have investigated these three general stages (and their numerous substages) in great detail, and have also attempted to demonstrate that a developmental "lesion" at a particular stage tends to give rise to a particular type of psychopathology. I will attempt to summarize this research, and then fit it explicitly with the spectrum model outlined in Part I. It is this integration or synthesis that will form the platform for the discussions in chapters [2] and [3].

The following section is necessarily technical and therefore somewhat abstruse. I have therefore included a fairly jargon-free, nontechnical summary, beginning on page 111. Those unfamiliar with psychoanalytic ego psychology may wish to skip to that summary now, and then come back and read as much of this section as desired.

The Developmental Dimensions of Psychopathology

During the past two decades, an explosion of theorizing and research has occurred in conventional psychoanalytic psychiatry, principally surrounding three closely related schools, generally known as psychoanalytic developmental psychology (Mahler, 1975; Kernberg, 1975; Blanck & Blanck, 1979), object-relations theory (Fairbairn, 1954; Winnicott, 1965; Guntrip, 1971), and self psychology (Kohut, 1971). The excitement and interest these schools have generated are apparent in such comments as that there has recently occurred a "quantum leap in the understanding of psychopathology" (Masterson, 1981); these advances represent "perhaps the major discovery of research into personality problems in this century" (Guntrip, 1971). Some of these discoveries are indeed monumental, and may of necessity become fundamental elements in any comprehensive psychology—including transpersonal psychology. Yet, taken in and by themselves, they possess certain grave limitations and distortions, upon which it would be unwise to base a *comprehensive* developmental psychology. What follows, then, is an attempt to outline the important aspects of these recent developments as well as what seem to be their limitations and even confusions.

The major breakthrough, so to speak, has come in the clinical investigation and treatment of the so-called borderline and narcissistic disorders. These disorders are in contrast to the classical psychoneuroses (hysteria, obsessive-compulsive neuroses, anxiety neuroses, etc.). The major difference between the psychoneuroses and the borderline-narcissistic disorders is that in the psychoneuroses, there is some sort of conflict or repression *within* the self-structure (the ego, for instance, *represses* some id impulse), whereas in the borderline and narcissistic conditions, there is too little self-structure to perform repression. On the contrary, the self-structure (or self-system) is so weak, so underdeveloped, so thin that its self and object representations merge or fuse; the self is overwhelmed by world-engulfment or fears of annihilation; or, alternatively, it treats objects and persons as mere extensions of its own grandiose world-fusion self. The term "borderline" means, roughly, that the syndrome is borderline between neuroses and psychoses; there is thus an overall continuum of increasing severity: neurotic, borderline neurotic, borderline, borderline psychotic, psychotic (Blanck & Blanck, 1979; Gedo, 1979; Tolpin, 1971).

Traditionally it had been thought that the borderline and narcissistic syndromes could not effectively be treated by standard psychoanalytic or psychotherapeutic techniques. Part of the recent "quantum leap," however, has involved the development of treatment modalities that have proven surprisingly effective with the borderline-narcissistic conditions. These treatment modalities developed out of three closely interrelated strands of research: (1) a detailed clinical description of the "archaic transferences" of borderline-narcissistic patients (spearheaded by Kohut [1971]); (2) sophisticated theoretical reformulations of the early stages (0–3 yrs) of development, and a consequent view of pathology as developmental arrest or distortion at qualitatively different levels of structural organization (Spitz, 1965; Jacobson, 1964; Mahler, 1975; Kernberg, 1976; Masterson, 1981, Blanck & Blanck, 1974); and (3) extremely meticulous observation and description of the earliest years of infant development (here the pioneering work of Margaret Mahler is recognized).

Because the research of Mahler and her associates has been so pivotal—not only in furthering our understanding of the earliest stages of self-development, but also in illuminating the etiology of the borderline-narcissistic syndromes—a brief outline of her key discoveries will be useful here.

Infant Development: The Work of Margaret Mahler

In almost two decades of what can only be called brilliant clinical research, Mahler concluded that the development of the self-structure in infants (0–3 yrs) generally proceeds through three phases: autistic, symbiotic, and separation-individuation, the last of which is divided into four subphases: differentiation, practicing, rapprochement, and consolidation, giving six overall stages. In chronological order, they are (all following quotes are from Mahler, 1975):

1. *Autistic phase* (0–1 month)—"The first weeks of extra-uterine life, during which the neonate appears to be an almost purely biological organism, his instinctual responses to stimuli being reflexive and thalamic. During this phase we can speak only of primitive unintegrated ego apparatuses and purely somatic defense mechanisms, consisting of overflow and discharge reactions, the goal of which is the maintenance of homeostatic equilibrium. The libido position is a predominantly visceral one with no discrimination between inside and outside." Mahler refers to this as a "closed monadic system" or a "primal undifferentiated matrix."

2. *Symbiotic phase* (1–5 months)—"From the second month on, the infant behaves and functions as though he and his mother were an omnipotent system—a dual unity within one common boundary." This is a "state of undifferentiation, of fusion with mother, in which the 'I' is not

yet differentiated from the 'not-I' and in which inside and outside are only gradually coming to be sensed as different." At this stage, the infant behaves as if it cannot even clearly distinguish its sensoriphysical body from the mother's and from the environment at large. "The essential feature of symbiosis is somatopsychic omnipotent fusion with the representation of the mother and, in particular, the delusion of a common boundary between two physically separate individuals."

3. *Differentiation subphase* (5–9 months)—This stage is marked by what Mahler calls "hatching": the infant's *sensoriphysical bodyself* "hatches" or wakes up from its previous, symbiotic, fused or dual unity with the mother and the sensoriphysical surround. At this stage, "all normal infants take their first tentative steps toward breaking away, in a *bodily sense,* from their hitherto completely passive lap-babyhood. . . . There are definite signs that the baby begins to differentiate his own [body] from the mother's body."

Notice that this particular differentiation is basically of the sensoriphysical bodyself from its surroundings, because the infant's mind (the newly emerging phantasmic or image level) and its feelings (the emotional-sexual level) are *not* yet differentiated from their surroundings. The infant exists as a distinct sensoriphysical bodyself but not as a *distinct* phantasmic-emotional self, because its emotional self-images and emotional object-images are still fused or merged. As we will see, it is only at the rapprochement subphase that this "psychological birth" or separation-differentiation occurs.

4. *Practicing subphase* (9–15 months)—This stage is significant because it seems to mark the peak of grandiose-exhibitionistic narcissism, with the world being, as Mahler puts it, "the junior toddler's oyster." "Libidinal cathexis shifts substantially into the service of the rapidly growing autonomous ego and its functions, and the child seems intoxicated with his own faculties and with the greatness of his own world. Narcissism is at its peak! He is exhilarated by his own abilities, continually delighted with the discoveries he makes in his expanding world, and quasi-enamored with the world and his own grandeur and omnipotence." According to Blanck and Blanck (1979), at this stage "the self continues to accumulate value by magical absorption of the larger world into its image." Technically speaking, self and object representations are still a fused unit.

5. *Rapprochement subphase* (15–24 months)—This stage, according to Mahler, is crucial to future development, for this is the stage in which

there occurs the first major differentiation of self and object representations. This means that a *separate and distinct phantasmic-emotional self* has finally emerged and clearly differentiated itself from its emotional-libidinal object representations. This, in other words, is "the psychological birth of the human infant." To conceptualize it within the basic structures, there is first simple birth; then "hatching," or the birth of a distinct sensoriperceptual bodyself; and then the rapprochement crisis, or the birth of a distinct phantasmic-emotional or "psychological" self.

Concomitant with this birth, there is a marked loss of the grandiose-omnipotent narcissistic fused self-and-object units of the previous (practicing) stage, and a correlative vulnerability to heightened separation anxiety and abandonment depression. "The narcissistic inflation of the practicing subphase is slowly replaced by a growing realization of [phantasmic-emotional] separateness and, with it, vulnerability. It often culminates in a more or less transient rapprochement crisis which is of great developmental significance," for the infant "must gradually and painfully give up the delusion of his own grandeur." Because there is now a separate self, there is now a separate other—the world is no longer its oyster. Researchers are fond of saying that at this stage, paradise has been lost.

But although the phantasmic-emotional body-mind of the infant is now differentiated from the "other," the infant's mind and body are themselves not yet differentiated; there is still mind-body fusion; it is only at the oedipal stage, as we will see, that the mind and body finally differentiate within the separate organism.

6. *Consolidation and emotional object constancy* (24–36 months)—This final subphase is the consolidation of the separation-individuation process and the attainment of "emotional-libidinal object constancy." It is normally marked by (1) a clear and relatively enduring differentiation of self and object representations; (2) the integration of part-self images into a whole-self representation (which includes both "good" and "bad" aspects of the self); and (3) the integration of part-object images into whole-object representations (which include both "good" and "bad" aspects of emotional-libidinal objects).

Such, then, are the six normal stages of the psychological birth of the human infant, as presented by Mahler.

The Fulcrum of Development: The Work of Blanck and Blanck

Mahler has presented extensive clinical evidence (1975) that infantile psychoses has as its major etiological factor a developmental "lesion" in the autistic-symbiotic phases (the infant fails to "hatch" or emerge as a separate sensoriphysical bodyself, but rather remains in the "closed monadic system" of the autistic phase or flounders in the "omnipotent dual unity" of the symbiotic phase).

However, Mahler believes the borderline syndromes have their major etiology in a rapprochement subphase lesion. The self-structure begins but fails to clearly differentiate-separate from the grandiose-omnipotent fused unit of the previous symbiotic and practicing subphases; this developmental arrest or lesion in self-structuralization leaves the borderline open to emotional engulfment, flooding, fusion panic, or self-and-object grandiosity. Because there are defects in self-structuralization at this primitive level of organization, the borderline does not have access to higher or neurotic defense mechanisms (repression, rationalization, displacement), but instead must rely on the primitive or less-than-neurotic defenses (particularly splitting, denial, introjection and projection).

On the other hand, as Blanck and Blanck (1979) summarize it, "If the symbiotic phase and the subphases of separation-individuation are experienced adequately, the child reaches the point of true identity—that of differentiation between self and object representations, and the capacity to retain the representation of the object independent of the state of need [that is the definition of 'emotional object constancy']. Structuralization proceeds to normalcy or, at worst, neurosis; borderline pathology is avoided." If this stage of separation-individuation is reached and resolved, the self-structure is then strong enough and individuated enough *to be able* to create a neurosis; the oedipal phase can then be engaged and either adequately resolved (normalcy) or misnavigated (psychoneuroses). On the other hand, if this separation-individuation phase is not adequately resolved, the individual self remains "less-than-neurotically structured," or borderline.

So central is this separation-individuation phase in general (and the rapprochement subphase in particular), that Blanck and Blanck (1979) call it "the fulcrum of development," and they represent it with a diagram (which they call "self-object differentiation"), similar to figure 3.

In effect, that diagram represents the major discoveries of the recent "quantum leap" in ego and object-relations theory. However, it can be further refined by including, not just the separation-individuation of the phantasmic-emotional self, but also the *previous* differentiation or "hatching" of the sensoriphysical bodyself. Blanck and Blanck (indeed, most developmental researchers) fail to adequately stress that these are two *qualitatively distinct* levels of differentiation, and thus should not be pictured as *one* continuum, as Blanck and Blanck do, but as two

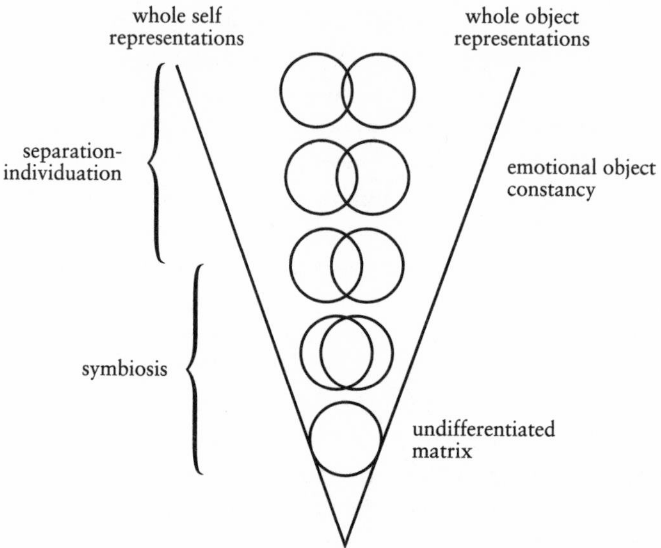

FIGURE 3. "Self-Object Differentiation" as Presented in Blanck & Blanck, 1979

distinct continua as shown in figure 4. Where the second fulcrum leads to *emotional* object constancy, the first fulcrum leads to *physical* object constancy.

The first fulcrum (autistic, symbiotic, and differentiating subphases) is the "hatching" stage, during which the self-system must negotiate the emergence of the physical and sensoriperceptual basic structures of existence. Should this hatching fail, the self remains locked in its own autistic-symbiotic orbit, unable, in the worst cases, to even differentiate its sensoriphysical self from the sensoriphysical surround (autistic and symbiotic psychoses); consequently it cannot advance to the second major fulcrum, that of phantasmic-emotional separation-individuation.

Should it negotiate this first fulcrum adequately, however, the sensoriphysical organism is adequately differentiated from the sensoriphysical surround. At this point, the self enters the second fulcrum of development, where it must negotiate the emergence and growth of the next major basic structures of existence, the emotional and phantasmic. This involves a differentiation, not between the organism and the environment, but within the organism itself—namely, a differentiation of internalized self-images from internalized object-images. This is represented in figure 4 by setting the second fulcrum on the left edge of the first fulcrum, as indicated by the arrow. The arrow also indicates that at this

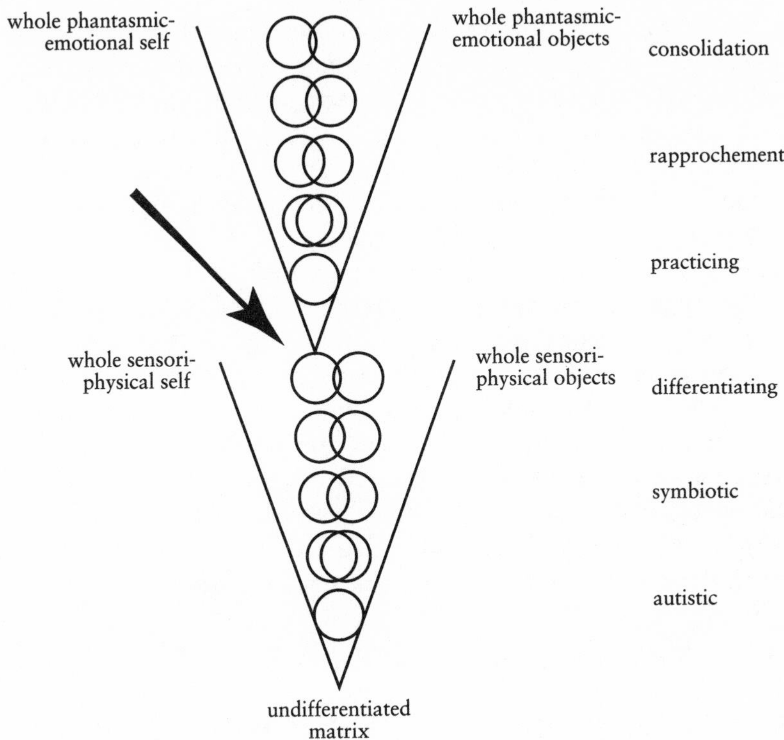

FIGURE 4. Self-Differentiation in Fulcrums 1 and 2

point there is a general *emergence* of the next, new and higher basic structures of existence, in this case, the phantasmic-emotional. It is exactly this new emergence that results in a new and higher fusion state, which itself must be separated-differentiated at a new and higher level of self-structuralization (in this case, the second fulcrum).

The work of Edith Jacobson (1964) as well as Mahler (1972) and Spitz (1965) bears out this interpretation. As Abend (1983) put it, "Jacobson's work stressed that at [the earliest or autistic-symbiotic] stage there is no clear differentiation between [the infant] as a separate [bodily] entity and the outside world. He may not as yet be aware that his own tension states come from his own body or that his gratifications and easing of psychological tension are afforded him by someone other than himself [this is during the first fulcrum]. Gradually, however, there must be a building up of *mental* [phantasmic] *images* of the self and the outside world [the emergence of the second fulcrum] along with *sensory* perceptions of the self and the other [the first fulcrum]. This later stage [the second fulcrum], however, is one during which the self-representation and the object-representation are likely to be distorted [merged or fused] as a result of projective and introjective mechanisms." The second fulcrum, in other words, involves a new, higher, and qualitatively different state of fusion (phantasmic-emotional) from that of the first (sensoriperceptual), and must be negotiated by a new, higher, and qualitatively different separation-differentiation process.

Finally, a note on the difference between *physical* object constancy (first fulcrum) and *emotional* object constancy (second fulcrum). Mahler (1975) herself accepts this distinction, and points out that physical "object permanence in Piaget's sense is a necessary, but not a sufficient, prerequisite for the establishment of libidinal object constancy." This difference is dramatically obvious in actual chronological development: physical object constancy, as Piaget (1977) has demonstrated, is achieved by around eighteen months, whereas emotional object constancy, according to Mahler, is rarely achieved before thirty-six months. Clearly, these are two different stages of structuralization.

The Spectrum of Developmental Fulcrums

We now reach a crucial question: Are there any other major fulcrums or critical nodal points of self-structuralization and self-differentiation? At this point, most object relations theories become vague and equivocal. Some of them seem to indicate major self-development is virtually over at thirty-six months. Others give scant attention to higher developmental fulcrums: "With adequate attainment of psychological birth, at approximately three years of age, the child is 'on the way to [emotional] object constancy.' While this is another beginning, not the end . . . , the first round is decisive to how secure subsequent rounds will be. Blos [1962] thinks that a second major development takes place in adolescence. We suggest that marriage can constitute another 'round' " (Blanck & Blanck, 1979).

This theoretical vagueness as to what exactly constitutes a "round" (or fulcrum) of self-development has dogged object-relations theory from its inception.[1] Vis-à-vis development as a whole, it is also very limiting to *define* "separation-individuation" as what occurs specifically during the rapprochement and consolidation subphases, and also say that it "continues" through "several, perhaps infinite, rounds throughout life" (Blanck & Blanck, 1979), with vague references to adolescence and marriage.

The psychoanalytic object-relations theorists appear to have so focused on the *particular* form the separation-differentiation process takes in the rapprochement and consolidation subphases, that they seem to have missed the idea that the "hatching" subphase (and not the rapprochement subphase) can be described as the *first* major round of separation-differentiation. However, they seem to have implicitly recognized this, in that they actually call that first fulcrum "the differentiation subphase."

Likewise, these theories have overlooked the fact that the oedipal phase itself can also be rather precisely defined as a fulcrum or separation-differentiation point. The oedipal phase—which can now be called the third major fulcrum of self-development—shares all of the abstract characteristics or defining marks of the first two fulcrums: it involves a process of increasing internalization, increasing structuralization and hierarchization, increasing separation-differentiation, and increasing integration. However, this process is now occurring on a new, higher, and qualitatively different level of organization, that of the *newly emerging* basic structures of the conceptual rep-mind, which bring the possibilities of a qualitatively different set of self-defenses (repression), self-needs, object relations, possible pathologies (psychoneuroses), and so on.

As we saw, at the completion of the separation-individuation subphases (the second fulcrum), the phantasmic-emotional self of the infant is differentiated from its surround, but the infant's mind (phantasmic and early symbolic) and its body (emotional-libidinal) are themselves *not yet differentiated from each other.* As the rep-mind (higher symbols and concepts) emerges, it initially shares this mind-body fusion. This is very clearly borne out by the works of Piaget (1977), Loevinger (1976), Broughton (1975), and others. Indeed, Freud himself announced, in *Inhibitions, Symptoms, and Anxiety* (1959), that a definitive differentiation of the ego from the id does not occur until around the time of the resolution of the oedipal stage. And that, exactly, is what is at stake in the third fulcrum: the differentiation/integration of the (rep) mind and the (emotional-libidinal) body. A developmental lesion at this fulcrum results in a *neurotic self-structure:* the central self remains fixated (morbid preservation) to certain bodily impulses, or it represses or dissociates (morbid negation) certain bodily impulses. If, however, this third fulcrum is adequately negotiated, the mind and body are clearly differentiated and integrated in the new and higher-order conceptual self-structure, with a new and higher internalization (superego), and the capacity for *conceptual object constancy*—the power to hold a *whole con-*

cept, or a class of properties, without confusing or collapsing its component members due to, e.g., libidinal desires. As Piaget (1977) has demonstrated, conceptual constancy does not emerge until around the sixth year of life, with such capacities as conservation-reversibility, i.e., holding conceptual properties despite physical-emotional displacement.

This third major fulcrum can now be added to the self-development diagram, as shown in figure 5, and this can all be simplified and schematically represented as in figure 6.

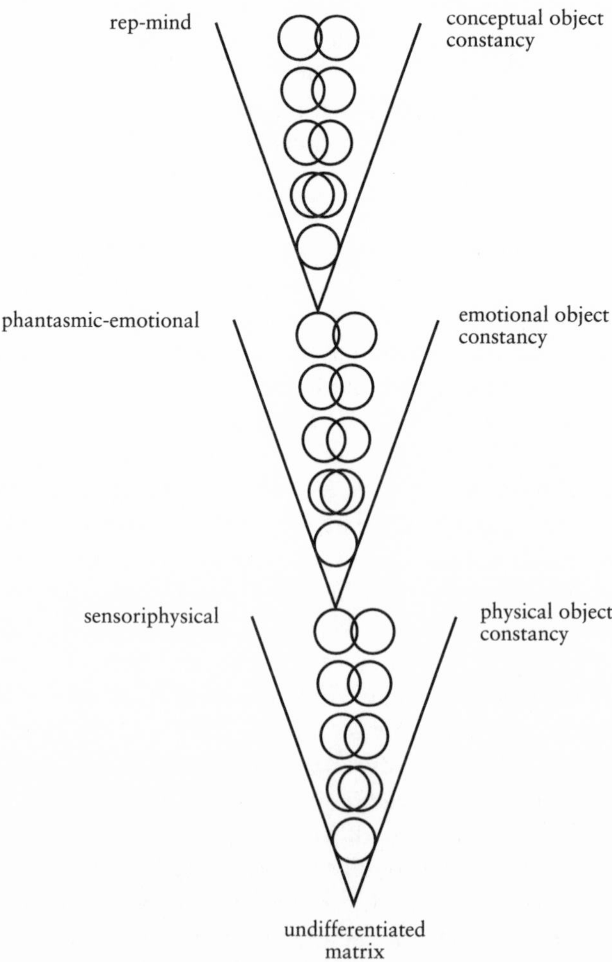

Figure 5. Self-Differentiation in Fulcrums 1–3

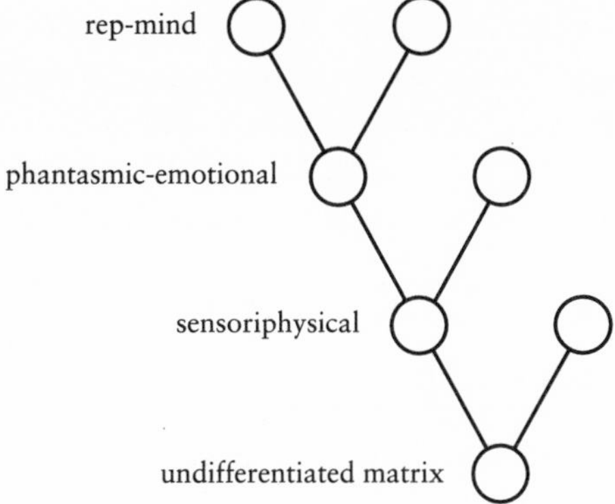

FIGURE 6. Self-Development Schematic for Fulcrums 1–3

The Combined Theories

The implications of combining psychoanalytic developmental psychology and object-relations theory with the basic structures or stages of consciousness may now be seen: *The first three fulcrums of self-development simply represent the self's climb up the first three rungs of the ladder of major basic structures* (depicted in figure 1).

At each fulcrum, the self identifies (normal preservation) with the corresponding basic structure, and thus is initially fused with, or undifferentiated from, that structure and its phenomenal objects. This is followed by a period of separation-differentiation (normal negation), wherein the self-system or self-structure learns to differentiate itself from both the *objects* of that level and the *subject* of the previous level (that is, it transcends its previous and exclusive subjective identification with the previous and lower basic structure). If at any fulcrum there is morbid preservation (fixation) or morbid negation (splitting, dissociation, repression), a characteristic pathology emerges, marked by the level of structural organization at which the lesion occurs.

As I said, these first three fulcrums and their associated pathologies (psychotic, borderline, and neurotic) correspond with the first three basic structures or rungs in the ladder or overall development (depicted in fig. 1). In the next chapter, I will suggest that the remaining basic structures or rungs (levels 4 through 9) each involve another and crucial fulcrum of self-development, and lesions at those fulcrums also generate specific and definable pathologies (which in turn respond to different treatment modalities or therapeutic interventions). In chapter [2] I will describe these higher fulcrums—their characteristics, their typical conflicts, and their corresponding pathologies; and then, in chapter [3], I will suggest the types of "therapies" that seem most appropriate for each.

But first we must return to the previous discussion and finish our account with the first three fulcrums and their associated pathologies. And this brings us to the work of Otto Kernberg.

The Conventional Hierarchy of Pathology: The Work of Otto Kernberg

In order to discuss the specific pathologies that characterize malformations at each of the fulcrums of self-development, it will help to use a few simple symbols to refer to the subphases of each fulcrum. In figure 7, *a* represents the initial fusion or undifferentiated state of each fulcrum; *b,* the process of separation-differentiation; *c,* the stable, differentiated, integrated self that emerges at the adequate negotiation of each fulcrum; and *d,* the correlative, differentiated-and-integrated object world of that fulcrum. (Thus, for example, "fulcrum-1a"—or simply F-1a—refers to the autistic phase; F-2b refers to the rapprochement subphase; F-2d refers to emotional object constancy; F-3b to the oedipal phase; F-3c to the stable rep-mind self-concept, and so on.) The developmental task of each fulcrum can now be stated simply: it involves a horizontal differentiation between *c* and *d,* and a concomitant, vertical differentiation of *c* and *a.* The latter is what I have elsewhere defined as "transcendence" (Wilber, 1980a).

Previous discussion briefly outlined Mahler's view of pathology throughout the first three fulcrums. But perhaps the most sophisticated and comprehensive map of pathology in these realms has been given by Otto Kernberg, who has presented a very influential and widely accepted "theory of (1) the origin of the basic 'units' (self-image, object-image, affect disposition) of internalized object relations, (2) the development of four basic stages in their differentiation and integration, (3) the relationship between failure in these developments and the crystallization of

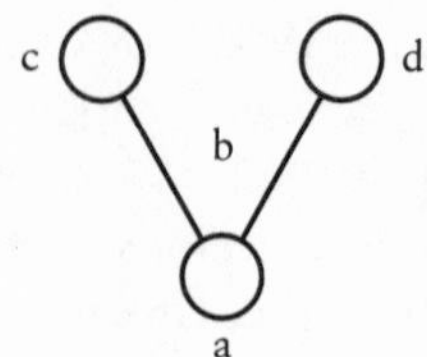

FIGURE 7. Subphases at Each Fulcrum of Self-Development

various types of psychopathology, and (4) the implications of this sequence of phases of general structural developments of the psychic apparatus" (1976).

Kernberg's stages of self-development and corresponding pathology are as follows (summarized by Abend, 1983):

> *Stage 1: Normal "Autism," or Primary Undifferentiated Stage.* This phase covers the first month of life and precedes the consolidation of the "good" undifferentiated self-object constellation. Failure or fixation of development at this stage is characteristic of autistic psychoses.
>
> *Stage 2: Normal "Symbiosis."* This phase extends from the second month of life to about six or eight months of age. There is a relative incompleteness of the differentiation of self and object representations from each other and a persisting tendency for defensive refusion of "good" self and object images when severe trauma or frustration determines pathological development. Pathological fixation of, or regression to, Stage 2 is characteristic of symbiotic psychosis of childhood, most types of adult schizophrenia, and depressive psychoses.
>
> *Stage 3: Differentiation of Self from Object-Representations.* This stage begins around the eighth month of life and reaches completion between the eighteenth and the thirty-sixth month. It ends with the eventual integration of "good" and "bad" self-representations into an integrated self concept [that should be "self-image"; concepts do not emerge until around the fourth year of life], and the integration of "good" and "bad" representations into "total" [whole, not part] object representations. Failures in development during this stage lead to the development of the borderline personality organization. [In this general category Kernberg includes borderline syndromes, addictions, narcissistic disorders, "as if" and antisocial personality disorders; what all of them have in common, he believes, is a failure to integrate "all good" and "all bad" self and object part-images, i.e., they are all primarily characterized by splitting.] During this stage an early constellation of defenses is brought into operation, centering on splitting or primitive dissociation and fostering the other early defenses of denial, primitive idealization, projective identification, omnipotence, and devaluation.
>
> *Stage 4: Development of Higher Level Intrapsychic Object*

> *Relations-Derived Structures.* This stage begins in the latter part of the third year of life and lasts through the entire oedipal period. The typical psychopathology of this stage is represented by the neuroses and "higher level" character pathology. Repression becomes the main defensive operation of this stage.
>
> *Stage 5: Consolidation of Superego and Ego Integration.* This is a [postoedipal] stage of development with the gradual evolution of ego identity.

It is obvious that Kernberg's developmental diagnostic scheme fits the first three fulcrums rather precisely, as shown in figure 8. Note that Kernberg's Stage 5 (F-3c), "the *consolidation* of superego and ego integration," is indeed a consolidation or integration, but it clearly is not to be confused with fulcrum-2c, the consolidation-integration of the phantasmic-emotional self, or fulcrum-1c, the consolidation-integration of the sensoriphysical self.

The substantial agreement between Kernberg's developmental-diagnostic stages and the first three fulcrums of self-development requires one refinement: Masterson (1981) has suggested that the narcissistic and borderline conditions, although very closely related, are developmentally distinct. According to Masterson, the borderline conditions do have their primary developmental lesion in the rapprochement subphase (F-2b), but the narcissistic conditions must have some aspect of their developmental lesion *before* that (i.e., in the practicing subphase, F-2a). The narcissistic conditions are marked by grandiose-self/omnipotent-object fused units, which characterize the practicing subphase (as Mahler put it, "Narcissism at its peak!"). The rapprochement subphase is marked by the breaking up or differentiation of the grandiose-omnipotent fused self-and-object units, and thus, Masterson believes, could not be the lesion point of the narcissistic disorders. As he puts it, "The fixation of the narcissistic personality disorders must occur before [the rapprochement crisis] because clinically the patient behaves as if the object-representation were an integral part of the self-representation—an omnipotent, dual unity. The possibility of the existence of a rapprochement crisis doesn't seem to dawn on this patient. The fantasy persists that the world is his oyster and revolves about him." The borderline, on the other hand, "behaves as if all life were one long, unresolvable rapprochement crisis." Thus, according to Masterson, fulcrum-2a: narcissistic; fulcrum-2b: borderline.

Notice that within each fulcrum there are, generally speaking, three subphases: subphase "a," which represents the undifferentiated base of the fulcrum; subphase "b," which represents the process of *vertical and horizontal* separation-differentiation; and the subphase "c/d," which represents the ideal resolution, consolidation, and integration of the newly differentiated self and object components. This is so in each of the three fulcrums—and therefore 9 subphases—examined thus far. These three fulcrums and their 9 subphases are listed in figure 8 for reference.

Figure 8, then, represents a summary of the "fit" between the conventional schools (e.g., represented by Kernberg and Mahler) and the first three rungs (and fulcrums) of the spectrum model presented in Part I. Let me repeat that these three fulcrums (and their associated pathologies) represent the three general stages in the prepersonal or prerational realms of overall development. This still leaves three general stages in the personal realms and three general stages in the transpersonal realms, as indicated in figure 9. In the next chapter I will go on to discuss these higher rungs and fulcrums and their associated pathologies, a discussion that will eventually take us into the contemplative and transpersonal dimensions of human growth and development.

Summary

This section has been somewhat technical and therefore, for the nonpsychoanalytically oriented reader, perhaps abstruse and off-putting. What I would like to do, therefore, is offer a brief, nontechnical summary of its central points.

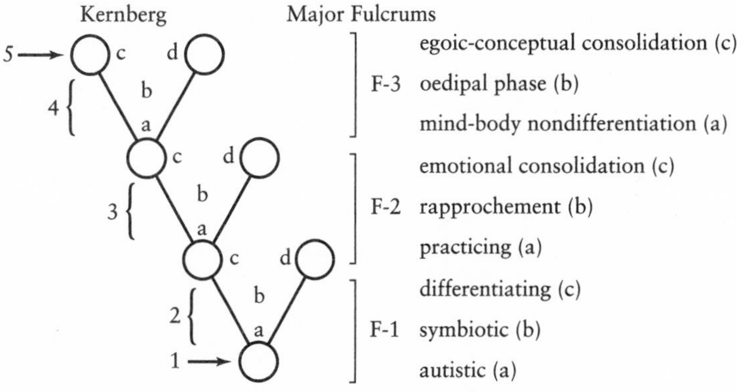

FIGURE 8. Fit of Kernberg Stages at Fulcrums 1–3

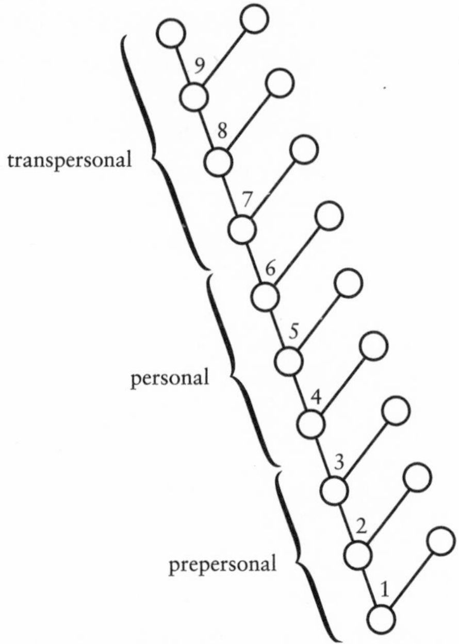

Figure 9. The Major Fulcrums of Self-Development

In this section we have examined the emergence of a *sense of self* in the human being, and we found that it proceeds through three general stages: the emergence of a *physical self* (0–1 yr), the emergence of an *emotional self* (1–3 yrs), and the emergence of a *mental self* (3–6 yrs). At each of these stages of growth, the individual must learn to distinguish the self from the environment, from others, and from other structures in its own psyche. If this differentiation fails, the individual remains "stuck" (fixated) at that stage, and a corresponding psychological disturbance generally results.

Thus, although the infant is born with a physical body, it does not yet possess a sense of being a distinct *physical self,* set apart from its environment and surroundings; it cannot easily distinguish inside from outside, or its own body from mother's. But sometime during the first year of life (typically 5–9 months), the infant learns to distinguish (or differentiate) its physical self from the physical environment, and a genuine sense of a distinct physical self emerges (this is appropriately called "hatching"). On the other hand, if this differentiation does not occur—usually due to severe and repeated trauma or other disturbing events—then the infant remains "stuck" in its prior undifferentiated or "fusion" state: inside and outside are fused and confused, hallucinatory thought processes may predominate, and severe anxiety or depression may result. This class of severe and primitive pathology is known as "psychoses."

Once the physical self has emerged and been established, the infant's *emotional self* begins to emerge and develop. Again, the infant possesses emotions probably from birth, but not a distinct and separate emotional self. Even after the first year of life, when the infant has (ideally) established a firm and distinct physical self, the infant's emotions are not yet clearly differentiated from the emotions of others (and particularly the mother). The infant imagines that what it feels, others are also feeling (this is called "narcissism"); its "emotional boundaries," so to speak, are still very fluid and shifting.

But sometime during the first and third year (the period 15–24 months seems most critical, and is called "rapprochement"), the infant learns to differentiate its emotional-psychological life from that of others (particularly the mother), and a stable, firm, individual emotional self emerges. A failure to achieve this "separation-individuation" leaves the individual with very weak emotional boundaries. The world then tends to "flood" the self, causing anxiety, depression, and severe thought disturbances—a class of pathology loosely referred to as "borderline" (because it is borderline between psychoses and neuroses).

Once the emotional self has emerged and been established, the child's *mental self* increasingly begins to emerge and develop, a process that is considerably aided by the acquisition of language. The mental self grows particularly rapidly from around the third to the sixth year, during which time the child learns not just to *feel* but to *think*—to verbalize, talk, and mentally control its behavior. But it might also learn that certain of its feelings and behaviors (particularly sexual and aggressive) are unacceptable to those around it, and it might try to "disown" or "repress" those feelings. In a sense, the mental self (and its thoughts) learns to repress the previous emotional self (and its feelings). If this repression is severe and prolonged, the repressed feelings may return in disguised and painful forms known as "neuroses" (such as phobias, compulsions, obsessions, hysterias, etc.).

Thus, during the first six or seven years of life, there are three particularly important "turning points" or "fulcrums" of self-development—the emergence of the physical self, the emotional self, and the mental self—each of which, if disturbed, may result in a particular type (or level) of pathology—psychoses, borderline, and neuroses. As we will particularly see in chapter [3], these pathologies are best treated by different types of therapies. In the neuroses, the individual is encouraged to "uncover" the repressed emotions and feelings and reexperience them more directly (these are called "uncovering techniques," such as classical psychoanalysis). In the borderline, on the other hand, it is not so much that the emotional self has been repressed, but that it hasn't yet fully emerged and been stabilized; the emotional boundaries are too fluid and shifting, and so the aim in therapy here is not to "uncover" anything but to *build up* a distinct and individuated sense of self (these techniques are therefore called "structure building techniques"). Finally, the very primitive pathologies (psychoses) are usually so severe that neither uncovering techniques nor structure building techniques are of much use, and the best that can usually be hoped for is some sort of stabilization using medication or, if necessary, custodial care.

We have seen the emergence of a physical self, then an emotional self, then a mental self, and these are the first three major "fulcrums" of self-development. In the next chapter, we will see that the mental self in turn goes through three major levels or fulcrums of development (concrete, formal, and integrative, or F-4, F-5, and F-6 for short), and then the self begins to become *transmental* (transrational or transpersonal) as it enters the contemplative or spiritual realms of development. Each of these higher levels and fulcrums also has its own potential pathologies and correlative treatment modalities, which we will discuss in detail in the chapter "Treatment Modalities."

Note

1. Object-relations theory is a general name for several schools of psychoanalytic theory that began to put emphasis not solely on the subject of development but on its relations with its object world. Classical libido psychology thus gave rise to two somewhat different schools of analytic theory: psychoanalytic ego psychology (Anna Freud, Heinz Hartmann) and object-relations theory (Fairbairn, Winnicott, Guntrip), the former stressing the subject of development, the latter, its objects (i.e., the former tends to emphasize nature, the latter, nurture [Gedo, 1981; Blanck & Blanck, 1974]). Most modern psychoanalytic schools use a combination of both theories, but, as Gedo points out, the two theories as generally presented are actually incompatible in fine point, and no one apparently has yet succeeded in satisfactorily uniting them in a coherent framework.

   The central reason, I believe, is that both schools contain certain confusions or reductionisms—holdovers from the "bad aspects" of libido psychology. Ego psychology, for instance, still tends to be bogged down in drive psychology; it has few theories of motivation that don't implicitly rely on libido (e.g., see Blanck & Blanck's [1979] attempt to reformulate motivation by reformulating the libido).

In my opinion, these approaches tend to overlook the fact that *each* basic structure might have its own intrinsic motivations, forces, or need-drives (for physical food, emotional food, conceptual food, spiritual food, etc.); that the self-system has its *own* drives (preserve, negate, ascend, descend); and that none of these should be confused with, derived from, or reduced to the others. Drive psychology tends to take the dynamics of *one* basic structure of existence (phantasmic-emotional) and make them the primary drives for all other basic structures *and* the self-system!

Object-relations theory, on the other hand, has attempted to present an adequate theory of motivation by making the templates of early object-relations the motivators of subsequent development. However, as Gedo has pointed out, not only is this a subtle form of reductionism, it *implicitly* amounts to a predominant reliance on environmental conditioning.

In my opinion, object-relations theory has also failed to clearly distinguish between two different types of "objects"—objects of the basic structures ("basic objects") and objects of the self-system ("self-objects"). *Basic objects* include physical objects, emotional objects, image objects, conceptual objects, rule objects, psychic objects, and subtle objects (there are no causal objects; the causal is the state of consciousness-without-an-object). These basic objects are the "levels of food" that correspond with the *basic structural needs* of each wave in the spectrum of consciousness—the need for physical food, the need for communicative exchange, the need for formal reflection, the need for spiritual engagement, and so on—real and genuine need-drives that reflect the *structural* demands or needs of each basic level of existence (Wilber, 1981b).

Self-objects, on the other hand, are basic objects that are appropriated by the self-system, at each stage of its development, as being most centrally important for (and sometimes constitutive of) its own sense of identity and selfhood. Self-objects, in other words, are basic objects that also serve as objects of primary concern for the *self* at each stage of its growth. If, for instance, I am thinking of a mathematical theorem, that theorem is a *formal basic object* of my mind; if I *invented* the theorem, however, and think of it as *mine,* or am very attached to it, then it is not just a basic object in my mind but a self-object in my ego. For an infant at the breast, the mother is not only a physical basic object providing food, but a self-object providing primary care and early identity information. The mother does not just feed the body, she feeds the self.

The self-objects, in other words, are basic objects that not only satisfy the basic structural needs, but also the correlated *self-needs* (see table 2). Using Maslow's hierarchy as an example, the basic structural need of, say, rung 5 is for formal-reflexive "food for thought," a real *need-drive* to think and to communicate and to exchange ideas; the corresponding self-need, however, is for reflexive self-esteem, and thus any basic objects of the formal-mind that also become important in one's own self-esteem needs become *self-objects*. Basic objects become self-objects when they are in any way associated with the "I," the "me," or the "mine."

Thus, there are basic structures and basic objects, and self-structures and self-objects. In my opinion, a failure to differentiate these objects lies at the heart of some of the confusions now plaguing object-relations theory. These confusions have recently been exacerbated by Kohut's introduction of what he calls "selfobjects" (without a hyphen), which I would define as self-objects that are experienced not as objects of the self-system but as *part* of the self-system, in which case they can indeed be called "selfobjects." Kohut's description of these selfobjects is an extremely important contribution to the field, but it has tended to add to the confusion as to what exactly constitutes an object, a self-object, and a selfobject.

Kohut has also suggested that self-development ("narcissistic development") proceeds independently of libidinal object development, which object-relations theorists usually claim is impossible, because self and object relations, they believe, must develop correlatively. Here, however, they are again overlooking the difference between basic objects and self-objects. Basic structures and basic objects develop correlatively, and self-structures and self-objects develop correlatively, but basic structures/objects and self-structures/objects do not necessarily develop correlatively. Libidinal development *as* libidinal is a basic structure development, and so of course it is largely independent of self-structure development, although, as we saw, at F-2 development they are *virtually* identical simply because the self-system, at F-2, is *identified* with the libidinal basic structure. For the same reason, we differentiate the oedipal stage, which is a phase of self-development, from the phallic stage, which is a libidinal basic structure development.

Although I cannot indicate in this short note how a spectrum approach might handle these and other related problems, perhaps enough has been said to indicate how a *nonreductionistic* approach to motivation, coupled with a distinction between basic structures/objects and self-structures/objects, might not only allow a reconciliation of ego and object psychology, but also allow room for the acceptance of the phenomenologically higher subjects *and* objects that appear in higher and contemplative development.

2

The Spectrum of Psychopathology

In the previous chapter, Wilber presented a brief outline of his spectrum model, and indicated how this model connects with the recent developments in psychoanalytic ego psychology. In effect, this covered the prepersonal or prerational range of development, with its three general stages, fulcrums, and correlative pathologies (psychotic, borderline, and neurotic). In this chapter, Wilber continues the account and discusses the intermediate or personal range of development (with its three general stages and pathologies) and the higher or transpersonal range of development (also with three general stages and pathologies). The result is an overall spectrum of pathology—from prepersonal to personal to transpersonal—that is comprehensive and specific.

THE FOLLOWING OUTLINE of the overall spectrum of psychopathology begins with a review of the first three fulcrums—which were introduced in the last chapter—and continues to fulcrum 9. For ease of presentation and reference, I have divided this chapter into three parts: Prepersonal, Personal, and Transpersonal, each consisting of three major fulcrums of self-development and the corresponding pathologies. I have simply listed the fulcrums (and their subphases) and noted the specific type(s) of pathology that are most characteristic of a developmental lesion at that phase or subphase. Needless to say, the standard cautions and qualifications about using such models of pathology should be kept in mind; i.e., no pure cases, the influence of cultural differences, genetic predispositions, genetic and traumatic arrests, and blended cases (see Abend, 1983; Gedo, 1981; Mahler, 1975).

Part I: The Prepersonal Pathologies

The "prepersonal" or "preconventional" pathologies are so named because this range of development involves the stages leading up to the emergence of an individuated-personal selfhood and its differentiation from prerational structures, impulses, primary process thought, and so forth. Consonant with recent research in this field (see chapter 3), I tend to see this range of development as consisting of *three general waves* of personality development and organization, which I have called F-1, F-2, and F-3, and whose general pathologies are psychotic, borderline, and neurotic. In the words of Jack Engler (see *Transformations of Consciousness,* chapter 1), "It is important to recognize that self-pathology does not depend on personality or character type, and still less on symptoms or symptom clusters. Almost all the commonly recognized personality *types* can occur at any level of personality *organization:* healthy, neurotic, borderline, or psychotic. Even the more pathological character types—schizoid, paranoid, infantile—can occur within a neurotic structure (Stone 1980). Stone has suggested that it is clinically more useful to think in terms of a continuum for each character or personality type as it varies from most to least pathological. He has accordingly proposed a promising three-dimensional model of personality typology which crosses personality type, level of personality organization and degree of constitutional or genetic loading. This distinction between structure and character is only beginning to become clear in clinical psychiatry and represents a breakthrough in psychodiagnostic understanding." I am in substantial agreement with Engler and Stone on this central issue.

Fulcrum-1

1A: Autistic Psychoses
1B/C: Symbiotic Infantile Psychoses
Most Adult Schizophrenia
Depressive Psychoses

This follows Kernberg and Mahler specifically.

Fulcrum-2

2A: Narcissistic Personality Disorders

The main clinical characteristics of the narcissistic personality disorder are grandiosity, extreme self-involvement and lack of

> interest in and empathy for others, in spite of the pursuit of others to obtain admiration and approval. The patient manifesting a narcissistic personality disorder seems to be endlessly motivated to seek perfection in all he or she does, to pursue wealth, power and beauty and to find others who will mirror and admire his/her grandiosity. Underneath this defensive facade is a feeling state of emptiness and rage with a predominance of intense envy.
>
> The narcissistic personality disorder must be fixated or arrested before the developmental level of the rapprochement crisis, since one of the important tasks of that crisis is not performed, i.e., the deflation of infantile grandiosity and omnipotence [i.e., the self-structure refuses to surrender "paradise"]. The intrapsychic structure of the narcissistic personality disorder preserves the infantile grandiosity and narcissistic link to the omnipotent object. (Masterson, 1981)

Specifically, the self- and object-representations of the narcissistic personality structure consist of a grandiose-self-plus-omnipotent-object fused unit. Other persons are *experienced,* according to direct clinical evidence, not as separate individuals (or as separate "whole objects") with rights and wishes of their own, but as extensions or aspects of the grandiose-exhibitionistic self, serving primary need gratification (Kohut, 1971). The sole function of the world is therefore to *mirror* the self's perfection. The omnipotent fused object representation contains all power, supplies, glory, etc.; the grandiose self-representation is one of being elite, superior, exhibitionistic, special, unique, perfect. The grandiose-self/omnipotent-object fused unit forms the central self; so airtight is this fused unit that it seemingly conceals the underlying empty-rageful-envious fused unit and its affect of profound abandonment depression. Should any object or person, however, fail to give the narcissistic individual what he or she is constantly seeking—namely a *mirroring* of his or her grandiose perfection—then the narcissistic individual reacts with rage, outrage, and humiliation. Typical defenses include devaluation, refusion, denial, avoidance, splitting (particularly of the grandiose-self/omnipotent-object fused unit from the empty/aggressive/depressive unit), and acting out (Kernberg, 1976; Kohut, 1971; Masterson, 1981).

2B: Borderline Personality Disorders

"The rapprochement crisis is crucial to the borderline, whose pathology can be seen as a reflection of his/her immersion in and inability to resolve it" (Masterson, 1981). Unlike the narcissistic structure, the borderline has achieved a partial or quasi-differentiation of self and object representations. A *separate* individual has started to emerge, but its structure is so tenuous or weak that it constantly fears engulfment by the other or abandonment by the other.

According to Masterson (1981) and Rinsley (1977), this splits the borderline structure into a helpless, dependent, compliant part-self with a clinging defense, and a "totally worthless," "rotten," "evil-to-the-core" part-self with a distancing or withdrawing defense. Associated with the compliant-clinging part-self is an all-good, rewarding, and protecting part-object, and associated with the "rotten-withdrawing" part-self is an all-bad, angry, attacking, and vengeful part-object.

The intrapsychic structure of the borderline is thus more complex than the narcissistic, because it has accomplished more differentiation; but these differentiations are not integrated, leaving the borderline with a series of fractured structures or part-units. The borderline thus typically oscillates between an almost total or chameleon-like compliance with others, which makes him/her feel "good," "accepted," or "safe," and a withdrawn and sullen distancing from others, who—now experienced as angry, vengeful, and denouncing—make him/her feel rotten, a worm, totally worthless, despicably bad (and occasionally suicidal). The one thing the borderline will not do is assert his or her own separation-individuation (Blanck & Blanck, 1979; Kernberg, 1975, 1976).

Fulcrum-3

3a: Borderline Neuroses

There are several different nosological terms for this set of conditions: pathological neuroses, high level borderline, neurosis with borderline features, borderline with neurotic features, etc. The general consensus, however, is simply that these conditions are either neurotic developments burdened with separation-individuation subphase deficiencies, or a part-regression to more borderline states in the face of too difficult neurotic-oedipal developments (Blanck & Blanck, 1974, 1979; Gedo, 1981).

Thus, to give only two examples, if genital sexuality is burdened with rapprochement subphase deficiencies, the person's understanding of sexual responses might be skewed in the direction of threats of entrapment or engulfment; if burdened with an unmetabolized need for narcissistic mirroring, then in the direction of triumph, possessive extension of self-grandiosity, or rageful-sadistic domination. The person characterized by neuroses-with-borderline-elements makes careful diagnosis and well-tailored treatment especially important, because appropriate interventions for similar symptoms on the neurotic level and the borderline level are often dramatically different.

3B: Psychoneuroses

Discussion of these well-known disorders—neurotic anxiety, obsessive-compulsive syndromes, neurotic depression, phobias, hysteria, hypochondriasis—can be limited here to comments about their significance and meaning in the overall spectrum. The lowest self-structures (autistic, symbiotic, and narcissistic) tend to be *monadic* in nature; the borderline structures, *dyadic;* and the psychoneurotic structures, *triadic.* In the monadic structures, there is basically one player on the stage—the self is either oblivious of the "other" (autistic), merged with the other (symbiotic), or part of an omnipotent dual unity with the other (narcissistic). As the monadic structure differentiates, self and other emerge as two distinct, if sometimes tenuous, units. There are now two players on the stage, self and (m)other, with all the joy and all the tragedy that that involves (Kohut [1977] calls this stage "Tragic Man").

At the dyadic stage, the infant is still more or less pregenital. It only has to negotiate the differentiation of self versus other; it does not have to negotiate the differentiation, within itself, of male versus female. Starting around age 2 or 3, however, the self awakens to its own gender identity, and this introduces three players on the stage: self, female-mother, and male-father. This development immensely enriches and complicates the situation. New capacities, new desires, new taboos, new object relations, a whole new set of conflicts—all come crashing onto the stage, with far-reaching, immensely complex implications.

In the dyadic (F-2) stage, the central self is a more or less stable phantasmic-emotional-libidinal structure. It is not so much that the self at this stage possesses a libido; rather, the self at this stage simply *is* a libidinal self (Guntrip, 1971): it is *identified* with the phantasmic-emotional basic structure. However, by the time we move from the F-2 dyad to the F-3 triad, the conceptual rep-mind has emerged and (ideally) *differentiated* from the libidinal body. The central or proximate self is *now* identified with, and exists as, a symbolic-conceptual structure, namely, the rep-mind *ego:* no longer a phantasmic-libidinal self, but a conceptual-egoic self.

The egoic self, therefore, has ideally accomplished three tasks: (1) it has horizontally differentiated from its new concept object-relations; (2) it has consolidated and integrated its own structure, which contains new and higher internalizations (superego); and (3) it has vertically differentiated from (or transcended) its previous self-stage (i.e., the libidinal self)—the *exclusively* libidinal self is *negated and transcended,* but the libido itself (or the id) *remains in existence* as a fundamental, appropriate, and necessary basic structure of existence.

But this overall process results in a *tripartite* structure of the fulcrum-3 self: ego-superego-id. Whereas, in the F-2 self, most conflict was interpersonal, in the F-3 self, most conflict is intrapersonal (or intrapsychic). If differentiation-and-integration is not clean or complete, there is war: superego vs. id (inhibition), id vs. ego (anxiety, obsession), superego vs. ego (guilt, depression). The triadic structure of conflict in the F-3 pathologies is one of the central diagnostic aids in differentiating them from the more dyadically structured pathologies of F-2 (and the monadic pathologies of F-1). Kohut calls this "Guilty Man" in contrast to "Tragic Man."

The triadic structure of the F-3 self also gives a major clue to the very meaning of the psychoneuroses in the overall spectrum of development and pathology. For the self is on its climb up the basic structures of existence, matter to body to mind to soul to spirit. The psychoneuroses stand at that great branch point where consciousness starts to move from a generally bodily existence to a generally mental existence, with all the rewards, and all the conflicts, that entails. The body belongs to nature, but the mind belongs to history; the body, to impulse; the mind, to reason. The body is merely subjective; the mind, however, is intersubjective, freely taking the role of *other subjects* in communicative exchange and symbolic discourse. The body constitutes a *merely present* feeling-self; the mind, on the other hand, supports a *temporal text-self*—a historic, hermeneutic, intentional, interpretive, meaningful, caring, moral, role-playing script-self.

The scripts and social roles of the F-3 or oedipal phase are, however, rather crude and simple, especially in comparison with those that are to follow. To begin with, the number and types of roles are fairly simple: child, parent, sibling. Further, the script-roles themselves are driven almost entirely (or at least predominantly) by merely libidinal agendas. The Oedipus complex is one of the earliest and most fundamental scripts of all (and it *is* a script, as Sophocles demonstrated), but it is a script whose roles are driven almost entirely by mere bodily desires. At the next fulcrum, the roles themselves shake off their merely bodily or libidi-

nal motives and assume their own higher function and status—and pathology.

Part II: The Personal Pathologies

Most conventional psychodynamic theorists tend to end their accounts of "serious" pathology at F-3, that is, at the oedipal phase and its resolution (or lack thereof). This is perhaps understandable; after all, the classic pathologies (from schizophrenia to hysteria) do seem to have their most disturbing etiologies in the first three fulcrums of self-development. But this by no means exhausts the spectrum of pathologies, not even the spectrum of "serious" or "profound" pathologies. Accordingly, researchers increasingly have begun to look at higher or "postoedipal" stages of development and their correlative vulnerabilities and dis-eases.

Take, for example, the whole notion of "role confusion." The very capacity for genuine role taking is a decisively postoedipal development (the capacity to take the role of other does not emerge, in any sophisticated fashion, until around age 7–8 yrs [Piaget, 1977; Loevinger, 1976], whereas the typical age of oedipal resolution is 6 yrs). Thus, one could theoretically resolve the oedipal conflict in a completely normal and healthy fashion, only to run aground on role confusion and identity confusion for reasons totally unrelated to oedipal conflicts or concerns. These seem to be entirely different levels (not just lines) of development, with entirely different conflicts and vulnerabilities. These conflicts are much more cognitive than psychodynamic in nature and origin, but can be just as debilitating and distressful. This whole range of cognitive, identity, and existential concerns, I call the "intermediate" or "personal" realm, and, based on recent research, I have divided it into three major levels (F-4, F-5, and F-6), which I call "cognitive-script," "identity," and "existential."

Fulcrum-4: The Role Self and Cognitive-Script Pathology

Fulcrum 4 begins to emerge as the central self transcends its exclusive identification with the rep-mind (and its oedipal projects) and begins to identify with the rule/role mind. The rule/role mind (or "conop"), as Piaget (1977) demonstrated, is the first structure that not only can imitate a role, but can actually *take* the role of others. This opens up an

entirely new dimension of object relations, with a new sense of self (Loevinger), a new set of self-needs (Maslow), a new moral sensibility (Kohlberg), a new mode of life and a new mode of death. In the F-3 pathologies (the psychoneuroses), the life/death (or preservation/negation) battles centered mostly on bodily concerns and impulses—desire for libidinal-body objects, fear of bodily loss (castration, mutilation, etc.). The life/death battles of the F-4 self, however, center more on its rules and roles—a desire to fit in, to belong, to find its place or role among other roles; to *understand* the *rules;* with a correlative fear of losing face, losing role, breaking the rules (Loevinger's conformist stage, Maslow's belongingness, Kohlberg's conventional, etc.).

By "script pathology" or "script neuroses" I have in mind, for example, the extensive work of Transactional Analysis on game theory and scripts, and communications theorists on role-taking (Selman & Byrne, 1974; Watzlawick, 1967). Obviously conceptual games and scripts (and their forerunners) reach back into F-3 development, but it is at F-4 that they assume a central and dominant influence. The preeminent defense mechanism of this stage is the "duplicitous transaction"—the individual overtly communicates one message (e.g., "I only want what's best for you") while covertly implying another ("Don't leave me"); if the covert message is pointed out, the individual strenuously denies it. The covert messages or hidden agendas are the key pathogenic structures in the F-4 self; if extreme, they result in an interior splitting or dissociation of the text-self, analogous to repression in F-3 and splitting in F-2. Script pathology and the reasons that it cannot be reduced to psychoneurotic pathology will be discussed in more detail in chapter [3].

Fulcrum-5: Identity Neurosis

The emergence of the formal-reflexive basic structure opens the possibility of F-5 self-development: a highly differentiated, reflexive, and introspective self-structuralization. The F-5 self is no longer unreflexively bound to social roles and conventional morality; for the first time it can depend on its own individual principles of reason and conscience (Kohlberg's postconventional, Loevinger's conscientious-individualistic, etc.). For the first time, too, the self can conceive *possible* (or hypothetical) futures (Piaget), with entirely new goals, new possibilities, new desires (life), and new fears (death). It can conceive possible successes, and possible failures, in a way never before imagined. It can lie awake at night, riveted with worries or elated by anticipation over all the possibil-

ities! It becomes a philosopher, a dreamer in the best and highest sense; an internally reflexive mirror, awestruck at its own existence. *Cogito, ergo sum.*

"Identity neurosis" specifically means all the things that can go wrong in the emergence of this self-reflexive structure. Is it strong enough to break free of the rule/role mind and stand on its own principles of conscience? Can it, if necessary, summon the courage to march to the sound of a different drummer? Will it dare to think for itself? Will it be overcome with anxiety or depression at the prospect of its own emergence? These concerns—which regrettably many object-relations theorists reduce to F-2 separation-individuation dimensions—form the core of the F-5 self and its identity pathology. Erikson (1959, 1963) has written perhaps the definitive studies on F-5 self-development ("identity vs. role confusion"). All that can be added here is the observation that *philosophical problems* are an integral part of F-5 development, and philosophical education an integral and legitimate part of therapy on this level (see the relevant section in chapter [3]).

Fulcrum-6: Existential Pathology

I must first distinguish between "existential" as a particular level of self-development (F-6) and "existential" as a particular conflict that can and does occur on *all* levels of self-development. The latter ("existential conflict") is simply one way to look at the life/death or preservation/negation battles that occur at each and every stage of self-development. Birth trauma, rapprochement crisis, separation-individuation, oedipal tragedies, role clashes, identity neuroses—these can all be described as "existential" in nature, simply because they involve profound and meaningful events in the course of human existence *(Dasein)*. The existential approach looks at each stage of development, not just in terms of its *content* (borderline, oedipal, etc.), but also from the *context* or categories of existence itself, or the various modes and stages of being-in-the-world. This is why the central dilemmas and drives of each stage of self-development can also be conceptualized as a life/death, preservation/negation, or existential concern, although the outward forms of this existential battle obviously vary from level to level. This is the approach of Boss (1963), Binswanger (1956), Yalom (1980), Zimmerman (1981), May (1977), and others, which I share in part.

Now the "existential level," as I use the term here, refers to a specific level of basic structure development ("vision-logic") and the correlative stage of self-development ("centaur"). It is termed "existential" for three reasons: (1) If the formal-reflexive mind is Descartes, the existential mind is Heidegger: his whole philosophy is marvelously saturated with this level of consciousness (as an actual discovery, not a merely subjective fabrication); (2) the self-structure of this level, as Broughton (1975) demonstrated, is one where "mind and body are both experiences of an integrated self." This personal mind-body integration—hence "centaur"—seems to be the goal of those therapies that explicitly call themselves "humanistic-existential." (This does not refer to many popular approaches that call themselves "humanistic" or "existential," but, in fact, are *pseudo*-humanistic/existential, and embody powerful techniques for regression to, and glorification of, the phantasmic-emotional or the narcissistic "paradise," which are mistakenly identified with "higher consciousness"); (3) this level is the *highest* level of consciousness that many authentic humanistic-existential approaches seem to acknowledge.

A review of the literature suggests that the major concerns of the F-6 or existential self are: personal autonomy and integration (Loevinger); authenticity (Kierkegaard, Heidegger); and self-actualization (Maslow, Rogers). Associated affects are: a concern for overall *meaning* in life (or being-in-the-world); a grappling with personal mortality and finitude; and finding a courage-to-be in the face of lonely and unexpected death. Where the formal-mind begins to conceive of life's *possibilities* and take flight in this new-found freedom, the existential mind (via vision-logic) *adds up* the possibilities and often finds this: personal life is a brief spark in the cosmic void. How the existential self handles the new potentials of autonomy and self-actualization, and how it grapples with the problems of finitude, mortality, and apparent meaninglessness—these are the central factors in F-6 pathology.

Common syndromes include:

1. *Existential depression*—a global-diffuse depression or "life-arrest" in the face of perceived meaninglessness.
2. *Inauthenticity*—which Heidegger (1962) defined as lack of profound awareness-acceptance of one's own finititude and mortality.
3. *Existential isolation and "uncanniness"*—a strong-enough self that nevertheless feels "not at home" in the familiar world.
4. *Aborted self-actualization*—Maslow (1971): "I warn you, if you deliberately set out to be less than you are capable of becoming, you will be deeply unhappy for the rest of your life."

5. *Existential anxiety*—the threatened death of, or loss of, one's self-reflexive modes of being-in-the-world (an anxiety that *cannot* occur prior to Fulcrums 5 and 6 because the very capacity for formal-reflection does not occur until then).

Not all cases of, e.g., "meaninglessness" are automatically to be considered as existential (in the specific sense of existential-level origin). Borderline abandonment depression and psychoneurotic depression, for instance, also produce affective states of meaninglessness. But existential ennui has a specific and unmistakable "flavor"; a strong and highly differentiated-integrated self-structure presents the symptom; it is a thoughtful, steady, concerned, profound depression; it has none of the "whining" of the borderline or the guilt of the psychoneurotic; it looks unflinchingly at the cosmos and then, for whatever reasons, despairs of finding any personal meaning. Interpretations of this depression on the basis of lower-level structures—psychoneurotic, borderline, or whatever—intuitively sound and feel "silly" or irrelevant to the concerned therapist. A classic example of genuine ennui is from Tolstoy (1929).

> The question, which in my fiftieth year had brought me to the notion of suicide, was the simplest of all questions, lying in the soul of every man: "What will come from what I am doing now, and may do tomorrow. What will come from my whole life?" Otherwise expressed—"Why should I live? Why should I wish for anything? Why should I do anything?" Again, in other words: "Is there any meaning in my life which will not be destroyed by the inevitable death awaiting me?"

Part III: The Transpersonal Pathologies

As with the prepersonal and personal realms, the transpersonal realm is here divided into three major waves of development and corresponding pathology, which I call psychic, subtle, and causal. I should like to emphasize, however, that the following discussion is a preliminary investigation. I have, in all cases, attempted to adopt a fairly neutral and balanced stance towards the different contemplative schools, but I realize that some of them might not agree with my particular wording or description of some of these higher stages or their possible pathologies.

Thus, if certain contemplative schools object to my use of the terms "psychic," "subtle," and "causal," I invite them to substitute more neutral terms, such as "beginning," "intermediate," and "advanced" stages of the practice, and then interpret the following according to their own tradition. I offer the following not as a series of dogmatic conclusions but as a way to open the discussion on a topic that has been sorely neglected by conventional and contemplative schools alike.

Fulcrum-7: Psychic Disorders

The emergence of the psychic basic structure brings with it the possibility of another wave of self-development and associated self-pathology. By "psychic pathology" (or "F-7 pathology") I mean specifically all the "lower-level" spiritual crises and pathologies that may (1) awaken *spontaneously* in almost any soul; (2) invade any of the lower levels of development during periods of severe stress (e.g., psychotic episodes); and (3) beset the *beginning* practitioner of a contemplative discipline.

1. The most dramatic psychic pathology occurs in the spontaneous and usually unsought awakening of spiritual-psychic energies or capacities. At best, these crises are elevating; at worst, they can be devastating, even to one who is securely anchored in a centauric self. The awakening of Kundalini, for instance, can be psychological dynamite. Excellent examples of these psychic pathologies can be found in Gopi Krishna (1972), John White (1979), and William James (1961).

2. One of the most puzzling aspects of transient schizophrenic breaks of psychotic-like episodes is that they often channel rather profound spiritual insights, but they do so through a self-structure that is neurotic, borderline, or even frankly psychotic (particularly paranoid schizophrenic). Anybody familiar with the *philosophia perennis* can almost instantly spot whether any of the elements of the particular psychotic-like episode have any universal-spiritual components, and thus fairly easily differentiate the "spiritual-channel" psychoses-neuroses from the more mundane (and often more easily treatable) pathologies that originate solely on the psychotic or borderline levels.

3. Beginning practitioner—Psychic pathologies besetting the novitiate include:

a) *Psychic inflation*—The universal-transpersonal energies and insights of the psychic level are exclusively applied to the individual ego or centaur, with extremely unbalancing results (particularly if there are narcissistic subphase residues in the self-structure).

b) *Structural imbalance due to faulty practice of the spiritual technique*—This is particularly common in the paths of purification and purgation; in kriya and charya yoga; and in the more subtle techniques, such as mantrayana. It usually manifests in mild, free-floating-anxiety, or in psychosomatic conversion symptoms (headaches, minor heart arrhythmia, intestinal discomforts, etc.).

c) *The Dark Night of the Soul*—Once the soul obtains a direct taste or experience of the Divine, with concomitant vision, ecstasy, or clarity, and that experience begins to fade (which it initially does), the soul may suffer a profound abandonment depression (*not* to be confused with borderline, neurotic, or existential depression; in this case, the soul *has seen* its meaning in life, its daemon or destiny, only to have it fade—that is the Dark Night).

d) *Split life-goals*—For example, "Do I stay in the world or retreat to meditation?" This can be extremely painful and psychologically paralyzing. It expresses one form of a profound splitting between upper and lower self-needs, analogous to text-splitting in script pathology, repression in psychoneuroses, etc.

e) *"Pseudo-duhkha"*—In certain paths of meditation (e.g., vipassana), where investigation into the very nature of the phenomena of consciousness is stressed, the early phase of awareness training (particularly the "stage of reflection") brings a growing realization of the painful nature of manifest existence itself. Where this realization becomes overwhelming—more overwhelming than the training itself is supposed to invoke—we speak of "pseudo-duhkha." Pseudo-duhkha is often the result of residual existential, psychoneurotic, or, more often, residual borderline contamination of the psychic fulcrum of development. The individual does not gain an understanding of the sourness of life; he or she simply goes sour on life. This psychic depression may be one of the most difficult to treat effectively, particularly because it is often backed by the rationalization that, according to (misunderstood) Buddhism, the world is *supposed* to be suffering. In such cases, more vipassana is exactly what is *not* needed.

f) *Pranic disorders*—This refers to a misdirection of kundalini energy in the early stages of its arousal. Various psychic (pranic) channels are over- or underdeveloped, crossed, or prematurely opened, e.g., "wind-horse" *(rLung)* disorders in Tibetan Buddhism. Pranic disorders are usually caused by improper visualization and concentration. They are particularly prevalent in raja yoga, siddha yoga, yoga tantra, and anu yoga. Dramatic psychosomatic symptoms are usually prevalent, including barely controllable muscle spasms, violent headache, breathing difficulty, etc.

g) *"Yogic illness" (Aurobindo)*—This disorder, according to Aurobindo, results when the development of the higher or psychic levels of consciousness puts an undue strain on the physical-emotional body. The great intensity of psychic and subtle energies, can, as it were, overload the "lower circuits," resulting (according to Aurobindo) in everything from allergies to intestinal problems to heart disorders.

Fulcrum-8: Subtle Disorders

The emergence of the subtle basic structure of consciousness brings with it the possibility of subtle-level self-development: a new and higher mode of self, with new object relations, new motivations, new forms of life, new forms of death—and new forms of possible pathology.

The two vulnerable points of F-8 pathology concern: (1) the differentiation-separation-transcendence of the previous mental-psychic dimension, and (2) the identification-integration-consolidation of the subtle-archetypal self and its object relations. Apparently, this pathology occurs most often in intermediate-to-advanced meditators. Some of its many forms:

1. *Integration-Identification Failure*—The subtle basic structure—which is conceived and perceived by different paths as a Being, a Force, an Insight, a Deity-Form, or a self-luminous Presence (all of which, for simplicity's sake, are referred to as Archetypal Presence or Archetypal Awareness)—is first apprehended, to put it metaphorically, "above and behind" mental-psychic consciousness. Eventually, as contemplation deepens, the self differentiates from its psychic moorings and ascends to an intuited identification with that Ground, Insight, Archetypal Presence or Awareness. "Gradually we realize that the Divine Form or Presence is our own archetype, an image of our own essential nature" (Hixon, 1978). This identity arises concomitantly with a beginning *witnessing* of the object relations of subtle consciousness—infinite space, audible illuminations *(nada)*, Brahma realms of ascended knowledge (in guru

yoga, this also includes an intuited identification with the guru and lineage as Archetypal Self). A *failure* to realize this Prior Identity-Awareness, *after* the practitioner is in fact structurally capable of it, is the central defining pathology of these syndromes, because it constitutes, at that point, a fracture between self and Archetype; in Christian terms, a pathology of the soul.

This fracture arises for one basic reason: to identify with and as Archetypal Presence or Awareness demands the *death* of the mental-psychic self. Rather than suffer this humiliation, the self *contracts* on its own separate being, thus fracturing the higher and prior archetypal identity. *Fragments* of Archetypal Presence then appear as *objects* of a still dualistic awareness, instead of whole Archetypal Presence acting as prior and intuited Subject of transcendental consciousness. In other words, instead of *being* Archetypal Awareness (as a subject), the self, in meditation, merely stares at fragments of it (as objects). Consolidation (8c) is not reached.

2. *Pseudo-nirvana*—This is simply the mistaking of subtle or archetypal forms, illuminations, raptures, ecstasies, insights, or absorptions for final liberation. This is not a pathology unless one is in fact pursuing causal or ultimate levels of consciousness, in which case the *entire* subtle realm and all its experiences, if clung to, are considered pathological, makyo, subtle illusions—Zen actually calls it the "Zen sickness."

3. *Pseudo-realization*—This is the subtle-level equivalent of pseudo-duhkha on the psychic. As vipassana meditation proceeds into the subtle levels of awareness, a stage of insight called "realization" arises (beyond which lies "effortless insight," the highest of the subtle-level developments). At the realization stage, *every* content of consciousness appears terrifying, oppressive, disgusting, painful, and loathsome; there is extreme physical pain and intense mental-psychic discomfort. However, this is not the pathology of this stage, but is *normalcy* at this stage, which involves an intense insight into the ultimately unsatisfactory nature of phenomena when viewed apart from noumenon. This intense pain and revulsion acts as the motivation to transcend all conceivable manifestation in nirvanic absorption. The pseudo-realization pathology occurs when that process fails to quicken and the soul is stranded on the shores of its own agony. Although Theravadin theorists might object to this terminology and its implications, it does seem that this pathology, in deep structure form, is identical to what was previously called a failure to engage Archetypal Awareness and its stable witnessing of all subtle-level object relations.

Fulcrum-9: Causal Disorders

The last major fulcrum of self-development has, for its two branches (c and d), the Formless or Unmanifest (9c), and the entire world of Form, or the Manifest Realm (9d). Normal development involves their proper differentiation (in the causal) and their final integration (in the ultimate). Pathology, on the other hand, results from miscarriages in either of these two crucial movements.

1. *Failure of Differentiation*—An inability to accept the final death of the archetypal self (which is simply the subtlest level of the separate-self sense) locks consciousness into an attachment to some aspect of the manifest realm. The Great Death never occurs, and thus Formless Consciousness fails to differentiate from or transcend the manifest realm. The fall into the Heart is blocked by the subtlest contracting, grasping, seeking, or desiring; the final block: desire for liberation.

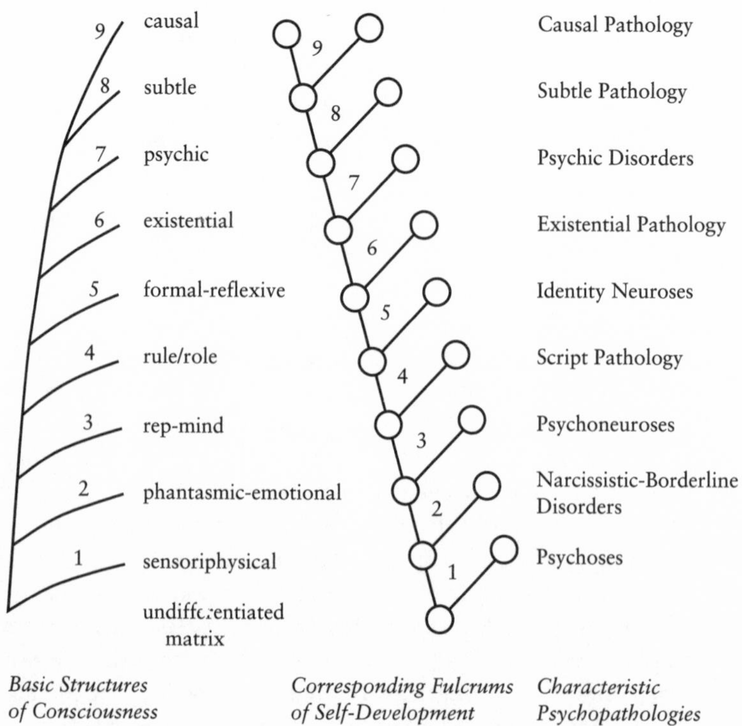

Figure 10. Correlation of Structures, Fulcrums, Psychopathologies

2. *Failure to Integrate, or Arhat's Disease*—Consciousness manages to differentiate itself from *all* objects of consciousness, or the entire manifest realm, to the extent that no objects even arise in awareness (jnana samadhi, nirvikalpa samadhi, nirvana). Although this is the "final" goal of some paths, in fact a subtle disjuncture, dualism, or tension now exists in consciousness, namely, between the manifest and the unmanifest realms. Only as this disjuncture is penetrated does the manifest realm arise as a modification of Consciousness, not a distraction from it. This is classic sahaj-bhava samadhi, the nondual union of Emptiness and Form.

Figure 10 is a schematic summary of the discussion thus far: the basic structures of consciousness, the corresponding fulcrums of self-development, and the possible pathologies that may occur at each fulcrum.

3

Treatment Modalities

In this chapter, Wilber concludes his presentation with a discussion of the various treatment modalities or therapeutic interventions that seem most appropriate for each of the major levels of psychopathology. In the closing section, he discusses the nature of narcissism, dreams, and psychotherapy/meditation, in light of the spectrum model.

WE HAVE SEEN that qualitatively different pathologies are associated with qualitatively different levels of self-organization and self-development. It might be expected, then, that a specific level of pathology would best respond to a specific type of psychotherapeutic intervention. In this section I would like to discuss those treatment modalities that seem best tailored to each type or level of self-pathology. Some of these treatment modalities were, in fact, specifically designed to treat a particular class of psychopathologies, and are often contraindicated for other syndromes.

Fulcrum-1 (Psychoses): Physiological Intervention

Most forms of severe or process psychoses do not respond well (or at all) to psychoanalytic therapy, psychotherapy, analytic psychology, family therapy, etc. (Greist, 1982)—despite repeated and pioneering efforts in this area (Laing, 1967). These disturbances seem to occur on such a primitive level of organization (sensoriperceptual and physiological) that only intervention at an equally primitive level is effective—namely, pharmacological or physiological (which does not rule out psychotherapy as an adjunct treatment [Arieti, 1967; Greist, 1982]).

Fulcrum-2 (Narcissistic-Borderline Disorders): Structure-Building Techniques

The central problem in the narcissistic and borderline syndromes is not that the individual is repressing certain impulses or emotions of the self, but that he or she does not yet possess a separated-individuated self in the first place (Blanck & Blanck, 1979). In a sense, there is not yet a repressed unconscious (or a "repression barrier") (Gedo, 1981). All the various thoughts and emotions are present and largely conscious, but there is considerable confusion as to *whom* these belong to—there is, in other words, a fusion, confusion, or splitting of self and object representations. The self is not yet strong enough or structured enough to "push" contents into the unconscious, and so instead simply rearranges the surface furniture. The boundaries between self and other are either blurred (narcissism) or very tenuous (borderline), and the self shuffles its feelings and thoughts indiscriminately between self and other, or groups all its good feelings on one subject (the "all-good part-object") and all its bad feelings on another (the "all-bad part-object") (Masterson, 1981).

Accordingly, the aim of therapy on this level is not so much to uncover unconscious drives or impulses, but to build structure. In fact, it is often said that the aim of therapy in these less-than-neurotically structured clients is to enable them to reach the level of neurosis, repression, and resistance (Blanck & Blanck, 1979). Therapy on the fulcrum-2 level thus involves the so-called "structure-building techniques," as contrasted with the "uncovering techniques" used to deal with repression and the psychoneuroses (Gedo, 1979, 1981; Blanck & Blanck, 1974, 1979).

The aim of the structure-building techniques, very simply, is to help the individual re-engage and complete the separation-individuation process (fulcrum-2) (Masterson, 1981). That involves an understanding (and undermining) of the two central defenses that the individual uses to prevent separation-individuation from occurring: projective identification (or fusion of self and object representations) and splitting (Kernberg, 1976; Rinsley, 1977). In projective identification (or merger defense), the self fuses its own thoughts and feelings (and particularly self-representations) with those of the other. Notice that the thoughts and feelings remain more or less conscious; they are not repressed, they simply tend to be fused or confused with those of the other. This inability to differentiate self and other leads to the self engulfing the world (narcissistic disorders) or the world invading and threatening to engulf the self (borderline disorders). In splitting, the particular thoughts and feelings also remain largely conscious, but they are divided up or compartmentalized in a rather primitive fashion. Splitting apparently begins in this way: During the first 6 months or so of life, if the mothering one soothes the infant, it forms an image of the "good mother"; if she disturbs it, an image of the "bad mother" forms. At this early stage, however, the self does not have the cognitive capacity to realize that the "good images" and the "bad images" are simply two different aspects of the *same* person (or "whole object"), namely, the real mother. As development continues, however, the infant must learn to integrate the "all-good part-object" and the "all-bad part-object" into a whole image of the object, which is *sometimes* good and *sometimes* bad. This is thought to be a crucially important task, because if there is excessive rage at the "all-bad part-object," the infant will not integrate it with the loving "all-good part-object" for fear it will harm the latter. In less technical language, the infant doesn't want to realize that the person it hates is also the person it loves, because the murderous rage at the former might destroy the latter. The infant therefore *continues* to hold apart, or split, its object world into all-good pieces and all-bad pieces (and thus over-react to situations as if they were a dramatic life and death concern, "all-good" or "all-bad") (Spitz, 1965; Jacobson, 1964; Kernberg, 1976).

In short, the F-2 pathologies result because there is *not enough structure* to differentiate self and object representations, and to integrate their part-images into a whole-self image and a whole-object world. The structure-building techniques aim at exactly that differentiation-and-integration.

It is very difficult to describe, in a paragraph, what these techniques involve. Briefly, we may say this: the therapist, keeping in mind the subphases of F-2 development, gently rewards all thrusts toward separation-individuation, and benignly confronts or explains all moves toward dedifferentiating and splitting. At the same time, any distortions of reality—caused by projective identification or splitting—are pointed out and challenged wherever feasible (this is known variously as "optimal disillusionment," "confrontation," etc.). A few typical therapist comments, paraphrased from the literature, illustrate this level of therapy: "Have you noticed how sensitive you are to even the slightest remark? It's as if you want the world to perfectly mirror everything you do, and if it doesn't, you become hurt and angry" (narcissistic mirror transference). "So far you haven't said a single bad thing about your father. Was he really all that good?"(splitting). "What if your husband leaves you? Would it really kill you?" (fear of separation abandonment). "Perhaps you have avoided a really intimate sexual relationship because you're afraid you will be swallowed up or smothered?"(fear of engulfment).

A common feature of the structure-building techniques is to help clients realize that they can *activate themselves,* or *engage separation-indi-*

viduation, and it will not destroy them or the ones they love. Sources on these techniques include Blanck & Blanck (1974, 1979), Masterson (1981), Kernberg (1976), and Stone (1980).

Fulcrum-3 (Psychoneuroses): Uncovering Techniques

Once a strong-enough self-structure has formed (but not before), it can repress, dissociate, or alienate aspects of its own being. The uncovering techniques are designed specifically to bring these unconscious aspects back into awareness, where they can be re-integrated with the central self. Readers may be familiar enough with these techniques, which include psychoanalysis proper (Greenson, 1967), much of Gestalt therapy (Perls, 1971), and the integrating-the-shadow aspect of Jungian therapy (Jung, 1971).

It is worth emphasizing here the importance of a more or less accurate initial diagnosis of the level of pathology involved, in each case, before intensive therapy begins (cf. Gedo, 1981; Masterson, 1981). It is of little use, for instance, to try to integrate the shadow with the ego-self if there is insufficient ego-self to begin with. The types of treatment modalities are characteristically different and often functionally opposed. In F-3 pathologies, for example, resistance is usually confronted and interpreted (as a sign of repression), but in the F-2 pathologies, it is often encouraged and assisted (as a sign of separation-individuation). Sources for such differential diagnosis include Kernberg (1975, 1976), Masterson (1981), Gedo (1981), and Blanck & Blanck (1974, 1979).

Fulcrum-4 (Script Pathology): Cognitive-Script Analysis

Most conventional psychodynamic theorists tend to end their accounts of "serious" pathology at F-3, that is, at the oedipal phase and its resolution (or lack thereof) (see, for example, Greenson, 1967). This is perhaps understandable; after all, the classic psychopathologies (from psychosis to hysteria) do seem to have their most disturbing etiologies in the first three fulcrums of self-development (cf. Abend, 1983; Kernberg, 1976). But this by no means exhausts the spectrum of pathologies, not even the spectrum of "serious" or "profound" pathologies. Accordingly, researchers increasingly have begun to look at higher or postoedipal stages of development and their correlative vulnerabilities and dis-eases.

Take, for example, the notion of "role confusion." The capacity for genuine role taking is a decisively post-oedipal development (the capacity to take the role of other does not emerge, in any sophisticated fashion, until around age 7–8 yrs [Piaget, 1977; Loevinger, 1976], whereas the typical age of oedipal resolution is 6 yrs). Thus, one could theoretically resolve the oedipal conflict in a completely normal and healthy fashion, only to run aground on role confusion and identity confusion, for reasons totally unrelated to oedipal conflicts or concerns. We are here dealing with different levels (not just lines) of development, with different conflicts and vulnerabilities. *These conflicts are much more cognitive than psychodynamic in nature and origin,* because at this point the self increasingly is evolving from bodily to mental levels of the spectrum.

One of Berne's (1972) contributions was the investigation of this crucial level of the self—the text self or script self—on its own terms, without reducing it to merely psychoneurotic or libidinal dimensions. He began with the tripartite ego (Parent-Adult-Child), which shows that he was starting at the F-3 level (and not F-1 or F-2), and then phenomenologically examined how this self took on more complex and intersubjective roles in an extended series of object relations. Similar but more sophisticated types of investigations have been carried out by cognitive role theorists (Selman, 1974), social learning theorists (Bandura, 1971), family therapists (Haley, 1968), cognitive therapists (Beck, 1979), and communications psychologists (Watzlawick, 1967). These closely related techniques, of whatever school, are referred to here as "cognitive-script analysis."

Probably the most prevalent or common pathologies are cognitive-script pathologies. These pathologies—and their treatment modalities—seem to break down into two very general classes, one involving the *roles* a person is playing, and one involving the *rules* the person is following. Though closely related, these two classes may be discussed separately:

1. *Role pathology*—This has been typically investigated by Transactional Analysis (Berne, 1972), family therapists (Nichols, 1984), and cognitive-role psychologists (Branden, 1971). The individual involved in role pathology is sending multi-level communicative messages, one level of which denies, contradicts, or circumvents another level. The individual thus possesses all sorts of hidden agendas, crossed messages, confused roles, duplicitous transactions, and so on. It is the job of the script

analyst to help separate, untangle, clarify, and integrate the various communicative strands involved in role-self pathology. The interior splitting of the text-self into overt versus covert communicative engagements (or into dissociated subtexts) is thus confronted, interpreted, and, if successful, integrated (a new and higher level of differentiation-integration).

2. *Rule pathology*—One of the central tents of cognitive therapy is that "an individual's affect and behavior are largely determined by the way in which he structures the world," and therefore "alterations in the content of the person's underlying cognitive structures affect his or her affective state and behavioral pattern" (Beck, 1979). In other words, an individual's cognitive schemas, configurations, or rules are a major determinant of his or her feelings and actions. Confused, distorted, or self-limiting rules and beliefs can be manifest in clinical symptoms; conversely, "through psychological therapy a patient can become aware of his distortions," and "corrections of these faulty dysfunctional constructs can lead to clinical improvement"(Beck, 1979). Similar cognitive approaches can also be found in such theorists as George Kelley (1955) and Albert Ellis (1973).

I do not mean to imply that cognitive-script therapy applies solely to F-4 pathology (it appears to have significant applications in the F-3, F-4, F-5, and F-6 range). It is simply that F-4 is the first major stage in which cognitive-script concerns fully develop and begin to differentiate themselves from the more psychodynamic concerns of the previous fulcrums. As in any developmental sequence, such early stages are particularly vulnerable to pathological distortions. Just as adult sexual dysfunctions can often be traced back to early Oedipal/Electra conflicts, many of the cognitive-script pathologies seem to have their genesis in the early (and possibly distorted or limited) rules and roles one learned when the mind *first* became capable of extended mental operations (i.e., during fulcrum-4). Thus, in addition to uncovering techniques, the pathogenic cognitive-script should ideally be attacked on its own level and in its own terms.

Fulcrum-5 (Identity Neurosis): Introspection

The holarchic model of pathology and treatment presented thus far is in substantial agreement with mainstream, conventional psychiatry. To cite one example, as far back as 1973 Gedo and Goldberg presented a hierarchic model composed of, as they word it, "five subphases and five therapeutic modalities. Each modality was tailored to deal with the principal problem characterizing a different subphase: introspection [formal-reflection] for the difficulties expectable in adult life, interpretation for the intrapsychic conflicts [psychoneuroses], 'optimal disillusionment' for archaic idealizations of others or self-aggrandizement [narcissistic mirroring], 'unification' for any failure to integrate one coherent set of personal goals [borderline splitting], and 'pacification' [pharmacological/custodial] for traumatic states."

With the exception of cognitive-script pathology and analysis, Gedo and Goldberg's model is, within general limits, quite compatible with the one I have thus far presented (i.e., F-1 to F-5). Pacification, either custodial or pharmacological, refers to F-1 pathology. "Optimal disillusionment"is a structure-building technique for the narcissistic disorders, and involves benign ways of letting the narcissistic self realize that it is not as grandiose or omnipotent as it thought or feared. "Unification" is a structure-building technique to overcome splitting, which is thought to centrally characterize F-2 pathology. "Interpretation" refers specifically to interpreting the resistances (repressions) and transferences manifested in the treatment of the F-3 pathologies (the psychoneuroses). And introspection, in this context, refers to the techniques used in dealing with the difficulties or problems that arise from F-5 development: the formal-reflexive-introspective self and its turmoils.

According to Gedo (1981), "The mode that reflects postoedipal phases of mental organization permits the analysand to apprehend his internal life through introspection, i.e., without the interpretation of defensive operations. In such circumstances, the role of the analyst is optimally confined to lending his presence to the procedure as an empathic witness." That is, the central and defining problems of F-5 development involve neither psychoneurotic repression nor immersion in pathogenic scripts, but the *emergence* and *engagement* of the formal-reflexive mind and its correlative, introspective self-sense (with its particular vulnerabilities and distresses). No amount of uncovering techniques or script analysis will suffice to handle these problems, precisely because these problems involve structures that transcend those lower levels of organization and thus present entirely new features, functions, and pathologies of their own.

This is not to say, of course, that F-5 pathology has no relation to the developments (or lack of them) at the previous four fulcrums. As we will see in a subsequent discussion of COEX systems, any previous subphase deficiencies, if not enough to arrest development entirely at a lower level, can and will invade upper development in specific and disturbing ways (cf. Blanck & Blanck, 1979; Mahler, 1975). In this case, for example, an individual with only partial F-2 (or separation-individuation) resolution may be very reluctant to engage the formal-reflexive mind, with its demanding call to individual principles of moral reasoning and conscience. The attempted engagement of the formal-reflexive mind might trigger abandonment-depression or separation anxiety.

Introspection may be considered simply another term for *philosophizing,* and it is philosophizing, by any other name, that seems to be the treatment modality of this level. However, I do not agree with Gedo that the therapist's job at this level is simply to be a silent empathic witness to the client's emergent philosophizing. To be merely silent at this point is to risk being absent (i.e., worthless). Gedo's psychoanalytic orientation may have instilled in him unwarranted fears of "contaminating" the client with countertransference material. But by Gedo's own definitions, *if* that occurs, it could only involve the interpretive modality, not the introspective. If the client is clearly in the introspective (not interpretive) modality, there is nothing to be lost, and much to be gained, by the therapist taking a more active role, becoming, in a sense, a co-educator or co-philosopher.

It is exactly at this level, then, that the therapist can engage the client in a *Socratic dialogue,* which engages, simultaneously, the client's formal-reflexive mind. (If, in this dialogue, lower-level residues surface, the therapist can revert to interpretation, structure-building, script analysis, etc.) As with any Socratic dialogue, the particular content is not as important as the fact that it engages, activates, draws out, and exercises the client's reflexive-introspective mind and its correlative self-sense (e.g., Loevinger's conscientious and individualistic). The therapist, then, need not overly worry about "contaminating" the client with his or her own philosophy; once engaged, the formal mind, by definition, will gravitate toward its own views, the birth of which the therapist may Socratically assist.

Fulcrum-6 (Existential Pathology): Existential Therapy

As introspection and philosophizing are engaged and matured, the basic, fundamental, or existential concerns of being-in-the-world come increasingly to the fore (cf. Maslow, 1968; May, 1958). Existential pathology occurs if these concerns begin to overwhelm the newly formed centauric self and freeze its functioning (Wilber, 1980a). These pathologies include, as we have seen, existential depression, angst, inauthenticity, a flight from finitude and death, and so forth.

How these existential pathologies are handled varies considerably from system to system; for some, it is a simple continuing and qualitative deepening of the introspective mode. But a central therapeutic commonality seems to be this: the *clearer* or more transparent the self becomes (via concernful reflection), or the more it can empty itself of egocentric, power-based, or inauthentic modes, the more it comes to an *autonomous* or *authentic* stance or grounding (Zimmerman, 1981). And it is this *grounding* in authenticity and autonomy that *itself* provides existential meaning in life, that combats dread and angst, and that provides a courage to be in the face of "sickness unto death" (Tillich, 1952; May, 1977). Authentic being, in other words, carries intrinsic (not extrinsic) meaning; it is precisely the search for extrinsic or merely external meaning that constitutes inauthenticity (and thus existential despair). Analysis of, and confrontation of, one's various inauthentic modes—particularly extrinsically oriented, nonautonomous, or death-denying—seems to be the key therapeutic technique on this level (Koestenbaum, 1976; Yalom, 1980; May, 1958; Boss, 1963).

These concepts of intrinsic *meaning* (or a new and higher level of interiorization) and the engagement of *autonomy* (or a new and higher level of self responsibility) seem to be the two central features emphasized by all genuine schools of humanistic-existential therapy. Further, their claim that this constitutes a higher level of development has substantial clinical and empirical research support—this is, for example, Loevinger's (1976) integrated/autonomous (as opposed to the previous conscientious/individualistic).

I should point out that when existential therapists speak of the self becoming a clearing or opening for the "Being" of phenomena, they do not mean that the self has access to, or opens to, any genuinely transcendental or timeless and spaceless modes of being. The self is an opening to Being, but that opening is strictly finite, individual and mortal. As far as they go, I agree with the existentialists; there is nothing timeless or eternal about the centauric self, and an acceptance of that fact is part of the very definition of authenticity. But to say this is the whole picture is to say the centauric self is the highest self, whereas, according to the *philosophia perennis,* there lie above it the entire realms of the superconscient. If this is correct, then at this point a denial of the possibility of spiritual transcendence would constitute a preeminent defense mechanism. It is my own belief that what the existentialists call autonomy is simply a higher interiorization of consciousness (see subsequent discussion); if this interiorization continues, it easily discloses psychic and subtle developments. The self is then no longer an opening to Being; it starts to identify with, and as, Being itself.

Fulcrum-7 (Psychic Pathology): The Path of Yogis

Da Free John (1977) has divided the world's great esoteric traditions into three major levels: the Path of Yogis, which predominantly aims for the psychic wave; the Path of Saints, which predominantly aims for the subtle wave; and the Path of Sages, which predominantly aims for the causal. That terminology will be used in the following sections, as I am in substantial agreement with his writings on these topics.

However, since these terms tend to have several different connotations, many not intended by Free John or by myself, one may also refer to these levels with more neutral terms, such as beginning, intermediate, and advanced; or ground, path, and fruition. I have tried to represent the various contemplative traditions evenly, but if it appears that my own preferences and biases are coloring any of the following discussions, I invite the reader to reinterpret them according to the terms, practices, and philosophies of his or her own particular path. My central point, no matter how it might be finally worded, is that contemplative development in general possesses three broad levels or stages (beginning, intermediate, and advanced); that different tasks and capacities emerge at each level; that different distortions, pathologies, or disorders may therefore occur at each level; and that these distortions or pathologies may best be treated by different types of "spiritual" therapy (some of which may also benefit from adjunct conventional therapies).

The following discussion of psychic (F-7) pathology parallels that of the preceding chapter, which outlined three general types—spontaneous, psychotic-like, and beginners.

1. *Spontaneous*—For pathology resulting from spontaneous and unsought awakening of spiritual-psychic energies or insights, there seem to be only two general treatment modalities: the individual must either "ride it out," sometimes under the care of a conventional psychiatrist who may interpret it as a borderline or psychotic break and prescribe medication, which often freezes the process in midcourse and prevents any further reparative developments (Grof, 1975); or the individual can *consciously* engage this process by taking up a contemplative discipline.

If the spontaneous awakening is of the kundalini itself, the Path of Yogis is most appropriate (raja yoga, kriya yoga, charya yoga, kundalini yoga, siddha yoga, hatha-ashtanga yoga, etc.). This is so for a specific reason: the Path of Saints and the Path of Sages, which aim for the higher subtle and causal realms, contain very little explicit teachings on the stages of psychic-kundalini awakening (e.g., one will look in vain through the texts of Zen, Eckhart, Saint John of the Cross, etc., for any mention or understanding of kundalini). If at all possible, the individual should be put in touch with a qualified yogic adept, who can work, if desired, in conjunction with a more conventional therapist (see, for example, Avalon, 1974; Krishna, 1972; Mookerjee, 1982; Taimni, 1975; Da Free John, 1977; White, 1979).

2. *Psychotic-like*—For genuinely psychotic or psychotic-like episodes with periodic but distorted spiritual components, Jungian therapy may be suggested (cf. Grof, 1975; White, 1979). A contemplative discipline, whether yogic, saintly, or sagely, is usually contraindicated; these disciplines demand a sturdy ego or centaur-level self, which the psychotic or borderline does not possess (Engler, 1984). After a sufficient period of structure-building (which most Jungian therapists are aware of), the individual may wish to engage in the less strenuous contemplative paths (e.g., mantrayana); see section on "Meditation and Psychotherapy."

3. *Beginning Practitioner*

a) *Psychic inflation*—This confusion of higher or transpersonal realms with the individual ego or centaur can often be handled with a subtler version of "optimal disillusionment," a continual separation of psychic fact from narcissistic fantasies (cf. Jung, 1971). If this repeatedly fails, it is usually because a psychic insight has reactivated a narcissistic-borderline or even psychotic residue. At that point, meditation should usually be stopped and, if necessary, structure-building engaged (either psychoanalytic or Jungian). If the individual responds to these, and eventually can understand the how and why of his psychic inflation, meditation can usually be resumed.

b) *Structural imbalance* (due to faulty practice of the spiritual technique)—The individual should verify this with the meditation teacher; these imbalances, which are not uncommon, point up how extremely important it is to undertake contemplative disciplines only under the guidance of a qualified teacher (cf. Aurobindo, n.d.; Khetsun, 1982).

c) *Dark Night of the Soul*—Reading accounts of how others have weathered this phase can be very helpful (see especially Saint John of the Cross, Underhill, Kapleau). In periods of profound despair, the soul may break into petitionary, as opposed to contemplative, prayer (to Jesus, Mary, Kannon, Allah, etc.); this need not be discouraged—it is prayer to one's own higher Archetype (cf. Hixon, 1978; Kapleau, 1965). It might be noted that no matter how profound the depression or agony of the Dark Night might be, the literature contains virtually no cases of its leading to suicide (in sharp contrast to existential or borderline depressions, for example). It is as if the depression of the Dark Night had a "higher" or "purgatorial" or "intelligent" purpose—and this, of course, is exactly the claim of contemplatives (see, for example, Saint John of the Cross, 1959).

d) *Split-life goals*—It is important (particularly in our society, and particularly at this point in evolution) that one's spiritual practice be integrated into daily life and work (as a bodhisattvic endeavor). If one's path is of exclusion and withdrawal, perhaps one ought to consider another path. In my opinion, the path of ascetic withdrawal all too often introduces a profound split between the upper and lower dimensions of existence, and, in general, confuses *suppression* of earthly life with transcendence of earthly life.

e) *Pseudo-duhkha*—Although the details of the treatment modality for this disorder may be worked out with the meditation teacher, the teacher is sometimes the worst person to consult in these particular cases. Spiritual teachers generally have no knowledge of the dynamics of borderline or psychoneurotic disorders, and their advice may be, "Intensify your effort!," which is precisely what triggered the problem in the first place. In most cases, the meditator should cease all meditation for a few months. If moderate-to-severe depression/anxiety persists, a borderline or psychoneurotic COEX might have been reactivated (see subsequent discussion), and appropriate structure-building or uncovering therapies might be engaged. It seems inadvisable for such an individual to continue intensive meditation until the particular subphase deficiencies have received appropriate attention.

f) *Pranic disorders*—These disorders are notorious for inducing hysterical-like conversion symptoms which, if left untreated, may induce genuine psychosomatic disease (cf. Da Free John, 1978; Chang, 1974; Evans-Wentz, 1971). They are best handled in conjunction with the yogic meditation teacher (and a physician if needed). Specifically suggested: kriya yoga, charya yoga, raja yoga and (more advanced) anu yoga (Khetsun, 1982; Rieker, 1971; Chang, 1974). Also, acupuncture performed by *qualified* practitioners may be very effective.

g) *Yogic illness*—The best "cure" is also the best prevention: strengthening and purifying the physical-emotional body: exercise, diet, restricted intake of caffeine, sugar, nicotine, alcohol, and social drugs (Aurobindo, n.d.; Da Free John, 1978).

Fulcrum-8 (Subtle Pathology): The Path of Saints

1. *Integration-Identification Failure*—The author is not aware of any treatment modality for this pathology except to engage (or intensify) the path of subtle-level contemplation (the Path of Saints), which, at this point, usually *begins* to involve some form of *inquiry,* overt or covert, into the *contraction* that constitutes the separate-self sense (Da Free John, 1978; Ramana Maharshi, 1972; Suzuki, 1970). It is said to be an actual *seeing* of that contraction, which is blocking subtle or transcendental awareness, that constitutes the therapeutic treatment for this particular disorder (much as, in psychoanalysis, one has to deal with the resistance first, then the content).

According to some traditions (e.g., Aurobindo, Christian mysticism, Hinduism), if this contraction or subtle-level resistance is not relaxed to a sufficient degree (it is not totally dismantled until the causal level), the consolidation and stabilization of the archetypal self will not be achieved, and the individual may then be inundated and overwhelmed by the tremendously powerful energies and dynamics released in the subtle realm—some Tantric texts speak of being "destroyed by luminosity" (e.g., Evans-Wenz, 1971); in Christian mystical terms, the soul damages itself by denying (resisting) God's love (or archetypal presence).

The common treatment modality for these disorders seems to include a *seeing* and then *understanding* of the subtle contraction or resistance to a larger transcendental awareness, a contraction that at bottom involves an inability to accept the death of the previous (or mental/psychic) self-sense and its attachments and desires—a case of morbid fixation or arrest at the mental/psychic level (which prevents transformation to the subtle; see, for example, Aurobindo, n.d.; Da Free John, 1978: Trungpa, 1976; Khetsun, 1982).

According to Hinduism and Buddhism, it is at this point, too, that one begins to encounter and understand the "deep-seated defilements" (root *kleshas* and *vasanas*) that not only obscure the next and higher stage of formless or unmanifest awareness, but ultimately give rise to all forms of human suffering and pathology, high or low (Deutsche, 1969; Feuerstein, 1975; Gard, 1962; Longchenpa, 1977).

2. *Pseudo-nirvana*—This mistaking of subtle illuminations and archetypal forms for ultimate enlightenment can only be handled by moving beyond these luminous forms to unmanifest or *formless cessation;* that is, by moving from subtle to causal level development. Many of the most sophisticated contemplative traditions have numerous "checking routines" that help the practitioner review the ecstatic, luminous, blissful, and "tempting" subtle experiences and thus eventually gain a distancing or nonattached stance toward this archetypal level (after, that is, it has been stably achieved in the first place) (Goleman, 1977; Da Free John, 1978; Khetsun, 1982; Trungpa, 1976).

3. *Pseudo-realization*—Unlike pseudo-duhka, which usually demands a halting of meditation, there is usually no cure for pseudo-realization except more meditation. The only thing more painful than continuing meditation is failing to continue meditation. Zen refers to this particular type of "Zen sickness" as being like "swallowing a red-hot iron ball" (Suzuki, 1970); it is apparently one of the few *disorders* for which one can *therapeutically* say, "Intensify your efforts!"

With most subtle-level pathologies, it apparently is not too late for adjunct psychotherapy, if, and only if, the therapist is sympathetic toward, and reasonably knowledgeable about, transcendental or spiritual concerns. The psychotherapeutic freeing of repressed emotional energies, for example, might be the crucial boost needed to negotiate subtle level integration. The structure-building techniques, while not without use, become increasingly less applicable at this stage, because most individuals with significant borderline deficiencies rarely develop to this stage.

Fulcrum-9 (Causal Pathology): The Path of Sages

1. *Failure to Differentiate*—According to teachings as diverse as Zen, Free John, and Vajrayana, this final differentiation or detachment (i.e., from all manifest form) involves a subtle but momentous collaboration on the part of the student and the teacher, which may be briefly (and

inadequately) described as follows: The teacher, at this point, resides within the "Heart"(or causal/unmanifest realm) of the student, and exerts a special "pull"; the student, in the final and root form of the separate-self sense (the archetypal self), is still standing in a subtly contracted form "outside" the Heart (i.e., resisting the final and total dissolution of the separate-self sense). The student and teacher "together," through an "effortless effort," release this stance, and the separate-self "falls" into the Heart. This "fall" into formless, unmanifest cessation or emptiness breaks all exclusive attachment to manifest forms and destinies, and Consciousness as Such (or Absolute Subjectivity) differentiates itself from all objects, high or low, and from all archetypal tendencies or root contractions (kleshas, vasanas, etc.). Repetition of this "fall"—or repeated "movement" from manifest to unmanifest and back again—"burns" the root inclinations and desires for contracted and separated modes of self existence. This fall is the "entrance" to the stages of enlightenment (conceived by Buddhism as ground, path, and fruition enlightenment, which may be thought of as the three subphases of the enlightened or "perfectly ordinary" estate).

2. *Failure to Integrate*—This "ultimate pathology" (a failure to integrate the manifest and unmanifest realms, or Form and Emptiness) results when the root kleshas and vasanas (or archetypal forms and inclinations) are seen *only* as defilements and not also as the means of *expression* or manifestation of unobstructed Wisdom (absolute Spirit or Being). The overcoming of this disjunction and the re-union or re-integration of emptiness-form and wisdom *are* the "supreme path," the path of "ordinary mind" (Maha Ati), "open eyes" (Free John), and "everyday mind" (Ch'an)—wherein all phenomena, high or low, exactly as they find themselves, are seen as already perfect expressions and seals of the naturally enlightened mind.

Figure 11 is a schematic summary of the basic structures of consciousness, the corresponding fulcrums of self-development, their characteristic pathologies, and the correlative treatment modalities.

Related Topics

In this section I would like to comment on differential diagnosis, connections to Grof's COEX systems theory, narcissism, dreams, and meditation/psychotherapy, in light of the full spectrum of development and pathology.

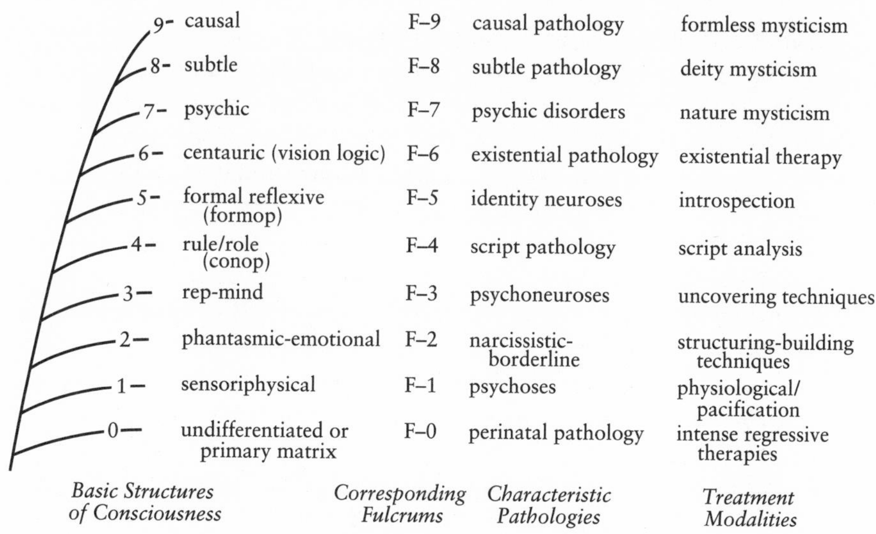

9- causal
F–9
causal pathology
formless mysticism
8- subtle
F–8
subtle pathology
deity mysticism
7- psychic
F–7
psychic disorders
nature mysticism
6- centauric (vision logic)
F–6
existential pathology
existential therapy
5- formal reflexive (formop)
F–5
identity neuroses
introspection
4- rule/role (conop)
F–4
script pathology
script analysis
3- rep-mind
F–3
psychoneuroses
uncovering techniques
2- phantasmic-emotional
F–2
narcissistic-borderline
structuring-building techniques
1- sensoriphysical
F–1
psychoses
physiological/pacification
0- undifferentiated or primary matrix
F–0
perinatal pathology
intense regressive therapies
Basic Structures of Consciousness
Corresponding Fulcrums
Characteristic Pathologies
Treatment Modalities

FIGURE 11. Correlation of Structures, Fulcrums, Psychopathologies, and Treatments

Differential Diagnosis

It is important to emphasize again the great care that should ideally be given to differential diagnosis, *particularly* in light of the full spectrum of human growth and development. For example, psychic anxiety, existential anxiety, psychoneurotic anxiety, and borderline anxiety are apparently very different phenomena with very different treatment modalities, and thus any effective and appropriate therapeutic intervention depends significantly on an accurate initial diagnosis. This, in turn, rests upon a skilled understanding of the entire spectrum of consciousness—an understanding of the overall waves of self-structuralization and the particular types of needs, motivations, cognitions, object relations, defense mechanisms, and pathologies that are specific and characteristic for each stage of structural development and organization.

Currently, models less comprehensive than the one proposed here are being used to diagnose and treat clients, with an apparent collapse of what seem to be very different diagnostic and treatment categories. For example, Kohut's two major diagnostic categories are Tragic Man (borderline) and Guilty Man (neurotic). His theory does not address spiritual pathologies, and therefore must reduce them all to lower-level concerns. Likewise, his conceptualization apparently requires the reduction of existential pathologies to borderline "Tragic Man," as if the only existential tragedy in the cosmos is separation of child from mother.

A major therapeutic confusion among various theorists stems from what I have called the "pre/trans fallacy" (Wilber, 1980b), which is a confusing of *pre*rational structures with *trans*rational structures simply because both are *non*rational. This confusion runs in both directions: prerational structures (phantasmic, magic, mythic) are *elevated* to transrational status (e.g., Jung), or transrational structures are *reduced* to prerational infantilisms (e.g., Freud). It is particularly common to reduce samadhi (subtle or causal subject-object identity) to autistic, symbiotic, or narcissistic-oceanic states. Likewise, Atman, the universal Self, is confused with the monadic-autistic F-1 self. Alexander (1931) even called Zen a training in catatonic schizophrenia. In my opinion, such theoretical (and therapeutic) confusions will continue to abound until the phenomenological validity of the full spectrum of human growth and development receives more recognition and study.

COEX Systems

Stanislav Grof (1975) has coined the term "COEX systems" to refer to "systems of condensed experience," which are developmentally layered or onion-like complexes in the psyche. This is an important concept and, although similar ideas abound in the literature, Grof has given the notion one of its clearest articulations.

Pathological COEX systems, as I see them, are simply the sum of the associated and condensed aspects of unmetabolized experiences or subphase deficiencies that result at any particular fulcrum of self-structuralization (cf. Guntrip, 1971; Kernberg, 1975). Starting at fulcrum-0, any particular subphase deficiency (provided it is not severe enough to derail development entirely at that point) is taken up—as a *dissociated pocket in the self-structure*—during the ongoing march of self-structuralization. At the next fulcrum, any subphase deficiencies or malformations likewise become split off and lodged in the self-structure, where—and this was pointed out by both Grof and Jung—they become condensed and associated with similar, previous subphase malformations. Not only do present-level malformations condense with previous ones, they tend to invade and contaminate the *subsequent* or higher-level fulcrums, skewing their development toward similar pathological malformations (quite apart from the malformations that might develop entirely due to their *own* subphase deficiencies). Like a grain of sand lodged in a pearl during its early formation, each subsequent layer tends to reproduce the defect on its own level. The result is a pathological COEX system, a multi-layered unit of associated and condensed subphase malformations, built up, fulcrum by fulcrum, and lodged, as split or dissociated subunits (or pockets of "unconscious, undigested experience") in the overall self-structure itself.

A presenting symptom, therefore, may be merely the tip of a more or less extensive pathological COEX system. The particular COEX might be compounded of residues from, say, F-5, F-3, and F-2 subphase deficiencies. One of the aims of psychotherapy in general is to re-contact and re-experience the particular undigested subphase residues, layer by layer if necessary, and thus help repair structural malformations—i.e., allow those aspects of the self-system, previously lodged and stuck in various lower subphase pockets, to be released or "freed-up" to *rejoin* the ongoing march of structural organization and development.

Narcissism

"Narcissism" is probably the most confused and confusing topic in the technical therapeutic literature. It has been given literally dozens of different and sometimes contradictory definitions; there are vague references to *levels* of narcissism (primary, secondary, tertiary, etc.); and finally, there is said to be normal narcissism and pathological narcissism. What are we to make of all this?

Most of these confusions can be cleared up if we (1) explicitly define the levels or stages of narcissism, and (2) recognize that each stage of narcissism has both normal and pathological dimensions.

To begin with, the term "narcissism," as it is used in the literature, has several major and quite different meanings. In a neutral or nonpejorative sense, "narcissism" is used to mean "self." "Narcissistic development," for instance, simply means "self-development." No negative connotations of egocentricity, grandiosity, or arrogance are implied. To say there are levels of narcissism or levels of narcissistic development means, in this usage, nothing more than that there are levels of self or levels of self-development. In this chapter, for instance, we have outlined nine major stages (each with three subphases) of "narcissism."

"Narcissism" is also used to mean "selfcentrism," or incapacity to take sufficient awareness of others. This, however, is not necessarily a pathological or morbid condition; in fact, it is usual to distinguish between "normal narcissism" and "pathological narcissism." Normal narcissism refers to the *amount of selfcentrism* that is *structurally inevitable* or normal at each stage of development. Thus, for example, primary narcissism (or incapacity to even recognize an object world) is inevitable or normal at the autistic stage. The grandiose-exhibitionistic self/object fusion is *normal* at the practicing subphase. Although this is often called "the narcissistic stage," as a matter of convention, it is universally recognized that the amount of narcissism (selfcentrism) at this stage is actually less than in the previous stage, because there is at least an awareness of objects, which the previous or primary narcissism lacked entirely.

The rep-mind stage is even less narcissistic or selfcentric than the grandiose stage, but it still possesses a substantial degree of selfcentrism (or narcissism), as Piaget demonstrated, simply because it cannot yet take the role of others. This narcissism decreases with the rule/role mind, since the role of others is now recognized, and decreases even further with the emergence of the formal-mind, which can increasingly escape its own subjectivism by *reflection* on alternative viewpoints.

But at this point a certain amount of selfcentrism still remains, according to the contemplative traditions, simply because a certain amount of the separate-self sense still remains. Even into the subtle realm, according to Da Free John, Narcissus (which is his term) is still present (though highly reduced) because there is still a subtle contraction inward on self and a consequent "recoil from relationship" (Da Free John, 1977).

So here is the first point: there are nine or so major levels of narcissism, *each of which is less narcissistic (less selfcentric) than its predecessor(s)*. Narcissism (selfcentrism) starts out at its peak in the autistic stage (primary narcissism); each subsequent fulcrum of development results in a reduction of narcissism, simply because at each higher stage the self transcends its previous and more limited viewpoints and expands its horizons increasingly beyond its own subjectivisms, a process that continues until narcissism (selfcentrism) finally disappears entirely in the causal realm (simply because the separate-self sense finally disappears).

Now, at each stage of this lessening-narcissistic development, there is not only the normal or healthy amount of structurally inevitable narcissism, there is the *possibility* of an abnormal, pathological, or morbid narcissism on that level. This pathological narcissism is usually a *defensive* measure; the self-structure of that level is overvalued and the self-objects of that level correlatively devalued, in order to avoid a painful confrontation with those self-objects (e.g., on the mental level: "So what if they disagree with me! Who are they anyway? I know what's going on here; they're all really a bunch of clowns," etc.). The result is an amount of narcissism (or selfcentrism) quite beyond what would be structurally inevitable and expectable *at that stage.* Theorists such as Mahler maintain that pathological narcissism may occur even at the earliest stages of self-development (i.e., F-1 and F-2).

In short, the "narcissistic defense" can theoretically occur at any stage of self-development (except the extreme end points), and involves an over-valuation of the self-structure of that stage and a correlative devaluation of the self-objects of that stage, as a defense against being abandoned, humiliated, hurt, or disapproved of by those objects. The narcissistic defense is not indicated merely by a very high self-esteem; if there is an equally high regard for self-objects, this is not narcissistic defense or pathology. It is the imbalance, the overestimation of self *as measured against* the devaluing of others, that marks the narcissistic defense.

It would be technically correct, then, and much less confusing, to define "narcissistic disorders" as the result of the narcissistic defense at *any level* of self-development. Thus, there is the normal narcissism of F-1, and the pathological (defensive) narcissism of F-1; there is a similar potential for normal and pathological narcissism at F-2, F-3, and so on, all the way up to and including the subtle fulcrum.

We could *also* speak of a "narcissistic disorder" if the *normal* narcissism of one stage is *not* outgrown at the *next* stage. In this case, narcissistic disorder would mean a developmental arrest/fixation at the normal narcissism of a particular lower level, and all we would have to do is specify which lower level is involved.

Unfortunately, however, the "narcissistic disorders"—and this is part of the extraordinary confusion surrounding this topic—have been solely defined as a developmental arrest at the normal narcissism of F-2. There is no way to reverse this general usage, and so I have followed it in the first part of this presentation; I will continue to use "narcissistic disorder" in the narrow sense to mean a pathological arrest/fixation at the normal narcissism of F-2.

To summarize: There are nine or so levels of narcissism, each of which is less narcissistic (less selfcentric) than its predecessor(s); each of which has a normal or structurally inevitable amount of narcissism (normal or healthy narcissism), and each of which can develop, as a defensive pathology, a morbid, overblown, or pathological narcissism. The "narcissistic disorders," in the broadest sense, refer to (1) the pathological narcissism that may develop on *any* level, and (2) a pathological arrest/

fixation to the normal narcissism of any *lower* level. In the narrowest sense—that of most present-day theory—a "narcissistic disorder" means an arrest/fixation at the normal narcissism of F-2.

Dreams and Psychotherapy

Dreams have long been held to be the "royal road to the unconscious," i.e., of great help in both the diagnosis and treatment of psychopathology. But given the nine or so levels of psychopathology, how might dreams best be used?

The practical theory of dream work that I have developed suggests the following: the manifest dream can be the latent carrier of pathology (or simply benign messages) from any or all levels, and perhaps the best way to work with the dream is to begin its interpretation at the lowest levels and progressively work upward. The *same* dream symbol in a single dream sequence could carry equally important material (pathological or healthy) from several different levels, and it is necessary to seek interpretations from *all* levels and see which ones elicit a responsive recognition in the individual. The therapist or analyst starts at the lowest levels—F-1 and F-2—and interprets significant dream symbols according to the meanings they might have on those levels. He/she watches for those interpretations that resonate with the client (usually by being emotionally charged), and then works through the charge surrounding each symbol. The dream is thus decathected or relieved of its emotional charge *at that level* (we "get its message"), and the interpretation then moves to the next level, reinterpreting each significant symbol according to its possible meanings on this new level (and so on up the spectrum).

Obviously in practice every single dream symbol cannot be interpreted from every single level—it would take hours or even days to do so. Rather, working from a general knowledge of the individual's overall self-structure and level of overall development, the therapist selects a few key symbols for each of, say, three or four most-suspected levels, and focuses on those. The more developed a person is, the higher the level of interpretation that is likely to also strike a responsive chord, although even the most highly developed individuals are by no means immune from lower-level messages (and frequently just the contrary—the lower levels are sometimes ones they have tended to ignore in their otherwise admirable ascent, a deficiency that dreams will not let them forget!).

The only way to indicate the apparent richness of this approach would be to present several cases with parallel interpretations across the various levels. Since that is beyond the scope of this short section, the following simple example may suffice to indicate the general thrust of this spectrum approach. A middle-aged woman presents a dream which contains a highly charged scenario composed of these central images: she is in a cave (associations: "hell," "death"); there is a silver-luminous pole leading from the cave to the sky ("heaven," "home"); she meets her son in the cave, and together they climb the pole ("release," "safety," "eternity").

What, for example, does the pole represent? From an F-1/F-2 level, it might represent a denial of the "all-bad" mother and a fusion or "umbilicus" to the safety of the symbiotic "all-good" mother (splitting). From an F-3 level, it might represent phallic/incestuous wishes. From an F-4 level, it might symbolize the means of more closely communicating with her son. From F-6, an escape or avoidance of existential death. And from F-7, the silver-lined kundalini sushumna (which is said to be the central channel in the spine leading from the first chakra of the physical-hell realms to the seventh chakra of liberation and release in the transcendental Self).

My point is that the pole might have simultaneously represented *all* of those. The dream symbol, being plastic, is apparently invaded and informed by any pressing issue or level of insistent pathology. Thus the way one might best deal with dreams is to start at the bottom and work up, resonating with the dream at each significant level. (We start at the bottom to insure that we don't take an unrealistic or "elevationist" stance, overlooking the unpleasant lower-level messages that might be involved; we don't *stop* with the lower levels, however, because we also want to avoid the "reductionist" stance, which violates the existential and spiritual dimensions of the human condition).

Meditation and Psychotherapy

Meditation, in my opinion, is not a means of digging back into the lower and repressed structures of the submergent-unconscious, it is a way of facilitating the *emergence,* growth, and development of the higher waves of consciousness. To confuse the two is to foster the reductionist notion, quite prevalent, that meditation is (at best) a regression in service of ego, whereas by design and practice it is a progression in transcendence of ego.

However, when a person begins intensive meditation, submergent-unconscious material (e.g., the shadow) frequently begins to reemerge or occasionally even erupt into consciousness. It is this "derepression of the shadow" that has contributed to the notion that meditation is an uncovering technique and a regression in service of ego. I believe this derepression does in fact frequently occur, but for a very different reason (possessing very different dynamics): Meditation, because it aims at developing or moving consciousness into higher levels or dimensions of structural organization, must break or disrupt the exclusive identification with the *present* level of development (usually mental-egoic). Since it is the *exclusiveness* of the identification that *constitutes* the repression barrier, its disruption, in whole or part, may release previously repressed material—hence the derepression. This happens very often in the initial stages of meditation, but it definitely seems to be a secondary by-product of the practice, not its goal, and certainly not its definition. (For a detailed discussion of this topic, see Wilber, 1980a, 1983.)

Can or should meditation be used in conjunction with psychotherapy? I believe that this depends largely on the type of meditation and on the level of pathology being treated by the particular therapy.

In general, meditation seems contraindicated in F-1 and F-2 pathologies. There simply isn't enough self-structure to engage the intense experiences that meditation practices occasionally involve. Not only does meditation not seem to help in these cases, it apparently can be detrimental, because it tends to dismantle what little structure the borderline or psychotic might possess. Meditation, in other words, tends to undo those intermediate-level self-structures that the borderline or psychotic is in need of creating and strengthening in the first place. Ironically, many individuals with F-2 pathologies are, according to Jack Engler (1983a), actually drawn to meditation, particularly its Buddhist forms, as a *rationalization* for their "no-ego" states. With Engler, I believe meditation is usually contraindicated in such cases.

Most forms of F-3 pathology, on the other hand, can apparently receive auxiliary benefit from meditation practice (cf. Carrington, 1975). I believe vipassana meditation, however, should be used with caution in cases of moderate-to-severe depression, due to the tendency to link psychoneurotic depression with pseudo-duhkha. The Path of Yogis can cause severe emotional-sexual upheavals, a fact that anyone undergoing F-3 therapy might consider before embarking upon that type of meditation. And in cases of psychoneurotic anxiety, Zen koan meditation—which frequently builds anxiety to an explosive peak—is probably contraindicated. But in general, most of the basic forms of meditation (following the breath, counting the breath, mantrayana, shikan-taza, ashtanga, etc.) can be an adjunct benefit to F-3 therapy. An added plus: the meditation itself will probably facilitate, as a by-product, the reemergence or derepression of various unconscious material, which can be worked on in therapy sessions.

Meditation may also be used with most forms of F-4 and F-5 pathologies, but there is a specific complication: someone caught in role-confusion or role-conformist pathology, or who is having a difficult time establishing formal self-identity, is particularly vulnerable to using meditation, and various meditation groups, in a cultic fashion, pledging allegiance to the particular meditative "in-group" as an acting out of unresolved identity neuroses. The resulting "cultic mentality" is extremely difficult to deal with therapeutically, because allegedly "universal-spiritual truths" are being used as an otherwise airtight rationalization for simple acting out.

Most forms of F-6 or existential pathologies, in my experience, usually show a positive response to meditation. Existential anxiety, unlike psychoneurotic anxiety, does not seem to be a contradiction for even the more strenuous meditation practices such as koan (cf. Kapleau, 1965); with existential depression, however, the duhka-intensifying meditations, such as vipassana, might be used with caution. Further, individuals with existential pathologies or persistent existential dilemmas usually find the whole philosophy behind contemplative endeavors to be salutory, pointing to a genuine and transcendental meaning to life's enterprise. Notice I said existential pathology; individuals at the normal existential level itself are frequently uninterested in (and suspicious of) meditation/transcendence—they think it is a deceptive form of death denial.

In sum: meditation is not primarily a structure-building technique, nor an uncovering technique, nor a script-analysis technique, nor a Socratic-dialoguing technique. It cannot substitute for those techniques, nor should it be used as a way to "spiritually bypass" (Welwood, 1984) any major work needed on those levels. In *conjunction* with analysis or therapy, however, it apparently can be very useful in most forms of F-3, F-4, F-5, and F-6 pathology, both because of its own intrinsic merits and benefits, and because it tends to "loosen" the psyche and facilitate derepression on the lower levels, thus contributing in an auxiliary fashion to the therapeutic procedures on those levels.

Meditation and Interiorization

The charge has been circulating, for quite some time now, in both psychoanalytic and popular literature, that meditation is a narcissistic withdrawal (Alexander, 1931; Lasch, 1979; Marin, 1975). I would in this section like to challenge that claim, using the definitions and findings of psychoanalysis itself.

In this chapter we have been discussing the *development* or *evolution* of consciousness. How, then, does psychoanalytic ego psychology define evolution? "Evolution, to [Heinz] Hartmann [the founder of psychoanalytic developmental psychology], is a process of progressive 'internalization,' for, in the development of the species, the organism achieves increased independence from its environment, the result of which is that '. . . reactions which originally occurred in relation to the external world are increasingly displaced into the interior of the organism.' The more independent the organism becomes, the greater its independence from the stimulation of the immediate environment" (Blanck & Blanck, 1974). Increasing development, for such psychoanalysts, is *defined* as increasing interiorization.

It does not follow, then, that such a theoretical orientation should applaud the increasing interiorization from body to ego-mind, but stand back aghast at the increasing interiorization from ego-mind to subtle-soul to causal-spirit (or meditation in general); but this is exactly what happens with a number of psychoanalytically oriented theorists (e.g., Alexander, 1931; Lasch, 1979) and with many popularly oriented writers who claim modern psychiatric support (e.g., Marin, 1975). This apparently occurs because, halfway up the Great Chain of increasing interiorization, these theorists begin to apply the term "narcissism." But we have seen that each higher level of development is marked by *less* narcissism. In other words, a perfectly acceptable psychoanalytic definition is: increasing development = increasing interiorization = decreasing narcissism. From which it follows that meditation, as an increasing development of interiorization, is probably the single strongest tool we have for decreasing narcissism.

This may sound paradoxical if one does not distinguish between two very different sorts of "insideness" or "internalness." Let us call these two sorts of internalness by the names "inside" and "interior." The first point is that each higher level of consciousness is experienced as being "interior" to its lower or preceding level, but *not* as being "inside" it. To give an example: the mind is experienced as being interior to the body, but not inside the body; if I eat some food, the food feels *inside* the body; or if I have a physical ache, that also feels *inside* the body; but there is no inside physical feeling, sensation, twitch, or twinge to which I can point and say, that is my mind. My mind, in other words, is not specifically felt as inside my body (as I am using the term), but is, somehow, felt to be rather vaguely "internal" to the body—and that feeling I call "interior."

The difference is simply that each level of consciousness has its own boundaries, with an inside and an outside; but a higher level is experienced as interior to the lower, not as literally inside it. These boundaries should not be equated, because they exist on different levels entirely. For example, the boundaries of my mind and the boundaries of my body are not the same. Thoughts can *come into* and *go out of* my mind without ever crossing the physical boundaries of my body.

Notice that because my mind is interior to my body, it can go beyond or escape the insides of the body. In my mind I can identify with a country, a political party, a school of thought; in intersubjective reflection I can take the role of others, assume their views, empathize with them, and so on. I could never do this if my mind were *only* and actually *inside* my body. Being interior to it, however, it can escape it, go beyond it, transcend it. This is why *interiorization* means *less narcissism*—one level, being interior to another, can go beyond it, which it could never do if it were really and solely *inside* it.

Likewise, the soul is interior to the mind; it is *not inside* the mind—the only thing inside the mind is thoughts, which is why introspecting the mind never reveals the soul. As thoughts quiet down, however, the soul emerges interiorly vis-à-vis the mind, and therefore can transcend the mind, see beyond it, escape it. And likewise, spirit is not inside the soul, it is interior to the soul, transcending its limitations and forms.

Apparently, then, theorists who claim that meditation is narcissistic imagine that meditators are going *inside* the mind; but they are rather going *interior* to it, and thus beyond it: less narcissistic, less subjectivisitic, less selfcentric, more universal, more encompassing, and thus ultimately more compassionate.

Conclusion

I would like to be very clear about what this presentation has attempted to do. It has not offered a fixed, conclusive, unalterable model. Although

I have at every point attempted to ground it in the theoretical and phenomenological reports of reputable researchers and practitioners, the overall project is obviously metatheoretical and suggestive, and is offered in that spirit. But once one begins to look at the full spectrum of human growth and development, an extraordinarily rich array of material becomes available for metatheoretical work; a variety of connections suggest themselves which were not apparent before; and a wealth of hypotheses for future research become immediately available. Moreover, different analytical, psychological, and spiritual systems, which before seemed largely incompatible or even contradictory, appear closer to the possibility of a mutually enriching synthesis or reconciliation.

This presentation has offered one such full-spectrum approach, more to show the strong possibilities than the final conclusions; if this type of model is useful in reaching better ones, it will have served its purpose. My point, rather, is that given the state of knowledge *already* available to us, it seems ungenerous to the human condition to present any models *less* comprehensive—by which I mean, models that do not take into account both conventional *and* contemplative realms of human growth and development.

References

Abend, S., Porder, M., & Willick, M. *Borderline patients: Psychoanalytic perspective.* New York: International Univ. Press, 1983.

Adler, G. *Dynamics of the self.* London: Conventure, 1979.

Aghiorgoussis, M. *La dilectique de l'image de Dieu chez Saint Basil Le Grand.* Unpublished doctoral dissertation. University of Louvain, France; School of Theology, 1964.

Akiskal, H. S., Djenderedijian, A. H., Bolinger, J. M., Bitar, A. H., Khani, M. D., & Haykal, R. F. The joint use of clinical and biological criteria for psychiatric diagnosis, II: Their application in identifying subaffective forms of bipolar illness. In H. S. Akiskal & W. L. Webb (Eds.), *Psychiatric diagnosis: Exploration of biological predictors.* New York: Spectrum Publications, 1978, 133–45.

Alexander, F. Buddhist training as an artificial catatonia. *Psychoanalytic Review,* 1931, *18,* 129–45.

Allison, J. Adaptive regression and intense religious experiences, *J. Nervous Mental Disease,* 1968, *145,* 452–63.

Allport, F. H. *Theories of perception and the concept of structure.* New York: Wiley, 1967 (1955).

Allport, G. *Becoming.* New Haven: Yale Univ. Press, 1955.

American Psychiatric Association. *Diagnostic and statistical manual of mental disorder.* 3rd Ed. Washington, D.C.: American Psychiatric Association, 1980.

Aquinas, T. *Summa theologiae.* 2 vols. New York: Doubleday/Anchor, 1969.

Arieti, S. *Interpretation of schizophrenia.* New York: Brunner, 1955.

———. *The intrapsychic self.* New York: Basic Books, 1967.

Arnold, M. B. Brain function in emotion: A phenomenological analysis. In P. Black (Ed.), *Physiological correlates of emotion.* New York: Academic Press, 1970a, 261–85.

———. Perennial problems in the field of emotion. In M. B. Arnold (Ed.), *Feelings and emotions.* New York: Academic Press, 1970b, 1969–85.

Assagioli, R. *Psychosynthesis: A manual of principles and techniques.* New York: Hobbs, Dorman, 1971

Athanasios, St. Migne. Patrologia Græcæ, 101B.

Aurobindo. *The life divine* and *The synthesis of yoga.* Pondicherry: Centenary Libary, XVIII-XXI, n.d.

Avalon, A. *The serpent power.* New York: Dover, 1974 (1931).
Baldwin, J. *Thought and things.* New York: Arno Press, 1975 (1906–15).
Bandura, A. *Social learning theory.* New York: General Learning Press, 1971.
———. Self-efficacy: Toward a unifying theory of behavioral change. *Psychological Review,* 1977, 34, 191–215.
Basil, St. Migne. *Patrologia Græcæ,* 20B, 29C, 30, 31, 32, 32B, 32C, 37A, 213D–216A, 864C, 908, 909, 909B,C.
———. (Phillip Shaff & Henry Wase, Trans.) Letters. *The Nicene and Post-Nicene fathers.* Vol. VIII. Grand Rapids, MI: 1955.
Beck, A., Rush, A., Shaw, B., & Emery, G. *Cognitive therapy of depression.* New York: Guilford Press, 1979.
Becker, E. *The denial of death.* New York: Free Press, 1973.
Bergin, A. E. Psychotherapy and religious values. *J. Consulting Clinical Psychology,* 1980, *48,* 95–105.
Berne, E. *What do you say after you say hello?* New York: Bantam, 1972.
Binder, H. *Die Helldunkeldeutungen im Psychodiagnostischem Experiment von Rorschach.* Zurich: Urell Fussli, 1932.
Binswanger, L. Existential analysis and psychotherpay. In F. Fromm-Reichmann & J. Moreno (Eds.), *Progress in psychotherapy.* New York: Grune & Stratton, 1956.
Blanck, G. & Blanck, R. *Ego psychology: Theory and practice.* New York: Columbia Univ. Press, 1974.
———. *Ego psychology II: Psychoanalytic developmental psychology.* New York: Columbia Univ. Press, 1979.
Blofeld J. *The tantric mysticism of Tibet.* New York: Dutton, 1970.
Bloomfield, H. H. Some observations on the uses of the Transcendental Meditation program in psychiatry. In D. W. Orme-Johnson & J. T. Farrow (Eds.), *Scientific research on transcendental meditation, Vol. I.* Weggis: M.E.R.U. Press, 1977.
Blos, P. *On adolescence: A psychoanalytic interpretation.* New York: Free Press, 1962.
———. The second individuation process of adolescence. *The Psychoanalytic Study of the Child,* 1967, 22, 162–86.
Bohm, D. Quantum theory as an indication of a new order in physics: Part B. Implicate and explicate order in physical law. *Foundations of Physics,* 1973, 2, 139–68.
Boorstein, S. The use of bibliotherapy and mindfulness meditation in a psychiatric setting. *J. Transpersonal Psychology,* 1983, *15,* 2, 173–9.
Boss, M. *Psychoanalysis and daseinsanalysis.* New York: Basic Books, 1963.
Bourguignon, E. The self, the behavioral environment, and the theory of spirit-possession. In Melford F. Spiro (Ed.), *Context and meaning in cultural anthropology.* New York: Free Press, 1965.
Bouyer, L. In Markey Perkins Ryan (Trans.), *Introduction to spirituality.* Collegeville, MN: Liturgical Press, 1961.
Bowlby, J. *Attachment and loss,* vol. 1: *Atttachment.* New York: Basic Books, 1969.
Bowlby, J. *Attachment and loss.* vol. 2, *Separation.* New York: Basic Books, 1973.

Boyer, L. & Giovacchini, P. *Psychoanalytic treatment of characterological and schizophrenic disorders.* New York: Aronson, 1967.

Boyer, L. B., Klopfer, B., Brawer, F. B. & Kawai, H. Comparison of the shamans and pseudoshamans of the Apache of the Mescalero Indian Reservation: A Rorschach Study. *J. Projective Techniques & Personnel Assessment,* 1964, *28,* 173–80.

Brainerd, C. J. The stage question in cognitive-developmental theory. *The Behavioral and Brain Sciences,* 1978, 2, 173–213.

Branden, N. *The psychology of self-esteem.* New York: Bantam, 1971.

Brandt, A. Self-confrontations. *Psychology Today,* Oct. 1980.

Brehm, J. W. *Responses to loss of freedom: A theory of psychological reactance.* Morristown, N.J.: General Learning Press, 1972.

Brock, S. St. Isaac of Ninevah and Syrian spirituality. *Sobornost,* 1975, 7, 2.

Broughton, J. The development of natural epistemology in adolescence and early adulthood. Doctoral dissertation, Harvard, 1975.

Brown, D. P. A model for the levels of concentrative meditation. *International J. Clinical and Experimental Hypnosis,* 1977, *25,* 236–73.

———. Mahāmudrā meditation: Stages and contemporary cognitive psychology. Doctoral dissertation, University of Chicago, 1981.

Brown, D. P. & Engler, J. The stages of mindfulness meditation: A validation study. *J. Transpersonal Psychology,* 1980, *12,* 2, 143–92.

Brown, D. P., Twemlow, S., Engler, J., Maliszewski, M. & Stauthamer, J. The profile of meditation experience (POME), Form II, Psychological Test Copyright, Washington, D.C., 1978.

Brunner, J. The course of cognitive growth. *American Psychologist,* 1964, *19,* 1–15.

———. Beyond the information given. Jeremy M. Anglin (Ed.), New York: Norton, 1973.

Caesarios. Migne. *Patrologia Græcæ,* 38, 1125.

Calef, V. A theoretical note on the ego in the therapeutic process. In. S. C. Post (Ed.), *Moral values and the superego concept in psychoanalysis.* New York: International Univ. Press, 1972.

Campenhausen, Hans Von. *The fathers of the Greek church.* New York: Pantheon, 1955.

Candelent, T., & Candelent, G. Teaching transcendental meditation in a psychiatric setting. *Hospital & Community Psychiatry,* 1975, *26,* 3, 156–59.

Carpenter, J. T. Meditation, esoteric traditions: Contributions to psychotherapy. *American J. Psychotherapy,* 1977, *31,* 394–404.

Carrington, P. & Ephron, H. Meditation as an adjunct to psychotherapy. In S. Arieti & G. Chrzanowski (Eds.), *The world biennial of psychotherapy and psychiatry,* 1975, 262–91.

Cayre, F. In W. Webster Wilson (Trans.), *Spiritual writers of the early church.* New York: Hawthorne, 1969.

Chang, G. *Teachings of Tibetan yoga.* Secaucus, N.J.: Citadel, 1974.

Chariton, Igumen of Valamo (Ed.). In E. Kadloubovsky and G. E. H. Palmer (Trans.), *Philokalia: The early church fathers.* London: Faber and Faber, 1967.

Chirban, J. T. *Human growth and faith: Intrinsic and extrinsic motivation in human development.* Washington, D.C.: University Press of America, 1981.

Chowdhury, U. *An Indian modification of the thematic appreciation test.* Calcutta: Sree Saraswaty Press Ltd., 1960.

Christou, Panagiotis "Γϱγόϱιος ὁ Παλαμάς." *Θϱησκευτική καί 'ΗΘική 'Εγκυκλοπαίδεια.* Athens, Greece: Martios, 1966.

Chrysostom, St. John. Migne. *Patrologia Græcæ,* 53, 56, 158D, 443, 443C.

Clement of Alexandria. Migne. *Patrologia Græcæ,* 9, 74, 140A, 277D.

Clifford, T. *Tibetan Buddhist medicine and psychiatry.* York Beach, ME: Samuel Weiser, 1984.

Growne, D. P. & Marlowe, D. A. A new scale of social desirability independent of psychopathology. *J. Consulting Psychology,* 1960, 24, 349–54.

Csikzentmihalyi, M. Play and intrinsic rewards. *J. Humanistic Psychology,* 1975, *15,* 3, 41–63.

Cyril of Alexandria. Migne. 74, 76, 276D, 277D, 1087.

Cyril of Jerusalem. Migne. *Patrologia Græcæ,* 33, 477, 836B.

Da Free John. *The paradox of instruction.* San Francisco: Dawn Horse, 1977.

———. *The enlightenment of the whole body.* San Francisco: Dawn Horse, 1978.

Dargyay, E. *The rise of esoteric Buddhism in Tibet.* New York: Weiser, 1978.

Dasgupta, S. *Obscure religious cults.* Calcutta: F. Klmukhopadhyay, 1946.

Davidson, R. J., Goleman, D. J., Schwartz, G. E. Attentional and affective concomitants of meditation: A cross-sectional study. *J. Abnormal Psychology,* 1976, *85,* 235–38.

Dean, S. R. Metapsychiatry: The interface between psychiatry and mysticism. *American J. Psychiatry,* 1973, *130,* 1036–38.

Deatherage, O. G. The clinical use of "mindfulness" meditation techniques in short-term psychotherapy. *J. Transpersonal Psychology,* 1975, *7,* 2, 133–43.

Deikman, A. J. Comments on the GAP report on mysticism. *J. Nervous Mental Disease,* 1977, *165,* 213–17.

Deutsche, E. *Advaita Vedanta.* Honolulu: East-West Center, 1969.

Dionysios the Areopagite. Translated by the Editors of the Shrine of Wisdom, *The mystical theology and celestial hierarchy.* Surrey, England: The Shrine of Wisdom, 1965.

Ducey, C. Rorschach experiential and representational dimensions of object relations: A longitudinal study. Unpublished doctoral dissertation, Harvard University, 1975.

Duval, S. & Wicklund, R. A. Effects of objective self-awareness on attribution of causality. *J. Experimental Social Psychology, 1973, 9,* 17–31.

Eliade, M. *Yoga: Immortality and freedom.* Princeton: Princeton Univ. Press, 1969.

Ellis, A. *Humanistic psychotherapy: The rational-emotive approach.* New York: McGraw-Hill, 1973

Engler, J. Vicissitudes of the self according to psychoanalysis and Buddhism: A spectrum model of object relations development. *Psychoanalysis and Contemporary Thought,* 1983a, *6,* 1, 29–72.

———. Buddhist Satipatthana-Vipassana meditation and an object relations model of therapeutic developmental change: A clinical case study. Unpublished dissertation, University of Chicago, 1983b.

———. Therapeutic aims in psychotherapy and meditation: Developmental stages in the representation of self. *J. Transpersonal Psychology,* 1984, *16,* 1, 25–61.

———. "The undivided self: Clinical case studies of object relations in Buddhist mindfulness meditation." In preparation (n.d.).

Epstein, M. & Topgay, S. Mind and mental disorders in Tibetan medicine. Unpublished manuscript.

Eriksen, C. W. Some temporal characteristics of visual pattern perception. *J. Experimental Psychology,* 1967, 74, 476–84.

Erikson, E. H. *Childhood and society.* New York: Norton, 1950, 1963.

———. Ego identity and the psychosocial moratorium. In H. L. Witmar & R. Kosinski (Eds.), *New perspectives for research in juvenile delinquency.* U.S. Children's Bureau, Publication #356, 1956, pp. 1–23.

———. *Identity and the life cycle.* New York: International Univ. Press, 1959.

Erikson, J. M. *Activity, recovery, growth: The communal role of planned activities.* New York: Norton, 1976.

Evans-Wentz, W. *Tibetan yoga and secret doctrines.* London: Oxford Univ. Press, 1971.

Exner, J. E. *The Rorschach: A comprehensive system.* New York: Wiley, 1974.

Fairbairn, W. *An object relations theory of the personality.* New York: Basic Books, 1954.

———. *Psychoanalytic studies of the personality.* New York, Basic Books, 1952.

Fenichel, O. *The psychoanalytic theory of neurosis.* New York: Norton, 1945.

Feuerstein, G. *Textbook of yoga.* London: Rider, 1975.

Fingarette, H. The ego and mystic selflessness. *Psychoanalytic Review,* 1958, *45,* 5–40.

Fischer, R. A. A cartography of the ecstatic and meditative states: The experimental and experiential features of a perception-hallucination continuum are considered. *Science,* 1971, *174,* 897–904.

Flavell, J. *The developmental psychology of Jean Piaget.* Princeton, N.J.: Van Nostrand, 1963.

———. Concept development. In P. Mussen (Ed.), *Carmichael's manual of child psychology.* Vol 1. New York: Wiley, 1970.

Fleming, J. Early object deprivation and transference phenomena: The working alliance. *Psychoanalytic Quarterly,* 1972, *10,* 439–51.

Fowler, J. W. *Stages of faith: The psychology of human development and the quest for meaning.* San Francisco: Harper & Row, 1981.

Frank, J. D. *Persuasion and healing: A comparative study of psychotherapy.* Baltimore: Johns Hopkins, 1961.

Frankl, V. *Man's search for meaning.* Boston: Beacon, 1963.

———. *The will to meaning.* Cleveland: New American Library, 1969.

French, A. P., Schmid, A. C., & Ingalls, E. Transcendental meditation, altered reality testing and behavioral change: A case report. *J. Nervous Mental Disease,* 1975, *161,* 1, 55–8.

Freud, A. *The ego and the mechanisms of defense.* New York: International Univ. Press, 1946.

———. The concept of developmental lines. In *The psychoanalytic study of the child.* New York: International Univ. Press. 1963, *8,* 245–65.

———. *Normality and pathology in childhood.* New York: International Univ. Press, 1965.

Freud, S. *Civilization and its discontents.* New York: W.W. Norton, 1930, 1961.

———. *Analysis terminable and interminable.* SE. London: Hogarth Press, 1937, vol. 23, pp. 209–53.

———. *Inhibitions, symptoms and anxiety.* SE. vol. 20. London: Hogarth Press, 1959 (1926).

———. *The ego and the id.* SE. vol. 19. London: Hogarth Press, 1961 (1923).

———. *An outline of psychoanalysis.* SE. vol. 23, London: Hogarth Press, 1964 (1940).

———. *A general introduction to psychoanalysis.* New York: Pocket Books, 1971.

Frey-Rohn, L. *From Freud to Jung.* New York: Delta, 1974.

Fromm, E., Brown, D., Hurt, S., Oberlander, J., Pfeiffer, G., & Boxer, A. The phenomena of self-hypnosis. *International J. Clinical Experiemental Hypnosis,* 1980.

Fromm, E., Oberlander, M. I., & Grunewald, D. Perception and cognitive processes in different states of consciousness: The waking state and hypnosis. *J. Projective Techniques & Personnel Assessment,* 1970. 34: 375–87.

Gard, R. *Buddhism.* New York: Braziller, 1962.

Gedo, J. *Beyond interpretation: Toward a revised theory for psychoanalysis.* New York: International Univ. Press, 1979.

———. *Advances in clinical psychoanalysis.* New York: International Univ. Press, 1981.

Gedo, J. & Goldberg, A. *Models of the mind: A psychoanalytic theory.* Chicago: Univ. of Chicago Press, 1973.

Geller, V. & Shaver, P. Cognitive consequences of self-awareness. *J. Experiemental Social Psychology,* 1976, *12,* 99–108.

Gilligan, C. *In a different voice.* Cambridge: Harvard Univ. Press, 1982.

Glueck, B. C., & Stroebel, C. F. Biofeedback and meditation in the treatment of psychiatric illnesses. *Comprehensive Psychiatry,* 1975, *16,* 303–21.

Goldberg, A. (Ed.). *Advances in self psychology.* New York: International Univ. Press, 1980.

Goldstein, J. *The experience in insight: A natural unfolding.* Santa Cruz: Unity Press, 1976.

Goleman, D. Meditation and consciousness: An Asian approach to mental health. *American J. Psychotherapy,* 1975, *30,* 41–54.

———. *The varieties of meditative experience.* New York: Dutton, 1977.

Goleman, D. & Epstein, M. Meditation and well-being: An Eastern model of psychological health. *ReVision,* 1980, *3,* 73–85.

Gottesman, I. I. & Schields, M. *Schizophrenia and genetics: A twin study vantage point.* New York: Academic Press, 1972.

Govinda, L. *The psychological attitude of early Buddhist philosophy.* New York: Samuel Weiser, 1974.

Graves, C. W. Levels of existence: An open system theory of values. *J. Humanistic Psychology,* 1970, *10,* 131–55.
Green, E., Green, A. & Walters, D. E. Voluntary control of internal states: psychological and physiological. *J. Transpersonal Psychology,* 1970, *2,* 1–26.
Greenson, R. *The technique and practice of psychoanalysis.* New York: International Univ. Press, 1967.
Gregory of Nyssa, St. In Jean Danielou and Herbert Musurillo (Eds.), *From glory to glory.* New York: Scribners, 1969.
———. Migne. *Patrologia Græcæ,* 44, 137, 184, 273A, 273B.
Gregory the Theologian, St. Migne. *Patrologia Græcæ,* 37, 77A.
Greist, J., Jefferson, J., & Spitzer, R. (Eds). *Treatment of mental disorders.* New York: Oxford Univ. Press, 1982.
Grof, S. *Realms of the human unconscious.* New York: Viking, 1975.
Group for the Advancement of Psychiatry (GAP). *Mysticism: Spiritual quest or psychic disorder?* New York: GAP (Publication 97), 1976.
Guénon, R. *Man and his becoming according to Vedanta.* London: Luzac, 1945.
Guenther, H. *Philosophy and psychology in the Abhidhamma.* Boulder: Shambhala, 1974.
Guntrip, H. *Personality structure and human interaction.* New York: International Univ. Press, 1961.
———. *Schizoid phenomena, object relations and the self.* New York: International Univ. Press, 1969.
———. *Psychoanalytic theory, therapy and the self.* New York, Basic Books, 1971.
Haley, J. *Strategies of psychotherapy.* New York: Grune & Stratton, 1963.
Haley, J. & Hoffman, L. (Eds.). *Techniques of family therapy.* New York: Basic Books, 1968.
Hanly, C. & Masson, J. A critical examination of the new narcissism. *International J. Psychoanalysis,* 1976, *57,* 49–65.
Hartman, H. *Ego psychology and the problem of adaptation.* New York: International Univ. Press, 1958.
Hebb, D. O. *The organization of behavior: A neuropsychological theory.* New York: Wiley & Sons, 1949.
Heidegger, M. *Being and time.* New York: Harper and Row, 1962.
Hilgard, E. R. Issues bearing on recommendations from the behavioral and social sciences study committee. *American Psychologist,* 1970, *25,* 5, 456–63.
Hixon, L. *Coming home.* New York: Anchor, 1978.
Hochberg, J. Attention, organization and consciousness. In D. Mostofsky (Ed.), *Attention: Contemporary theory and analysis.* New York: Appelton-Century, 1970.
Hoffman, J. E. A two-stage model of visual search. *Perception and Psychophysics,* 1979, *25,* 319–27.
Holt, R. & Havel, J. A method for assessing primary and secondary process in the Rorschach. In M. A. Rickers-Ovsiankina (Ed.), *Rorschach psychology.* New York: Wiley, 1960.
Horner, A. J. *Object relations and the developing ego in therapy.* New York: Jason Aronson, 1979.

Horney, K. *Neurosis and human growth.* New York: Norton, 1950.
Horton, P. C. The mystical experience as a suicide preventative. *American J. Psychiatry, 1973, 130,* 294–96.
———. The mystical experience: Substance of an illusion. *J. American Psychoanalytic Association,* 1974, *22,* 364–80.
Hugel, F. von *The mystical element in religion.* London: Dent, 1908.
Hume, R. (Trans.). *The thirteen principle Upanishads.* London: Oxford Univ. Press, 1974.
Huxley, A. *The perennial philosophy.* New York: Harper & Row, 1944.
Ickes, W. J., Wicklund, R. A., & Ferris, C. B. Objective self-awareness and self-esteem. *J. Experimental and Social Psychology,* 1973, *9,* 202–19.
Ikegami, R. Psychological study of Zen posture. In Yoshiharu Akishige (Ed.), *Psychological studies on Zen.* Tokyo: Zen Institute of Kamazawa University, 1970, 105–33.
Irenaeos, St. Migne. *Patrologia Græcæ,* 1105A, C.
Isaac the Syrian. Οἱ 'Ασκητικοί τοῦ 'Ισάχ. Athens, Greece.
Jacobi, J. *The psychology of C.G. Jung.* London: Routledge & Kegan Paul, 1942.
Jacobson, E. *The self and the object world.* New York: International Univ. Press, 1964.
James, W. *Principles of psychology,* 2 vols. New York: Dover, 1950 (1890).
James, W. *The varieties of religious experience.* New York: Colliers, 1961 (1901).
John Climacos, St. In Archmandite Lazarus Moore (Trans.), *The ladder of divine ascent.* Willets, CA: Eastern Orthodox Press, 1959.
John of Damascus, St. Migne. *Patrologia Græcæ,* 94, 95, 97A, 924A, 1037C.
John of the Cross. *The dark night of the soul.* Garden City, NY: Anchor, 1959.
Jonas, H. *The gnostic religion.* Boston: Beacon, 1958.
Jung, C. G. *The undiscovered self.* New York: Mentor, 1957.
———. *Analytical psychology: Its theory and practice.* New York: Vintage, 1961.
———. *Man and his symbols.* New York: Dell, 1964.
———. *The portable Jung.* J. Campbell (Ed.). New York: Viking, 1971.
Kabat-Zinn, J. An outpatient program in behavioral medicine for chronic pain patients based on the practice of mindfulness meditation. *General Hospital Psychiatry,* 1982, 4, 33–47.
Kalef, M. The negation of ego in Tibetan Buddhism and Jungian psychology. *J. Transpersonal Psychology,* 1983, *15,* 2, 103–24.
Kapleau, P. *The three pillars of Zen.* Boston: Beacon, 1965.
Kasamatsu, A. & Harai, T. An electroencephalographic study on the Zen meditation (Zazen). *Folia Psychiatry Neurologica Japonica,* 1966, *20,* 315–36.
Kastenbaum, R. & Aisenberg, R. *Psychology of death.* New York: Springer, 1972.
Kelley, G. *The psychology of personal constructs,* vols. 1 & 2. New York: Norton, 1955.
Kennedy, R. B. Self-induced depersonalization syndrome. *American J. Psychiatry,* 1976, *133,* 1326–28.
Kernberg, O. Borderline personality organization. *J. American Psychoanalytic Association,* 1967, *15.*

———. The treatment of patients with borderline personality organization. *International J. Psychoanalysis,* 1968, *49,* 600–19.

———. Prognostic considerations regarding borderline personality organization. *J. American Psychoanalytic Association,* 1971, *19.*

———. Treatment of borderline patients. In P. Giovacchini (Ed.), *Tactics and techniques in psychoanalytic therapy.* New York: Science House, 1972.

———. *Borderline conditions and pathological narcissism.* New York: Jason Aronson, 1975.

———. *Object relations theory and clinical psychoanalysis.* New York: Jason Aronson, 1976.

———. The structural diagnosis of borderline personality organization. In P. Hartocollis (Ed.), *Borderline personality disorders.* New York: International Univ. Press, 1977, 87–122.

Kernberg, O., et al. Psychotherapy and psychoanalysis: Final report of the Menninger Foundation's psychotherapy research project. *Bulletin Menninger Clinic,* 1972, *36* (1/2).

Kety, S., Rosenthal, D., Wender, P. H., *et al.* Mental illness in the biological and adoptive families of adopted schizophrenics. In D. Rosenthal & S. Kety (Eds.), *The transmission of schizophrenia.* Oxford: Pergamon Press, 1968, 345–62.

Kehtsun Sangpo Rinbochay. *Tantric practice in Nying-Ma.* Ithaca, NY: Gabriel/Snow Lion, 1982.

Khan, Inayat. *The soul: whence and whither.* New York: Sufi Order, 1977.

Kierkegaard, S. *Fear and trembling* and *The sickness unto death.* New York: Doubleday/Anchor, 1953.

———. *The concept of dread.* Princeton: Princeton Univ. Press, 1957.

Klein, D. F. Psychopharmacology and the borderline patient. In J. E. Mack (Ed.), *Borderline states in psychiatry.* New York: Grune and Stratton, 1975, 75–92.

Klein, M. *The psychoanalysis of children.* London: Hogarth Press, 1932.

———. Notes on some schizoid mechanisms. In M. Klein, *Envy and gratitude and other works, 1946–1963.* New York: Delacorte Press/Seymour Lawrence, 1946, 1–24.

Klopfer, B. & Boyer, L. B. Notes on the personality structure of a North American Indian shaman: Rorschach interpretation. *J. Projective Techniques & Personnel Assessment,* 1961, *25,* 170–78.

Koestenbaum, P. *Is there an answer to death?* New York: Prentice-Hall, 1976.

Kohlberg, L. *Essays on moral development,* vol. 1. San Francisco: Harper & Row, 1981.

Kohut, H. Forms and transformations of narcissism. *J. American Psychoanalytic Association,* 1966, *5,* 389–407.

———. *The analysis of the self.* New York: International Univ. Press, 1971.

———. *The restoration of the self.* New York: International Univ. Press, 1977.

Kohut, W. & Wolf, E. S. The disorders of the self and their treatment. *International J. of Psychoanalysis,* 1978, *59,* 4, 413–425.

Kornfield, J. The psychology of mindfulness meditation. Unpublished doctoral dissertation, The Humanistic Psychology Institute, 1976.

———. *Living Buddhist masters.* Santa Cruz: Unity Press, 1977.

———. Intensive insight meditation: A phenomenological study. *J. Transpersonal Psychology,* 1979, *11,* 1, 41–58.

Kris, E. The psychology of caricature. *International J. Psychoanalysis,* 1936, *17:* 285–303.

Krishna, G. *The secret of yoga.* London: Turnstone Books, 1972.

Krivoshine, Basil. The ascetic and theological teaching of Gregory Palamas. *Eastern Churches Quarterly,* 1955.

Lacan, J. *Language of the self.* Baltimore: Johns Hopkins Univ. Press, 1968.

Laing, R. D. *The politics of experience.* New York: Ballantine, 1967.

Lasch, C. *The culture of narcissism.* New York: Norton, 1979.

Lazarus, A. A. Psychiatric problems precipitated by transcendental meditation. *Psychological Reports,* 1976, *39,* 601–02.

Leeper, R. W. The motivational and perceptual properties of emotions as indicating their fundamental character and role. In M. B. Arnold (Ed.), *Feelings and emotions.* New York: Academic Press, 1970, 151–85.

Leggett, T. *The tiger's cave.* London: Routledge and Kegan Paul, 1964.

Levinson, D. J. *et al. The seasons of a man's life.* New York: Knopf, 1978.

Levinson, P. Religious delusions in counter-culture patients. *American J. Psychiatry,* 1973, *130,* 1265–69.

Lichtenberg, J. The development of the sense of self. *J. American Psychoanalytic Association,* 1975, *23.*

Loevinger, J. *Ego development.* San Francisco: Jossey-Bass, 1976.

Loewald, H. W. On the therapeutic action of psychoanalysis. *International J. Psychoanalysis,* 1960, *41,* 16–33.

———. *Psychoanalysis and the history of the individual.* New Haven: Yale Univ. Press, 1978.

Longchenpa. *Kindly bent to ease us.* 3 vols. H. Guenther (Trans.). Emeryville, CA: Dharma Press, 1977.

Lossky, V. In Asheleigh Moorhouse (Trans.), *The vision of God.* Clayton, WI: Faith Press, 1963.

Lowen, A. *The betrayal of the body.* New York: Macmillan, 1967.

Luk, C. *Ch'an and Zen teaching.* 3 vols. London: Rider, 1962.

Luthe, W. *Autogenic training: Research and theory.* New York: Grune & Stratton, 1970.

McCarthy, T. *The critical theory of Jürgen Habermas.* Cambridge, Mass.: MIT Press, 1978.

Maddi, S. The existential neurosis. *J. Abnormal Psychology,* 1967, 72.

Mahasi Sayadaw. *Progress of insight.* Kandy: Buddhist Publ. Society, 1965, 1973.

———. *Practical insight meditation.* Santa Cruz: Unity Press, 1972.

Mahler, M. *On human symbiosis and the vicissitudes of individuation.* New York: International Univ. Press, 1968.

———. On the first three subphases of the separation-individuation process. *International J. Psychoanalysis,* 1972, *53,* 333–38.

Mahler, M., Pine, F., & Bergman, A. *The psychological birth of the human infant.* New York: Basic Books, 1975.

Maliszewski, M., Twemlow, S., Brown, D., & Engler, J. A phenomenological typology of intensive meditation: A suggested methodology using the questionnaire approach. *Re-Vision,* 1981, 4.

Marin, P. The new narcissism. *Harper's,* Oct. 1975.

Marmor, J. Recent trends in psychotherapy. *American J. Psychiatry,* 1980, *137,* 409–16.

Maslow, A. *Motivation and personality.* New York: Harper & Row, 1954.

———. *Toward a psychology of being.* New York: Van Nostrand Reinhold, 1968.

———. *The further reaches of human nature.* New York: Viking, 1971.

Masterson, J. F. *Treatment of the borderline adolescent: A developmental approach.* New York: Wiley, 1972.

———. *The narcissistic and borderline disorders.* New York: Brunner/Mazel, 1981.

Masterson, J. (Ed.). *New perspectives on psychotherapy of the borderline adult.* New York: Brunner/Mazel, 1978.

Masterson, J. F., & Rinsley, D. B. The borderline syndrome: The role of the mother in the genesis and psychic structure of the borderline personality. *International J. Psychoanalysis,* 1975, *56,* 163–77.

Masterson, J. F., & Rinsley, D. B. The borderline syndrome: The role of the mother in the genesis and psychic structure of the borderline personality. Revised and reprinted in R. F. Lax, S. Bach, & J. A. Burland (Eds.), *Rapprochement: The critical subphase of separation-individuation.* New York: Jason Aronson, 1980, 299–329.

Maupin, E. Individual differences in response to a Zen meditation exercise. *J. Consulting Psychology, 1965, 29: 139–45.*

May, R. *Love and will.* New York: Norton, 1969.

———. *The meaning of anxiety* (rev. ed.). New York: Norton, 1977.

May, R., Angel, E., & Ellenberger, H. (Eds.). *Existence.* New York: Basic Books, 1958.

Mayman, M. Measuring introversiveness on the Rorschach Test: The fabulization scale. Unpublished manuscript, Aug., 1960.

———. Reality contact, defense effectiveness and psychopathology in Rorschach form-level scores. In Klopfer, B., Meyer, M. & Brawer, F. (Eds.), *Developments in the Rorschach technique III: Aspects of personality structure.* New York: Harcourt Brace Jovanovich, 1970, 11–46.

Mayman, M. & Voth, H. M. Reality closeness, phantasy, and autokinesis. *J. Abnormal Psychology,* 1969, *74,* 635–41.

Mead, G. *Mind, self, and society.* Chicago: Univ. Chicago Press, 1934.

Meyendorff, J. *A study of Gregory Palamas.* London: Faith Press, 1964.

———. *Eastern Christian thought.* Washington, D.C. and Cleveland, OH: Corpus Books, 1969.

———. *St. Gregory Palamas and Orthodox spirituality.* Crestwood, NY: St. Vladimir's Press, 1974.

———. *Byzantine theology.* New York: Fordham University, 1975.

Meyer, J. *Death and neurosis.* New York: International Univ. Press, 1975.

Mishra, R. (Trans.). *Yoga sutras (The textbook of Yoga psychology),* by Patañjali. Garden City, NY: Anchor Press, 1973.

Monk of the Eastern Church. *Orthodox spirituality—An outline of the Orthodox ascetical and mystical tradition.* London: SPCK, 1968.
Mookerjee, A. *Kundalini.* New York: Destiny Books, 1982.
Mukerjee, R. (Trans.). *The song of the self supreme (Astavakra Gita).* San Francisco: Dawn Horse, 1971.
Murphy, G. *Human potentialities.* New York: Basic Books, 1958.
Nagera, H. *Early childhood disturbances, the infantile neuroses, and the adult disturbances.* New York: International Univ. Press, 1966.
Narada. *A manual of Abhidhamma.* Kandy: Buddhist Publication Society, 1975.
Naranjo, C. *The one quest.* New York: Viking, 1972.
Naranjo, C., & Ornstein, R. E. *On the psychology of meditation.* New York: Viking, 1971.
Neisser, U. *Cognitive psychology.* Englewood Cliffs, N.J.: Prentice-Hall, 1967.
———. *Cognition and reality.* Ithaca: Cornell Univ. Press, 1976.
Nemiah, J. Dissociative disorders. In A. Freedman, H. Kaplan & B. Sadock (Eds.), *Comprehensive textbook of psychiatry* (3rd ed.). Baltimore: Williams and Wilkins Co., 1980.
Neumann, E. *The origins and history of consciousness.* Princeton: Princeton University Press, 1954.
Nichols, M. *Family therapy.* New York: Gardner Press, 1984.
Nyanamoli, B. (Trans.). *Visuddhimagga: The path of purification by Buddhaghosha.* 2 vols. Boulder, CO: Shambhala, 1976.
Nyanaponika. *The heart of Buddhist meditation.* New York: Samuel Weiser, 1973.
Nyanatiloka. *A Buddhist dictionary.* Colombo: Frewin & Co., Ltd., 1972.
Origen. Φιλοχαλία τῶν 'Ιερώυ Νηπιχωυ Volume II. Athens, Greece: 1893.
Osrow, M. The syndrome of narcissistic tranquillity. *International J. of Psychoanalysis,* 1967, 45, 573–83.
Otto, R. *Mysticism East and West.* New York: Macmillan, 1932.
———. *The idea of the holy.* New York: Oxford, 1969.
Peck, R. & Havighurst, R. *The psychology of character development.* New York: Wiley, 1960.
Pelletier, K. R. Influence of transcendental meditation upon autokinetic perception. *Perceptual and Motor Skills,* 1974, 39, 1031–34.
Perls, F. *Gestalt therapy verbatim.* New York: Bantam, 1971.
Piaget, J. *The essential Piaget.* Gruber & Voneche (Eds.). New York: Basic Books, 1977.
Podvoll, E. M. Psychosis and the mystic path. *Psychoanalytic Review,* 1979, 66, 571–90.
Pratyabhijnahrdayam. J. Singh (Trans.). Delhi: Motilal Banarsidass, 1980.
Pribram, K. Feelings as monitors. In M. B. Arnold (Ed.), *Feelings and emotions.* New York: Academic Press, 1970, 41–53.
———. Toward a holonomic theory of perception. In S. Ertel & L. Kemmler (Eds.), *Gestalt-theorie in der Modern Psychologie (Gestalt theory in modern psychology).* Cologne: Erich Wergenroth, 1974.
Rama, S., Ballentine, R. & Ajaya, S. *Yoga and psychotherapy.* Glenview, Ill.: Himalayan Institute, 1976.

Ramana Maharshi. *The collected works.* London: Rider, 1972.
Rapaport, D. The theory of attention cathexis: An economic and structural attempt at the explanation of cognitive processes. In Merton M. Gill (Ed.), *The collected papers of David Rapaport.* New York: Basic Books, 1967, 778–94.
Rehyer, J. Electroencephalogram and rapid eye movements during free imagery and dream recall. *J. Abnormal Psychology,* 1969, 74, 574–82.
Reynolds, D. *Morita therapy.* Berkeley: Univ. California Press, 1976.
Rieff, P. *The triumph of the therapeutic.* New York: Harper & Row, 1966.
Rieker, H. *The yoga of light.* San Francisco: Dawn Horse, 1971.
Rinsley, D. An object relations view of borderline personality. In Hartocollis, P. (Ed.), *Borderline personality disorders.* New York: International Univ. Press, 1977, 47–70.
———. Dynamic and developmental issues in borderline and related "spectrum" disorders. *Psychiatric Clinics of North America,* 1981, 4, 1: 117–31.
Rizzuto, A. M. *The birth of the idea of God.* Chicago: Univ. Chicago Press, 1978.
———. *The birth of the living God.* Chicago: Univ. Chicago Press, 1979.
Rogers, C. *On becoming a person.* Boston: Houghton Mifflin, 1961.
Runions, J. E. The mystic experience: A psychiatric reflection. *Canadian J. Psychiatry,* 1979, 24, 147–51.
Sannella, L. *Kundalini—psychosis or transcendence?* San Francisco: H. S. Dakin, 1976.
Schachter, S. The assumption of identity and peripheralist-centralist controversies in motivation and emotion. In M. B. Arnold (Ed.), *Feelings and emotions.* New York: Academic Press, 1970, 111–21.
Schafer, R. *A new language for psychoanalysis.* New York: International Univ. Press, 1976.
Schaya, L. *The universal meaning of the Kabbalah.* Baltimore: Penguin, 1973.
Scheir, M. F. Self-awareness, self-consciousness, and angry aggression, *Journal of Personality,* 1976, 44, 627–44.
Scheir, M. F. & Carver, C. S. Self-focused attention and the experience of emotional attraction, repulsion, elation, and depression. *J. Personality and Social Psychology,* 1977, 35, 625–36.
Schneider, W. & Shiffrin, R. M. Controlled and automatic information processing: I. Detection, search, and attention. *Psychological Review,* 1977, 84, 1–66.
Schuon, F. *Logic and transcendence.* New York, Harper & Row, 1975.
Segal, H. *Introduction to the work of Melanie Klein.* New York: Basic Books, 1974.
Selman, R., & Byrne, D. A structural analysis of levels of role-taking in middle childhood. *Child Development,* 1974, 45.
Seraphim of Sarov, St. In Franklin Jones (Ed.), *Saint Seraphim of Sarov.* Los Angeles: Dawn Horse Press, 1973.
Shafii, M. Silence in the service of the ego: Psychoanalytic study of meditation. *International J. of Psychoanalysis,* 1973, 54, 431–43.
Shapiro, D. Zen meditation and behavioral self-control strategies applied to a case of generalized anxiety. *Psychologia,* 1976, 19, 134–38.
Shapiro, D. H & Giber, D. Meditation and psychotherapeutic effects: Self-regulation

strategy and altered state of consciousness. *Archives General Psychiatry,* 1978, *35,* 294–302.

Simon, H. A. An information processing theory of intellectual development. In W. Kessen and C. Kuhlman (eds.), *Thought in the young child. Monographs of the Society for Research in Child Development,* 1962, 27, no. 2 (whole no. 83).

Singer, J. L. & Antrobus, J. S. Daydreaming, imaginal processes, and personality: A normative study. In Peter Sheehan (Ed.), *The function and nature of imagery.* New York: Academic Press, 1972.

Singh, K. *Naam or word.* Tilton, NH: Sant Boni Press, 1974.

———. *Surat Shabd yoga.* Berkeley: Images Press, 1975.

Smith, H. *Forgotten truth.* New York: Harper & Row, 1976.

Smith, J. C. Psychotherapeutic effects of TM with controls for expectation of relief and daily sitting. *J. Consulting Clinical Psychology,* 1976, 44, 630–37.

Speck, R. & Attneave, C. *Family networks.* New York: Pantheon, 1973.

Spitz, R. *A genetic field of ego formation.* New York: International Univ. Press, 1959.

———. *The first year of life.* New York: International Univ. Press, 1965.

Stace, W. T. *Mysticism and philosophy.* New York: Lippincott, 1960.

Stephanou, Eusebius A. *Charisma and gnosis in Orthodox thought.* Fort Wayne, IN: Logos Ministry for Orthodox Renewal, 1976.

Sterba, R. F. The fate of the ego in analytic therapy. *International J. Psychoanalysis,* 1934, *15,* 117–26.

Sternberg, S. High-speed scanning in human memory. *Science,* 1966, *153,* 652–54.

Stone, M. H. *The borderline syndromes: Constitution, personality and adaptation.* New York: McGraw-Hill, 1980.

Straus, J. Diagnostic models and the nature of psychiatric disorder. *Archives General Psychiatry,* 1973, *29,* 444–49.

Sullivan, H. *The interpersonal theory of psychiatry.* New York: Norton, 1953.

Suzuki, D. T. *Studies in the Lankavatara Sutra.* London: Routledge & Kegan Paul, 1968.

———. *Essays in Zen Buddhism.* 3 vols. London: Rider, 1970.

Suzuki, Shunryu. *Zen mind, beginner's mind.* New York: Weatherhill, 1970.

Taimni, I. *The science of yoga.* Wheaton: Quest, 1975.

Takakusu, J. *The essentials of Buddhist philosophy.* Honolulu: Univ. Hawaii Press, 1956.

Tart, C. T. Scientific foundations for the study of altered states of consciousness. *J. Transpersonal Psychology,* 1971, *3,* 93–124.

———. *States of consciousness.* New York: Dutton, 1975a.

———. *Transpersonal psychologies.* New York: Harper & Row, 1975b.

Tatian, Migne. *Patrologia Græcæ,* 6, 837B.

Theodoret of Cyrus, Migne. *Patrologia Græcæ,* 80, 104B, 105B, C.

Thondup, Tulku. *Buddhist civilization in Tibet.* Santa Cruz, Calif.: Maha Siddha Nyingmapa Center, 1982.

Tillich, P. *The courage to be.* New Haven: Yale Univ. Press, 1952.

Tolpin, M. On the beginnings of a cohesive self. *The psychoanalytic study of the child,* 1971, 26 (New York: Quadrangle Books).

———. Discussion of "Psychoanalytic developmental theories of the self: An integration" by Morton Shane and Estelle Shane. In A. Goldberg (Ed.), *Advances in self psychology.* New York: International Univ. Press, 1980, 47–68.

Tolstoy, L. *My confession, my religion, the gospel in brief.* New York: Scribners, 1929.

Tompkins, S. *Affect, imagery and consciousness.* Vols. 1–2. New York: Springer, 1962–63.

Trungpa, C. *The myth of freedom.* Berkeley: Shambhala, 1976.

Tucci, G. *Minor Buddhist texts, Part II: First Bhavāna krama of Kamalaśila.* Rome: Instituto Italian Perg, 1958.

Turner, H. J. M. St. Gregory of Nyssa as a spiritual guide for today. *Eastern Churches Review,* 1975, 7, 1.

Ullman, M. & Krippner, S., with Alan Vaughan & Gardner Murphy. *Dream telepathy.* New York: Macmillan, 1973.

Underhill, E. *Mysticism.* New York: Meridian, 1955.

Vahia, H. S., Doengaji, D. R., Jeste, D. V. *et al. Psychophysiologic therapy based on the concepts of Patanjali. American J. Psychotherapy,* 1973, 27, 557–65.

Vaillant, G. E. Theoretical hierarchy of adaptive ego mechanisms. *Archives General Psychiatry,* 1971, 24, 107–18.

———. *Adaptation to life.* Boston: Little, Brown and Co., 1977.

Vajiranana, P. *Buddhist meditation in theory and practice.* Kuala Lumpur: Buddhist Missionary Society, 1975.

Van Nuys, D. Meditation, attention, and hypnotic susceptibility: A correlational study. *International J. Clinical and Experimental Hypnosis,* 1973, *21,* 59–69.

Varenne, J. *Yoga and the Hindu tradition.* Chicago: Univ. Chicago Press, 1976.

Venkatesananda (Trans.). *The supreme yoga.* Australia: Chiltern, 1981.

Vivekananda. *The Yogas and other works.* S. Nikhilananda (Ed.). New York: Ramakrishna-Vivekananda Center, 1953.

Wallace, A. F. C. Cultural determinants of response to hallucinatory experience. *Archives General Psychiatry,* 1970, *1,* 58–69.

Walsh, R. Initial meditative experiences: I. *J. Transpersonal Psychology,* 1977, 9, 2, 151–92.

———. Initial meditative experiences: II. *J. Transpersonal Psychology,* 1978, *10,* 1, 1–28.

———. Meditation. In R. Corsini (Ed.), *A handbook of innovative psychotherapies.* New York: Wiley, 1980a.

———. The consciousness disciplines and the behavioral sciences: Questions of comparisons and assessment. *American J. Psychiatry,* 1980b, *137,* 663–73.

———. Speedy Western minds slow slowly. *ReVision,* 1981, 4, 75–7.

Walsh, R., & Roche, L. Precipitation of acute psychotic episodes by intensive meditation in individuals with a history of schizophrenia. *American J. Psychiatry,* 1979, *136,* 1085–86.

Watkins, J. G. & Stauffacher, J. C. An index of pathological thinking in the Rorschach. In P. M. Lerner (Ed.), *Handbook of Rorschach scales.* New York: Internat. Univ. Press, 1975.

Watzlawick, P., Beavin, J., & Jackson, D. *Pragmatics of human communication.* New York: Norton, 1967.

Wensink, A. J. *Mystical treatises by Isaac of Nineveh.* Wiesbaden, Germany: 1969.

Werner, H. *Comparative psychology of mental development.* New York: International Univ. Press, 1964 (1940).

White, J. *Kundalini, evolution and enlightenment.* New York: Anchor, 1979.

Wilber, K. *The spectrum of consciousness.* Wheaton: Quest, 1977.

———. A developmental view of consciousness. *J. Transpersonal Psychology,* 1979, *11.*

———. *The Atman project.* Wheaton: Quest, 1980a.

———. The pre/trans fallacy. *ReVision,* 1980b, 3, 51–73.

———. Ontogenetic development: Two fundamental patterns. *J. Transpersonal Psychology,* 1981a, *13,* 33–59.

———. *Up from Eden.* New York: Doubleday/Anchor, 1981b.

———. *A sociable god.* New York: McGraw-Hill, 1982.

———. *Eye to eye.* New York: Doubleday/Anchor, 1983.

———. The developmental spectrum and psychopathology; Part I, stages and types of pathology. *J. Transpersonal Psychology,* 1984, *16,* 1, 75–118.

———. *System, self, and structure.* In preparation. [See *Integral Psychology,* CW 4.]

Wilde, J. & Kimmel, W. (Eds.). *The search for being.* New York: Noonday, 1962.

Winnicott, D. *Collected papers.* New York: Basic Books, 1958.

———. *The maturational process and the facilitating environment.* New York: International Univ. Press, 1965.

Yalom, I. *Existential psychotherapy.* New York: Basic Books, 1980.

Yogeshwarand Saraswati. *Science of soul.* India: Yoga Niketan, 1972.

Young, P. T. Affective processes. In M. B. Arnold (Ed.), *The nature of emotion.* New York: Penguin Books, 1969, 222–37.

Zaehner, R. L. *Mysticism, sacred and profane.* New York: Oxford, 1957.

Zetzel, E. A developmental approach to the borderline patient. *American J. Psychiatry,* 1971, *127,* 7, 43–47.

Zimmerman, M. *Eclipse of the self.* Athens: Ohio Univ. Press. 1981.

Zubek, J. P. (Ed.), *Sensory deprivation: Fifteen years of research.* New York: Appleton-Century-Crofts, 1969.

PARADIGM WARS

An Interview with Ken Wilber

Q: I don't think I've heard a word more used or overused in the past decade than "paradigm." What exactly is a paradigm?

A: The term was introduced about thirty years ago [as of 1989] by sociologist Thomas Kuhn, in a very influential book called *The Structure of Scientific Revolutions.* A paradigm, as Kuhn used the term, had a very precise meaning. He did not use it the way most people do now, particularly New Agers, as a type of "supertheory" or "worldview." He meant it as a specific social practice or exemplar—a type of injunction or experiment. But it has recently come to mean, in the popular mind, a type of massive overview, supertheory, or worldview.

Q: So, does this mean that paradigms don't exist?

A: Well, worldviews definitely exist. In that sense, Freud had a new paradigm, a new supertheory. I know several people who are working on a "new paradigm," in the sense of a new worldview. Jay Ogilvy and Peter Schwartz, for example, are working on a book tentatively called *The Politics of Paradigms.* They feel that we are at present undergoing a paradigm shift that is becoming apparent in all sorts of fields and disciplines. Markley and Harman have published *Changing Images of Man,* in which they trace the historical development of various major worldviews. They, too, believe we are in the midst of a paradigm shift. And there's Marilyn Ferguson and Fritjof Capra and so on. . . .

I am a great fan of both Ogilvy and Schwartz, and I think there are excellent and even brilliant points in their position. But I don't believe anything like the consensus they are talking about exists in the various disciplines. I agree with Markley and Harman that we need a new image of man, and I roughly agree with what they think that image should be: It would be evolutionary or developmental, would allow for higher and spiritual states of being; it would be inclusive rather than exclusive, eclectic in methodology, and would study subjective as well as objective states; it would include values, and would be hierarchical, comprehensive, and unified. I just don't think that this new image is having much impact—and won't have—for decades, maybe centuries.

The point is that the world is just now entering, fully and completely, the mental dimension. The great "paradigm shift" has already happened—it's the "Third Wave," the "Information Age," the computer revolution. It will take us several hundred years to work through that, to collectively "peel off" the mental, before we are ready for a genuinely spiritual paradigm, a genuinely comprehensive and transcendental paradigm. So there is a new paradigm—not in the strong sense of Kuhn but in the loose sense, as "worldview." But it's already happened—and it's mental, not spiritual. It's global mental, not transcendental spiritual.

Q: So there is a new paradigm—but not in the strong sense first suggested by Kuhn. Some people are suggesting that in fact your work describes that paradigm. Dr. C. M. Kleisen of the Netherlands has written: "Adopting the view of reality that [Wilber] presents would re-shape science in many different disciplines and many different ways. It not only opens up completely new areas of research, notably the transpersonal, but also provides new perspectives and suggests new questions and approaches in already existing disciplines, notably the 'human sciences,' and seems to offer a new explanatory framework for recent new developments and thinking in diverse fields of scientific investigation, e.g., in the fields of physics, biology, the human sciences, but also in fields like creativity, intuition, imagination and inspiration, at the moment still considered rather esoteric. And, potentially at least, Wilber's transcendental paradigm provides explanations for a whole class of well established facts of experience which must, under the current paradigm, remain unexplained. Also, it introduces new ways of knowledge acquisition and accumulation into science, like at the time of Galileo. . . ." Sounds like the new paradigm.

A: What Dr. Kleisen says about the implications of these ideas is accurate, but that's not the point. The point is that these ideas simply are not having a revolutionary impact on the *entire world,* nor are they likely to for decades, if then. I would love to see the world enthusiastically embrace a more integral paradigm; I think it's comprehensive, balanced, and sane, and does justice to the full spectrum of human existence. But I honestly do not think the world is ripe for collective spiritual anything. Some people, yes. But part of the implication of a "paradigm" is that it has a worldwide impact, at all levels of society. *If* these ideas were adopted on a worldwide basis, there might be major and beneficial changes. The question is, will they be widely adopted in the foreseeable future? I don't think so.

Q: You're saying, in effect, that the world's not ready for an integral and spiritual philosophy.

A: I would just say that the word has other tasks that it must accomplish first, on the mental dimension, before it can collectively move to the spiritual dimension. That's not a put-down. The world has got to do what the world has got to do. Just as we had to farm the physical—by learning agriculture and then industry—before we could collectively move to the mental, so now we have to farm the mental—information and computers and technology—before we go beyond it to the spiritual. All in its own time. Frankly, I think the world is moving along at a handsome clip.

Q: You suggest that there are different paradigms (in the general sense) at each level of development—that different worldviews emerge and then dissolve as we evolve through the spectrum of consciousness.

A: Yes, that's right. Each stage of development, each evolutionary emergence, introduces new dimensions of existence, new modes of knowing, new desires, new fears, new perceptions, new modes of space and time, new motivations, new moral sensibilities, and so on. So one of the things I've tried to do, in several books, is trace out exactly the type of worldview or paradigm that is most characteristic of each of the waves of development.

Q: Would you explain this, stage by stage?

A: I usually describe a simple version of the spectrum—matter, mind, and spirit—or a slightly expanded version—matter, body, mind, soul, and spirit. Each of those levels subdivides into several sublevels.

The material level I'll leave as just one level for this discussion. You could, however, divide this level into subatomic particles, atoms, molecules, and so on, but this isn't necessary here. In human beings, the material level is the level of the physical body, including its physiology, biochemistry, nutrition, muscular and skeletal system, and so on.

The vital-body level I subdivide into three sublevels: sensation, perception, and impulse or emotion. Because these are still fairly junior levels of development, we tend to share them with other animals. For example, we share sensation and perception with reptiles and amphibians, and we share rudimentary emotions (or "paleoemotions") with other mammals. This is why, in the triune model of the brain, the two lowest levels are called the reptilian brain and the paleomammalian brain. The third and highest, the neocortex, is distinctly human, or mental—which is our next level, mind.

Mind is divided into five sublevels—image, symbol, concept, rule, and meta-rule. An *image* is a mental representation that represents its object by more-or-less "looking like" that object. For example, if you close your eyes and form a mental image of a tree, that image looks more or less like a real tree. It's a fairly simple mental operation—the simplest, in fact. Images start to emerge, in an infant, at around seven months. Next up in the mental dimension is *symbol.* A symbol, unlike an image, is a non-pictorial representation, usually but not always verbal, that denotes an object without looking like it. For example, I name my dog Fido; but the word "F-i-d-o" does not look like the real Fido at all. Yet the word does very effectively denote Fido. Thus, it's a harder (and higher) mental task than simple images. Symbols start to emerge in the infant at around eighteen months, with the word "no." Next is *concepts,* which denote, not just one object, like Fido, but a class of objects, like "dog." "Dog" refers to all possible dogs, it refers to a class. This is a concept; it doesn't just denote, it connotes. Concepts start to emerge at around three to four years. Next is a *rule.* A rule is not just a symbol or a concept. It is an *operation,* what Piaget called "concrete operational thought." An operation would include things like adding, dividing, multiplying, and so forth. Rules also involve an understanding of social rules and roles I am expected to play. So rules are very important. They begin to emerge at around age seven in most children. Finally, in the mental realm, there is *meta-rule,* or what Piaget called "formal operational thought." Formal operational thought *operates on* rules and mental objects. It is "thought about thought." It's abstract, but it's also very "dreamy," in the sense that it can envision all sorts of possibilities. Most importantly—and this is crucial—it has *perspective.* It can put itself in someone else's shoes; it has a tolerant and pluralistic outlook; it can perform hypothetico-deductive or experimental work (the first structure that can do so); and it can be highly introspective. This is, roughly, what we would call "rationality" or "reason." In most people, it emerges between eleven and fifteen years of age.

At this point, I add a stage. You can think of it as the highest of the mental or the lowest of the soul; it doesn't matter. I call it "the existential" or "the centaur" level. This level is marked by *vision-logic* or unifying logic that *operates on* formal operational thought, and thus produces comprehensive and inclusive and holistic systems. The previous level, the rational, tends to be divisive and analytic, but this level is inclusive and additive. I call it "centaur" because it is the first level where the "human mind" and "animal body," ordinarily at odds, are integrated into a single whole, like the mythic centaur. As Loevinger and Broughton and several others have demonstrated, this is the first level where, to quote Loevinger, "mind and body are both experiences of an integrated self." That "integrated personal self" is the centaur.

Now we shift into the soul or subtle dimensions. I divide the soul realm into two major realms, the psychic and the subtle. The psychic is the beginning of genuinely transcendental or spiritual development. Paranormal events or siddhi can occur here, but they don't have to. The psychic dimension is simply the beginning dimension of spiritual involvement, whatever form that might take. The psychic dimension operates by panoramic and panenhenic *vision.* While vision-logic must laboriously reason out holistic connections, vision sees the connections almost instantly. Aurobindo has written extensively on vision-logic and vision, and I am following him in this regard.

Then, we have the subtle dimension itself. The subtle is the home of the archetypes, in the Platonic, Buddhist and Augustinian sense. It is also the realm of audible illuminations, spiritual illumination, nada, shabd, experiential realms of ascended knowledge (Brahmaloka) and expanded awareness. This is the soul proper, the highest point of individual identity, beyond which lies total release of the knot of the soul in absolute spirit itself. And that's the final level, the level of spirit. Following Vedanta, I also call it the causal level, since it is the cause and support of all the lesser levels. Sometimes the causal is described, by the various traditions, as being the ultimate level itself, completely unmanifest and formless. But at other times it is taken to be merely the subtlest level of manifestation, containing all the subtler archetypes, and pure spirit lies beyond the causal (turiya). Context alone can tell you which use is intended. Technically, I therefore divide it into the "low" and "high" causal, but we needn't go into that here.

Q: The map you have just given us is not just your "invention," but is a synthesis of over fifty other systems, East and West.

A: Yes, it is a kind of "master template," based on most of the world's great religious and psychological systems. It takes each system, compares and contrasts it with the others, and then uses each to fill in the holes or gaps in the others. The result, I believe, is a fairly comprehensive system of cross-cultural validity, or at least plausibility.

Q: Okay, so now we are going to go into the different worldviews or "paradigms" of each of these levels?

A: Yes, each level has a different perspective on reality. I often use the metaphor of a ladder for the spectrum, and every rung in the ladder has a different view of the surrounding area. If you climb a big ladder, you get a "higher" angle on the world with every rung. That's exactly what happens in development, psychological as well as historical. The major worldviews are the archaic, the magic, the mythic, the rational, the existential, the psychic, the subtle, and the causal. These are correlated with waves of development. If you just have matter, sensation, perception, emotion, and image—the earliest levels—then your worldview is archaic. If you add symbols and concepts, your worldview shifts to magic. Add rules, or concrete operational thought, and magic gives way to mythic. Add formal operational thought, and mythic gives way to rational. Add vision-logic, and the rational gives way to the existential. And so on . . . and then the psychic (with vision), then the subtle (with archetype), and finally the causal (with unmanifest). So each of the major waves of development has its own peculiar and distinctive worldview or paradigm.

So you already know what it's like to go through a paradigm shift, because at each stage of an individual's own growth and development, he or she goes through one. As an average adult, you have *already* gone from the archaic paradigm to the magical paradigm to the mythical paradigm to the mental or rational paradigm.

Catastrophe is always right around the corner, and that is why we have so many casualties along the way. The entire Freudian psychology, for example, is nothing but an understanding of the first two or three major paradigm shifts in the psyche, which occur in childhood, and an understanding of how those revolutions get messed up, and how developmental snarls continue to wreak havoc in the adult.

Q: So let's start with the archaic and magic, and work up.

A: Okay. The archaic is particularly marked by its dim awareness of dualities—subject versus object, or inside versus outside. There is no evidence, for example, that the infant can tell where its self ends and the environment begins. The infant is one with the mother, one with the world. This is *not* a mystical state. The mystical state is being one with all the rungs in the ladder, material, emotional, mental, and spiritual. The archaic state is just a material fusion, just a union with the first rung. As Piaget put it, "The self is here material, so to speak . . ." And, phylogenetically, this dreamy immersion in physical nature was probably the state of "dawn man," and is probably behind all the Eden myths of being one with nature in a kind of physical paradise. Of course, that Eden must be surrendered before any further growth or development can occur.

Q: When the archaic is surrendered, then the magical emerges.

A: Yes. And in modern day individuals, if the archaic is not surrendered—if there is a fixation at the archaic stage due to repeated trauma or frustration or physiological malfunction—then the result is often the various types of psychosis, such as schizophrenia. The individual can't tell where his body stops and the chair starts, he hallucinates, the boundary between self and other collapses, and so forth. There is nothing paradisiacal about this at all. But for most people, between the ages of two and four, the archaic winds down and the magical worldview begins to emerge. And it does so simply because symbols and concepts begin to emerge. The young child awakens as a separate individual—not in the sense of an introspective person, but in the sense of a bodily self-sense differentiated from the environment in general and the mother in particular.

Q: Why is it called "magical"?

A: Because the self and the physical world are just barely differentiated, they remain very close and "magically involved" with each other. The images and symbols that represent things are often still fused and confused with the things they represent. In voodoo, for example, if you stick a pin in a doll, that is the same thing as hurting the actual person. This is the basis of "magic"; to manipulate a symbol is to magically control or manipulate the object it represents. Also, there is a lot of narcissistic grandiosity at this level. Because the self was just recently "one with" the world, it thinks it can control or lord over the entire world. As Margaret Mahler put it, "Narcissism at its peak!" All magical stories are full of magical feats—you can fly through the air, you can zap a person just by pointing your finger at them, you can materialize anything you want out of thin air, and so on.

Q: But don't you believe in miracles, for example?

A: Sure. But actual miracles are rare, and we have to account for the billions of occasions where people think they can fly but can't. That's magic. In the early years of growth it's natural, normal, and perfectly healthy. It was also perfectly healthy for grown men and women two hundred thousand years ago, when magic was the highest level that evolution had reached. But today, if this structure is not surrendered—if it is repeatedly traumatized or frustrated, or if there is a physiological malfunction—then the result is a whole class of emotional problems known as "borderline," meaning borderline between psychosis and neurosis.

Q: So what about the mythic level?

A: In most children, the magic structure subsides and the mythic begins to emerge at around ages five to seven, with the emergence of the next basic structure, the "rule" or "role" structure, the concrete operational structure. A fascinating shift occurs at this point. The self is continuing to learn to differentiate itself from the environment, with greater and greater clarity. So its narcissism and its omnipotence continue to *decrease.* The self no longer thinks that it can order the world around, or fly, or materialize things. So it transfers that magical belief to real or imaginary figures in the environment. I can no longer move the world around, but God can! So a whole panoply of gods and goddesses and spirits and demons—all understood in a terribly concrete fashion—come onto the scene. The other thing about concrete-literal myth is that it often has a narrative structure, unlike magic. Magic is dominated by impulse and images, with a few symbols and concepts, so it tends to be present-centered. You *do* magic, poof! But you *tell* myths; they are often *stories.* The self tells stories and understands itself by its stories, because of the roles it has and the rules it follows. So magic is "poof!" but myth is "Once upon a time . . ."

Q: So you disagree with Jung's belief that myths are essentially religious?

A: This is a very complicated issue. Let me just say that I believe Jung often confused transrational archetypes with prerational mythic forms, and this confusion distorted his understanding of spirituality. But that really is another story. . . . Now I'm talking about the concrete-mythic structure of development. And while *some* spiritual insights might be expressed through the mythic structure, by far the largest portion of the mythic structure is prerational, concrete, nonspiritual and nontranscendental—and that's what I'm referring to now. If the mythic level is not surrendered—if it is traumatized or frustrated—the result is various types of neurosis. Speaking simplistically, fixation/disruption at the archaic level produces psychoses, at the magic level, borderline, and at the mythic level, neurosis. Neurosis is an unconscious myth; it's a false and distortive story you subconsciously tell yourself, such as "I'm no good, I'm worthless. If I do that, God will punish me. If I desire sex I'm bad and should feel guilt. The forces that be are going to punish me for this," and so on. Neurosis is all the pain and anxiety and guilt and depression that we generate by telling ourselves false and distorted stories, or myths.

This is why the cognitive approach to most neurosis is so effective: you find out the stories or myths that people are telling themselves and, using reason—the next higher stage—you disrupt the myths. You demonstrate that they simply are not true, that the preponderance of evidence clearly shows they are false. This can be hard, because all us neurotics are attached to our myths—"Neurosis is a private religion," said Otto Rank—and we are fearful of giving them up. The mythic idea is that God will get you if you stop believing. What's more, if you dig deeply into most of your myths, you'll often find little leftover seeds of magic as well. You think, "I hate that person" then the next day that person drops dead of a heart attack, and you feel terrible. To the magic structure, a thought is the same as a deed. Magic and myth are never going to go away entirely; the point is just not to be dominated by them. When myth—as I am using the term—starts to dominate, neurosis is not far behind.

Q: How does the rule/role mind support the mythic structure?

A: Technically, a rule is a sophisticated cognitive operation that allows you, for example, to multiply numbers, or divide them.

Q: Could you give some concrete examples?

A: If you take a child of seven or eight, someone who has just developed the rule mind, and you tell them *A* is greater than *B,* and *B* is greater than *C,* the child will be able to tell you that *A* is therefore greater than *C.* The preoperational or magic child cannot do that. Or take this: if you get a short fat glass and a tall thin glass, fill the first glass with water, then pour that water into the second glass, the preoperational child will say the tall glass has more water, even though the exact same amount of water was in both glasses and he's standing right there watching. He does not have a rule that allows him to mentally conserve volume. The mythic child does, and will immediately tell you that both glasses have the same amount of water.

Q: And what about "roles"?

A: If you take a preoperational (or magical) child, and put a ball that is half red and half green between you and the child, with one color facing the child, and then ask "What color do you see?" the child will tell you what color he's looking at, say, red. You then turn the ball half way around, and the child correctly says "green." The child knows that the ball has two colored halves. Now, with the green half facing the child, you say, "What color am *I* looking at?" and the child will say "green." In other words, the child cannot mentally put himself in your place, he *cannot take the role of other.* But when the rule/role mind emerges, around age seven, the child will immediately give the right answer. The child's moral sense switches from "impulsive" or "whatever I want" to what is called "conformist" or "conventional." This is due to the emergence of the rule/role mind.

Q: How does the rule/role mind support a mythic worldview?

A: We usually think of the mythic structure as wildly imaginative and dreamlike, and the rational level as dry and unimaginative. In fact it is exactly the opposite. The mythic structure, despite all its gods and goddesses, its demons and spirits, is in fact very concrete and literalistic. *It believes these myths as a matter of concrete fact,* not as symbolic and visionary. Moses really did part the Red Sea, Christ really was born from a virgin, God really did rain bread down from heaven, and so on. Very concrete and very unimaginative, as James Fowler's research demonstrates. This is *concrete* operational thinking. You can see this not only in the world's great myths, but in the very actions of the mythic child. Take the mythic child, for example, put three glasses in front of him, each containing different clear liquids, and tell him, "Two of these liquids, when mixed together, will turn red. How can you find the right two?" The mythic child will carefully and laboriously go through each combination of two liquids. He will sit there and actually begin mixing the various liquids together. But a formal operational child, age fifteen or so, will simply tell you, "I'd try A with B, then A with C, then B with C." In other words, he can *mentally picture all the possibilities.* Unlike his mythic predecessor, he can dream up solutions and not have to do them in concrete fact. It is in adolescence that real dreaming and youthful idealism—seeing all the possibilities, all the "what ifs"—first appear. This is a major cognitive revolution, the overthrow of concrete myth for symbolic reason and nonliteralistic dreaming. This is meta-rule.

Q: So why do we think that myth is so freeing, or has so much freedom, if in fact it is so bound and tied to the concrete?

A: Because *we* look at it from the vantage point of reason. That is, we take the freedom of reason and mix it with the fantastic aspects of myth, and the result is a romantic notion of myth as imaginative, free, and transcendental. But when you are actually *in* the mythic structure it's nothing of the sort. It's hardheaded, concrete, and pretty unimaginative. It's fundamentalist.

Q: What about the rational structure itself?

A: As we were saying, it's the first structure to understand possibilities, or "what if" and "as if" statements—technically, this is called hypothetico-deductive. This is the structure that discovered science, medicine, physics, because it is the first structure willing to experiment. Two, it is self-reflexive and introspective; it is the first structure strong enough to look at itself, at least in some aspects. This can be frightening. And three, it understands perspective, or pluralism. It understands that "truth" is not always cut and dried, a concrete event with only one way to look at it, but that truth is based on one's perspective and is open to different interpretations. A keen sense of interpretive truth—technically called "hermeneutics," the science of interpretation—comes into existence. This does not happen in the mythic structure because its capacity for perspective is just beginning; it can take the role of others but it cannot equally hold and balance them all in mind, which is what rational perspectivism does. This is why mythic believers—fundamentalists, for example—simply will not allow any truth other than their own. They simply cannot way, "All religions offer different and valuable perspectives on God." They can only say, "My way is absolutely the only way." And they actually think they'll be eternally damned if they don't believe that. It's rather dangerous and belligerent—holy war time.

Q: So what happens if you get stuck at the rational level? At the archaic level it was psychosis; at magic, borderline; at mythic, neurosis* What happens if you get stuck at the rational?

A: By and large, nothing, because the rational is the stage that evolution at large has now reached. So most people stop here. No higher structure—psychic or subtle or causal—will *automatically* start to emerge. If you want to go beyond the rational, you're on your own. You have to fight, and work, and struggle mightily.

But if you run into problems *on* the rational level, the result is an "identity crisis." Once you are no longer defined merely by society's roles and rules, who are you? Many people in our society face an identity crisis, because *left to their own devices,* they are unsure of who they are. This is a battle for *autonomy* and *self-esteem.*

Q: If you surrender the rational worldview, what replaces it?

A: You could regress, which often happens. You resurrect some sort of concrete myth or belief system, and hang onto it for dear life. As the joke has it, "I've given up looking for truth, now I'm just trying to find

---

*I am, in this simple account, combining F-3 and F-4.

a good fantasy." Whenever the good reason and goodwill of men and women is battered, myths often come running in to replace it.

Q: So, let's assume that development continues to go forward, not backward.

A: If you do move forward, you go beyond an exclusive belief in rationality. Rationality itself can remain, and has some important tasks to do, you're just not stuck in it. If you surrender the purely rational paradigm, a more existential-humanistic worldview starts to emerge. This has three very specific and unmistakable characteristics. One is the mind-body integration or organismic unity which I call "centaur." Developmental studies have repeatedly confirmed a mind-body integration at this point. Two, it is marked by what I have called "vision-logic." At the rational level, remember, for the first time we can take account of *possibilities,* we can experiment, we can dream of alternatives, we can actually imagine different and possible worlds. Now vision-logic adds up these possibilities, and sees them in a holistic or visionary fashion. Aurobindo described this much better than I can. He called it the "higher mind"—which can "freely express itself in single ideas, but its most characteristic movement is a mass ideation, a system or totality of truth-seeing at a single view; the relations of idea with idea, of truth with truth . . . self-seen in the integral whole." Three, this level has a conspicuously "existential" flavor. Vision-logic "adds up all the possibilities," and what it finds is: life is a brief spark in a totally uncaring universe. In a sense that's absolutely right. You see, when you give up magic and myth, and your comfortable and smug scientific rationality, then where will you be safe? Who or what will protect you? You have given up all the consolations of childhood and adolescence, but have not yet discovered the refuge of higher spirituality and genuine mysticism. So there is a certain brave "man is the measure of all things" attitude about this stage. Most importantly, this stage demands that we come to terms with our *finitude* and *mortality.* No parental god will save us from death. We have to face that by ourselves, completely and totally alone. This is why the existentialists said that "God is dead." The *mythic* god is dead. And this is also why the existentialists, Heidegger for example, define "inauthentic" as someone who—I think this is a more or less direct quote—"has not the constant and profound realization of lonely and unexpected death." The existentialists therefore offer profound analysis of the "immortality symbols" we use to deny our death, to avoid awareness that, as William James put it, the skull will in fact grin at the banquet. The existentialists—from Kierkegaard, Nietzsche, and

Dostoyevsky to Karl Jaspers, Martin Buber, Paul Tillich, and Rollo May—bring great sanity to human affairs.

Q: So the existential level, in a sense, is the clearing house for higher or spiritual development, even if, at that level, it looks like spirit doesn't exist at all.

A: Actually, the rational and the existential levels combine to strip us of childish and adolescent approaches to Spirit. They clean out the magical and mythical notions of Spirit as a cosmic parent who doles out rewards for belief or eternal damnation for non-belief. You can be at the existential level and still believe in Spirit. You might, for example, believe in mystical Christianity, which accurately reflects the subtle and causal dimensions. But you are still going to have to strip away any remaining magical and mythical beliefs about Spirit before you can actually progress into a more mature realization of Spirit. And this is hard. You get in a really life-threatening situation, and you will probably find yourself bargaining with God. That's magic and mythic plea-bargaining. But that god no longer exists. We have to realize that if we are to prepare for a mature and authentic relationship with Spirit. Nobody will save you but you. You alone have to engage your own contemplative development. There is all sorts of help available, and all sorts of good agency to quicken this development, but nobody can do it for you. And if you do not engage this development, and on your deathbed you confess and scream out for help to God, nothing is going to happen. Spiritual development is not a matter of mere belief. It is a matter of actual, prolonged, difficult growth, and merely professing belief is meaningless and without impact. It's like smoking for twenty years, then saying, "Sorry, I quit." That will not impress cancer. Reality, in other words, is not interested in your beliefs; it's interested in your actions, what you actually do, your actual karma. And this is why infantile and childish views of God, once appropriate, are so detrimental for mature spirituality.

Q: It's ironic that the existentialists are viewed as antispiritual, since they seem to be playing John the Baptist to Christ, preparing the way to actual spiritual descent.

A: Yes. But remember that a fair number of extremely influential existentialists were (and are) what they themselves call "theistic existentialists," such as Tillich and Jaspers. And they are right on target, I believe. God has to be reinterpreted, not as a big daddy or cosmic parent, but as the Ground of Being (Tillich) or radical Mystery (Jaspers). They didn't have a very good understanding of contemplative development, so I believe that their views are limited to the existential level and its basic structures. But as far as they go, they seem to be right on.

Q: "As far as they go"—I've noticed you use that phrase a lot when referring to many theorists.

A: Well, I think virtually every theorist has something important to tell us, and our job is to incorporate all these truths into a more encompassing vision. At the same time, many of them deny or ignore the higher stages of development and dimensions of reality, so their views are often partial and incomplete. So I try to appreciate them "as far as they go," and then supplement their insights with those of others who have gone further.

Q: Could you briefly discuss the moral sense of each of these stages?

A: Yes, Kohlberg found for men, and Gilligan for women, that people go through three major stages of moral development: preconventional, conventional, and postconventional. And those stages are, basically, the magic, the mythic, and the rational. The preconventional moral stage is a type of Hell's Angels morality—reality is what I say or wish it to be, I do whatever the hell I want, nobody messes with me, and so on. Something is morally wrong if and only if I get caught. This is called "preconventional" because it doesn't recognize conventions or rules. It's very narcissistic. This is the magical structure.

Q: All that changes at the mythic—or conventional—level.

A: The mythic level, with its rule/role mind, understands very clearly that there are roles to be imitated and rules to be obeyed, and it gladly goes along. In fact, it often goes overboard. It is so preoccupied with rules and roles, with "fitting in," that it becomes virtually incapable of challenging the roles or the rules. It becomes, that is, a complete conformist. "My country right or wrong." Kohlberg calls this the "good boy/nice girl" stage; Loevinger, the "conformist stage"; Maslow, the "conventional stage." This is the mythic level, the concrete operational level. This is a fairly unimaginative structure, conforming to whatever is around it. It does not understand possibilities or alternatives or "what ifs."

Q: I see. The rational structure *can* envision possibilities, so it becomes postconventional.

A: Yes. Because the rational structure can conceive other ways than the present way of doing things, it can decide for itself whether the conventional way is the best. As Kohlberg describes the postconventional structure, one might end up following conventional morals or not. The point is that conventions are given critical scrutiny based on logic and reason, on universal principles of moral reasoning. This postconventional stance is greatly helped by the rational structure's capacity for introspection and self-reflexiveness. You can actually "look within" and decide what's right or wrong, not just look without and do what others say. Most of our moral heroes—Thoreau, Gandhi, Martin Luther King—are heroes to us precisely because they looked within, and hearing the sound of a different drummer, courageously marched to it. This is postconventional at its awe-inspiring best.

Q: Now Kohlberg added a final and highest stage, didn't he? He called it the "universal-spiritual."

A: Yes. This is to his everlasting credit. The spiritual dimension is the next up, but these higher dimensions—psychic, subtle, and causal—are so rare that it's almost impossible to get much data on them. So Kohlberg understandably just lumped them all together as "universal-spiritual."

Q: It has always struck me as odd that the existential level would lie right next to the psychic level. They seem so antithetical, so different, that I don't see how psychological development could move smoothly from one to the other.

A: That is actually no different from what happens at all sorts of other stages. For example, look at Loevinger's stages of ego development, which are widely regarded as being fairly accurate. Her stages are: symbiotic, impulsive, self-protective, conformist, conscientious-conformist, conscientious, individualistic, autonomous, and integrated. Those stages, incidentally, are basically the archaic (symbiotic), the magical (impulsive and self-protective), the mythic (conformist and conscientious-conformist), the rational (conscientious and individual), and the existential (autonomous and integrated). But notice the shift, for example, from the self-protective to the comformist. These are diametrically opposed stances. You go from being a Hell's Angel to being a conformist good boy/nice girl. Every child goes through that, and does it in about a six-month period. Then, after you make that amazing switch, almost an about-face, and you become a nice conformist, then the next stage is up: the conscientious, the individualistic, the postconventional. Again, diametrically opposed. From slavish conformity to individualistic freedom of choice. Far from the existential/psychic shift being an oddity, it's simply another example of the "dialectic of development": each level eventually runs into its opposite (what Hegel calls its "negation"); the thesis runs into its antithesis, and these are eventually combined (or transcended) in a new and higher synthesis. But that's development. Each succeeding level has both something in continuity with its predecessor, and something extremely different. That's what makes development so fraught with tension and conflict and anxiety.

Q: Okay. Now, to return to the main topic, we have left the psychic, the subtle, and the causal worldviews or paradigms. Want to briefly fill those in?

A: We can do this fairly quickly, I think. Da Free John has written extensively on the worldviews of these three subsets of the overall spiritual dimension. As he points out, the worldviews of the psychic, subtle, and causal are, respectively, that of the yogi, the saint, and the sage. Or, as I have described it, there are three different types or levels of genuine spirituality or mysticism: there is nature (or psychic) mysticism, there is theistic (or subtle) mysticism, and there is nondual (or causal) mysticism, and that correlates with the yogi, the saint, and the sage.*

Q: Maybe we better take them one at a time.

A: Okay. The yogic worldview is the first step beyond existentialism. It uses or strenuously develops the gross body and mind—exactly like existential-humanists do—but it does so in order to move beyond the gross body and mind toward the subtle dimensions of existence. All the yogic techniques, the pranayama, the hatha yoga postures, and so on, are ways to "yoke" the physical bodymind and begin to transcend it, get free of it. If there are actual mystical experiences at this stage, they tend not to be "vertical" transformations to subtle or causal levels, but rather "horizontal" expansions of awareness—in other words, finding a union with the manifest world of nature, and not actually finding a "higher world" in God and Spirit. Aurobindo was pretty clear on this, as were Sri Ramana Maharshi, Evelyn Underhill and others. So the psychic level is typically the level of nature mysticism, and pantheistic mysticism, or a "horizontal religion," a horizontal expansion, ecological expansion, one with the physical or natural world. Again, very correct and useful as far as it goes. When you first break through the existential level, one of the first types of religious experience that you have tends to be of nature mysticism—you're sitting there, looking around, feeling perfectly isolated, alone, finite, and mortal, and maybe you're looking at a sunset or something, and all of a sudden—wham!—you're one with the sunset, one with the ocean, one with the whole scene. You realize, in a very concrete and real fashion, that there is most definitely something beyond your "skin-encapsulated ego," as Watts would say, you realize that there is

*I am here treating causal and nondual as one.

a higher or spiritual and unified dimension, and that you partake of that union in your very being, that you are one with all of nature, all of what you see. This is usually a profoundly shattering and liberating experience, liberating you from the rational-existential knot of existence. This is the introduction to the spiritual dimension.

Unfortunately, a lot of people stop here, or, in any event, they over-idealize this pantheistic nature mysticism. The psychic dimension *is* a new paradigm, and moving from the rational-existential to the psychic is a major cognitive revolution, another dialectic of development, but it is just another moment on the way, and not some ultimate worldview. It should be appreciated and accommodated, and then quietly let go.

Q: Which is what happens when you move to the subtle level?

A: Ideally, yes. The subtle level is the worldview of the "saint," and the source of theistic mysticism, the direct relation to the soul to God/Goddess. There is still a subtle dualism between self (soul) and other (God). So the soul communes with God, or the soul finds a union with God, or the soul might even temporarily find an identity with God. But the soul remains intact and ultimately separate, communing with its higher or divine dimensions or God. But the great advantage of the subtle level over the psychic level is that it understands that there is a spiritual dimension above or beyond mere nature, or what you can see with your physical senses. It is not just a union with the physical world, but also a union with the subtle world, which is invisible to the senses, invisible to nature. This is the transcendental mysticism of the saints. Saints have halos not because they're moralistic, but because the subtle level consists of levels and "rings"—literally—of audible illuminations (nada, shabd) and divinity revealed as light, at and around the sixth and seventh chakra, or the crown of the head, so saints are universally depicted with halos of divine light around their heads. This is not symbolic; this is exactly what they perceive. That is a direct communion or union with the Divine.

Q: That's very clear. Agree or not, that's quite interesting. Okay, and finally, the causal?

A: The causal is the worldview of the sage; it is nondual mysticism. Both the yogi and the saint, you see, are engineering higher experiences. As subjects, they are looking at the higher levels as objects. But the sage is not interested in experiences; the sage is not interested in being a subject looking at higher objects. The sage is interested in dissolving the subject altogether, transcending the subject-object dualism entirely, and thus in being liberated from the fate of being a separate-self sense, which is necessarily a fate of pain, fear, separation, time, history, and death. The sage doesn't want to see God—although there is nothing wrong with that—the sage wants to get rid of the separate "seer" altogether. And this is why sages, unlike saints, are always depicted as completely average or normal or ordinary. Saints have light shining from their heads, they have siddhi or paranormal powers, people flock around them, try to touch them. But sages largely go unnoticed. They have transcended the separate-self sense so entirely that they are not particularly noticeable. D. T. Suzuki used to sign his letters *"wu shih,"* which means "nobody special." That's the sage's paradigm. Ordinary life, and ordinary reality, freed of the separate-self sense, is itself ultimate reality. "How wonderful, how transcendental this! I chop wood, I carry water," goes one of the most famous Zen koans.

Now sometimes sages will consent to teach, and go public—mostly out of compassion for you and me—and so they become "big deals." But that is not what the sage is all about. Anyway, this is nondual mysticism, mysticism that finally and totally transcends the subject/object or self/other duality. This is the final paradigm shift, and as far as we can tell, the ultimate cognitive revolution. This is the return *of* Spirit, *to* Spirit, *as* Spirit, as Hegel would say. Or, to use several Zen phrases: this is the Great Death of the separate-self sense; this is the Great Liberation; this is finding out who you are before your parents were born; this is seeing your Original Face. And in Christian terms, this is the alpha and omega of all development; in our terms, the final paradigm.

Q: But do you think the "final paradigm" is actually "final"? Do you think this realization, the realization of the sages, the realization of the causal, do you think that this is unchanging and forever invariant?

A: No, not like that. Hegel actually went from thinking that "enlightenment" was an end state, a final product, to seeing it as an eternal process. The great Japanese meditation master, Dogen Zenji, had probably the greatest line ever on spiritual development. It manages to pack virtually everything you can say about spiritual development into four lines. Dogen said, "To study Buddhism"—but I'm going to take the liberty of changing the word "Buddhism" to "mysticism," because that is what it really refers to—"To study mysticism is to study the self. To study the self is to forget the self. To forget the self is to be one with all things. To be one with all things is to be enlightened by all things, and this traceless enlightenment continues forever."

In other words, enlightenment is a process, not an end state, not a product. It goes on forever. . . . "And this traceless enlightenment continues forever. . . ." That is the testimony, the confession of the world's great sages. And in that sense, and that sense only, you have the final paradigm, which continues forever as process. . . . And it does not involve some sort of New Age hoopla and narcissism and me-ness and oh-boy. It involves "wu shih" . . . nobody special. Nobody special . . . you see?

A WORKING SYNTHESIS OF TRANSACTIONAL ANALYSIS AND GESTALT THERAPY

ABSTRACT: *By supplying the necessary theoretical link between the predominantly Gestalt concepts of retroflection and projection, a basic core is provided for the fundamental synthesis of Gestalt Therapy and Transactional Analysis. This synthesis suggests that the ego states of Parent and Child correspond in most cases to particular forms of retroflection and projection. The* present *activities of retroflection and projection take as their vehicles of expression the Parent and Child, which are by and large the products of* past *experience. Transactional Analysis and Gestalt therapy are thus two complementary approaches to the same psychodynamic factors, and hence a synthesis of their best elements should prove stronger than either alone.*

TWO SCHOOLS of humanistic psychology today enjoying wide popularity are Transactional Analysis and Gestalt Therapy, the former associated with Eric Berne (1961, 1964, 1972) and Thomas Harris (1969), the latter with Fritz and Laura Perls (Perls, 1969a, 1969b; Perls et al., 1951; see also Fagan, 1970; Polster, 1974; Pursglove, 1968). Much of the success of Transactional Analysis seems to lie in its utter simplicity and the basic directness of its approach, while the success of Gestalt Therapy stems from the powerful and fundamental changes of growth it facilitates in those who endure it with awareness.*

Because of the simplicity of Transactional Analysis and the power of Gestalt Therapy, many people—therapists, educators, laypeople—have been using the two procedures together, either alternating between the two or using a more or less adequate synthesis of both. There is certainly good reason to attempt such a synthesis, and—barring a few theoretical differences—I believe a working synthesis of Transactional Analysis and Gestalt Therapy is indeed possible, a synthesis which combines the speed and simplicity of T. A. with the power and depth of Gestalt.

We can begin our synthesis on a solid foundation if we realize that Transactional Analysis and Gestalt Therapy generally agree that the personality is a tripartite structure. Early on, Freud himself had proposed a three-way structural division of the psyche: the superego (with subdivisions of ego-ideal and conscience); the ego proper; and the id, closely associated with the infantile ego (Blum, 1953; Fenichel, 1972). Despite the fact that the theoretical underpinnings of the two newer schools of psychotherapy differ somewhat from the Freudian, they both agree that the individual's personality structure contains three more or less distinct subpersonalities. Transactional Analysis refers to them as the Parent, the Adult, and the Child; while to Gestalt Therapy they are the Topdog, the centered self, and the Underdog.

Such appears to be the tripartite division of the personality. There is the superego, the Parent, the Topdog, whose nucleus is composed of the internalized demands and judgments of parents and other authority figures. There is the infantile ego, the Child, the Underdog, consisting of all the feelings of helplessness and dependence that the person felt as a child. Finally, and fortunately, there is the mature ego, the Adult, the authentic self, capable of seeing present reality and capable of basing its decisions on objective facts and not on the threats of the Parent/Topdog nor the archaic fears of the Child/Underdog.

But to bring out this Adult and firmly establish it, the person has to free himself of the continuing choice to operate in his modes of Parent or Child—and just this is the aim of therapy. In Transactional Analysis this "freeing-up of the Adult" is based on a simple principle—since the tapes of the Parent and Child are recorded permanently in your brain,

---

*My own formal position is that of spectrum psychology (Wilber, 1975). The approach suggested here is directed toward the Shadow/Ego Level.

you cannot erase them. But if you can learn to spot and clearly recognize in yourself the Parent tapes as well as the Child tapes, you can choose to turn them off! In short, you can learn to "stay in the Adult."

Thus, as a person begins Transactional Analysis, she learns the fundamentals of the Parent-Adult-Child scheme, and then she applies them to her present transactions. She begins to spot the signals that indicate her "Parent is hooked," such as the furrowed brow, pursed lips, the pointing index finger, usually accompanied by such verbal pronouncements as "Now you're in real trouble"; "Never let me see you doing that again!"; "How dare you!"; "I can't for the life of me . . ." The individual also begins to recognize the clues that her "Child is hooked," such as tears, pouting, whining voice, temper tantrums, and feelings of anxiety, fearfulness, inferiority, and so on. As the individual starts to get a real feel for her Parent and Child, she will further discover that both the Parent and the Child can be "aimed" in one of two basic directions. The Parent, for example, can direct its demands and pronouncements *outwardly* toward others, but it can also direct its threats and punishments *inwardly* toward the Child in the person. Likewise, the Child can be aimed *inwardly* toward the threats of its own Parent or *outwardly* toward the threats of the Parents in others. And all in all, this gives individuals *four basic patterns* in which they can operate if they refuse to stay in the Adult. (I mention this seemingly trivial point because it will actually turn out to be of great significance in our synthesis of Transactional Analysis and Gestalt Therapy.)

The fact that individuals can step back and reflect on which tapes are now playing and which direction they are aimed—just that is the therapeutic agent. For in objectively and rationally identifying the Parent and the Child in both self and others, they are necessarily operating in the Adult! And therapy is simply a day-to-day strengthening of the Adult and a silencing of the archaic Child and Parent.

Now the aim of Gestalt Therapy is similar, in that it, too, tries to free up the personality from the overbearing influence of the Topdog/Parent and the Underdog/Child. But since, according to Gestalt Therapy, these "two clowns" have their genesis in impasse situations where self-potential is abandoned in favor of environmental support, Gestalt Therapy aims directly at recovering that lost potential. Now the major mechanisms that a person uses to throttle, avoid, and surrender his own potentials are those of introjection, retroflection, and projection—mechanisms we will soon explain in detail. It is precisely by working through these "mechanisms of avoidance" that Gestalt Therapy restores to the individual his potentials for growth, thus freeing his energies from the clutches of the Topdog and Underdog.

It is expressly the strengths of these two therapeutic systems that we wish to combine and utilize. We have already examined briefly the structure of the psyche according to both schools, and concluded that both would generally agree the personality to be a tripartite system—composed of Parent/Topdog, Adult/Authentic self, and Child/Underdog—whose basis was laid in times past but whose functioning is reactivated and purposefully maintained in the present. Hence, it is not so much with past "causes" but with present transactions that therapy must chiefly concern itself. Having briefly reviewed the structure of the personality, we will now focus our attention on its dynamics, for it is in this arena that neurotic battles are fought, and hence it is just here that we must seek our synthesis if it is to be of any real value in the therapeutic process.

Let us begin by looking more closely at the Child/Underdog. According to Transactional Analysis, the predominant feelings residing in everybody's Child are ones of frustration, anxiety, and fear. And just because the tapes recorded in the Child are *permanent,* they can replay at almost any time in a person's current transactions, given the right stimulus. A person might, for example, be in the midst of an economic crisis, or someone might make a snide remark to him, or he might not get his way in a given situation, or any number of such instances. "These 'hook the Child', as we say, and cause a replay of the original feelings of frustration, rejection, or abandonment, and we relive a latter-day version of the small child's primary depression. Therefore, when a person is in the grip of feelings, we say his Child has taken over" (Harris, 1969, pp. 48–49).

But recall that according to Gestalt Therapy, the Child/Underdog is simply a position we take today in times of stress or impasse, where environmental support is not forthcoming and authentic self-support is not yet realized. Because this self-support is not yet achieved, the person feels totally resourceless, lacking potential, helpless—in short, she feels NOT OK. And in an attempt to assuage her NOT OK feelings, she throws herself into a manipulative frenzy, seeking to mobilize in others that which she fails to find in herself. Hence, instead of realizing her own resources, she looks to the environment for them. Yet it's important to realize that *when the Child is hooked, a person's potentials do not just up and leave her, they do not evaporate, they are not and could not be lost*—they are only abandoned, surrendered, projected. In other words, according to Gestalt, the person's potentials are definitely available, but only in the form of projections!

Thus we come to our first preliminary synthesizing rule: *When the Child is hooked, we look for projections.*

Projection is the basic mechanism associated with the Child. No matter that the fundamental data of the Child was recorded when the person was three years old—the point is that *if* the Child is hooked now, the individual feels himself to lack the potential and the resources necessary to the task. But that potential is not thereby abolished or obliterated—it is merely projected and exists fully and completely in the projections. As Perls (1969b) explains, "Much material that is our own, that is part of ourselves, has been dissociated, alienated, disowned, thrown out. The rest of our potential is not available to us. But I believe most of it *is* available, but as projections." Thus the potential is indeed present, but as projections, and we rediscover our "lost" resources—*and hence facilitate staying in the Adult*—by reowning our projections. The person whose Child is hooked does feel helpless, not because he lacks the necessary resources, but because he projects them, attributes them to everybody else. Thus, when the Child is hooked, we look for just those projections. In this area of therapy, the strength of Transactional Analysis is the ease with which it spots the Child; the strength of Gestalt is the ease with which it spots the projections. The wise therapist will use both, for the hooking of the Child and the projecting of potentials are flip sides of the same coin.

One of the aims of Transactional Analysis is to learn to recognize every signal and recording from the NOT OK Child so as to be able to turn off those tapes. If, for example, I am very upset and hurt "because of" some seemingly cruel remark made to me, I can learn to pause and realize, "Oh, those feelings of hurt and shame are simply my NOT OK Child." That realization alone often brings immediate relief. Recognizing my uncomfortable feelings to be the replay of some NOT OK Child tapes, I am not caught up in them, I am not overwhelmed by them. In other words, I am learning to simply shut them off.

But—as many Transactional Analysts agree—sometimes the tapes just don't want to shut off. And under those circumstances it's almost impossible to stay in the Adult. The reason the person refuses to stay in the Adult is that he doesn't see how he is going to muster the potential, the resources, the strength to do so. In a sense, he *actively clings* to the position of the NOT OK Child because that is the only way he knows to cope.

This is the point where the very strength of Gestalt Therapy shows itself, and thus we may look to Gestalt for some complementary insights. The Child tapes won't turn off because they are associated with a projection, a bit of "unfinished business" that will clamor for attention until the gestalt is closed and the business finished. Conversely, in assimilating that projection one yanks the support out from under the position of the Child. Furthermore, to integrate projections it is not necessary to ask *why* one projects, but rather to discover *how* one projects. If you regain the simple awareness of how you now project, then you are spontaneously free to cease. In Transactional Analysis terms, if you discover not *why* you activated the Child tapes, but *how* you turned them on, *then* you are in a position to turn them off. It's almost as if you had, in the dark, inadvertently turned on a radio switch while you were trying to sleep, and the machine is now blaring away at full blast. To pause, reflect, and search out possible reasons for why you turned it on does you no good whatsoever—you could sit there and theorize forever . . . with the radio accompanying you. On the other hand, if you can find out *how* you turned it on—where the switch is and how it operates—then you can easily turn it off.

We will return shortly to the *how* of projections—what I would like to emphasize at this point is that I believe the reowning of projections is in fact precisely what occurs in Transactional Analysis as the person learns to spot the Child and then stay in the Adult. For what does the person who habitually comes on as the NOT OK Child actually feel as she learns to stay in the Adult? She feels a gradual discovery of her strength, her potential, and her resources—resources she didn't think she possessed when operating as the Child. By continually learning to stay in the Adult, she is simply learning to discover and act on her own potentials, and not surrender them by falling back into the archaic circuits of the NOT OK, resourceless, helpless Child.

But this is precisely the point where the complementary insights of Gestalt Therapy are so useful, for Gestalt accurately spots just which potentials the person is surrendering when she comes on as Child! For these potentials are present as projections, and thus the projections of the Child mark out exactly what potentials need to be returned to the person as she learns to stay in the Adult. In short, the activation of the Adult *is* the reowning of projected potential. Transactional Analysis proceeds through the former, Gestalt through the latter—but they certainly can be used conjointly. By learning to spot the Child, *and then the projections,* the person's ability to switch to the position of Adult is greatly facilitated, for she understands exactly what potentials she will be mobilizing as the Adult. She knows what to look for. She begins to see just *how* she activates the Child. And thus she starts to understand the corollary to the first basic synthesizing rule: to stay in the Adult is to refuse to project.

So let us now proceed—as promised—to explore more systematically this mechanism of projection. Projections, to repeat, are facets of the personality not recognized as one's own but instead alienated and thus perceived as if they resided in other people. For example, a person who tends to approach people sexually can, for various reasons, try to avoid this impulse. But since the impulse is nevertheless definitely present, he cannot actually abolish it, he can only attempt to disown it. Doing so, he feels that *he* lacks that nasty impulse, but since he knows only too well that *somebody* has a hell-of-a-lot of sex on the mind, he has only to pick a candidate. And anybody will do, as long as he finds at least one. Suddenly, come to think of it, the world looks full of perverts, most of whom are out to rape him personally! And he feels NOT OK.

Projections are easily spotted, for they are aspects of people or things that strongly *affect* where they would otherwise *inform*. Thus, what I see in other people is more or less correct if it only informs me, but it is likely a projection if it strongly affects me—and that is the crucial difference. So if we are overly attached to somebody (or something) on the one hand, or if we avoid or hate someone on the other, then we are respectively shadow-hugging or shadow-boxing.

Since projections are actually disidentifications or alienations of some facets of self, in therapy we must do just the opposite—we take back, identify with, reown our projections. "So what we are trying to do in therapy is step-by-step to *reown* the disowned parts of the personality until the person becomes strong enough to facilitate his own growth. Everything the person disowns can be recovered, and the means of this recovery is understanding, playing, becoming these disowned parts" (Perls, 1969b, pp. 37–38). As I said, these disowned parts are very obvious—they are things, people, or events in the environment that affect and disturb us, and hence ones we energetically resist and avoid. So initially there seems to be a bonafide conflict between the person and his environment, a real individual vs. environmental feud. But by identifying with the disturbing elements of the environment, playing in fantasy as if he actually were those elements, the person soon realizes that the conflict is really between facets of himself. The battle is not between me and thee, but me and me—thee just got in the way.

We can say, then, that during Gestalt Therapy, all conflicts between self and environment are reduced to a prior conflict between self and self. Now in a broad sense (and I will clarify this in a minute), these conflicts between self and self are nothing but *retroflections*. Thus, the initial movements of Gestalt Therapy are concerned with *converting or reducing all projections to retroflections*. And it is to the undoing of retroflections that Gestalt Therapy then directs its attention.

Perls, Hefferline, and Goodman explain retroflections as follows:

> To retroflect means literally "to turn sharply back against." When a person retroflects behavior, he does to himself what originally he did or tried to do to other persons or objects. He stops directing various energies outward in attempts to manipulate and bring about changes in the environment that will satisfy his needs; instead, he redirects activity inward and *substitutes himself in place of the environment* as the target of behavior. To the extent that he does this, he splits his personality into "doer" and "done to." (Perls et al., 1951)

Most retroflections are done consciously; the person is perfectly aware that he is actively holding in an impulse—such as the urge to scream—perhaps until a more favorable time or place. The person, under these circumstances, knows both that *he* is doing the inhibiting and *how* he is doing the inhibiting. But in many cases the inhibitions have become habitual and thus are performed almost totally unconsciously. The person forgets how he inhibited or retroflected the impulse, and hence he can't release it. The impulse is no longer temporarily suppressed, but chronically repressed.

Nevertheless, the impulse does not thereby vanish—it must have some sort of outlet, and denied direct expression in the environment, it takes as its object the next best thing, namely, the person himself. A person who chronically retroflects anger turns that anger back on himself and then clobbers himself with his own energies. Someone who retroflects her critical attitude finds that she is perpetually criticizing herself, punishing herself, beating herself. A student trying to work a math problem and not succeeding, slaps himself and pounds his thigh as he retroflects his mobilized aggression.

It is in just this fashion that the personality is split into a "doer" and a "done to," with the "done to" receiving the blows originally meant for the environment. It's very much as if I started out to pinch someone but instead turned that activity back and pinched myself. This is retroflection, and it necessarily splits the personality into two sides: the pincher versus the pinched. Thus we see there are always two poles in a retroflection: the pincher side of the retroflection is experienced as the *active* doer, powerful, inhibiting, forceful; while the pinched side of the retroflection is experienced as a more *passive* done to, helpless, inhibited, powerless.

Now in most retroflections, the person is at least vaguely aware with which of the two sides he is associated. The frustrated golfer who begins screaming at himself, "You stupid SOB, why can't you learn to putt!" experiences himself as the active doer. On the other hand, the person who develops severe headaches when she knows she'd rather scream will feel herself as a rather passive done-to, a "victim" of her headaches and not the active cause of them.

At this point the reader might feel that these two sides of the personality are beginning to look very familiar. They are, in fact, merely different aspects of the same old "two clowns" we have already discussed. The pincher, the active doer side of the retroflection, is very intimately associated with the Topdog/Parent; and the pinched, the passive done-to side, is closely connected with the Underdog/Child. (Note, in this connection, Perl's statement, "So the topdog and underdog strive for control. Like every parent and child, they strive with each other for control. The person is fragmented into controller and controlled.") This intimate connection is borne out by several other factors.

Recall that in retroflection, an impulse is interrupted and diverted from its original object back onto the self. But why, let us ask, is the impulse diverted in the first place? There are, of course, numerous auxillary "causes" retroflection, but the very root of the difficulty lies in the introjected Parent (Perls, 1951, pp. 146, 203; Perls, 1969a, p. 223). It is the Parent/Topdog with its "wall of conscience," its shoulds and shouldnots, that actively retroflects any of the impulses deemed unworthy. It's almost as if the Parent were a mirror off which the impulse is reflected back onto the person himself. But the side of the person toward which the impulse is directed will necessarily feel that it *lacks* that impulse, that it is its victim, a helpless and innocent bystander. And this is, of course, the Child/Underdog. Overall, it looks very much as if the original impulse is retroflected off the Parent onto the Child.

Thus, we have our second preliminary synthesizing rule: *When the Parent is hooked, we look for retroflections.*

Retroflections come in all flavors. A few of the more common are narcissism (retroflected affection), depression (anger), hypochondria (inspection), self-pity (pity), masochism (cruelty), compulsiveness (drive). As we mentioned, once a retroflection has occurred, and the personality is split into the active pincher and the passive pinched, the individual can—and usually does—associate himself more closely with one of the two sides. Sometimes, for the same retroflected impulse, the emotional tone of one pole is dramatically different from that of the other. For example, if a person retroflects his hostility and associates with the doer side, he feels active self-hate; but if he associates with the done-to side, he feels passive depression. So the retroflections I've just listed will, of course, change their tone a bit depending upon which pole the person associates with. In general, the more the impulse is inhibited, the more completely the person will associate with the passive, done-to side of the retroflection; that is, the more he will feel a NOT OK Child being beaten by his Parent.

Regardless of which pole a person associates herself with, to undo retroflections she has generally to begin by contacting and taking back the active pole. She has to assume responsibility for the impulses contained in the active pole by getting the feel of precisely *how* she turns that impulse back on herself. For once she feels exactly how she retroflects, then—for the first time—she is in a position to reverse the retroflection and redirect her energies back into the environment.

Again, I believe that just this reversal of retroflections actually occurs in Transactional Analysis as a person learns to shift from the mode of the Parent to that of the Adult. When the individual can say with certainty and feeling, "My Parent is hooked and is riding my Child," then he can view his predicament objectively and rationally—he has engaged his Adult. By that very action he quits beating and criticizing himself and, significantly, he thereby frees that energy for a critical appraisal of the environment and his transactions with it.

However, as with the Child, there are stubborn cases in which the Parent just won't shut off. And it is expressly here that Gestalt can add its complementary insights, offering the Transactional Analyst an alternative to the Freudian "why?" The individual can't shut off the Parent because he hasn't developed an adequate feel of *how* he himself hooks his Parent, of how he himself retroflects. For while the nucleus of the Parent/Topdog was undoubtedly formed in early years, *its strength is supplied by nothing other than the energies of present-day retroflections.* Where the Transactional Analysis spots and deals with the Parent, Gestalt tackles the retroflections—two sides of the same therapeutic process.* And as the Individual comes to understand just that fact, he learns the corollary to the second basic synthesizing rule: to stay in the Adult is to refuse to retroflect.

Perhaps this is the point to mention a most crucial event that occurs in the process of retroflection. Once an impulse is retroflected, it generally changes its form to *con-form* to its new object, the self. An impulse to hit an object or person is carried out with a striking motion in the arm, shoulder, and fist. Should that impulse be retroflected, however, the person doesn't so much smash himself in the face as he locks and immobilizes those muscles of the arm, shoulder and fist. He doesn't keep striking himself, he freezes himself. Nevertheless, this is still a type of attack on himself, but the impulse has merely con-formed to its new object: his body. The result is stalemate, spasm—vast amounts of energy committed to dynamic inaction. In such fashion, constructive biological aggression, when retroflected, con-forms into destructive self-aggression; or lively curiosity con-forms into morbid introspection. It is only when the retroflection is reversed that the con-formed impulse is released, given true expression, and thus *trans-formed* back into its original and less destructive dimensions. This trans-formation is important for the individual to understand, or he will likely refuse to turn outward the impulses that seem so obviously destructive. If he understands, however, that their reversal trans-forms them, he will be able to experiment with staying in the Adult where before he refused to do so.

One other point here: a retroflected impulse does not really find an adequate object in the self—that is to say, a con-formed impulse is never completely satisfied. On the theory that something is better than nothing, the Parent will nevertheless keep directing blows at the Child—but this is a poor substitute (cf. Freudian "substitute gratifications"). As such, the con-formed impulse frequently intensifies its strength in an effort to find true and satisfactory expression ("return of the repressed"). A retroflector thus tends to increase his retroflecting activity. And all of these retroflections, it should be further noted, are not bound up with just emotional impulses; on the contrary, personal traits, feelings, ideas, characteristics, convictions—all can be and usually are interwoven with retroflected impulses and emotions.

Thus, for example, a person who retroflects hostility will feel a mo-

---

*Both T.A. and G.T. stress the dissolving, or rather assimilating, of introjections, and this is not to be overlooked in therapy. Because of the agreement of the two schools on this point, I am not emphasizing it here.

ment of self-reproach and self-hate. If this activity becomes chronic, however, the person will start to invent reasons for her self-hatred in order to make sense of her behavior. She will come to feel her self-hatred "justified" because she's too poor, or too fat, or too old, or too sick, or too dumb—any intelligible reason will do. The active side hates the passive side—the Parent beats the Child—"because" it's such-and-such. On the other hand, there are some cases in which the traits or ideas may be said to preceed the retroflection. A person who is, for instance, rather heavyset, may indeed retroflect hostility back on himself, due to unkind cultural introjects, and hate with an unbridled passion his body. Which actually precedes which is not so much the point—rather, I wish only to emphasize that ideas, traits, characteristics, and concepts are frequently bound up with retroflected emotions and con-formed impulses.

We will presently return to the undoing of retroflections, but first let us investigate the precise relation of retroflection to projection. This investigation is necessary for the final form of our synthesis of Transactional Analysis and Gestalt Therapy. For by grasping the actual relation between the mechanism of retroflection and the mechanism of projection—a relation that I have never seen stated in any of the literature—we will also be able to expand and extend upon the first two preliminary synthesizing rules. In this expansion, we will be able to subdivide these two basic rules, resulting in a more comprehensive synthesis.

We have seen that all projections can be reduced to retroflections, and that this is exactly how Gestalt Therapy proceeds. But theoretically, how is this possible? What is the connection? I would like to suggest that the connecting link between retroflection and projection is just this: all projections are actually projected retroflections. Projection is simply the next step after retroflection on a continuum of alienation, and for this very reason can and should be reduced back to retroflection during therapy.

We can approach this as follows. Recall that retroflection results in the splitting of the personality into an active pincher-and-doer (associated with the Parent), and a passive pinched-and-done-to (associated with the Child), with the individual usually associating himself more closely with one or the other side. Now not only can the person associate more-or-less with one side of the retroflection, he *can totally repress, and thus project, the other side,* so that the projected side now appears to belong not to him but to the environment. Further, the projected pole of the retroflection *bears the same functional relation to the remaining pole as it did in the original retroflection*—a fact that allows us to easily unravel the projection.

For example, the sexual impulse. A person who, through frustration, shame or conscience chronically retroflects his sexual desires will take himself as the object of his sexual activities. His only direct sexual outlet will be masturbation. Now while it is true that he may reach intense orgasms this way—principally because he's minding his own business—glowing satisfaction eludes him, because he's now operating on a con-formed impulse. If he associates with the active pole of the retroflection, he is likely to have fantasies of seducing or even raping someone; if he associates more with the passive side, he might have fantasies of being seduced or raped. But if he projects the active-doer side, he will feel himself to totally lack any sexual impulses, but everybody out there has strange designs on him! He is likely to be prudish or perhaps frigid, and should sex happen to come his way he can at best dutifully submit. But should he project the passive done-to side of himself, he becomes the wolf—he actively seeks to regain the alienated aspects of himself by uniting sexually with those onto whom he projects them. Of course, that never really provides the sought-after satisfaction, because the wolf (who thinks he's "oversexed") is acting on a con-formed impulse instead of the trans-formed one. For this reason his sexual affairs are unstable and unsatisfactory, each one being rather transitory as he chases forever onward after his own shadow, making love to himself with the help of any willing human mirror.

Thus we see that in retroflection, a person can associate with one or the other side of that retroflection; and further, this process, carried to extremes, results in the actual projection of the dissociated pole. To use the terms of Transactional Analysis, in retroflection we merely associate with the Parent or Child; in projection we cast out the Parent or Child, and perceive it in the environment. *But at all times the two poles maintain the same functional relation and direction to one another.*

Thus, to give another example of this entire process, with emphasis on the maintenance of the same functional relation of the poles, let's take the impulse of a person to *reject,* on valid grounds, those things or people in the environment rightly deserving of some criticism. If the impulse is retroflected, and the person associates more with the active Parent side of the retroflection, she will constantly criticize herself: a self-criticism complex. If she associates more with the passive done-to side, she will begin to develop a creeping inferiority complex, as her Child buckles under the tortuous criticisms of the Parent. Now if she projects the Parent, she is left only with her Child, and she sees her Parent instead everywhere in the environment, especially in policemen, teachers, or other authority figures. The world is constantly out to get her—and she develops a persecution complex. If, however, she projects the Child, she is left identified with only the Parent, continually criticizing not so much the Child traits of others as her own projected Child traits she imagines she sees in others. This can result in anything from annoyance to prejudice.

We can therefore establish the following continuum of alienation: expression to suppression to retroflection to projection. And in therapy, we simply reverse the order, starting with projection.

Fritz Perls (1969a, p. 237) used to say that projection was the mechanism whereby an individual converts organismic activity into passivity, "I act on this" into "This acts on me," "I happen to things" into "Things happen to me." While this is certainly true, it applies mainly to only one of the two major classes of projection, namely, the projected Topdog/Parent. When this occurs, a person's active approach to the environment is indeed converted into a re-active response to the environment. But an individual can also project the passive side of a retroflection, and then he is apt to respond to these projected facets in a most violently active manner, shadow-boxing his way through the valleys of his own reflections.

To start with the former, recall the genesis of this class of projections: an impulse spontaneously arises (e.g., I desire to pinch someone); this impulse is interrupted and retroflected (I pinch myself); the active pole of this retroflection is projected (Others are pinching me). Now when a person forgets *how* he is pinching himself, this is retroflection—he is aware, however vaguely, that *he* is pinching himself, but he doesn't quite know how he's doing it and thus he can't stop. But when the individual then forgets not only *how* the retroflection is accomplished but also that it is *he* who is doing it, this is projection—he isn't pinching himself, the world is! Conversely, when he sees that *he,* not someone else, is pinching himself, he has taken back the projection; when he further sees *how* he is pinching himself, he has mastered the retroflection. He is finally free to pinch others—but now with a trans-formed impulse, not a harsh con-formed one.

Projections might show up in dreams, in other people, in things or events. In all cases, they are simply the hooks upon which the projections are hung. These things then seem to pinch him—people are hurting him, laughing at him, staring at him, rejecting him, chasing him, hating him

. . . In Gestalt Therapy, the person will likely be asked to initiate a dialogue, in fantasy, between himself and the person who seems to be pinching him. By playing both parts and identifying completely with the "pinching person," the individual comes to realize that it is *he* who is really doing the pinching to himself, In effect, the individual has taken back the projected Parent/Topdog; his projections have been reduced to the prior retroflections.

The person understands that he is hurting himself, and now—to undo this retroflection—he must regain the feel of *how* he is accomplishing this feat. So he plays the role of the pincher, the Topdog/Parent. In fact, he plays it up—he is asked to increase the symptom, to exaggerate it, to harden his pinching. No longer is he trying to fight the symptom, he is trying to increase it! "As long as you fight a symptom, it will become worse. If you take responsibility for what you are doing to yourself, how you produce your symptoms, how you produce your illness, how you produce your existence—the very moment you get in touch with yourself—growth begins, integration begins" (Perls, 1969b, p. 178).

As long as the person is fighting the symptom, he is tacitly assuming that it is not he who is producing it—and that means nothing other than that he is out of touch with the side of himself that *is* doing the pinching. To try to silence the symptom is only to try to silence responsibility for it, and that is precisely what started the problem in the first place. Besides, the symptom contains the con-formed impulse, and thus to fight the symptom is to further alienate the impulse which seeks expression. Instead, the person is asked to get into the symptom, exaggerate it, increase it—for he is, by that very activity, assuming responsibility for it. He is learning *how* he actually produces his symptoms by consciously *trying* to produce them.

As the person is thus playing the pincher, the Topdog/Parent, exaggerating his symptoms, getting the feel of himself as a retroflector, a squeezer, a pincher—he is asked to "make the rounds" *while playing the Topdog*. That is, while playing the dictatorial and imperious Super Mouse, he addresses the members of the group (or some person in fantasy), doing unto them what he has heretofore been doing so unmercifully unto himself. But a strange thing has now happened—by this very act he has reversed the retroflection, and is aiming his impulses toward the original object: the environment. And although the impulse thus directed outward might at first be rather harsh—because it is the conformed impulse he's used to aiming at himself—it softens quickly as it is trans-formed back into its original dimensions.

With this additional understanding of retroflection and projection, we are in a position to draw up our final synthesizing conclusions. Our study of Gestalt Therapy showed us that there are two major classes of retroflection (associated with the active pole and the passive pole), and two major classes of projections (projection of active pole and of passive pole), giving in all a total of *four basic patterns of avoidance.* But recall that Transactional Analysis also acknowledges four major patterns of refusing to stay in the Adult (Parent aimed inwardly, Parent aimed outwardly, Child aimed inwardly, Child aimed outwardly). In fact, these are both the same four patterns of irresponsibility, and Transactional Analysis and Gestalt Therapy embody complementary therapeutic approaches to just these four patterns. Understanding this, we can now set out all four major synthesizing rules:*

1. When the Child is hooked and aimed outwardly, we look for a projection; specifically, we look for the projection of the active pole of the retroflection, the Parent/Topdog.
2. When the Parent is hooked and aimed inwardly, we look for a retroflection; specifically, the person is associated more or less with the active pole of the retroflection.
3. When the Parent is hooked and aimed outwardly, we look for a projection; specifically, we look for the projection of the passive pole of the retroflection, the Child/Underdog.
4. When the Child is hooked and aimed inwardly, we look for a retroflection; specifically, the person is associated more or less with the passive pole of the retroflection.

With regard to each of these four modes, to "stay in the Adult" is to assume responsibility for that mode of avoidance and thus to refuse to operate in it unconsciously. In this sense, therapy is simply a day-to-day strengthening of that responsibility.

From a practical standpoint, a person beginning therapy (either self, dyad, or group) can grasp the fundamentals of Parent-Adult-Child within the hour: that she has Parent and Child tapes, as well as the ability to function as the Adult; that in times of stress and impasse she

*There are certainly numerous variations on these four basic patterns; e.g., the Child is not always associated with the passive pole. But these do seem to me to be the four most basic and most prevalent patterns—most others can be reduced to one of these four.

chooses to turn off the Adult and reactivate the Parent or Child tapes. She can learn to recognize and thoroughly differentiate the Parent, Child, and Adult. This understanding alone, when matured, is often quite helpful, for to the extent she can stay in the Adult, retroflections and projections—as we explained—*tend* to fall away of themselves. At any rate, she can then proceed to develop the understanding that she herself is turning on the tapes of the Parent or Child. To the extent this understanding crystallizes, her projections are reduced to retroflections. Consequently, she can then actively begin to explore just *how* it is that she turns on the tapes—and thus, she is then free to turn them off, releasing and re-directing the previously retroflected energies. This basic procedure is supported by a comprehensive understanding of the four basic rules suggested above; and, should the therapist or individual wish, can be supplemented by script or game analysis.

The reason I have not mentioned game analysis in this synthesis is that I fully agree with Harris (1969) that successful game analysis usually rests upon an accurate structural analysis. Thus, game analysis—in psychotherapy at least—is often secondary to structural and transactional analysis, and in our synthesis it is secondary to a grasp of the four synthetic patterns outlined above. It is in this deeper level of individual psychology that we have sought a fundamental synthesis, and thus, should game analysis be deemed necessary, it can then be carried out as an extension of the four basic patterns of avoidance. We need only note that in duplex transactional games, the psychological level of the game rests upon one (or more) of these four basic patterns.

Thus, to give only one example, we can look at that most famous of games, "If It Weren't For You," or IWFY for short. In my opinion, the person who is "it" in IWFY is psychologically operating from pattern number one. That is, the person is a self-frustrator but, projecting the active pole of that retroflection, feels that not *he* but the world is holding him back. He knows that somebody is holding him back, but since it obviously isn't him, it must be somebody else. And he needs a volunteer. He will even, if necessary, actively seek out a "hook" for the projection lest he be faced with his own self-frustrating activities. The Child is in control, looking externally for its own frustrating Parent.

In the most notorious variation of IWFY, namely Marital Style, enter the spouse: and there, out in the environment, in the form of the dearly beloved, the individual beholds nothing other than his own alienated shadow, his own frustrator tendencies. "The *nerve* of that fink, holding *me* back from such-and-such!" The individual, of course, feels—

superficially at least—that such-and-such is really what he wants to do above all else, and that he would do just that with a passion, "if it weren't for you." If the spouse, the intended hook of the projection, swallows it line and sinker, the game is under way. The spouse will probably respond from pattern number three, "Don't you dare try such-and-such, you can't handle it!" Or, the spouse might act from pattern number four, "You're right, I am a fink." At any rate, the point I wish to emphasize is that in all transactions, if a person reacts to, for example, another person coming on as Child, he is really reacting to his own *projected* Child, or facets of that Child. This is often overlooked by Transactional Analysts because the projection might be a perfect fit and thus escape detection. Nevertheless, in all cases a person can have insight into another's motivations only by analogy with *his own* feelings.

Now the spouse might instead refuse the projection. The spouse might respond from the position of the Adult with "Go ahead, great idea!" This instantly places the individual in a quandary, for he still knows *somebody* is holding him back, but since it's not the spouse, who could it be? The person is left, we might say, with his projection dangling. He could, at this point, begin to reown his projection by converting it to its prior retroflection, translating "If It Weren't For You" into "If It Weren't For Me." More likely he will try to maintain the projection by switching to another game, such as "Why Don't You—Yes But," and ending up with, "Ain't It Awful." The projection of the active pole of the retroflection is simply transferred to new hooks until it gets a sucker to bite. The social payoff of the game is the "catch and kill"; the psychological payoff is the maintenance of a mechanism of avoidance.

With all of this, it is worthwhile to keep in mind Harris' conclusion:

> It is my firm belief from long observation of this phenomenon that game analysis must always be secondary to Structural and Transactional Analysis. Knowing what game you are playing does not, *ipso facto,* make it possible for you to change. (Harris, 1969, pp. 150–51)

What does make change possible is an understanding and implementation of Transactional Analysis, or Gestalt Therapy, or—in my opinion—a working synthesis of both. And that is exactly what I have tried to present in this paper—a pragmatic synthesis of the best elements of Transactional Analysis and Gestalt Therapy that provides a simple but powerful therapeutic system.

References

Berne, E. *Transactional Analysis in Psychotherapy.* New York: Grove Press, 1961

———. *Games People Play.* New York: Grove Press, 1964

———. *What Do You Say after You Say Hello?* New York: Grove Press, 1972

Blum, G. *Psychoanalytic Theories of Personality.* New York: McGraw-Hill, 1953

Fagan J., & Shepherd, I. L. (eds.). *Gestalt Therapy Now.* New York: Harper & Row, 1970

Fenichel, O. *Psychoanalytic Theory of Neuroses.* New York: Norton, 1972

Harris, T. A. *I'm OK—You're OK.* New York: Avon, 1969

Perls, F. S. *Ego, Hunger, and Aggression.* New York: Vintage, 1969a

———. *Gestalt Therapy Verbatim.* Lafayette: Real People Press, 1969b

Perls, F. S.; Heferline, R.; & Goodman, P. *Gestalt Therapy.* New York: Dell, 1951

Polster, E., & Polster, M. *Gestalt Therapy Integrated.* New York: Vintage, 1974

Pursglove, P. (ed.). *Recognitions in Gestalt Therapy.* New York: Harper & Row, 1968

Wilber, K. *Psychologia Perennis:* The Spectrum of Consciousness. *Journal of Transpersonal Psychology* 7, 2 (1975): 105–33

WHAT IS TRANSPERSONAL PSYCHOLOGY?

ABRAHAM MASLOW—who is generally regarded as the modern founder of transpersonal psychology—pointed out that there are now "Four Forces" in the field of psychology: (1) behaviorism, or objective-empirical (and therefore often physicalistic) approaches; (2) psychoanalysis, or psychodynamic and psychosexual approaches; (3) humanistic, or existential and mental-intentional approaches; and (4) transpersonal, or spiritual and transcendental approaches. In a sense, the four major forces of psychology deal, respectively, with the first four of the seven chakras—the physical-vital, the emotional-sexual, the mental-intentional, and the beginning-spiritual. Each of the "four psychologies," then, has something very important, very necessary, very significant—and very limited—to tell us, and thus each should be approached, in my opinion, with a mind both open-appreciative and critical-evaluative.

In a sense, however, transpersonal psychologists have always attempted to do just that. In other words, it is not quite accurate to say that transpersonal psychology is interested solely or even predominantly in the fourth chakra. Transpersonal psychology is *theoretically* interested in *all* stages of life or levels of consciousness, one through seven. It accepts the valid aspects of the first three stage-schools of psychology, and it then attempts to bridge or unite them, theoretically, with the three higher stage-schools of development (e.g., yogis, saints, and sages).

Now I emphasized the word "theoretically" for an important reason: Transpersonal psychology is *not* a praxis, not a way of life or a complete psychospiritual discipline—it is not, that is, a genuinely transformative path leading individuals to the Radiant Ground and Goal of all development. But to criticize transpersonal psychology on that score alone would be to miss the point entirely. No genuine transpersonal psychologist I know considers himself or herself a guru, master, or adept—and those that do have always ended up looking a bit silly. No, most transpersonal psychologists (I would say around 70 percent) themselves are practitioners of a particular path—yogic, saintly, sagely—and are fully cognizant of the difference between level 3/4 *theoria* and level 5/6/7 *praxis.*

Rather, the aims of transpersonal psychology are more modest, but not, therefore, less important. I would generally state them as follows: (1) To render spirituality theoretically acceptable to the "other" or "lower" schools of psychology. By presenting mental (chakra 3) models that persuasively and comprehensively include the higher or spiritual stages of adaptation, transpersonal psychology forces schools such as psychoanalysis to reconsider their reductionistic dismissal of transcendental possibilities. (2) When it comes to "psychotherapy," transpersonal psychologists act much like "General Practitioners" (GPs) in medicine. Medical GPs know enough about organic brain disorders, for example, to recognize the condition when they see it and recommend a competent brain surgeon. Just so with "spiritual GPs"—they might treat lower-level disorders themselves (using standard psychotherapeutic procedures for which they were trained), but when it comes to upper-level disorders (chakras 5/6/7), they recommend competent masters. Genuine transpersonal psychologists never attempt "brain surgery" themselves. Rather, they recommend that the client see a competent spiritual Adept—perhaps Buddhist, perhaps Christian, perhaps Hindu, perhaps Jewish, and so on, each therapist having his or her own favorite teachers.

Transpersonal psychology, then, is not a total psychospiritual or completely transformative path (despite the claims made by some of its advocates); it is not a way of ultimate liberation or radical transcendence. Nor, on the other hand, is it a reductionistic, positivistic, spirit-denying psychology. Rather, it is a theoretical approach that, standing precisely between the upper and the lower hemispheres of existence, is attempting to get each to talk to, not at, the other.

That, I think, is the genuine service that transpersonal psychologists are performing, quite apart from the individual work they are doing on their own chosen spiritual paths. The genuine transpersonalists (and there are many) have no illusions about what they, *as* transpersonal psychologists, are doing—which is, we might say, to make room in the *minds* or the *psyches* of men and women for an intellectual acceptance of God—at which point, as always, the work of the genuine Adepts and Masters can more easily begin. Transpersonal psychologists are, in plain language, apologists for the soul, gnostic intermediaries whose function is made necessary by the fact that, incredibly enough, modern psychology has forgotten its own soul, its own *psyche*(!), which has always been held to be the intersection of the Temporal and the Eternal—that still point in the Heart where the Divine resurrects the Mortal and tacitly announces a new Destiny in Consciousness. They sit silent at the crossroads and point; no more, no less.

TWO HUMANISTIC PSYCHOLOGIES?

A Response

ABSTRACT: *In response to certain questions raised by John Rowan (1989), Wilber suggests that there are indeed two humanistic psychologies, one of which is open to the spiritual, transcendental, or transpersonal dimensions in men and women, and one of which is not. This response includes a defense of transpersonal psychology against certain charges (notably by Rollo May) that it is, in effect, a product of unrealistic or wish-fulfillment thought, that it is out of touch with the evil side of men and women, and that "transpersonal experiences" themselves are at best imaginary. The article concludes with a defense of mysticism in general, pointing out that its claims are based on experiential evidence and thus are no more or less verifiable than any other experiential knowledge claims, including those of empirical science.*

BECAUSE JOHN ROWAN'S (1989) questions touch on Rollo May's criticism of transpersonal psychology, I'll take this opportunity to answer my old friend Rollo May at length. Since this will be an open letter, I'll restate John Rowan's questions.

First of all, Rowan states that humanistic psychology has traditionally been known as the psychology that postulates "one great force of growth that pushes forward all the time, and leads us, unless we resist, into self-actualization. This was the view of the two great classics, Maslow and Rogers, and subscribed to in various ways by Perls, Moreno, Assagioli, Lowen. . . ." And he then quotes Maddi's *Personality Theories:* "They [humanistic psychologists] assume only one basic force in man. Therefore, life is not considered to be a compromise, but rather the process of unfolding of the one force. I have called the position exemplified by these theories the fulfillment model. . . . If the force is the tendency to express to an ever greater degree the capabilities, potentialities, or talents based on one's genetic constitution, then we are confronted with the actualization version. . . ."

Rowan then points out that the "one great force" theories have recently come under fire, for different reasons, by *humanistic* theorists such as Alvin Mahrer (1978), Rollo May (1982), Geller (1982, 1984), and Friedman (1982). Rowan wonders if the theory of self-actualization is necessary or even useful for humanistic psychology.

The concept of self-actualization, of course, is a very old one; it was given perhaps its best explanation by Aristotle. I think, however, that the idea of self-actualization as "the one and only force" is a misleading abstraction. I do happen to believe that there is an overall or overarching spiritual telos or eros, a self-evolution through self-transcendence, *but* this "single force" only manifests itself *as* the various levels of development, so in concrete terms there are as many "forces" in humans as there are levels or structures of development and evolution. Thus, for example, spiritual telos manifests itself on the material plane as hunger, on the biological plane as sex, on the mental plane as desire for communicative exchange, and so forth. So spiritual telos, although "one" in an abstract sense, is plural in any concrete or actual sense, and the drive to transcendence, growth, development, or evolution is always expressed by and as the emergence of the next higher concrete drive. This leaves plenty of room for conflict and compromise between the various expressions, something the "pure" self-actualization models persistently have difficulty explaining.

Thus speaking of "one basic drive in man" is a misleading and lopsided way of describing the growth process, and it leads to problems that are mostly generated by the inadequate formulation itself. Moreover, since the manifest world is usually composed of oppositions or dualities, I believe there is another overall general drive or "force" existing in the opposite direction, namely, thanatos (or what in the East is known as involution; we might call it regression). Like its opposite, thanatos always expresses itself as a concrete drive (whether hunger, sex, power, etc.); it simply involves the choice of a lower-level need to the exclusion of a higher. This drive, I believe, is implicated in all pathology (as fixation, regression, arrest), although again, each specific case involves its own particular and concrete drives and pathological choices.

I believe it is the somewhat glib and "airy fairy" references, on the part of many humanistic writers (including, on occasion, Maslow and Rogers), to "one basic force in man" that has so annoyed the likes of Mahrer and May. As far as it goes, I agree with them (although for very different reasons), but I'll return to this in a moment.

John Rowan also raises the question, are our potentials actually "drives" or are they, as Mahrer maintains, nothing but "choices"? Mahrer says "there is no great force, there is no spiritual path, there is nothing to lead us forward or in any direction. There is only choice." I believe this is largely a semantic problem: if you say there are nothing but choices, then I am allowed to say that a person is therefore driven to choose, and thus reintroduce some form of drive theory.

Of course, one can always say that as long as something is strictly potential, it can exert no force or drive, because the definition of "potential" is "not present or active." But the whole point about human potentials is that they drive to become actual or manifest, and those potentials, to the extent that they begin to manifest themselves, are definitely experienced as drives, as emergent forces or intentions. We can say, for example, that a newborn baby has the potential for language, but I don't think the newborn therefore decides it's time to learn language. The potential for language is not a choice. Rather, as Chomsky points out, language simply arrives, it shows up whether wanted or not, and it introduces a host of new drives and forces in the psyche. These are experienced as real drives! Language is very pushy.

I believe the evidence clearly supports the thesis that our higher structural potentials exist in precisely the same way as language, sex, hunger, or any of the other structural drives of men and women. The "only choices" view, on the other hand, is inadvertently reverting to a behavioristic learning model, a tabula rasa theory of mind, which today carries not much weight. More regrettably, it overlooks the large amount of research on the cross-cultural existence of the stages of spiritual development. These stages are not choices, they are structures (the choice is whether to engage them or not).

In the "one force" debate, then, I side with May/Mahrer. In the "potentials as drives," I side with Maslow/Rogers.

The final issue revolves around—well, it can be put many ways: the problem of spiritual transcendence, the problem of evil, the problem of just how far human potentials go (or, where does human stop and divine begin?). Or again, it is the problem of the relation between humanistic and transpersonal psychology. Is transcendence of conventional selfhood possible, or are such notions basically defense mechanisms designed to shield us from our mortality and finititude? If spiritual transcendence is possible, then what happens to evil? This all touches, of course, on Rollo May's recent attack on transpersonal psychology (1986).

Now it is often thought that there are only two major sides to these issues: the existential-humanistic on the one hand, and the transcendental-transpersonal on the other. The distinction "humanistic/transpersonal" is obviously a very important one, but I will try to show that there are two other distinctions that in fact have been just as important, and sometimes more important, in the recent debates between, for example, Rogers (1982a, 1982b) and May (1982), or May and the transpersonalists (1986). The first distinction is based on one's stance toward evil (the realists vs. the idealists). The second is based on one's stance toward spirit or divinity (atheistic, theistic, or mystical). Along with the humanistic/transpersonal, that gives us three major distinctions, each of which cuts at right angles to the others, generating a grid of different overall theoretical stances. I'll elaborate on these three distinctions and then show how they can help clarify many of the debates now occurring.

The two basic stances toward evil depend upon how much weight one gives to evil in the lives and motivations of men and women. The first camp—which I will call the "realist"—tends to assign evil a rather high priority; this camp believes that evil is a very real force in the world, that men and women are constantly underrating the extent and brutality of evil, and that consequently men and women end up caught in evil by their very denial of its pervasiveness. (Notice that when and if realists become bitter and jaded, they tend to slide into cynicism, and a kind of cruel pessimism—call them the "cynics.")

The second camp—which I will call "idealist"—tends to downplay the importance of evil; this camp believes that although evil may occasionally play an important role in human affairs, it is subordinate to an overall "good," that darkness or evil is not an actual ontological presence but merely the absence of light, an absence that is ended with higher growth. (Notice that when this camp looses its critical faculty, it tends to degenerate into a total and complete flakiness, evidenced in a type of mindless giddiness and a sweetness-and-light view of the world—colloquially referred to as "goofs" or "flakes.")

The second distinction—atheistic/theistic/mystical—concerns the issue of the human soul and its relation to divine spirit (assuming such exists). The three stances are

a. There is no divine or transcendental spirit, so there is no problem ("atheistic").
b. The human soul and the divine spirit exist and may commune with each other, but they are ultimately separate ontological entities ("theistic").
c. At the summit of human growth there exists a supreme identity of soul and spirit, an identity that can be directly intuited or apprehended under certain circumstances ("mystical").

We now come to the last major distinction, that between "humanistic" and "transpersonal." For the time being, I will simply define "humanistic" as "primarily interested in the human being, soul, or psyche" and transpersonal as "primarily interested in the human soul and divine spirit (psyche and pneuma)." (I will return to the issue of whether or not "transpersonal" is a real category.)

So we have three different overall scales: (1) realist/idealist (with their degenerate counterparts, cynic/flake), (2) atheistic/theistic/mystical, and (3) humanistic/transpersonal. Subtracting self-contradictions and redundancies (e.g., there is no "atheistic transpersonal") gives us about a dozen major different theoretical camps or subcamps. Rollo May, for example, is a theistic realist humanist, Perls was an atheistic idealist humanist, Maslow was a mystical idealist transpersonalist, Sartre was an atheistic realist humanist, and so forth.

Using these three general distinctions, instead of just one, makes it easier to understand the conflicts that have arisen not only between humanists and transpersonalists, but within each discipline as well. Let me give a few examples of these conflicts, then I'll give my own opinions on each.

The debate between Rollo May and Carl Rogers is a classic case of realist humanist versus idealist humanist. May sees evil as "nascent in all of us, though covered over with a veneer of civilization," whereas Roger sees evil as primarily the result of aborted or warped growth. A similar conflict exists within transpersonal schools between the realist transpersonalists and the idealist transpersonalists. The former maintain that in the *manifest* world evil is a real and ineradicable force (relative evil is transcended in the absolute, but so is relative good); the latter maintain that evil is only the result of not realizing the absolute, and that all of manifestation can theoretically be good. It is the latter or idealist stance that can degenerate into the flake or everything-is-love-and-light school, which particularly irritates realists of all types.

Within the realist humanist camp there is a historically important and long-standing debate between the atheists and the theists. The atheistic realist humanists—Feuerbach and Sartre being the best known—tend to view theistic humanists, even realistic theistic humanists (which Rollo May is), as being ultimately antihumanistic and antiperson. Feuerbach, for example, views all reference to spirit or deity as nothing but a projection of as-yet-unrealized human potentials; theism is the last refuge of an oppressed humanity. For this reason, the atheistic realist humanists are often Marxists.

Realist humanists of almost all types frequently refer to themselves as "existentialists" (in deliberate contrast to transcendentalists and essentialists). Accordingly there are both theistic existentialists (May, Tillich, Marcel) and atheistic existentialists (Sartre). This category explains the existence of what otherwise might appear a contradiction: existentialist Marxism, pioneered by Sartre.

Within the transpersonal schools, both East and West, there is a long-standing debate between the theists and the mystics. Theistic transpersonalists—Saint John of the Cross, Suso, Ramanuja, and so forth—believe that human soul and divine spirit can share a "spiritual marriage" or "divine communion," but there is no point at which they are one and identical. The mystical transpersonalists—Meister Eckhart, Shankara, Chih I, and so forth—believe that there is a point in development where, without in any way obliterating the boundary between human soul and divine spirit, the boundary can be transcended and a "supreme identity" revealed, where "each is both" while paradoxically remaining perfectly themselves.

At this point I should explicitly identify my own position as realist mystical transpersonal. That is, I believe evil is inherent in the manifest world and can be lessened but not eradicated; that the belief that relative evil can be eradicated is itself a prime cause of evil; that the absolute is nondual, or beyond *both* good and evil (not just evil); that the human soul and divine spirit share a common ground (or godhead) without obliterating their respective differences; and that that godhead can be directly intuited under certain circumstances.

Let me now comment specifically on Rollo May's recent attacks on humanism of a Rogerian sort and transpersonalism of any sort, for there are actually two *other,* hidden debates going on here. The first is realist versus idealist. May, being a realist, doesn't like idealist theories of any sort—humanist or transpersonal being irrelevant. A realist myself, I happen to agree with those aspects of May's critiques. I think I can understand his irritation at the idealist schools, because in fact many of them, humanistic and transpersonal both, during the 1970s degenerated into goofs and flakes of one sort or another. Sometimes, though, May seems so irritated that he slides from realist to cynic, and some of his self-discussions sound like they are between not realist and idealist, but cynic and flake.

Where May begins to err, and err badly, is in his assumption that all transpersonalists are idealists. This turns out to be the first of several major obfuscations. The criticism he leveled at Rogers' idealism he now tries to level at the whole of transpersonalism, and of course it won't work, because many transpersonalists are staunch realists (in fact, the vast majority are, since the realist or nondualist tradition includes most of the perennial philosophers, East and West). They would concur entirely with May's statement: "[William James] agreed with Jung and Nietzsche that the concept of good can never exclude the concept of evil; in fact, they belong together." Incredibly, however, May fails to mention that James, Jung, and Nietzsche each believed—along with the perennial philosophers of virtually all cultures—that there existed a spiritual dimension that itself was "beyond good and evil." This "beyond" is one of the basic areas studied by transpersonalists. And precisely *because* the personal or manifest world is always marked by dualities such as good/evil, one of the meanings of "transpersonal" is "beyond dualism" (e.g., Sanskrit *advaita*). May, on the other hand, seems to acknowledge only dualistic thought, and so he denies the very existence of anything "beyond" his own categories.

Most surprising to me was what amounts to May's orthodox theism and his apparent denial, or at least misunderstanding, of mysticism. *The* classic and standard argument of the theologians against the mystics is that the mystics confuse soul and spirit, that they deny the boundary between the human and the divine (or, as May would have it, "confuse both psychology and religion"). When Christ was being stoned by his fellows, he asked, "Why do you stone me; is it for bad works?" The reply came: "No, it is for blasphemy, since you, being a man, make yourself out God." Mystics from that time on have been, in the West, crucified for this so-called blasphemy.

Christ's response to the charge of blasphemy is interesting. He said, "Does it not say in your own scriptures that you are all Sons of God? Why then stone me?" In other words, Christ's experience of the supreme identity of soul and spirit ("I and the Father are One") is something that is freely available to all, or, as Saint Paul would have it, "Let this consciousness be in you which was in Christ Jesus, that we all may be one. . . ." Greek theologians would work this out by saying that Christ was one person with two natures—he was both fully human and fully divine, without confusing either. What the orthodox theologians would not allow, however, was that anybody other than Christ could have that experience. In other words, Christ-consciousness is *not* available to anyone else. Every mystic, of course, starting with Christ, disagreed with exactly that point.

The same conclusion can as easily be reached using the Trikaya doctrine of Buddhism or the Brahman-Atman doctrine of Hinduism. The essential point is that soul and spirit share a common ground of being, and that ground can be directly prehended or intuited without in any way obliterating the boundary between them. When Buddha gained enlightenment it didn't mean he ceased to be human; it meant he also realized the aspect of his being that is divine (or Bodhi-minded), a realization that all of his followers have been invited to repeat.

It is admittedly difficult to find acceptable terms for defining states that partake of both finite and infinite, form and emptiness, time and eternity, soul and spirit. We could indeed use terms such as *mystical humanistic,* because what is being transcended is not, as May believes, humanness per se but conventional humanness (what the Christian mystics call "the natural man"). It has long been recognized, for example, that *mystical humanism* is a fairly good term for Taoism and Zen. However, when Maslow and Sutich founded the Fourth Force, the term *humanistic* already had a rather specific and definite meaning—it referred to what was being done by Rogers, May, Matson, Murray, Frankl, the early Maslow, and so forth. They needed a new term to refer to states of being that included but went beyond conventional humanism; for better or worse, the term chosen was *transpersonal.*

May's concern is that, among other things, "transpersonal psychology" is a contradiction in terms, like saying "transpsychological psychology." This is a legitimate but carping criticism. As Huston Smith points out in *Forgotten Truth,* what we really need is a term like *pneu-*

matology instead of *psychology* (to indicate the study of spirit or pneuma in men and women, and not just the study of soul or psyche in men and women). Since we're stuck with *psychology,* we prefix it with *transcendental* or *transpersonal.*

May seems to misunderstand the meaning of *transcendence* itself; as far as I can tell, he either confuses it with obliteration or negation, or relegates it to the imaginal. But as Hegel pointed out, to transcend or supersede is "at once to negate and to preserve." In other words, transcendence both goes beyond (or negates) and includes (or preserves) the given. *Transpersonal* in this sense means "that which goes beyond and includes the conventional personality." It does *not* mean "to obliterate or skip over the personality." "Grace," said Saint Thomas, "*perfects* nature, not obliterates it."

That is precisely why the word *transpersonal* has a paradoxical ring to it—"beyond but including the personal." Many of the terms traditionally used to refer to self-transcendence have a similar ring to them. What about Nietzsche's *Übermensch*—literally, the "Overman"? It is very similar to Emerson's "Overself" and Aurobindo's "Overmind." What about the Greek translation of the Christian conversion: *metanoia,* literally "beyond one's mind," or the Buddhist doctrine of *anatta,* "without separate self?" Over-, trans-, beyond-, beside-, without-, meta-, even para-: We just happened to choose *trans-*. Instead of man, mind, nous, self, psyche, or soul, we chose *person.* So what is this big controversy about?

Finally, I would like to address the issue of whether anything like transcendence is even possible, for although May at least says he "believes in the value of Transcendence," many of his existentialist cohorts do not (e.g., Irv Yalom). The mystics, of course, claim that transcendence is not a theoretical postulate but a direct experience (or even permanent adaptation), and indeed most critics acknowledge that the mystics base their claims on certain experiences they have had. But the critics then move to invalidate the cognitive status of these experiences using one of several standard ploys:

1. The mystical experience is not valid knowledge because it is ineffable and therefore incommunicable.
2. The mystical experience, which seems so certain to the mystic, could in fact simply be mistaken; the mystics might think they are becoming one with the ground of being, but that doesn't necessarily mean that's what's actually happening; no knowledge can be absolutely certain.

3. The mystical vision could in fact be schizophrenic.
4. At the very least, the mystical notion of living "in eternity" is a defense mechanism designed to shield one from the horrors of mortality and finititude.
5. The mystical experience is not real knowledge because it is not empirical.

To which it can be replied:

1. The mystical experience is indeed ineffable, or not capable of being entirely put into words; like any experience—a sunset, eating a piece of cake, listening to Bach's music—one has to have the actual experience to see what it's like. We don't conclude, however, that sunset, cake, and music therefore don't exist or aren't valid. Further, even though the mystical experience is largely ineffable, it *can* be communicated or transmitted, namely, by taking up spiritual practice under the guidance of a spiritual master or teacher (much as judo can be taught but not spoken; as Wittgenstein would have it, the mystical "can be shown but not said").

2. I would agree that mystical experiences are in principle no more certain than any other direct experiences, but far from pulling down the mystics' claims, that argument actually elevates their claims to a status equal to all other experiential knowledge, a status I would definitely accept. In other words, this argument against mystical knowledge actually applies to all forms of knowledge based on experiential evidence (including empirical sciences). I think I'm looking at the moon, but I could be mistaken; physicists think electrons exist, but they could be mistaken; critics think *Hamlet* was written by a historical person called Shakespeare, but they could be mistaken; and so on. How do we find out? We check it against more experience—which is also exactly what the mystics have historically done, checking and refining their experiences over the decades, centuries, and even millennia (a track record that makes modern science look like a johnny-come-lately). The point is that, far from tossing out the mystics' claims, this argument actually (and correctly) gives their claims exactly the same status as informed experts in any other field that relies on evidence to decide issues.

3. I don't think anybody doubts that a few mystics might also manifest some schizophrenic elements, and that some schizophrenics might also evidence mystical insights, but I don't know any authority in the

field who believes mystical experiences are basically and primarily schizophrenic hallucinations. I know a fair number of nonauthorities who think so, and it's hard to convince them otherwise in a short space, so let me just say that the spiritual and contemplative practices used by mystics (such as prayer or meditation) can be fairly strong, but they simply are not strong enough to take wholesale numbers of normal, healthy, adult men and women and turn them, in the space of a few years, into flurridly hallucinating schizophrenics. Zen Master Hakuin left behind him eighty-three fully transmitted students, who together revitalized and organized Japanese Zen. Eighty-three hallucinating schizophrenics couldn't organize a trip to the toilet, let alone Japanese Zen.

4. If "living in eternity" is merely believed in, as an idea or a hope, then it is frequently part of a person's "immortality project," a system of defenses designed magically to ward off death and promise an expansion or continuation of life (as I tried to explain in *Up from Eden* and *A Sociable God*). But the *experience* of timelessness is not an idea or a wish; it is a direct apprehension, and we can treat that direct experience in one of three ways: claim it is hallucinatory (see #3 above), claim it is mistaken (see #2 above), or accept it as it announces itself to be, a direct experience of timelessness (subject, of course, to further experiential refinement).

5. If by *empirical* you mean "experiential," then mysticism is definitely empirical and can be empirically validated. If by *empirical* you mean "amenable to verification by the senses or their extensions," then mysticism is not empirical—and neither are mathematics, logic, literature, most philosophy, psychoanalysis, and so forth—all of which, like mysticism, are largely transempirical.

In short, none of the five standard arguments against mysticism really stands up to sustained criticism or modern scholarship, from which it seems to follow that those who react to mysticism are doing so out of either conceptual misinformation or emotional prejudice. Personally, I think that although Rollo May professes to value transcendence, he simply has gotten so fed up with the (pseudo)idealists, goofs, and flakes that he has short-circuited and come out swinging blindly. This is perhaps understandable; I am periodically gripped with similar feelings.

So, to return to John Rowan's initial question, it appears that there are indeed two humanistic psychologies: One is at least open to the transpersonal or transcendental in men and women, the other is not. Maslow and Rogers (and, I'm sure, Mahrer) have definitely allowed for, or even embraced, the transpersonal. As Rowan himself suggests, Rogers and especially Maslow explored not only the centaur (or existential humanistic dimension) but also the subtle (or transpersonal and self-transcending) realms of human experience. This pioneering, broad-spectrum approach occasionally and understandably gave their theories a rambling or sprawling appearance. On the other hand, theorists such as May, Perls, and Maddi have confined their researches to the existential-humanistic realm. This focusing of attention on the centaur usually gives their theories a "tighter" or "purer" appearance, as Rowan notes, but I think that's fine.

In my own scheme of human development, growth moves through a dozen or so waves, from body to ego-mind to centaur to transcendental (see, for example, *Transformations of Consciousness*). Prior to the advent of humanistic psychology, most behavioral theories were either body-based (behaviorism) or ego-based (psychoanalysis). It seems to me that it took great courage for the early humanistic psychologists to go beyond ego-level psychologies (which accepted an intractable mind/body dualism and identified self with the rational, willful, linguistic mind) toward more genuinely centaur-based theories (wherein both mind and body are experiences of an integrated and often spontaneous organismic self, or "centaur").

I think it also took great courage for some of these same theorists to continue their research, pursuing it beyond centaur toward the transpersonal. I think history will record that the two great psychological revolutions of our time have been the move from ego to existential and from existential to transpersonal. I'm truly sorry my friend Rollo May couldn't join us for the second half of the ride, especially after helping so much with the first.

References

Bakan, D. (1982). "On Evil as a Collective Phenomenon." *Journal of Humanistic Psychology* 22(4).

Friedman, M. (1976). "Aiming at the Self: The Paradox of Encounter and the Human Potential Movement." *Journal of Humanistic Psychology* 16(2).

———. (1982). "Comments on the Rogers-May Discussion of Evil." *Journal of Humanistic Psychology* 22(4).

Geller, L. (1982). "The failure of Self-Actualization Theory: A Critique of Carl Rogers and Abraham Maslow." *Journal of Humanistic Psychology* 22(2).

———. (1984). "Another Look at Self-Actualization." *Journal of Humanistic Psychology* 24(2).

Maddi, S. (1968). *Personality Theories.* Homewood, Ill.: Dorsey.

Mahrer, A. (1978). *Experiencing: A Humanistic Theory of Psychology and Psychiatry.* New York: Brunner/Mazel.

May, R. (1982). "The Problem of Evil: An Open Letter to Carl Rogers." *Journal of Humanistic Psychology* 22(3).

———. (1986). "Transpersonal Psychology." *APA Monitor* 17(5): 2.

Rogers, C. (1982a). "Notes on Rollo May." *Journal of Humanistic Psychology* 22(3).

———. (1982b). "Reply to Rollo May's Letter to Carl Rogers." *Journal of Humanistic Psychology* 22(4).

Rowan, J. (1989). "Two Humanistic Psychologies or One? *Journal of Humanistic Psychology* 27(2).

Wilber, K.; Engler, J.; & Brown, D. (1986). *Transformations of Consciousness: Conventional and Contemplative Perspectives on Development.* Boston: Shambhala.

SHELDRAKE'S THEORY OF MORPHOGENESIS

PERHAPS THE MOST persistent problem in developmental biology concerns morphogenesis, or the coming into being of form, because the actual form of an organism—its pattern, its shape, its spatiotemporal order—cannot be predicted or even accounted for in terms of its constituent material parts. To give the simplest example: a protein is a long chain of molecules that, based on the properties of the molecules themselves, could easily fold into any number of energetically equivalent forms, and yet, in living systems, they are always found folded in only one way. That is, one form is always selected from numerous equivalent possibilities, and yet, on the basis of mass and energy considerations, no one form should be preferable to any other. The same puzzle is found, a fortiori, in larger and more complex organic systems. No known physical laws can account for the form these systems take. So what *does* account for it?

Aside from the mechanistic approach, which purports to explain the problem by ignoring it, there have been three major attempts to account for morphogenesis. One is the vitalist approach, pioneered at the turn of the century by Driesch (1914). This theory, influenced in part by Aristotelean ideas, maintains that each organic system possesses a characteristic vital force that, as entelechy, guides and shapes the form of the organism. This theory, admirable as a first attempt, suffered mostly from its vagueness, and consequently was replaced in the 1920s by various forms of organismic theory, influenced largely by the works of Whitehead, Smuts, and the Gestalt psychologists. "Vital force" was replaced by the more sophisticated and precise concept of the "morphogenetic field," which is said to guide the actual form or pattern of the organism's material and energetic components, much as a magnetic field will guide and shape iron filings placed within it. Thus, as is well known, if one removes a section of a growing embryo, the embryo will regenerate the section. It does so, according to this theory, because the morphogenetic field of the embryo drives it to replenish, not merely its lost matter, but its lost form. That is, the embryo has, in addition to its material-energetic laws (governed by the standard laws of physics), a holistic drive to reform the whole (a drive to "closure" governed by the morphogenetic field, which itself is not governed or explained by physical laws).

The theory of morphogenetic fields was pioneered by Waddington (1975) largely under the (then unacknowledged) influence of Whitehead. But Waddington wavered on the exact nature of the morphogenetic field; in fact, he hinted that it could probably be explained on the mere basis of physico-chemical properties. René Thom (1975), in his famous catastrophe theory, took up Waddington's ideas and gave them a powerful and impressive reformulation in terms of topographical mathematics. Despite the undeniable contribution of Thom, however, his theory attempts only to describe morphogenesis, not explain it, and thus the how and the why of these fields remained untouched.

Goodwin (1979), on the other hand (and this is the third of the major approaches), takes the Platonic view that these fields are actually archetypal and timeless forms that are forever or transcendentally given but only become actualized in the course of historical development or evolution. This at least gives a possible explanation of the existence and purpose of these fields, but it has the awkward side-effect of implying that, since all forms are timelessly given, there is no actual creativity or genuine novelty anywhere in the universe. It seems, in fact, a subtle form of determinism.

Enter Rupert Sheldrake (1981) and his theory of formative causation. Sheldrake accepts wholeheartedly the theory of morphogenetic fields, but unlike Waddington and Thom, he wishes to explain these fields (not just describe them), and unlike Goodwin, he believes that these fields themselves can develop. They are not timelessly given but rather are themselves effected and molded by past morphogenetic fields. The idea, simply, is that once a particular form comes into existence, it will have a *causal* effect on all subsequent, similar forms; and thus the more a particular form *has been* replicated, the more likely it *will be* replicated in the future. This causal influence of one form on another Sheldrake calls "formative causation" (similar to Aristotle's formal causation), and the actual means of this causation Sheldrake calls "morphic resonance."

To return to the example of protein folding: According to Sheldrake, the first time in evolution that a particular protein was generated, it could potentially have folded into any number of energetically equivalent forms, but by chance it settled into one form. However, the next time this protein was generated, anywhere in the world, it would, according to Sheldrake, have a significantly elevated tendency or probability of settling into this *same* form, simply by virtue of morphic resonance and formative causation from the morphogenetic field of the first protein. As more and more proteins eventually adopted similar forms, this set up a very powerful formative causation that, in effect, forced all subsequent (and similar) proteins to take on the same form. An original contingency has become, via repetition, a virtual necessity. The morphogenetic field of this protein now governs the form of the protein, but it is not a field that is given from the beginning. Far from being an archetypal law, it is rather more like a habit, or cosmic memory. Indeed, for Sheldrake, all of the laws (or formal regularities) of the world have been built up, over successive generations, by morphic resonance and formative causation. Put succinctly, the probability that a given form will occur in the present is a function of the number of times a similar form has occurred in the past. That probability field is exactly the basis of the morphogenetic field. (This view is, as far as it goes, apparently similar to that of Peirce, who held that natural laws are actually habits built by probabilities, and not immutable givens.)

However, what makes Sheldrake's theory so radical is that formative causation postulated to act in a nonlocal fashion; that is, it operates instantaneously across space and time. Once a particular form has been learned by a system, it will be more easily learned by a similar system anywhere else in the world, without any spatiotemporal contact. And, in fact, Sheldrake points out that there is already a fair amount of circumstantial evidence supporting this. For example, it is well known that it is extremely difficult to crystallize complex organic compounds for the first time, but once it has been done in any laboratory, it is more easily (more rapidly) done in others. It has also been shown that once rats learn to negotiate a particular maze in one part of the world, rats elsewhere learn that maze more rapidly. And this, according to Sheldrake, is because of nonlocal morphic resonance and formative causation.

This is obviously a bold and innovative hypothesis. Fortunately, Sheldrake has carefully explained just how this hypothesis can be empirically tested (one can, for instance, set up protein crystallization experiments around the world). Further, these experiments would allow us to distinguish, for example, between Goodwin's theory and Sheldrake's: If the form of each subsequent generation of the protein is crystallized more easily, without any cross-contact, that would rebuff Goodwin's proposition that these forms are changelessly given from the start, and support Sheldrake's hypothesis of cumulative conditioning and formative causation. We must await, then, the results of these experiments.

In the meantime, however, we might speculate on the implications and nature of the hypothesis itself. I for one agree entirely on the existence of morphogenetic fields. In addition to the evidence of developmental biologists, there is much corroborative evidence from the fields of developmental psychology and sociology (a morphogenetic field is, in fact, a homolog of what psychologists and anthropologists would call a "structure," which is defined, not by its components, but by its overall form or pattern, and this holistic pattern governs its constituent components). Certain theoretical objections, however, might be raised against Sheldrake's contentions that (1) these fields are entirely abstract, without any energy of any sort; (2) these fields are nonlocal in character; and (3) there are no archetypal or changeless forms involved in evolution itself. To take them in order:

1. To say that morphogenetic fields are entirely formal or abstract, that they are without any type of mass or energy, but that they somehow influence, indeed govern, mass and energy, raises that ancient and intractable dualism: How can nonmatter affect matter? This looks suspiciously like a new ghost in the old machine, no matter that these ghosts are said causally to interact. I am not a priori against this dualism, but somehow it just doesn't compel. And this is reinforced by the fact that most of the analogies that Sheldrake uses are based on *energetic* fields: the magnet and its fields of force, for example. Even the idea of morphic resonance is taken from sonic fields (two strings vibrating at the same pitch).

It is therefore possible—I would say probable—that morphogenetic fields are not completely formal but rather possess some sort of very subtle energy, and it is the influence of these subtler energies on the denser ones that constitutes the formative capacity of morphogenetic fields. This idea also fits with the more traditional view that, for example, the biological morphic field is composed of a subtle energy ("bioenergy" or "prana"), and it is the *subtlety* of this energy that imposes—and thus appears *as*—the *form* of the grosser energies. This view at least obviates the dualism. Sheldrake himself says that form cannot exist without energy, and energy cannot exist without form. It is therefore difficult to see how formative causation could act without a correlative energetic causation.

Now one of the reasons that Sheldrake makes such a sharp distinction between form and energy (or formative causation and energetic causation) is that the two seem to follow (or display) different laws. Sheldrake gives the example of a flower: If you burn a flower to ashes, the mass-and-energy of the flower is conserved, but the form or pattern of the flower is simply destroyed (i.e., energy is conserved, form isn't). But by Sheldrake's own theory this is not quite true. The form of the flower, in fact, must be retained in something like cosmic memory if it is to subsequently influence similar forms via morphic resonance and formative causation. A form that was *totally* destroyed, that ceased to exist absolutely, could not have any effect whatsoever on subsequent form. In other words, Sheldrake's own theory, which denies the conservation of form, in fact demands *some sort* of subtle formal conservation, analogous (but not identical) to energetic conservation. Formal conservation seems exactly what formative causation is all about. If this is so, Sheldrake has implicitly hit upon a profound and novel truth.

2. Another reason Sheldrake wishes to sharply separate formative causation and energetic causation is that some of the examples he is considering (e.g., protein crystallization) seem to act across space and time (i.e., nonlocally), and no known type of energetic causation can do so. Fortunately, the experiments Sheldrake has proposed will go a long way in helping decide this issue. My point is simply that, even if these experiments disprove Sheldrake's nonlocal formative causation, they will not disprove morphogenetic fields themselves, which may just as easily operate in subtle yet still more or less local ways. In fact, most of the known cases of information transfer (i.e., form transfer) definitely occur *in* space and time, not outside space and time (thus, even in Sheldrake's favorite analogy of form transfer, that of a telephone or radio, the transmission takes place *in* space-time). Even if there are occasional nonlocal transfers (as in Bell's theorem), nonetheless the bulk of information transfers that we know of is local, and we still must explain *that*. It seems to me that much (not all) of Sheldrake's nonlocal formative causation might as easily be explained as subtle local formative causa-

tion. In other words, Sheldrake might be drastically overstating the case that all formative causation must be nonlocal. Rather, the typical case seems to be as follows: each moment bequeaths its energy-mass and its form to subsequent moments, which add their own unique (creative) characteristics and then bequeath that whole package (form and content) to the next moment, and so on indefinitely, so that each event would eventually and ultimately be interconnected with all other events, but not necessarily in an instantaneous and nonlocal fashion. This, anyway, seemed to be Whitehead's view (he believed in prehensive unifications, but they were unifications of actual space-time occasions, which are not instantaneously nonlocal).

3. Sheldrake, in the line of Spencer, Ward, Schelling, Bergson, Dilthey, and so on, keenly understands the importance of historicism or developmentalism in the nature of the world. He is thus suspicious of those theoreticians who tend to see all truths, all forms, all entities as being somehow timelessly implanted in the world from the start. (It should be said that we are not talking about the possibility of a radically timeless and *formless* Ground of Being or Godhead; we are talking about the nature of created *forms,* and whether or not *they* are rigidly unchanging. As for a transcendental Ground of Being, Sheldrake has made it quite clear that he believes in such). In particular, Sheldrake was deeply influenced by Bergson's idea of *creative* evolution, and Bergson's critique of those who, once a new form has emerged, deny its genuinely creative import by claiming it was really there all along in potential or hidden form. This would include, of course, Goodwin's archetypal interpretation of morphogenetic fields. Sheldrake thus takes the stance that perhaps it would be better to see all forms, all entites, as being products of past development, on the one hand, or creative emergence, on the other. But timeless, unchanging categories—that Sheldrake denies.

I would certainly agree on the importance of evolution and creativity, but perhaps Sheldrake goes too far in his disavowal of archetypal givens. For instance, by Sheldrake's own theory, there are certain categories that *must be the case* in order for his theory itself to be true, and these a priori categories are in fact archetypal. For example, Sheldrake sees the world as composed of energy and form; he sees energy causing energy and form causing form; he sees development occurring; and he sees creativity as essential. And *all* of those—energy, form, causation, development, creativity—are seen to be present everywhere, timelessly, from the start. They are therefore archetypal by his own standards, at least for *this* universe (which is not to say that prior to this universe they were necessary). Even Whitehead, the champion of process reality, believed in the existence of what he called "eternal objects" (shape, color, etc.). In short, there seem to be at least certain deep structures to this cosmos that are everywhere invariant, but its particular surface structures seem everywhere variable (learned, habitual, developmental, etc.). I think Sheldrake's hypothesis of formative causation is a substantial addition to our possible understanding of how the latter (i.e., the developmental) components might in fact develop, although it tells us nothing about the former or archetypal components.

(Some critics have faulted Sheldrake for not explaining why or how new forms emerge, and while that is an understandable criticism, it is unfair. Sheldrake himself clearly and carefully explains that his theory is only meant to explain how certain forms are replicated once they emerge. He believes in the creative emergence of new forms, but does not purport to explain it. I am simply adding that his theory does not and in fact cannot address the creativity of new forms simply because creativity itself is archetypal, a category his specific theory does not explicitly recognize.)

A small side issue, but one that is sure to be raised: It is often said that the phenomena of black holes—in which all known laws and forms are suspended—proves that no patterns can be archetypal. Perhaps. I myself don't find that argument very convincing. For we arrive at the properties of a black hole on the basis of calculations generated from present physical laws. If those laws are themselves suspect—due to the existence of black holes—then so are the properties attributed to those black holes by the present physical laws. This amounts to saying that the present physical laws suggest that there are no present physical laws. It's like writing a book claiming that there is no such thing as writing. I'm perfectly willing to admit that black holes are completely weird phenomena, but I'm not prepared to admit that they are *absolutely* without properties (physicists, after all, have managed to explain them in gruesome detail), and those properties—strange as they may be—are simply a subset of the archetypal givens of this universe.

It might seem that, given these reservations, I am not all that impressed with Sheldrake's efforts. In fact, however, for various reasons I find his hypothesis to be one of the most innovative, careful, and refreshing scientific presentations of the last decade, especially among what is known as "New Age" science (i.e., the attempted synthesis of empirical science and transcendental traditions). For one, it is written in an extremely meticulous and clear fashion. It shares none of the ambiguous and half-baked (or should one say fully baked?) notions that seem to define the typical "new paradigm" confessions, most of which are neither science nor art, but a dodge. Further, Sheldrake does not subscribe to the fashionable notion that physics somehow has a corner on truth; in fact, he shuns exclusively physical approaches and, following Whitehead and Bergson, looks to living or biological systems for more fundamental (or "higher") truth claims. Unlike Pribram, Zukav, the early Capra, and so on, Sheldrake refuses to see physical interactions as paradigmatic for the universe, and his reasons for this refusal are a classic and eloquent explanation of the inherent limitations of extrapolating from physics and chemistry to the Entire World. Finally, since he claims this as a scientific theory, he does what most New Age scientists fail to do: Along the lines of Sir Karl Popper, he proposes ways, not to *prove* his theory (anybody can dream up supposed proofs), but to potentially *disprove* his theory, which helps to define a scientific hypothesis. Despite my interim agnosticism about his conclusion (agnosticism he scientifically shares), I am tempted to say that, in Rupert Sheldrake, we have the emergence of one of the first genuinely "New Age" scientists, and, in the spirit of his own philosophy, this is a creative emergence I happily applaud.

References

Baldwin, J.M. (1902). *Development and Evolution.* New York: Macmillan.

Bergson, H. (1911). *Creative Evolution.* London: Macmillan.

Driesch, H. (1914). *History and Theory of Vitalism.* London: Macmillan.

Goodwin, B. C. (1979). "On Morphogenic Fields." *Theoria to Theory* 13: 109–14.

Popper, K. (1965). *Conjectures and Refutations.* London: Routledge & Kegan Paul.

Sheldrake, R. (1981). *A New Science of Life.* Los Angeles: J. P. Tarcher.

Thom, R. (1975). *Structural Stability and Morphogenesis.* Reading, Mass.: Benjamin.

Waddington, C. (1975). *The Evolution of an Evolutionist.* Edinburgh: Edinburgh University Press.

Whitehead, A. N. (1969). *Process and Reality.* New York: Macmillan.

Introduction to *THE HOLOGRAPHIC PARADIGM AND OTHER PARADOXES*

OVER THE PAST THREE YEARS or so, an extraordinary dialogue (and debate) occurred in the pages of *ReVision Journal.* Its topic: perhaps the first serious and sustained look at the interface of "real science" (e.g., physics and physiology) and "real religion" (e.g., mysticism and transcendence), a topic that more than one scholar has termed "epochal." This book is the product and content of that dialogue.

The general, historical dialogue between science and religion itself goes back a long way—at least to Plato, Aristotle, and Plotinus (although "science" didn't mean quite the same thing then as it does now). Previously, however, the discussions usually centered on the *differences* between science and religion, their conflicts, their competing and apparently irreconcilable truth-claims (with an occasional strained discussion on a possible armistice and some sort of peaceful, if edgy, coexistence).

But here, rather suddenly, in the 1970s, were some very respected, very sober, very skilled researchers—physicists, biologists, physiologists, neurosurgeons—and these scientists were not talking *with* religion, they were simply *talking religion,* and more extraordinarily, they were doing so in an attempt to explain the hard data of science itself. The very *facts* of science, they were saying, the actual data (from physics to physiology) seemed to make sense only if we assume some sort of implicit or unifying or transcendental ground underlying the explicit data.

Why this is so is exactly the topic of this book. For the moment, however, let us simply note that, for various sophisticated reasons, these researchers and theoreticians from the "hard sciences" were saying that, without the assumption of this transcendental, spaceless, and timeless ground, the data themselves, the very results of their laboratory experiments, admitted of no cogent explanation. Moreover—and here was the shock—this transcendental ground, whose very existence seemed necessitated by experimental-scientific data, seemed to be identical, at least in description, to the timeless and spaceless ground of being (or "Godhead") so universally described by the world's great mystics and sages, Hindu, Buddhist, Christian, Taoist. And it was *that* idea, unprecedented and far-reaching, that sparked and defined our dialogue.

Different investigative currents came together in this dialogue. There was, first, the pioneering research of Stanford neurosurgeon Karl Pribram, whose book *Languages of the Brain* is already acknowledged as a modern classic. As will be explained in the following pages, Pribram's studies in brain memory and functioning led him to the conclusion that the brain operates, in many ways, like a hologram. A hologram is a special type of optical storage system that can best be explained by an example: if you take a holographic photo of, say, a horse, and cut out one section of it, e.g., the horse's head, and then enlarge that section to the original size, you will get, not a big head, but a picture of the *whole* horse. In other words, each individual part of the picture contains the whole picture in condensed form. The part is in the whole and the whole is in each part—a type of unity-in-diversity and diversity-in-unity. The key point is simply that the *part* has access to the *whole.*

Thus, if the brain did function like a hologram, then it might have access to a larger whole, a field domain or "holistic frequency realm" that transcended spatial and temporal boundaries. And this domain, reasoned Pribram, might very likely be the same domain of transcendental unity-in-diversity described (and experienced) by the world's great mystics and sages.

It was approximately at this time that Pribram became aware of the works of English physicist David Bohm. As we will see, Bohm's work in subatomic physics and the "quantum potential" had led him to the conclusion that physical entities which seemed to be separate and discrete in space and time were actually linked or unified in an implicit or underlying fashion. In Bohm's terminology, under the *explicate realm* of separate things and events is an *implicate realm* of undivided wholeness, and this implicate whole is simultaneously available to each explicate part. In other words, the physical universe itself seemed to be a gigantic hologram, with each part being in the whole and the whole being in each part.

It was at this point that the "holographic paradigm" was born: the brain is a hologram perceiving and participating in a holographic universe. In the explicate or manifest realm of space and time, things and events are indeed separate and discrete. But beneath the surface, as it were, in the implicate or frequency realm, all things and events are spacelessly, timelessly, intrinsically, one and undivided. And, Bohm and Pribram reasoned, the quintessential religious experience, the experience of mystical oneness and "supreme identity," might very well be a *genuine* and *legitimate* experience of this implicate and universal ground.

In some ways, the paradigm seemed to mark the culmination of a discernible historical trend: ever since the "quantum revolution" of fifty years ago, various physicists have been finding intriguing parallels between their results and certain mystical-transcendental religions. Heisenberg, Bohr, Schroedinger, Eddington, Jeans, even Einstein himself all held a mystical-spiritual view of the world. With the great influx of Eastern religions to the West (beginning principally with D. T. Suzuki's *Essays in Zen Buddhism*), these parallels were drawn with increasing clarity and forcefulness. On a popular level, Alan Watts began to use modern physics and systems theory to explain Buddhism and Taoism. A more scholarly approach was *The Medium, the Mystic, and the Physicist,* by Lawrence LeShan. But perhaps no book more captured the interest of scholars and laypeople alike as Fritjof Capra's enormously successful *The Tao of Physics.*

All of these researchers—Pribram, Bohm, Capra—were part of our dialogue. Other voices joined in: Stanley Krippner on parapsychology, Kenneth Pelletier on neurophysiology, Sam Keen on the "cosmic connection," John Welwood on psychology, Willis Harman on the new science, John Battista on information theory and psychiatry, and many others. Special mention, however, should be made of the contributions of Marilyn Ferguson and Renée Weber. Marilyn Ferguson—whose most recent book, *The Aquarian Conspiracy,* is an important contribution to this whole topic—was instrumental (via *Brain/Mind Bulletin*) in initiating the general dialogue itself. And Renée Weber, besides contributing numerous articles and ideas herself, very skillfully conducted interviews with Bohm and with Capra that aided immeasurably in clarifying the central issues.

What follows is not, of course, the only types of dialogues possible between science and religion—far from it. But judging from the evidence, the theories and ideas represented in the following pages have generated as much or more excitement and enthusiasm as any. Nor is there any doubt that the ideas of such theorists as Pribram, Bohm, and Capra represent some of the most serious and sophisticated attempts to directly interface "hard science" with spiritual or transcendental realities. One may agree or disagree with the new paradigm—and both pro and con arguments are well-represented in this volume. And "the" paradigm itself actually has all sorts of different interpretations—some researchers have found it necessary to introduce hierarchical and evolutionary dimensions to the paradigm; other researchers have found, not a strict identity between science and mysticism, but merely some important analogs; still others have questioned whether a new *mental* map or paradigm, no matter how apparently unified, can actually lead to a *transcendence* of the mind itself (which is the real aim of genuine mysticism).*

But my point: agree or disagree with the new paradigm(s), one conclusion unmistakably emerges: at most, the new science demands spirit; at least, it makes ample room for spirit. Either way, modern science is no longer *denying* spirit. And *that* is epochal. As Hans Küng remarked, the standard answer to "Do you believe in Spirit?" used to be, "Of course not, I'm a scientist," but it might very soon become, "Of course I believe in Spirit. I'm a scientist."

*[For my critique of the holographic paradigm, see *The Eye of Spirit* (CW 7), chap. 9; the Introduction to *Quantum Questions*, in this volume; and especially *Eye to Eye* (CW 6), chaps. 5 and 6.]

from

QUANTUM QUESTIONS

Preface

THE THEME OF THIS BOOK, if I may briefly summarize the argument of the physicists presented herein, is that modern physics offers no positive support (let alone proof) for a mystical worldview. Nevertheless, every one of the physicists in this volume was a mystic. They simply believed that if modern physics no longer objects to a religious worldview, it offers no positive support either; properly speaking it is indifferent to all that. The very compelling reasons why these pioneering physicists did not believe that physics and mysticism shared similar worldviews, and the very compelling reasons that they nevertheless *all* became mystics—just that is the dual theme of this anthology. If they did not get their mysticism from a study of modern physics, where *did* they get it? And why?

It is not my aim in this volume to reach the New Age audience, who seem to be firmly convinced that modern physics automatically supports or proves mysticism. It does not. But this view is now so widespread, so deeply entrenched, so taken for granted by New-Agers, that I don't see that any one book could possibly reverse the tide. It was, I believe, with every good intention that this "physics-supports-mysticism" idea was proposed, and it was with every good intention that it was so rapidly and widely accepted. But I believe these good intentions were misplaced, and the results have been not just wrong but detrimental. If today's physics supports mysticism, what happens when tomorrow's physics replaces it? Does mysticism then fall also? We cannot have it both ways. As particle physicist Jeremy Bernstein put it, "If I were an Eastern mystic the last thing in the world I would want would be a reconciliation with modern science, [because] to hitch a religious philosophy to a contemporary science is a sure route to its obsolescence." Genuine mysticism, *precisely* to the extent that it is genuine, is perfectly capable of offering its own defense, its own evidence, its own claims, and its own proofs. Indeed, that is exactly what the physicists in this volume proceed to do, without any need to compromise poor physics in the process.

No, the audience I would like to reach is the same audience these physicists wanted to reach: the orthodox, the established; the men and women who honestly believe that natural science can and will answer all questions worth asking. And so, in that orthodox spirit, I would simply ask, you of orthodox belief, you who pursue disinterested truth, you who—whether you know it or not—are molding the very face of the future with your scientific knowledge, you who—may I say so?—bow to physics as if it were a religion itself, to you I ask: what does it mean that the founders of your modern science, the theorists and researchers who pioneered the very concepts you now worship implicitly, the very scientists presented in this volume, what does it mean that they were, *every one of them, mystics?*

Does that not stir something in you, curiosity at least? Cannot the spirit of these pioneers reach out across the decades and touch in you that "still, small point" that moved them all to wonderment?

The last thing these theorists would want you to surrender is your critical intellect, your hard-earned skepticism. For it was exactly through a sustained use—not of emotion, not of intuition, not of faith—but a sustained use of the critical intellect that these greatest of physicists felt absolutely compelled to go beyond physics altogether. And as we will see in the following pages, they left a trail, clear enough, for all sensitive souls to follow.

INTRODUCTION

Of Shadows and Symbols

BEYOND THE CAVE

PHYSICS AND MYSTICISM, physics and mysticism, physics and mysticism . . . In the past decade there have appeared literally dozens of books, by physicists, philosophers, psychologists, and theologians, purporting to describe or explain the extraordinary relationship between modern physics, the hardest of sciences, and mysticism, the tenderest of religions. Physics and mysticism are fast approaching a remarkably common worldview, some say. They are complementary approaches to the same reality, others report. No, they have nothing in common, the skeptics announce; their methods, goals, and results are diametrically opposed. Modern physics, in fact, has been used to both support and refute determinism, free will, God, Spirit, immortality, causality, predestination, Buddhism, Hinduism, Christianity, and Taoism.

The fact is, every generation has tried to use physics to both prove and disprove Spirit—which ought to tell us something right there. Plato announced that the whole of physics was, to use his terms, nothing more than a "likely story," since it depended ultimately on nothing but the evidence of the fleeting and shadowy senses, whereas truth resided in the transcendental Forms beyond physics (hence "metaphysics"). Democritus, on the other hand, put his faith in "atoms and the void," since nothing else, he felt, had any existence—a notion so obnoxious to Plato that he expressed the strongest desire that all the works of Democritus be burned on the spot.

When Newtonian physics ruled the day, the materialists seized upon physics to prove that, since the universe was obviously a deterministic machine, there could be no room for free will, God, grace, divine intervention, or anything else that even vaguely resembled Spirit. This seemingly impenetrable argument, however, had no impact whatsoever on the spiritually minded or idealistic philosophers. In fact, they pointed out, the second law of thermodynamics—which unequivocably announces that the universe is winding down—can mean only one thing: if the universe is winding down, something or somebody had to have previously wound it up. Newtonian physics doesn't disprove God; on the contrary, they maintained, it proves the absolute necessity of a Divine Creator!

When relativity theory entered the scene, the whole drama repeated itself. Cardinal O'Connell of Boston warned all good Catholics that relativity was "a befogged speculation producing universal doubt about God and his creation"; the theory was "a ghastly apparition of Atheism." Rabbi Goldstein, on the other hand, solemnly announced that Einstein had done nothing less than produce "a scientific formula for monotheism." Similarly, the works of James Jeans and Arthur Eddington were greeted by cheers from the pulpits all over England—modern physics supports Christianity in all essential respects! The problem was, Jeans and Eddington by no means agreed with this reception, nor in fact with each other, which prompted Bertrand Russell's famous witticism that "Sir Arthur Eddington deduces religion from the fact that atoms do not obey the laws of mathematics. Sir James Jeans deduces it from the fact that they do."

Today we hear of the supposed relation between modern physics and Eastern mysticism. Bootstrap theory, Bell's theorem, the implicate order, the holographic paradigm—all of this is supposed to prove (or is it disprove?) Eastern mysticism. In all essential respects it is simply the same story with different characters. The pros and cons strut their wares, but what remains true and unchanged is simply that the issue itself is extremely complex.

In the midst of this melange, then, it seemed a good idea to consult the founders of modern physics on what *they* thought about the nature of science and religion. What is the relation, if any, between modern physics and transcendental mysticism? Does physics bear at all on the issues of free-will, creation, Spirit, the soul? What *are* the respective roles of science and religion? Does physics even deal with Reality (capital *R*), or is it necessarily confined to studying the shadows in the cave?

This volume is a condensed collection of virtually every major statement made on those topics by the founders and grand theorists of modern (quantum and relativity) physics: Einstein, Schroedinger, Heisenberg, Bohr, Eddington, Pauli, de Broglie, Jeans, and Planck. While it would be asking too much to have all these theorists precisely agree with each other on the nature and relation of science and religion, nevertheless, I was quite surprised to find a very general commonality emerge in the worldviews of these philosopher-scientists. While there are exceptions (as we will see), certain strong and common conclusions were reached by virtually every one of these theorists. I will return to these general conclusions in a moment and state them more carefully and precisely, but by way of first approximation, we can say this: these theorists are virtually unanimous in declaring that modern physics offers no positive support whatsoever for mysticism or transcendentalism of any variety. (And yet they were *all* mystics of one sort or another! The reason for *that* will be one of the central questions of this section.)

According to their general consensus, modern physics neither proves nor disproves, neither supports nor refutes, a mystical-spiritual worldview. There *are* certain similarities between the worldview of the new physics and that of mysticism, they believe, but these similarities, where they are not purely accidental, are trivial when compared with the vast and profound differences between them. To attempt to bolster a spiritual worldview with data from physics—old or new—is simply to misunderstand entirely the nature and function of each. As Einstein himself put it, "The present fashion of applying the axioms of physical science to human life is not only entirely a mistake but has also something reprehensible in it."[1] When Archbishop Davidson asked Einstein what effect the theory of relativity had on religion, Einstein replied, "None. Relativity is a purely scientific theory, and has nothing to do with religion"—about which Eddington wittily commented, "In those days one had to become expert in dodging persons who were persuaded that the fourth dimension was the door to spiritualism."[2]

Eddington, of course, had (like Einstein) a deeply mystical outlook, but he was absolutely decisive on this point: "I do not suggest that the new physics 'proves religion' or indeed gives any positive grounds for religious faith. . . . *For my own part I am wholly opposed to any such attempt.*"[3] Schroedinger—who, in my judgment, was probably the greatest mystic in this group—was just as blunt: "Physics has nothing to do with it. Physics takes its start from everyday experience, which it continues by more subtle means. It remains akin to it, does not transcend it generically, it cannot enter into another realm."[4] The attempt to do so, he says, is simply "sinister": "The territory from which previous scientific attainment is invited to retire is with admirable dexterity claimed as a playground of some religious ideology that cannot really use it profitably, because its [religion's] true domain is far beyond anything in reach of scientific explanation."[5]

Planck's view, if I may summarize it, was that science and religion deal with two very different dimensions of existence, between which, he believed, there can properly be neither conflict nor accord, any more than we can say, for instance, that botany and music are in conflict or accord. The attempts to set them at odds, on the one hand, or "unify them," on the other, are "founded on a misunderstanding, or, more precisely, on a confusion of the images of religion with scientific statements. Needless to say, the result makes no sense at all."[6] As for Sir James Jeans, he was simply flabbergasted: "What of the things which are not seen which religion assures us are eternal? There has been much discussion of late of the claims of ["scientific support" for "transcendental events"]. Speaking as a scientist, I find the alleged proofs totally unconvincing; speaking as a human being, I find most of them ridiculous as well."[7]

Now it cannot be claimed that these men were simply unaware of the mystical writings of the East and West; that if they simply read *The Dancing Wu-Li Masters* they would all change their minds and pronounce physics and mysticism to be fraternal twins; that if they knew more about the details of the mystical literature they would indeed find numerous similarities between quantum mechanics and mysticism. On the contrary, their writings are positively loaded with references to the Vedas, the Upanishads, Taoism (Bohr made the yin-yang symbol part of his family crest), Buddhism, Pythagoras, Plato, Berkeley, Plotinus, Schopenhauer, Hegel, Kant, virtually the entire pantheon of perennial philosophers, and they still reached the above-mentioned conclusions.

They were perfectly aware, for instance, that a key tenet of the perennial philosophy is that in mystical consciousness subject and object become *one* in the act of knowing; they were also aware that certain philosophers claimed that Heisenberg's Uncertainty Principle and Bohr's Complementarity Principle supported this mystical idea, because, it was said, in order for the subject to know the object, it had to "interfere" with it, and that proved that the subject-object duality had been transcended by modern physics. *None of the physicists in this volume believed that assertion.* Bohr himself stated quite plainly that "the notion of complementarity does in no way involve a departure from our position as detached observers of nature. . . . The essentially new feature in the analysis of quantum phenomena is the introduction of a *fundamental distinction between the measuring apparatus and the objects under investigation* [his ital.]. . . . In our future encounters with reality we shall have to distinguish between the objective and the subjective side, to make a division between the two."[8,9] Louis de Broglie was even more succinct: "[It has been said that] quantum physics reduces or blurs the dividing region between the subjective and the objective, but there is . . . some misuse of language here. For in reality the means of observation clearly belong to the objective side; and the fact that their reactions on the parts of the external world which we desire to study cannot be disregarded in microphysics neither abolishes, nor even diminishes, the traditional distinction between subject and object."[10] Schroedinger—and keep in mind that these men firmly acknowledged that in mystical union subject and object are one, they simply found no support for this idea whatsoever in modern physics—stated that "the 'pulling down of the frontier between observer and observed' which many consider [a] momentous revolution of thought, to my mind seems a much overrated provisional aspect without profound significance."[11]

Accordingly, for the reasons that these theorists rejected the "physics-supports-mysticism" view, we will have to look elsewhere than the alleged fact that they were unacquainted with mystical literature or experience. And even if their knowledge of, say, Taoism, could be shown to be deficient, their critique would still, I believe, be absolutely valid. Further, this critique (which I will present in a moment) is not affected one way or another by any particular advances in physics; it is a logical critique that cuts at right angles to any possible new discoveries. This critique is simple, straightforward, and profound; at one stroke, it cuts across virtually everything written on the supposed parallels between physics and mysticism.

Briefly, the critique is this. The central mystical experience may be fairly (if somewhat poetically) described as follows: in the mystical consciousness, Reality is apprehended directly and immediately, meaning without any mediation, any symbolic elaboration, any conceptualization, or any abstractions; subject and object become one in a timeless and spaceless act that is beyond any and all forms of mediation. Mystics universally speak of contacting reality in its "suchness," its "isness," its "thatness," without any intermediaries; beyond words, symbols, names, thoughts, images.

Now, when the physicist "looks at" quantum reality or at relativistic reality, he is *not* looking at the "things in themselves," at noumenon, at direct and nonmediated reality. Rather, the physicist is looking at *nothing but a set of highly abstract differential equations*—not at "reality" itself, but at mathematical symbols of reality. As Bohr put it, "It must be recognized that we are here dealing with a *purely symbolic procedure.* . . . Hence our whole space-time view of physical phenomena depends ultimately upon these abstractions."[12] Sir James Jeans was specific: in the study of modern physics, he says, "we can never understand what events are, but must limit ourselves to describing the patterns of events in mathematical terms; no other aim is possible. Physicists who are trying to understand nature may work in many different fields and by many different methods; one may dig, one may sow, one may reap. But the final harvest will always be a sheaf of mathematical formulae. These will *never* describe nature itself. . . . [Thus] our studies can never put us into contact with reality."[13]

What an absolute, radical, irredeemable difference from mysticism! And this critique applies to any type of physics—old, new, ancient, modern, relativistic, or quantum. The very nature, aim, and results of the approaches are profoundly different: the one dealing with abstract and mediate symbols and forms of reality, the other dealing with a direct and nonmediated approach to reality itself. To even claim that there are direct and central similarities between the findings of physics and mysticism is necessarily to claim the latter is fundamentally a merely symbolic abstraction, because it is absolutely true that the former is exactly that. At the very least, it represents a profound confusion of absolute and relative truth, of finite and infinite, of temporal and eternal—and that is what so repelled the physicists in this volume. Eddington, as usual, put it most trenchantly: "We should suspect an intention to reduce God to a system of differential equations. That fiasco at any rate [must be] avoided. However much the ramifications of [physics] may be extended by further scientific discovery, they cannot from their very nature trench on the background in which they have their being. . . . We have learnt that the exploration of the eternal world by the methods of physical science leads not to a concrete reality but to a *shadow world of symbols,* beneath which those methods are unadapted for penetrating."[14]

Physics, in short, deals with—and can only deal with—the world of shadow-symbols, not the light of reality beyond the shadowy cave. Such, as a brief first approximation, is the general conclusion of these theorists.

But why, then, did *all* of these great physicists embrace mysticism of one sort or another? Obviously, there is *some* type of profound connection here. We have seen that this connection does *not* lie, according to these theorists, in a similarity of worldviews between physics and mysticism, nor a similarity in aim or results; between shadow and light there can be no fundamental similarity. So what forced so many physicists out of the cave? What, in particular, did the *new* physics (quantum and relativistic) tell these physicists that the old physics failed to mention? What, in brief, was the crucial difference between the old and new physics, such that the latter tended much more often to be conducive to mysticism?

There is, once again, a general and common conclusion reached by the majority of the theorists in this volume, and best elucidated by Schroedinger and Eddington. Eddington begins with the acknowledged fact that physics is dealing with shadows, not reality. Now the great difference, he says, between the old and the new physics is not that the latter is relativistic, non-deterministic, four-dimensional, or any of those sorts of things. The great difference between old and new physics is both much simpler and much more profound: both the old and the new physics were dealing with shadow-symbols, *but the new physics was forced to be aware of that fact*—forced to be aware that it was dealing with shadows and illusions, not reality. Thus, in perhaps the most famous and oft-quoted passage of any of these theorists, Eddington eloquently states: "In the world of physics we watch a shadowgraph performance of familiar life. The shadow of my elbow rests on the shadow table as the shadow ink flows over the shadow paper. . . . The frank realization that physical science is concerned with a world of shadows is one of the most significant of recent advances."[15] Schroedinger drives the point home: "Please note that the very recent advance [of quantum and relativistic physics] does not lie in the world of physics itself having acquired this shadowy character; it had ever since Democritus of Abdera and even before, *but we were not aware of it; we thought we were dealing with the world itself*."[16] And Sir James Jeans summarizes it perfectly, right down to the metaphor: "The essential fact is simply that *all* the pictures which science now draws of nature, and which alone seem capable of according with observational fact, are *mathematical* pictures. . . . They are nothing more than pictures—fictions if you like, if by fiction you mean that science is not yet in contact with ultimate reality. Many would hold that, from the broad philosophical standpoint, the outstanding achievement of twentieth-century physics is not the theory of relativity with its welding together of space and time, or the theory of quanta with its present apparent negation of the laws of causation, or the dissection of the atom with the resultant discovery that things are not what they seem; it is the general recognition that we are not yet in contact with ultimate reality. We are still imprisoned in our cave, with our backs to the light, and can only watch the shadows on the wall."[17]

There is the great difference between the old and new physics—both are dealing with shadows, but the old physics didn't recognize that fact. If you are *in* the cave of shadows and don't even know it, then of course you have no reason or desire to try to escape to the light beyond. The shadows appear to be the whole world, and no other reality is acknowledged or even suspected—this tended to be the philosophic effect of the old physics. But with the new physics, the shadowy character of the whole enterprise became much more obvious, and sensitive physicists by the droves—including all of those in this volume—began to look beyond the cave (and beyond physics) altogether.

"The symbolic nature of physics," Eddington explains, "is generally recognized, and the scheme of physics is now formulated in such a way as to make it almost self-evident that it is a partial aspect of something wider." However, according to these physicists, about this "something wider" physics tell us—and can tell us—nothing whatsoever. It was exactly this radical failure of physics, and not its supposed similarities to mysticism, that paradoxically led so many physicists to a mystical view of the world. As Eddington carefully explains: "Briefly the position is this. We have learnt that the exploration of the external world by the methods of physical science leads not to a concrete reality but to a shadowy world of symbols, beneath which those methods are unadapted for penetrating. Feeling that there must be more behind, we return to our starting point in *human consciousness*—the one centre where more might become known. There [in immediate inward consciousness] we find other stirrings, other revelations than those conditioned by the world of symbols. . . . Physics most strongly insists that its methods do not penetrate behind the symbolism. Surely then that mental and spiritual nature of ourselves, known in our minds by an intimate contact transcending the methods of physics, supplies just that . . . which science is admittedly unable to give."[18]

To put it in a nutshell: according to this view, physics deals with shadows; to go beyond shadows is to go beyond physics; to go beyond physics is to head toward the metaphysical or mystical—and *that* is why so many of our pioneering physicists were mystics. The new physics contributed nothing positive to this mystical venture, except a spectacular failure, from whose smoking ruins the spirit of mysticism gently arose.

A Closer Look

I should like, in this section, to look more closely at the relation between science and religion, their nature, methods, and domains. It must be emphasized, however, that in this section, unlike the previous section, I am not necessarily representing the views of the physicists in this volume; these are more or less my own ideas, which will, I believe, help clarify the issues in this anthology. And while many, perhaps most, of the physicists included herein would probably agree with most of what I have to say, nevertheless we are now dealing, not with generalities or commonalities, but with specific details and terminology, about which each physicist had his own particular and often idiosyncratic views. I will often indicate the points with which the various physicists would agree, and those points with which they would probably disagree.

There is, first of all, the very meaning of the word "science." We are, of course, free to define "science" any way we wish, as long as we are consistent, and, in fact, much of this "science-and-religion" argument consists of nothing more than a jockeying for definitions selected in advance to produce precisely the conclusion desired. Thus, for instance, if you define science simply as "knowledge," then contemplative religion becomes a form of science—becomes, in fact, the highest science (this approach is often taken by present-day Eastern masters, who continually speak of the science of yoga, the science of meditation, the science of creative intelligence, and so on). Physics then becomes a branch of that all-encompassing Tree of Science, and we're off and running with *The Medium, the Mystic, and the Physicist.*

On the other hand, if you define science as "empirical-sensory knowledge, instrumentally validated," then virtually all forms of religion become nonscientific. You then have one of two paths open: (1) view religion as a perfectly valid form of *personal* faith, values, and belief not open to scientific scrutiny—these are said to be two different but equally legitimate domains between which there can properly be neither conflict nor compromise nor parallels (this view was pioneered by Kant and

Lotze, and has many adherents to this day, including some of the physicists in this volume, such as Planck, Einstein, and Eddington); (2) view religion as non-scientific in the purely pejorative sense, as a superstitious relic of magical and primitive thinking (Comte), or a defense mechanism expiating guilt and anxiety (Freud), or an opaque ideology institutionalizing alienation (Marx), or a debilitating projection of men's and women's inward and humanistic yearnings (Feuerbach), or a purely private emotional affair, harmless in itself but not deserving the title "knowledge" (Quine, Ayer, and the positivists).

Now *all* of that confusion, you see, rests in large measure on how you define "science." The issues are so complex and subtle that if we don't specify precisely what we mean by "science" (and later, by "religion"), then statements about the relation between the two become silly at best, sinister at worst. Personally, I am now at the point that, if a popular writer makes some sweeping statement about the "new science" and "spirituality," I have no idea whatsoever about what they might mean, and all I feel certain of is that they don't, either.

Since this entire anthology is, in fact, devoted to the themes of "science and religion," I don't see that we have any choice except to examine very carefully what we mean, or *can* mean, by the word "science" and the word "religion." My somewhat dreary editorial task, then, for the next few pages, is to play the role of linguistic analyst, that most banal of all philosophic activities. I shall try to make the operation as painless as possible.

Start with "science." As I said, we are free to define "science" any way we wish, as long as we are consistent. But it seems to me that at the very least we must distinguish between the *method* of science and the *domain* of science. The *method* of science refers to the ways or means that whatever it is we call science manages to gather facts, data, or information, and manages to confirm or refute propositions vis-à-vis that data. Method, in other words, refers to ways in which "science" (still unspecified) manages to gather knowledge.

Domain, on the other hand, simply refers to the types of events or phenomena that become, or can become, objects of investigation by whatever it is we mean by science. "Method" refers to the epistemology of science, while "domain" refers to its ontology.

Let me give a crude analogy. Say we are exploring Carlsbad Caverns in the dark of night. We take a flashlight with us—that is our means or our method of gaining knowledge (or of "shedding light" on the various caves), and the caves are the different objects or domains that we will investigate and illuminate with our methodology, with our flashlight. One cave might contain buried treasure of gems and gold, another might contain nothing but mud and bats—the point is that the same flashlight might discover very different types of objects, and we don't want to confuse these objects simply because the same flashlight was used to find them.

Instead of asking vaguely "What is science?," let us therefore ask "What is a scientific *method?*" and "What is a scientific *domain?*" As for scientific method, general science texts seem to be in agreement: a method of gaining knowledge whereby *hypotheses* are *tested* (instrumentally or experimentally) by reference to *experience* ("data") that is potentially *public,* or open to *repetition* (confirmation or refutation) by peers. In bare essentials, it means that the scientific method involves those knowledge-claims open to *experiential* validation or refutation.

Notice that this definition—which we will accept for the moment—correctly makes no reference to the domain or objects of the scientific method. If there is a way to test a knowledge-claim *in whatever domain* by appeal to open experience, then that knowledge can properly be called "scientific."

This definition, correctly I believe, does *not* say that only sensory or physical objects are open to scientific investigation—that would be like claiming that our flashlight can be used in only one cave. There is nothing in that definition that prevents us from legitimately applying the term "scientific" to certain specifiable knowledge-claims in the realms or domains of biology, psychology, history, anthropology, sociology, and spirituality. Indeed, that is exactly what the Germans mean by "geist-science," the science of mental and spiritual phenomena, and what we Americans mean by the human or social sciences.

The point is that because this definition correctly concerns only method and makes no reference to object-domains, the dividing line between "scientific" and "nonscientific" is *not* between physical and metaphysical; the dividing line is between experientially testable and non-testable (or merely dogmatic) pronouncements, the former being exposed to confirmation/refutation based on open experience, the latter being based on evidence no more substantial than the "because-I-tell-you-so" variety. If "science" were restricted to "physical-sensory" object-domains, then mathematics, logic, psychology, and sociology could not be called "scientific," in that the central aspects of those domains are non-sensory, non-empirical, non-physical, or meta-physical occasions.

There is, for instance, a way to *test* the truth-value of a mathematical theorem, but this test is based, not on *sensory* evidence, but on *mental* evidence, namely, the inward *experience* of the mental *coherence* of the train of logical propositions, an inwardly-experiential coherence that can be checked by the minds of other equally trained mathematicians, an inwardly experiential coherence (not correspondence) that has nothing to do with physical-sensory evidence. (The correspondence, or lack of it, can also be tested by reference to evidence, either mental or sensory as the case requires.) The point is that "test by experiential evidence" does *not* mean merely "test by physical-sensory evidence" (a point we will soon elaborate), and that is exactly why mathematics, logic, psychology, and so forth are properly called "sciences."[19]

Having seen that "scientific method" applies to experientially testable knowledge-claims as opposed to nontestable, dogmatic proclamations (which *may* be valid, but on grounds we will have to call by something other than the term "scientific"), we can now ask, "To what *domain(s)*, then, is the scientific method applicable?" But let us ask first, "What domains *are* there?" That is, what realms of experience, or modes of being, or aspects of reality are even available, in the first place, to which the "scientific method" may or may not be applicable? In other words, what *ontology* shall we accept? How many caves are there in the universe that we may go exploring with our flashlight?

I am not going to make a long drawn-out argument over this; for the purposes of this presentation, I shall simply assume the basic ontology of the perennial philosophy; specifically, as summarized by Lovejoy, Huston Smith, René Guénon, Marco Pallis, Frithjof Schuon, et al., and as embraced (in whole or in part) by modern thinkers such as Nicolai Hartmann, Samuel Alexander, Whitehead, Aurobindo, Maritain, Urban, etc. Nor am I going to haggle over terms; God, Godhead, Absolute, Ultimate, Being, Spirit, life, consciousness, psyche, soul—those terms can mean pretty much whatever you want them to. My purpose lies in a different direction.

Here, then, is our working ontology—the so-called "Great Chain of Being" (see diagram).

Running up the diagram, I have appended a general name to each domain; running down the diagram, I have listed a representative discipline that generally (but not necessarily exclusively) takes as its object of study that particular domain. The numbers simply refer to the levels, and the letters I will explain in a moment. I might also mention that some versions of the Great Chain give anywhere from three to twenty

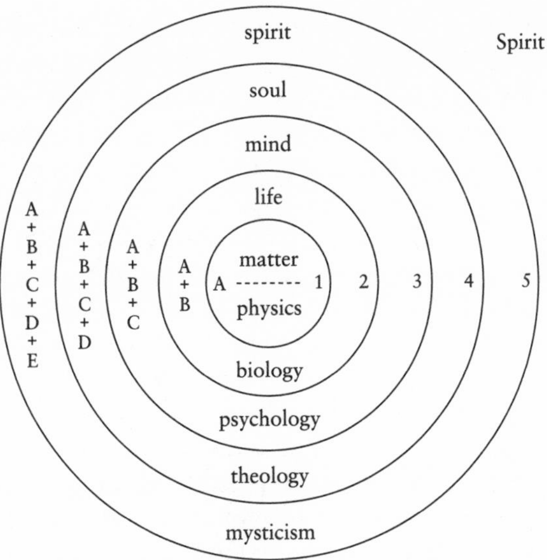

or more levels; this simple five-level scheme will adequately serve our purposes.

The general meaning of the terms "matter," "life," and "mind" might be fairly obvious, but let me say a word or two about "soul" and "spirit." The soul-realm, as I will use the term, refers to the realm of Platonic Forms, archetypes, personal deity-forms (yidam, ishtadeva, archangelic patterns, and so forth). In the soul-realm, there is still some sort of subtle subject-object duality; the soul apprehends Being, or communes with God, but there still remains an irreducible boundary between them. In the realm of spirit (level 5), however, the soul *becomes* Being in a nondual state of radical intuition and supreme identity variously known as gnosis, nirvikalpa samadhi, satori, kensho, jnana, etc. In the soul-realm, the soul and God commune; in the spirit-realm, both soul and God unite in Godhead, or absolute spirit, itself without exclusive boundaries anywhere.

Already, however, we run into grave semantic difficulties with the word "spirit," for there is virtually no way we can discuss the realm of spirit without involving paradox. Spirit itself is not paradoxical; it is, strictly speaking, beyond all characterization and qualification whatsoever (including that one). Because spirit is, so to speak, the ultimate limit of the nested hierarchy of Being, it enters our verbal formulations in apparently contradictory or paradoxical ways (as Kant, Stace, Nagarjuna, and others have pointed out). This becomes problematic, however, *only* if we forget to include *both* sides of the paradox in our verbal formulations.

Let me give a few examples. Notice that each level in the Great Chain *transcends but includes* its predecessor(s). That is, each higher level contains functions, capacities, or structures not found on, or explainable solely in terms of, a lower level. The higher level does not violate the principles of the lower, it simply is not exclusively bound to or explainable by them. The higher transcends but includes the lower, and *not vice versa,* just as a three-dimensional sphere includes or contains two-dimensional circles, but not vice versa. And it is this "not-vice-versa" that establishes and constitutes nested hierarchy. Thus, for example, life transcends but includes matter, and not vice versa: biological organisms contain material components, but material objects do not contain biological components (rocks don't genetically reproduce, etc.). This is also why, for example, in the study of biology one uses physics, but in the study of physics one does not use biology.*

Thus, life transcends but includes matter; mind transcends but includes life; soul transcends but includes mind; and spirit transcends but includes soul. At that point, however, asymptotic at infinity, we have reached a paradoxical limit: spirit is that which transcends everything *and* includes everything. Or, in traditional terms, spirit is both completely transcendent to the world and completely immanent in the world—and there is the most notorious (and unavoidable) paradox of spirit.

On the one hand, then, spirit is the *highest* of all possible domains; it is the Summit of all realms, the Being beyond all beings. It is the domain that is a subset of no other domain, and thus preserves its radically transcendental nature. On the other hand, since spirit is all-pervading

*How does the Great Chain metaphor relate to the shadow and cave metaphor? Very simply: the *levels* of the Great Chain are the *levels of the shadow-objects* in the cave, for some shadow-objects are obviously *closer* to the opening than others, which constitutes the *hierarchy* of the levels. The levels of the Great Chain are thus levels of decreasing shadow and increasing light, culminating at the opening to spirit (level 5), whereupon we realize there was always and *only* spirit, even at the lowest levels (although this can only be *realized* at the highest.) This does not mean that the levels of manifestation are pure illusion or pure unreality, for they are all manifestations of Being and, therefore, bathe, in various degrees, in its glory. It is just that the higher levels, being closer to the opening, need (as Bradley put it) less and less supplementation to pass into the Absolute. The fact that *all* things are God, but some things are more God than others—that is another version of the paradoxicality of Being.

and all-inclusive, since it is the set of all possible sets, the Condition of all conditions and the Nature of all natures, it is not properly thought of as a realm set apart from other realms, but as the Ground or Being of *all* realms, the pure *That* of which all manifestation is but a play or modification. And thus spirit preserves (paradoxically) its radically immanent nature.

Now I labor on this apparently trivial point for what is really a very important reason. Because spirit can legitimately be referred to as both perfectly transcendent and perfectly immanent, then if we aren't extremely careful which meaning we wish to convey, we can play fast and loose with statements about what is or is not the realm of spirit. Thus, for example, if we emphasize solely the transcendental nature of spirit, then religion (and spirit) are obviously "out of this world" and have absolutely nothing in common with earth-bound science. Any attempt to identify spirit with the manifest world of nature is, in this truncated view, charged with the ugly epithet of "featureless pantheism," and theologians are all in a tither to explain that "dragging God into the finite realm" supposedly abolishes all values and actually destroys any meaning we could attach to the word "God" or "spirit."

On the other hand, if we commit the equal but opposite error and emphasize solely the immanent nature of spirit, then not only are science and religion compatible, but science becomes a subset of religion, and "The more we know of things [science], the more we know of God [religion]" (Spinoza). Attempts to place God or Spirit in any sort of transcendental "realm beyond" are met with howling charges of "dogmatism" and "nonsensicality," and all congratulate themselves on solving the transcendental Mystery, whereas all they have done is ignore it.

Much of this confusion would evaporate if we (1) acknowledge the necessary paradoxicality of verbal formulations of spirit, and (2) simply indicate which aspect of spirit—transcendent or immanent—we mean at any given time. This is not a philosophical nicety; it is an absolutely crucial prerequisite to making any meaningful statement about the role and relation of science and religion.

For my part, then, when I wish to refer to spirit in its transcendental aspect—as the highest dimension or summit of being—I will use "spirit" or "spiritual realm" with a small "s," to indicate that the spiritual realm (level 5) is a realm that in some very significant ways is *different* from, or *transcendent* to, the realms of matter, life, mind, and soul. Specifically, I mean this: we said that each level transcends but includes its predecessor(s). If matter (level 1) has the characteristic of *A*, then biological life (level 2) can be represented as *A* + *B*, where *B* stands for all those capacities found in living organisms but not in inanimate matter (such as food consumption, metabolism, sex, motor functions, and so on). Mind (level 3) is then *A* + *B* + *C*, where *C* represents all those capacities found in psychological systems but not in biological or material systems (such as ideas, concepts, values, insights, and so on). Likewise, the soul-realm is *A* + *B* + *C* + *D*; and the spiritual realm (with a small "s") is *A* + *B* + *C* + *D* + *E*. Thus, when we speak of "exploring the spiritual realm" or "the characteristics of the spiritual realm," we mean exactly those functions, capacities, and aspects (represented by *E*) that are found in the spiritual realm and nowhere else (such as jnana, nirvikalpa samadhi, nirguna Brahman, and so on).

If we were allowed to speak of the "science of spirit" (we haven't yet addressed that issue), all we would mean is the "scientific investigation of those events that constitute class *E*." In that sense, spiritual science would definitely be significantly different from, but not at all antagonistic toward, physical science (study of class *A*), biological science (study of class *B*), psychological science (study of class *C*), and so on. Nothing whatsoever would be gained by trying to mix or confuse these sciences, or claim they are all "really one," or lump them together indiscriminately—that, again, would be like claiming that the gold in one cavern is the same as the mud in another because the same flashlight discovered both.

Now, when I wish to refer to the all-pervading, all-embracing, radically *immanent* aspect of spirit, I will use "Spirit" with a capital *S*, to indicate that Spirit is not the highest level among other levels but rather is the Ground or Reality of *all* levels, and thus could have no specific qualities or attributes itself, other than being the "isness" (tzu jan) or "suchness" or "thatness" (tathata) of all possible and actual realms—in other words, the unqualifiable Being of all beings, not the qualifiable being of any particular beings, and certainly not class *E* as opposed to class *A*, *B*, *C*, or *D*. (In the diagram of the Great Nest of Being, Spirit is represented, not by level 5, but by the paper on which the entire diagram is drawn).*

---

*This paradox is exactly why most of the physicists in this volume will talk about some sort of "unity" between physics and mysticism (or the realms of matter and spirit), and yet often in the same sentence completely deny it. What they are doing, consciously or unconsciously, is reflecting the paradoxical nature of spirit/Spirit. As spirit (small *s*), it is the *highest* dimension (and therefore quite divorced from physics), and as Spirit (large *S*), it is the *common* Ground (and therefore "underlying"

As regards Spirit (not spirit), the important point is that Spirit is neither One nor Many, neither infinite nor finite, neither whole nor part—for *all* of those are supposed *qualifications* of Spirit, and thus could at best apply to spirit, not Spirit. This is exactly the Buddhist doctrine of shunyata ("nonqualifiability"), the negation of all negations. And in particular notice that Spirit is *not* One, not Wholeness, not Unity—*neti, neti*—for all of those are dualistic concepts, possessing meaning only in contrast to their opposites.

Now there is a legitimate meaning to, for example, "Wholeness"—namely, the sum Totality of everything in existence, levels 1–5. But that Wholeness or Totality, it must be emphasized, has precisely nothing to do with Spirit, which is radically, completely, absolutely, and equally immanent in and as every single particular anywhere in existence. Thus, seven things do not contain more Spirit than three things, and wholeness is not more Real than partialness. "Wholeness" does have an important applicability on the transcendental side of the paradox—for example, any biological object possesses more wholeness than any material object, and thus *is closer to the spiritual realm but not closer to Spirit.* I mention this so that we don't fall into the positivistic error of equating Spirit with Totality or Wholeness, an error that, it seems to me, is quite popular nowadays, and under whose auspices many an outrageous philosophical sleight-of-hand has been perpetrated.*

I think we have enough tools now to return to our original questions and attempt closure.

---

physics in a "unitary" fashion). Thus Eddington, as summarized by Cohen: "Professor Eddington's main thesis, so far as it has bearing upon religion, is the existence of two worlds, one to which scientific 'laws' apply, and another world, to which scientific laws have no application. But there is, he admits, 'a kind of unity between the material and the spiritual worlds . . . but to those who have any intimate acquaintance with laws of chemistry and physics [and here comes the paradoxical denial], the suggestion that the spiritual world could be ruled by laws of an allied [or so-called parallel] character, is as preposterous as the suggestion that a nation could be ruled by the laws of grammar.' " This type of paradoxicality is rampant in the works of Einstein, Eddington, Schroedinger, Bohr, Heisenberg—indeed, in virtually all of the theorists in this volume. That, as I believe, is exactly as it should be; problems arise only if we ignore or forget that inherent paradoxicality. I am simply trying to make it conscious and explicit, so it doesn't befuddle an already difficult enough situation.

*This is why Zen, for example, emphatically denies that Spirit is one, or whole, or an underlying unity or identity. As D. T. Suzuki put it: "Followers of identity are to be given the warning: they are ridden by concepts" (*Zen and Japanese Culture*). Zen says, if anything, that Spirit is "not-two, not-one!"

What do we mean by "religion"?

In *A Sociable God* I presented nine equally legitimate uses of the term "religion"; for our much simpler purposes, we can say that the type of religion we are discussing in this volume is that which has—or claims to have—direct access to levels 4 and 5 (and especially 5). The question then becomes, does that type of religion (or spirituality) deserve the status of knowledge? Can it claim *valid* knowledge? Or even more specifically, does it deserve the status of *scientific* knowledge? From our previous discussion, we know that what the question really means is this: are religious phenomena (phenomena of levels 4 and 5) such that they can become a proper *domain* for the scientific *method?*

My own conclusion is that all domains (levels 1–5) contain certain features or deep structures that are open to scientific investigation, because *all* domains are open to *experiential* disclosure. There is religious *experience* just as certainly as there is psychological experience and sensory experience. In that sense, we can speak of the science of religion just as legitimately as we speak of the science of psychology, biology, or physics.

Now by "religious experience" I mean the direct apprehension, in consciousness, of those phenomena we have called class *D* and class *E,* or the domains of soul and spirit. The central feature of those domains are not only experienceable, they are *public,* because consciousness can be *trained* to apprehend those domains (this training is called meditation or contemplation), and a trained consciousness is a public, shareable, or intersubjective consciousness, or it couldn't be trained in the first place. Simply because religious experience is apprehended in an "interior" fashion does not mean it is merely private knowledge, any more than the fact that mathematics and logic are seen inwardly, by the mind's eye, makes them merely private fantasies without public import. Mathematical knowledge is public knowledge to all equally trained mathematicians; just so, contemplative knowledge is public knowledge to all equally trained contemplatives. The preposterous claim that all religious experience is private and noncommunicable is stopped dead by, to give only one example, the *transmission* of Buddha's enlightenment all the way down to the present-day Buddhist masters.

This does not mean that all so-called "religious knowledge" passes the scientific (experiential and public) test. Dogmatic assertions, idiosyncratic preferences, personal and intentionally private beliefs, and nontestable theological claims—these may or may not be valid, but they are not scientifically demonstrable or refutable; they are, that is, nonscientific or non-testable knowledge-claims. On the other hand, virtually all the Eastern texts on meditation and yoga, and virtually all the Western texts on contemplation and interior prayer, can legitimately be called *scientific treatises* dealing (principally) with levels 4 and 5; they contain rules and *experiments,* which, if followed correctly, disclose to consciousness phenomena (or data) of the classes we have called *D* and *E,* phenomena that can be as easily checked with (confirmed or refuted by) equally trained peers as geometric theorems can be checked with (confirmed or refuted by) other equally trained mathematicians.

What about the conflict or battle between science and religion?

There *is* a real, genuine, and important battle here, I believe, but it is not properly stated as a battle between science and religion.

To begin with, we have seen that there is a difference between "domain" and "method," and thus we are really dealing with two completely different scales, so to speak. On the one hand, there are the natural and important differences between the lower and upper domains of existence. On the other hand, there are the natural and important differences between genuine or verifiable and dogmatic or nonverifiable knowledge-claims.

Unfortunately, when these scales are confused or equated, then science comes to mean "lower *and* genuine," and religion comes to mean "upper *and* nonsensical." The battle, thus stated, can *never* be resolved, because both parties are half-right and half-wrong. Properly speaking, there is no battle whatsoever between the lower and upper dimensions of reality (since the latter transcend but include the former). There is, however, a very real battle between genuine versus nonsensical knowledge-claims, but this battle is *not* a battle between lower and upper domains of existence. It is a battle that reappears on *every* realm of existence (levels 1–5) and concerns knowledge-claims that are open to experiential test versus those that are dogmatic and nonverifiable (or nonrefutable).

Thus, if by "science" you mean the study of the lower, base, or natural levels of existence (usually 1/2/3), and if by "religion" you mean an approach to the upper, higher, or "supernatural" levels (usually 4/5), then the only *real* battle is between genuine science and bogus science, and between genuine religion and bogus religion ("genuine" meaning "experientially verifiable/refutable"; "bogus" meaning "dogmatic, nonexperiential, nonverifiable/refutable"). *There is bogus or pseudo-science just as much as there is bogus or pseudo-religion,* and the only worthwhile battle is between genuine and bogus, not between science and religion.

Accordingly, both genuine science and genuine religion are allied against pseudo, nonexperientially grounded, dogmatic knowledge-claims (which infect all domains), which is why, at this point, we can just as easily refer to this methodological alliance as the science of physics, the science of biology, the science of psychology, and the science of religion (or spirituality). Here "science" refers not to any particular domain, high or low, but to a methodology based on experiential evidence and not dogmatic assertions, a methodology we want to apply to all genuine knowledge-claims on all levels; this is what we mean by the terms "higher" or "spiritual" or "geist" *sciences.* In no case, however, is there a genuine battle between science and religion, only a battle between experiential science and religion versus dogmatic science and religion.

Are the methods of the mental or spiritual sciences the same as those of the physical sciences?

Yes and no. Yes, in that the central methodological criterion—namely, that all knowledge-claims ultimately be settled on the basis of direct appeal to experience—is identical in all the genuine sciences, physical, biological, psychological, and spiritual. No, in that each domain has quite different characteristics, and thus the actual application of the scientific method in each domain takes on the form, as it were, of that domain.

For example, one of the dominant characteristics of the physical realm is its extension in space-time. The easiest way to deal with extension is to *measure* it; thus, measurement is very prominent in the physical sciences (this aspect of the physical sciences was discovered independently by Kepler and Galileo, in 1605, and so they are properly referred to as the fathers of modern physical science). By the time we get to the mental-psychological level, however, quantity and extension largely give way to quality and intention; therefore, quantitative measurement, although still applicable in certain areas, is not nearly so prominent. A typical knowledge-claim in the physical sciences is, "A proton has two thousand times the mass of an electron," whereupon we proceed to test the claim through complicated instrumental procedures.

On the other hand, a typical knowledge-claim in the mental realm is, "The meaning of *Hamlet* is such and such," which we then *test* in the hermeneutic circle (or the intersubjective realm of communicative exchange) of those who have read and studied *Hamlet.* Bad interpretations can be rebuffed by the hermeneutic circle, thus assuring a quasi-objective status for all genuine truth-claims. But here we are not so much judging extension as we are intention, so measurement plays a minor role.

Likewise, a typical knowledge-claim in the spiritual realm is, "Does a dog have Buddha-nature?" There is a specific, repeatable, verifiable, experiential test and answer to that question—a bad answer can most definitely be refuted—but it has virtually nothing to do with physical measurement or mental intentionality.[20]

This overall approach, then, assures us of a unity-in-diversity of the knowledge quest: a unity in methodological criteria, or a unity in knowledge itself, underlying a diversity in its objects, or a diversity in its particular applications. Put somewhat poetically: unity in *knowledge* underlying diversity of *phenomena.* I say "poetically," because if we push that statement very hard, it will collapse in paradox (simply because it ultimately ascribes to Spirit the qualification of "underlying unity," which violates *shunyata*). But let us temporarily ignore that in order to ask the central question of this anthology: with reference to the actual data or phenomena of physics and mysticism, are there any important parallels? In other words,

Are there any significant parallels between the phenomena disclosed by physics and those disclosed by mysticism?

Here we are not discussing the abstract, central criteria of all genuine sciences, whether physical or psychological or mystical—we have already said that those share a similar form. We are discussing the findings, the results, the data, the phenomena of the physical and mystical sciences, and asking whether *those* share any significant parallels. And there, whether we define mysticism as knowledge of spirit or as knowledge of Spirit, the answer is still "None (or at best, a few rather trivial ones)." *This is exactly the same conclusion we reached in the first section of this essay,* the conclusion that reflected the common or majority agreement of the physicists included in this volume, although we arrived at it by entirely different means. Then we took a rather steep or drastic approach, following the course of most of the physicists themselves. In light of our more extended discussion in this section, we can reach the same conclusion by a slower yet steadier route.

First, if by mysticism we mean a direct and experiential knowledge of the spiritual realm (level 5), then of course there will be some sort of parallels between the findings of physics and mysticism, simply because we can expect some sort of similarities, however meager, between levels 1 and 5. But these similarities are rather trivial when compared with the profound differences between these dimensions of Being (as I will explain in a moment), and, further, overemphasizing these parallels invites a total confusion of the two object-domains in question.

The parallels themselves—to judge from popular expositions—usually boil down to some sort of statement about "all things being mutually interrelated in a holistic way." But if that statement is not outright wrong, it is still trivial. Personally, I believe it to be wrong: all things are not mutually or symmetrically or equivalently interrelated; in the realm of manifestation, hierarchical and asymmetrical relationships are, as we have seen, at least as important as mutual or equivalent relationships. In the realm of time, for instance, the past has affected the present but the present has no effect on the past (e.g., what Columbus did most definitely affects you, but what you do has no effect on Columbus; there is nothing mutual in that relationship at all).

But even supposing that statement is true, it is still trivial, for it tells us nothing the old physics couldn't tell us. According to Newtonian physics, everything in the universe was related to everything else by instantaneous action-at-a-distance, a holistic concept if ever there was one. (Incidentally, there is an excellent book on the new physics—Heinz Pagel's *The Cosmic Code*[21]—which is the only book I can unreservedly recommend on the topic. In addition to a superb explanation and discussion of the new physics, it points out—correctly I believe—that Newtonian physics is actually much closer in many ways to Eastern mysticism than is quantum physics.) I could go on in this fashion, examining each of the supposed parallels between the findings of the new physics and those of mysticism, but the conclusion would be the same: where the alleged parallels are not simply the result of over-generalizations or foggy semantic conclusions, they are either downright wrong or trivial.

And if, finally, by mysticism we mean a direct knowledge of and as Spirit (or Ground), there are no parallels whatsoever between physics (old or new) and mysticism, for the simple reason that Spirit as Ground has no qualities with which it can be compared, contrasted, or paralleled. In order to compare Spirit with, say, the findings of physics, Spirit has to be assigned *some sort* of qualifications or set-apart characteristics, at which point it ceases absolutely to be Spirit.

But aren't physics and mysticism simply two different approaches to the same underlying Reality?

No, no, yes, and no. If by "Reality" you mean spirit (or level 5), then physics and mysticism are not dealing with the same reality at all, but with two very different levels or dimensions of reality, a confusion of which is wholly unwarranted.

If by "Reality" you mean Spirit as Ground, then no valid comparisons can be stated at all, and only Wittgenstein's commandment remains: "Whereof one cannot speak, thereof one must be silent."

If by "underlying Reality" you mean the Totality of everything that is, then obviously physics and mysticism are parts or aspects of that Totality; all you have done is invent a trivial tautology. I am rather perversely in favor of the shock value that that tautology has on orthodox scientists, but unfortunately (and quite correctly), when they investigate it more closely, they find only bogus scientific claims supporting allegedly mystical claims, which, in the long run, helps neither genuine science nor genuine mysticism.

Finally, if by "one underlying Reality" you explicitly mean Spirit, then you are attributing the particular quality of "oneness" to Spirit, which is exactly, as we have seen, the way *not* to think about Spirit. And yet it is usually that attribution that is at the heart of the considerable success of the popular "physics/mysticism" books. When Charles II was asked to explain the popularity of a rather obscure preacher, he replied, "I suppose his nonsense suits their nonsense."

Before we leave this topic, let me give a concrete example to make my somewhat difficult semantic distinctions as clear as possible. We have seen that each level in the Great Nest transcends but includes its predecessor, such that level 1 could be represented as A, level 2 as $A + B$, level 3 as $A + B + C$, and so on. There are more significant parallels between level 1 and 2, or 2 and 3, or 3 and 4, than there are between, say, 1 and 4 or 1 and 5—simply because the former are "closer" in terms of structural similarities and number of shared characteristics. But my point: physics has combed the material realm (level 1) and found four—and only four—major "forces": gravitational, electromagnetic, strong nuclear, and weak nuclear. By the time we reach level 2, or biological systems, we still have those four forces in effect, but we have *added* the forces of food-desire, sex-desire, water-desire, motor capacity, plus other rather elementary drives commonly called instincts. As we move to the psychological (level 3), we *add* the forces or motivations of jealousy, hope, envy, pride, guilt, remorse, justice, artistic endeavor, morality—to name a very few. And in the spiritual realms (4 and 5), we have the added forces of universal love, compassion, grace, skillful means, radical intuition, the ten *paramitas*—to also name a very few.

Now there is a legitimate type of endeavor that attempts to isolate certain commonalities between *all* these forces, but already you can see how extremely careful we must be in this endeavor. After all, there are (as far as we know) only four forces operating on level 1; by the time we reach level 5, we have added hundreds, perhaps thousands, of new and different operative forces, and whatever parallels we find between the four physical forces and the hundreds or thousands of higher forces will obviously be of the most meager variety imaginable. *I am absolutely in favor of that endeavor;* it is simply that every effort I have seen in this direction (including General System Theory) turns out to be either wrong (i.e., based on category errors) or trivial (i.e., noncommitally abstract), and personally, I suspect that most of the genuine parallels (we call them "analog laws") will be, as I also said, rather meager.

And so that, to summarize, is why virtually all of the physicists in this volume concluded that, no matter how you slice the ontological pie, the findings of modern physics and mysticism have very little in common, other than the trivial tautology that they are all different aspects of the same reality.

But—and I should like to end on this note—every physicist in this volume was completely in favor of interdisciplinary dialogue. After intensively studying all their works for this anthology, I personally believe they would disagree with virtually all of the popular books on "physics-and-mysticism," but they would wholeheartedly applaud and support those efforts to come to terms with, we might say, the fundamental quantum questions of existence. The individuals in this volume were physicists, but they were also philosophers and mystics, and they couldn't help but muse on how the findings of physics might fit into a larger or overall worldview. I would estimate that, despite the fact (or actually because of the fact) that their common conclusion was that the domains of physics and mysticism have little in common, nonetheless, ninety percent of this volume contains ideas and opinions generated precisely by the dialogue between these two extreme limits of the Great Nest of Being. All of that, it is my own belief, is exactly as it should be. Their aim was to find physics *compatible* with a larger or mystical worldview—not confirming and not proving, but simply not contradicting. All of them, in their own ways, achieved considerable success.

Settle back now for some of the finest dialogues between physics and philosophy and religion ever authored by the human spirit.

Note

In the preface I said that the attempt to "prove" mysticism with modern physics is not only wrong but actually detrimental to genuine mysticism. Now the attempt itself is perfectly understandable—those who have had a direct glimpse of the mystical *know* how real and how profound it is. But it is so hard to convince skeptics of this fact, that it is extremely tempting and appealing to be able to claim that physics—the "really real" science—actually supports mysticism. I, in my earliest writings, did exactly that. But it *is* an error, and it is detrimental, meaning, in the long run it causes much more harm than good, and for the following reasons: (1) It confuses temporal, relative, finite truth with eternal timeless truth. Fritjof Capra has, I believe, considerably modified his views, but in *The Tao of Physics,* for instance, he put much stake in bootstrap theory (which says there are no irreducible things, only self-consistent relationships) and equated this with the Buddhist mystical doctrine of mutual interpenetration. But nowadays most physicists believe there are irreducible things (quarks, leptons, gluons) that arise out of broken symmetries. Does Buddha therefore lose his enlightenment? To repeat Bernstein, "To hitch a religious philosophy to a contemporary science is a sure route to its obsolescence." And *that* is detrimental. (2) It encourages the belief that in order to achieve mystical awareness all one need do is learn a new worldview; since physics and mysticism are simply two different approaches to the same reality, why bother with years of arduous meditation? Just read *The Tao of Physics.* This was obviously not Capra's intent, merely one of the unforeseen effects. (3) In the greatest irony of all, this whole approach is profoundly *reductionistic.* It says, in effect: since all things are ultimately made of subatomic particles, and since subatomic particles are mutually interrelated and holistic, then all things are holistically one, just like mysticism says. But all things are *not* ultimately made of subatomic particles; all things, including subatomic particles, are ultimately made of God. And the material realm, far from being the most significant is the least significant: it has less Being than life, which has less Being than mind, which has less Being than soul, which has less Being than spirit. Physics is simply the study of the realm of least-Being. Claiming that all things are ultimately made of subatomic particles is thus the most reductionistic stance imaginable! I said this is ironic, because it is exactly the opposite of the obviously good intent of these New Age writers, who are trying to help mysticism while in fact they have just sunk it. The extreme (but often subtle and hidden) reductionism of this view horrifies even orthodox philosophers and scientists. Stephen Jay Gould, for instance, in a very thoughtful and sympathetic review of Capra's *The Turning Point,* finally stood back aghast: "Consider the peculiarity of that last sentence: 'the subatomic particles—and therefore, ultimately, all parts of the universe. . . .' The self-styled holist and antireductionist [i.e., Capra] is finally caught in his own parochialism after all. He has followed the oldest of the reductionist strategies. As it is with the structure of physics, so it must be, by extrapolation, with all of nature. You don't exit from this [reductionistic] trap by advocating holism at the lowest level. The very assertion that this lowest level, whatever its nature, represents the essence of reality, *is* the ultimate reductionist argument." Gould then goes on to point out that modern biology, psychology, and sociology work with "entities in a sequence of levels with unique explanatory principles emerging at each more inclusive plateau. This hierarchical perspective must take seriously the principle that phenomena of one level cannot automatically be extrapolated to work in the same way as others." In other words, modern orthodox scientists and philosophers are simply rediscovering the Great Chain of Being! But it is embarrassing, to say the least, for them to have to point out the blatant reductionism in the New Age "antireductionists." And this is *detrimental,* as I said, because it further alienates and polarizes the orthodox theorists who, I believe, really want to be open to hierarchical-transcendentalism, if it is presented carefully and nonreductionistically. As it is now, most new-age approaches simply irritate the orthodox, not because these approaches are mystical but, to the contrary, because they are so reductionistic! Thus Gould, who started out his review of *The Turning Point* by saying that "This enormously right-minded general theme surely wins my approval," ended it with: "I found myself getting more and more annoyed with his book, with its facile analogies, its distrust of reason, its invocation of fashionable notions. In some respects, I feel closer to rational Cartesians [he despises them] than to Capra's California brand of ecology" (*New York Review of Books,* March 3, 1983). I think Gould is too harsh on Capra; my point is that Capra is one of the most careful of the new-age writers, and yet even his approach is reductionistic enough to shock poor Gould into apoplexy. And the attempt continues: Arthur Young thinks absolute spirit is a photon. But wait! French physicist Jean Charon, in *The Unknown Spirit,* has just demonstrated that spirit is an electron! And, as I now write this, *God and the New Physics* has just been released. . . .

References

1. Interview contained in M. Planck, *Where Is Science Going?* (New York: Norton, 1932), p. 209.
2. Sir Arthur Stanley Eddington, *The Nature of the Physical World* (New York: Macmillan, 1929).
3. Sir Arthur Stanley Eddington, *New Pathways in Science,* (New York: Macmillan, 1935), pp. 307–8.
4. Erwin Schroedinger, *Science, Theory, and Man* (New York: Dover, 1957), p. 204.
5. Erwin Schroedinger, *Nature and the Greeks* (Cambridge University Press, 1954), p. 8.
6. Quoted in W. Heisenberg, *Physics and Beyond* (New York: Harper and Row, 1971), pp. 82–83.

7. J. Jeans, in A. Einstein et al., *Living Philosophies* (New York: Simon & Schuster, 1931), p. 117.
8. Niels Bohr, *Atomic Physics and Human Knowledge* (New York: Wiley, 1958), p. 74.
9. Quoted in W. Heisenberg, *Physics and Beyond,* p. 88.
10. Louis de Broglie, *Matter and Light* (New York: Dover, 1946), p. 252.
11. *E. Schroedinger, Nature and the Greeks,* p. 15.
12. N. Bohr, *Atomic Theory and the Description of Nature* (Cambridge University Press, 1961), p. 77.
13. Sir James Jeans, *Physics and Philosophy,* pp. 15–17.
14. A. Eddington, *The Nature of the Physical World,* p. 282.
15. Ibid.
16. E. Schroedinger, *Mind and Matter* (Cambridge University Press, 1958).
17. Sir James Jeans, *The Mysterious Universe* (Cambridge University Press, 1931), p. 111.
18. A. Eddington, *Science and the Unseen World* (New York: Macmillan, 1929).
19. I have dealt with all this in greater detail; see K. Wilber, *Eye to Eye* (New York: Doubleday/Anchor, 1983) [CW3].
20. Ibid.
21. H. Pagels, *The Cosmic Code* (New York: Bantam, 1982).

Biographical Sketches

The following sections are the headnotes to the selections collected in Quantum Questions, *included here to provide a summary of the contents.*

Werner Heisenberg (1901–1976)

In the summer of 1925, suffering from a bout of hay fever and exhausted from wrestling with the perplexities of atomic spectral lines, Werner Heisenberg—then only twenty-four years old—took a short vacation from the Physics Institute at Gottingen University, where he was studying with Max Born, and traveled to the hills of Helgoland. There, in one fevered day and night, he invented what was to be known as matrix quantum mechanics. With the help of Max Born, Pascual Jordan, Paul Dirac, and Wolfgang Pauli, matrix quantum mechanics was formalized (one of the results of which was the famous Heisenberg Uncertainty Principle, which, in plain language, says that the more we know about half of the subatomic world, the less we can know about the other half). Erwin Schroedinger, working independently and along different lines, developed a wave mechanics; these two formalisms were quickly shown to be equivalent, and, almost at one stroke, modern quantum mechanics was born. In 1932 Heisenberg was awarded the Nobel Prize in Physics for his crucial and brilliant contributions.

The selections are taken from *Physics and Beyond* (New York: Harper and Row, 1971), *Across the Frontiers* (New York: Harper and Row, 1974), and *The Physicist's Conception of Nature* (New York: Harcourt and Brace, 1955). Heisenberg's central point is that physics can only make statements "about strictly limited relations that *are only valid within the framework of those limitations* [his italics]." If we want to go beyond physics, however, and begin to philosophize, then the worldview that can most easily *explain* modern physics is that not of Democritus but of Plato. Heisenberg was an excellent philosopher (probably, with Eddington, the most accomplished in this volume), and a metaphysician or mystic of the Pythagorean-Platonic variety. Capable of being rigorously analytical and empirical, he nonetheless despised mere positivism—or the attempt to be *only* analytical and empirical—and thus in the opening section, Heisenberg, Pauli, and Bohr lament the attempt of philosophy to ape physics.

Erwin Schroedinger (1887–1961)

At about the same time that Heisenberg et al. were developing matrix mechanics, Erwin Schroedinger independently discovered a form of "wave mechanics" that was quickly shown to be equivalent to, but in many respects simpler and more elegant than, the matrix mechanics. It was therefore "Schroedinger's wave equation" that soon became the heart of modern quantum mechanics and its most widely used mathematical tool. For this seminal work, Schroedinger was awarded the 1933 Nobel Prize in Physics.

The selections are taken from *My View of the World* (Cambridge University Press ["C.U.P."], 1964), *Mind and Matter* (C.U.P., 1958), *Nature and the Greeks* (C.U.P., 1947). Schroedinger's mystical insight, I believe, was probably the keenest of any in this volume, and his eloquence was matched only by Eddington's. The last selection (chapter 10), in particular, contains some of the finest and most poetic mystical statements ever penned, and stands eloquently as its own remark.

Albert Einstein (1879–1955)

Albert Einstein is generally regarded, quite simply, as the greatest physicist ever to have lived. His contributions to physics are legion: special and general relativity theory, quantum photoelectric effect, Brownian movement theory, the immortal $E = mc^2$. He was awarded the Nobel Prize in Physics in 1921.

The selections are taken from *Ideas and Opinions* (New York: Crown Publishers, 1954). Einstein's mysticism has been described as a cross between Spinoza and Pythagoras; there is a central order to the cosmos, an order that can be directly apprehended by the soul in mystical union. He devoutly believed that although science, religion, art, and ethics are necessarily distinct endeavors, it is wonderment in the face of "the Mystery of the Sublime" that properly motivates them all.

Prince Louis de Broglie (1892–1987)

Louis de Broglie is best known for his theory of "matter waves," the crucial formulations of which he presented in two papers of September 1923, while he was still a student. These papers became part of his doctoral thesis, a copy of which was sent to Einstein, who, much impressed, widely circulated the ideas. Erwin Schroedinger heard of de Broglie's thesis—that moving electrons produce waves—and that directly led him to develop the Schroedinger wave equations so central to quantum mechanics. The actual existence of matter waves was experimentally verified in 1927, and two years later de Broglie received the Nobel Prize in Physics.

The selections are taken from *Physics and Microphysics* (New York: Pantheon, 1955). In the first section, de Broglie argues (as did Einstein) that all genuine science is motivated by what, in fact, are spiritual ideals. But science itself cannot pronounce on these ideals, and thus, in the second section, he argues that, in addition to science, we need "a supplement of the soul."

Sir James Jeans (1877–1946)

Sir James Jeans was a mathematician, physicist, and astronomer. He made fundamental contributions to the dynamical theory of gases, the mathematical theory of electromagnetism, the evolution of gaseous stars, the nature of nebulae—to name a few. He was knighted in 1924 and went on to become one of the most popular and prominent philosophers of science.

The selection is taken from *The Mysterious Universe* (Cambridge University Press, 1931). Sir Jeans concludes that, since we can only understand the physical world through mathematics, then we might rightly conclude that, to use his favorite phrase, "God is a mathematician, and the universe begins to look more like a great thought than a great machine."* He makes it very clear he is talking now as a philosopher, not a scientist, but his Pythagorean mysticism inspires a style that manages to embrace both with delight, rigor, and wit.

MAX PLANCK (1858–1947)

It was Max Planck's bold, brilliant, daring, and wholly unprecedented leap of genius that, in 1900, ushered in the entire quantum revolution, for it was Planck who hit upon the idea that nature is not continuous,

---

*We don't have to agree with everything Jeans said in order to point out that the idea of the physical realm being a "materialization of thought" has extremely wide support from the perennial philosophy. As Huston Smith points out in *Forgotten Truth,* the perennial philosophy has always maintained that matter is a crystallization or a precipitation of mind (ontologically, not chronologically). Actually, this "precipitation" process runs throughout the Great Chain of Being. With reference to the diagram in the Introduction [see page 259], we can explain it like this: If you start with the spiritual realm (level 5) and *subtract E,* you get soul; if you then *subtract D,* you get mind; subtract C and you get life; subtract *B* and you get matter. This *subtraction process* is a progressive precipitation of the lower from the higher, a process called "involution"; each junior dimension is thus a *reduced subset* of its senior dimension. The reverse of this subtraction, precipitation, or involution process is simply *evolution,* or the unfolding of successively senior dimensions from their prior or involuntary enfoldment in the lower domains (where they exist, as Aristotle would have it, in potentia, although nothing in the lower gives any evidence that a higher can break through it and emerge transcendentally beyond its domains). This is why evolution, vis-à-vis the lower, is an *addition* or *creative emergence* of successively higher domains from (or rather through) the junior dimensions. Involution, we may speculate, gave rise to the "Big Bang," where the material realm blew into existence via a concrete precipitation of the higher (although at this point still ontologically implicit) realms, and the universe has been evolving back or upwards ever since, producing thus far matter, then life, then mind (and in some saints and sages, a *conscious* realization or concrescence of soul and the spirit).

The significant point: every physicist in this volume was profoundly struck by the fact that the natural realm (levels 1 and 2) obeys in some sense the laws or forms of mathematics, or, in general, obeys some sort of archetypal mental-forms (which reside at levels 3 and 4). But that is exactly what would be expected if the natural realms are a reduced subset or precipitate of the mind-soul realms; the child obeys its ontic parents. Heisenberg and Pauli looking for the archetypal forms which underlie the material realm; de Broglie claiming mind-forms had to precede (ontically) matter forms; Einstein and Jeans finding a central mathematical form to the cosmos—all of that becomes perfectly understandable in this light.

Because the natural realms are a *reduced* subset of, or are ontically *less than,* the mental-soul realms, then all fundamental natural processes can be essentially represented mathematically, but not all mathematical forms have a material applica-

but rather comes in discrete packets or quanta. Justly regarded as the father of modern quantum theory, Planck was awarded the Nobel Prize in Physics in 1918.

Of Planck, who was deeply respected and loved by all his colleagues, Albert Einstein had these memorable words: "The longing to behold harmony is the source of the inexhaustible patience and perseverance with which Planck has devoted himself to the most general problems of our science, refusing to let himself be diverted to more grateful and more easily attained ends. I have often heard colleagues try to attribute this attitude of his to extraordinary will-power and discipline—wrongly, in my opinion. The state of mind which enables a man to do work of this kind is akin to that of the religious worshipper or the lover; the daily effort comes from no deliberate intention or program, but straight from the heart. There he sits, our beloved Planck, and smiles inside himself at

---

tion. That is, of the almost infinite number of mathematical schemes existing implicitly in the mental-soul realms, only a rather small, finite number actually crystallize or precipitate in and as the material realm. Put another way, because the material realms are ontically much less than the mental, only the relatively *simpler* mental-soul forms show up in, or precipitate as, the material realm. And this leads exactly to *the* guiding principle that every one of these physicists followed in trying to discover the mental laws governing material phenomena: of all possible mathematical schemes that might explain physical data, *choose the simplest and most elegant.* Einstein put it perfectly: "Nature is the *realization* [crystallization or precipitation] of the simplest conceivable mathematical ideas." This does not mean that matter *is* an idea, pure and simple; it means that whatever Matter is, is a reduced, subtracted, or condensed version of whatever Idea is. Matter is a Platonic shadow, if you wish, but a shadow that, as Jeans says, bears *some* of the forms of the ontically higher domains, in this case, mathematical forms.

Finally, this explains why all these physicists maintained that mathematical laws cannot be deduced from mere sensory-physical-empirical data: you cannot deduce or derive the higher from the lower. To *check* whether a particular mathematical scheme correctly applies to some physical realm, we must use the physical senses (or their instrumental extensions); to *find* that mathematical scheme in the first place, however, we use mind and only mind. What we are doing (using the eye of reason) is searching through the mental universe to see which schemes or forms might have crystallized in and as this particular physical universe (which we then check with the eye of flesh). Thus the criteria for establishing the truth of a physical theory: vis-à-vis mind, it must be *coherent* (free of self-contradiction); vis-à-vis physical data, it must *correspond* (match or fit evidence); if two theories equally meet those criteria (which happens very often), then choose the simpler and more elegant. The empiricists want only correspondence theories of truth; the idealists, only coherence theories; whereas both are equally important, and simple elegance or beauty the final crown. I think this is why Heisenberg so often quoted "The simple is the seal of the true" and "Beauty is the splendor of the truth."

my childish playing-about with the lantern of Diogenes. Our affection for him needs no thread-bare explanation. May the love of science continue to illumine his path in the future and lead him to the solution of the most important problems in present-day physics, which he has himself posed and done so much to solve."

The selections are taken from *Where is Science Going?* (New York: Norton, 1932).

Wolfgang Pauli (1900–1958)

In terms of sheer intellectual brilliance, Wolfgang Pauli was probably second to no physicist of this or any period (according to Max Born, Pauli's genius exceeded even that of Einstein). Intellectual sloppiness or logical inconsistency would bring down the wrath of Pauli on the poor soul unfortunate enough to be its author. He was a brilliant and ruthless critic of ideas, and virtually every physicist of his generation looked to the mind of Wolfgang Pauli as one of *the* mandatory tests to pass if a theory had any chance of survival. Pauli's own positive contributions were profound and numerous, including the famous "exclusion principle" and the prediction of the existence of the neutrino some two decades before it was discovered. He received the Nobel Prize in Physics in 1945.

In spite of, or rather precisely because of, Pauli's analytical and intellectual brilliance, he insisted that rationality had to be supplemented with the mystical. I had originally planned to include in this section Pauli's essay, "The Influence of Archetypal Ideas on Kepler's Construction of Scientific Theories," which sets forth his Platonic-Pythagorean worldview, and which was written in collaboration with C. G. Jung. But his lifetime friend and colleague Werner Heisenberg wrote a beautiful summary of Pauli's position, which is not only briefer but considerably more elegant reading, and so I have presented that instead ("Wolfgang Pauli's Philosophical Outlook," chap. 3 in *Across the Frontiers*).

Sir Arthur Eddington (1882–1944)

Sir Arthur Eddington made important contributions to the theoretical physics of the motion, evolution, and internal constitution of stellar systems. He was one of the first theorists to grasp fully relativity theory, of which he became a leading exponent. No mere armchair theorist, Eddington led the famous expedition that photographed the solar eclipse which offered the first proof of Einstein's relativity theory. For his outstanding contributions, he was knighted in 1930.

The selections are taken from *Science and the Unseen World* (New York: Macmillan, 1929), *New Pathways in Science* (New York: Macmillan, 1935), and *The Nature of the Physical World* (New York: Macmillan, 1929). Of all the physicists in this volume, Eddington was probably the most eloquent writer; with Heisenberg, the most accomplished philosopher; and with Schroedinger, the most penetrating mystic. Moreover, he possessed an exquisite intellectual wit, evidenced on almost every page of his writings (it sometimes takes the reader a while to realize just how humorous Eddington is being, so set your mind in that direction now). I have divided his topics into three rough sections, the first dealing with the shadowy limitations of physical science, the second with the necessity to equate the reality behind the shadows with *consciousness* itself, and the third, his famous defense of mysticism.

SOCIOCULTURAL EVOLUTION

Sociocultural Evolution

IN THE WAKE of my most recent books, *Up from Eden* and *A Sociable God*, a few criticisms have been raised. Dick Anthony has gathered these together, added his own, and presented them in a privately circulated paper. This is my response.[1]

PART I: PROGRESS AND EVOLUTION

The Idea of Progress

I have rarely, if ever, used the term "progress"; I have used the terms "development" and "evolution." There is a big difference: "progress" tends to imply that development is necessarily and in all ways a positive or beneficial affair, an idea I absolutely reject. "Evolution" or "development," on the other hand, implies that, in the course of the emergence or growth of various phenomena, there is indeed a discernible differentiation and increase in certain structures and functions, but these increases *can* be used malevolently as well as benevolently. I do believe in development or evolution—biological, psychological, sociological, and religious; but I do not automatically equate this with "progress" or "enlightenment." As I tried to demonstrate in *Up from Eden*, "We tend to be much too glib about our rise up from the apes, imagining each new evolutionary step as a wonderful leap forward that brought new potentials, new intelligence, and new abilities. That is in one sense quite true, but it is equally true that each new evolutionary step forward brought new responsibilities, new terrors, new anxieties, and new guilts. . . . In short, there is a price to be paid for every increase in consciousness, and only that perspective, I believe, can place humankind's evolutionary history in the proper context. Most of the accounts of humanity's evolution err to one side or the other of that equation. They either overemphasize the growth aspect, seeing human evolution as nothing but a series of great advances and great leaps forward, thereby ignoring the fact that evolution is not a happy-go-lucky series of sweetness-and-light promotions but a painful process of growth. Or they tend to the opposite direction and, seeing the agony and despair of humankind, look back nostalgically to that lost Eden of innocence, prior to self-consciousness, wherein humanity slumbered with the beasts in blissful ignorance. This view tends to see every evolutionary step out of Eden as being a crime. With very persuasive evidence, they show that war, hunger, exploitation, slavery, oppression, guilt, and poverty largely came into existence with the rise of civilization and culture and man's increasing 'evolution.' Primal man, on the whole, suffered few of those problems—thus, if modern, civilized man is a product of evolution, then please give us less of it. . . . What I am saying is that, in the main, both views are correct."

In other words, I most definitely believe in development or evolution, but I do not automatically equate this with so-called "progress," for there are "good" *and* "bad" aspects to any developmental sequence. In individual psychological development, for example, a three-year-old child does not yet possess the capacity for higher or formal reasoning (abstract-conceptual thought). When this capacity emerges (usually during adolescence), it can be used to engage in philosophy, sociology, abstract science, and so on (some of the "good" aspects of higher cognitive development); but it can also be used to plot revenge, to malevolently oppress others, to harbor intricately or conceptually evil designs (some of the potentially "bad" aspects of higher development not found at lower stages). Moreover, the faculties of higher development—in this example, reasoning—*can* be used to deny or *repress* the appropriate, necessary, and useful aspects of those functions that have already emerged at previous stages of development—such as free or spontaneous expression of prerational or bodily impulses and feelings (which the three-year-old child certainly possesses).

What I object to is this: with any developmental sequence, taking only the potentially "bad" aspects of increasing development and then using them either to damn the idea of development altogether or to embrace some sort of pseudo-romantic notion of a "lost Eden," a notion that all evolution is somehow necessarily decadent. This view, which is in my opinion a rather easy and cheap theoretical game to play, results from comparing only the "good" aspects of a lower stage with the potentially "bad" aspects of a higher stage and then summarily damning the idea of evolution altogether.

I have, up to this point, been discussing "evolution" in rather vague terms; I shall now endeavor to be more precise. To begin with, there seem to be four general theoretical stances toward "human evolution" itself (whether psychological, sociological, historical, or religious):

1. Decadence theories (e.g., Klagess)—Human evolution is viewed as being, for the most part, a devolutionary movement, with each "advance" actually involving a weakening or loss of vital faculties and their replacement by thinly rationalized substitutes.
2. Progress theories (e.g., Comte)—Human (anthropological) evolution is a progressive advancement marked almost entirely by positive gains and benefits that render previous stages and previous accomplishments largely worthless; previous stages are "primitive" in a pejorative sense, or are judged, not so much on their own merit, but as being "proto-scientific" or "crude" attempts at rational-technological endeavors.
3. Static theories (e.g., Lévi-Strauss)—These theories, in effect, tend to deny that profound qualitative social evolution occurs at all; i.e., the cognitive-emotional deep structures of human beings are viewed as being roughly the same everywhere, and roughly from the earliest times (traditional structuralism and traditional ethnomethodology, for example). "Primitive" thought forms and relations are viewed as being different from, but just as rich and complex as, modern thought forms. While cultural and anthropological changes are obviously admitted, the notion of ontically "higher" or "lower" stages of development is felt to be largely meaningless, and attempts to "evaluate" or "rank" psychosocial structures are usually charged with "ethnocentric bias."
4. Evolutionary theories (e.g., Habermas)—Human (cultural) development is viewed as a process of psychosocial evolution, generally governed by a developmental-logic, and generally (not always) showing increasing differentiation, increasing complexity of organization, qualitatively different modes of adaptation, etc. According to these theories, it is possible to speak of (and define) "higher" and "lower" stages of development, but every stage is viewed as a necessary, useful, or stage-specific event;

higher stages are "higher" only in the abstract, so that an automatic equation of evolution with progress is ruled out from the start.

These theories, although often adhered to individually or exclusively, are not necessarily incompatible in all respects. I am in some cases an evolutionary theorist, but I also believe that certain periods and certain aspects of evolutionary development show genuine progress; other periods, I believe, have shown definite decadence, decay, or regression. I further believe that, once they have emerged and solidified, the deep structures of a particular stage-level of psychosocial development are more or less universal and cross-cultural (and "static" or synchronic in that sense), although these deep structures themselves emerge only in the course of historical development or evolution, and, therefore, are very much molded by those temporal currents (they are a type of evolutionary memory or habit). These four views, then, are not radically distinct or necessarily incompatible; I have incorporated aspects of all of them in my overall view.

Dick Anthony, however, in attacking my view as one of "pure progress," lumps together all "progress theories" with all "evolutionary theories," and, in the rather easy task of dismissing naive progress theories, he seems to equally condemn all evolutionary theories. I know of no contemporary researcher who believes in simple progress theories. These theories were in vogue at the time of Comte, Tylor, and Frazer, but the two world wars, the threat of nuclear holocaust, impending ecological disasters, etc., have long ago put an end to all such happy notions of unadulterated progress.

But does this condemn *all* social evolutionary theories? Dick seems to think so. These theories, he confidently states, have "fallen on hard times recently. Most contemporary social theory is opposed to it." And much of my work, therefore, being evolutionary in nature, "would not be accepted by most contemporary social thinkers and scholars of religion. . . ."

While it is very true that a self-contradictory stance of radical egalitarianism and nonranking is sweeping many academic departments (self-contradictory because it claims itself to be the correct or better stance when no stance is supposed to be correct or better in the first place; it ranks nonranking as better than ranking), nonetheless some of the most promiment contemporary social and religious theorists rather courageously remain evolutionalists in the face of the leveling pressure. In order to clarify my own position, I will comment on some of the more notable examples.

Robert Bellah

Bellah's paper "Religious Evolution" is a classic delineation of five stages of religious evolution: primitive, archaic, historic, early modern, and modern. In *Up from Eden*, I roughly delineated seven major structure-stages of consciousness evolution (to date): archaic, magic, early mythic, late mythic, early rational, middle rational, and late rational; these stages match very closely with those of Bellah, though we naturally differ in details and emphasis, and though we developed our schemes independently. Bellah is not a cultural relativist (nor am I); nevertheless, he does reject the attempt to deduce values from this socioreligious evolutionary process ("I am not a relativist and I do think judgements of value can reasonably be made between religions, societies, or personalities. But the axis of that judgement is not provided by social evolution and if progress is used in an essentially ethical sense, then I for one will not speak of religious progress"). Rather, Bellah defines evolution "at any system level as a process of increasing differentiation and complexity of organization that endows the organism, social system, or whatever the unit in question may be with greater capacity to adapt to its environment, so that it is in some sense more autonomous relative to its environment than were its less complex ancestors . . . at each stage the freedom of personality and society has increased relative to the environing conditions. . . . This scheme of religious evolution has implied at almost every point a general theory of social evolution. . . ."

The fact that freedom, autonomy, and adaptive capacity increase at each stage of development sounds to me suspiciously as if some values are in fact embedded in evolution (as I believe). But I should only like to emphasize that, according to Bellah, "since it has been clear for a long time that levels of social and cultural complexity are best understood in an evolutionary framework, it seems inevitable that religion too must be considered in such a framework."

Jürgen Habermas

In my opinion, the most sophisticated sociologist now writing is Jürgen Habermas, and he has, among many other things, presented a very powerful "theory of social evolution." My own sociological writings have been deeply influenced by Habermas, and although I am far from being a strict Habermasian, I would like to briefly mention a few of his more cogent points and how I have recast or reconstructed them in my own works.

Habermas is generally regarded as the foremost theorist of the sociological school of "Critical Theory." "Critical," as Bleicher points out, "should be here taken to mean mainly the appraisal of existing states of affairs in view of standards that derive from the knowledge of something better that already exists as a potential or a tendency in the present." Although Habermas is deeply indebted to hermeneutics, he believes, contra traditional hermeneutics, that there exist external, universal, or "quasi-transcendental" standards by which the *level* of social evolution and communicative exchange can be adjudicated or "appraised." Part of these "quasi-transcendental" criteria (or "narrative foils") involve evolutionary or developmental *cognitive structures*, similar (but not identical) to those advanced by Piaget in cognitive developmental psychology. "The stimulus that encouraged me to investigate normative structures from the point of view of developmental logic," he writes, "also came from Piaget's genetic [evolutionary] structuralism, that is, from a conception which has overcome the traditional structuralist front against evolutionism [i.e., its traditional "static" or synchronic commitment] and has assimilated motifs of the theory of knowledge from Kant to Peirce."

Habermas argues—correctly, I believe—that neither hermeneutics nor functionalism can operate effectively without a theory of social evolution (contrary to many of their own expectations). "What is demanded is a level of analysis at which the connection between normative structures and steering problems becomes palpable. I find this level in a historically oriented analysis of social systems, which permits us to ascertain for a given case the range of tolerance within which the goal values of the system might vary without its continued existence being critically endangered. Ranges of variation for structural change obviously can be introduced only within the framework of a theory of social evolution." Furthermore, "Characterizations of contemporary society as industrial, post-industrial, technological, scientized, capitalist, late-capitalist, state-monopolistic, state-capitalistic, modern, post-modern, etc. spring from just as many developmental models that connect the present social formation with earlier ones."

As McCarthy points out, Habermas's "version of a theory of social evolution—relying as it does on a distinction among structural patterns, empirical learning mechanisms, and contingent boundary conditions—requires neither unilinearity, nor necessity, nor continuity, nor irreversibility in history." That, of course, removes it from any version of progress theories.

Notice, however, that "there is one feature of traditional philosophic conceptions of history that . . . is retained in Habermas's theory of social evolution: teleology. The very term *evolution* implies a conception of cumulative processes in which a direction can be perceived. Even if one does not subscribe to the necessity and irreversibility of evolutionary processes, any talk of directionality or hierarchical ordering seems to presuppose criteria of historical progress." In my own system, this telos is spiritual (or a drive toward increasing authenticity of Being); for Habermas, the telos is unrestrained communicative exchange (which, in my opinion, is simply the form that authenticity takes in the intermediate levels of evolution [levels 9–10, see below]; Habermas is correct in positing the necessity of telos, but his version of telos, I believe, is not radical enough to support the amount of work he wishes it to do; in other words, Habermas has set his teleological sights much too low—set them, in fact, at rationality, not spirituality). But the only point I would like to emphasize is that neither Habermas's nor my view of telos and developmental levels involves automatic progress theories. As only one example, Habermas points out that

> the amount of exploitation and repression by no means stands in inverse relation to these developmental levels. Social integration that is achieved through kinship relations and secured (in cases of conflict) through preconventional legal institutions belongs, from a developmental-logical perspective, to a lower stage than social integration that is achieved through relations of domination and secured (in cases of conflict) through conventional legal institutions. At the same time, despite this progress, the exploitation and repression that is *necessarily practiced* in political class societies must be regarded as a regression in comparison to the less considerable social inequalities that are *allowed* in kinship systems.

Thus, there is a "dialectic of progress"—although each new and higher level of psychosocial evolution or learning is generally released from the defining problems or conflicts of the previous social formation, it also introduces new problems that, in fact, may be of greater intensity.

As Habermas puts it, "The dialectic of progress manifests itself in the fact that with the acquisition of new problem-solving capacities new problem situations come to consciousness [compare *Eden*: "There is a price to be paid for every increase in consciousness"]. Thus we can attempt to interpret social evolution around those problems that are first called forth by evolutionary achievements."

Habermas traces (reconstructs) social evolution through several different developmental stages. The precise nature of these stages need not concern us; suffice it to say that, because he has explicitly pointed out the *general* correlations of his model with those of Loevinger, Piaget, and Kohlberg—as have I—that the general and substantial agreement of our two models is quite apparent (with the major exception that I have added several higher or spiritual-contemplative levels not recognized by Habermas, and I have grounded telos in *those* levels, not the rational-communicative or intermediate levels). I should also point out that Habermas's views are not ultimately dependent on those of Loevinger, Piaget, Kohlberg, etc.; it is simply that his own analyses (and mine) have found interesting convergences with those theorists (whose validity I will independently examine in a later section).

It is important to notice carefully the theoretical justifications for this developmental-evolutionary approach, for that is largely what is at stake in this discussion. Although Habermas has written extensively on this topic, the best short summary is given by Thomas McCarthy, and is worth quoting at length.

> The leading idea is that social evolution can be comprehended as a *learning process*, not in the sense of behavioristic psychology—which, Habermas feels, is not complex enough to grasp more than peripheral learning mechanisms—but in the sense of cognitive developmental psychology. Central to this approach is the notion of a *developmental logic* that incorporates a distinction between formally characterized levels of learning and the learning processes that are possible at each level. Drawing on these ideas, Habermas construes organizational principles of society as sociostructural innovations that institutionalize developmental-logical levels of learning; they establish the structural conditions for technical and practical learning processes at particular stages of development. Principles of organization [deep structures] circumscribe ranges of possibility [surface structures] within which institutional systems can vary, productive forces

> can be developed and utilized, and system complexity and steering capacity can be increased. The concrete embodiments of these abstract principles are the "institutional nuclei" that function as relations of production and determine the dominant form of social integration (for example, kinship relations in primitive societies, the political order in traditional societies, the economic system in liberal capitalist societies). Social evolution can then be thought of as a bidimensional learning process (cognitive/technical and moral/practical), the stages of which can be described structurally and ordered according to a developmental logic.

Although this must be carefully qualified, such a developmental logic, in the abstract, specifies:

> An irreversible sequence of discrete and increasingly complex developmental stages, whereby no stage can be passed over and each higher stage implies or presupposes the previous stages. (This does not exclude regressions, overlaps, arrested developments, and the like). Stages are constructed wholes that differ qualitatively from one another; phase-specific schematic can be ordered in an invariant and hierarchically structured sequence; no later phase can be attained before earlier ones have been passed through, and elements of earlier phases are preserved, transformed, and reintegrated in the later. In short, the developmental-logical approach requires the specification of a hierarchy of structured wholes in which the later, more complex, and more encompassing developmental stages presuppose and build upon the earlier.

I had embarked upon a similar project long before I learned of Habermas's work; indeed, *Up from Eden* was conceived and completed with only the most cursory knowledge of and reference to Habermas (*A Sociable God*, on the other hand, devotes an entire chapter to him). But it is instructive that, although we started from quite different directions and disciplines, and with quite different resources and orientations, we both arrived at an essentially compatible core thesis: a developmental logic, the notion of "quasi-universal" and hierarchic structure-stages, the "dialectic of progress" (as a "dialectic of suffering"), phase-specific schematic, etc.

There is, of course, only one way such a developmental-structural theory of social evolution can succeed—namely, in a careful distinction between the "quasi-universal" or *deep structures* of a level of development and the contingent, variable, or *surface structures* of that stage. Although Habermas rarely uses those terms, nor are his ideas on the topic precisely those of my own, he nevertheless has clearly recognized and responded to the problem—"the idea being [as McCarthy continues] that the universals of social evolution and the ordering principles of a developmental logic must be formulated at a level abstract enough to avoid social and historical specificity. Within such a general framework, it might then be possible to take account of this specificity in terms of particular empirical mechanisms, initial and boundary conditions, and so forth. In other words Habermas is proposing the combination of a genetic-structural level of analysis with an empirical-historical level of analysis in order to meet both developmental-logical and empirical conditions of adequacy."

Toward this end, Habermas utilizes the concept of a "social formation" and the hypothesis that any given social formation is determined by a fundamental principle of organization (i.e., deep structure, or basic limiting and defining principle). As he words it,

> By principle of organization I understand those innovations which become possible through learning processes that can be reconstructed in a developmental logic, and which institutionalize a new societal level of learning. The organizational principle of a society circumscribes ranges of possibility; in particular, it determines within which structures changes in the system of institutions are possible; to what extent the available productive capacities can be socially utilized or the development or new productive forces can be stimulated; and thereby also to what degrees system complexity and steering performances can be heightened. A principle of organization consists of such abstract regulations that within the social formation determined by it several functionally equivalent modes of production are permitted.

To these deep structures or basic principles of organization are added, by historical contingencies (or other nonuniversal determinants), the particular surface structures that give the social formation its final and recognizable form. As McCarthy points out, "Habermas emphasizes that the rationally reconstructible, hierarchical patterns of increasingly comprehensive structures of rationality describe only the 'logical space' within which structural formation takes place. Whether and when new structures are formed, however, depends on contingent circumstances. If this distinction is made, there is no need to impute necessity and irreversibility to the course of history. . . . On the basis of what has been accomplished in this area, [Habermas] wants now to distinguish between the universal and the particular components in the foreknowledge of adult members of society. To the former belong the universal structures of cognitive, linguistic, and interactive competence acquired in socialization processes in general; to the latter belong the everyday views and standards of rationality particular to given life-worlds. Social inquiry involves the explicit reconstruction of both components; this reconstructed foreknowledge can be used (together with assumptions concerning empirical mechanisms) in the explanation of social processes."

And, finally, to summarize this summary, McCarthy brings out the following very central and germane points:

> The research program he is proposing has, Habermas contends, distinct advantages over competing evolutionary approaches. For one thing, it does not restrict attention to the synchronic analysis of existing structures as purely structuralist approaches tend to do but requires an investigation of structure-forming processes as well. For another, it focuses attention—as functionalist neoevolutionism (espoused by Parsons, Lenski, and Luhmann, for example) does not—on variety-producing mechanisms at both the individual and societal levels. A specification of systems problems and of functionally equivalent possible solutions does not of itself *explain how* a social system actually acquires the capacity to solve these problems. The recourse to learning processes is meant precisely to explain why some systems expand their problem-solving capacity, while others fail in the face of similar problems. Furthermore, the directional criteria of progress typically invoked by neoevolutionists (for example, increase in system complexity or steering capacity through differentiation, functional specification, integration, and so on) are inadequate [as I will discuss in connection with "higher worlds" or "developmental wholes"]. Even at the level of biological evolution, an increase in the complexity of bodily organi-

> zation or mode of living may be an evolutionary dead-end. What is needed here is a determination of the "inner logic" of a series of morphological changes or an expansion of reaction potential [such as, in my view, relative autonomy and functional communion].

This developmental-structural-evolutionary vantage allows Habermas to complement (not replace) historical-hermeneutics with a more critical-normative approach. I think this is very important: "Viewing cognitive development on the social level as a learning process is essential to the critique of knowledge if this is to provide us with standards that are not merely language- or culture-relative. After having embraced a number of fundamental hermeneutic insights, Habermas could distance himself from what he took to be the inherently situational and relativistic character of a purely hermeneutic approach only by further developing the theoretical side of critical theory. The construction of a general interpretive framework made it possible to pursue a 'theoretically' or 'systematically generalized history' and thus to mitigate the radically situational character of a purely hermeneutic approach. To this extent, the 'initial situation' to which hermeneutic interpretation is bound would be theoretically grounded and thus less radically context-dependent. And he could locate different cultural expressions (such as worldviews and moral and legal systems), at one or another structurally defined level of development." And that, of course, is the program I had already embarked upon in *Eden*.

Neo-evolutionists

Two of my favorite social theorists are Niklas Luhmann—arguably the world's greatest social systems theorist—and Gerhard Lenski. Their work was mentioned above, in relation to Habermas's criticisms (which I share) of the limitations of systems theory and functionalism as complete or well-rounded theories. At the same time, this is not to dismiss the important contributions of these fields—and these two theorists in particular. My opinion is that any theory that does not take their work into account, and include their essential points, is severely restricted in its scope.

I will return to the notion of psychosocial evolution and discuss such theorists as Huston Smith, James Fowler, Jean Gebser, and Carol Gilligan. But in order to make fruitful comparisons with my system, we first need a very brief summary of it.

The Spectrum Approach

1. The Basic Structures

The simplest way to summarize my work in sociology is to say that, just as cognitive developmental psychology has partially informed the sociology of Habermas, so transpersonal developmental psychology has partially informed my own sociology. That accounts for the many similarities—and also the important differences—in our views. In the preceding section I have outlined the similarities; I'll now touch on the basic differences, most of which arise because Habermas's psychological model is, in my opinion, limited in its nature, scope, and range. In particular, since transpersonal psychology offers a specifically nonreductionistic approach to the psychology of religion, it affords by analogy the opportunity for a genuinely nonreductionistic approach to the sociology of religion, an approach I tried to take in *A Sociable God*.

In the transpersonal model of psychological development that I have proposed, the structures or formations of the psyche are divided into two general types: the *basic structures* and the *transition structures* (what I also call "levels" and "lines"). The basic structures are those structures that, once they emerge in development, tend to remain in existence as relatively autonomous units or subunits in the course of subsequent development (they are "holons" in the Leibniz-Koestler sense). Transition structures, on the other hand, are phase-specific and phase-temporary structures that tend to be more or less entirely replaced by subsequent phases of their own development. Where particular basic structures tend to be subsumed, included, or subordinated in subsequent development, particular transition structures tend to be negated, dissolved, or replaced by subsequent development (I will give some examples below). Negotiating these structural developments is the *self-system*, which is the locus of identification, volition, defense, organization, and "metabolism" ("digestion" of experience at each level of structural development).

Here, very briefly, are some of the postulated basic structures of existence. (For the higher structures, instead of giving a description or explanation, which would be too detailed for this presentation, I have simply listed, as only one example, Aurobindo's corresponding levels of superconscient development):

1. Matter—insentient (nonbiologically reproducing) physical substratum

2. Sensation—protoplasmic "irritability" or biological "reactivity"
3. Perception—zoological registration of sensations
4. Emotion—emotional-sexual (libidinal) impulse and instinct
5. Image—pictorial representation
6. Symbol—nonpictorial denotation
7. Concept—nonpictorial connotation
8. Rule—concrete-operation
9. Meta-rule—formal-operation
10. Vision—"higher mind" (Aurobindo)
11. Psychic—"illumined mind"
12. Subtle—"intuitive mind"
13. Causal—"overmind"
14. Absolute—"supermind/satchitananda"

These basic structures are conceived not only as structures and organizing principles of psychosocial growth, but also as fundamental *ontological dimensions* of existence—they are, in fact, a modern, updated version of the Great Nest of Being—matter to body to mind to subtle-soul to causal-spirit.

It is very difficult, in a short presentation, to give much force to my hypothesis (and my conclusion) that those basic structures are some of the central or "quasi-universal" structures of being and consciousness. I have developed this thesis in some half-dozen books, drawing on several disciplines, and grounded in the philosophia perennis in both ancient and modern forms (e.g., Plato to Whitehead, Shankara to Nicolai Hartmann, Plotinus to Aurobindo), and the reader may consult those if he or she wishes. I will only say that it is the conclusion of this research that the *deep structures* of those basic structures are essentially similar wherever they appear in human development and evolution (and whether they are part of psychological, sociological, religious, etc. formations). I am fully aware of, and quite sympathetic toward, the general hermeneutic tradition that stresses the difficulty (or even impossibility) of escaping traditional or culture-bound "prejudices" in any sort of "transcultural" fundamentals; nonetheless, and quite in spite of that, I have attempted to abstract the deep structures in a way that is really *deep*, i.e., "free of cultural specificity." Thus, for example, an "image" (level 5) is an image whether it appears in China, India, or Mexico; its surface structures, however, (contents, modes of expression, etc.) vary considerably from culture to culture (and thus not only are culturally bound but can only be hermeneutically disclosed).

My hypothesis, then, is that the deep structures of the basic structures are largely cross-cultural invariants or "quasi-universals," by which I mean relatively enduring and relatively unchanging structures or patterns, essentially similar wherever they appear. I do not believe it is necessary to postulate them as eternally fixed Platonic Forms, Whiteheadian eternal objects, or Husserlian essences; even "physical laws" may be merely relatively unchanging physical "habits," as Peirce, Sheldrake, and others have maintained. This relatively unchanging and basically similar character is what I mean by "quasi-universal"; the whole sequence of basic structures, to my mind, is more like a living habit-pattern than a fixed mechanism. But whether one argues that the deep structures of the basic structures are eternally fixed or relatively unchanging is incidental to my central thesis that they are essentially similar wherever they appear, and thus constitute, among other things, the cross-cultural or quasi-invariant skeletal backbone of psychosocial evolution.

It is the deep structures of the basic structures that are governed and disclosed by a developmental logic. The surface structures of the basic structures, however, usually vary from culture to culture, tradition to tradition, society to society, and thus are governed and disclosed by historic-hermeneutic circumstances and contingencies. Since psychosocial evolution (indeed, evolution in general) is always a combination of deep and surface features, this undercuts the merely idealistic attempt to *deduce* via logical necessity the whole of evolutionary development, because, even though the deep structures are developmentally invariant, the surface structures are historically contingent (this is not to say that surface structure development follows no rules or patterns, only that those patterns seem everywhere largely culture-specific and thus theoretically nondeducible). It also undercuts the merely materialist (and functionalist) attempt to explain historical development on the basis of changing surface structure formations, since no amount of variable surface structure patterning could announce or define a next higher or emergent level of organization altogether.

When it comes to critical-normative statements about psychosocial displays, there are thus at least two dimensions of adjudication involved—one is vertical and involves deep structures; the other is horizontal and involves surface structures. With the deep structures we may speak of higher or lower, more evolved or less evolved, according to the dictates of developmental logic. Within any given basic deep structure, however, there are several possible, equally functional formations or arrays of surface structures, no one of which can be said to be higher or lower vis-à-vis a developmental logic, since each possible array is at the same ontic level. The question here is not whether one formation is higher or lower than another, but rather how any particular formation functions "horizontally." Is it well integrated or poorly integrated? Does it offer legitimate meaning? What *is* that meaning? Does it achieve pattern maintenance, tension regulation, etc? In short, what are its latent/manifest functions and meanings, and how well are they served by this particular psychosocial formation, system, or array of surface structures?

The vertical dimension I refer to as "authenticity"; the horizontal dimension, "legitimacy." And I have suggested that developmental-structuralism (or psychosocial evolution) can best adjudicate authenticity; that hermeneutics can best adjudicate manifest and/or individual legitimacy; and that functionalism can best adjudicate latent and/or collective legitimacy. These are by no means cut-and-dried distinctions, but they do give an indication of one of the ways I have attempted to bring together developmental-structuralism, hermeneutics, and functionalism in a relatively coherent system.

2. Transition Structures

Allow me to finish this brief account by mentioning the transition structures. These structures, recall, are ones that are not included and subsumed in subsequent development but tend instead to be negated, dissolved, or replaced by subsequent development. Take, for example, the works of Piaget and Kohlberg (and ignoring, for the moment, the truth status of their theories). Piaget's cognitive structures are, for the most part, basic structures (the very general correlations are: sensorimotor is level 2/3, preconceptual preoperational is 5/6, conceptual preoperational is 7, concrete operational is 8, and formal operational is 9). Once these levels come into existence, they remain in existence during subsequent development; in fact, each level becomes, in Piaget's system, the operand or "object" of the next higher level. Thus, a person at, say, basic level 8, has *simultaneous* access to, and use of, levels 1 through 7; they are all still present, and all still (ideally) performing their necessary and appropriate tasks and functions.

Kohlberg's moral stages, however, are largely phase-specific *replacement* structures: someone at, say, moral stage 3 does not simultaneously act equally from stage 1. Stage 3 *replaced* stage 2 which replaced stage 1, and so on. Although the moral transition structures depend on or "rest on" the basic cognitive structures (as both Piaget and Kohlberg have pointed out), the two otherwise refer to rather different types of structures (i.e., basic and transitional).

Let me give a simple metaphor I often use to explain this distinction. The basic structures are like the rungs in the ladder of existence; the self-system is the climber of the ladder; and the different perspectives, interactions, and views of reality that are constructed at each rung are the transition structures. As the self-system evolves or develops from, say, rung 4 to rung 5, the more limited view of rung 4 is *replaced* by the broader view from rung 5, but rung 4 itself *remains* in existence as a necessary basic structure or support for subsequent development.

I have suggested that the transition structures include, among other things: affects, morals (e.g., Kohlberg/Gilligan), needs (e.g., Maslow), self-identity (e.g., Loevinger), defenses (e.g., psychoanalytic hierarchy of defenses), interpersonal competence (e.g., Selman), and types of world-views (e.g., Gebser), among others. These are often referred to as *developmental lines*. Thus, through the 14 or so basic structures or basic *levels* of the spectrum of consciousness (or Great Nest of Being), pass at least a dozen different developmental *lines*. These lines develop relatively independently through the spectrum, so that a person can be at, say, a very high level of cognitive development, a medium level of interpersonal development, and a low level of emotional development. This underscores just how uneven and nonlinear overall development can be. Although the individual developmental or evolutionary lines themselves almost always follow a specific sequence of unfolding—they follow the available levels of the spectrum of consciousness (e.g., preconventional to conventional to postconventional)—nonetheless *overall development*, or the "sum total" of the various lines, *follows no set sequence whatsoever.* This is yet another reason that a developmental view cannot be equated with a progress view. Overall development is certainly not a "linear" affair, a charge that is often leveled at this approach, a charge that can only be sustained by an ignorance of the subtleties involved.

Since *worldviews* are often associated with "religion" in the broadest sense, I will give a brief explanation of this aspect of my hypothesis. The idea itself is simple: hermeneutically speaking, what would the world look like from each of the basic rungs of existence? (Or, if you prefer, what type of psychosocial worldview would be co-created by self and other, given, as raw materials, a particular basic structure?) I believe a fairly precise analysis-report (in *deep structural* terms) is possible; for convenience sake, I usually group these worldviews into a half-dozen or so easily recognizable sets, with the lowest levels loosely and collectively referred to as "archaic."

With reference to the first five worldviews: as I explained in *Up from Eden*, I had independently hit upon essentially identical worldviews as had the great Jean Gebser, and in deference to his pioneering work, I often use his terminology. But Gebser's highest stage, "integral-aperspectival" (my centauric "vision-logic"), is actually just the beginning of at least three or four higher stages of genuinely spiritual development (psychic, subtle, causal, nondual), all of which Gebser clumsily collapses into the integral. With that exception, I am in substantial agreement with the studies of this remarkable man.

Basic Structure(s)	*Corresponding Worldview*
Physical (1), sensation (2), perception (3), emotion (4), image (5)	Archaic
Image (5), symbol (6), concept (7)	Magic
Concept (7), rule (8)	Mythic
Meta-rule (9)	Mental (rational)
Vision-logic (10)	Existential (centauric)
Psychic (11)	Yogic (shamanic, panenhenic)
Subtle (12)	Saintly
Causal (13)	Sagely

Selecting a single term to represent an entire worldview is always a dicey proposition, and a few critics have understandably reacted to my (and Gebser's) choice of terms for the various worldviews. Let me say, then, that what I mean by "magic," "mythic," "saintly," and so on, is carefully explained in *Eye to Eye* and *Up from Eden*; you are free to use any terms you wish to exemplify these worldviews; the ones I have chosen simply seem to me to best capture the "flavor" of each level. But I mean nothing so naive as that anything that is simply called a "myth" automatically belongs to the "mythic level," or that all forms of so-called "rationality" are to be plopped, without further ado, into the "rational level." I will return to an explanation of these worldviews in a subsequent section.

3. PSYCHOSOCIAL EVOLUTION

In *The Atman Project*, *Eye to Eye*, and "The Developmental Spectrum and Psychopathology,"[2] I have traced the evolution of these (and other) basic and transition structures in present-day psychological development; in *Up from Eden* and *A Sociable God* I traced similar (deep structural) developments in anthropological and social formations. As for the theory of social evolution outlined in those books, the central points are as follows.*

The material substratum of existence, as the "lowest" ontic dimension, is the canvas on which social evolution (indeed, evolution at large) is written. As each higher basic structure or ontic level emerges—starting with sensations—the material substratum at the site of the emergence is *complexified* in certain characteristic ways (with sensations: protein macromolecules and nuclei acids; with perceptions: rudimentary neuronal nets; with emotion-impulses: spinal networks with brain stems, and so on). These material complexifications are, as it were, both the record of, and the support for, the higher and interior levels of development.

With the beginning of the more specifically humanoid levels of development (images and symbols, or levels 5 and 6), these material complexifications take on an external form known as *institutions.* This means specifically that in social formations and interactions, we must examine not only the forms of the higher levels as they immediately present themselves in everyday activity (thoughts, feelings, ideas, emotions, speech acts, etc.), but also as they become embedded or institutionalized in material complexifications (an image in a painting, an emotion in a poem, an idea in a text, an operation in a steel mill, a formal logic in a computer circuit, etc.). In archeology this is all-important, of course, because all we have left are material complexifications or institutionalized remnants from which we must attempt to read, hermeneutically, the nature and type of higher and interior levels—emotions, images, symbols, concepts, rules, etc., as well as their worldviews (magic, mythic, rational, and so on)—that informed and molded the particular materialized artifact. An interrelated system of psychosocial patterns, as they become embedded in recognizable physical complexifications, I call a material institutionalization.

Here is my point: As each senior dimension emerges, it rests upon—but is not caused by—its junior dimension, and therefore a *distortion* in a lower dimension *inclines* (but does not cause) the higher dimension to

*[The rest of this section, although it does not use these terms, is an early argument for the importance of including all four quadrants in historical analysis, and especially the LR quadrant, or material social institutions.]

reproduce the distortions on its own domain and in its own surface structures. A distorted higher domain, in turn, can inform and embed (causally) its own distortions in a lower level, right down, finally, to alienated and alienating materialized complexifications which institutionalize these illegitimacies (which in turn developmentally predispose subsequent consciousness to reproduce the distortions, and so on). In social evolution, then, we want to trace, among other things: (1) the higher and interior levels of psychosocial interaction, (2) their material institutionalizations, and (3) the interaction between the two.

Thus, for example, I have tried to suggest (I am putting this all very simplistically) that hunting is a material institutionalization of aspects of the image-symbol level of consciousness (with its "magic" worldview); farming is a material institutionalization of aspects of the concept-rule level (with its "mythic" worldview); the industrial complex is a material institutionalization of aspects of the formal-operational level (with its "rational" worldview), and so on—with the proviso that the influences of exterior base and interior consciousness on each other are quite mutual. Individuals born in, say, an industrial society are thus, from birth, *already* resting upon a material base that will (1) incline their consciousness to rise to the level that informed the base; (2) incline them to reproduce, along the way, any distortions or illegitimacies institutionalized in the base.

This, I believe, is the proper relation between the "base" (material) and the "superstructure" ("everything else"). It is not, as in orthodox Marxism, that the base *determines* the superstructure. It is rather that *horizontal* (surface-structure) developments in the base incline (but do not cause) horizontal developments of the superstructure to reproduce analogous arrays (legitimate or illegitimate) in their own surface structures, and incline *vertical* (deep structure) development to rise to the highest average level that informed the base in the first place.

Orthodox Marxism outlines five social-material developments: primitive, ancient, feudal, capitalist, socialist. I believe the structural sequence of this (or any other display) is, as I have said, partially dependent upon historic-contingent circumstances that can only be reconstructed after the fact, not rigidly predicted or deduced prior to it. The Marxist "deduction" of the five or so stages of development of material modes of production looks fairly accurate, not because they hit upon an invariant-universal law of the stages of *material* unfoldment (dialectical materialism), but because the invariant (*after* the fact) universal *vertical* stages of psychosocial evolution—with their associated needs, functions, worldviews (e.g., archaic, magic, mythic, rational, humanistic)—left *their* modes materially institutionalized in the physical-economic forms that the Marxists call primitive, ancient, feudal, capitalistic, socialistic (to speak very generally).

Thus, I believe, for any theory of psychosocial evolution, the developments of the material base are very significant, *not* because they represent the highest or most important level, but precisely because they represent the lowest level—the end or stopping off point for all downwardly institutionalizing processes, and the beginning point for all upward ontogenetic developments—the broad canvas on which is graphically recorded all the texts of higher-level developments, enfolded and structurally inserted in the material complexifications of the base.

For actual psychosocial evolution, this has one other very important implication. Major social transformations—shifts in "epochs" or "eras" (however conceived)—have never been initially caused or produced by a new mode of production or a new material complexification. "The great technical inventions have not produced, but only accompanied new epochs." Rather, one individual, or a small group of individuals, conceived an idea (a particular image, symbol, concept, rule, etc.) that, whether realized or not, could potentially be of collective import; this idea began circulating at its own level, where it effected the harbinger of potential transformation; eventually another individual/small group (occasionally the same as the originators) conceived a practical way to embody or materially institutionalize the original idea, thus making it part of the lowest and therefore most commonly accessible level; the idea itself (whether legitimate or illegitimate) thus became an institutionalized component of the base; and therefore all subsequently born humans in the vicinity of the base, whether or not they understood or even wished to understand the original idea, had their own ontogenetic development automatically (nonvolitionally) rested, in part, upon this materialized idea, which then acted to: (1) move consciousness to the basic level on which the original idea emerged, and (2) reproduce the surface array (legitimate or illegitimate) embodied in the original idea.

Thus, for example, when farming was invented, it first emerged as a conceived idea (either the idea was deliberately planned, or it emerged in response to the accumulated contradictions and limitations of the previous productive stage, or its discovery was purely accidental—either way, it still had to be recognized before implemented); this idea was subsequently embodied or materially institutionalized in the form of the plow, the domesticated oxen, the ownership plot, irrigation, and so forth. Individuals who, for developmental or other reasons, could never themselves conceive or have conceived the original idea, were thus made privilege to (or, in the case of alienating arrays, bondage to) ideas they never necessarily comprehended or voluntarily initiated.

In this fashion, material complexifications of the base play a prime role, not in initially producing transformations, but in carrying and embodying transformative powers—ideas, concepts, rules, visions, etc. —perhaps never clearly grasped by the masses that are subsequently so transformed. In just this way, for example, computers are today the material institutionalizations of certain aspects of the formal-operational mind—carriers of the "third wave" of cultural transformation, irrevocably changing the lives of millions of people who have not or could not understand the ideas informing that base. One may, of course, interpret this for the better or for the worse, depending on one's own theoretical hopes and fears; my simpler point is that any theory of psychosocial evolution ought to pay a peculiar type of attention to the material complexifications and institutionalizations of overall development, not because they are in themselves ontically senior or privileged, but because of all the paradoxical repercussions that result from their being the lowest and therefore most readily accessible template of all higher-level evolution.

A side note: Most "New Age" writers, prophesying a great coming global transformation, center their works almost solely on the superstructure—new ideas, visions, psychic-subtle insights, new paradigms, etc. So "airy" do their analyses become that they seem to forget entirely that, in manifest evolution, the material realm is an enduring basic structure, not a transition structure (even Buddhas have to eat). The "Aquarian Age" will still have to rest upon a characteristic material complexification or set of material institutionalizations—hopefully saner than the rationalized ones now dominant. But until New Agers begin to examine how their visions will become institutionalized in the base, and how these institutionalizations can best be effected, the New Age will remain dust in the wind.

Huston Smith

Finally, in a defense of psychosocial evolution, we can turn to some of the modern "religious authorities," which Anthony claims would disavow my general developmentalism. Certain authorities most definitely would, particularly the static structuralists (Eliade, Campbell), but their views are far from the consensus, nor can they themselves withstand much scrutiny.

I begin with a "hard case"—hard because he ended the most prophetic chapter of his most important book with the quite unequivocal announcement that "the wave of the future will be a return to the past. 'There is only the fight to recover what has been lost. . . .' 'I sing the songs of olden times with adoration.'" This does not bode well for an evolutionary stance. I am speaking, of course, of Huston Smith, author of *The Religions of Man*, and arguably the most respected religious scholar now alive.

But, in fact, there has recently been a subtle change, or at least a shift in emphasis, in Smith's thought. Like many religious scholars, faced with the de facto development from mythic to rational involvements, Smith originally flirted with a decadence view of human evolution ("After all, myths recount devolution more than evolution, and we know for a fact that later human forms are not necessarily more advanced: Steinheim man preceded Neanderthal but was [allegedly] more 'evolved.' " When pressed for actual evidence of overall devolution, Smith's response is uncharacteristically anemic: "If it be asked, 'Where, then, are the remains of these "giants who walked the earth in those days"?' it might be answered that in his beginnings, when he stood close to provenient spirit, man was ethereal to the point of leaving less in the way of ossified remains"). The same book (*Forgotten Truth*) contained a scathing indictment of Teilhard de Chardin's views, ostensibly because they confused science and religion, but also, one suspects, because Teilhard de Chardin's views are evolutionary, not devolutionary.

It was therefore with considerable integrity that, about five years later, Smith delivered his Georgetown address, "A Footnote on Teilhard de Chardin." While still lamenting Teilhard de Chardin's confusion of scientific and religious statements, Smith acknowledged that "If I were to rewrite *Forgotten Truth*, I would omit the . . . scathing [sections on] Teilhard de Chardin's *The Phenomenon of Man*. . . . So I use this occasion to voice my regrets that in alluding to Teilhard in the past I was so occupied with the problems he posed for me [confusion of science and religion] that I had not then the wit to see how his vision can be read constructively."

But even in *Forgotten Truth*, this "constructive [evolutionary] vision" pops up all over the place. I take the time to give a few quotes because, remember, this is an originally "decadence theorist" reflecting, from a religious view, on the *nature* of overall evolution. So what does he see in it? And from an "academic religious" stance?

> The history of nature shows [and he here quotes Michael Polanyi's *Personal Knowledge*] "a cumulative trend of changes tend-

> ing toward higher levels of organization. . . . At each successive stage of this epic process we see arising some novel operations not specifiable in terms of the preceding level."

In this idea of evolutionary-emergence, Smith concludes, Polanyi "is on sure ground. . . . *Far from denying life's progression, tradition* [the world's great religious traditions] *provides a reason for it*: Microcosm mirrors macrocosm, earth mirrors heaven. But mirrors invert. The consequence here is that that which is first in the ontological order appears last in the temporal order" (my italics). In other words, the higher the domain, the later it manifests in evolution. On balance, Smith concludes, "The evolutionary sequence is not denied."

Huston has never been consistent on this issue. He seems to believe that evolution (or the evolutionary sequence) occurred for fifteen billion years up to humans, then promptly stopped unfolding. Nature's productions all evolve, human productions all do not. Strange dualism. But let us end with the fact that on occasion Huston states: the evolutionary sequence is not denied.

James Fowler

James Fowler is the leading empirical investigator of "religious faith"—its nature, dynamic, and development. Without going into detail, we may simply note that Fowler's research has led him to the conclusion that faith develops or evolves through seven major stages: (1) undifferentiated, (2) projective-magical, (3) mythic-literal, (4) synthetic-conventional, (5) individual-reflective, (6) conjunctive, and (7) universalizing. As Professor Joel Funk has demonstrated, these stages match very closely my own (or rather, match the transitional stages and worldviews correlated with each basic structure): Fowler's stage 1 is my archaic; stage 2, magical; stage 3, early mythic-membership; stage 4, late mythic-membership; stage 5, formal-reflexive; stage 6, integrative-vision. Fowler's highest stage is simply the beginning of four higher stages in my own scheme; other than that, the fit between our models is quite close. Fowler's research data is massive; that he found it necessary to adopt an evolutionary-developmentalism is, in my opinion, very significant.

Aurobindo

Bringing Aurobindo into the discussion at this point might seem almost redundant; everybody knows he is an evolutionist. But I would like to mention a few not irrelevant points in regard to his work. When I first began writing in this field, I was in fact a devolutionist. It was my firm opinion (following Eliade, Norman O. Brown, Campbell, etc.) that the best possible interpretation of all the existing evidence pointed toward a view of devolution (or, at best, a static or synchronic situation). In fact, I began research for *Eden* with the intention of trying to show that a devolutionist perspective was at least as believable as an evolutionary one. All those "myths of devolution," of a "golden age," simply could not, I believed, be radically ignored. I subsequently found what I believe is the best explanation for the existence of those concrete (not symbolic) myths (they embody the painful move "up" from subconsciousness to selfconsciousness, not a decadent move "down" from superconsciousness to selfconsciousness), but the transition to that evolutionary perspective was a very difficult period for me. And the straw that broke the theoretical camel's back was Aurobindo.

I would not call myself a strict follower of Aurobindo, but I do think what he accomplished is quite staggering and in many ways unparalleled. The reasons I find Aurobindo's case to be particularly illuminating, and the reasons I give his work what might seem a disproportionate weight, are three: (1) he was, by all accounts, a highly enlightened sage; (2) he was deeply trained in both Eastern and Western schools of thought; (3) he was one of the first modern sages to carefully examine the evolutionary and anthropological evidence offered by Western science and compare it with the traditional ideas and thought of Eastern wisdom. His conclusions were thus not easy for me to casually dismiss: "An evolution of consciousness is the central motive of terrestrial existence. The evolutionary working of Nature has a double process: an evolution of material forms [the "base"], an evolution of the soul ["super-structure"]." Aurobindo would agree in principle, I believe, with virtually everything I wrote above about the relationship between the material base and the higher structures of consciousness. But his central point is this: "The spiritual evolution obeys the logic of a successive unfolding; it can take a new decisive main step only when the previous main step has been sufficiently conquered: even if certain minor stages can be swallowed up or leaped over by a rapid and brusque ascension, the consciousness has to turn back to assure itself that the ground passed over is securely annexed to the new condition. It is true that the conquest of the spirit supposes the execution in one life or a few lives of a process that in the ordinary course of Nature would involve a slow and uncertain procedure of centuries or even of millennia: but this is a question of the speed with which the steps are traversed; a greater or concentrated speed does not eliminate the steps themselves or the necessity of their successive surmounting."

I have written extensively on the correlations of Aurobindo's stages of consciousness evolution with my own postulated basic structures; I will not here repeat my arguments and explanations, but will simply list these correlations.

Basic Structures	*Aurobindo's Stages*
1. Matter	Physical subconscient
2. Sensation	Sensation
3. Perception	Perception
4. Emotion	Vital-emotional
5. Image	
6. Symbol	Will-mind (lower conceptual mind)
7. Concept	
8. Rule	Sense-mind (a concrete-based mind)
9. Meta-rule	Reasoning-mind (not concrete-based)
10. Vision-logic	Higher-mind (mass network/vision)
11. Psychic	Illumined-mind
12. Suble	Intuitive-mind
13. Causal	Overmind
14. Absolute	Supermind/Satchitananda

Da Free John

Da Free John is an enlightened Western adept; he is also possessed of a keen and prolific philosophic mind. Central to his teaching is the idea that there are at least seven major universal "stages of life"; these stages are inherent structural potentials of the human condition, essentially similar wherever they appear; they generally unfold in a developmental sequence (with all sorts of spirals and regressions possible). As his own community has frequently acknowledged, the model I have presented is fully compatible with Da Free John's.

Objections to Evolution Theory

Bellah, Habermas, Luhmann, Lenski, Aurobindo, Gebser, Fowler, etc.—to say, then, that the notion of evolutionary development is completely rejected is simply nonsense, although many incoherent and self-contradictory alternatives are flourishing like fleas. Rather, I think the more naive aspects of progress theories have, in recent times, been replaced by more realistic and accurate theories of psychosocial evolution, ones that include a "dialectic of suffering" as well as a "dialectic of advance."

Some scholars, of course, are still very wary of evolutionary theories of any variety; the reasons for this, I believe, include the following:

1. Pseudo-evolutionary theories involving "genetic superiority" or "elite races" have been used to justify the most outrageously barbaric acts (Nazis, Ku Klux Klan, etc.).

2. A humanistic-secular-rational stance tends to be radically egalitarian; any suggestion of "higher" or "lower" development is misconstrued as a condemnatory judgment and reacted to with alarm.

3. The rich variety of surface structures in different cultures has tended to obscure the possible similarities in deep structures; the problem has simply been that, for these deep structures, scholars did not initially look *deep enough*. Various groupings of surface structures were mistaken for quasi-universal deep structures; when these groupings were shown to be culturally specific, the whole idea of quasi-universal deep structures was dismissed—quite prematurely, in my opinion—and various forms of hermeneuticism took center stage, where they assumed a significance out of all proportion to their undeniably important but otherwise limited contributions.

4. In psychology, where developmentalism dominates most fields except behaviorism, sequences of developmental stages are fairly easy to demonstrate. In social systems, however—and therefore in sociology itself—developmentalism (or social evolution) is a much more complex and difficult task (both theoretically and practically). In any given social system, at any given time, its component individuals may be at any number of partially circumscribed but otherwise rather different developmental stages, and thus the social system as a whole cannot be branded as being at a particular, discrete, obvious, monolithic stage of social evolution, nor can its system behavior be reduced to or derived from the sum of its individual components or personal vectors. Rather, we can at best introduce such sociological concepts as:

   a. *average-expectable level of adaptation*—the level of individual psychosocial development reached by the largest number of peoples in a given social system (more precisely, we can distinguish between mean-expectable and median-expectable; though I cannot discuss it here, I believe both of those carry significant and specifiable meaning)

b. *average steering-level of adaptation*—the level of moral-decision making consistently evidenced by governing or steering bodies in a social system or subsystem
c. *highest-expectable level of superconscient adaptation*—the highest levels of transcendental realization consistently reached by the most developed adepts in a given social system
d. *average, common, or most collectively defining level of worldview*—the level *from which* the most culturally legitimate and legitimating worldviews are derived, irrespective of the level *on which* they are accepted

And so on through literally dozens of similar variables. These concepts are not, of course, as precise as their counterparts in psychology, but they are far from being useless on that account. In *Eden*, for instance, I traced the historical evolution of "average-expectable" and "highest-expectable" modes of psychosocial and religious interaction, with, I believe, some very illuminating results. My point is simply that the notorious complexity of social systems has tended to make developmental analyses seem impossible, whereas all it has actually done is render them statistical (as is most modern science; in fact, I have often thought the stage theorists in psychology, such as Loevinger or Kohlberg, ought not to treat the individual self as a single monolithic entity located at *one* stage or another, but rather as a miniature social system of numerous personae, many of which exist at different levels of moral-cognitive development, with the ego or central self being the average-expectable level of consciousness for this miniature community; this would immediately obviate many of the problems in the stage conception, such as the self's notorious tendency to give responses quite removed from the stage "it" is supposed to be at; those responses would simply represent, for example, the opposition party in the ego's steering committee).

5. Because the time span between profound social transformations (or change in deep structures) is usually measured in centuries or millennia, it is very difficult for sociologists to actually *observe* a transformation occurring, which makes it very easy to forget that the idea of social evolution might have an importance on a larger, not smaller, scale. Small-scale sociology has thus tended to overlook developmentalism. (In a similar vein, I have always found it ironic that no biologist has ever seen the emergence or evolution of a species, and yet none of them doubts that it occurred and is occurring.) By most accounts, there have

not been more than three or four *profound* transformation in humankind's history (which I would equate roughly with the transition in *average-expectable worldviews* from archaic to magic to mythic to mental, along with their characteristic material institutionalizations). Many sociologists therefore understandably assume that such "speculations" on social evolution do not at any rate effect their present observational and theoretical activities. I agree with Habermas, however, that even the explicitly nonevolutionary sociological theories in fact implicitly assume a developmental theory (modern, postmodern, industrial, post-industrial, etc.), and these theories ought to be made explicit and subject to discourse.

6. The simple confusion of all naive "progress theories" with all "psychosocial evolution theories" made the latter automatically appear monolithic, linear, elitist, racist, fascist, etc., etc.

7. All evolutionary theories are said to "marginalize" various minorities. (But that, of course, doesn't mean that these theories are wrong, only that we don't like them—which means we *can* alter the marginalizing activity while still realistically recognizing evolution and development. In fact, the only thing that truly stops marginalizing activity is interior development and consciousness evolution, from preconventional to conventional to postconventional domains of universal pluralism. Evolution is the only cure for marginalization, and those who fight evolution institutionalize marginalization.)

For some or all of those reasons, some scholars have avoided psychosocial evolution theories and concentrated instead on functional and hermeneutic issues. My own approach has been to try to introduce developmental issues, *not* to the exclusion of functional and hermeneutic issues, but *alongside* them. It is that gesture of balance, I believe, that is essential.

Part II: Reason, Myth, and Religion: Legitimate versus Authentic

In Anthony's original critique, after scolding me for my developmentalism, he rattles off a series of a dozen or so one-line critiques. It's hard to know how to respond to these; it's like sparring with a sociological Henny Youngman. I'll explicitly answer most of them here and pick up the others in subsequent discussion. Anthony imputes the following beliefs to me, which he criticizes or rejects:

1. "Wilber is epistemologically objectivist." If by "objectivist" Anthony means "empiric-analytic," this is not true; I have outlined at least five major modes of knowledge, only one of which is empiric-analytic (the most central one is phenomenological-hermeneutic, and the most important one is gnostic). If by "objectivist" he means I believe in radically culture-free knowledge claims, this is also not true, as I have explained above (every deep structure has surface structure components that are themselves historically, hermeneutically, or culturally bound; I do believe deep structures, once solidified, are quasi-universal, and that the denial of universals requires itself at least one universal; in part III of this response, I specifically address the issue of "culture-free rationality"). If by "objectivist" Dick means "nonsubjectivistic," I do believe valid truth-claims are potentially independent of particular subjects, though not necessarily of subjects per se.

2. "There are objectively identifiable communities of spiritually advanced psychotechnicians who are in command of the knowledge base which epistemologically grounds transpersonal theories." "Objectively identifiable" and "psychotechnicians" are presumably pejorative; that aside, and keeping in mind the way I use "objective," the statement is essentially correct.

3. "The fear of death (rather than, for instance, the fear of sin, i.e., of embodying negative value) is the primal human motive." I have no idea where Dick got that one. I have postulated motivations (or dynamics) for each of the basic structures; I have postulated motivations (or dynamics) for each of the transition structures; and I have postulated motivations (or dynamics) for the self-system. In the latter, I have suggested four such motivations, one of which is fear of death. But "death" is defined as loss of any value, identification, or attachment of the self-system at *any* given point in its history. If virtue ("goodness") is part of how the self-system at some point construes its own identity, then loss of *that* virtue (or "sin") *is* what I mean by "death" in that case. There are as many potential "deaths" as there are potential self-identifications (and thus "death" for a male might be "loss of autonomy" whereas "death" for a female might be "loss of relationship").

4. "Reason excels emotion in developmental terms." This is a point on which Dick has consistently misinterpreted and oversimplified my

position. First of all, I have postulated that each basic level of consciousness has, among other things, a specific mode of space, time, cognition ("knowing"), conation ("motivation"), and affect (or "feeling" in general). In *The Atman Project*, I outlined these five lines for each of a dozen or so major levels of consciousness development. Thus, the level I sometimes call "emotional-sexual" (prana, libido, bioenergy, élan vital, etc.) has particular and characteristic affects, *but so does* the image level, the symbol level, the concept level, the rule level, and so on, all the way up to the ananda or "transcendental bliss" of the causal realm. In other words, each level has its own feelings, affects, or emotions (in the broad sense), with one level—the pranic—being referred to as impulsive or emotional (in the narrow sense), simply because that level (level 4) is the first where simple sensations and perceptions give way to more full-fledged (but still developmentally primitive) emotions per se (which Arieti calls "protoemotions," such as rage, pleasure, and rudimentary or physiological tension, all related, more or less, to emotional-libidinal impulses). The affect-feelings (or emotions in the broad sense) of the mental-rational level were given in *The Atman Project* as "concept-affects, dialogue-emotions, especially guilt, desire, pride, love, hatred." The affect-feelings of the transpersonal levels include universal love, compassion, bliss, and so forth.

In short, there are higher and lower feelings corresponding with higher and lower cognitions.

5. "Devolution and evolution are the only alternatives with respect to analyzing cultural and religious history. He [Wilber] ignores the class of synchronic [given, unchanging] cultural theories. Most structuralist theories (e.g., de Saussure, Lévi-Strauss, Chomsky, etc.) are synchronic rather than diachronic [developmental] as Wilber's is." That is not my view, as we have already seen. I believe that various deep structures, *once they emerge and settle as habits*, are then everywhere largely synchronic (I believe certain functional invariants—of translation, transformation, and the self-system—are also largely synchronic). However, I believe that the static structuralists mentioned by Anthony have, in exclusively stressing some of these synchronic features, overlooked the equally important diachronic features: developmental emergence, the historic-contingent nature of surface structures, the transcendent function that everywhere surprises and upsets static synchronicities, etc. My model is a strong integration of both static-synchronic and developmental-diachronic.

6. "Societies can be successfully integrated by rationality alone." My view was (and is) that formal-operational consciousness is as capable, or more capable, of integrating societies as is concrete-operational (mythic-literal) consciousness. Neither Dick nor I believe that any final or genuinely stable integration of society can occur without (or until) the descent of supramental, transcendental, or authentic spiritual awareness, a situation that I believe has never collectively existed in the past, but might exist in the future as and if psychosocial evolution continues beyond its merely mythic and rational exchanges.

Perhaps I might say a word or two on my use of the terms "myth" and "mythic." "Myth" obviously has a variety of meanings:

a. Most commonly, it is used in contrast to "reality" to mean "any fictitious story; any imaginary person or thing spoken of as though existing" (*Webster's*).
b. It is also commonly used to mean "a traditional story of unknown authorship, serving to explain some phenomenon of nature, the origin of man, etc.: myths usually involve the exploits of gods and heroes" (*Webster's*).
c. "Myth" can also be used in a broader context to mean any pattern or system of images, symbols, concepts, rules, etc. that confers or carries *meaning* (not confirmable beyond itself) for all those who exchange its units (and are thus bound and identifiable, in part, by that exchange). Let us call this "Myth" with a capital *M*; in this sense, religion might be Myth, *but so is* science, philosophy, and logic (in that their own basic assumptions cannot themselves be proven or demonstrated, but can nevertheless be used to construct and carry meaning in certain social exchange patterns). In this sense, too, a psychologist might speak of individual pathology as a failure to find or create an adequate personal Myth (e.g., constructs theory), and sociologists might speak of the power of collective Myths to stabilize or destabilize a social action system. In all these cases, "Myth" is referring, in part, to the legitimating power (as I have defined it) of a particular individual or collective worldview. In this usage, there are archaic Myths, magic Myths, mythic Myths, rational Myths, psychic Myths, and so on.
d. In addition to the above meanings of the word "myth"—each of which we are free to use so long as we specify which is implied—I have added a developmental definition of the term. Myth, in this

specific sense, refers to the *type* of worldview that develops when the cognitive capacities of concepts and rules are added to those of images and symbols, but *prior* to those of meta-rules.

This thesis is developed at length in *Eye to Eye* and *Eden*. To give a brief summary (confined, for the moment, to an abstract description of present-day ontogenetic development): the emergence of images (around 7 months) and symbols (around 1½ yrs) transforms the archaic, undifferentiated, or subject-object fusion state into the magical or proto-differentiated state, where the subjective world begins to be differentiated from the object world. This differentiation, however, is far from clean or complete; "inner" and "outer" remain partially fused and confused: images are animistically merged with the objects they represent (and thus, to manipulate the image is to magically affect the object); members of a class are interchangeable with other members (displacement) and whole classes are conflated with individual members (condensation)—in short, Sullivan's "parataxic," Arieti's "paleologic," Piaget's "preoperational," Freud's "primary process," etc. —all of which result when images and symbols, not yet under constraint of concepts and rules, act according to their own phase-specific devices, which, for convenience, I call "magical."

With the emergence of concepts and rules (or concrete operations), the magical worldview is gradually transformed into the mythic worldview. The differentiation between inner and outer is mostly complete, and thought forms can thus begin to concretely operate on the world. But because thought cannot yet operate on thought itself (meta-rule or formal-reflexive), thought forms tend to be physicalized or concretized; concrete gods, goddesses, heroes, forces, or spirits *operate on* the world (just as concrete thoughts operate on the environment); "concrete supernaturalism" might well describe this stage (cf. Fowler). Condensation and displacement of the previous stage are transformed into concrete-linguistic metaphor and metonym (Lacan); magical animism is transformed into concrete supernaturalism; and magical subjective manipulation is transformed into concrete supernatural interventionism. And all of this, for short, I refer to as a mythic worldview (it actually appears to have several different substages, but that need not concern us here).

The emergence of meta-rules or formal-operational thought—the capacity *of* thought to operate *on* thought—transforms the mythic worldview into the rational worldview. Consequently—if I may broaden the context—mythology is transformed into philosophy, mythic religion is transformed into rational theology, concretistic science is transformed into hypothetico-deductive science, monolithic membership (conventional) is transformed into pluralistic intersubjectivism (postconventional)—or, in short, rational Myths replace mythic Myths. And my specific claim vis-à-vis social integration or legitimating power is that rational Myths are, all other things considered equal, as effective or indeed more effective in this regard than mythic Myths, simply because of the greater degree of differentiation-integration offered by the rational structure itself.

7. "Civil religion can at best be 'legitimate.' It could not possibly be 'authentic.' " It *could* be if the average-expectable level of structural adaptation of "civility" rose from mythic-rational levels to psychic-subtle levels, which has never happened in American society, is not happening now, and likely will not happen for some time yet. Until then, civil religion is at best legitimate, not authentic. I do not believe that civil religion, in *any* of its forms (prophetic or celebratory) described by Bellah, is or ever was authentic (as I have defined those terms), although it has enjoyed various and often very high degrees of legitimacy.

But perhaps I should repeat the definitions of legitimacy and authenticity, since many readers react to these terms with connotations I do not intend. Legitimacy is a "horizontal" scale or measure of integrative power and meaning conferred or carried by a particular array of surface structures within a particular deep structure, *as measured against* the amount of integrative-meaning of other comparable surface structure arrays (or, theoretically, as against the total potential that could be supported by that particular deep structure). Legitimacy, in short, is a hermeneutic-functional variable.

Authenticity, on the other hand, is a "vertical" or developmental scale, as measured against those levels that can be shown to have preceded or succeeded, in developmental terms and by a developmental logic, any given stage. *In this sense*, magic is more authentic than archaic, mythic is more authentic than magic, rational is more authentic than mythic, subtle and causal are more authentic than rational, and so on. In calling this scale "authenticity," I definitely mean to imply an evolutionary value that is the Ground and Telos of the developmental-logic itself, namely, transcendental Spirit or Absolute Consciousness as Such—Brahman-Atman, Dharmakaya, Godhead, Keter—such that each evolutionary stage, since it requires (as Bradley would put it) less and less supplementation to pass into the Absolute, is more and more authentic.

As I was tracing out the developmental-logic from archaic to magic to mythic to rational to humanistic to psychic to subtle to causal, I was struck by a great irony, which I might introduce as follows: If you describe these various worldviews to the average person, and then ask them to pick one that sounds the most "religious," they will frequently say the "mythic"—Zeus guiding Ulysses, Jehovah smiting Egyptians, Moses parting the Red Sea, Indra slaying Vritra—that's "really religious stuff." This choice is reinforced by the fact that the descriptions and practices of the transcendental or superconscient stages of development do not always sound "religious"; there may be no mention of god(s), goddess(es), supernatural interventions and the like; rather, they frequently sound like some sort of exotic or higher psychology—there are abundant references to Higher Self, mental concentration, levels of insight, deepening awareness, and so forth, but no "really religious" references to deities, fates, daemons, and so on. Theravadin Buddhism, for instance, has so little mention of those terms that some scholars have even claimed it is not a religion at all, and one may search in vain through Zen for any mention of God, Creator, etc. (Zen speaks simply of the discovery of one's own True Self that is no-self). Now I happen to believe that those systems are definitely religions; I'm simply suggesting that one of the reasons why some people deny that Buddhism is a religion is that it has so few mythic Myths, which we naively tend to associate with "really religious."

Furthermore, many superconscient sages scornfully attack all such "mythic-religious" terms and beliefs as being, not transrational or genuinely transcendental, but as being prerational, childish magic and myth: "Such is the root of conventional religion, in which dependence on the parent agency is projected on all relations to Infinity, where we install the cultic Deity of our childhood, the archetypal and immortal Parent, and spend our days alternately pleading for the fulfillment of our needs and turning away, in adolescent fashion, to doubts and the consolations of functional fulfillments themselves. Those who are still critically burdened by their childish dependency look to the Spiritual Master, and to the Divine, as an objective, independent 'Other' or Parent, a Source that is also a perfect Agent. Such individuals must be awakened to the egoic illusion in their own approach, since it will prevent their Realization of the Truth [Absolute Spirit, Condition, Self]." (Da Free John).

Here is my point: because mythic Myths instinctively or naively seem "really religious" to many people, then: when progressive rationality began its attack on the previous mythic (or "really religious") structures;

when Nietzsche proclaimed that God-as-Parent is dead; when "religious" institutional steering choices increasingly gave way to rational "secular" ones; when, in short, mythic Myths began to give way to rational Myths, many spiritually oriented scholars became increasingly alarmed, because the whole movement looked "antispiritual"—the death of God! the decline of Religion! oh my God! (no answer).

And I said this was *ironic*, because the whole movement from mythic Myths to rational Myths is part of the evolutionary movement *on the way* toward spirit, not away from it. Put differently (and using these terms only as I have defined them), there is more spirit (and thus more authentic religion) in even secular reason than in mythic religion (which is why, I believe, Einstein said that in this day and age, the only truly religious people were the scientists).

But, of course, the vaunted "decline of religion" *in general* (religious dimension in Durkheim's sense), which was predicted by the early positivists and feared by the theologians, simply has not come to pass, because *both* the prediction and the fear arose in part from that reflex and naive identification of religion with mythic religion, which *has* declined in legitimating power under the attack by rationality and rational Myths (as Bellah put it, "The unexamined magical and religious conceptions of nonliterate or semiliterate strata, what used to make up the bulk of the religious life in any society, has come more and more under conscious inspection and critical evaluation. . . . This has involved the erosion of numerous beliefs and practices, some formerly considered essential to orthodoxy . . .").

But the demise of mythic religion does not spell the demise of religion per se. Not only does that naive identification overlook the religious dimension of rationality itself, it is blind to the even more authentic engagements lying yet beyond reason: the visionary religion of a universal humanity (postconventional centauric); the psychic religion of yogic illumination and cosmic connection (panenhenic nature mysticism); the saintly religion of actual transcendental *union* with the Divine (theistic myticism); and the sagely religion of radical *identity* with the Divine itself (formless mysticism). But where such higher endeavors were, in the past, always the province of a select and isolated few (a few shamans, a few saints, a few sages), they are slowly becoming the province of a wider number of individuals, as the average mode of cultural evolution begins to run into those higher levels glimpsed in the past only by a growing-tip few (the grain of truth, otherwise pathetically overblown, in the idea of a "New Age").

Reason itself, which is more developmentally authentic than magic or myth, is nevertheless considerably less authentic than, say, subtle or causal adaptations, or genuinely transcendental, transrational, and transpersonal engagements. And that is why, to return to our original point, I believe that the civil religion—which was, in my opinion, a combination of mythic Myths, rational elaborations and additions to those Myths, and an exceedingly minor dose of psychic-subtle insights—was simply not a very authentic religious engagement, even though, I repeat, it was often extremely legitimate.

I realize Bellah has refined his position, but his paper "Civil Religion in America" gives most of the necessary information. "The God of the civil religion . . . is also on the austere side, much more related to order, law, and right than to salvation and love. . . . He is actively interested and involved in history, with a special concern for America. [Quoting Jefferson:] 'I shall need, too, the favor of that Being in whose hands we are, who led our fathers, as Israel of old, from their native land and planted them in a country flowing with all the necessaries and comforts of life.'"

All of that—the watchful Parent, the emphasis on merely conventional law-and-order morality as a cosmic or universal principle, the concretistic supernatural interventionism, the petitionary intent—all of that suffices to announce that this is a mythic-membership, or at best, mythic-rational, *level* of belief system. There is nothing radically or experientially transcendental or transpersonal in any of that—nor in any of the quotes or explanations Bellah gives—and thus, although I know what he means by this, I have simply never agreed with his conclusion that "the civil religion at its best is a genuine apprehension of universal and transcendent religious reality."

As the prime example of "civil religion at its best," Bellah gives Abraham Lincoln. Lincoln was an extraordinary individual (and my favorite president), but there is no evidence whatsoever that Lincoln was installed at, say, a subtle or causal level of structural adaptation. I should say, rather, that he was an example of rational-humanistic adaptation, embued with vision-logic's humanistic universalism, and expressing his religion in humanistic, sometimes rationalistic, and occasionally mythic modes (although this by no means rules out intimations of—not permanent experiences of—highly or genuinely transcendental modes, as I try to explain in *A Sociable God*). Thus, if Bellah wishes to say that civil religion at its best is (or was) a dim intimation or intuition of psychic or subtle religious realities *expressed* in mythic-rational forms that themselves have no power to transform one to a genuine experience or apprehension of psychic-subtle reality *itself*, then I would agree; but that is precisely my definition of a legitimate, not authentic, religion, and it *serves* integration-translation, not transformation-transcendence.

Aside from that, I think Bellah's discussion of civil religion is extremely important, *precisely* because it draws out the legitimacy ("horizontally religious") dimension of each and every level of development, however "secular" it might otherwise appear. It is just that, in my opinion, Bellah tends to confuse or conflate legitimacy and authenticity; that is, he does not adequately differentiate the horizontal religious dimension (which seeks to meaningfully integrate a worldview) from the vertical religious dimension (which seeks to radically transform it). Any merely integrative or legitimating worldview (i.e., any yoking of meaning and motivation is a unified-coherent worldview, *irrespective* of how small or large, high or low, the world so unified might be) is therefore thought to be "universal," "genuinely transcendental," etc.—a confusion of legitimacy and authenticity.

This is borne out, I believe, by Bellah's definition of religion itself: "the most general mechanism for integrating meaning and motivation in action systems." That, in my opinion, is a definition of the legitimating function of a religious system; its degree of authenticity, on the other hand, might be defined as "the most general mechanism for destroying and resurrecting, or radically transforming, meaning and motivation in action systems."

I suspect that Bellah is aware of these distinctions; I'm simply suggesting that he does not sufficiently stress them. Due, perhaps, to this hermeneutic-functional bias, he tends to judge religious systems predominantly in terms of their success at legitimation or integration—in his own words, at how well they "bring together the coherence of the whole of experience." But what that overlooks is the fact that what constitutes the "whole of experience" varies drastically from level to level of development, and integrating the whole of experience at one level (legitimacy) is quite different from moving to a different level altogether (authenticity). In short, Bellah would do well to take more seriously his own work on *levels* of religious evolution.

Let me use an example to say the same thing from a slightly different angle. A completely integrative-meaningful-coherent magic worldview is just as legitimate, for its purposes, as any integrative-meaningful-coherent mythic or rational or subtle (etc.) worldview; it might even be more legitimate ("function better"). But it is still not as *authentic* (as I have defined the term), because, *even if it meaningfully integrated every element of its world*, there would still be, *above* its world, higher elements ("higher worlds," if you wish)—higher subjects, objects, cognitions, feelings, motivations, etc.—that simply cannot, developmentally speaking, even be *seen* at or by that level, and thus that level needs more supplementation than its senior levels in order to pass into the Absolute—and thus it is, however you wish to conceive it, and by whatever terms you wish—*less authentic*, even if, on its own level, it was quite legitimate.

Part III: Rationality and Rationalization

The Protestant Ethic and "Rationalization"

Anthony draws on Weber's characterizations of the Protestant Ethic, an ethic that Anthony likes very much, it seems. In this interpretation, the original Protestant Ethic implies that "(1) Spiritual status and worldly status have no relationship to each other; (2) history is not progressive—all worldly history is dominated by delusion or original sin, it is all equally 'fallen'; (3) God determines man's salvation or lack of it and his will has no effect; (4) it is more spiritual to sacrifice individual for collective ends." Anthony (following Weber) believes that this Protestant Ethic eventually degenerated or was perverted—by a weakening or "rationalization" process—into the Success Ethic: "(1) Greater spiritual stature will cause greater worldly power and status; (2) the idea of Progress; (3) belief in autonomy and free will; (4) utilitarian individualism." These, he believes, are a "perversion or degradation of Protestant spirituality."

The situation, I believe, is not nearly that simple, because the Protestant Ethic was, in part and from the start, a repressive/dissociative structure, which tended to sever higher and lower dimensions of existence in a Manichean flight from matter and life. The Protestant Ethic, in fact, confused the repression of earthly life with the transcendence of earthly life. Mythic mentality in flight from life and body—there was a central part of the Protestant Ethic, whatever else its authentic contributions might have been.

In my opinion, the Success Ethic was, *in part*, an attempt to rectify the developmental miscarriages embedded in the Protestant Ethic. Mythic staticism was replaced by (admittedly naive) progress; conventional-collective (and often herd) morality was opened, at least in a few places, to the idea of individual autonomy and volition (however naive that also might have been); rigid determinism gave way to creative initiative. I am no great fan of the Success Ethic (and its spiritual consequentialism); I just don't think it was merely the dirty little boy Dick would have us believe. In fact, I believe the contrary case can be put with at least equal vigor: the Success Ethic, apart from its vulgarities and banalities (of which there were many), was part of the first great assault of rational-industrial Myths on feudal-mythic Myths. As I would put it, a legitimate worldview (with all its relative perfections) was in the painful process of being replaced by a potentially more authentic but initially much less legitimate worldview (with all its relative imperfections). Dick romantically focuses on the rash of sudden illegitimacies and bastard sons and screams "devolution"; I focus on the potential authenticities and the actual parents and see possible "evolution" as well.

Anthony's difficulties stem, in my opinion, directly from some of the inadequacies in the (otherwise admirable) Weberian system. Weber was writing, in part, in the great tradition of the German Romantics, and, as such, wished to incorporate the *nonrational* elements of existence into a theory of social action. This he attempted to do with the concepts of *meaning* and *charisma*. That is all well and fine. The problem goes back to the German Romantic tradition itself, which, from Novalis to Schleiermacher, divided experience into two great realms—the rational and the nonrational—and then emphasized the nonrational as the door to genuine transcendental and religious experience. This dichotomy between the rational and the nonrational is, as I have repeatedly tried to demonstrate, the great bane of spiritual theorists, simply because, on the nonrational side, it fails to consistently distinguish between *pre*rational experiences and *trans*rational experiences. Prerational and transrational are indiscriminately lumped together as one great nonrational or so-called "experiential" domain (the doorway to "genuine religious experience"), and every movement of "rationality" then appears as a move down or away from "experiential" or "spiritual" purity, whereas that is *only* the case when the experience in question is transrational; when it is prerational, the movement toward reason is progressive, not decadent. There is, in other words, a vast difference between "rationalization" (one definition of which might be a move downward from transrational spirit into the mere forms of reason) and "rationality" (or a move upward, via reason, from prerational experience and impulsivity). Weber does not consistently make that distinction, and so he is never quite sure which way is up and which way is down. When prerational and transrational are lumped together as nonrational, then there is precisely nothing left to do with rationality except give it the short end of the stick, whereas, in at least half the cases, it is a distinct improvement on its predecessors, no matter how admittedly partial and incomplete reason (even at its best) will always be.

"Culture-Free" Rationality

According to Dick, I believe in a radically culture-free rationality, and, further, I place it, as a separate stage, between (mythic) religion and (transpersonal) mysticism. And, he concludes, "I don't know what to say about this. It sort of floors me. It seems the singlemost problematic aspect of Wilber's system. 'Rationality' is notoriously hard to define in any culture-free sense." Not so fast, my friend. Those who deny any and all culture-free rationality claim that their arguments are true for any and all cultures—that is, they themselves use culture-free rationality to deny its existence. Since they are in fact using a culture-free rationality, let me explain how and why I also use it.

First, a few things about "stages" themselves, toward which I take a view most developmentalists would find rather relaxed, considering the weight I attach to the general idea itself. For instance, I do not believe it is necessary, perhaps not even possible, to know or precisely determine the actual number and types of structure-stages that might exist. I do not, however, think that that detracts one whit from the descriptive or explanatory powers of the stage-model. For example, Arieti gives the basic structures as (roughly): physiostates, sensations, perceptions, protoemotions, images, endocepts, symbols, and concepts. Notice that his series, as far as it goes, is quite similar to mine, with the exception of endocepts (or "preconceptual felt-knowledge"). I happen to believe in the existence of endocepts (they are the cornerstone of Gendlin's "felt meaning," but they do not exist, as Gendlin thinks, at the centauric level, but at the typhonic, as Arieti shows; in other words, they are premind/body differentiation, not post-mind/body differentiation), and I believe (with Arieti) that they are quasi-universal basic structures, but I rarely list them unless they are immediately relevant to the discussion.

But there is a more serious question involved here, namely, how many basic structures are there in fact? Not how many do I wish to include, but how many *could* I include with reasonable certainty? For instance, the level I have simply called "the subtle" actually contains, according to some traditions, anywhere from three to ten discrete levels. The question then becomes, are these levels actually quasi-universal deep structures or merely tradition-bound surface structures? At this point, I feel we simply do not have enough information to decide, and thus our decisions on these types of issues (how to divide or subdivide levels) are somewhat arbitrary, but that does not render them useless: the stage-model claim is simply that, in any developmental sequence, certain classes of behavior stably emerge only after certain other classes, and if some of those classes are eventually found to contain other discrete classes, then we have simply enriched our understanding of the sequence, we have not denied it. Thus, for example, Jane Loevinger initially postulated four stages of ego development; refined research subsequently led her to conclude that there are at least ten stages.

As of this writing, I personally believe that one can reasonably postulate approximately two dozen basic structures or developmental *levels* of consciousness (through which a dozen or more different developmental *lines* move relatively independently—such as the lines of cognition, motivation, morals, affects, creativity, esthetics, self-sense, and so on. I am here, however, focusing on the basic levels or basic structures themselves). In most of my writings, I usually group the basic levels into seven to ten of the most important, simply for ease of presentation (in this paper I am using fourteen). But my central point is that it is not theoretically sloppy to assume a casual stance toward the "actual number" of stages; even if, for example, someone discovered a basic cognitive structure between symbols and concepts, it still would not alter the fact that symbols emerge *before* concepts, and concepts emerge only *after* symbols—and it is that relative "before" and "after" that constitutes one of the central claims of developmental theories. If the before and after relation of class *r* and class *z* can be demonstrated to be cross-culturally invariant, then we are (for the moment) justified in suspecting that, at some level of analysis, there are quasi-universal deep structures involved, irrespective of how many classes may or may not subsequently be found in between them.

The pressing question then is, how can we be sure that a given basic structure actually has a quasi-universal deep structure and that is not simply a particular culture-bound array of surface structures? Traditionally, developmentalists have used several criteria for establishing that a particular array has, at its base, a quasi-universal deep structure. The most common is that "Stages may be viewed as existing in some objective sense to the extent that the behaviors associated with them emerge in an order that cannot be altered by environmental factors."* And I am claiming that the basic structures I have presented satisfy that criterion. No matter how much reinforcement you use, you *cannot* get rules to emerge before sensations.

That various classes of phenomena emerge in an order that cannot be altered by environmental factors *is* to say that those classes possess an invariant (quasi-universal) structure, or else their sequence could definitely be altered by contingent factors. In other words, invariant sequence means quasi-universal class structures are involved at some level, or the sequence would not (and could not) be invariant; wobble in the structure would mean wobble in the sequence (which is precisely a definition of surface structure).

Now, virtually all developmentalists acknowledge that "decisions about how to slice up the stream of behavioral change are based on external criteria such as economy and elegance. Hence, there might be several different models that could be posited, all of which would be equally valid descriptions or change in the organism." This does not mitigate the possible quasi-universal nature of the different stage-structures; it simply says that, if you slice the stream from this particular angle, you will always see the same basic phenomena, in the same order, wherever the stream appears.

Likewise, researchers usually agree that there are no precise demarcation lines between stages; the situation appears more like a rainbow, with each color shading into the others, which nevertheless does not prevent us from recognizing that orange is different from blue.

And finally, most developmentalists acknowledge that the task of stage definition is a process whereby "We select certain instants in the course of dynamic change, take 'snapshots' of the system at those instants, and use these snapshots as descriptions of the system at a particular stage of development." Different series of snapshots are obviously possible, and each series usually tells us something important; but if the shots effectively "catch" a deep structure, the order between the phenomena in those shots will be invariant, and vice versa: we have a "stage."

Part of the developmentalist's task, then, is to describe or define, to whatever degree possible, the nature of these stages. Some developmentalists use factor analysis (Royce), some use mathematics (Piaget), some use information processing (Klahr and Wallace), some use more literary

*[See *Transformations of Consciousness,* Introduction, for the sources of the quotations in this section.]

or verbally descriptive methods (Erikson). In my own particular slicing of the developmental stream, I have almost always preferred the literary-descriptive method (even though I have often been moved to postulate a particular stage by researchers using other methods), simply because most other approaches are usually tied to some state-of-the-art schematizations that tend, apart from their initial usefulness, to go obsolete fairly quickly.

As for the stage in question—that of "rationality"—let me explain exactly how and why I came to postulate it, and exactly what I mean by it.

When I first entered this field I was particularly struck by the fact that, as Huston Smith demonstrated, all of the world's great traditions maintained that there were at least four or five hierarchical dimensions or levels of existence: physical, emotional, mental, subtle ("soul"), and spirit, with each senior realm, as it were, including but transcending its juniors. It soon became obvious, from a closer look at both the more sophisticated religious systems and the wealth of Western psychological data, that each of those general realms could in fact be greatly subdivided and still carry quasi-universal import.

The mental sphere, it initially seemed to me, could be divided into *images* (pictorial representation; a mental image of a tree looks more or less like a real tree), *symbols* (nonpictorial representation; the word-symbol "Rover" does not look like the real dog), and *concepts* (a symbol that represents a class of objects—"dog" means all dogs, not just Rover)—and thus, for me, "rational" (as the "highest" mental level) meant "conceptual"; beyond the "conceptual-rational" mind was the beginning of the transmental or subtle dimensions of existence.

However, a deepening study of developmental psychology (particularly but not solely Piaget) convinced me that concepts were not the highest mental constructs (and that, in fact, concepts, when left to their own devices, produce rather primitive or "irrational" worldviews). Beyond concepts are *rules* or operations; a concept can form classes, but operations can combine classes, divide them, multiply them, and so forth. And *meta-rules* can operate on rules themselves. I therefore concluded that the mental domain consisted of at least five major structures: images, symbols, concepts, rules (concrete-operations, or mental operations tied to concrete phenomena), and meta-rules or formal-reflexive thought (thought operating on thought). I was struck to subsequently find Aurobindo's descriptions of these last two stages to be very similar to mine (one of the things that had originally put me off about Aurobindo was that he seemed to have too many stages—sense-mind, will-mind, thought-mind, reasoning-mind, etc. I figured he was making it all up as he went along; it is only recently that I have come to appreciate the extraordinary sophistication of what he was doing; I have no idea where he got that precision—it certainly wasn't from Western psychologists, most of whom, during Aurobindo's time, made distinctions no more complicated than "primary" and "secondary" mental processes).

Now whatever it is that level 9 refers to—assuming it is there—I call by various names: formal-rational, formal-reflexive, meta-rule (or operations on operations), reason, perspectival rationality, or simply rationality. Piaget calls it formal-operational thought, and he has defined it technically as a mathematical lattice generating the sixteen binary propositions of formal logic. I am not convinced that that particular mathematization is the best way to slice and define the developmental stream at that point. As Annette Karmiloff-Smith (a Genevan Piagetian) has conceded, "In all events, a distinction must be drawn between, on the one hand, the idea that there exist certain fundamental qualitative changes that might be described as 'stages,' and, on the other hand, the particular mathematical formalization chosen to represent them. Piaget's formalization (an adaptation of the Bourbaki system) merely reflects the state of the art in the 1950s. Since then, Piaget and his colleagues have considered other formalizations." I prefer the literary description-definition (which Piaget has also used) of "thought operating on thought" (just as I prefer, for the concrete-operational stage, "thought operating on environment," and for the preoperational, "thought representing environment"). Piaget's mathematical description of thought operating on thought might not be a universal description of that stage but a culture-bound description of its most common form in civilized Europe.[3] But however we define those three particular stages, the evidence is overwhelming *that* they are there, although exactly *what* they are is described differently by different researchers.

Thought-operating-on-thought would structurally be expected to involve several related features or classes of behavior, which thought-operating-on-environment would find difficult or impossible: it would be highly reflexive; it would have the capacity for sustained introspection; and it would be able to conceive hypothetico-deductive possibilities. I believe the great bulk of research data supports those claims, and supports the existence of that general stage itself. In fact, Piaget's detractors have almost never attacked his literary descriptions of this stage or its existence; they have attacked (with some justification) his particular mathematical definitions, his claim that his stages are explanatory rather than descriptive, his claim that formal-operational is the highest stage, his "too strict" or "discrete" conception of a stage, his view of the particular dynamics of development. But even his most thoughtful critics—such as Brainerd—have concluded that "Piaget's stages are perfectly acceptable as descriptions of behavior."

Thus, with those particular qualifications in mind, and with the understanding that my definition of this stage is not strictly Piagetian, I believe it is reasonable to conclude, based on available evidence, that thought-operating-on-thought (however otherwise it might be conceived) is a quasi-universal deep structure, essentially similar whether it appears in American, India, Japan, or Malaysia, the specific forms of which, however, are largely culture-bound and historically contingent. I also conclude that thought-operating-on-thought does not emerge in present-day ontogenetic development, if it emerges at all, until around adolescence; that it did not emerge historically in any significant fashion prior to the first millennium BCE; that it finally became a central and dominating structure of the so-called industrial or modern era; and that it itself is now in process of giving way to its successor(s).

There are other, more philosophic reasons for believing that thought-operating-on-thought is a genuine and meaningful stage phenomenon. The whole idea of the evolution of consciousness involves the notion that each basic structure of development *transcends* but *includes* its predecessor. Even Piaget realized the broader meaning of what he was doing: "These overall structures are integrative and noninterchangeable. Each results from the preceding one, integrating it as a subordinate structure, and prepares for a subsequent one, into which it is sooner or later itself integrated." What is the whole of one stage becomes a part of the next; the subject of one stage becomes an object of the next—and so on. As each stage of consciousness transcends its predecessor, it can, for just that reason, prehend it, be aware of it, *operate on it*. It was by thought, in the broadest sense, that men and women could transcend, and thus operate on, the immediate physical environment and the immediate dictates of the physical body (impulse control, volition, technics, etc.). Thought-operating-on-thought simply represents the point that consciousness finally *begins* to transcend thought itself, and thus can *operate on* thought. It represents the point that, so to speak, the whole mental realm starts to become, not merely a subject of awareness, but an object of awareness. It is the beginning of the transcendence of mind, on the way toward supramental developments.

I think this perspective helps to explain, among many other things, the profound shifts in modern philosophy. Traditional philosophy tended to simply assume that thought and language were transparent tools with which to grasp reality; that is, thought and language were unproblematically subjects. One of the single greatest shifts in modern philosophy involved language becoming the *object* of sustained philosophical reflection; thought-operating-on-thought became increasingly aware of the structure of its own existence. The results: linguistic analysis, hermeneutics, structuralism, and semiotics, all of which, I maintain, are consistent with the phenomena that would be expected to emerge at this stage of evolution.

Kohlberg and Gilligan

As for Kohlberg's stages, Dick trots out all the well-worn objections; in this case, however, I happen to agree with a few of them. The single greatest problem with *some* aspects of Kohlberg's descriptions of moral "deep structures" is simply that, in my opinion, he did not go *deep enough*. Some aspects of his deep structures, in other words, seem to be subculture-biased arrays of surface structures (though that does not, as we will see, warrant tossing out his entire or general schema). Carol Gilligan, in particular, has written a moving and believable critique of Kohlberg's system, charging it with, in effect, sexism.

Since Dick puts much stock in Gilligan's account, it is important to realize what, in fact, Gilligan has tried to accomplish. She has *not* challenged the notion that moral transition structures rest on cognitive basic structures; she has *not* challenged the general Piagetian tradition; and, most importantly, she has *not* challenged Kohlberg's basic scheme of preconventional, conventional, and postconventional stages of moral development. In fact, Gilligan simply presents her own three hierarchical stages of moral development in women, and these are explicitly stated as being the female *correlate* of Kohlberg's more male-oriented discoveries. She concludes that "the sequence of women's moral judgement proceeds from an initial concern with survival [preconventional] to a focus on goodness [conventional] and finally to a reflective [thought-operating-on-thought] understanding of care as the most adequate guide to the resolution of conflicts in human relationship." She summarizes these stages as *selfish*, *care*, and *universal care*.

Gilligan consistently refers to her highest stage as "postconventional meta-ethical"; she defines it as being *able* to subject conventional moral standards to reflective considerations. Her major conclusion is simply that, whereas men progress through the three major stages or moral development in terms of rights and justice, women develop through the same stages in terms of care and responsibility. For example, "In the development of a postconventional ethical understanding, women come to see the violence inherent in inequality, while men come to see the limitations of a conception of justice blinded to the differences in human life."

These three general hierarchical stages also happen to be virtually identical to the ones postulated by Piaget's own (relatively unknown) moral studies, which Gilligan quotes with approval ("Piaget describes a three-stage progression through which constraint turns into cooperation and cooperation into generosity.") Further, all of these researchers—Piaget, Kohlberg, and Gilligan—agree that these three general moral stages rest on the three basic structures we have called thought-representing-environment, thought-operating-on-environment, and thought-operating-on-thought. (None of these researchers, however, includes the higher moral stages of the superconscient levels, 10–14, which apparently progress through the various stages of, to use the Buddhist version: arhat morality to bodhisattva morality to the "crazy wisdom" of the siddha or free adept; I try to outline these stages in *System, Self, and Structure*).[4]

The service that Gilligan has rendered is simply to suggest (and partially demonstrate) that certain lines of development might take different forms in men and women, and that, consequently, we must carefully guard against sexist "deep structuring." I agree entirely; but far from "tossing out" Piaget's or Kohlberg's basic schemas or general ideas, Gilligan has offered substantial supporting evidence for them.

I, like Dick, find Gilligan's work very exciting; I had always suspected—based on the fact that in kundalini yoga, each of the seven stages of consciousness evolution is said to have solar and lunar components—that each basic structure of development might have male and female aspects. Gilligan's account is the first clear demonstration, to my knowledge, of precisely how this might occur.

Freud

Dick's critique of Freud is rather wild and random; I don't know who or what he means by the "modern Freudians." Sullivan? Kohut? Kernberg? Mahler? Arieti? Gedo? Masterson?—those are the so-called "Freudians" that have most directly influenced my own work. How the data of those researchers reflect "the false universality of antisocial hyperindividualized human nature" is simply not spelled out, though I must say I was left shuddering at the thought that so devastating an epithet should fall on anybody.

As for modern psychoanalytic theory being "hyper-individual" or "antisocial," I'm sure Dick is aware that object-relations theory (also known as interpersonal theory) arose precisely to emphasize that, as both Fairbairn and Winnicott put it, the organism seeks above all else, not individual impulse discharge, but to *establish relationships*; psychological symptoms are symptoms of disturbed relationships; and disturbed relationships take quite different forms in different societies (as emphasized by Horney, Sullivan, Fromm, etc.). Dick's ideas on "modern psychiatry" seem frozen somewhere in the 1930s, despite (or perhaps because of) his sojourn in the halls of Freudian academe.

My own criticism of "Freud" (i.e., modern object-relations theory, psychoanalytic ego and developmental psychology, and Kohutian self psychology) runs in the opposite direction. I believe that, because modern psychiatry does not recognize higher, existential, and transpersonal dimensions of awareness, that it sooner or later—in theory and especially in practice—stultifies higher growth. Instead of allowing consciousness to go transverbal and transmental, it mistranslates higher and supramental impulses downwardly into obsessively verbal and rational dimensions, thus effectively preventing higher growth. In short, I believe modern psychiatric theory is not so much wrong as it is very limited and partial, and it is those "correct but partial" aspects that I have tried to incorporate in my model.

Kierkegaard

Of all the people I might choose to lead a theoretical assault on anybody, Kierkegaard would be the last. I happen to be a great fan of Kierkegaard (particularly for taking Schelling's notion of "positive philosophy" and turning it into the first important steps toward an existential philosophy). I even wrote a long paper ("Kierkegaard's Passion")[5] on the important contributions of the man. But to be indicted by Kierkegaard is the easiest thing in the world to arrange, because Kierkegaard can be used to indict anybody who recognizes a class of events. Even worse, Kierkegaard himself condemned all verdicts on his own thought, since all such attempts, he felt, reflect only the critic's own existence. He feared and predicted his work would fall into the hands of the professors; and here he is, snug in Dick's hands, being solemnly inflicted on me.

I'll make this brief: Kierkegaard's central difficulty, in my opinion, is that he wants to define truth solely in terms of the *way* it is apprehended, *and* he wants to define it in terms of *what* is apprehended; this inconsistency is elevated to the exalted status of "paradox" and used to cap his whole system.

That this is so is all too obvious if we look at Kierkegaard's position vis-à-vis emotion, reason, and spirit. It is true, as Dick says, that Kierkegaard does not want to elevate reason above sensory-feeling. But it is equally true that he wants to! That is why, in *Stages on Life's Way*, he clearly refers to them as *ranked* stages: esthetic stage, ethical-reasoned stage, and religious-spiritual stage. Here, of course, Kierkegaard is very close to McDougall, Kohlberg, Gilligan, Piaget, etc.

Kierkegaard maintains both positions because—in blind anti-Hegelian reaction—he wishes to maintain that there can be no (objective) criteria for making choices, *and* that the ethical stage *is* superior to the esthetic (precisely because in the former, but not the latter, the role of choice is consciously acknowledged—a nice definition of Kohlberg's and Gilligan's postconventional). This is a blatant and crude inconsistency, not an earth-shaking paradox.

And, anyway, to return specifically to Dick's charges, for someone who just blasted the Freudians for "antisocial hyperindividualism," Kierkegaard is the last name to be theoretically marching behind. Kierkegaard's subjectivistic, antisocial, isolationist fantasies are supposedly "authentic" and "concrete" and "existential," whereas the interpersonal theorists reflect a "false universality of antisocial and hyperindividualized human nature." This is a very strange line of attack.

What I hear Dick saying, through Kierkegaard, is that there is a very real danger of taking any system of thought and turning it, in effect, into an objective idol. With that, I agree entirely. Dick feels that some people take my system and make it into a be-all and end-all, as if Emptiness could ever be radically objectified in mental-linguistic forms. And so let me say, for the record, that that is not at all the way I view my own work. Not only do I hold *all* of it in provisional status, the so-called "highest" state is specifically "defined" as Formless, Mystery, Unknowing, Divine Ignorance, etc., radically beyond any particular objective phenomena, including *any* mental models, that might parade by in the face of formless Infinity. All such models have, at best, what the Hindus and Buddhists would call "relative truth" as opposed to "absolute truth," and much of my writing has been devoted to just that point. If certain individuals insist on misusing my work in this fashion, all I can do is decry it, and repeat again the words from the Preface to *The Atman Project*: the model that follows is of relative use but is "finally a lie in the face of that Mystery which only alone is."

"Normal Consciousness" and "Culture-Free Reason"

1. As for my "failure to differentiate faith and belief," I refer Anthony to *Eden*, *Atman*, and *Eye to Eye*, where the life/death dialectic of each stage of development is highly emphasized, and to the chapter in *A Sociable God* entitled "Belief, Faith, Experience, and Adaptation," where precisely those distinctions are made.

2. "He [Wilber] and his fellow theorists have transcended culture by means of rationality." Nobody has transcended culture by means of rationality; rather, thought-operating-on-thought can become more aware of the impact of its own cultural settings and the relative nature of many of its own perspectives, *precisely* because it can be more reflectively aware of the structure of its own operations (some aspects of which, by comparison, can be seen to be quasi-universal). In both of these ways reason can begin to escape its own provincialism, but that is a far cry from transcending culture per se.

As Dick realizes, I take a more culturally relativistic stance than, e.g., Kohlberg. I do not believe reason (or rationality) per se transcends its own cultural manifestations or preconceptions. I believe, rather, that consciousness in the mode of reason transcends *its own previous* stages of development *in that culture*. In other words, Kohlberg's postconventional stage does not transcend culture per se, it merely transcends the conventional level of culture; it can to some degree operate or reflect on its own conventional operations, and thus to that degree transcend *that level* of its own cultural embeddedness, but it does not thereby transcend cultural embeddedness altogether. For example, it does *not* transcend the new and subtler level of cultural interactions that *constitute* the postconventional *community* of *reflexive* intersubjective exchange.

The very term "postconventional" *correctly* implies that reflective morality transcends nonreflective embeddedness in conventional norms; it *erroneously* implies that the postconventional individual stands freely above all culture, suspended in mid-air, whereas in fact the postconventional individual is now embedded in a *new and subtler culture of reflexive communicative exchange*, whose surface structures mold and are molded by the particular cultural interactions at *that* level of psychosocial development. Those surface-structure (or cultural) constraints can be *lessened* by a hermeneutic-interaction with different cultures or cultural arrays (which is one of the purposes of hermeneutics), but the deep structure constraints can be *transcended* only by a further vertical development within consciousness itself.

Thus, to my mind, it is not a simple affair of "transcending culture" or "not transcending culture." It is rather a complex affair of progressively transcending various possible levels of cultural interaction, with the "final" or "absolute" transcendence of culture occurring *only* at the transcendence of manifestation itself. Each higher level is relatively "freer" vis-à-vis *its own previous stages*, but is *not* thereby free of the surface structures or relational exchanges that embody the deep structure of its own higher level of adaptation, and is therefore not free of culture at *that* level [i.e., each level has all four quadrants].

3. Dick himself believes that "normal consciousness can be viewed in its universal or general form only if you have a place to view it which is outside of it, i.e., transcendence." Here Dick seems to assume there are only two states of consciousness, normal and perfectly transcendental. But if there are over a dozen stages of consciousness, each of which significantly transcends its predecessors, then significant-general statements can be made by each stage vis-à-vis its predecessor. Dick seems to fall into the notion that no generalized knowledge is possible without recourse to absolute (transcendental) knowledge, in which case it would be impossible to genuinely know anything until we know everything. Why Dick reverts to Hegelianism at this point is puzzling, to say the least.

Moreover, Dick's position confuses *collective* with *transpersonal* (a confusion perfected by the Jungians). We can determine, by mundane empiric-analytic inquiry, that the human body everywhere (universally or collectively) possesses ten toes, but that does not mean that if I experience my toes I am having a transcendental-mystical experience. Likewise, the simple statement that certain deep structures are quasi-universal does not imply or demand a radically transcendental stance.

6. Dick defines *true rationality* as "detachment." I understand what he's driving at here, and in a sense I agree—only that, as previously noted, I see each stage of development as being a mini-transcendence (or mini-detachment) from its predecessor(s). Rationality (thought-operating-on-thought) is simply the first major point where mind itself starts

to become quasi-objective, and thus consciousness has a general "feel" we would recognize as "nonattachment" (which I prefer to "detachment"; the latter tends to connote antifeeling, morbid distancing, alienation, etc., which is a mark of rationalization, not rationality).

As for my failure to explore in depth the distinction between rationality and rationalization, Dick is quite right. Other than being reasonably certain that the distinction exists, and that other researchers have often overlooked it, I have not pursued the topic. So I might start with this: rationalization is the illegitimate use of rationality, just as emotionalism or sentimentalism is the illegitimate use of emotion, hedonic indulgence is the illegitimate use of sensation, and so forth. From a psychological view, these illegitimacies (or inappropriate, nonfunctional uses of structural potentials) almost always arise as defense mechanisms, ways to shield the self-system from disintegration (death) through compensatory overuse of a particular structural advantage.

It seems, then, that rationalization, as a defense mechanism (in the broadest sense), can be used to: (1) defend (or "rationalize") lower or emotional-sexual repressions; (2) elevate, reify, or promote a merely rational worldview into a universalistic dogma (e.g., science into scientism); (3) dilute, repress, or "transform-downward" a spiritual-transcendental insight into the mere forms of the rational mind. In other words, "true rationality" can be used to approach the premental, mental, and transmental domains; if defensively misused in any of those approaches, it degenerates into, respectively, the three rationalizations just listed.

I agree entirely with Dick when he states that *both* forms of reason (rationality and rationalization) have played crucial roles in the course of modern Western civilization, and that a truly balanced account would trace the effects (and, where possible, the causes) of both strands. I would be particularly interested in tracing the material institutionalizations of degenerate rationalizations, and their subsequent effects on the course of average-mode consciousness.

5. As for Rorty's brilliant and befuddled book, a few brief comments: from the start Rorty, in my opinion, muddles the distinction between conversation and inquiry; this forces him into a vague coherence theory of truth, which forces him to see not only all philosophy but all natural science as being merely "what we can agree on these days." This, of course, fits the prejudices of any relativist, except that the project itself is so ultimately self-contradictory. Rorty himself pulls back from its logical

implications and falls into a watered-down pragmatist view of truth ("watered-down" because pragmatist theories presuppose something in the external world which will rebuff improper inquiries, and for Rorty there are no inquiries, only conversations). In my own epistemology, I have tried to strike a balance between correspondence and coherence theories of truth; at the very least, I have never found either type of theory alone to be sufficient, and this certainly applies to Rorty's edifications.

Transrational Religion and Its Trivialization

1. Dick claims no stage model can work for spirituality. In response, I will simply report the research findings of Maliszewski, Twemlow, Brown, and Engler, who, after hermeneutic comparisons between key Buddhist, Hindu, and Christian meditative texts, concluded: "The interesting overview that emerged as a result of these analyses was that, upon close inspection of the classical texts, the sequence of experiences reported within the . . . traditions did *not* vary greatly from one meditation system to the next. . . . The major traditions we have studied in their original languages present an unfolding of meditation experiences in terms of a stage model. The models are sufficiently similar to suggest an underlying common invariant sequence of stages [deep structure], despite vast cultural and linguistic differences as well as different styles of practice [surface structure]."

I have carefully included the stages of this study in my own model, and correlated them with other "higher developmentalists." The point is, this approach is far from impossible, let alone useless or trivial. On the contrary, models that do not take this extensive research into account are unreliable.

2. I appreciate Dick's pointing out how difficult the higher stages of development can be, and how rare their accomplishment is. But I do not believe they are quite as rare as Dick maintains. Rather, I believe the majority of contemplative traditions—from Vedanta to Zen to Vajrayana—agree that fairly rapid transformation is *possible* (Zen, Siddha Yoga, and Dzogchen Vajrayana maintain that if you are drawn to practice in this lifetime, you *can* achieve enlightenment in the same lifetime). Dick, apparently, believes that that is impossible; I do not.

3. "History as Illusion"—Nowhere is the importance of interdisciplinary dialogue more obvious than in the notion that history is, pure

and simple, an "illusion." Dick is approaching sociology with the religious presumption that, according to the perennial philosophy, history is an illusion (or "completely fallen"; this is one of the reasons he seems to like the Protestant Ethic and does *not* like the notion of evolution). While there are indeed many texts of the perennial philosophy that can be so interpreted, I do not think the case is that easily settled.

First of all, the idea that the "perennial philosophy" is all *that* perennial is becoming increasingly dubious; at the very least, we must distinguish between radical, formless, and timeless Truth (which in that sense is perennial or eternal, but without form or utterance), and the mere *forms* of Truth (which are temporal and historical). And while formless Truth itself is timeless, the forms of truth are, I believe, historical and evolutionary. Successive forms of evolution are increasingly capable of realizing the formless Ground of all levels of evolution, such that Godhead might therefore best be conceived as both the *Goal* of evolution (the telos of its own Self-realization) and the everpresent *Ground* of evolution (or the Condition of all evolving conditions).

In any event, Spirit or Godhead, when apprehended by the mind, is a paradox: both Goal and Ground, Source and Summit, Alpha and Omega. *From the view of Ground*, history *is* pure illusion. Since God is equally and wholly present at every point of time, then history can neither add to nor subtract from God's omnipresence. *From the view of Summit or Goal*, however, history *is* the unfolding of God to Itself, or the movement from subconscious to selfconscious to superconscious modes; only the latter or superconscient mode can *directly realize* an everpresent unity with God-as-Ground, and thus the latter *alone*, of all the modes, is the direct realization *of* God *by* God. From that point of view, history is the unfolding of God to Itself, an unfolding that appears to us, through a glass darkly, as evolution. From this side of the paradox, history is no mere illusion, *it is the very substance of this drama and the very means of its enactment.*

Thus, to maintain that history is mere illusion is to take a very univocal (nonparadoxical) and dualistic view of Spirit; it is to cling to the timeless One and deny the temporal Many; it is to hide in Spirit-as-contemplated and not see Spirit-in-action; it is to see only Spirit transcendent and not also Spirit immanent. Even Whitehead maintained that God has two natures, primordial and consequent. And this, I think, is why so many *modern* sages are embracing the general notion of evolution as being a more adequate *form* for the comprehension of Spirit-in-action (Schelling, Hegel, Free John, Aurobindo, Teilhard de Chardin,

Hazrat Inayat Khan, Meher Baba's "progressive" statements, etc.). To the question "Why didn't the ancient sages speak of evolution?" these modern sages might answer, "Because, in archaic times, collective evolution had not yet arrived at highly self-conscious forms—evolution was not yet reflexively aware of its own existence—and thus the general *idea* of evolution was not available as a *form* through which superconscient realization could easily express itself."

4. "Words from a perfect master have meaning but when paraphrased by others they lose that meaning." Dick knows that I agree with that; I just don't think they lose *all* meaning. But I am profoundly suspicious of *any* statements about the transrational levels; I have referred to all such attempts—including my own—as "mandalic" (poetic-paradoxical) *at best*; I have said that what these higher stages mean can only be fully understood by actual personal transformation. But this is not to condemn to idolatry any and all discussions of the higher domains. A menu is an obstacle only if one tries to eat it instead of the meal.

I think rational discussions of transrational domains—however partial, limited, and constrictive—serve a useful if intermediate function, if for no other reason than that we live in a "rationalized" society that itself will initiate such discussion quite beyond our protests. But to understand the radical limitations of mental forms does not mean to cease using them, and if certain my "followers" insist on confusing my "mandalic maps" with the territory itself, I can do nothing except repeat again all the warnings for such "translative" (as opposed to transformative) endeavors.

I have also—in *Eye to Eye* and *A Sociable God*—voiced this protest to my transpersonal colleagues, some of whom are attempting to construct "hermeneutic maps" of the transrational domains with a univocal precision I find ludicrously impossible and self-serving; and while I am obviously in sympathy with such "mandalic map" constructions, all of them can *only* be, as Zen would put it, fingers pointing at the moon. Some of my colleagues, alas, imagine they have captured the lunar landscape itself, and *that*, both Dick and I would agree, is preposterous.

I do believe, however, that *some* things about the transrational domains can be hinted at with a skillful but controlled use of reason, just as a painter can, with a skillful use of a 2-D canvas, convey the feeling of a 3-D perspective. This is what I attempt to do with my sketches of the higher or transrational levels of development, and this is where hermeneutic-mandalic maps are useful. The sources of these maps are not my own personalistic ideas; they are composites taken from the mystical traditions themselves—particularly Vajrayana, Zen, and Theravadin Buddhism; Vedanta; Kashmir Shaivism; Christian mysticism; Kabbalah; Sufism; neo-Confucianism; and such "individuals" as Plotinus, Chih I, Free John, Aurobindo, Gurdjieff, and—I must remind Dick of this—Meher Baba (Chart I in *God Speaks* outlines seven planes of consciousness, from gross to mental to infinite, culminating in God-consciousness, yet another version of the Great Nest of Being). In my own spiritual practice, I have been fortunate enough to glimpse some of these realms, and I have been careful to set into words only those general aspects that do not seem, in my own experience, to be violently distorted by utterance. But, anyway, if discussing the transrational is a sin, then both Dick and I are bound for hell, where, I'm sure, the discussion will continue unabated.

Notes

1. In the following, when I say, for example, "According to Anthony, my presentation fails in such and such a way," it is not necessarily Dick's criticism but merely one that he is repeating. Likewise, when I criticize "Dick Anthony," it is not necessarily his own views I am challenging. I will try to indicate specifically when a criticism is Anthony's.
2. Published in the *Journal of Transpersonal Psychology* 16, no. 1 (1984), pp. 75–118, and reprinted as chapters 3, 4, and 5 of *Transformations of Consciousness*.
3. Thus, I have never been comfortable with Piaget's matrix mathematics used to define the concrete operational stages, either. What I appreciate about Piaget is that, where most pyschologists (such as Arieti) simply described cognitive development up to concepts, Piaget's brilliant research showed that what was loosely said to be "conceptual thinking" actually breaks down into at least three different types or stages-preoperational (preop), concrete operational (conop), and formal operational (formop). (Preop is part of conop, but it is common to treat them as separate stages.) Both conop and formop Piaget defined in a very specific fashion, using either mathematical formalisms or binary propositions. But my point is, whether or not we agree with his mathematical definitions, the fact remains that preop, conop, and formop are quite different types of thinking, and this is a profoundly important discovery. My preference, as indicated, is for the literary description-definition of these types as, respectively: thought representing environment, thought operating on environment, and thought operating on thought. This does not preclude Piaget's mathematical formalisms, but neither is it tied to them.
4. [See *Integral Psychology* in this volume.]
5. *ReVision* 6, no. 1 (Spring 1983), pp. 81–85.

DEATH, REBIRTH, AND MEDITATION

SOME TYPE OF REINCARNATION DOCTRINE is found in virtually every mystical religious tradition the world over. Even Christianity accepted it until around the fourth century CE, when, for largely political reasons, it was made anathema. Many Christian mystics today, however, accept the idea. As the Christian theologian John Hick pointed out in his important work *Death and Eternal Life,* the consensus of the world's religions, including Christianity, is that some sort of reincarnation occurs.

Of course, the fact that many people *believe* something does not make it true. And it is very difficult to support the idea of reincarnation by appealing to "evidence" in the form of alleged past-life memories, because in most cases these can be shown to be only a revival of subconscious memory trace from *this* life.

Yet this problem is not as serious as it might at first appear, because the doctrine of reincarnation, as used by the great mystical traditions, is a very specific notion: It does *not* mean that the *mind* travels through successive lives and therefore that under special conditions—for example, hypnosis—the mind can recall all of its past lives. On the contrary, it is the *soul,* not the mind, that transmigrates. Hence, the fact that reincarnation cannot be proven by appeal to memories of past lives is exactly what we should expect: Specific memories, ideas, knowledge, and so on, belong to the mind and do not generally transmigrate. All of that is usually left behind, with the body, at death. (Perhaps a few specific memories can sneak through every now and then, as the cases recorded by Professor Ian Stevenson and others suggest, but these would be the exception rather than the rule.) What transmigrates is the soul, and the soul is not a set of memories or ideas or beliefs.

Rather, according to most branches of the perennial philosophy, the soul has two basic defining characteristics: First, it is the repository of one's "virtue" (or lack thereof)—that is, of one's karma, both good and bad; second, it is one's "strength" of awareness, or one's capacity to "witness" the phenomenal world without attachment or aversion. This second capacity is also known as "wisdom." The accumulation of these two—virtue and wisdom—constitutes the soul, which is the only thing that transmigrates. So, when people claim to be "remembering" a past life—where they lived, what they did for a living, and so on—they are probably not, according to any major religion or branch of the perennial philosophy, remembering any actual past lives. Only Buddhas (or tulkus), it is said, can usually remember past lives—the major exception to the rule. Even the Dalai Lama has said he cannot remember his past lives, which should perhaps serve as a reminder to those who think they can.

Reincarnation as a Spiritual Hypothesis

But if ostensible past-life memories are not good evidence for reincarnation, what other type of evidence could there be to support the doctrine? Here we should remember that the perennial philosophy in general allows three major and different types of knowledge and its verification: sensory or empirical knowledge; mental or logical knowledge; and spiritual or contemplative knowledge. Reincarnation is not primarily a sensory or a mental hypothesis; it cannot easily be explained or verified using sensory data or logical deduction. It is a spiritual hypothesis, which is to be tested with the eye of contemplation, not with the eye of flesh or the eye of mind. So, although we will find little ordinary evidence to convince us about reincarnation, once we take up contemplation and become fairly proficient at it, we will start to notice certain obvious facts—for example, that the witnessing position, the soul position, begins to partake of eternity, of infinity.

There is a timeless nature about the soul that becomes perfectly obvious and unmistakable: one actually begins to "taste" the immortality of the soul, to intuit that the soul is to some extent above time, above history, above life and death. In this way one becomes gradually convinced that the soul does not die with the body or the mind, that the soul has existed before and will exist again. But this usually has nothing to do with specific memories of past lives. Rather, it is a recollection of that aspect of the soul that touches spirit and is therefore radically and perfectly timeless. In fact, from this angle it becomes obvious that, as the great Vedantic seer Shankara put it, "The one and only transmigrant is the Lord," or absolute Spirit itself. It is ultimately Buddha-mind itself, the One and Only, that is appearing as all these forms, manifesting itself as all these appearances, transmigrating as all these souls. In the deeper stages of contemplation, this realization of eternity, of spirit as undying and indestructible, becomes quite palpable.

Yet, according to the perennial teachings, it is not *merely* the Absolute that transmigrates. If the soul awakens, or dissolves in spirit, then it no longer transmigrates; it is "liberated," or it realizes that, as spirit, it is reincarnated everywhere, as all things. But, if the soul does not awaken to spirit, if it is not enlightened, then it is reincarnated, taking with it the accumulation of its virtue and wisdom, rather than specific recollections of its mind. And this chain of rebirths continues until these two accumulations—virtue and wisdom—finally reach a critical point, whereupon the soul becomes enlightened, or dissolved and released in spirit, thus bringing individual transmigration to an end.

Even Buddhism, which denies the absolute existence of the soul, acknowledges that the soul has a relative, or conventional, existence, and that this relatively or conventionally existing soul does transmigrate. When the Absolute, or shunyata, is directly experienced, the relative transmigration—and the separate soul—comes to an end. One might think, however, that a Buddhist would object to our use of the word *soul* in this context, since this term generally has the connotation of something that is indestructible or everlasting—a connotation that seems to be incompatible with the Buddhist idea that the soul has only a relative and temporary existence. A closer look at the teachings of the perennial philosophy, however, will resolve this apparent contradiction.

According to the perennial tradition, the soul is indeed indestructible, but when it fully discovers spirit, its own sense of separateness is dissolved or transcended. The soul still remains as the individuality, or expression of the particular person, but its being or center shifts to spirit, thus dissolving its illusion of separateness. And this doctrine accords almost exactly with the highest teachings of Buddhism—the anuttara-tantra yoga, or "highest Tantra teaching"—according to which there exists at the very center of the heart chakra, in each and every individual, what is technically called "the indestructible drop" (or luminosity). As the Vajrayana teaches, it is this indestructible drop that transmigrates. Further, it *is* indestructible; even Buddhas are said to possess it. The indestructible drop is said to be the seat of the very subtle "wind" *(rLung)* that supports the "very subtle [or causal] mind," the mind of enlightenment, or one's spiritual essence. Hence, Buddhism agrees with the perennial philosophy: The indestructible drop is the soul, the continuum, as I have defined it.

Stages of the Dying Process: Dissolution of the Great Chain of Being

The various branches of the perennial philosophy agree, in a general way, about the stages of the dying process and the experiences that accompany these stages: Death is a process in which the Great Chain of Being "dissolves," for the individual, "from the bottom up," so to speak. That is, upon death, the body dissolves into mind, then mind dissolves into soul, then soul dissolves into spirit, with each of these dissolutions marked by a specific set of events. For example, body dissolving into mind is the actual process of physical death. Mind dissolving into soul is experienced as a review and "judgment" of one's life. Soul dissolving into spirit is a radical release and transcendence. Then the process "reverses," so to speak, and based upon one's accumulated karmic tendencies, one generates a soul out of spirit, then a mind out of soul, then a body out of mind—whereupon one forgets all the previous steps and finds oneself reborn in a physical body. According to the Tibetans, the whole process takes about forty-nine days.

The Tibetan tradition contains the richest, most detailed phenomenological description of the stages of the dissolution of the Great Chain during the dying process. According to the Tibetans, the *subjective experiences* that accompany each of what are said to be eight stages of the dissolution are know technically as: "mirage," "smokelike," "fireflies," "butter lamp," "white appearance," "red increase," "black near-attainment," and "clear light." In order to understand these terms, we need a somewhat more precise and detailed version of the Great Chain. So, instead of our simplified version of body, mind, soul, and spirit, we will use a slightly expanded version: matter, sensation, perception, intention, cognition, psychic, subtle, causal (or formless unmanifest), and spirit (or ultimate).

The first stage of the dying process occurs when the aggregate of form, or matter—the lowest level of the great chain—dissolves. There are said to be five *external* signs of this: the body loses its physical power; one's vision becomes unclear and blurred; the body becomes heavy and feels like it is "sinking"; life goes out of the eyes; and the body's complexion loses its luster. The *internal* sign, which occurs spontaneously with these outer signs, is a "miragelike appearance," a type of shimmering, watery image, such as appears in a desert on a hot day. This is said to occur because, technically, the "wind" *(rLung)* of the "earth" element has dissolved in the "central channel" and the "water" element thus predominates—hence, the watery or miragelike appearance.

Next, the second aggregate, that of sensation, dissolves. Again there are five external signs: One ceases to have bodily sensations, pleasant or unpleasant; mental sensations cease; bodily fluids dry up (the tongue becomes very dry, for example); one no longer perceives external sounds; and inner sounds (buzzing in the ears, for example) also cease. The internal sign associated with this second dissolution is a "smokelike appearance," which is like a fog. Technically, this is said to occur because the "water" element, which caused the miragelike appearance, is dissolving into the "fire" element—hence the smoky appearance.

The third stage is the dissolution of the third level or aggregate, that of perception or discernment. The five external signs: One can no longer recognize or discern objects; one can no longer recognize friends or family; the warmth of the body is lost (the body becomes cold); one's inhalation becomes very weak and shallow; and one can no longer detect smells. The internal sign spontaneously accompanying this stage is called "fireflies," which is described as an appearance like a bunch of fireflies or cinder sparks from a fire. Technically, this is said to occur because the "fire" element has dissolved and the "wind" element now predominates.

The fourth stage is the dissolution of the fourth level or aggregate, that of intention (or "intentional formations"). The five external signs of this dissolution: One can no longer move (because there are no impulses); one can no longer recollect actions or their purposes; all breathing stops; the tongue becomes thick and blue and one can no longer speak clearly; and one can no longer experience tastes. The internal sign of this is a "butter-lamp appearance," described as looking like a steady, clear, bright light. (At this point we can start to see similarities with the near-death experience, which I will discuss further below).

To understand the fifth and subsequent stages of the dissolution process, it is necessary to know a little Tantric physiology. According to Vajrayana, all mental states—gross, subtle, and very subtle (or causal)—are supported by corresponding "winds," or energies, or life forces, (*prana* in Sanskrit, *rLung* in Tibetan). When these winds dissolve, their corresponding minds also dissolve. Stage five is the dissolution of the fifth level or aggregate, that of cognition, or gross consciousness itself. As the Vajrayana teachings make clear, however, there are many levels of consciousness. These levels are divided into what are called the gross mind, the subtle mind, and the very subtle mind, each of which dissolves in order, producing specific signs and experiences. So, stage five is the dissolution of the gross mind, along with the "wind" that supports it. There is then no gross conceptualization, no ordinary mind, left.

During this fifth stage, after the last of the gross mind dies away and the first of the subtle mind emerges, one experiences a state called "white appearance." This is said to be a very bright, very clear white light, like a clear autumn night brilliantly lit by a shimmering full moon. To understand the cause of this white appearance, however, we have to introduce the Tibetan notion of *thig–le,* which means, roughly, "drops" or "essence." According to Vajrayana, there are four drops, or essences, that are particularly important. One, the white drop, is said to be located at the crown of the head; one receives it from one's father, and it is said to represent (or to actually be) bodhichitta, or enlightenment-mind. The second, the red drop, one receives from one's mother; it is located at the naval center. (The white drop is also said to be connected with semen, the red drop with [menstrual] blood, but the point is that men and women have both, equally.) The third, which is called "the drop that is indestructible for this life," is located at the very center of the heart chakra. This drop is, so to speak, the essence of this particular lifetime of the individual; it is one's "continuum," which stores all the impressions and understandings of this particular life. And *inside* this "drop that is indestructible for life" is the fourth drop, "the drop that is eternally indestructible or forever indestructible." This is the indestructible drop that remains forever—that is, it is indestructible through this life, indestructible through death and the dying process, indestructible through the bardo, or intermediate state between death and rebirth, and through rebirth itself. This drop even remains through enlightenment and is, in fact, the very subtle wind that serves as the "mount," or basis, of enlightenment being. As mentioned before, even Buddhas are said to possess this eternally indestructible drop.

So, what we have seen so far is the dissolution of all the gross winds and the gross minds associated with them. The first subtle mind has thus emerged—that of "white appearance"—and it is "riding" a correspondingly subtle wind, or subtle energy. Now, the actual cause of this mind of white appearance is said to be the descent of the white drop, or bodhichitta, from the crown to the heart chakra. Usually, it is said, the white drop is held at the crown chakra by constricting knots and winds of ignorance and gross-level clinging and grasping. But at this stage of the dying process, the gross mind has dissolved, so the knots around the crown chakra naturally loosen, and the white drop descends to the indestructible drop at the heart chakra. When it reaches it, the mind of white appearance spontaneously arises.

Incidentally, if these Tibetan explanations of the phenomena in question sound a bit far-fetched, we should remember that there is a tremendous amount of contemplative evidence supporting the existence of the various experiences said to occur during the dying process. The *experiences* themselves are real and seem largely incontrovertible, but there is plenty of room to argue with the traditional Tibetan account of what actually causes them. (I'll return to this point shortly.) Here I am merely describing the straight Tibetan version as a point of departure.

Nevertheless, we should also keep in mind that, unlike our own Western culture, traditional cultures like the Tibetan live with death constantly; people die in their homes, surrounded by family and friends. The actual stages of the dying process have thus been observed thousands, even millions of times. And when we add the further fact that the Tibetans possess a rather sophisticated understanding of the spiritual dimension and its development, the result is an incredibly rich store of knowledge and wisdom about the actual dying process *and* how it relates to the spiritual dimension, to spiritual development, to karma and rebirth, and so on. Clearly, it would be foolish for an investigator to toss out the massive data that this tradition has accumulated.

But, to continue with the stages of the dying process. At stage six, the subtle mind and its wind dissolve, and an even subtler mind, called "red increase," emerges. Red increase is also an experience of brilliant light; but in this case, it is an experience like a clear autumn day pervaded by bright sunlight. Technically, this is said to occur because the gross life-supporting winds have dissolved, and thus all the knots and constrictions around the navel, which were holding the red bodhichitta, or red drop at the navel, are released or unloosened, and the red drop rises up to the indestructible drop at the heart. When it reaches it, the mind of red increase spontaneously arises.

Stage seven is said to be the dissolution of the subtle mind of red increase and the emergence of an even subtler mind and wind, called "the mind of black near-attainment." In this state, all consciousness ceases, all manifestation dissolves. Further, there is a cessation of all of the specific consciousnesses and energies that were developed in this life. The experience is said to be one of a completely black night, with no stars, no light. It is called "near-attainment" because it is "nearing" the final attainment, so to speak; it is nearing the clear light void. This level, in other words, can be thought of as the highest of the subtle or the lowest of the causal, or as the unmanifest dimension of spirit itself. Technically, this "blackness" is said to occur because the white drop from above and the red drop from below now surround the indestructible drop, thus cutting off all awareness.

In the next and final stage, however—in stage eight—the white drop continues downward and the red drop continues upward, thus freeing or opening the indestructible drop. Then, it is said, a period of extraordinary clarity and brilliant awareness results, which is experienced like an extremely clear, bright, and radiant sky, free from any type of blemish, any clouds, any obstructions. This is the clear light.

Now, the mind of clear light is said to be not a subtle mind, but a very subtle mind, and it mounts a correspondingly very subtle wind or energy. This very subtle or "causal" mind and energy are, in fact, the mind and energy of the eternally indestructible drop. This is the causal body, or the ultimate spiritual mind and energy, the Dharmakaya. At this point, the eternally indestructible drop sheds the lifetime indestructible drop, all consciousness ceases, and the soul, the eternally indestructible drop, commences the bardo experience, or the intermediate states that will eventually lead to rebirth. The white drop continues downward and appears as a drop of semen on the sexual organ, and the red drop continues upward and appears as a drop of blood at the nostrils. Death, finally, has occurred, and the body can be disposed of. To do so before this has occurred makes one karmically guilty of murder, because the body is still alive.

Stages of the Rebirth Process

What we have seen so far is the progressive dissolution of the Great Chain, in an individual's case, starting at the bottom and working up. Matter, or form, dissolved into body (or into sensation, then perception, then impulse), and body dissolved into mind, into the gross mind. The gross mind then dissolved into the subtle mind, or soul realms, and the soul then reverted to causal or spiritual essence. Now, at this point, the process will be reversed, depending on the karma of the soul—on the accumulation of virtue and wisdom that the soul takes with it. Thus, the bardo experience is divided into three basic realms, or stages, and these stages are simply the realms of spirit, then mind, then body and matter. The soul, according to its virtue and wisdom, will either recognize, and thus remain in, the higher dimensions, or it will not recognize them—indeed, will actually flee from them—and thus will end up running "down" the Great Chain of Being until it is forced to adopt a gross physical body and hence be reborn.

At the point of actual or final death—which is what we have been calling the eighth stage of the overall dying process—the soul, or the eternally indestructible drop, enters what is called the chikhai bardo, which is nothing other than spirit itself, the Dharmakaya. As the *Tibetan Book of the Dead* states, "At this moment, the first glimpsing of the Bardo of the Clear Light of Reality, which is the infallible Mind of the Dharmakaya, is experienced by all sentient beings."

This is the point where meditation and spiritual work become so important. Most people, according to the *Tibetan Book of the Dead,* cannot recognize this state for what it is. In Christian terms, they do not know God and thus they do not know when God stares them in the face. In fact, they are at this point one with God, entirely and totally in a supreme identity with Godhead. But unless they recognize this identity, unless they have been contemplatively trained to recognize that state of divine Oneness, they will actually flee from it, driven by their lower desires and karmic propensities. As W. Y. Evans-Wentz, the first translator of the *Tibetan Book of the Dead,* put it: "Owing to unfamiliarity with such a state, which is an ecstatic state of non-ego, of [causal] consciousness, the average human being lacks the power to function in it; karmic propensities becloud the consciousness-principle with thoughts of personality, of individualized being, of dualism, and losing equilibrium, the consciousness-principle falls away from the Clear Light."

So the soul contracts away from Godhead, from Dharmakaya, away from the causal. Indeed, it is said that the soul actually seeks to escape from the realization of divine Emptiness and "blacks out," so to speak, until it awakens in the next lower realm, which is called the chonyid bardo, the subtle dimension, the Sambhogakaya, the archetypal dimension. This experience is marked by all sorts of psychic and subtle visions, visions of gods and goddesses, dakas and dakinis, all accompanied by dazzling and almost painfully brilliant lights and illuminations and colors. But again, most people are not used to this state and have no idea about transcendental light and divine illumination, so they actually flee these phenomena and are attracted by the lesser or impure lights that also appear.

Thus, the soul again contracts inwardly, tries to get away from these divine visions, blacks out again, and wakes up in what is called the sidpa bardo, the gross-reflecting realm. Here the soul eventually has a vision of its future parents making love, and—in good old-fashioned Freudian style—if it is going to be a boy it feels desire for the mother and hatred for the father, and if it is going to be a girl it feels hatred for the mother and attraction to the father. (So far as I can tell, this is the first detailed explanation of the Oedipal/Electra complex—about a thousand years ahead of Freud, as Jung himself pointed out.)

At this stage, it is said, the soul—because of its jealousy and envy—"steps in" in its imagination to separate the father and mother, to come between them; but the result is simply that it really does come between them—that is, it ends up being reborn to them. It now has desire, aversion, attachment, hatred, and a gross body: In other words, it is a human being. It is at the lowest stage of the Great Chain, and its own growth and development will be a climb back up the stages that it has just denied and fled from; its evolution is, so to speak, a reversal of the "fall." How far it gets back up the Great Chain of Being will determine how it handles the dying process and the bardo states when it is again time to shed its physical body.

Interpretation of the Subjective Death and Rebirth Experiences

The contemplative evidence strongly suggests that the data, the phenomenological *experiences* that accompany the dying process—for example, the "white appearance," the "red increase," the "black near–

attainment"—exist and are very real. Further evidence of their reality is found in the fact that they seem to have actual ontological referents in the higher dimensions of the Great Chain of Being. The three experiences just mentioned, for instance, refer respectively to what I have called the psychic, the subtle, and the causal levels of consciousness. In my opinion, then, the levels are real, and thus the experiences of those levels are themselves real. But this does not mean that individuals' experiences of these levels cannot be quite different.

For example, a Buddhist would probably experience the "white appearance" as a type of emptiness or shunyata experience, whereas a Christian mystic might see it in the form of a saintly presence, possibly Christ himself, or a great being of light. But this is as it should be. For, until the "lifetime indestructible drop"—the accumulated impressions and beliefs gathered throughout this lifetime—actually dissolves (at what we have called stage seven), it will color and mold all of one's experiences. A Buddhist will therefore tend to have a Buddhist experience, a Christian will have a Christian experience, a Hindu will have a Hindu experience, and an atheist will probably be extremely confused. All this is what we should expect. It is only at stage eight, at the clear light void, or pure Godhead, that one's personal interpretations and subtle beliefs are shed and a direct realization of pure reality itself, as clear light, is given. Hence, the Tibetan explanation of the data is not the only account possible. It is, however, one among several very important reflections or perspectives on the process of dying, death, and rebirth, rooted in a profound grasp of the Great Chain of Being, both going "up" (meditation and death) and going "down" (bardo and rebirth).

NEAR-DEATH EXPERIENCE AND THE STAGES OF THE DYING PROCESS

The most common phenomenon in Western reports of the near–death experience (NDE) is the experience of passing through a tunnel and then seeing a brilliant light, or meeting a great being of light—a being that has incredible wisdom and intelligence and bliss. The particular individual's religious belief does not matter here; atheists have this experience as often as true believers. This fact, in itself, tends to corroborate the idea that, in the dying process, one does contact some of the subtler dimensions of existence.

From the standpoint of the Tibetan model we have been discussing, the "light" reported in NDEs, depending on its intensity or its clarity, could be the level of the butter lamp, the white appearance, or the red increase. The point is that, at this point in the death process, the gross mind and body, or the gross winds and energies, have dissolved, and thus the subtler dimensions of mind and energy begin to emerge, which are characterized by brilliant illumination and mental clarity and wisdom. So it is not surprising that people universally, regardless of belief, report the experience of light at this point. Many people who report NDEs believe that the light they have seen is absolute spirit. If the Tibetan model is accurate, however, then what people see during the NDE is not exactly the highest level. Beyond white appearance or red increase is black near-attainment, then clear light, then the bardo states.

The experience of the subtle-level light is very pleasant—in fact, amazingly blissful. And the next level, the very subtle or causal, is even more so. Indeed, people who have had NDEs report that they have never experienced anything as peaceful, as profound, as blissful. But we need to keep in mind that all of the experiences up to this point are molded by the "lifetime indestructible drop"; hence, as we have already noted, Christians might see Christ, Buddhists see Buddha, and so on. All this makes sense, because the experiences of these realms are conditioned by one's present life experiences. But then, at stage eight, the "lifetime indestructible drop" is shed, along with all the personal memories and impressions and specifics of this particular life, and the "eternally indestructible drop" moves out of the body and into the bardo state. And thereupon commences the bardo ordeal—a real nightmare unless one is very familiar with these states through meditation.

The dying experience and the NDE are actually a lot of fun, in a sense: It is universally reported that, after one gets over the terror of dying, the process is blissful, peaceful, extraordinary. But when the "ascent" is completed, the "descent," or bardo, begins—and there's the rub. Because at that point, all of one's karmic propensities, all of one's attachments, desires, and fears, actually appear right before one's eyes, so to speak, just as in a dream, because the bardo is a purely mental or subtle dimension, like a dream, where everything one thinks immediately appears as a reality.

Thus, one does not hear about this "downside" to the death process from the NDE people. They are just tasting the early stages of the overall process. Nevertheless, their testimony is powerful evidence that this process does in fact occur. It all fits with a fairly remarkable precision.

Moreover, it is not possible to explain away their testimony by claiming that all of them have studied Tibetan Buddhism; in fact, most of them have not even heard of it. But they have essentially similar experiences as the Tibetans because these experiences reflect the universal and cross-cultural reality of the Great Chain of Being.

Meditation as Rehearsal for Death

Where does meditation fit into all of this? Every form of meditation is basically a way to transcend the ego, or die to the ego. In that sense, meditation mimics death—that is, death of the ego. If one progresses fairly well in *any* meditation system, one eventually comes to a point of having so exhaustively "witnessed" the mind and body that one actually rises above, or transcends, the mind and body, thus "dying" to them, to the ego, and awakening as subtle soul or even spirit. And this is actually experienced as a death. In Zen it is called the Great Death. It can be a fairly easy experience, a relatively peaceful transcendence of subject-object dualism, or—because it is a real death of sorts—it can also be terrifying. But subtly or dramatically, quickly or slowly, the sense of being a separate self dies, or is dissolved, and one finds a prior and higher identity in and as universal spirit.

But meditation can also be a rehearsal of actual bodily death. Some meditation systems, particularly the Sikh (the Radhasoami saints) and the Tantric (Hindu and Buddhist), contain very precise meditations that mimic or induce the various stages of the dying process very closely—including stopping the breath, the body becoming cold, the heart slowing and sometimes stopping, and so forth. Actual physical death is then not much of a surprise, and one can then much more easily use the intermediate states of consciousness that appear after death—the bardos—to gain enlightened understanding. The point of such meditations is to be able to recognize spirit, so that when the body, mind, and soul dissolve during the actual dying process, one will recognize spirit, or Dharmakaya, and abide as that, rather than flee from it and end up back in samsara again, back in the illusion of a separate soul, mind, and body; or to be able, if one does choose to reenter a body, to do so deliberately—that is, as a bodhisattva.

These death-mimicking meditations are not actually life threatening; the body is not really dying, or going through the concrete death stages themselves. Rather, it is like holding one's breath to see what it is like:

One does not stop breathing forever. But some of the states that can be induced by these meditations are powerful imitations of the real thing. One's heartbeat, for example, can actually stop for an extended period, as can the breath. This, for example, is how it is possible to tell that the "winds" have entered and are remaining in the central channel. One is "imitating" death, but doing so by actually—if temporarily—dissolving the same winds that are dissolved in death. Thus it is a very concrete and very real imitation.

How exactly do the various winds or energies described in Tantra relate to meditation? The central idea of all Tantra, whether Hindu, Buddhist, Gnostic, or Sikh, is that every mental state, or every state of consciousness—in other words, every level in the Great Chain of Being—also has a specific supporting energy, *prana,* or wind. (We have already examined the Tibetan version of this doctrine.) Thus, if one dissolves that particular wind, one will dissolve the mind that is supported by it. Hence, if one can gain control over these winds or energies, one can transcend the minds that "ride" them. This is the general notion of pranayama, "breath" or "wind" control. But also, since mind rides wind, wherever one puts the mind, its winds tend to gather. So, for example, if a meditator concentrates very intensely on the crown chakra, then wind, or energy, will tend to gather there and then dissolve there.

This means that mind, at whatever level, has a measure of control over the winds associated with it. Hence, by mental training and concentration, one can learn to gather winds or life energies at particular places, then dissolve them there. And that dissolution is said to be the same type of process that occurs at death. So one is actually experiencing, in a very concrete way, what happens when all the various winds dissolve at death—beginning with the gross winds, then continuing as the subtle winds dissolve, leaving the very subtle or causal wind and the mind of clear light that rides it. By inducing these experiences of the dying process by one's own free will, then, when actual death comes, one knows exactly what the dissolution of the winds is going to produce.

This type of practice also gives one the ability to prolong each state, particularly the subtler states, such as those of white appearance, red increase, black near-attainment, and clear light, because one has already more or less mastered them. Then, at the actual final point of death, at what we have been calling the eighth stage—as one enters the chikhai bardo, the Dharmakaya—one can remain there if one chooses. That clear-light state is very clear and obvious and easy to recognize, because one has seen it many times in meditation and in the mind of one's guru;

hence, one cleaves to that and is thus released from the necessity of rebirth. (One might, however, still choose to be reborn in a physical body in order to help others reach this understanding and freedom—just as in a lucid dream one can consciously control what appears.)

A common technique for gathering and dissolving winds at a particular spot in the body is to concentrate on the "red drop" at the navel center (the source of what is called the tummo fire). One simply concentrates on that object—visualized as a fiery red drop, the size of a small pea—until one can remain concentrated, with unbroken attention, for thirty or forty minutes or so. At that point, the energies of the body will be so concentrated in that area that breathing will subside and become very soft, almost imperceptible. All of the winds or energies of the body are being withdrawn from their ordinary work and concentrated there. Hence, it is very similar to these winds dissolving, or being withdrawn, as occurs in actual death. So if one continues to meditatively concentrate, it is said that one will begin to experience all the signs of the dying process, in order, including the miragelike appearance, the smoke appearance, the fireflies appearance, and the butter-lamp appearance.

At this point, as the winds or energies of the body begin to gather and dissolve at the heart, as in actual death, one will experience the levels of the subtle mind, the mind of white appearance, then red increase, then black near-attainment. Then, through the power of one's meditation and spiritual blessings, all winds or energies will finally dissolve in the indestructible drop at the heart, and one will experience the clear-light void, the ultimate spiritual dimension and realization. In short, this type of meditation is a perfect mimicking of the dying process. And again, the whole point is that by familiarizing oneself with the clear light, by developing meditative wisdom and virtue, then upon actual death, one can remain as the clear light and thus recognize final liberation.

This type of mediation is obviously a very intense ordeal, almost gymnastic in its demands. Not all meditation is this exacting, nor is this the only contemplative path that can traverse the entire upper reaches of spiritual development. But the importance of the anuttaratantra class of meditation, which I just outlined, is the incredibly rich phenomenological descriptions that it gives of an overall contemplative path that uses *both* the mind's awareness and the body's energies to plumb the depths of the human spirit.

Although most meditative paths are not this demanding, most do in fact follow a similar, general, overall course of unfolding (see *Transformations of Consciousness*). There is the initial rising above the gross ego, experienced as a release from the confines of the separate-self sense and its obsessive sufferings. This initial release—depending on the specifics of the path and the person—might be experienced as a type of cosmic consciousness or nature mysticism, as an initial arousal of kundalini energy beyond the conventional realm, as an awakening of paranormal powers, or as an interior experience of blissful luminosity, to name a common few. If consciousness continues to move through the subtle and into the causal, all of those experiences continue to intensify, to the point that they are all dissolved or reduced to pure formlessness, to the causal unmanifest, to an Emptiness prior to all form, a Silence prior to all sounds, an Abyss prior to all being, a Godhead prior to God. The soul reverts to spirit and is released into formless infinity, timeless eternity, unmanifest absorption, radiant emptiness. Consciousness resides as the unmoved Witness, the formless mirror mind, impartially reflecting all that arises, utterly indifferent to the play of its own patterns, thoroughly quiet in the face of its own sounds, wholly nonattached to the forms of its own becoming. And then, in the final mystery, the Witness dies into everything that is witnessed, Emptiness is realized not other than Form, the mirror mind and its reflections are not two, Consciousness awakens as the entire World. The sound of a waterfall on the distant horizon, the sight of a gentle misty fog, the crack of lightning in a late night storm, somehow say it all. The subject and object, the human and divine, the inner and the outer, by any other names, are simply and only One Taste.

STAGES OF MEDITATION

An Interview with Ken Wilber

Q: We would like you to describe the experiences of several stages of meditation. But first, tell us about meditation itself—the different types and how they work.

A: It is common among scholars to divide meditation into two broad categories, called "concentration" and "awareness" (or "insight") meditation. Or "opened" and "closed." For example, let's say you are looking at a wall that has hundreds of dots painted on it. In concentration meditation, you look at just one dot, and you look at it so fiercely that you don't even see the other dots. This develops your powers of concentration. In awareness training, or insight meditation, you try to be as aware of all the dots as you can be. This increases your sensitivity, awareness, and wisdom, in that sense.

In concentration meditation, you put your attention on one object—a rock, a candle flame, your breathing, a mantra, the heart prayer, and so on. By intensely concentrating on a single object, you as subject gradually become "identified" with that object. You start to undercut subject/object dualism, which is the basis of all suffering and illusion. Gradually, higher and higher realms of existence, leading toward the ultimate or nondual dimension, are all made obvious to you. You transcend your ordinary self or ego, and find the higher and subtler dimensions of existence—the spiritual and transcendental.

However, this is reaching the higher dimensions by "brute force," so to speak. And although concentration meditation is said to be very important, by itself it doesn't uproot our tendencies to create dualism in the first place. In fact, it just ignores them, it tries to bypass them. It focuses on one dot and ignores all the others. Concentration meditation can definitely show us some of the higher realms, but it can't permanently install us at those higher realms. For that, you have to look at all the dots. You have to investigate all of experience, with detachment, nonjudgmentalism, equanimity, and crystal clear awareness.

Q: That's insight or awareness meditation.

A: Yes, that's right. The Buddhists call concentration meditation *shamatha* and awareness meditation *vipassana,* or *dhyana* and *prajna.* The former leads to samadhi, or one-pointed concentration, the latter to satori, or transcendental awareness and wisdom.

The point about any of these meditation practices—and there are others, such as visualization, koan, contemplative prayer, and so on—the point is that they are all actually doing two important things. One, they are helping to still the discursive, rational-existential mind, the mind that has to think all the time, the mind that has to chatter to itself all the time and verbalize everything. It helps us quiet that "monkey mind." And once the monkey mind quiets down a bit, it allows the subtler and higher dimensions of awareness to emerge—such as the psychic, the subtle, the causal, and the ultimate or nondual. That is the essence of genuine meditation. It is simply a way to continue evolution, to continue our growth and development.

The Psychic Level

Q: Could you describe the levels of meditation, and how they are experienced? What actually happens at each stage?

A: When you practice meditation, one of the first things your realize is that your mind—and your life, for that matter—is dominated by largely subconscious verbal chatter. You are always talking to yourself. And so, as they start to meditate, many people are stunned by how much junk starts running through their awareness. They find that thoughts, images, fantasies, notions, ideas, concepts virtually dominate their awareness. They realize that these notions have had a much more profound influence on their lives than they ever thought.

In any case, initial meditation experiences are like being at the movies. You sit and watch all these fantasies and concepts parade by, in front of your awareness. But the whole point is that you are finally becoming aware of them. You are looking at them impartially and without judgment. You just watch them go by, the same as you watch clouds float by in the sky. They come, they go. No praise, no condemnation, no judgment—just "bare witnessing." If you judge your thoughts, if you get caught up in them, then you can't transcend them. You can't find higher or subtler dimensions of your own being. So you sit in meditation, and you simply "witness" what is going on in your mind. You let the monkey mind do what it wants, and you simply watch.

And what happens is, because you impartially witness these thoughts, fantasies, notions, and images, you start to become free of their unconscious influence. You are looking at them, so you are not using them to look at the world. Therefore you become, to a certain extent, free of them. And you become free of the separate-self sense that depended on them. In other words, you start to become free of the ego. This is the initial spiritual dimension, where the conventional ego "dies" and higher structures of awareness are "resurrected." Your sense of identity naturally begins to expand and embrace the cosmos, or all of nature. You rise above the isolated mind and body, which might include finding a larger identity, such as with nature or the cosmos—"cosmic consciousness," as R. M. Bucke called it. It's a very concrete and unmistakable experience.

And, I don't have to tell you, this is an extraordinary relief! This is the beginning of transcendence, of finding your way back home. You realize that you are one with the fabric of the universe, eternally. Your fear of death begins to subside, and you actually begin to feel, in a concrete and palpable way, the open and transparent nature of your own being.

Feelings of gratitude and devotion arise in you—devotion to Spirit, in the form of the Christ, or Buddha, or Krishna; or devotion to your actual spiritual master; even devotion in general, and certainly devotion to all other sentient beings. The bodhisattva vow, in whatever form, arises from the depths of your being, in a very powerful way. You realize you simply have to do whatever you can to help all sentient beings, and for the reason, as Schopenhauer said, that you realize that we all share the same nondual Self or Spirit or Absolute. All of this starts to become obvious—as obvious as rain on the roof. It is real and it is concrete.

The Subtle Level

Q: So what about the next general stage, the subtle level?

A: As your identity begins to transcend the isolated and individual bodymind, you start to intuit that there is a Ground of Being or genuine Divinity, beyond ego, and beyond appeals to mythic god figures or rationalistic scientism or existential bravery. This Deity form can actually be intuited. The more you develop beyond the isolated and existential bodymind, the more you develop toward Spirit, which, at the subtle level, is often experienced as Deity Form or archetypal Self. By that I mean, for example, very concrete experiences of profound Light, a Being of Light, or just of extreme clarity and brilliance of awareness.

The point is that you are seeing something beyond nature, beyond the existential, beyond the psychic, beyond even cosmic identity. You are starting to see the hidden or esoteric dimension, the dimension outside the ordinary cosmos, the dimension that transcends nature. You see the Light, and sometimes this Light literally shines like the light of a thousand suns. It overwhelms you, empowers you, energizes you, remakes you, drenches you. This is what scholars have called the "numinous" nature of subtle spirit. Numinous and luminous. This is, I believe, why saints are universally depicted with halos of light around their heads. That is actually what they see. Divine Light. My favorite reading from Dante:

Fixing my gaze upon the Eternal Light
I saw within its depths,
Bound up with love together in one volume,
The scattered leaves of all the universe.
Within the luminous profound subsistence
Of that Exalted Light saw I three circles
Of three colors yet of one dimension
And by the second seemed the first reflected
As rainbow is by rainbow, and the third
Seemed fire that equally from both is breathed.

That is not mere poetry. That is an almost mathematical description of one type of experience of the subtle level. Anyway, you can also experience this level as a discovery of your own higher self, your soul, the Holy Spirit. "He who knows himself knows God," said Saint Clement.

Q: And the actual experience itself?

A: The actual experience varies. Here is one example: Say you are walking downtown, looking in shop windows. You're looking at some of the merchandise, and all of a sudden you see a vague image dance in front of your eyes, the image of a person. Then all at once you realize that it is your own reflection in the shop window. You suddenly recognize yourself. Your recognize your Self, your higher Self. You suddenly recognize who you are. And who you are is—a luminous spark of the Divine. But it has that shock of recognition—"Oh, that!"

It's a very concrete realization, and usually brings much laughter or much tears. The subtle Deity form or Light or Higher Self—those are all just archetypes of your own Being. You are encountering, via meditative development, and beginning a direct encounter with Spirit, with your own essence. So it shows up as light, as a being of light, as nada, as shabd, as clarity, numinosity, and so on. And sometimes it just shows up as a simple and clear awareness of *what is*—very simple, very clear. The point is that it is aware of all the dots on the wall. It is clearly aware of what is happening moment to moment, and therefore transcends the moment. It transcends this world, and starts to partake of the Divine. It has sacred outlook, however it might be expressed. That's the subtle—a face to face introduction to the Divine. You actually participate in Divinity, and in the awareness and wisdom of Divinity. It is a practice. It can be done. It has been done, many times.

THE CAUSAL LEVEL

Q: That's very clear. So what about the next level, the causal?

A: You're sitting there, just witnessing everything that arises in the mind, or in your present experience. You are trying to witness, equally, all the dots on the wall of your awareness. If you become proficient at this, eventually rational and existential dots die down, and psychic dots start to come into focus. Then, after a while, you get better at witnessing, so subtler objects or dots start to show up. These include lights and audible illuminations and subtle Deity forms and so on. If you continue simply witnessing—which helps you disidentify from lower and grosser forms, and become aware of the higher and subtler forms—even subtle objects or subtle dots themselves cease to arise. You enter a profound state of nonmanifestation, which is experienced like, say, an autumn night with a full moon. There is an eerie and beautiful numinosity to it all, but it's a "silent" or "black" numinosity. You can't really see anything except a kind of silvery fullness, filling all space. But because you're not actually seeing any particular object, it is also a type of Radical Emptiness. As Zen says, "stop the sound of that stream." This is variously known as shunyata, as the Cloud of Unknowing, Divine Ignorance, Radical Mystery, nirguna ("unqualifiable") Brahman, and so on. Brilliant formlessness, with no objects detracting from it.

It becomes obvious that you are absolutely one with this Fullness, which transcends all worlds and all planes and all time and all history. You are perfectly full, and therefore you are perfectly empty. "It is all things and it is no things," said the Christian mystic Boethius. Awe gives way to certainty. That's who you are, prior to all manifestation, prior to all worlds. In other words, it is seeing who or what you are timelessly, formlessly.

That's an example of the causal level; that's jnana samadhi, nirvikalpa samadhi, and so on. The soul, or separate-self sense, disappears, and God or separate Deity form disappears, because both—soul and God—collapse into formless Godhead. Both soul and God disappear into the Supreme Identity.

The Nondual Level

Q: So that leaves the nondual level.

A: In the previous causal level, you are so absorbed in the unmanifest dimension that you might not even notice the manifest world. You are discovering Emptiness, and so you ignore Form. But at the ultimate or nondual level, you integrate the two. You see that Emptiness appears or manifests itself as Form, and that Form has as its essence Emptiness. In more concrete terms, what you are is all things that arise. All manifestation arises, moment by moment, as a play of Emptiness. If the causal was like a radiant moonlit night, this is like a radiant autumn day.

What appear as hard or solid objects "out there" are really transparent and translucent manifestations of your own Being or Isness. They are not obstacles to God, only expressions of God. They are therefore empty in the sense of not being an obstruction or impediment. They are a free expression of the Divine. As the Mahamudra tradition succinctly puts it, "All is Mind. Mind is Empty. Empty is freely-manifesting. Freely-manifesting is self–liberating."

The freedom that you found at the causal level—the freedom of Fullness and Emptiness—that freedom is found to extend to all things, even to this "fallen" world of sin or samsara. Therefore, all things become self-liberated. And this extraordinary freedom, or absence of restriction, or total release—this clear bright autumn day—this is what you actually experience at this point. But then "experience" is the wrong word altogether. This realization is actually of the nonexperiential nature of Spirit. Experiences come and go. They all have a beginning in time, and an end in time. Even subtle experiences come and go. They are all wonderful, glorious, extraordinary. And they come, and they go.

But this nondual "state" is not itself another experience. It is simply the opening or clearing in which all experiences arise and fall. It is the bright autumn sky through which the clouds come and go—it is not itself another cloud, another experience, another object, another manifestation. This realization is actually of the utter fruitlessness of experience, the utter futility of trying to experience release or liberation. All experiences lose their taste entirely—these passing clouds.

You are not the one who experiences liberation; you are the clearing, the opening, the emptiness, in which any experience comes and goes, like reflections on the mirror. And you are the mirror, the mirror mind, and not any experienced reflection. But you are not apart from the reflections, standing back and watching. You *are* everything that is arising moment to moment. You can swallow the whole cosmos in one gulp, it is so small, and you can taste the entire sky without moving an inch.

This is why, in Zen, it is said that you cannot enter the Great Samadhi: it is actually the opening or clearing that is ever-present, and in which all experience—and all manifestation—arises moment to moment. It seems like you "enter" this state, except that once there, you realize there was never a time that this state wasn't fully present and fully recognized—"the gateless gate." And so you deeply understand that you never entered this state; nor did the Buddhas, past or future, ever enter this state.

In Dzogchen, this is the recognition of mind's true nature. All things, in all worlds, are self-liberated as they arise. All things are like sunlight on the water of a pond. It all shimmers. It is all empty. It is all light. It is all full, and it is all fulfilled. And the world goes on its ordinary way, and nobody notices at all.

Foreword to *YOGA: THE TECHNOLOGY OF ECSTASY* by Georg Feuerstein

IT IS A GREAT PLEASURE, indeed honor, to write this foreword. I have been a fan of Georg Feuerstein ever since I read his classic *Essence of Yoga*. His subsequent works simply reinforced my belief that in Georg Feuerstein we have a scholar-practitioner of the first magnitude, an extremely important and valuable voice for the perennial philosophy, and arguably the foremost authority on Yoga today.

In the East, as well as in the West, there tend to be two rather different approaches to spirituality—that of the scholar and that of the practitioner. The scholar tends to be abstract, and studies world religions as one might study bugs or rocks or fossils—merely another field for the detached intellect. The idea of actually practicing a spiritual or contemplative discipline rarely seems to dawn on the scholar. Indeed, to practice what one is studying is held to interfere with one's "objectivity"—one has become a believer and therefore nonobjective.

Practitioners, on the other hand, although admirably engaged in an actual discipline, tend to be very uninformed about all the various facets of their tradition. They may be naive about the cultural trappings of their particular path, or about its actual historical origins, or about how much of their path is essential truth and how much is simply cultural baggage.

Rare, indeed, to find a scholar who is also a practitioner. But when it comes to writing a book on Yoga, this combination is absolutely essential. A treatise on Yoga can be trusted neither to the scholars nor the practitioners alone. There is an immense amount of information that must be mastered in order to write about Yoga, and therefore a scholar is needed. But Yoga itself is born in the fire of direct experience. It must be engaged, and lived, and practiced. It must come from the head, but equally from the heart. And this very rare combination is exactly what Georg brings to this remarkable topic.

The essence of Yoga is very simple: it means *yoking* or *joining*. When Christ said, "My yoke is easy," he meant "My yoga is easy"—whether East or West, Yoga is the technique of joining or uniting the individual soul with absolute Spirit. It is a means of liberation. And it is therefore fiery, hot, intense, ecstatic. It will take you far beyond yourself; some say it will take you to infinity.

Therefore, choose your guides carefully. The book you now hold in your hands is, without a doubt, the finest overall explanation of Yoga now available, a book destined to become a classic. And for a simple reason: it comes from both the head and the heart, from impeccable scholarship and dedicated practice. In this sense, it is much more perceptive and accurate than the works of, say, Eliade or Campbell.

Enter now the world of Yoga, which is said to lead from suffering to release, from agony to ecstasy, from time to eternity, from death to immortality. And know that on this extraordinary tour, you are indeed in good hands.

Foreword to *CLINICAL STUDIES IN TRANSPERSONAL PSYCHOTHERAPY* by Seymour Boorstein

THERE SEEM TO BE three general phases—each lasting about a decade—that new schools of psychology go through in the course of their own growth and development: the first phase is one of innovation and extreme enthusiasm; the second, one of hard work and conceptual labor; the third, one of general acceptance and assimilation by mainstream schools (assuming it achieves any sort of acceptance at all). The first phase tends to be more enjoyable; the second phase, more productive; and the third, more rewarding.

I believe Transpersonal Psychology is now beginning its second major phase. It is moving from the enjoyable phase to the productive phase—the phase that, because it is marked by more intellectual rigor and integrity, is all the more vital and productive and, therefore, in its own way, all the more exciting.

The first phase began about twenty-five years ago [as of 1986], with the pioneering work of Huxley, Maslow, Watts, Sutich, and the founding of the *Journal of Transpersonal Psychology*. The atmosphere was one of electric excitement; the enthusiasm, almost palpable. There were grand visions in the air. Meditation, yoga, psychedelics, biofeedback—all had combined to literally blow open the field of psychology and introduce it to heights of consciousness—and depths of consciousness—never before dreamt of by Western science. The enthusiasm and excitement of this first phase was evidence of, and testament to, the genuine power that the new field of Transpersonal Psychology had tapped into and unleashed. No Western scientists had ever explored such vast new fields of mind and consciousness. We were all pioneers; we were both the subjects and the objects of our own investigations; above all, we were enthusiastic. The New Age lay before us.

I believe that giddy, happy time is over. If Transpersonal Psychology is to enter its second and more productive phase, that raw energy and enthusiasm must now be channeled, via coherent and systematic ideas, into a comprehensive and unified framework.

Above all, I believe this comprehensive framework must reach out to, and embrace, the orthodox and mainstream schools of psychology, and it must do so in a very rigorous and detailed fashion. It seems to me that only in this way can Transpersonal Psychology become the truly comprehensive school that it rightfully claims to be. Freudian psychoanalysis became the dominant school of psychiatry for half a century, not because it displaced earlier schools, but because it so effectively encompassed them that it rendered them almost superfluous. Freudian psychoanalysis, in other words, took as its foundation the then existing schools of psychology and psychiatry, and, by effectively incorporating their essential insights into its own system, became the dominant school of psychiatry for the next half-century.

I believe the same "grand synthesis" can and must now be accomplished by Transpersonal Psychology. And that means we must take very seriously the idea that orthodox psychiatry and psychology have already laid a viable foundation, but it is up to us to incorporate this foundation and then build on it to develop it into a much more comprehensive and transpersonal orientation.

One of the main tasks before us, then, in our productive phase, is the building of bridges between Transpersonal Psychology and the more orthodox, mainstream schools. There are, in my opinion, four major orthodox schools with which Transpersonal Psychology must contend: (1) Behaviorism—including not only classical and operant behaviorism, but also the more modern schools of cognitive behaviorism, social learning theory, and self-regulating management; (2) Neurophysiological psychology—including neuropharmacology, brain research, and physiological psychology; (3) Psychoanalytic Psychiatry—including psychoanalytic ego psychology, object-relations theory, and self psychology; and (4) Cognitive Developmentalism—including the work of Piaget, Kohlberg, Gilligan, Loevinger, Graves, and Arieti.

In approaching these four major orthodox schools, we can take one of two views: we can assume the orthodox schools, because they lack a transpersonal perspective, are essentially wrong in most respects and therefore need to be replaced in toto by Transpersonal Psychology; or we can assume the orthodox schools are more or less correct as far as they go, but need to be supplemented with Transpersonal Psychology.

For various reasons, I think the second view is the only possible way to proceed. That is, I believe the major orthodox schools are essentially correct as far as they go, but they need desperately a supplement of the soul. They are correct but partial, and thus the job of Transpersonal Psychology is to build upon that orthodox foundation a more comprehensive, viable, and adequate psychology, one that includes not only mind and body but soul and spirit.

I believe this approach is the correct one with respect to all four orthodox schools—the behavioristic, the physiological, the psychoanalytic, and the developmental. With Behaviorism we can easily accept the central role of reinforcement theories and self-regulating strategies, but we must add the notion of higher levels or dimensions of reinforcement. An event becomes a reinforcer not only if it satisfies physical and emotional needs, but also if it satisfies mental, psychic, and spiritual needs, which are every bit as real as—indeed, more real than—the need for material food or sex. Our job is to incorporate behaviorism, not deny it.

Likewise, we can easily accommodate the central tenet of Physiological Psychology, namely, that every state of consciousness has a physiological correlate and that psychopathology may be (in whole or part) a physiological dysfunction partially correctable by pharmacological agents. Large sectors of modern psychiatry have, in fact, abandoned the strictly psychoanalytic model and embraced the physiological model—the so-called "medical model"—because its clinical results are so immediate and palpable—certain classes of anxiety, depression, phobias, and thought disorders yield almost immediately to pharmacological management. This medical or physiological model has been further bolstered by major breakthroughs in the understanding of neurotransmitter pathways and functions (such as acetylcholine, norepinephrine, the endorphins, and so forth). Underlying this entire enterprise is the assumption that each specific state of consciousness—and therefore, each specific psychopathology—has a specific physiological correlate, and, therefore, can be manipulated at a pharmacological level. All of this rests on the mapping and correlating of states of consciousness with their particular physiological substates.

Transpersonal Psychology would simply add that there is a whole spectrum of higher or transcendental states of consciousness; that the physiological correlates of those states can and should be mapped; and that those states might also be triggered, at least temporarily, by pharmacological action. Moreover, Transpersonal Psychology can do this without embracing the psycho-neural identity theory (which is a blatant form of reductionism); to say that higher states of consciousness leave their footprints in the physiological substratum is not to say these higher states are their footprints.

The third major orthodox school that Transpersonal Psychology should eventually embrace is the Psychoanalytic school. Unfortunately, psychoanalytic theory seems so profoundly antithetical to spiritual concerns that most transpersonal psychologists avoid it entirely. But, again, I believe the more accurate view is that psychoanalysis is not entirely incorrect nor inaccurate; rather, it contains some very important but very partial truths, and our task as transpersonal theorists is to incorporate these partial truths into a much more encompassing and adequate discipline.

Likewise with the fourth major orthodox school, that of Cognitive Developmentalism. Here, our job has been easy: we have agreed with the developmentalists that consciousness develops through a series of stages or structures. We have simply added that there are demonstrably higher stages of conscious development than those recognized by the orthodox. And this has been easy, as I said, because developmental-logic itself announces the necessity of higher, transcendental, or transpersonal states. Developmental-logic rests happy nowhere short of Infinity.

Here, then, is the task of Transpersonal Psychology in its second major phase, its productive phase: if Transpersonal Psychology is genuinely a psychology of Totality or Wholeness, then it must be able to foster a broad integration or general synthesis of the four major orthodox schools, by showing each school to be a correct but partial aspect of a larger truth; and it must then use this integration as the foundation upon which a more properly transcendental, spiritual, or transpersonal model can profitably be built.

I do not think this synthesis of orthodox schools is as formidable as might at first appear. Donald Hebb has already provided us with a key integrating link between the behavioristic and physiological models, namely, the idea of synaptic facilitation. A behavioristic-reinforcing event is a synaptic facilitating event. And Piaget has already provided us with a key integrating link between behaviorism and cognitive development, namely, the idea that an event can be reinforcing only if it can be assimilated by the organism, and that levels of development are, therefore, actually levels of allowable reinforcers.

What remains, for the "grand synthesis," is an incorporation of modern psychoanalytic theory. I think the broad outlines of how to integrate psychoanalysis with the other major orthodox schools is reasonably straightforward: as consciousness develops through its various stages of allowable reinforcers, a developmental miscarriage (a maladaptive self-regulation, reinforcement, or synaptic facilitation) will result in a particular type or class of psychopathology. In other words, different levels of developmental miscarriage (or maladaptive reinforcement or synaptic facilitation) would result in qualitatively different types of psychopathology (which, in turn, would yield broadly to different types of pharmacological intervention). Different stages of cognitive development mean different levels of allowable reinforcers and different levels of psychopathology (each accompanied by a distinctive physiological footprint or synaptic array).

Modern psychoanalytic theory recognizes three general levels of psychopathology: psychotic, borderline, and neurotic. I have suggested adding the broad classes of existential pathologies and transpersonal pathologies. In other words, the entire spectrum of consciousness can also be viewed as a spectrum of possible pathologies, with each level possessing a distinct and different type of possible pathology requiring distinct and different treatment modalities.

What is now so urgently needed is exactly this type of interfacing between psychoanalytic developmental models and a broader transpersonal approach. In my opinion, this is the last major interface needed before Transpersonal Psychology can effect its comprehensive foundation. There are, to my mind, three researchers in particular who are doing pioneering work in this area: Jack Engler, Dan Brown, and Seymour Boorstein. Examples of the work of Engler and Brown can be found in *Transformations of Consciousness*. This book is Boorstein's approach.

One of the central ideas of this book is that as consciousness develops from prepersonal to personal to transpersonal modes, different types of pathologies can arise, each requiring a different type of treatment modality. Of the five major classes of psychopathology—namely, psychotic, borderline, neurotic, existential, and transpersonal—Seymour discusses the impact of meditation of four of them: psychotic, borderline, neurotic, and existential. This book makes three important points: (1) in general, the treatment modalities for these pathologies are quite different; (2) in general, intensive meditation is contraindicated for the more severe and primitive pathologies (psychotic and borderline); and (3) there are, however, certain cases of primitive pathologies that appear to be helped by meditation (or other transpersonal exercises). Exactly what that means and how that occurs will remain a central point of theoretical debate for years to come.

Transpersonal Psychology has completed its first phase; we are now moving into the second or productive phase. In many ways, I think this phase is more exciting and even more visionary than the first. I believe extraordinary theoretical and clinical breakthroughs now lie in our collective grasp. If we meet the challenges ahead with intellectual integrity and rigor, I believe Transpersonal Psychology will take its rightful place as the sanest, the most basic, and the most comprehensive psychology yet to appear. If there is only one Self—and there is—there is only one psychology. That Self is transpersonal; and so, therefore, is that psychology.

IN THE EYE OF THE ARTIST

Art and the Perennial Philosophy

FOREWORD TO *SACRED MIRRORS: THE VISIONARY ART OF ALEX GREY*

ACCORDING TO the perennial philosophy—the common mystical core of the world's great spiritual traditions—men and women possess at least three different modes of knowing: the eye of flesh, which discloses the material, concrete, and sensual world; the eye of mind, which discloses the symbolic, conceptual, and linguistic world; and the eye of contemplation, which discloses the spiritual, transcendental, and transpersonal world. These are not three different worlds, but three different aspects of our one world, disclosed by different modes of knowing and perceiving.

Moreover, these three modes of knowing, these three "eyes," are not simply given to a person all at once. Rather, they unfold in a developmental sequence from the lower to the higher. In the first two years of a baby's life, sensorimotor intelligence—the eye of flesh—develops and evolves to disclose a material world of "object permanence," of solid surfaces and colors and objects, as well as the sensorimotor body's own feelings and emerging impulses. In the following decade or two, the eye of mind will increasingly emerge and develop, disclosing in its turn the world of ideas, symbols, concepts, images, values, meanings, and intentions. If development continues beyond the mind via meditative disciplines or mystical experience, then the eye of contemplation opens and discloses the world of soul and spirit, of subtle energies and insights, of radical intuition and transcendental illumination.

The eye of flesh tends to disclose a prepersonal, preverbal, preconceptual world, a world of matter and bodies. The eye of mind tends to disclose a personal, verbal, and conceptual world, a world of ego and mind. And the eye of contemplation tends to disclose a transpersonal, transverbal, transegoic world, a world of luminous soul and spirit. The first realm made visible to perception is composed of *sensibilia,* or phenomena that can be perceived by the body. The second realm is composed of *intelligibilia,* or objects perceived by the mind. The third realm consists of *transcendelia,* or objects perceived by the soul and spirit. These three overall realms, from matter/body to ego/mind to soul/spirit, are collectively referred to in various contemplative traditions as the Great Chain of Being.[1]

When it comes to a critical theory of art based on the perennial philosophy, then, the immediate question is: What eye, or eyes, is the particular artist using? Of course, the artist's medium is usually sensibilia, or various material substances (paint, clay, concrete, metal, wood, etc.). The critical question, however, is this: Using the medium of sensibilia, is the artist trying to represent, depict, or evoke the realm of sensibilia itself, or the realm of intelligibilia, or the realm of transcendelia? In other words, to the standard question "How competent is the artist in depicting or evoking a particular phenomenon?" we add the crucial ontological question: "Where on the Great Chain of Being is the phenomenon the artist is attempting to depict, evoke, or express?"

We have, then, two important but different scales of critical evaluation for any work of art: (1) How well does it succeed on its own level? (2) How high is that level?

The great achievement of European art in the last thousand years was the convincing depiction of the realm of sensibilia. Not much more than five hundred years ago the rules of perspective became widely known and utilized in painting, embodying a discovery and an understanding of the actual geometry of the material-sensible world (as in, for example, Renaissance art). Painting became increasingly *realistic,* or empirical, tied to the concrete sensory world; the eye of flesh and its bodily perspective. Even religious art tended to be concrete and literal. Depictions of the Virgin Birth, the Ascension, the parting of the Red Sea—all were portrayed as actual, concrete facts, not as symbolic, figurative, or conceptual. In other words, even most "religious" art was tied to the realm of concrete sensibilia.

All of that would begin to change with the coming of modern art. If the first great achievement of European art was to perfect the depiction of sensibilia, the second great achievement was to rise above it and begin to depict the various realms and aspects of intelligibilia, of symbolic and abstract and conceptual and phenomenological art and its rules. The media would still be sensibilia, but the depicted object no longer would be bound by the rules or perspectives of matter; it would not follow the contours of matter, but of mind. No longer Nature, but Psyche. No longer realistic, but abstract. Not things, but thoughts. Not Euclidean, but Surrealistic. Not representational, but impressionistic or expressionistic. Not literal and concrete, but figurative and symbolic.

Starting with Paul Cézanne, whom Matisse called "the master of us all," we see the fixed perspectivism of the material-sensible world broken down and superseded by an emotional-psychological participation (intelligibilia), not mere representation (sensibilia). With Kandinsky, arguably the father of abstract art, we see the full emergence, if not perfection, of intelligibilia over sensibilia; of the condensed potency of the abstract over the mere imitation of Nature's forms. As Kandinsky put it, "It must become possible to hear the whole world as it is without represential interpretation."[2] That is, seeing not with the eye of flesh, but with the eye of mind.

Cubism began as a type of geometry of natural form, but quickly became a vehicle for essential impressionism, an act of attention not just to outer objects but also to inward mental forms and patterns. "This is the art of painting new structures out of elements borrowed not from the reality of sight, but from the reality of insight,"[3] as one critic expressed it.

Perhaps no one articulated the need to go from mere Nature to more than Nature better than Piet Mondrian. "As the natural becomes more and more automatic, we see life's interest fixed more and more on the inward. The life of *truly modern* man is directed neither toward the material for its own sake nor toward the predominantly emotional [matter/body]: rather, it takes the form of the autonomous life of the human [psyche] becoming conscious. . . . Life is becoming more and more *abstract.* The truly modern artist *consciously* perceives the abstractness of the emotion of beauty. . . . In the vital reality of the abstract, the new man has transcended the feelings of nostalgia. . . . There is no escaping the tragic, so long as our vision of nature is naturalistic [tied to sensibilia]. That is why a deeper vision is essential."[4] Deeper than sensibilia is intelligibilia, and deeper still, is transcendelia. Mondrian and Kandinsky were pioneers in both.

The point was to free the mind from the confines of nature, and thus to free art from photographic realism, while at the same time plumbing the depths of the psyche and giving artistic expression to that extraordinary search.

The art of the mind, of depicting the geometries of thought and the patterns of psyches, the art of intelligibilia clothed in sensibilia, was found in an inward, not solely outward, direction. It was an act of attention to the inner subject as well as to the outer object, and conveyed the interrelationship between the two. In it, the patterns of thought interrelated with the patterns of things. Although these patterns or essences depend in part on looking inwardly with the mind's eye, they are not merely subjective or idiosyncratic, but rather, to the extent that they resonate truly in a work of art, reflect the larger patterns of reality itself. As Brancusi almost screamed out: "They are imbeciles who call my work abstract; that which they call abstract is the most realist, because what is real is not the exterior form but the idea, the essence of things."[5] As Hegel and Schelling would put it, "The ideal is real, and the real is ideal."

By exploring the realm of intelligibilia, modern artists were able to return to the ground of sensibilia with new insights and radically novel approaches. The Cubists brought a completely new understanding to form, while Seurat, Delaunay, and Matisse brought a new revelation of color. Matisse, for example, freed color from the constraints of nature. As he forcefully put it, "The Beaux Arts masters told their students: 'Copy nature stupidly.' Throughout my entire career I have reacted against this attitude. . . . Color exists in itself, possesses its own beauty. . . . I understood then that one could work with expressive colors which are not necessarily descriptive colors."[6] Color could be expressive of intelligibilia, not just descriptive of sensibilia. The point, then, was to stay firmly rooted in sensibilia—not to deny nature or repress it; but to reach through or beyond sensibilia to intelligibilia, to the essence of mind, idea, and intention, and to clothe them in the "plastic" of the material or natural realm; and further, through introspection and intuition of the patterns of mind and intelligibilia, to return afresh with new and radical insights into the form and color and essence of sensibilia itself.

We now reach the third and most crucial evolutionary movement: the emergence in art not just of body or of mind, but moreover of spirit, and the correlative depiction in art not just of sensibilia and intelligibilia, but also of transcendelia.

Not that the spiritual hadn't been portrayed before in art, but in the West its flowering had always been fragile. Early Christian icons, with their simplified forms floating on golden fields of "light," were sacred symbols of the incarnation of the Word. When Christianity adopted the figurative, naturalistic style of secular art, it replaced the symbolic icon with a fundamentalist form of realism that specialized in the literal depiction of spiritual events such as the resurrection. There is nothing transcendental in fundamentalist "facts" that wish to claim the dubious status of empirical sensibilia.

Contrary to prevailing tendencies of realism in European art, there has been a sporadic Western "tradition" of mystical and visionary painting over the last nine hundred years. Early evidence of this visionary symbolist art can be found in the twelfth century in the work of Hildegard of Bingen. She was a powerful abbess who created a major text explaining the symbols of her visions and had the visions illustrated or illuminated. These beautiful works are surely forms of transcendelia.

Michelangelo, a Neoplatonist, was trying to symbolically express through his art a spiritual ideal clothed in material form. As he said, ". . . it is not sufficient merely to be a great master in painting and very wise, but I think that it is necessary for the painter to be very moral in his mode of life, or even, if such were possible, a saint, so that the Holy Spirit may inspire his intellect."[7] Hieronymous Bosch created a unique world of highly symbolic, imaginative vistas of heavens and hells intended to reinforce the spiritual faith of his viewers. The poet and visionary artist William Blake wrote in the *Marriage of Heaven and Hell:*

> If the doors of perception were cleansed
>   every thing would appear to man as it is, infinite.
> For man has closed himself up, till he sees all things
>   through narrow chinks of his cavern.[8]

To Blake, painting had nothing to do with copying from nature, but was an art of divine imagination:

> Shall Painting be confined to the sordid drudgery of facsimile representations of merely mortal and perishing substances, and not be as poetry and music are, elevated into its own proper sphere of invention and visionary conception? No, it shall not be so! Painting, as well as poetry and music, exists and exults in immortal thoughts.[9]

The nineteenth-century symbolist painter Delville wrote that he intended to evoke, "the great universal life . . . which rules and moves the universe, beings and things, mortals or immortals, in the infinite rhythm of Eternity."[10] And in the twentieth century the painter Pavel Tchelitchew's works moved through the visionary, symbolic levels of consciousness to mystical abstractions reflecting deep transcendental levels of being and light.

There were also artists throughout the history of European art who depicted images of sensibilia but, like the Zen landscapists, reached a state of contemplative absorption which dissolved the boundary between subject and object and opened a channel to immanent transcendelia. The pre-Renaissance master Fra Angelico was a monk and a painter. His works were intended for the contemplation of other monks and are filled with a devotional intensity which raises them high on the Great Chain. Rembrandt was good at creating the illusion of space in his painting, but he was *great* precisely because he also revealed a dimension of the human soul. He revealed character and a living, spiritual presence in all his portraits and the self-portraits in particular. The spirit in the flesh, this is what we see—not a mound of material sensibilia, but a soul timelessly peering through matter. Van Gogh let the rhythms of the cosmos, a universal energy, resonate through his works. His landscapes are saturated with spirit. In the twentieth century, Ivan Albright has conveyed in his magical hyperrealist paintings a sense of the awesome and infinite dimension of the immanent Divine. These artists had powers of concentration, imagination, or mystic reverie that gave them glimpses of divinity and enabled them to create visionary or representational images that evoke a world beyond sensibilia and intelligibilia.

Many of the pioneers in modern abstraction, such as Kandinsky, Mondrian, Malevich, Klee, and Brancusi, felt that a new spirituality in art would have to be Spirit approached directly and immediately, not in the mythic forms of the religious mind or with representational imagery, but through direct intuition and contemplative realization. They felt that they had in fact pushed beyond the individual mind and body and discovered, through their art, a genuine and powerful approach to Spirit itself. They were disclosing and portraying not just sensibilia, or intelligibilia, but transcendelia.

Art was to be not just the technical skills of observation and execution, or creativity, but a method of spiritual growth and development on the part of the artists. True art, according to Kandinsky, must involve the cultivation of the soul and spirit: "The artist must train not only his eye but also his soul, so that it can weigh colors in its own scale and thus become a determinant in artistic creation."[11]

If artists are to "be the servants of Spirit," he said, then they must grow and develop their own souls to a point at which they are capable of directly intuiting the spiritual dimension. In order to see (let alone artistically convey) Spirit, the eye of contemplation must first be opened, and this opening—Kandinsky's "revelation of Spirit illumined as if by a flash of lightning"[12]—discloses newer, higher, and wider dimensions of existence.

In the artist's own spiritual growth and development, ever subtler experiences, emotions, and perceptions would come into view, and it was the artist's duty to portray these subtler experiences (transcendelia), and thus to evoke them and encourage them in those who witness with care the finished work.

We have said that sensibilia is the realm of the prepersonal, intelligibilia the realm of the personal, and transcendelia the realm of the transpersonal. That is, the body and nature are preverbal, preconceptual, and therefore pre-egoic and prepersonal. The mind is verbal, conceptual, and symbolic, and therefore forms the basis of ego and individuality. But Spirit, being universal, is beyond body and mind—it is transverbal, transegoic, transindividual. It exists at a point where the soul touches eternity and transcends the prison of its own involvement.

The more consciousness evolves, the more it grows beyond the narrow bounds of the personal ego, the more it touches the transpersonal and universal Divine. Thus it is no accident that Mondrian states: "All art is more or less direct aesthetic expression of the universal. This *more or less* implies degrees [of development or evolution]. . . . A great heightening of subjectivity is taking place development in man—in other words a *growing, expanding consciousness*. Subjectivity ceases to exist only when the mutation-like leap is made from individual existence to universal existence." Thus, he concludes, "The new culture will be that of the mature individual; once matured, the individual will be open to the universal and will tend more and more to unite with it"[13]—a common conclusion of mystics the world over.

According to modern masters such as Malevich, Franz Marc, Paul Klee, Brancusi, and others, true and genuine art, the highest art, involved, first, the development or growth of the artist's own soul, right up to the point of union with universal Spirit and transcendence of the separate self or individual ego; and second, the artistic depiction/expression of this spiritual dimension, particularly in such a way as to evoke similar spiritual insights on the part of observers.

There remains the difficult question: Did these great modern masters succeed? Did they succeed, not only in freeing intelligibilia from sensibilia, but also in freeing transcendelia itself and bringing it down into "plastic form"? Did they discover and portray not just body-nature and psyche-mind, but also Spirit?

My own conclusion is that, at best, the pioneering effort has just begun. I think the clear and definite accomplishment of these masters was to free intelligibilia from the confines of sensibilia, to save mind from engulfment in matter. A flash of lightning, yes; a new dawn, no. But the beginning has been made, and a powerful new direction for the future spiritual art has been charted. A genuine search has begun for what Franz Marc called "symbols that belong on the altars of a future spiritual religion."[14]

If, as many modernists thought, true art is the manifestation of Spirit, and if Spirit is seen most clearly with the eye of contemplation, and if meditation is one of the surest ways to open the contemplative eye, it follows that the truest and purest art will be contemplative art, art born in the fire of spiritual epiphany and fanned by meditative awareness.

This, of course, is precisely the idea behind many of the great Asian works of art, from Tibetan thangkas to Zen landscapes to Hindu iconography. The best of these works of art stem directly from the meditative mind. The artist/master enters meditative samadhi, or contemplative union, and from the union of the subject and the object, the "subject" then "paints" the "object," although all three—painter, painting, and object—are now one indivisible act ("He who cannot become an object cannot paint that object").[15] Precisely because the painting is executed in this nondual state of subject/object union or transcendence, it is spiritual in the deepest sense. It springs from the dimension of nondual and universal Spirit, which transcends (and thus unites) both subject and object, self and other, inner and outer. These artworks serve one main purpose: they are supports for contemplation. By gazing on the artwork, the viewer is invited to enter the same meditative and spiritual state that produced it. That is, the viewer is invited to experience nonduality, the union of the subject with all objects and the discovery of universal or transcendental awareness, in an immediate, simple, and direct fashion. This is the purest reason why one views art in the first place; *art created in this nondual awareness offers direct access to nondual Spirit.*

The secret of all genuinely spiritual works of art is that they issue from nondual or unity consciousness, no matter what "objects" they portray. A painting does not have to depict crosses and Buddhas to be spiritual. This is why, for example, Zen landscapes are so profoundly sacred in their texture, even if they are "just landscapes." They issue from a nondual awareness or unity consciousness, which is itself Spirit. At the height of transcendence, Spirit is also purely immanent and all-pervading, present equally and totally in each and every object, whether of matter, body, mind, or soul. The artwork, no matter what the object, becomes transparent to the Divine, and is a direct expression of Spirit.

The viewer momentarily *becomes* the art and is for that moment released from the alienation that is ego. Great spiritual art dissolves ego into nondual consciousness, and is to that extent experienced as an epiphany; a revelation, release or liberation from the tyranny of the separate-self sense. To the extent that a work can usher one into the nondual, then it is spiritual or universal, no matter whether it depicts bugs or Buddhas.

A critical theory of art based on the perennial philosophy would thus demand at least two scales. On the horizontal scale would be included all the elements on a given level that influence a work of art. These elements include everything from the artist's talent and background, socioeconomic facts and psychological factors, to cultural influences. The vertical scale, according to the perennial philosophy, cuts at right angles to all these earthly facts and deals with the ontological dimension of Being itself. This vertical scale would have several components summarized by the question, Where on the Great Chain of Being is the work itself situated?

The great artists of the modern era kept alive the quest for the sacred and the search for Spirit, while all about them the cultural world was succumbing to scientific materialism. For this we are forever in their debt. The next great movement in Western art is waiting to be born. It will not be of the body, or the mind, but of the soul and spirit. Thus we await with much anticipation the great artistic symbols "that belong on the altars of some future spiritual religion."[16]

So I write this essay for my long-time friend Alex Grey, who is attempting to unite in his art the realms of sensibilia, intelligibilia, and transcendelia. His *Sacred Mirrors* series takes the viewer from the gross physical plane of the body, through the subtler etheric-mental-psychic planes of one's being, to the spiritual-transcendental Clear Light Void at the core of every being. Like the best of Alex's work, this series helps the self become transparent to itself, thus facilitating transcendence.

Alex has inherited the modern masters' desire to manifest a spiritual essence through art. However, his own historical and stylistic roots emerge more from a metaphysical visionary tradition which can be traced back through Blake and Fludd to nineteenth-century symbolists like Delville and Klimt, and artists in this century such as Tchelitchev and Fuchs.

These visionary artists shared similar spiritual intentions with the early modernists, but sought to merge the immanent (representational) aspects of the Divine with the transcendental (abstract/nonrepresentational) aspects. Alex's work is a rich amalgam that includes references to ancient Hindu and Tibetan Buddhist sources as well as contemporary scientific and medical illustration. The detailed precision of his work arises from an obsession to experience and communicate the multidimensional nature of the self and the transformative and evolutionary potential of consciousness.

Alex's work places him in a very small group of important contemporary artists; through his art he aspires to all three realms—reaching from matter, to mind, to spirit—in itself a very rare ideal.

NOTES

1. The Great Chain is often said to consist of five, seven, or even more levels of being and knowing; my own model presents over two dozen carefully defined ontological levels. (See K. Wilber, *The Atman Project;* Wilber, Engler, and Brown, *Transformations of Consciousness.)* For the purposes of this foreword, the simple three-level division will suffice, but it should be kept in mind that a theory of art based on the Great Chain of Being can be much more precise than three levels.
2. Quotations are from Roger Lipsey's *An Art of Our Own* (Boston: Shambhala Publications, 1988), which I strongly recommend as the best introduction to the subject of art and the spirit. See also *The Spiritual in Art: Abstract Art 1890–1985* (New York: Abbeville Press, 1986).
3. Lipsey, *An Art of Our Own.*

4. Ibid.
5. Ibid.
6. Ibid.
7. Robert Clements, editor, *Michelangelo: A Self-Portrait* (Englewood Cliffs, N.J.: Prentice-Hall, 1963), p. 67.
8. Anthony Blunt, *The Art of William Blake* (New York: Columbia University Press, 1959), p. 23.
9. Ibid.
10. Jean Delville, *The New Mission of Art: A Study of Idealism in* Art (London: Francis Colmer, 1910).
11. Lipsey, *An Art of Our Own.*
12. Ibid.
13. Ibid.
14. Ibid.
15. Ibid.
16. Ibid.

Foreword to *LORD OF THE DANCE: THE AUTOBIOGRAPHY OF A TIBETAN LAMA* by Chagdud Tulku

CHAGDUD TULKU RINPOCHE came to America in 1979 and has resided here ever since. But from the time of his birth in Eastern Tibet, in 1930, to his arrival in the States, a story has unfolded as remarkable as any I have heard. This book is that story.

First, I want to set Rinpoche's story in some sort of context, for there are many things he simply will not tell you, even though this is his autobiography. He will not speak of his seemingly boundless compassion, a compassion that to us, his students, defines his very being. He will not talk of his profound awareness of the absolute nature of mind, an awareness he seems to be living and transmitting twenty-four hours a day. He will not tell you of the thousands and thousands of people whom he has served as teacher, spiritual master, physician, and friend. He will give little hint that he is renowned as a scholar, artist, and poet. Few of his remarkable accomplishments over the past decades—especially those in the West—will you find in this autobiography, and you cannot know from his narrative that this man has enhanced the lives of an incredible number of people through his profound transmission of the spiritual path.

When Rinpoche arrived in Los Angeles on October 24, 1979, he and his wife-to-be, Jane, first went to San Francisco. In mid-1980 he was asked to visit Eugene, Oregon, in order to teach an overview of Tibetan medicine to a group of American doctors. At the request of His Holiness Dudjom Rinpoche he remained in the Eugene area as a resident lama of Yeshe Nyingpo, the name given to Dudjom centers in the United States. Several years later, responding to students who wanted to ensure that there would be a seat in the West for future Chagdud incarnations, Rinpoche established the Chagdud Gonpa Foundation.

The original Chagdud Gonpa, founded in 1131, is one of the few monasteries in Eastern Tibet to have survived the Communist Chinese invasion. Chagdud Tulku Rinpoche, as the sixteenth incarnation of the original founder of that monastery, set up the first seat of Chagdud Gonpa in the West at River House (later renamed Dechhen Ling) in Cottage Grove, Oregon. There, as in all Chagdud Gonpa centers, instruction was offered in the methods and wisdom of Tibetan Buddhism, including the arts, philosophy, and meditation practices of the Vajrayana Buddhist tradition.

In the fall of 1988 Rinpoche and his students acquired 286 acres in northern California's Trinity Mountains, and Rigdzin Ling, Chagdud Gonpa's main center, was born. The heart of the development at Rigdzin Ling will be a traditional Tibetan Buddhist temple, or *lha khang* (literally, abode of deities), which will include an extensive display of Vajrayana sculpture and decorative arts.

Presently, the Chagdud Gonpa Foundation has seven centers on the West Coast as well as centers in Brazil and Switzerland. Rinpoche's other projects include the Mahakaruna Foundation, which provides support for poor and infirm Tibetans in the refugee communities of India and Nepal; the Tibetan Library, which purchases and preserves rare and irreplaceable Tibetan texts; and Padma Publishing, dedicated to making the works of the Nyingma tradition available in English, as well as translating and editing Rinpoche's own teachings. He has also created major Buddhist statues in the United States and has trained several Westerners in Tibetan art.

Rinpoche travels constantly, stopping only to lead retreats. To those who urge him to slow down, he explains, "I am still gathering my students. Perhaps some of the dharma seeds I plant now will ripen in future lifetimes. Vajrayana bonds are very strong and are not dissolved by the illusory displays of death and birth. We meet and meet again until ultimately we recognize that we are inseparable in enlightened buddha nature."

When Rinpoche's family, students and friends began asking him to write down the experiences that make up this volume, he saw no reason to record his life. He said that he did not want to write the usual Tibetan *namtar,* an account of a lama's life in which human failings are glossed over by the sheen of spiritual attainment. Although Rinpoche is a *tulku,* a recognized incarnation of a highly realized lama, he himself teaches that tulkus, being born into the realm of humans, must deal with very human issues in establishing the continuity of their spiritual path from one life to another. The essential attributes of a tulku combine a powerfully directed intention to work for the welfare of all living beings with the meditative realization to sustain this intention throughout this life and through the turmoil of the intermediate state between death and rebirth.

The combination of pure intention and great realization that produces a tulku also produces an extraordinary life, as Rinpoche demonstrates, and the requests that he write his story persisted until he finally yielded to them and began this book. He did not emphasize the achievements that have so defined his experience, but mostly his human foibles and his mistakes, using these to make teaching points, essentially at his own expense.

Anybody who knows Rinpoche will realize that he would write his story in no other way. Never mind that he is one of the greatest living masters of Dzogchen, the Great Perfection, the highest Buddhist teachings. Never mind that he took the groundbreaking step of fully ordaining a Western woman as a lama or that he is one of the first Tibetan masters to take Westerners completely into his confidence and trust, and to train them according to the teachings of the Great Perfection. Never mind that all of his students have unlimited access to him literally twenty-four hours a day. None of this has made its way into the following pages. Although Rinpoche teaches many categories of Vajrayana Buddhism, his realization of the Great Perfection informs his presentation of every level of teaching and is at the heart of his transmission.

Of the three major categories of the Buddha's teachings, the first, Hinayana, emphasizes the basic meditation practices of concentration and insight, and sets as its goal liberation from suffering through renunciation and cutting all attachment. The second, Mahayana, emphasizes the path of compassion and selfless motivation to work for the benefit of sentient beings until all are enlightened. The third, Vajrayana, emphasizes the revelation of mind's true nature, using many skillful methods of which the Great Perfection is the highest and most direct.

Rinpoche's life demonstrates how Great Perfection realization becomes thoroughly integrated with the conduct of daily activities. Mind's boundless, absolute nature, nakedly apparent to him in moments of visionary experience as a young child, became the central thrust of his spiritual path thereafter in finding teachings that would allow him to stabilize those glimpses. Throughout his last turbulent period in Tibet following the violent conquest by the Chinese communists and during the difficulties of being a refugee in India and Nepal, there was a profound continuity in his spiritual perspective and a deep, powerful current of compassion. In one of his published teachings he says:

> The key to all is pure-heartedness, one's own selfless aspirations, one's pure motivation. Your actions and those of another may not be so different; the difference is in the heart, in the motivation for what you do. And that's what makes all the difference in the outcome of your actions in the world. You must have the purity of your own heart, the purity of your own stance and intentions toward others and the world around you. This is the seed of all inner peace.

When one is in the presence of Chagdud Rinpoche, one is aware that this is a large-scale human being, a man of great qualities, humor and sincerity. As one of his students put it:

> Sometimes he flashes forth with words that have a stunning impact, like a lightning bolt. Then, after the shock comes a freshness, like the clean air that follows a thunderstorm. The whole environment of one's being feels purified. As for Rinpoche, he is immovable. His love is still there. His kindness is still there. The incomprehensible vastness of his mind that holds all the phenomena of our own is still there.

Asked why he finally wrote his autobiography after ignoring requests to do so for many years, he replied, "My life is a lesson in impermanence, and impermanence is the foremost teacher of the spiritual practitioner." Chagdud Tulku's story can be read on many levels—as a colorful, often humorous adventure story; as an inner, spiritual journey; and as a teaching on how one person attains the perspective of absolute truth amid life's uncertainty. As such it is both inspiring and encouraging, and highly relevant to anyone who seeks ultimate meaning in this time of dire prediction.

Foreword to *HEALING THE SPLIT: MADNESS OR TRANSCENDENCE?* by J. E. Nelson

JOHN NELSON HAS written an enormously impressive, profound, and important book, which takes as its simple starting point the fact that Spirit exists. This might seem an utterly obvious place to begin, except for the fact that Dr. Nelson is a member in good standing of the mainstream psychiatric community. And modern psychiatry, for all the relative good it has managed to accomplish, is still by and large totally ignorant of the spiritual and transpersonal dimensions of human experience. This is all the more curious in that psychiatry, whatever else its mission, has been understood from its inception to the science of the soul. And yet on the subject of the human soul and spirit modern psychiatry has been strangely silent.

Even worse, most of the genuine human experiences of transcendental spirit have been not merely ignored but rather violently pathologized by modern psychiatry. The easiest way to be labeled schizophrenic in our society is to let it be known that you feel that in the deepest part of your being you (and all sentient beings) are one with infinite Spirit, one with the universe, one with the All—an insight that every wisdom culture the world over has held to be not the depths of mental illness but the pinnacle of human understanding. This intuition of the Supreme Identity, shared by all beings, is for such cultures not the ultimate pathology but the ultimate liberation.

The Supreme Identity of the human soul and the transcendental Divine is the cornerstone of the perennial philosophy and the defining insight of the world's greatest mystics and philosophers. As Aldous Huxley put it, "*Philosophia perennis*—the metaphysic that recognizes a divine Reality substantial to the world of things and lives and minds; the psychology that finds in the soul something similar to, or even identical with, divine Reality; the ethic that places man's final end in the knowledge of the immanent and transcendent Ground of all beings—the thing is immemorial and universal."

Erwin Schroedinger, the founder of modern quantum mechanics and himself a profound mystic, explained that if you carefully look through the world's great spiritual and mystical literature, you will find "many beautiful utterances of a similar kind. You are struck by the miraculous agreement between humans of different race, different religion, knowing nothing about each other's existence, separated by centuries and millennia, and by the greatest distances that there are on our globe." This perennial philosophy, as Arthur Lovejoy pointed out, "has, in one form or another, been the dominant philosophy of the larger part of civilized mankind through most of its history" and has been embraced "by the greater number of speculative minds and religious teachers." And so Alan Watts draws the obvious conclusion:

> Thus we are hardly aware of the extreme peculiarity of our own position, and find it difficult to recognize the plain fact that there has otherwise been a single philosophical consensus of universal extent. It has been held by men and women who report the same insights and teach the same essential doctrine whether living today or six thousand years ago, whether from New Mexico in the Far West or from Japan in the Far East.

The only major culture to ignore or devalue the perennial philosophy has been, alas, our own modern culture of secular materialism and brutish scientism, which has by and large, from the eighteenth century onward, been dominated by that which can be perceived by the senses and manipulated by measurement. The concept of the Great Chain of Being—according to which men and women have at least five major levels of being: matter, body, mind, soul, and spirit—was reduced to mere matter and body. First spirit, then soul, and then mind were rejected by modern psychology and psychiatry, with the disastrous result that men and women were held to be nothing more than sophisticated bundles of material atoms in vaguely animate bodies. Thus our modern "science of the soul," almost from the start, has been a science merely of the physical and bodily components of the entire human being—a reductionistic cultural catastrophe of the first magnitude.

In recent times, however, the school of humanistic psychology has succeeded in reintroducing mind to psychology, thus supplementing and surpassing the empirical-physicalistic schools of behaviorism and the instinctual-bodily-emotional schools of psychoanalysis. And even more recently, transpersonal psychology has gone further still, and reintroduced the dimensions of soul and spirit. The result is a comprehensive or full-spectrum view of human psychology that includes matter, body, mind, soul, and spirit, in both their normal and pathological manifestations.

The aim of transpersonal psychology, then, is to give a psychological presentation of the perennial philosophy and the Great Chain of Being, fully updated and grounded in modern research and scientific developments. It fully acknowledges and *incorporates* the findings of modern psychiatry, behaviorism, and developmental psychology, and then adds, where necessary, the further insights and experiences of the existential and spiritual dimensions of the human being. We might say it starts with psychiatry and ends with mysticism.

That is exactly the value of *Healing the Split*. It presents one version of a full-spectrum model of human growth and development that incorporates the vast richness of modern psychiatry and neuroscience and then supplements it with transcendental and spiritual dimensions. And one of its chief attractions, as I have said, is that it is authored by a member in good standing of the mainstream psychiatric community. In this regard Dr. Nelson joins the ranks of such pioneering transpersonal psychiatrists as Stanislav Grof, Stanley Dean, Roger Walsh, Edward Podvoll, and Seymour Boorstein. It is an utterly welcome addition, for John Nelson discusses these topics with insight, clarity and, above all, I think, a truly heartfelt compassion, genuine and tender and compelling.

Not all of his theoretical conclusions, of course, will be accepted by all transpersonal theorists. The field is young, and there is plenty of room for healthy disagreements. Although this is somewhat technical, I think the following points of potential disagreement should be very briefly spelled out, because they are rather important:

1. Dr. Nelson's use of the term "the Spiritual Ground" is, I believe, slightly misleading. He speaks of the Spiritual Ground—that is, infinite Spirit—as "interacting" with the ego or the individual self; he speaks of "the energies of the Ground" and of "the relentless pressure of the Ground." But infinite Spirit, precisely because it is infinite, doesn't *interact* with anything. That which is infinite is not set apart from anything, including the ego, but rather pervades equally all that is, as the water of the ocean pervades each wave. We don't say that water interacts with waves; rather, each and every wave is a *form* of water, just as each and every manifest thing is a form of Spirit. There is no separation between the finite and the infinite such that any "interaction" could occur (interaction happens only between finite events). Likewise, infinite Spirit does not contain "energies" or exert "pressure," any more than water exerts pressure on waves. To maintain that the Ground is set apart from the ego and interacts with it is a very subtle but pernicious form of dualism (a mistake, I believe, that Nelson inherited from Michael Washburn's otherwise perceptive and important writings).

2. Rather, Nelson is using the term *Spiritual Ground* in a very loose sense to mean all the various higher levels and dimensions generally referred to as spiritual or transpersonal. As he says, the Ground is actually "composed" of various bands or wavelengths. These higher bands or levels are sometimes referred to as the psychic, the subtle, and the causal dimensions of existence, but even they are not to be confused with the ultimate or infinite spirit itself, which is no particular level or dimension at all, but rather the reality or suchness of each and every level. Thus, when Dr. Nelson speaks of the interaction of the Ground with the ego or the individual self, he is really speaking of the interaction of one of the subtler levels of existence (psychic, subtle, or causal, which he calls, respectively, the fifth, sixth, and seventh stages of development) with the ego or individual self. Indeed, most of what Nelson refers to as the Ground is really the psychic or beginning dimension of transpersonal existence, which does interact with the ego, and does contain energies, and does exert pressure on the ego (none of which the infinite does).

3. In particular, the infantile self is not "more open" to infinite Spirit than is the adult self. In fact, the opposite is true. The infantile self is embedded in the material and bodily levels of development, and because its self-boundaries are very weak and fluid, it is open to a dramatic and enormous influx, not from Spirit, but from the immense material and biological energies of those early levels, from the overwhelming

energies of élan vital, prana, libido. The fact that these energies are overwhelming does not mean they are spiritual.

Nelson (following Washburn) maintains that the infantile self is one with infinite Spirit (albeit unselfconsciously). But infinite Spirit is one with *all* levels—matter, body, mind, soul—and thus if the infantile self were one with Spirit (in a way that the ego-mind is not), it would also *have* to be one with *all* levels. But that is impossible, since in the infantile self the symbolic, mental, logical, and conceptual levels haven't emerged yet. No, the infantile self is one with, or fused with, the biomaterial world in general and the mothering one in particular. I believe this early stage is just as important as Dr. Nelson maintains that it is, but not because it is more in touch with Spirit, but because it is lost in the lower, oceanic spheres of existence, with feeble and easily overwhelmed self-boundaries. And, in fact, the material and bodily levels are *less* in touch with Spirit than are the mental levels, which are less in touch than the soul levels.

4. Dr. Nelson speaks of the fifth level of development as the home of creative genius and the sixth level as the home of paranormal abilities. While these are fine as a first approximation, they are slightly problematic. Most transpersonalists do not see creativity or paranormal abilities as an actual *stage* of growth, because a stage by definition is something that everybody *must* proceed through invariably. And it is simply not the case that all mystics, even if enlightened, *necessarily* go through a period of highly developed paranormal abilities. Most, in fact, do not. Rather, creativity and paranormal abilities may or may not develop at various stages of growth, and are not themselves a *particular* stage of growth.

These are all important points, I think. But in the larger view, they are also just nitpicking. John Nelson has succeeded in writing an important and helpful book, which has gone further than any other, I think, in directly grounding transpersonal psychology in the research of modern medical psychiatry, neuroscience, and psychiatric psychotherapy. If this type of book were required reading in all psychiatric schools in this country, we would soon be rejoining the ranks of a common humanity that has unmistakably found in the human soul "something similar to, or even identical with, divine Reality." And John Nelson will have helped that long-overdue return to basic sanity in a major, profound, and compassionate way.

Foreword to *THE FABRIC OF THE FUTURE: WOMEN VISIONARIES ILLUMINATE THE PATH TO TOMORROW* Edited by M. J. Ryan

THE FABRIC OF THE FUTURE is truly an extraordinary book, profound, wise, far-ranging, visionary, compassionate, often brilliant, always moving. And a book whose forty or so contributors are all women.

This in itself is not the least surprising. What is surprising, and more than a bit depressing, is that the vast wisdom of this rich diversity of female voices has to be presented in a book, instead of being an already accepted part of the fabric of the culture at large. And yet just that situation is, in a sense, the theme of this volume: The fabric of the future will necessarily incorporate the rich diversity of female voices, and it will do so in a more gracious, graceful, and generous fashion than does today's world, if livable future we are to have at all.

On the one hand, of course, men and women share a vast array of common and universal experiences: we are all born, we all die, and in between we laugh and love and loathe and cherish; we play, and work, and fight, and fear. We breathe the same air, are sustained by the same Earth, have our heads in the same sky, and wonder all about it. More technically, there appear to be many linguistic, cognitive, biological, and affective universals, which remind us daily that we are, finally, a common humanity interrelated with global commons and all of Gaia's inhabitants.

But within those profound commonalities, there are wonderful differences: between cultures, between individuals, and between the sexes. And we seem to be at an extraordinary and auspicious moment in human evolution, where many of these rich differences, previously undervalued or even devalued altogether, are now being unleashed. And this certainly seems to be true of those values that have traditionally been called "feminine."

Some theorists, of course, prefer not to speak of a difference between "male" and "female" values, believing that any differentiation between the sexes will simply lead, in the long run, to further disenfranchisement of women; and thus it is imperative that we solely emphasize gender equity, equal rights, and sexual equality. While I think that is mandatory as a *legal* agenda (all individuals, regardless of race, creed, or gender, stand equal before the law), surely there is room, within that legal freedom, to recognize and cherish the many values traditionally known as "female," if for no other reason than that those values are precisely ones that the modern world has so insistently overlooked. And values that, therefore, a future evolution will incorporate in a more balanced and graceful tomorrow.

This book, beautifully assembled by M. J. Ryan, is a radiant blueprint for just such a future, womb of a wisdom too long unheard, a call to a tomorrow that embraces us all with care and compassion and grace.

Foreword to *THE MISSION OF ART* by Alex Grey

ALEX GREY MIGHT BE the most significant artist alive. In a world gone postmodern, bereft of meaning and value, cut loose on a sea of irony and indifference, Alex is taking a stunning stand: there is a God, there is Spirit, there is a transcendental ground and goal of human development and unfolding. Higher realities are available to us—that is the message of Alex Grey's art and words in this book. He has set himself the extraordinary task of depicting, in art, these higher truths, and here encourages all artists to find their own unique means of serving art's abiding mission.

This is art in its original and highest meaning: the subjective revelation of Spirit. When an artist is alive to the spiritual domains, he or she can depict and convey those domains in artistic rendering, which wrestles Spirit into matter and attempts to speak through that medium. When great artists do so, the artwork then reminds us of our own higher possibilities, our own deepest nature, our own most profound ground, which we all are invited to rediscover. The purpose of truly transcendent art is to express something you are not yet, but that you can become.

And this is exactly what Alex does in his truly stunning art. His work, like all great transcendental art, is not merely symbolic or imaginary: it is a direct invitation to recognize and realize a deeper dimension of our very own being. In the eternal trinity of the good, the true, and the beautiful, art, while it can be good and true, has always staked out the domain of the beautiful. Alex's art is deeply, profoundly, beautiful, the surest sign that it is on the trail of Spirit.

I myself have one other personal test of great art: when you first look at it, it simply takes your breath away. One of the great pleasures in my life is showing people Alex's art for the first time: they always gasp, wonderfully. You can almost see them thinking: perhaps there is more to reality, and to myself, than I thought. That is the great, profound, extraordinary service that Alex's art serves: it calls us beyond ourselves, it takes us beyond ourselves, to a transpersonal land where Spirit is real, where God is alive, where Buddha smiles and the Tao sings, where our own original face shines with a glory that time forgot and space cannot recall. We are confronted with the best that we can be, the deepest we can feel, the highest we can see, and so we go away from Alex's vision a little better than we were a minute before.

This places Alex in a rather extraordinary lineage of Western painters whose art is saturated with Spirit. Let us, with all due reverence, bow down deeply when we even hear these names: Hildegard, Michelangelo, Angelico, Bosch, Blake, Rembrandt, Delville, van Gogh, Mondrian, Malevich, Klee, Brancusi, Marc, Klimt, Kandinsky, Fuchs, Tchelitchev, and Alex Grey.

Foreword to *COMING HOME: THE EXPERIENCE OF ENLIGHTENMENT IN SACRED TRADITIONS* by Lex Hixon

"ENLIGHTENMENT IS the awakening to our primal harmony or, in another mystical language, to our rootedness in the Divine."

Thus begins what is, in my opinion, the single best introductory book ever written on the world's great mystical traditions. As Lex Hixon himself makes quite clear, *Coming Home* is not an attempt at an academic survey or a textbook of the historical and doctrinal details of each of the great wisdom traditions. There are many excellent books that already serve this function (Huston Smith's *The World's Religions,* for example). Nor is this book an attempt at a philosophical justification of the mystical or enlightened state (W. T. Stace's *Mysticism and Philosophy* accomplishes this brilliantly). Nor is it even a general anthology culled from the various traditions. Such anthologies—Aldous Huxley's *The Perennial Philosophy* is still the best—are important because they demonstrate that however different the various wisdom traditions might outwardly appear, they nevertheless inwardly share certain profound and cross-cultural insights into the nature of absolute Spirit or Godhead. And the supreme insight shared by all of the great traditions is simply this: absolute Spirit or Godhead is the ultimate source, essence, and identity of each and every individual being. Absolute Spirit is one's own True Nature or Original Face, which is the face of the cosmos as well. There is only Spirit; and so these anthologies eloquently proclaim.

Important and extremely valuable as these approaches are, Lex Hixon's approach cuts at right angles to all of them, not replacing or displacing, but complementing them. He simply assumes the truth of divine Spirit as manifested in and through the various wisdom traditions, and then, instead of telling you all the historical details and doctrines of the various traditions, he invites you to release yourself into Spirit as it manifests itself through each of these traditions. Each chapter is thus devoted to a particular path, from Taoism to Krishnamurti, from Zen to Plotinus, from Vedanta to Sufism. While each essay gives enough historical background to orient the reader, the real purpose is to talk you into the contemplative awareness that is the mystical heart of each tradition but that is itself beyond all talk. The intent is to use thinking to tease us out of thinking, to dive to the very heart of the particular path, and to allow us to release ourselves into the openness and illumined nature of the very Divine itself. Lex Hixon is not primarily interested in doctrine, dogma, or ideas about Spirit, however relevant they all might be, but rather in the vulnerable, open, empty, illumined, and direct experience or realization of Spirit itself, standing free at the Heart, outshining the world, radiant to infinity. It is this timeless awareness that he wants us to glimpse.

Because Spirit manifests itself only in and as the world of form—of apparently separate things and apparently different events, of seeming separation and isolation and alienation—it is in this diverse world that we must begin our search for the One beyond the Many, our Primordial Ground. Therefore, we need a vehicle, a *yana,* to take us to the formless shore beyond, even if the final realization is only that no vehicle was necessary or even possible. It is for this purpose that the world's great mystical paths have come into existence. They are not beliefs, not theories, not ideas, not theologies, and not doctrines. Rather, they are vehicles; they are experiential *practices.* They are experiments to *perform* (and thus see "through form"). They are something to *do* and then *be,* not something to merely think and then believe. Ultimately, there are no mystical doctrines or beliefs whatsoever; there are only mystical experiences and insights, all springing directly and immediately from the flow of one's own primordial experiencing in this very moment, illuminating all that is, like sunlight on the clearest of crystal autumn days.

This is the genius of Lex Hixon's book. He does not dwell on the forms, doctrines, and details of the various traditions, essential as they most definitely are. Rather, he takes us gently but almost immediately to the unending *conclusion* of each and every path—the mood and experience of enlightenment itself. Using the terms and sometimes the actual practices of each of the particular vehicles that he is discussing, he invites us, in each chapter, to release all forms, concepts, names, and thoughts, and to tacitly acknowledge and actually *feel* that which is always prior to thought and sensation—namely, our own primordial experiencing or basic awareness, the presence and flow of Spirit itself.

This fundamental and universal consciousness, you and all beings possess fully at every moment. It is your simple and bare awareness in this moment *before* you manipulate it, name it, judge it, or in any way fiddle with it. It is always the case prior to your attempts to grasp it. And therefore, ultimately, there is no path to this primary, basic, and ultimate consciousness. There is no way to walk to your own feet. Rather, the various traditions provide ways to exhaust the seeking mind, to exhaust the effort to grasp in time that which is eternal, to exhaust the attempts to grasp in space that which is infinite, and to exhaust the "great search" for Spirit so that Spirit itself may shine forth of its own accord. As Eckhart said, "God is closer to me than I am to myself." God or Spirit is simply your ultimate Self or Consciousness now lighting the words on this page—a Self (or no-self) that is one and undivided in all sentient beings.

This enlightened understanding and realization is what each of the world's great wisdom traditions attempts to transmit to those who would consent to perform the great experiment in their own souls. And it is the timeless conclusion of this mystical experiment that Lex Hixon presents throughout this book. In each chapter he takes us from surface thinking and the world of will and seeking and forms, to a deeper or contemplative understanding, itself devoid of form, seeking, restriction, or knowing. In that openness, flashes of enlightened mind can shine forth, taking you so radically beyond yourself that you actually discover your True Self or Original Nature, which is as close as your present experiencing and your own basic awareness in this very moment. To abide as that Awareness in the simplicity and luminosity of the present, without will or effort, is to be ushered into a magical world you never left, and to understand what it means to be "coming home," a homecoming that is said to lead from time to eternity and from death to immortality.

Coming Home is a simple, brilliant book. It explains and epitomizes the best of the world's great mystical traditions. By centering on the heart of enlightenment, it blazes the path of no-path. In the traditional Tibetan gesture of welcome, gratitude, and deep appreciation, I touch my forehead to that of my friend Lex Hixon—he who is "rooted in the Divine," as this book so eloquently testifies.

Foreword to *TEXTBOOK OF TRANSPERSONAL PSYCHIATRY AND PSYCHOLOGY*

Edited by Bruce Scotton, Allan B. Chinen, and John R. Battista

BIOLOGICAL AND MEDICAL SCIENTISTS are now in the midst of intensive work on the Human Genome Project, the endeavor to map of all of the genes in the entire sequence of human DNA. This spectacular project promises to revolutionize our ideas of human growth, development, disease, and medical treatment, and its completion will surely mark one of the greatest of advances in human knowledge.

Not as well known, but arguably more important, is what might be called the Human Consciousness Project, the endeavor, now well under way, to *map the entire spectrum of the various states of human consciousness* (including, as well, realms of the human unconscious). This Human Consciousness Project, involving hundreds of researchers from around the world, involves a series of multidisciplinary, multicultural, multimodal approaches that together promise an exhaustive mapping of the entire range of consciousness, the entire sequence of the "genes" of awareness, as it were.

These various attempts, which you will see amply represented in the following pages, are rapidly converging on a "master template" of the various stages, structures, and states of consciousness available to men and women. By comparing and contrasting various multicultural approaches—from Zen Buddhism to Western psychoanalysis, from Vedanta Hinduism to existential phenomenology, from Tundra Shamanism to altered states—these approaches are rapidly piecing together a master template—a spectrum of consciousness—using the various approaches to fill in any gaps left by the others.

Although many of the specifics are still being intensively researched, the overall evidence for the existence of this spectrum of consciousness is already so significant as to put it largely beyond serious dispute. The existence of these various structures and states of consciousness is based upon careful experimentation and consensual validation. From such gatherings of consensual and documented data, firmly anchored in appropriate validity claims, the spectrum of consciouses is constructed.

This spectrum appears to range from prepersonal to personal to transpersonal experiences, from instinctual to egoic to spiritual modes, from subconscious to self-conscious to superconscious structures, from prerational to rational to transrational states. And it is this all-inclusive spectrum of consciousness upon which transpersonal psychiatry and psychology are primarily based.

The word "transpersonal" simply means "personal plus." That is, the transpersonal orientation explicitly and carefully includes all of the facets of personal psychology and psychiatry, but then *adds* those deeper or higher aspects of human experience that transcend the ordinary and the average—experiences that are, in other words, "transpersonal," or "more than the personal," or personal plus.

Thus, in the attempt to more fully, accurately, and scientifically reflect the entire range of human experience, transpersonal psychiatry and psychology take, as their basic starting point, the entire spectrum of consciousness.

In the following chapters, you will see the most important approaches to this spectrum outlined. You will also see the diverse methodologies that have evolved to address (and assess) the different dimensions of this spectrum—including empiricism, phenomenology, representational models, hermeneutical interpretations, meditative states, and so on—but with all of them oriented toward careful verification and justification procedures. The transpersonal orientation is, in all cases, geared toward consensual *evidence,* evidence that can be confirmed or rejected by a community of the adequate (the all-important fallibist criterion for genuine knowledge accumulation).

You will also see that this spectrum develops. Like all complex living systems, the spectrum of consciousness grows and evolves. It moves, in the most general sense, from subconscious to self-conscious to superconscious modes, or prepersonal to personal to transpersonal capacities, not in a linear fashion, but in a series of flowing waves. And you will see some of the more important models that have been proposed to account for this extraordinary growth and development of human consciousness.

Precisely because the spectrum of consciousness develops, various "mis-developments" can occur at any stage of this unfolding. As with any living entity, pathology can occur at any point in growth. Thus, the spectrum of consciousness is also a spectrum of different types of possible pathologies: psychotic, borderline, neurotic, cognitive, existential, spiritual. And, as you will clearly see in this volume, transpersonal psychiatry and psychology have developed a sophisticated battery of treatment modalities that address these different types of pathologies.

Because transpersonal psychiatry and psychology are dedicated to a careful and rigorous investigation into the entire spectrum of consciousness, they naturally find themselves allied with other transpersonal approaches, ranging from transpersonal ecology to transpersonal philosophy, transpersonal anthropology to transpersonal sociology. And you will find in the following pages an impressive collection of essays touching on these various fields. The point, of course, is that if the entire spectrum of consciousness is accurately acknowledged and taken into account, it will dramatically alter each and every discipline it touches. And this, indeed, is part of the extraordinary interest and excitement that the transpersonal orientation has generated in numerous disciplines.

The editors of this book—Bruce Scotton, Allan Chinen, and John Battista—have done a superb job in presenting a balanced, thoughtful, and inclusive cross-section of virtually every aspect of transpersonal studies, with appropriate emphasis, of course, on the psychological and psychiatric dimensions. It is a brilliant and pioneering effort that will no doubt become an indispensable standard in the field, and for which the editors deserve the highest praise.

It is such remarkable inclusiveness, I think, that especially announces the transpersonal orientation. If nothing human is alien to me, then neither should it be alien to our sciences of the mind, the soul, the psyche, the possible human. How could orthodox psychology ignore, dismiss, or pathologize the further reaches of human nature? How could positivistic science reduce it all to a pile of frisky dirt?

Looking deeply into our world, deeply into ourselves, deeply into our brethren, is there really nothing more to be found than a bunch of material atoms hurling through the void? Is there not more in heaven and earth than is dreamt of in that philosophy? Are there not depths and heights that awe and inspire, that bring us to our knees, that stun us with the beauty of the sublime, the radiance of the real, the truth and goodness of a spiritual domain that outshines our loveless ways? Are these not part of the extraordinary spectrum of human possibilities?

Transpersonal psychiatry and psychology are dedicated to the assumption that there is decidedly more than the conventional approaches assume. That the spectrum of consciousness is vast indeed. That there is in fact a "personal plus." And, in addition to the undeniable importance of personal psychology, it is especially the nature of that plus, that depth, that height, that transpersonal psychiatry and psychology are dedicated to exploring.

Foreword to *DRINKING LIGHTNING* by Philip Rubinov-Jacobson

ART. ITS DEFINITIONS are legion, its meanings multiple, its importance often debated. But amid the many contradictory definitions of art, one has always stood the test of time, from the Upanishads in the East to Michelangelo in the West: art is the perception and depiction of the Sublime, the Transcendent, the Beautiful, the Spiritual. Art is a window to God, an opening to the Goddess, a portal through which you and I, with the help of the artist, may discover depths and heights of our soul undreamt of by the vulgar world. Art is the eye of Spirit, through which the Sublime can reach down to us, and we up to It, and be transfigured and transformed in the process. Art, at its best, is the representation of your very own soul, a reminder of who and what you truly are, and therefore can become.

Philip Rubinov-Jacobson is a true artist, one in whom the Sublime is at work. But, as Phil explains in this book, the spiritual impulse—the artistic impulse—is at work in every act of creativity. Art can be a way to awaken that creative and spiritual process, and hone it to a fine degree. That is what Phil has done in his own life, and what he shows the reader how to do in the following pages.

This is a wonderful book, ripe with the wisdom of an artist in whom the creative fire is alive, touched by the Gods and Goddesses of a realm that the conventional mind too often fails to see, enraptured by the vision of a beauty too painful to pronounce. Art, as the eye of Spirit, is the royal road to your own soul, and this book is nothing less than a road map for that extraordinary adventure.

Foreword to *SHADOWS OF THE SACRED: SEEING THROUGH SPIRITUAL ILLUSIONS* by Frances Vaughan

Frances Vaughan is the wisest of the Wise Women I know. Such a wonderful concept: the woman who is wise, the woman who has more wisdom, perhaps, than you or I, the woman who brings a special knowledge, a graceful touch, a healing presence, to her every encounter, for whom beauty is also a mode of knowing and openness a special strength—a woman who sees so much more, and touches so much more, and reaches out with care, and tells us that it will be all right, this woman who is wise, this woman who sees more.

The woman from whom we all can learn. I suppose there are some in our society who object to distinguishing between male and female persons; the gender wars are intense nowadays, and any "differences" ascribed to men and women are looked upon suspiciously, as perhaps a prelude to some oppressive agenda. The "differences" between male and female are just so much propaganda, the argument goes, designed to keep women barefoot, pregnant, and in the kitchen. But if the differentiation between the male and female value sphere is an oppressive plot, it goes back to day one. From the earliest foraging cultures to the first horticultural societies, and from there to the great agrarian Empires that ran from the Aztecs and Incas to the Khans and Ottomans, Romans and Greeks, Egyptians, and Chinese: in virtually all known societies to date, the male and female value spheres were indeed thought to be quite different. Some of these societies—such as the horticultural planting communities ruled by the Great Mother—valued the female sphere more or less equally with the male sphere (as did many earlier foraging societies.) Other cultures—particularly the agrarian Empires and the cultures of horse and herding—placed an almost exclusive emphasis on the male value sphere: the deities were purely male and the values were those of the warrior or princely aristocrat (the "patriarchy").

Looking back on history, we moderns feel sadness, sometimes outrage, that some cultures so disproportionately championed the male sphere over the female sphere, but the point for now is that, regardless of emphasis, in all of these cultures (foraging to horticultural to agrarian, matrifocal or patrifocal)—in all of these cultures, the male and female values spheres were crisply differentiated, and these differences show a surprising consistency—sometimes monotonously so—across cultures.

And indeed, in recent times, the radical feminists, the spiritual feminists, and the ecofeminists, in their own various ways, have all embraced the female value sphere as indeed embodying a universal sphere of values, a sphere significantly different from the male sphere, and a sphere that has been severely undervalued during the last several thousand years of agrarian/herding/patriarchal cultures. And there is much truth to this, I think.

But what, indeed, are these values, in both the male and female sphere? Perhaps the simplest way to summarize the evidence is in terms of the two major types of love—Eros and Agape—and the two major types of action—agency and communion. Eros is the love of the lower reaching up for the higher, always ascending, always yearning for more, always seeking, often recklessly, restlessly, for more; whereas Agape is the love of the higher reaching down to the lower, embracing it in compassion and acceptance, tenderness and care (thus Eros tends always to aim high, for the sky and Heaven, and Agape always reaches down and embraces gladly the body and the Earth). Agency is a type of action and being that stresses the individual, the separate and autonomous agent, the isolated, the singular; whereas communion stresses relationship, network, linking, joining.

It's not that one form of love or action is better or nobler or more desirable than the other. It's more the primordial yin and yang: interpenetrating each other, relying on each other, generating each other, and—ideally—balancing each other.

Without in any way pigeonholing men and women, or implying that distinctions are etched in concrete, the evidence strongly suggests that, across cultures and virtually from day one, the female value sphere has been pictured as emphasizing Agape and communion, whereas the male sphere has been seen as emphasizing agency and Eros.

And, indeed, these are the main differences in values that Carol Gilligan, for example, has detected in men and women's responses to moral dilemmas: males have a tendency to emphasize individual rights and legalistic justice (agency), whereas females tend to emphasize care and responsibilities (communion). Likewise, the theological ("thealogical") and spiritual feminists have tended to summarize the entire thrust of "feminine spirituality" as "the Divine embodied" (Agape incarnate!), bringing heavenly wisdom down and into relationships, into the Earthbody, into the day-to-day living of the Divine (whereas most forms of "male spirituality," from shamans to yogis and saints, have almost always sought "journeys" to the "other world," the upward yearning Eros looking for ways beyond the everyday Earthbody, for their kingdom is not of this world.)

Every single major world religion (Christianity, Islam, Judaism, Hinduism, Buddhism, and even later Taoism) arose during the time of the great agrarian empires (and/or the horse and herding cultures). Which means that *every single major world religion* arose in a climate that highly valued the male sphere of Eros and agency (go off in a cave, or into the desert by yourself, and ascend!)—and thus they either indirectly devalued, or frankly oppressed, the female value sphere of Agape, of Earthbody, of communion with nature and with others, of embodiment, and most of all, of *being-in-relationship*.

This, of course, does not mean that the great patriarchal wisdom traditions have nothing to teach us, any more than it means we shouldn't use the wheel because a man invented it. It does mean, however, that there is a whole value sphere yet to be, literally, unearthed in the modern era. The great traditions do not need to be simply jettisoned—that would be catastrophic—but they need desperately to be supplemented.

And that means, above all, that we are desperately in need of, yes, the Wise Woman.

Frances is such a one: the woman who brings wisdom into the world and does not flee the world for wisdom somewhere else. The woman who teaches individuality, but set in its larger and deeper contexts of communion: communion with others, with body, with Spirit, with one's own higher Self, the Spirit that manifests its very being in relationships. And that is how I think of Frances most often: the wise woman who teaches sane and sincere relationship, the woman who sets us in our deeper contexts, this wise woman whom I am proud to know.

But it is not just as a Wise Woman that Frances comes to us. When historians from Toynbee to Whyte remarked that the introduction of Buddhism to the West would likely be regarded by future generations as one of the great turning points in civilization, I think they were onto something important. Perhaps Buddhism per se will not become a culture-wide movement, but the point, I think, is that the introduction or discovery (or rediscovery) of some form of genuinely *transpersonal endeavor* is crucial to the future of Western culture.

In the West, where psychology and psychiatry have completely replaced religion as the dominant sciences of the soul, it is the school of transpersonal psychology that carries most clearly the banner of genuine contemplative spirituality. Drawing on the great mystical and contemplative traditions (but not limited to them), transpersonal psychology weaves ancient insights with modern psychotherapeutic techniques, creating a unique synthesis and amalgam of ancient wisdom and modern knowledge.

And Frances is one of the relatively few transpersonal psychologists actually "in the trenches," as it were—working with clients, day to day, on a professional basis. Not only has she been trained in several contemplative traditions (from Christian to Zen to Hindu and Sufi), and not only has she received her "orthodox" training from the highly regarded California School of Professional Psychology, but she brings that combined wisdom to the actual day-to-day details of the therapeutic situation.

The book you are holding in your hands is, so to speak, dispatches from the front lines, which is why it is so incredibly important as a document. It is what Frances and her clients have taught each other about sane living, sane relationships, care and compassion, dignity and grace, in and through the most difficult of times that bring people to the office of a therapist, looking for a kind ear and a sense of gentle direction. They have lost their way a bit, in this society that doesn't particularly care, perhaps even lost their soul, and they come quietly and confused, and can you help me, please?

In the type of transpersonal practice that Frances (and a handful of others) are attempting to forge, we see the emergence of whatever it was that Toynbee and White recognized as so crucial: some sense of the transpersonal, some sense of the Mystery of the Deep, some context beyond the isolated me, that touches each and every one of us and lifts us from our troubled and mortal selves, this contracted coil, delivers us into the hands of the timeless and very Divine, and gracefully releases us from ourselves; where openness melts defenses and relationship grounds sanity, where compassion outpaces the hardened heart and care outshines despair: this is the opening to the Divine that Frances teaches each of us.

One of Frances's clients once told her that she (Frances) had helped to midwife, to deliver, her soul. I think that somehow says it all. To midwife the Divine—already present in each, but perhaps not shining brightly; already given to each, but perhaps not noticed well; already caring for the world, but perhaps forgotten in all the rush: this opening also Frances teaches us.

Like all dispatches from the front, the following notes are not linear. They are not in the form of a logical argument where one enters the tunnel at point A and is coerced through an argument to come out at point B. They sometimes meander, these notes. They sometimes bounce around. They follow the contours of real-life terrain; they are conversations with her clients, conversations she is having with us as well, following the ups and downs of real thought and genuine dialogue, and not the stiff lines of geometric proof.

And so, if I may suggest, let these note wash over you, wash through you, and follow gently the curves of terrain, and don't force it into a linear argument. It is through a new and strange and wonderful landscape, this transpersonal journey, and your tour guide has seen it all, and lived it all, and lived to tell the tale. And there, just there, is the definition of the Wise Woman.

Let us both, you and I, take the hand of the Wise Woman, and walk with her through the land of our own soul, and listen quietly to the tale she has to tell. And know that a surer pair of hands we are not likely to find in this lifetime.

PATHS BEYOND EGO IN THE COMING DECADE

THERE ARE SEVERAL exciting developments in spiritual or transpersonal studies that I believe will be particularly important in the coming decade, and I would like briefly to outline them.* They involve research into: *states* of consciousness and *structures* of consciousness; cross-cultural investigations of contemplative paths and patterns; situating spirituality in the larger currents of the postmodern world; a rereading of world philosophies, religions, and psychologies from a genuinely transpersonal perspective; a continued study of the relation of the various "breaks from normality" (i.e., the relation of psychoses and mysticism); the excruciatingly difficult problem (still) of the relation of mind and body; more precise mappings of the developmental spectrum of consciousness (in its conventional, contemplative, and pathological dimensions); the relation of Jungian and transpersonal psychology; a finer theoretical understanding of the relation of "marginal groups" (such as the transpersonal) to the "larger forces" of world development and technological advance; the relation of the spiritual domain to the three great "Others" or neglected domains of the world's religions (namely, body, nature, woman); the relation of nature and Spirit; the relation of theory and practice; and, most importantly, continued work in the "grand theories" or "integral studies" aimed at a synthesis of the spiritual dimension with all of the various conventional disciplines (anthropology, medicine, ecology, economics, the humanities, etc.).

* [This was written in 1992.]

To take them in that order:

1. *States and structures.* There are two dominant paradigms now governing transpersonal studies: altered states of consciousness and developmental structures of consciousness. Both of these two paradigms have their archetypal representation in Vedanta, where a distinction (and correlation) is made between the five major sheaths or *structures* (koshas) of consciousness (matter, body, mind, higher mind, universal mind) and the three major *states* of consciousness (gross, subtle, and causal realms, experienced in waking, dreaming, and deep sleep states). Vedanta maintains that a given state of consciousness can support several different structures; Aurobindo added the insight that structures, but not states, develop (thus, the infant has access to all three major states of waking, dreaming, and sleeping, but it has access to only the *lowest* structures of the gross realm; the higher structures have not yet developed).

The research agenda is: what is the relation of states (which can be prepersonal, personal, and transpersonal) to structures (which are also prepersonal, personal, and transpersonal)?

As it is now, there has been little work done on how to integrate these two paradigms, and in many ways they appear incompatible: structures are cumulative and integrative, states are discrete and exclusionary. I suggest that the answer will involve the notion that developmental structures are the permanent unfolding or actualization, or coming into stable manifestation, of that which is only *temporarily* experienced in an altered state. To the extent that temporary and discrete states become actualized (and not just passing), they must enter the stream of development and "obey" its patterns. Mapping and explaining these transformations will be one of the major breakthrough areas in transpersonal studies.

2. *Cross-cultural studies of contemplative development*: Much pioneering work has been done in this area, but much more awaits the future researcher. Of particular importance is the careful phenomenological descriptions of contemplative states/structures (with all the difficulty involved in describing often transverbal realities). An extremely important question in this area is: can the same developmental-logic governing the unfolding of conventional stages of cognition, conation, morals, affects, and so forth, be shown to apply to the higher states/structures as well? Is there a unity to evolution and development? I believe there is, but *if not*, then what does that say about the unity of Spirit and its unfolding (or lack thereof)?

3. *Situating transpersonal studies in the larger currents of postmodernism*: There are now four main intellectual currents in the humanities of the "postmodern world," all struggling for supremacy: the classical Enlightenment-humanists, the deconstructionist "anti-thinkers" (Derrida), the "critical interpretives" (Foucault), and "communicative ethics" (Habermas).

Enlightenment humanism is marked by a belief in the power of instrumental rationality to discover any and all truths capable (and worthy) of being known, and a belief in the power of such rational truth to set men and women free, both personally and politically. However noble these aspirations, they have historically tended to degenerate into a "disenchanted" and fragmented worldview, with the domains of art, morality, and science radically divorced from each other and from individuals' lives, and with a rather blind faith that technological rationality can solve the resultant dilemmas.

In response to this fractured and rather limited rational worldview (traditional "modernism" and "humanism"), there have arisen three broad "postmodern" movements, as I mentioned: the deconstruction of Jacques Derrida, the neostructuralism of Michel Foucault, and the universal pragmatics of Jürgen Habermas. All of them are united by a critique of instrumental rationality and a critique of the isolated and autonomous ego (the foundation of humanism); they believe that truth is historically and linguistically situated (and not simply universally given); and they show a great concern with ethical action in a world that can no longer ground its truth-claims in mechanistic rationality and positivism.

Deconstruction attempts to demonstrate that linguistic rationality ("logocentrism"), which has marked much of Western philosophy (and civilization), is internally self-contradictory: it undermines its own position whenever it is applied to itself (e.g., the criterion for empirical truth is not itself empirical). This deconstruction of logocentrism is said to open up new pathways of moving beyond a rigidly dualistic rationality. Foucault's analysis of knowledge as structures of power, and his demonstration that various worldviews or "epistemes" have abruptly emerged throughout history, have both had an effect similar to deconstruction: they undermine thoroughly the traditional humanistic/rational assumptions about the world, about truth, about ethics. And Jürgen Habermas (whom many consider the world's greatest living philosopher) has attempted to move beyond instrumental rationality—and beyond the isolated and autonomous ego—by emphasizing "communicative ethics," or the ways in which human beings attempt to understand each other in a community of mutual exchange and mutual respect.

All of these postmodern movements are indeed post-ego movements. In fact, they often explicitly refer to their projects as the "death of the ego-philosophies" or "the death of the subject-philosophies." And while all of this is very encouraging from a transpersonal perspective, the "death of the ego" that they are referring to does not mean an opening to a genuine spiritual or transpersonal dimension, but rather the transformation from a narrow, instrumental, rational egoic worldview to a multiperspective, organic, relational, and socially-situated bodymind (what I have called the "vision-logic" of the "centaur," which is still a separate-self sense, but "better" than the previous "ego"—postmodernism is "moving in the right direction").

But all of these postmodern movements contain explicit criticisms of any sort of mystical transcendentalism, of pure presence, of trans-historical realities. So a crucial topic for the coming decade will be: Where are spiritual and transpersonal studies situated in these postmodern currents, and how can transpersonal studies answer their sharp criticisms? I would suggest that all of these postmodern theories *already* display hidden transcendentalism, and this needs only to be pointed out so that they themselves can then be situated in the spectrum of transpersonal development. In other words, deconstruction can be deconstructed (à la Nagarjuna), Foucault can be situated in his own episteme, and even Habermas has held open the possibility that there are still higher stages of development yet to unfold (which is the province of transpersonal developmental studies). For conventional academic concerns in the humanities, *this* question—"What comes after the subject?," or "What comes after the ego?"—will be the hot-bed of theoretical action.

4. *Reconceptualizing world philosophies from a spiritual or transpersonal perspective.* The virtually uncontested assumption of modern Western intellectuals is that anything "spiritual" or "transcendental" is simply a "theory" or a mere "ideology," and thus history is read as a chronicle of shifting ideologies whose only grounding is the relative cultural legitimation given to them by particular (and equally shifting and relative) cultures. But what if *some* transcendentals are in fact direct experiences and direct disclosures that, although mediated by language, are in some important ways extra-linguistic or cross-cultural? A diamond will cut a piece of glass, no matter what words we use for "diamond," "cut," and "glass"—and there is abundant evidence that a soul

can experience God, no matter what words we use for "soul," "experience," and "God."

History, then, would have to be entirely re-read as a chronicle of the growth and accumulation of true transcendental experiences filtered through various ideologies, and not merely reduced to one ideology among others. This would completely revolutionize our concepts of human potentials and divine possibilities, and place the growth of spiritual knowledge correctly alongside any other genuine advances.

5. *The relation of psychosis and mysticism.* This always fascinating topic is significant not just in itself, but for several vitally important and related topics: creativity and madness, normalization and marginalization, ordinary and extra-ordinary potentials, personal breakdown and personal breakthrough. The important field of *spiritual emergency network* is also intimately connected with this topic. Too many people diagnosed with psychotic breaks seem to be undergoing a spiritual emergency, and the details of these crises desperately need further investigation (not to mention the relation of spirituality to addictions, depressions, anxieties, and so forth). This whole topic is also related directly to how we conceptualize "the" unconscious (demons, gods, infrarational, superrational, all of the above?). The continued mapping and conceptualization of the unconscious will be one of the most important and fruitful areas of transpersonal research in the coming decade.

6. *The relation of brain states and mind states.* This perennial question affects transpersonal and spiritual studies much more than most fields, simply because the "separation" or "gap" between the two (exterior matter and interior awareness) is "greater" in this area. After all, some spiritual experiences carry the overwhelming conviction that consciousness is prior to any manifestation (that it is eternal, timeless, and unbounded). How does this "unbounded consciousness" relate to a purely finite, bounded, temporal brain?

Whatever we decide, this issue cannot be avoided. For the transpersonalist, the seemingly innocuous question of the relation of mind (consciousness) and body (matter) is in fact the ultimate question of the relation of Emptiness and Form, Infinite and finite, Spirit and world. My own feeling is that this conundrum can be solved—not with the eye of flesh or with the eye of mind—but only with the eye of contemplation. Including meditative and contemplative states in orthodox research will result in exciting breakthroughs in the coming decade.

7. *How do any "consciousness states" relate to material-physiological "brain states"?* On a more specific level, how do actual states and structures of consciousness relate to specific brain states? Initial studies in this field have centered on major states of consciousness and their correlation with gross brain wave patterns, PET scans, and so forth, usually showing that some meditative states show an increase in alpha/theta activity or deep delta patterns, and so on.

I believe that major breakthroughs will occur in electronically inducing brain-wave patterns that are in some ways similar to meditation (such as deep theta/delta), and that the machines to do this will become widely available commercially—and I believe nobody will become "enlightened" from this, precisely because brain and mind are not *merely* identical, and enlightenment occurs in the mind (consciousness), not just in the brain (although changes occur there also). What this research will show us, I believe, is that certain brain states more easily allow certain consciousness states, but do not determine them. Exactly what this relationship is will be a major field of research, and will become a profound tool for exploring the mind/body problem.

8. *Continued mappings of the developmental spectrum, in conventional, contemplative, and pathological dimensions.* This is a crucial endeavor, made all the more pressing by the urgent need to clarify the relation between structures and states. If the transpersonal or contemplative stages and structures of consciousness also have specifiable pathologies (which I believe is the case), continuing to map these pathologies will be extremely important. Also, an enormously rich field awaits in the mapping and the clarification of the transpersonal stages of moral development, cognition, motivation, worldviews, affect, and so forth.

Transpersonal developmental studies are still one of the most promising and important areas of research. Unlike states of consciousness, which are temporary and noninclusive, structures of consciousness can be studied using a *reconstructive science* (precisely as used by Gebser, Piaget, Gilligan, Kohlberg, Habermas, Graves, etc.). A reconstructive science does not postulate the existence of structures in an a priori or merely theoretical fasnion, but rather studies those individuals who have *already* demonstrated a *competence* in the particular task (whether linguistic, cognitive, moral, contemplative, etc.). It then reconstructs, *after the fact*, the components and stages of development that lead up to the competence (Buddha, in a sense, simply reconstructed the steps he went through to gain his enlightenment, and presented them as a reconstructive science that could be tried and verified—or rejected—by a community of experimenters). Since reconstructive sciences reconstruct after the fact, they are not open to charges of a priori metaphysics, and, further, their claims can be subjected to nonverification (the so-called "fallibility criterion"). That transpersonal developmental psychology is a reconstructive science (which it is) means also that it is open in many ways to the fallibility criterion of any true science. This is by far the single strongest argument the transpersonalist can present to the conventional community.

In the coming decade, transpersonal developmental studies will especially focus, I believe, on the relation of developmental *levels* of consciousness (the spheres in the Great Nest of Being, from matter to body to mind to soul to spirit) and the various developmental *lines* moving through those levels (lines such as cognitive, moral, affective, interpersonal, spiritual, etc.). This is *the* crucial area for future research.

9. *The relation of Jungian theory to transpersonal theory.* This is an enormously complicated and delicate topic. For almost half a century, the Jungian paradigm has been the major—and only—viable theory of transpersonal psychology. I personally believe that the Jungian and neo-Jungian model has many strong points—and many weak points—and that this debate will in fact be one of the most heated areas of discussion in the coming decade, simply because so many people are involved in its outcome. But in any event the dialogue between the Jungian model and the general transpersonal field will continue to be a source of rich mutual stimulation and challenge, and will go hand in hand with the extremely important and even larger dialogue of transpersonal psychology with the other major forces of psychology.

10. *The relation of "marginal" to "normal" groups in social evolution.* A large number of transpersonalists believe that many of the world's critically pressing problems, from social fragmentation to environmental crisis, can only be "solved" by a widespread transpersonal transformation. I personally do not believe that this is so, but in either case, a cogent theory of how marginal knowledge (such as the transpersonal) becomes normalized, or conventionally accepted, needs to be worked out and thoroughly checked by then rereading history using that model. Work in this area is virtually nonexistent, and yet without it any claim to "world transformation" (or even the claim that transpersonal theory can have a world influence) is simply more ideology.

My own feeling is that a theory of world transformation will cover the intricate relations between the material-technological-economic base of any society and its worldviews, legitimation strategies, and consciousness states/structures, not in order to reduce the latter to the former (à la Marxism), but to understand their mutual influence and nonreducible realities [i.e., the four quadrants]. This field is virtually wide open.

11. *The relation of the three "Others" (body, nature, woman) to the Great Traditions.* The fully developed Wisdom Traditions (such as Christianity, Hinduism, Buddhism, Judaism, Islam, aspects of Taoism) all arose in a climate of discourse that tended to devalue the body, nature, and women. All three of these "Others" were often equated with evil, temptation, samsara, or illusion. How can women today develop any faith in the Great Traditions when most of their tenets were developed almost exclusively by men?

And is not the alienation of women historically parallel to the alienation of the body and nature? And is not this global alienation now showing up in the environmental crisis? Far from "saving" us, are not the Great Traditions the root of a crisis that very well might kill us all?

These are crucial questions for any contemplative/transpersonal discipline, and they need to be faced squarely. The Great Traditions do indeed emphasize an Ascending and Transcendental current; but many of them also contain an equal emphasis on the Descending and Immanent nature of Spirit. The Tantric traditions, for example, recommend a union of the Transcendental and Ascending God (Shiva) with the Immanent and Descending Goddess (Shakti), a union that is found in the nondual Heart, and a union that emphasizes equally the masculine and feminine faces of Spirit.

Nonetheless, I believe that the entire pantheon of the Great Traditions will, in the coming years, have to be scrutinized thoroughly and "scrubbed clean" of the universal alienation of the three "Others"—nature, body, woman—but in a way that does not throw out the baby with the bathwater. To simply reject everything the Traditions have to tell us would be catastrophic; as I said, might as well refuse to use the wheel just because a man invented it. But this field, too, will yield an enormous number of insights in the coming decade.

Related to this is:

12. *The "Other" of nature in relation to Spirit.* I mention this as a separate issue simply because of the pressing nature of the global environmental crisis. There is no doubt in my mind that the purely Ascend-

ing (or Gnostic) Traditions, which see the manifest world merely as illusion, have indeed contributed to a set of cultural prejudices that have allowed a despoliation of the Earth.

And once again I believe that we will have to turn to the Tantric traditions, East and West, for some indication of integrative intent. These Traditions universally see the finite realm (Earth and all) as a perfect manifestation of Spirit, not as a detraction from Spirit, and thus they celebrate and honor embodiment, descent, immanence, the feminine, the Earthbody values.

The "secret" relation of the Ascending (transcendent) and Descending (immanent) aspects of Spirit was given by Sri Ramana Maharshi (among many others):

> The world is illusory
> Brahman alone is real
> Brahman is the world.

A comprehensive Spirituality thus includes both of these two great currents (Ascending and Descending, masculine and feminine, Heaven and Earth, God and Goddess). Seeing that the world is illusory is the Transcendental or Ascending current (the current overemphasized by the Gnostic/Theravadin/Yogic traditions almost everywhere they appeared). Seeing that Brahman is the world is the Immanent or Descending current which embraces all manifestation as a Perfect Gesture of the Divine.

Either one of those currents taken in and by itself is catastrophic. We have seen the disasters of overemphasizing the masculine Ascending current. We are now privileged to watch the disasters of those movements trying to equate the finite world with the Infinite. We are now in a furry of Descending theories, from deep ecology to ecofeminism to Earth-bound and geocentric revivals, all of which happily confuse shadows with Source. These Descending endeavors, as crucially important as they are, are nonetheless in their own ways just as lopsided and dualistic and fragmented as their merely Ascending counterparts.

The work for the coming decade is to find a way to unite and honor both of these currents—Ascending and Descending, the One and the Many, Emptiness and Form, Wisdom and Compassion, God and the Goddess—without reducing one to the other or privileging one over the other.

13. *The relation of theory and practice.* Transpersonal studies in themselves are not necessarily a spiritual practice, although, of course,

the two are intimately connected. The nature of this connection will be a crucial topic in the coming decade.

There are any number of practices that induce or open one to the transpersonal or spiritual dimension—meditation, shamanic techniques, Goddess rituals, kundalini exercises, holotropic breathwork, psychedelics, deep psychotherapy, biofeedback and electronic induction, the various yogas (from devotion to work), contemplative prayer, life itself. It is from the community of those who have displayed a *competence* in any of these fields that the reconstructive science of transpersonal psychology draws its subjects. The *theory* of transpersonal psychology depends upon those who have *practiced* and achieved competence in a transpersonal/spiritual discipline.

Ideally, then, a transpersonal researcher will also have some sort of personal spiritual practice (a "participant observer"). How to separate—and relate—the theory and the practice will thus remain a pressing issue. This is complicated by the fact that transpersonal theory attempts to abstract from the various disciplines those universal factors that seem to be the common or key ingredients in each, but one still has to practice a *particular* discipline to attain competence.

Further, the various disciplines are themselves evolving in today's global village and postmodern world, as Buddhism meets science and Yoga meets the computer. This has rendered problematic many aspects of the traditional disciplines, such as the role of the guru, facets of the disciplines that seem to be merely cultural artifacts, the sexism in many of the traditions, and so forth.

I believe it is crucial for a transpersonal researcher to have a personal spiritual discipline. But the exact relation of theory and practice will remain an extremely important topic for discussion and shared insights, as the transpersonal field finds its way into the twenty-first century.

14. *Grand theories and Integral Studies.* The transpersonal field is uniquely situated to synthesize and integrate the various fields in humanity's knowledge-quest, simply because it is the one field that is particularly dedicated to exploring, honoring, and acknowledging the full spectrum of human (and divine) consciousness, or all the dimensions of men and women's experience—sensory, emotional, mental, social, spiritual. Transpersonal studies, then, actually evolve into *integral studies*, or the attempt to explore, elucidate, and integrate every level and line in the condition human and divine.

Integral studies appear to be the only truly global studies now in existence, studies that span the entire spectrum of human growth and aspiration. The coming decade, I have no doubt, will witness the emergence of integral studies as a truly comprehensive field of human endeavor. And although I do not think that the world is entering anything resembling a "new age" or "transpersonal transformation," I do believe that integral studies will always be that one beacon to men and women who see Spirit in the world and the world in Spirit.

INTEGRAL PSYCHOLOGY

Consciousness, Spirit, Psychology, Therapy

Note to the Reader

A DAYLIGHT VIEW

THE WORD *psychology* means the study of the psyche, and the word *psyche* means mind or soul. In the *Microsoft Thesaurus*, for *psyche* we find: "self: atman, soul, spirit; subjectivity: higher self, spiritual self, spirit." One is reminded, yet again, that the roots of psychology lie deep within the human soul and spirit.

The word *psyche* or its equivalent has ancient sources, going back at least several millennia BCE, where it almost always meant the animating force or spirit in the body or material vehicle. Sometime in sixteenth century Germany, *psyche* was coupled with *logos*—word or study—to form *psychology*, the study of the soul or spirit as it appears in humans. Who actually first used the word *psychology* is still debated; some say Melanchthon, some say Freigius, some say Goclenius of Marburg. But by 1730 it was being used in a more modern sense by Wolff in Germany, Hartley in England, Bonnet in France—and yet even then psychology still meant, as the *New Princeton Review* of 1888 defined it, "the science of the psyche or soul."

I once started taking notes for a history of psychology and philosophy that I was planning on writing. I had decided to do so because, in looking at most of the available history of psychology textbooks, I was struck by a strange and curious fact, that they all told the story of psychology—and the psyche—as if it abruptly came into being around 1879 in a laboratory in the University of Leipzig, headed by Wilhelm Wundt, who indeed was the father of a certain type of psychology anchored in introspection and structuralism. Still, did the psyche itself just jump into existence in 1879?

A few textbooks pushed back a little further, to the forerunners of Wundt's scientific psychology, including Sir Francis Galton, Hermann von Helmholtz, and particularly the commanding figure of Gustav Fechner. As one textbook breathlessly put it, "On the morning of October 22, 1850—an important date in the history of psychology—Fechner had an insight that the law of the connection between mind and body can be found in a statement of quantitative relation between mental sensation and material stimulus." Fechner's law, as it was soon known, is stated as $S = K \log I$ (the mental sensation varies as the logarithm of the material stimulus). Another text explained its importance: "In the early part of the century, Immanuel Kant had predicted that psychology could never become a science, because it would be impossible to experimentally measure psychological processes. Because of Fechner's work, for the first time scientists could measure the mind; by the mid-nineteenth century the methods of science were being applied to mental phenomena. Wilhelm Wundt would take these original and creative achievements and organize and integrate them into a 'founding' of psychology."

Every textbook seemed to agree that Gustav Fechner was one of the major breakthrough figures in the founding of modern psychology, and text after text sang the praises of the man who figured out a way to apply quantitative measurement to the mind, thus finally rendering psychology "scientific." Even Wilhelm Wundt was emphatic: "It will never be forgotten," he announced, "that Fechner was the first to introduce exact methods, exact principles of measurement and experimental observation for the investigation of psychic phenomena, and thereby to open the prospect of a psychological science, in the strict sense of the word. The chief merit of Fechner's method is this: that it has nothing to apprehend from the vicissitudes of philosophical systems. Modern psychology has indeed assumed a really scientific character, and may keep aloof from all metaphysical controversy."[1] This Dr. Fechner, I presumed, had saved psychology from contamination by soul or spirit, and had happily reduced the mind to measurable empirical doodads, thus ushering in the era of truly scientific psychology.

That is all I heard of Gustav Fechner, until several years later, when I was rummaging through a store filled with wonderfully old philosophy books, and there, rather shockingly, was a book with a striking title—*Life after Death*—written in 1835, and by none other than Gustav Fechner. It had the most arresting opening lines: "Man lives on earth not once, but three times: the first stage of his life is continual sleep; the second, sleeping and waking by turns; the third, waking forever."

And so proceeded this treatise on waking forever. "In the first stage man lives in the dark, alone; in the second, he lives associated with, yet separated from, his fellow-men, in a light reflected from the surface of things; in the third, his life, interwoven with . . . universal spirit . . . is a higher life.

"In the first stage his *body* develops itself from its germ, working out organs for the second; in the second stage his *mind* develops itself from its germ, working out organs for the third; in the third the *divine* germ develops itself, which lies hidden in every human mind.

"The act of leaving the first stage for the second we call Birth; that of leaving the second for the third, Death. Our way from the second to the third is not darker than our way from the first to the second: one way leads us forth to see the world outwardly; the other, to see it inwardly."

From body to mind to spirit, the three stages of the growth of consciousness; and it is only as men and women die to the separate self that they awaken to the expansiveness of universal Spirit. There was Fechner's real philosophy of life, mind, soul, and consciousness; and why did the textbooks not bother to tell us *that*? That's when I decided I wanted to write a history of psychology, simply because "Somebody has *got* to tell."

(Tell that the notion of the unconscious was made popular by von Hartmann's *Philosophy of the Unconscious*, which was published in 1869—thirty years before Freud—and went into an unprecedented eight editions in ten years, and von Hartmann was expressing Schopenhauer's philosophy, which Schopenhauer himself explicitly stated he derived mostly from Eastern mysticism, Buddhism and the Upanishads in particular: under the individual consciousness lies a cosmic consciousness, which for most people is "unconscious," but which can be awakened and fully realized, and this making conscious of the unconscious was men and women's greatest good. That Freud directly took the concept of the id from Georg Groddeck's *The Book of the It*, which was based on the existence of a cosmic Tao or organic universal spirit. That . . . well, it is a long story, all of which powerfully reminds us that the roots of modern psychology lie in spiritual traditions, precisely because the psyche itself is plugged into spiritual sources. In the deepest recesses of the psyche, one finds not instincts, but Spirit—and the study of psychology ought ideally to be the study of *all* of that, body to mind to soul, subconscious to self-conscious to superconscious, sleeping to half-awake to fully awake.)

Fechner did indeed make extraordinary contributions to empirical and measurable psychology; his *Elements of Psychophysics* is justly regarded as the first great text of psychometrics, and it fully deserves all the accolades psychologists from Wundt onward gave it. Still, the whole point of Fechner's psychophysics was that spirit and matter were inseparable, two sides of one great reality, and his attempts to measure aspects of the mind were meant to point out this inseparability, not reduce spirit or soul to material objects, and certainly not to deny spirit and soul altogether, which seems to have nonetheless been its fate in the hands of less sensitive researchers.

Fechner maintained, as one scholar summarized it, "that the whole universe is spiritual in character, the phenomenal world of physics being merely the external manifestation of this spiritual reality. Atoms are only the simplest elements in a spiritual hierarchy leading up to God. Each level of this hierarchy includes all those levels beneath it, so that God contains the totality of spirits. Consciousness is an essential feature of all that exists. . . . The evidences of soul are the systematic coherence and conformity to law exhibited in the behavior of organic wholes. Fechner regarded the earth, 'our mother', as such an organic besouled whole."[2]

Fechner himself explained that "as our bodies belong to the greater and higher individual body of the earth, so our spirits belong to the greater and higher individual spirit of the earth, which comprises all the spirits of earthly creatures, very much as the earth-body comprises their bodies. At the same time the earth-spirit is not a mere assembly of all the spirits of the earth, but a higher, individually conscious union of them." And the earth-spirit—Fechner was giving a precise outline of Gaia—is itself simply part of the divine-spirit, and "the divine-spirit is one, omniscient and truly all-conscious, i.e., holding all the consciousness of the universe and thus comprising each individual consciousness . . . in a higher and the highest connection."[3]

But this does not mean the obliteration of individuality, only its completion and inclusion in something even larger. "Our own individuality and independence, which are naturally but of a relative character, are not impaired but conditioned by this union." And so it continues up the nested hierarchy of increasing inclusiveness: "As the earth, far from separating our bodies from the universe, connects and incorporates us with the universe, so the spirit of the earth, far from separating our spirits from the divine spirit, forms a higher individual connection of every earthly spirit with the spirit of the universe."[4]

Fechner's approach to psychology was thus a type of *integral approach*: he wished to use empirical and scientific measurement, not to deny soul and spirit, but to help elucidate them. "To regard the whole material universe as inwardly alive and conscious is to take what Fechner called the *daylight view*. To regard it as inert matter, lacking in any teleological significance, is to take what he called the *night view*. Fechner ardently advocated the daylight view and hoped that it could be supported inductively by means of his psychophysical experiments."[5]

Well, it appears that the night view has since prevailed, yes? But there was a period, roughly during the time of Fechner (1801–1887) to William James (1842–1910) to James Mark Baldwin (1861–1934), when the newly emerging science of psychology was still on speaking terms with the ancient wisdom of the ages—with the perennial philosophy, with the Great Nest of Being, with the Idealist systems, and with the simple facts of consciousness as almost every person knows them: consciousness is real, the inward observing self is real, the soul is real, however much we might debate the details; and thus these truly great founding psychologists—when their real stories are told—have much to teach us about an integral view, a view that attempts to include the truths of body, mind, soul, and spirit, and not reduce them to material displays, digital bits, empirical processes, or objective systems (as important as all of those most certainly are). These pioneering modern psychologists managed to be both fully scientific and fully spiritual, and they found not the slightest contradiction or difficulty in that generous embrace.

This is a book about just such an integral psychology. While attempting to include the best of modern scientific research on psychology, consciousness, and therapy, it also takes its inspiration from that integral period of psychology's own genesis (marked by such as Fechner, James, and Baldwin, along with many others we will soon meet). This volume began that day in the wonderful old-book store, and the shocked recognition that Fechner's true story had rarely been told, and my subsequent historical research. The result was a very long textbook in two volumes, which includes a discussion of around two hundred theorists, East and West, ancient and modern, all working, in their own way, toward a more integral view; and it contains charts summarizing around one hundred of these systems.[6] For various reasons I have decided to publish it first in a very condensed and edited form—this present book—along with most of the charts (see charts 1 through 11, beginning on page 627).

As such, what follows is merely the briefest outline of what one type of integral psychology might look like. It attempts to include and integrate some of the more enduring insights from premodern, modern, and postmodern sources, under the assumption that all of them have something incredibly important to teach us. And it attempts to do so, not as a mere eclecticism, but in a systematic embrace, with method to the madness.

But the major aim of this book is to help start a discussion, not finish it; to act as a beginning, not an end. The reason I decided to publish this book in outline form first was to share an overview without crowding it with too many of my own particular details, and thus spur others to jump into the adventure: agreeing with me, disagreeing with me; correcting any mistakes that I might make, filling in the many gaps, straightening out any inadequacies, and otherwise carrying the enterprise forward by their own good lights.

For teachers using this as a text, and for the serious student, I have included extensive endnotes. In fact, this is really two books: a fairly short, accessible text, and endnotes for the dedicated. As usual, I recommend skipping the notes until a second reading (or reading them by themselves after the first). The notes do two things in particular: flesh out the outline with some of my own details (especially for students of my work), and make a series of specific recommendations for further readings, by other scholars, on each of the major topics. Thus teachers, for example, might consult some of these other texts (as well as their own favorites), make photocopies and hand-outs for the class, and thus supplement the main outline with any number of more specific readings. Interested laypersons can follow the notes to further reading in any of the areas. These recommendations are not exhaustive, only representative. For the recommended books on transpersonal psychology and therapy, I took a poll of many colleagues and reported the results.

I have not included a separate bibliography; the references on the charts alone are over a hundred pages. But today it is easy enough to get on the Internet and search any of the large booksellers for the various publications (which is why I have not included publisher's information either). Likewise, I have often simply listed the names of some of the more important authors, and readers can do a book search to see which of their books are available.

I personally believe that integral psychology (and integral studies in general) will become increasingly prevalent in the coming decades, as the academic world gropes its way out of its doggedly night view of the Kosmos.

What follows, then, is one version of a daylight view. And, dear Gustav, this one is for you.

K.W.
Boulder, Colorado
Spring 1999

PART ONE

GROUND

The Foundation

PSYCHOLOGY IS THE STUDY of human consciousness and its manifestations in behavior. The *functions* of consciousness include perceiving, desiring, willing, and acting. The *structures* of consciousness, some facets of which can be unconscious, include body, mind, soul, and spirit. The *states* of consciousness include normal (e.g., waking, dreaming, sleeping) and altered (e.g., nonordinary, meditative). The *modes* of consciousness include aesthetic, moral, and scientific. The *development* of consciousness spans an entire spectrum from prepersonal to personal to transpersonal, subconscious to self-conscious to superconscious, id to ego to Spirit. The *relational* and *behavioral* aspects of consciousness refer to its mutual interaction with the objective, exterior world and the sociocultural world of shared values and perceptions.

The great problem with psychology as it has historically unfolded is that, for the most part, different schools of psychology have often taken one of those aspects of the extraordinarily rich and multifaceted phenomenon of consciousness and announced that it is the only aspect worth studying (or even that it is the only aspect that actually exists). Behaviorism notoriously reduced consciousness to its observable, behavioral manifestations. Psychoanalysis reduced consciousness to structures of the ego and their impact by the id. Existentialism reduced consciousness to its personal structures and modes of intentionality. Many schools of transpersonal psychology focus merely on altered states of consciousness, with no coherent theory of the development of structures of consciousness. Asian psychologies typically excel in their account of consciousness development from the personal to the transpersonal domains, but have a very poor understanding of the earlier development from prepersonal to personal. Cognitive science admirably brings a scientific empiricism to bear on the problem, but often ends up simply reducing consciousness to its objective dimensions, neuronal mechanisms, and biocomputer-like functions, thus devastating the lifeworld of consciousness itself.

What if, on the other hand, *all* of the above accounts were an important part of the story? What if they all possessed true, but partial, insights into the vast field of consciousness? At the very least, assembling their conclusions under one roof would vastly expand our ideas of what consciousness is and, more important, what it might become. The endeavor to honor and embrace every legitimate aspect of human consciousness is the goal of an *integral psychology.*

Obviously, such an endeavor, at least at the beginning, has to be carried out at a very high level of abstraction. In coordinating these numerous approaches, we are working with systems of systems of systems, and such a coordination can only proceed with "orienting generalizations."[1] These cross-paradigmatic generalizations are meant, first and foremost, to simply get us in the right ballpark, by throwing our conceptual net as wide as possible. A logic of inclusion, networking, and wide-net casting is called for; a logic of nests within nests within nests, each attempting to legitimately include all that can be included. It is a vision-logic, a logic not merely of trees but also of forests.

Not that the trees can be ignored. Network-logic is a dialectic of whole and part. As many details as possible are checked; then a tentative big picture is assembled; it is checked against further details, and the big picture readjusted. And so on indefinitely, with ever more details constantly altering the big picture—and vice versa. For the secret of contextual thinking is that the whole discloses new meanings not available to the parts, and thus the big pictures we build will give new meaning to the details that compose it. Because human beings are condemned to meaning, they are condemned to creating big pictures. Even the "anti-big picture" postmodernists have given us a very big picture about why they don't like big pictures, an internal contradiction that has landed them in various sorts of unpleasantness, but has simply proven, once again, that human beings are condemned to creating big pictures.

Therefore, choose your big pictures with care.

When it comes to an integral psychology—a subset of integral studies in general—we have an enormous wealth of theories, research, and practices, all of which are important trees in the integral forest. In the following pages, we will be reviewing many of them, always with an eye to an integral embrace.

Elements of my own system, developed in a dozen books, are summarized in charts 1a and 1b. These include the structures, states, functions, modes, development, and behavioral aspects of consciousness. We will discuss each of those in turn. We will be drawing also on premodern, modern, and postmodern sources, with a view to a reconciliation. And we will start with the backbone of the system, the basic levels of consciousness.

1

The Basic Levels or Waves

The Great Nest of Being

A truly integral psychology would embrace the enduring insights of premodern, modern, and postmodern sources.

To begin with the premodern or traditional sources, the easiest access to their wisdom is through what has been called the perennial philosophy, or the common core of the world's great spiritual traditions. As Huston Smith, Arthur Lovejoy, Ananda Coomaraswamy, and other scholars of these traditions have pointed out, the core of the perennial philosophy is the view that reality is composed of various *levels of existence*—levels of being and of knowing—ranging from matter to body to mind to soul to spirit. Each senior dimension transcends but includes it juniors, so that this is a conception of wholes within wholes within wholes indefinitely, reaching from dirt to Divinity.

In other words, this "Great Chain of Being" is actually a "Great Nest of Being," with each senior dimension enveloping and embracing its juniors, much like a series of concentric circles or spheres, as indicated in figure 1. (For those unfamiliar with the Great Nest, the best short introduction is still E. F. Schumacher's *A Guide for the Perplexed*. Other excellent introductions include *Forgotten Truth* by Huston Smith and *Shambhala: The Sacred Path of the Warrior* by Chögyam Trungpa, who demonstrates that the Great Nest was present even in the earliest shamanic cultures).[1] The Great Nest of Being is the backbone of the peren-

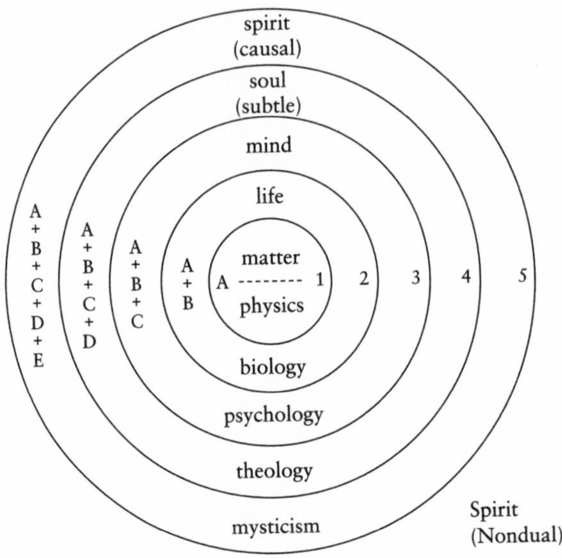

FIGURE 1. *The Great Nest of Being.* Spirit is both the highest level (causal) and the nondual Ground of all levels.

nial philosophy, and it would therefore be a crucial ingredient of any truly integral psychology.

For the last three thousand years or so, perennial philosophers have been in nearly unanimous and cross-cultural agreement as to the general levels of the Great Nest, although the number of divisions of those levels has varied considerably. Some traditions have presented only three major levels or realms (body, mind, and spirit—or gross, subtle, and causal). Others give five (matter, body, mind, soul, and spirit). Still others give seven (e.g., the seven kundalini chakras). And most of the traditions also have very sophisticated breakdowns of these levels, often giving 12, 30, even 108 subdivisions of the levels of being and knowing that can be found in this extraordinarily rich Kosmos.

But many of the perennial philosophers—Plotinus and Aurobindo, for example—have found around *a dozen levels of consciousness* to be the most useful, and that is roughly what I have presented in the charts (pp. 627–47).[2] My basic levels or basic structures are listed in the left column in all the charts. These are simply the basic levels in the Great Nest of Being, each transcending and including its predecessors—whether we use a simple five-level scheme (matter, body, mind, soul, spirit) or a slightly more sophisticated version (such as the one I have presented in the charts, and which I will explain as we proceed: matter, sensation, perception, exocept, impulse, image, symbol, endocept, concept, rule, formal, vision-logic, vision, archetype, formless, nondual).

To introduce a useful term: these basic levels are *holons* of consciousness. A holon is a whole that is part of other wholes. For example, a whole atom is part of a whole molecule, a whole molecule is part of a whole cell, a whole cell is part of a whole organism, and so on. As we will see throughout this volume, the universe is fundamentally composed of holons, wholes that are parts of other wholes. Letters are parts of words which are parts of sentences which are parts of entire languages. A person is part of a family which is part of a community which is part of a nation which is part of the globe, and so on.

Since each holon is embraced in a larger holon, holons themselves exist in nested hierarchies—or *holarchies*—such as atoms to molecules to cells to organisms to ecosystems. The Great Nest is simply a big picture of those levels of increasing wholeness, exactly as indicated in figure 1.[3] In short, the *basic levels* are the basic holons (stages, waves, spheres, nests) in the Great Nest of Being.

I use all three terms—basic *levels*, basic *structures*, and basic *waves*—interchangeably, as referring to essentially the same phenomenon; but each has a slightly different connotation that conveys important information. "Level" emphasizes the fact that these are *qualitatively* distinct levels of organization, arranged in a nested hierarchy (or holarchy) of increasing holistic embrace (each level transcending but including its predecessors, as shown in fig. 1). "Structure" emphasizes the fact that these are enduring *holistic patterns* of being and consciousness (each is a holon, a whole that is part of other wholes). And "wave" emphasizes the fact that these levels are not rigidly separate and isolated, but, like the colors of a rainbow, infinitely shade and grade into each other. The basic structures are simply the basic colors in that rainbow. To switch metaphors, they are the waves in the great River of Life, through which its many streams run.

There is nothing linear or rigid about these various waves. As we will abundantly see, individual development through the various waves of consciousness is a very fluid and flowing affair. Individuals can be at various waves in different circumstances; aspects of their own consciousness can be at many different waves; even subpersonalities in an individual's own being can be at different waves. Overall development is a very messy affair! The basic levels or basic waves simply represent some of the more noticeable bends in the great River of Life, nothing more, nothing less.

Charts 2a and 2b (pages 628–30) outline the basic levels or basic waves as conceived in a dozen different systems East and West. We will be discussing many others as we proceed. But it should be realized from the start that these levels and sublevels presented by the perennial sages are *not* the product of metaphysical speculation or abstract hair-splitting philosophy. In fact, they are in almost every way the codifications of *direct experiential realities*, reaching from sensory experience to mental experience to spiritual experience. The "levels" in the Great Nest simply reflect the full spectrum of being and consciousness available for direct experiential disclosure, ranging from subconscious to self-conscious to superconscious. Moreover, the discovery of these waves, over the years, has been communally generated and consensually validated. The fact that wherever they appear, they are often quite similar, sometimes almost identical, simply tells us that we live in a patterned Kosmos, and these richly textured patterns can be—and were—spotted by intelligent men and women in almost every culture.

Each senior dimension in the Great Nest—from matter to body to mind to soul to spirit—transcends and includes its juniors, so that living bodies transcend but include minerals, minds transcend but include vital bodies, luminous souls transcend but include conceptual minds, and radiant spirit transcends and includes absolutely everything. Spirit is thus both the very highest wave (purely transcendental) and the ever-present ground of all the waves (purely immanent), going beyond All, embracing All. The Great Nest is a multidimensional latticework of love—eros, agape, karuna, maitri—call it what you will, it leaves no corner of the Kosmos untouched by care nor alien to the mysteries of grace.

That point is as important as it is often forgotten—Spirit is fully transcendent and fully immanent. If we are to try to conceptualize Spirit at all, we should at least try to respect both points. These are shown in figure 1, where the highest sphere represents transcendental spirit (which is written with a small *s* to indicate that it is one level among other levels, albeit the highest), and the paper itself represents immanent Spirit as the equally present Ground of all the levels (with a capital *S* to indicate that it has no other). The patriarchal religions tend to emphasize the transcendental "otherworldly" aspect of spirit; and the matriarchal, neopagan religions tend to emphasize the fully immanent or "thisworldy" aspect of Spirit. Each of them is important, and a truly integral view would find ample room for both. (The context will determine which aspect of spirit/Spirit I mean, but both are always implied.)

The Great Holarchy of Being and Knowing: such is the priceless gift of the ages. This is the core of the perennial philosophy, and, we might say, it is the part of the perennial philosophy that has empirically been found most enduring. The evidence continues overwhelmingly to mount in its favor: human beings have available to them an extraordinary spectrum of consciousness, reaching from prepersonal to personal to transpersonal states. The critics who attempt to deny this overall spectrum do so—not by presenting counterevidence—but simply by refusing to acknowledge the substantial evidence that has already been amassed; the evidence, nonetheless, remains. And the evidence says, in short, that there exists a richly textured rainbow of consciousness, spanning subconscious to self-conscious to superconscious.

At the same time, the fact that the perennial philosophers were the first to spot many of the colors in this extraordinary rainbow doesn't mean that modernity and postmodernity must come mute to the meeting. Nobody elucidated the nature of concrete and formal operational thinking like Piaget. And the ways in which some aspects of the early stages can be repressed—well, it took a Freud to really spell those out. Modernity and postmodernity are not without their geniuses; the perennial philosophy is not without its limitations and inadequacies; a more complete spectrum of consciousness will necessarily include and balance all of their insights and discoveries. But the general nature of the waves in the great River of Life: the perennial philosophers were often right on the money.

I will often refer to the perennial philosophy (and the Great Nest) as the "wisdom of premodernity." This is not pejorative. Nor does it mean that you can find no trace of the perennial philosophy in modernity or postmodernity (although, frankly, it is rare). It simply means that the perennial philosophy originated in what we call premodern times. Also—and this is an important point that often confuses people—to say that premodernity had access to the entire Great Nest of Being does not mean that everybody in premodernity was fully awakened to every level in the Great Nest. In fact, the shamans, yogis, saints, and sages who had awakened to the higher levels of soul and spirit were always extremely rare. The average individual (as we will see in chapter 12) spent much of his or her time at prerational, not transrational, levels of consciousness. Still, "wisdom" means the *best* that any era has to offer, and sensitive scholars have often found that the perennial philosophers—from Plotinus to Shankara to Fa-Tsang to Lady Tsogyal—are a storehouse of extraordinary wisdom.

Reaching out to them is more than an embrace of some important truths. It is a way to affirm our continuity with the wisdom of the ages; a way to acknowledge our own ancestors; a way to transcend and include that which went before us, and thus flow with the current of the Kosmos; and most of all, a way to remind ourselves that even if we are standing on the shoulders of giants, we are standing on the shoulders of GIANTS, and we would do well to remember that.

What I have tried to do, therefore, in presenting the basic waves of the Great Nest, is to look first to the perennial philosophy for the general contours of the various levels; and then to significantly supplement that understanding with the many refinements (and sometimes corrections) offered by modernity and postmodernity. Take Aurobindo, for example (see chart 2b). Notice that he referred to the intermediate levels as the lower mind, the concrete mind, the logical mind, and the higher mind. Aurobindo gave verbal descriptions of all of these basic structures, which are very useful. But those intermediate levels are also the structures that have been intensely investigated by Western developmental and cognitive psychology, and backed with considerable amounts of clinical and experimental evidence. I have therefore tended to use, for the intermediate levels, terms taken from that research, such as the rule/role mind, concrete operational thinking, and formal operational thinking. But all of these various codifications of the developmental levels are simply different snapshots taken from various angles, using different cameras, of the great River of Life, and they are all useful in their own ways. (Of course, blurred or bad photos are not very useful, and we can reject any research that doesn't measure up to decent standards. I have tried to include, in the charts, only the work of great photographers.)

In all of the charts, the correlations I have given among the various stages and theorists are very general, meant only to get us in the right ballpark (and initiate more refined and careful correlations). Still, many of these correlations have been given by the theorists themselves, and on balance I believe most of them are accurate to within plus-or-minus 1.5 stages. This is true for the higher (transpersonal) stages as well, although the situation becomes more difficult. First of all, as we approach the upper reaches of the spectrum of consciousness, orthodox Western psychological research begins to abandon us, and we increasingly must draw on the great sages and contemplatives, East and West, North and South. Second, cultural surface features are therefore often dramatically different, making the search for any cross-cultural deep features more demanding. And third, few practitioners of one system are conversant with the details of others, thus fewer cross-systematic comparisons have been made. Nonetheless, substantial and impressive studies, some of which we will see below, have made a great deal of headway in these important correlations, and I have reported many of these results in the charts. That there is a general cross-cultural *similarity* of these higher, transrational, transpersonal stages is a sure sign that we are photographing some very real currents in a very real River.

The Great Nest Is a Potential, Not a Given

It is not necessary to picture the basic structures or basic holons as being permanently fixed and unchanging essences (Platonic, Kantian, Hegelian, or Husserlian). They can, in part, be understood as habits of evolution, more like a Kosmic memory than a pregiven mold.[4] But either way, a crucial point remains: the fact that the great yogis, saints, and sages have *already* experienced many of the transpersonal realms (as we will see) shows us unmistakably that we *already* have the potentials for these higher levels present in our own makeup. The human organism and its brain, in its present form, has the capacity for these higher states. Perhaps other states will emerge in the future; perhaps new potentials will unfold; possibly higher realizations will dawn. But the fact remains that *right now* we have at least these extraordinary transpersonal realms already available to us. And whether we say that these higher potentials have been eternally given to us by God, or that they were first created by the evolutionary pioneering saints and sages and then bequeathed to the rest of us as morphogenetic fields and evolutionary grooves, or that they are Platonic Forms forever embedded in the Kosmos, or that they showed up by blind dumb chance mutation and vapidly mindless natural selection, doesn't change in the least the simple fact that those higher potentials are now available to all of us.

The basic structures or basic holons that I generally present—and that are listed in the far-left column in each of the charts—represent a master template taken from premodern, modern, and postmodern sources, using each to fill in the gaps in the others. For comparison, charts 2a and 2b show some of the basic levels as conceived in other systems. Under the "General Great Chain" I have listed the most common five: matter, body (in the sense of living, vital bodies, the emotional-sexual level), mind (including imagination, concepts, and logic), soul (the supraindividual source of identity), and spirit (both the formless ground and nondual union of all other levels). These levels, as I said, are like colors in a rainbow, so I have drawn them overlapping. But even that is misleading; a more accurate representation would be a series of concentric spheres, with each senior sphere enfolding and embracing its juniors (as in fig. 1). The model here is not rungs in a ladder each piled on top of the other, but holons in a holarchy like atoms/molecules/cells/organisms, with each senior enfolding its juniors.

At the same time—and this cannot be emphasized too strongly—the higher levels in the Great Nest are *potentials*, not absolute givens. The lower levels—matter, body, mind—have already emerged on a large scale, so they already exist full-fledged in this manifest world. But the higher structures—psychic, subtle, causal—are not yet consciously manifest on a collective scale; they remain, for most people, potentials of the human bodymind, not fully actualized realities. What the Great Nest represents, in my opinion, is most basically a great *morphogenetic field* or *developmental space*—stretching from matter to mind to spirit—in which various potentials unfold into actuality. Although for convenience I will often speak of the higher levels as if they were simply given, they are in many ways still plastic, still open to being formed as more and more people coevolve into them (which is why, as I said, the basic structures are more like Kosmic habits than pregiven molds). As these higher potentials become actualized, they will be given more form and content, and thus increasingly become everyday realities. Until then, they are, in part, great and grand potentials, which nonetheless still exert an undeniable attraction, still are present in many profound ways, still can be directly realized by higher growth and development, and still show a great deal of similarity wherever they appear.[5]

Structures and States

The most classic, and probably the oldest, of the sophisticated versions of the Great Nest is that of Vedanta (chart 2b), which also includes the extremely important distinctions between states, bodies, and structures. A *state* means a state of consciousness, such as waking, dreaming, and deep sleep. A *structure* is a sheath or level of consciousness, of which the Vedanta gives five of the most important: the material level, the biological level, the mental level, the higher mental, and the spiritual. A *body* is the energetic support of the various states and levels of mind, of which Vedanta gives three: the gross body of the waking state (which supports the material mind); the subtle body of the dreaming state (which supports the emotional, mental, and higher mental levels); and the causal body of deep sleep (which supports the spiritual mind).[6]

Notice that a given state of consciousness—such as waking or dreaming—can in fact house several different structures or levels of consciousness. In Western terms we would say that the waking *state* of consciousness can contain several quite different *structures* of consciousness, such as sensorimotor, preoperational, concrete operational, and formal operational. In other words, although states of consciousness are important, structures of consciousness give much more detailed information about the actual status of any individual's growth and development, and thus a full-spectrum approach would want to include both states and structures.

In my own system, the *structures* are of two major types: the basic structures (which we have already introduced) and the structures in the various developmental lines (which we will examine below). Structures, in both psychology and sociology, are simply *stable patterns* of events. Psychological structures can be divided and subdivided in numerous ways—deep and surface, levels and lines, enduring and transitional—and I use all of those distinctions.[7] But, as I said, I most often use only two: the structures in the basic levels of consciousness (such as sensation, impulse, image, rule, formop, vision-logic, psychic, subtle, etc.) and the structures in the developmental lines of consciousness (such as the stages of cognition, affect, needs, morals, and so on). In short, structures are the *holistic patterns* that are found in both the *levels* of development and the *lines* of development.

The major *states* are also of two general types: natural and altered. The *natural states of consciousness* include those identified by the perennial philosophy—namely, waking/gross, dreaming/subtle, and deep sleep/causal. According to the perennial philosophy, the waking state is the home of our everyday ego. But the dream state, precisely because it is a world created entirely by the psyche, gives us one type of access to states of the soul. And the deep sleep state, because it is a realm of pure formlessness, gives us one type of access to formless (or causal) spirit. Of course, for most people, the dream and deep sleep state are less real, not more real, than waking reality, which is true enough from one angle. But according to the perennial philosophy, these deeper states can be entered with full consciousness, whereupon they yield their extraordinary secrets (as we will see). In the meantime, we can simply note that the perennial philosophy maintains that waking, dreaming, and deep sleep states offer one type of access to the gross ego, the subtle soul, and causal spirit, respectively.

(I often subdivide the subtle states into a lower or "psychic" realm and the "subtle" realm proper, because the lower subtle or psychic, lying as it does right next to the gross realm, often involves an intense embrace or sense of union with the entire gross realm, as in *nature mysticism*; whereas the subtle proper so transcends the gross realm that it usually involves purely transcendental states of *deity mysticism*. The causal, of course, is the realm of unmanifest cessation, and is the home of *formless mysticism*. Integrating all of them is *nondual mysticism*. We will be examining all of these higher, transpersonal realms throughout this book, so most questions about their exact meaning will be cleared up by further reading.)

The importance of these three (or four) natural states is that every human being, at no matter what stage or structure or level of development, *has available the general spectrum of consciousness*—ego to soul to spirit—at least as temporary states, for the simple reason that all humans wake, dream, and sleep.

An *altered state of consciousness* is a "non-normal" or a "nonordinary" state of consciousness, including everything from drug-induced states to near-death experiences to meditative states.[8] In a *peak experience* (a temporary altered state), a person can briefly experience, while awake, any of the natural states of psychic, subtle, causal, or nondual awareness, and these often result in direct *spiritual experiences* (such as nature mysticism, deity mysticism, and formless mysticism; see below). *Peak experiences can occur to individuals at almost any stage of development.* The notion, then, that spiritual and transpersonal states are available only at the higher stages of development is quite incorrect.

Nonetheless, although the major states of gross, subtle, causal, and nondual are available to human beings at virtually any stage of growth, *the way in which those states or realms are experienced and interpreted* depends to some degree on the stage of development of the person having the peak experience. This means, as I suggested in *A Sociable God*, that we can create a grid of the types of spiritual experiences that are generally available to individuals at different stages of growth.

For example, let us simply call the earlier stages archaic, magic, mythic, and rational. A person at any of those stages can have a temporary peak experience of the psychic, subtle, causal, or nondual. This gives us a grid of around sixteen different types of spiritual experiences.

To give a few examples: A person at the magic stage of development (which cannot easily take the role of other) might have a subtle-level peak experience (of, say, a radiant God-union), in which case that person will tend to experience God-union as applying only to himself (since he cannot take the role of other and thus realize that all people—in fact, all sentient beings—are equally one with God). He will thus tend to suffer massive ego-inflation, perhaps even psychotic in its dimensions. On the other hand, a person at the mythic level (which has expanded identity from egocentric to sociocentric, but which is very concrete-literal and fundamentalist) will experience subtle God-union as being a salvation that is given, not exclusively to him (as the egocentric does), but exclusively to those who embrace the particular myths ("If you want to be saved, you must believe in my God/dess, which is the one and only true Divinity"); thus this person might become a born-again fundamentalist, set upon converting the entire world to his or her version of a revealed God. The subtle-level experience is very real and genuine, but *it has to be carried somewhere*, and it is carried, in this case, in an ethnocentric, fundamentalist, mythic-membership mind, which dramatically limits and ultimately distorts the contours of the subtle domain (as did, even more so, the previous egocentric stage). A person at the formal-reflexive level would tend to experience subtle God-union in more reason-based terms, perhaps as rational Deism, or as a demythologized Ground of Being, and so on.

In other words, a given peak experience (or temporary state of consciousness) is usually *interpreted* according to the general stage of development of the individual having the experience. This gives us, as I said, a grid of around sixteen very general types of spiritual experience: psychic, subtle, causal, and nondual states poured into archaic, magic, mythic, and rational structures. In *A Sociable God* I gave examples of all of these, and pointed out their importance (and we will return to them later in this book).[9]

But all of those peak experiences, no matter how profound, are merely temporary, passing, transient states. In order for higher development to occur, those *temporary states must become permanent traits*. Higher development involves, in part, the conversion of altered states into permanent realizations. In other words, in the upper reaches of evolution, the transpersonal potentials that were only available in temporary *states* of consciousness are increasingly converted into enduring *structures* of consciousness (states into traits).

This is where *meditative states* become increasingly important. Unlike natural states (which access psychic, subtle, and causal states in the natural sleep cycle, but rarely while awake or fully conscious) and unlike spontaneous peak experiences (which are fleeting), meditative states access these higher realms in a deliberate and prolonged fashion. As such, they more stably disclose the higher levels of the Great Nest, higher levels that eventually become, with practice, *permanent realizations.*[10] In other words, psychic, subtle, causal, and nondual states can all become *enduring structures in one's own makeup,* which is why those labels (psychic, subtle, causal, and nondual) are also used to refer to the highest of the *basic structures* in the Great Nest of Being. As they emerge permanently in an individual's development, their potentials, once available only in passing states, become enduring contours of an enlightened mind.

The Basic Levels in Other Systems

As I said, charts 2a and 2b give the Great Nest and its basic structures or levels as conceived in some other systems. I am not claiming that these are all identical structures, levels, or waves, only that they share many important similarities across a developmental space, and this *developmental space*, we will see, is what is so interesting—and so important for an integral psychology.

It appears that the oldest of any of these systems originated in India and thereabouts, perhaps as early as the first or second millennium BCE (although tradition claims a much older date). The chakra system, the Vedanta sheaths and states, the Buddhist vijnanas, the Kashmir Shaivite vibratory levels, and Aurobindo's superconscient hierarchy all come out of this historically unsurpassed river of consciousness research. Following soon thereafter, and possibly due to migration (but just as likely due to the universal existence of these potentials), the Mesopotamian/Middle Eastern river begins its mighty journey, which would include Persian, North African, Palestinian, and Grecian streams. The most influential of these would unfold as the Neoplatonic tradition, represented by currents from Plotinus to Kabbalah to Sufism to Christian mysticism (all of which are represented on the charts).

Although it has become fashionable among pluralistic relativists to bash the perennial philosophy (and anything "universal" other than their own universal pronouncements on the importance of pluralism), a less biased look at the evidence shows a rather striking set of very general commonalities among the world's great wisdom traditions. And why should this surprise us? The human body everywhere grows 206 bones, two kidneys, and one heart; and the human mind everywhere grows the capacities for images, symbols, and concepts. Likewise, it seems, the human spirit everywhere grows intuitions of the Divine, and these, too, show many similarities in deep, not surface, features. Some traditions were more complete than others; some were more precise. But putting them all together gives us a general map of the incredibly wide spectrum of human possibilities.

At this point, people who are uncomfortable with level and stage conceptions tend to become suspicious: is consciousness and its development really just a series of linear, monolithic stages, proceeding one after another, ladder-like fashion? The answer is, not at all. As we will see, these basic waves in the Great Nest are simply the general levels through which numerous different developmental lines or streams will flow—such as emotions, needs, self-identity, morals, spiritual realizations, and so on—all proceeding at their own pace, in their own way, with their own dynamic. Thus, overall development is absolutely not a linear, sequential, ladder-like affair. It is a fluid flowing of many streams through these basic waves. We will soon examine many of these streams. But first we need to finish our account of the basic waves and their emergence.

Dates of Emergence of the Basic Waves

In the far-left column of chart 3a, I have included the average ages of emergence of the basic structures of consciousness up to the formal mind. Research suggests that these ages are relatively similar for most people in today's world, simply because—I have hypothesized—collective development or evolution on the whole has reached the formal level (whereas levels higher than the formal, which collective evolution has not reached, must be accessed by one's own efforts—again, in part because they are higher potentials, not givens).[11]

The traditions often divide life's overall journey into the "Seven Ages of a Person," where each age involves adaptation to one of the seven basic levels of consciousness (such as the seven chakras: physical; emotional-sexual; lower, middle, and higher mental; soul; and spirit), and each of the seven stages is said to take seven years. Thus, the first seven years of life involve adaptation to the physical realm (especially food, survival, safety). The second seven years involve adaptation to the emotional-sexual-feeling dimension (which culminates in sexual maturation or puberty). The third seven years of life (typically adolescence) involves the emergence of the logical mind and adaptation to its new perspectives. This brings us to around age twenty-one, where many individuals' overall development tends to become arrested.[12] But if development continues, each seven-year period brings the possibility of a new and higher level of consciousness evolution, so in chart 3a I have listed in brackets these general ages next to the higher basic structures. Of course, these are the most general of generalizations, with exceptions abounding, but they are rather suggestive.

Why "seven ages" and not, say, ten? Again, exactly how to divide and subdivide the number of colors in a rainbow is largely a matter of choice. However, the perennial philosophers and psychologists have found that, no matter how many minute subdivisions we might make for various purposes (such as perhaps thirty for very specific and detailed stages of certain types of meditation), nonetheless there is a sense in talking about *functional groupings* of the basic waves in the Great Nest. That is, there is a sense in which the material levels and sublevels (quarks, atoms, molecules, crystals) are all material and not biological (none of them can sexually reproduce, for example). Likewise, there is a sense in which the mental levels and sublevels (images, symbols, concepts, rules) are all mental and not, say, psychic or subtle. In other words, even if we find it useful on occasion to distinguish dozens (or even hundreds) of minute gradations in the colors of a rainbow, there is also good reason to say there are basically just six or seven major colors in most rainbows.

This is what the perennial philosophy means by the "Seven Ages of a Person" or the seven main chakras or basic structures. For various reasons, I have found that although around two dozen basic structures can be readily identified (e.g., form, sensation, perception, exocept, impulse, image, symbol, endocept, concept, rule . . .), nonetheless they can be condensed into around seven to ten *functional groupings* which reflect easily recognizable stages (as we will see throughout this volume). These functional groupings of basic structures I represent with some very general names, which are also listed on the left column in the all charts: (1) sensorimotor, (2) phantasmic-emotional (or emotional-sexual), (3) rep-mind (short for the representational mind, similar to general preoperational thinking, or "preop"), (4) the rule/role mind (similar to concrete operational thinking, or "conop"), (5) formal-reflexive (similar to formal operational, or "formop"), (6) vision-logic, (7) psychic, (8) subtle, (9) causal, and (10) nondual.[13] Again, these are simple orienting generalizations, but they offer us a convenient way to deal with a great deal of data and evidence. But none of these generalizations need stop us from using maps that are either more detailed or more simplified, as the occasion warrants.

Cognitive Development and the Great Nest of Being

The Great Nest is actually a great holarchy of being and knowing: levels of reality and levels of knowing those levels. That is, the perennial philosophers found both ontology and epistemology to be important, as inseparable aspects of the great waves of reality. Modernity found it necessary to differentiate ontology and epistemology, which would have been quite welcome had modernity or postmodernity completed the development and *integrated* those differentiations, whereas all that happened was that those differentiations completely fell apart; and modernity, trusting only its own isolated subjectivity, embraced epistemology alone, whereupon ontology fell into the black hole of subjectivism, never to be heard from again.

The Great Chain, to the degree modernity recognized it at all, thus became merely a hierarchy of levels of knowing—that is, *a hierarchy of cognition*, such as investigated by Piaget. That is not so much wrong as it is terribly partial, leaving out the levels of reality that would ground the cognition (or, just as sadly, acknowledging only the sensorimotor level of reality, to which all cognition must be faithful in order to be judged "true"). Nonetheless, if for the moment we focus just on cognition—and because it is certainly true that the Great Chain is in part a great spectrum of consciousness—the question then becomes: in individuals, *is the development of the Great Chain the same as cognitive development?*

Not exactly. To begin with, you certainly can think of the Great Nest as being, in part, a great spectrum of consciousness, which it is. One of the dictionary definitions of "cognitive" is "relating to consciousness." Therefore, in dictionary terms anyway, you could think of the development of the Great Nest (which in individuals involves the unfolding of higher and more encompassing levels of consciousness) as being generally quite similar to cognitive development, as long as we understand that "cognition" or "consciousness" runs from subconscious to self-conscious to superconscious, and that it includes interior modes of awareness just as much as exterior modes.

The problem, as I was saying, is that "cognition" in Western psychology came to have a very narrow meaning that excluded most of the above. It came to mean *the apprehension of exterior objects.* All sorts of "consciousness" or "awareness" (in the broad sense) were therefore *excluded* (e.g., emotions, dreams, creative visions, subtle states, and peak experiences). If the *contents* of consciousness were not some sort of *objective-empirical object* (a rock, a tree, a car, an organism), then that consciousness was said *not* to possess cognitive validity. So much for all the really interesting states and modes of consciousness.

In the hands of such as Piaget, the meaning of cognition was narrowed even further, to types of logico-mathematical operations, which were claimed to underlie all other developmental lines in all other domains. At that point, consciousness as "cognition" had been reduced to perceiving nothing but the flat and faded surfaces of empirical objects (what we will be calling "flatland"). Put simply, any awareness that saw something other than the world of scientific materialism was not a true awareness, was not a "true" cognition.

In that sense, the development of the Great Nest in individuals is most certainly *not* a "cognitive development." And yet, if we look a little closer at the Piagetian scheme—and at what most subsequent psychologists have meant by "cognitive development"—we can find some very interesting (and very important)—if limited—similarities.

First of all, the Western psychological study of cognitive development still involves the study of some sort of *consciousness*, however narrow and restricted on occasion. Thus, what Piaget studied as formal operational thought—which was conceived as a mathematical structure (the INRC grouping)—is one legitimate way to slice the stream of consciousness at that point, but it hardly exhausts the snapshots we can take of consciousness at that particular bend in the River. Numerous other and equally valid perspectives exist for defining consciousness at that stage, from role taking to epistemological styles to worldviews to moral drives. But in focusing on cognitive development, Piaget was at least highlighting the central importance of *consciousness development*, even if in a sometimes narrow way.

That importance is underscored by the fact that, when specific developmental lines are studied—such as moral development, self development, and role-taking development—it has almost always been found that *cognitive development is necessary (but not sufficient) for these other developments*. In other words, *before* you can develop morals, or a self-perspective, or some idea of the good life, you have to be able to consciously register those various elements in the first place. Consciousness is thus necessary, but not sufficient, for these other developments.

And that is exactly the claim of the Great Nest theorists. The levels of the Great Nest (the basic structures of consciousness) are the levels through which the various developmental lines will proceed, and without the basic waves, there is nothing for the various boats to float on. This is why the basic structures (whether conceived as the sheaths in Vedanta, the levels of consciousness in Mahayana, the ontological levels of the sefirot of Kabbalah, or the stages of the soul's growth toward God in Sufism) are the backbone, the crucial skeleton, on which most other systems hang.

Thus, although they can by no means be equated, cognitive development (as studied by Western psychologists) is perhaps the closest thing we have to the Great Chain or the spectrum of consciousness (at least up to the levels of the formal mind; beyond that most Western researchers recognize no forms of cognition at all). For this reason—and while keeping firmly in mind the many qualifications and limitations—I sometimes use cognitive terms (such as conop and formop) to describe some of the basic structures.

Still, because cognitive development does have a very specific and narrow meaning in Western psychology, I also treat it as a separate developmental line apart from the basic structures (so that we can preserve the ontological richness of the basic holons, and not reduce them to Western cognitive categories). Charts 3a and 3b are correlations of the basic structures with the cognitive stages disclosed by various modern researchers.

One of the most interesting items in those charts is the number of Western psychologists who, based on extensive empirical and phenomenological data, have detected several stages of *postformal* development—that is, stages of cognitive development beyond linear rationality (i.e., beyond formal operational thinking, or formop). Although "postformal" can refer to any and all stages beyond formop, it usually applies only to mental and personal, not supramental and transpersonal, stages. In other words, for most Western researchers, "postformal" refers to the first major stage beyond formop, which I call *vision-logic*.[14] As shown in charts 3a–b, most researchers have found two to four stages of postformal (vision-logic) cognition. These postformal stages generally move beyond the formal/mechanistic phases (of early formop) into various stages of relativity, pluralistic systems, and contextualism (early vision-logic), and from there into stages of metasystematic, integrated, unified, dialectical, and holistic thinking (middle to late vision-logic). This gives us a picture of the *highest mental domains* as being dynamic, developmental, dialectical, integrated.

Few of those researchers, however, move into the *transmental* domains (of psychic, subtle, causal, or nondual occasions—transrational and transpersonal), although many of them increasingly acknowledge these higher levels. For the contours of these levels we must often rely, once again, on the great sages and contemplatives, as several of the charts make clear.

In this regard, a hotly disputed topic is whether the spiritual/transpersonal stages themselves can be conceived as higher levels of cognitive development. The answer, I have suggested, depends on what you mean by "cognitive." If you mean what most Western psychologists mean—which is a mental conceptual knowledge of exterior objects—then no, higher or spiritual stages are *not* mental cognition, because they are often supramental, transconceptual, and nonexterior. If by "cognitive" you mean "consciousness in general," including superconscious states, then much of higher spiritual experience is indeed cognitive. But spiritual and transpersonal states also have many other aspects—such as higher affects, morals, and self-sense—so that, even with an expanded definition of cognitive, they are not *merely* cognitive. Nonetheless, "cognition" in the broadest sense means "consciousness," and thus cognitive developments of various sorts are an important part of the entire spectrum of being and knowing.

THE COGNITIVE LINE

Charts 3a and 3b list some of the best-known and most influential researchers in cognitive development. Piaget's studies are pivotal, of course. Even with all of their shortcomings, Piaget's contributions remain a stunning accomplishment; certainly one of the most significant psychological investigations of this century. He opened up an extraordinary number of avenues of research: following the pioneering work of James Mark Baldwin (see below), Piaget demonstrated that each level of development has a different worldview, with different perceptions, modes of space and time, and moral motivations (discoveries upon which the work of researchers from Maslow to Kohlberg to Loevinger to Gilligan would depend); he showed that reality is not simply given but is in many important ways constructed (a structuralism that made possible poststructuralism); his *méthode clinique* subjected the unfolding of consciousness to a meticulous investigation, which resulted in literally hundreds of novel discoveries; his psychological researches had immediate influence on everything from education to philosophy (Habermas, among many others, stands greatly in his debt). Few are the theorists who can claim a tenth as much.

The major inadequacy of Piaget's system, most scholars now agree, is that Piaget generally maintained that cognitive development (conceived as logico-mathematical competence) is the only major line of development, whereas there is now abundant evidence that numerous different developmental lines (such as ego, moral, affective, interpersonal, artistic, etc.) can unfold in a relatively independent manner. In the model I am presenting, for example, the cognitive line is merely one of some two dozen developmental lines, none of which, as lines, can claim preeminence. (We will examine these other lines in the next chapter.)

But as for the cognitive line itself, Piaget's work is still very impressive; moreover, after almost three decades of intense cross-cultural research, the evidence is virtually unanimous: Piaget's stages up to formal operational are universal and cross-cultural. As only one example, *Lives across Cultures: Cross-Cultural Human Development* is a highly respected textbook written from an openly liberal perspective (which is often suspicious of "universal" stages). The authors (Harry Gardiner, Jay Mutter, and Corinne Kosmitzki) carefully review the evidence for Piaget's stages of sensorimotor, preoperational, concrete operational, and formal operational. They found that cultural settings sometimes alter the *rate* of development, or an *emphasis* on certain aspects of the stages—but not the stages themselves or their cross-cultural validity.

Thus, for sensorimotor: "In fact, the qualitative characteristics of sensorimotor development remain nearly identical in all infants studied so far, despite vast differences in their cultural environments." For preoperational and concrete operational, based on an enormous number of studies, including Nigerians, Zambians, Iranians, Algerians, Nepalese, Asians, Senegalese, Amazon Indians, and Australian Aborigines: "What can we conclude from this vast amount of cross-cultural data? First, support for the universality of the structures or operations underlying the preoperational period is highly convincing. Second, the qualitative characteristics of concrete operational development (e.g., stage sequences and reasoning styles) appear to be universal [although] the rate of cognitive development . . . is not uniform but depends on ecocultural factors." Although the authors do not use exactly these terms, they conclude that the deep features of the stages are universal but the surface features depend strongly on cultural, environmental, and ecological factors (as we will later put it, all four quadrants are involved in individual development). "Finally, it appears that although the rate and level of performance at which children move through Piaget's concrete operational period depend on cultural experience, children in diverse societies still proceed in the same sequence he predicted."[15]

Fewer individuals in any cultures (Asian, African, American, or otherwise) reach formal operational cognition, and the reasons given for this vary. It might be that formal operational is a genuinely higher stage that fewer therefore reach, as I believe. It might be that formal operational is a genuine capacity but not a genuine stage, as the authors believe (i.e., only some cultures emphasize formal operational and therefore teach it). Evidence for the existence of Piaget's formal stage is therefore strong but not conclusive. Yet this one item is often used to dismiss *all* of Piaget's stages, whereas the correct conclusion, backed by enormous evidence, is that all of the stages up to formal operational have now been adequately demonstrated to be universal and cross-cultural.

I believe the stages at and beyond formop are also universal, including vision-logic and the general transrational stages, and I will present substantial evidence for this as we proceed. At the same time, as we will see when we get to the discussion on childhood spirituality (in chapter 11), the early stages are exactly the stages of Piaget's studies that have consistently held up to cross-cultural evidence. This will help us to see these early stages in a more accurate light, I believe.

As for the cognitive line itself, its overall study has been fruitfully carried forward by Michael Commons and Francis Richards, Kurt Fischer, Juan Pascual-Leone, Robert Sternberg, Gisela Labouvie-Vief, Herb Koplowitz, Michael Basseches, Philip Powell, Suzanne Benack, Patricia Arlin, Jan Sinnott, and Cheryl Armon, to name a prominent few (all of whom are represented on the charts).[16]

Although there are important differences between these researchers, there are also many profound similarities. Most of them have found that cognitive development moves through three or four major stages (with numerous substages): sensorimotor, concrete, formal, and postformal.

The sensorimotor stages usually occur in the first two years of life, and result in a capacity to perceive physical objects. Cognition then slowly begins to learn to represent these objects with names, symbols, and concepts. These early symbols and concepts tend to suffer various sorts of inadequacies (objects with similar predicates are equated; there is more water in a tall glass than in a short one, even if it is the same water; concepts are confused with the objects they represent; and so on). These inadequacies lead to various sorts of "magical" displacements and "mythical" beliefs. This is why, on all the charts, you will see so many researchers referring to these early stages with names like magic, animistic, mythic, and so on.

This is *not* to say that all magic and all myths are merely early cognitive inadequacies, but that some of them clearly are—if I eat the eye of a cat, I will see like a cat; a rabbit's foot brings good luck; if I don't eat my spinach, God will punish me, etc. There is a world of difference between mythic symbols taken to be concretely and literally true—Jesus really was born from a biological virgin, the earth really is resting on a Hindu serpent, Lao Tzu really was nine hundred years old when he was born—and mythic symbols imbued with metaphor and perspectivism, which only come into existence with formal and postformal consciousness. Unless otherwise indicated, when I use the word "mythic" it refers to preformal, concrete-literal mythic images and symbols, some aspects of which are in fact imbued with cognitive inadequacies, for these myths claim as empirical fact many things that can be empirically disproved—e.g., the volcano erupts because it is personally mad at you; the clouds move because they are following you. These preformal mythic beliefs, scholars from Piaget to Joseph Campbell have noted, are always egocentrically focused and literally/concretely believed.

For the same reason, these early stages are referred to by names such as preconventional, preoperational, egocentric, and narcissistic. Because children at the sensorimotor and preoperational stages cannot yet easily or fully take the role of other, they are locked into their own perspectives. This "narcissism" is a normal, healthy feature of these early stages, and causes problems only if it is not substantially outgrown (as we will see).

As cognitive capacity grows, these researchers generally agree, consciousness begins more accurately to relate to, and operate on, the sensorimotor world, whether that be learning to play the violin or learning to organize classes in order of their size (although many "mythic adherences" still remain in awareness). These *concrete operations* are carried out by *schemas* and *rules*, which also allow the self at this stage to adopt various *roles* in society, and thus move from the egocentric/preconventional realm to the sociocentric/conventional.

As consciousness further develops and deepens, these concrete categories and operations begin to become more generalized, more abstract (in the sense of being applicable to more and more situations), and thus more universal. *Formal operational* consciousness can therefore begin to support a *postconventional* orientation to the world, escaping in many ways the ethnocentric/sociocentric world of concrete (and mythic-membership) thought.

Although, largely under the onslaught of anti-Western cultural studies (with a strong relativistic prejudice), "rationality" has become a derogatory term, it is actually the seat of an extraordinary number of positive accomplishments and capacities (including the capacities used by the antirational critics). Rationality (or reason in the broad sense) involves, first and foremost, the capacity to take perspectives (hence Jean Gebser calls it "perspectival-reason"). According to Susanne Cook-Greuter's research, preoperational thinking has only a first-person perspective (egocentric); concrete operational adds second-person perspectives (sociocentric); and formal operational goes further and adds third-person perspectives (which allow not only scientific precision but also impartial, postconventional, worldcentric judgments of fairness and care). Thus reason can "norm the norms" of a culture, subjecting them to criticism based on universal (non-ethnocentric) principles of fairness. Perspectival-reason, being highly reflexive, also allows sustained introspection. And it is the first structure that can imagine "as if" and "what if" worlds: it becomes a true dreamer and visionary.

As important as formal rationality is, these researchers all acknowledge the existence of yet higher, *postformal* stages of cognition—or a higher reason—which takes even more perspectives into account (fourth- and fifth-person perspectives, according to Cook-Greuter). Bringing together multiple perspectives while unduly privileging none is what Gebser called *integral-aperspectival*, which involves a further deepening of worldcentric and postconventional consciousness. There is general agreement that these postformal (or vision-logic) developments involve at least two or three major stages. Growing beyond abstract universal *formalism* (of formop), consciousness moves first into a cognition of dynamic relativity and *pluralism* (early vision-logic), and then further into a cognition of unity, holism, dynamic dialecticism, or universal *integralism* (middle to late vision-logic), all of which can be seen quite clearly on charts 3a and 3b (and others we will discuss later).[17]

As "holistic" as these vision-logic developments are, they are still mental realm developments. They are the very highest reaches of the mental realms, to be sure, but beyond them lie supramental and properly transrational developments. I have therefore included Sri Aurobindo and Charles Alexander as examples of what a full-spectrum cognitive developmental model might include. (In chapter 9, we will investigate this overall cognitive line as it moves from gross to subtle to causal.) Notice that Aurobindo uses decidedly cognitive terms for almost all of his stages: higher mind, illumined mind, overmind, supermind, and so on. In other words, the spectrum of consciousness is in part a spectrum of genuine cognition, using "cognition" in its broadest sense. But it is not just that, which is why Aurobindo also describes the higher affects, morals, needs, and self identities of these higher levels. But his general point is quite similar: cognitive development is primary and is necessary (but not sufficient) for these other developments.

Summary

Such, then, is a brief introduction to the basic levels in the Great Nest of Being. The Great Nest is simply a great *morphogenetic field* that provides a *developmental space* in which human potentials can unfold. The basic levels of the Great Nest are the basic waves of that unfolding: matter to body to mind to soul to spirit. We saw that these basic levels (or structures or waves) can be divided and subdivided in many legitimate ways. The charts give around sixteen waves in the overall spectrum of consciousness, but these can be condensed or expanded in numerous ways, as we will continue to see throughout this presentation.

Through these general waves in the great River, some two dozen different developmental streams will flow, all navigated by the self on its extraordinary journey from dust to Deity.

2

The Developmental Lines or Streams

THROUGH THE BASIC *levels* or waves in the Great Nest, flow some two dozen relatively independent developmental *lines* or streams. These different developmental lines include morals, affects, self-identity, psychosexuality, cognition, ideas of the good, role-taking, socio-emotional capacity, creativity, altruism, several lines that can be called "spiritual" (care, openness, concern, religious faith, meditative stages), joy, communicative competence, modes of space and time, death-seizure, needs, worldviews, logico-mathematical competence, kinesthetic skills, gender identity, and empathy—to name a few of the more prominent developmental lines for which we have some empirical evidence.[1]

These lines are "relatively independent," which means that, for the most part, they can develop independently of each other, at different rates, with a different dynamic, and on a different time schedule. A person can be very advanced in some lines, medium in others, low in still others—all at the same time. Thus, *overall development*—the sum total of all these different lines—shows no linear or sequential development whatsoever. (It is that fact which finally undid the Piagetian scheme.)

However, the bulk of research has continued to find that *each developmental line itself* tends to unfold in a sequential, holarchical fashion: higher stages in each line tend to build upon or incorporate the earlier stages, no stages can be skipped, and the stages emerge in an order that cannot be altered by environmental conditioning or social reinforcement. So far, considerable evidence suggests that this is true for all of the developmental lines that I mentioned.[2]

For example, in the widely regarded text *Higher Stages of Human Development* (edited by Charles Alexander and Ellen Langer), the works of thirteen top developmental psychologists—including Piaget, Kohlberg, Carol Gilligan, Kurt Fischer, Howard Gardner, Karl Pribram, and Robert Kegan—are presented, and of those thirteen, all of them except one or two present models that are hierarchical in part, including Gilligan for female development. These conclusions are based on massive amounts of experimental data, not merely on theoretical speculations. This is not to say that all of these developmental lines are *only* hierarchical; many of their features are not (see below). But crucial aspects of all of them appear to be hierarchical in important ways. Furthermore, there is a general consensus that no matter how different the developmental lines might be, not only do most of them unfold holarchically, *they do so through the same set of general waves*, which include: a physical/sensorimotor/preconventional stage, a concrete actions/conventional rules stage, and a more abstract, formal, postconventional stage.[3]

In learning to play a musical instrument, for example, one first physically grapples with the instrument and learns to relate to it in a sensorimotor fashion. One then learns to play a simple song or two, gradually mastering the concrete operations and rules of using the instrument. As one becomes proficient in playing the musical keys and scales, the skills become more abstract, and one can increasingly apply the abstract skills to new and different songs. Almost all of the developmental lines—from cognitive to ego to affective to moral to kinesthetic—proceed through those three broad stages. If we allow for the fact that there might be yet higher or transpersonal stages of development, and if we simply call all of those "post-postconventional," then that would give us four broad stages, levels, or waves—sensorimotor, conventional, postconventional, and post-postconventional (precon to con to postcon to post-postcon)—through which most of the developmental lines proceed.

And what are those four broad waves? Nothing but a simplified version of the Great Nest of Being, moving from body (sensorimotor) to mind (conventional and postconventional) to spirit (post-postconventional). Of course, those four broad stages are just a succinct summary of what research has found; in most of the cases—cognitive, self, and moral, for example—development actually goes through five, six, seven or more stages, and in virtually every case, those stages, as far as they go, match in a very general fashion the levels in the Great Nest.

In other words, the reason that most of the developmental lines proceed through a largely universal, invariant, holarchical sequence is that they are following the largely universal, invariant, Great Holarchy of Being—they are following the general morphogenetic field so clearly suggested in the charts. *The Great Nest is most basically that general morphogenetic field or developmental space.* It simply represents some of the basic waves of reality that are available to individuals; and as different talents, capacities, and skills emerge in individuals, they tend to follow, in a general way, the contours of the Great Nest, they migrate through that developmental space. Again, it is not that these levels are etched in concrete or set in stone; they are simply some of the stronger currents in the great River of Life; and when pieces of wood are dropped in that River, they tend to follow the currents already operating. Just so for the individual potentials that emerge in human development: they tend to follow the currents in the great River of Life, they follow the waves in the Great Holarchy. This, at any rate, is what the preponderance of empirical evidence has consistently suggested.

But to return to an equally important point: the various streams, even if they migrate across a similar field, do so in a relatively independent manner. A person can be highly evolved in some lines, medium in others, and low in still others. This means, as I said, that overall development follows no linear sequence whatsoever.

All of this can be represented as in figure 2, which is what I call an "integral psychograph." The levels in the Great Nest are shown on the

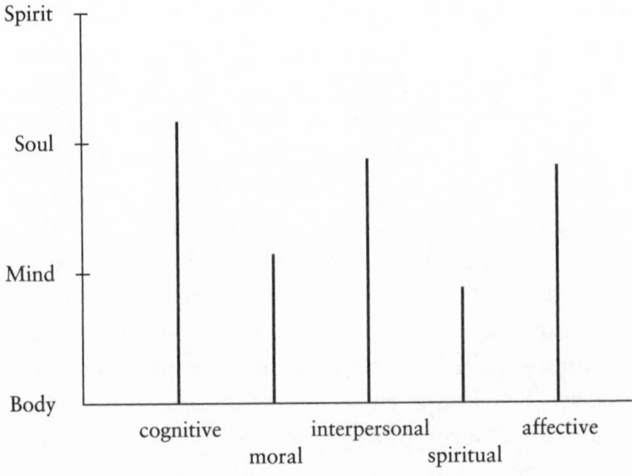

FIGURE 2. *The Integral Psychograph*

vertical axis, and through those levels run the various lines. (Of the two dozen or so lines, I give five as examples: cognitive, moral, interpersonal, spiritual, and affective. I have listed "spirit" both as the highest level, and as a separate developmental line, reflecting the two most common definitions of "spirituality" [see chapter 10]). Since the Great Nest is actually a holarchy (as shown in fig. 1), we can more accurately represent the integral psychograph as in figure 3.

This does not mean that all, or even most, of the important aspects of development are hierarchical. In my system, each basic structure or wave actually consists of both hierarchy (or increasing holistic capacity) and heterarchy (or nonhierarchical interaction among mutually equivalent elements). The relation *between* levels is hierarchical, with each senior level transcending and including its juniors, but not vice versa (molecules contain atoms, but not vice versa; cells contain molecules, but not vice versa; sentences contain words, but not vice versa), and that "not vice versa" establishes an *asymmetrical hierarchy of increasing holistic capacity* (which simply means that the senior dimension embraces the junior, but not vice versa, so that the senior is more holistic and encompassing). But *within* each level, most elements exist as mutually equivalent and mutually interacting patterns. Much of develop-

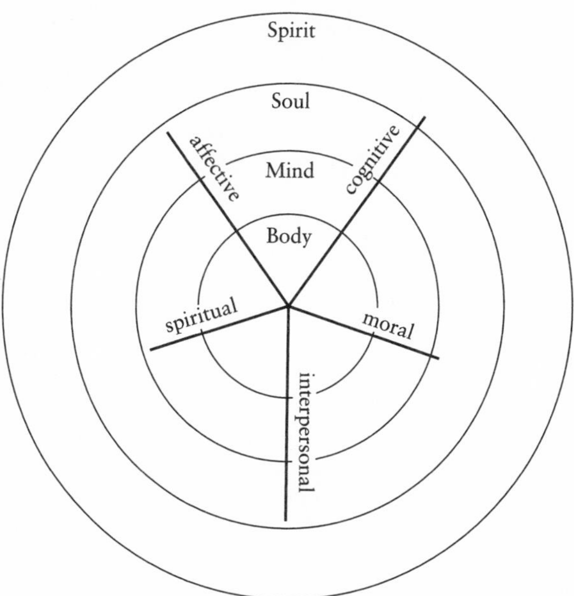

FIGURE 3. *The Integral Psychograph as a Holarchy*

ment—at least half of it—involves various types of nonhierarchical, heterarchical processes of competence articulation and application. These nonhierarchical processes, of course, are not indicated on the charts, which focus on migratory development; but their profound importance should not on that account be forgotten.

Thus *holarchy*, as I use the term, includes a balance of both *hierarchy* (qualitatively ranked levels) and *heterarchy* (mutually linked dimensions). Theorists who attempt to use only one or the other of those types of relations have consistently failed to explain development at all.

We will return to the nature of the developmental streams and give several examples. But first, a look at the self that is navigating those streams.

3

The Self

LEVELS AND LINES are navigated by the self. Although I will subdivide that simple scheme in a moment, those three items—the basic waves, the developmental streams, and the self as the navigator of both—appear to be central to an integral model. We have examined the basic levels or waves, and we will shortly return to the developmental lines or streams and examine them more closely. But at this point we need to look at the self, and the role it plays in the overall evolution of consciousness.[1]

The Self as the Navigator of the Waves and Streams

If you get a sense of your self right now—simply notice what it is that you call "you"—you might notice at least two parts to this "self": one, there is some sort of observing self (an inner subject or watcher); and two, there is some sort of observed self (some objective things that you can see or know about yourself—I am a father, mother, doctor, clerk; I weigh so many pounds, have blond hair, etc.). The first is experienced as an "I," the second as a "me" (or even "mine"). I call the first the *proximate self* (since it is closer to "you"), and the second the *distal self* (since it is objective and "farther away"). The both of them together—along with any other source of selfness—I call the *overall self.*

These distinctions are important because, as many researchers have noted—from Sri Ramana Maharshi to Robert Kegan—during psychological development, *the "I" of one stage becomes a "me" at the next.* That is, what you are identified with (or embedded in) at one stage of development (and what you therefore experience very intimately as an "I"), tends to become transcended, or disidentified with, or de-embedded at the next, so you can see it more objectively, with some distance and detachment. In other words, the *subject* of one stage becomes an *object* of the next.

For example, a young infant is identified almost solely with its body—the body is the infant's self or subject (the proximate I), and thus the infant cannot really stand back and objectively observe its body. It simply *is* a bodyself, and as a body it looks at the world. But when the infant's verbal and conceptual mind begins to emerge, the infant will start to identify with the mind—the mind becomes the self or subject (the proximate I), and the infant can then, for the first time, start to see its body objectively (as a distal object or "me")—the body is now an object of the new subject, the mental self. Thus, the subject of one stage becomes an object of the next.

(And, the perennial philosophers add, at the very upper reaches of the spectrum of consciousness, your individual I—your separate self or inner subject—becomes an object of the ultimate I, which is none other than radiant Spirit and your own true Self. According to the mystics, you are one with God as ultimate Subject or pure Consciousness—a pure Emptiness that, as absolute Witness, I-I, or Seer, can never itself be seen, and yet paradoxically exists as Everything that is seen: the Spirit that transcends all—and thus can never be seen—and includes all—and thus is everything you are looking at right now. We will pursue this in chapter 8.)

The *overall self*, then, is an amalgam of all of these "selves" insofar as they are present in you right now: the proximate self (or "I"), the distal self (or "me"), and at the very back of your awareness, that ultimate Witness (the transcendental Self, antecedent Self, or "I-I"). All of those go into your sensation of being a self in this moment, and all of them are important for understanding the development or evolution of consciousness.

Precisely because the overall self contains several different streams (and all sorts of *subpersonalities*, which we will discuss below), the overall self does *not* show a sequential or stage-like development. However, modern research has consistently shown that *at least one aspect of the self does undergo relatively sequential or stage-like development, and that is the proximate self.*[2] Jane Loevinger, for example, in some highly respected and widely repeated research (including in non-Western countries), has found substantial evidence that "ego development" proceeds through almost a dozen stages of clearly recognizable growth (up to what I call the centaur; see chart 1a). What Loevinger calls "ego development" is quite similar to what I refer to as proximate-self development.[3] And proximate-self development is, in my view, at the very heart of the evolution of consciousness. *For it is the proximate self that is the navigator through the basic waves in the Great Nest of Being.*

The basic structures or basic waves themselves are devoid of a sense of self. This point has been made by perennial philosophers from Plotinus to Vasubandhu to Padmasambhava to Saint Teresa. The basic structures are simply the waves of being and knowing that are available to the self as it develops toward its highest potentials. Each time the self (the proximate self) encounters a new level in the Great Nest, it first *identifies* with it and consolidates it; then disidentifies with it (*transcends* it, de-embeds from it); and then includes and *integrates* it from the next higher level. In other words, the self goes through a *fulcrum (or a milestone) of its own development.* These major milestones of self development have been investigated by researchers such as James Mark Baldwin, Clare Graves, Jane Loevinger, John Broughton, Erik Erikson, Susanne Cook-Greuter, Don Beck, and Robert Kegan, to name a prominent few, all of whom are represented on the charts. (Again, these researchers are not investigating identical currents, but simply currents that run close together in the Great River and thus share certain similarities—similarities in the nature of the proximate-self sense.)

To say that the self has identified with a particular wave in the Great Rainbow does not, however, mean that the self is rigidly stuck at that level. On the contrary, the self can be "all over the place" on occasion. Within limits, the self can temporarily roam all over the spectrum of consciousness—it can regress, or move down the holarchy of being and knowing; it can spiral, reconsolidate, and return. Moreover, because the self at every stage of its development has fluid access to the great natural states of consciousness (psychic, subtle, causal, and nondual), it can have temporary peak experiences of any or all of those transpersonal realms, thus momentarily leaping forward into greater realities.

Still, empirical evidence has consistently demonstrated that the self's *center of gravity*, so to speak, tends to hover around one basic level of consciousness at any given time. This means, for example, that if you give individuals a test of ego development, about 50 percent of their answers will come from one level, and about 25 percent from the level immediately above or below it. In my view, the reason this happens is that, each time the self identifies with a particular level of consciousness, it experiences the loss of that level as a death—literally, as a type of death-seizure, because the very *life* of the self is identified with that level.[4] Letting go of that level is therefore experienced only with great difficulty. In fact, I believe that each of the major milestones of self-development is marked by a difficult life-death battle, involving the death (or the disidentifying with, or the transcendence) of each level, which can often be quite traumatic (see chart 1a; we will examine these milestones or fulcrums of self-development in chapter 8).[5] The only reason the self eventually accepts the *death* of its given level is that the *life* of the next higher level is even more enticing and ultimately satisfying. The self therefore disidentifies with (or de-embeds from) its present level, "dies" to an exclusive identity with that level, and identifies with (or embraces and embeds in) the life of the next higher level, until its death, too, is accepted. (And according to the perennial philosophy, when all deaths have been died, the result is only God, or an awakening to the what the Sufis call the Supreme Identity of self and spirit.)

The proximate self, then, is the navigator of the waves (and streams) in the great River of Life. It is the central source of identity, and that identity expands and deepens as the self navigates from egocentric to sociocentric to worldcentric to theocentric waves (or precon to con to postcon to post-postcon levels of overall development)—an identity that ranges from matter to id to ego to God.

(Incidentally, when we say that identity expands from, say, egocentric to sociocentric to worldcentric, this does not mean that somebody at the worldcentric or postconventional level has no ego at all; on the contrary, somebody at worldcentric has a very mature ego. It simply means that the person can take *multiple perspectives* no longer confined to *just* his own ego, and thus he can make moral judgments based on the considerations of fairness, justness, and care, regardless of race, color, sex, or creed. He will still act in his own self-interest where that is appropriate, but the sphere of his consideration is immeasurably expanded, and his own self-interest will increasingly include the interests of others, since they fall into the orbit of his own expanded identity. See chapter 9, section "Morals.")

As the central navigator through the Great Nest, the self is the locus of such important functions as *identification* (what to call "I"), *will* (or choices that are free within the constraints and limitations of its present level),[6] *defenses* (which are laid down hierarchically),[7] *metabolism* (which converts states into traits),[8] and most important of all, *integration* (the self is responsible for balancing and integrating whatever elements are present).[9] (As for the Buddhist objections to the self, see endnote).[10]

Conclusion

What each of us calls an "I" (the proximate self) is both a *constant function* and a *developmental stream*. That is, the self has several *functional invariants* that constitute its central activity—it is the locus of identity, will, metabolism, navigation, defenses, and integration, to name the more important. And this self (with its functions) also undergoes *its own development* through the basic waves in the Great Nest (the stages of which we will examine in chapter 8: material self to bodily self to mental self to soul self to selfless Self). Especially significant is the fact that, as the locus of integration, the self is responsible *for balancing and integrating all of the levels, lines, and states in the individual.*

In short, the self as navigator is a juggling act of all of the elements that it will encounter on its extraordinary journey from subconscious to self-conscious to superconscious—a journey we will soon follow in detail.

4

The Self-Related Streams

THE SELF NAVIGATES through the basic waves of the Great Nest by using the self's capacity to *identify* with each wave and ride it to some sort of completion. The self has the capacity to intimately identify with a level of consciousness, become competent at that level, and then disidentify with it (and integrate it) in order to step up to the next higher and wider sphere and identify with it (and so on until its capacity for growth is exhausted).

Each time the self's center of gravity orbits around a new level of consciousness, it has, of course, a new and different outlook on life. Precisely because each basic level in the Great Nest has a different architecture, the self at each level *sees a different world*: it faces new fears, has different goals, suffers new problems. It has a new set of needs, a new class of morals, a new sense of self. I call all of those developmental lines the *self-related lines or streams*, because they are all intimately connected with the self and its extraordinary journey through the great waves.

Thus, there are the developmental lines in general (cognitive, affective, aesthetic, kinesthetic, mathematical, etc.), and, as a subset of those, there are the developmental lines that are especially and intimately associated with the self, its needs, its identity, and its development—and those are the self-related lines.

In fact, the self-related stages are generated, in part, precisely from the self's *identifying with a particular level of consciousness*. To give a simplistic example: when the self identifies with the conventional mind (when the self's major level of consciousness is late conop), its sense of self (à la Loevinger) is a *conformist role*, its moral sense (à la Kohlberg) is starting to become *conventional*, and its major need (à la Maslow) is for *belongingness* (you can see these on the charts). All of those specific roles, morals, and needs come into play when the self's center of gravity is at the late rule/role mind, and they are supported largely by the *exclusive identification* of the self with that level of consciousness.[1] From that particular level in the Great Spectrum, that is what the world looks like.

Many of those stages—such as morals, self-identity, and self-needs—are listed in charts 4a–c and 5a–c. Charts 4a-c contain the self-related stages that are most intimately connected with *self identity* (such as Loevinger's ego development and Erikson's psychosocial stages), and charts 5a–c contain the self-related stages of *morals and perspectives*, or the different types of outlook (and worldviews) that the self has at each of the basic levels of consciousness. We will discuss them in that order.

The Self-Stages (Charts 4a–c)

Early pioneers in the study of the stages of self-development (and those who have considerably influenced my own view) include James Mark Baldwin, John Dewey, G. H. Mead, C. Cooley, Anna Freud, Heinz Werner, Edith Jacobson, Harry Stack Sullivan, Heinz Hartmann, Rene Spitz, Erich Neumann, Edward F. Edinger, Clare Graves, and Erik Erikson.[2] More recent theorists (also instrumental in my view) include Jane Loevinger, John Broughton, Otto Kernberg, Jacques Lacan, Heinz Kohut, Margaret Mahler, James Masterson, Robert Kegan, and Susanne Cook-Greuter (among others to be discussed).

Erikson, coming from within the psychoanalytic tradition, posed such a profoundly far-reaching extension of its concepts that it actually helped to undermine psychoanalytic reductionism. His "psychosocial stages," ranging from birth through adolescence to old age, struck an immediately sympathetic cord not only with the public but with many other researchers—he was clearly on to something of importance. In Erikson's scheme, quite reminiscent of the "seven ages of a person," there are seven or eight major ages (or stages) of a person's life (see chart 4a). Echoing a truth that was already beginning to surface from Baldwin's and Piaget's studies (and which was explicit in the German Idealists' vision, which greatly influenced both Baldwin and Piaget), each stage of development sees a different world—with different needs, different tasks, different dilemmas, different problems and pathologies. Instead of reducing all of life's problems to something that went wrong in the first age of a person, there are six or seven other ages, equally important, sometimes more important. Erikson's highest stages were not quite transpersonal (they were often horizontal unfoldings of a personal sort);[3] still, it would never be quite as easy to reduce all significant life events to the first age of a person.

Clare Graves was one of the first (along with Baldwin, Dewey, and Maslow) to take a developmental scheme and show its extraordinary applicability in a wide range of endeavors, from business to government to education. Graves proposed a profound and elegant system of human development, a system that subsequent research has refined and validated, not refuted. "Briefly, what I am proposing is that the psychology of the mature human being is an unfolding, emergent, oscillating spiraling process marked by progressive subordination of older, lower-order behavior systems to newer, higher-order systems as man's existential problems change. Each successive stage, wave, or level of existence is a state through which people pass on their way to other states of being. When the human is centralized in one state of existence"—that is, when the self's *center of gravity* hovers around a given level of consciousness—"he or she has a psychology which is particular to that state. His or her feelings, motivations, ethics and values, biochemistry, degree of neurological activation, learning system, belief systems, conception of mental health, ideas as to what mental illness is and how it should be treated, conceptions of and preferences for management, education, economics, and political theory and practice are all appropriate to that state."[4]

Graves outlined around seven major "levels or waves of human existence," ranging from autistic, magical, and animistic, through sociocentric/conventional, to individualistic and integrated, as shown in chart 4c. As is usually the case with Western researchers, he recognized no higher (transpersonal) levels, but the contributions he made to the prepersonal and personal realms were profound.

It should be remembered that virtually all of these stage conceptions—from Abraham Maslow to Jane Loevinger to Robert Kegan to Clare Graves—are based on extensive amounts of research and data. These are not simply conceptual ideas and pet theories, but are grounded at every point in a considerable amount of carefully checked evidence. Many of the stage theorists that I am presenting (such as Piaget, Loevinger, Maslow, and Graves) have had their models checked in first-, second-, and third-world countries (as we saw with Piaget). The same is true with Graves's model; to date, it has been tested in over fifty thousand people from around the world, and there have been no major exceptions found to his scheme.[5]

Of course, this does not mean that any of these schemes give the whole story, or even most of it. They are all, as I said, partial snapshots of the great River of Life, and they are all useful when looking at the River from that particular angle. This does not prevent other pictures from being equally useful, nor does it mean that these pictures cannot be refined with further study. What it does mean is that any psychological model that does not include these pictures is not a very integral model.

Graves's work has been carried forward, refined, and significantly extended by Don Beck. *Spiral Dynamics*, written with his colleague Christopher Cowan (they founded the National Values Center), is a superb application of developmental principles in general (and Gravesian ones in particular) to a wide range of sociocultural problems. Far from being mere armchair analysts, Beck and Cowan participated in the discussions that lead to the end of apartheid in South Africa (and then went on, using the same developmental principles, to design the "hearts and minds" strategy for the South African rugby union team, which won the 1995 World Cup). The principles of Spiral Dynamics have been fruitfully used to reorganize businesses, revitalize townships, overhaul education systems, and defuse inner-city tensions. Beck and Cowan have had this extraordinary success because, in a world lost in pluralistic relativism, they have brought the clarity—and the reality—of dynamic developmentalism.

The situation in South Africa is a prime example of why the idea of developmental levels (each with its own worldview, values, and needs) can actually reduce and even alleviate social tensions, not exacerbate them (as critics often charge). Spiral Dynamics sees human development as proceeding through eight general value MEMES or deep structures: *instinctive* (uroboric), *animistic/tribalistic* (typhonic-magic), *power gods* (magic-mythic), *absolutist-religious* (mythic), *individualistic-achiever* (rational-egoic), *relativistic* (early vision-logic), *systematic-integrative* (middle vision-logic), and *global-holistic* (late vision-logic), as shown in chart 4b. These are not rigid levels but fluid and flowing waves, with much overlap and interweaving, resulting in a meshwork or dynamic spiral of consciousness unfolding.

The typical, well-meaning liberal approach to solving social tensions is to treat every value as equal, and then try to force a leveling or redistribution of resources (money, rights, goods, land) while leaving the values untouched. The typical conservative approach is take its particular values and try to foist them on everybody else. The developmental approach is to realize that there are many different values and worldviews; that some are more complex than others; that many of the problems at one stage of development can only be defused by evolving to a higher level; and that only by recognizing and facilitating this evolution can social justice be finally served. Moreover, by seeing that each and every individual has all of these MEMES potentially available to them, the lines of social tension are redrawn: not based on skin color, economic class, or political clout, but on the *type* of worldview from which a person, group of persons, clan, tribe, business, government, educational system, or nation is operating from. As Beck puts it, "The focus is not on types *of* people, but types *in* people." This removes skin color from the game and focuses on some of the truly underlying factors (developmental values and worldviews) that generate social tensions, and this is exactly what happened to help dismantle apartheid in South Africa.[6]

(We will return to Beck at the end of this chapter for some fascinating examples, so if these sections on self development seem dry and abstract, they will hopefully come alive with numerous examples and applications.)

Jane Loevinger's impressive research focused specifically on ego development (see chart 4a); it brought a great deal of precision to the field and sparked an explosion of further developmental studies. She found that ego (proximate-self) development moves through about ten discernible stages, the names of which tend to tell the story: autistic, symbiotic, impulsive, self-protective, conformist, conscientious-conformist, conscientious, individualistic, autonomous, and integrated. Her research has been repeated in several different cultures now, and continues to garner wide support. Susanne Cook-Greuter has refined and extended Loevinger's research, and is forging her own original and important model of self development (chart 4c).[7]

Robert Kegan (chart 4c) seems to be everybody's favorite developmentalist (count me in). He discusses a broad range of developmental issues with insight, exactitude, sensitivity, and care. Kegan's approach is especially important, in my view, because he so clearly elucidates the nature of embedding (identifying) and de-embedding (transcending), which marks each major wave of self development. His books *The Evol-*

ving Self and *In Over Our Heads* show why a developmental approach is so important (and why Kegan is everybody's favorite son).

Juan Pascual-Leone brings a much-needed Continental (hermeneutic, phenomenological, dialectical) orientation to developmental studies, weaving together the work of Piaget, Jaspers, Husserl, Scheler, Merleau-Ponty, and Heidegger (who have likewise influenced my view)—plus his own highly original formulations—into a powerful system of dynamic dialecticism (charts 3b and 4b).[8]

John Broughton's research is of great significance, I believe, especially in terms of delineating the developmental stages of self and its epistemology (chart 4a). Following the lead of James Mark Baldwin (see below), Broughton has contributed not only a good deal of important research, but a much-needed series of theoretical counterbalances to the narrowness of the Piagetian tradition.[9]

As examples of researchers who follow the self-stages into the transpersonal domains, I have included Rudolf Steiner (chart 4b), Michael Washburn (4a), and Jenny Wade (4a); Stan Grof's levels can be seen in chart 2a.[10] Steiner (1861–1925) was an extraordinary pioneer (during that "genesis period" of Fechner, Jung, James, etc.) and one of the most comprehensive psychological and philosophical visionaries of his time. The founder of anthroposophy, he authored over two hundred books on virtually every conceivable subject.[11] Michael Washburn has presented a very clear version of a Romantic view of higher development involving a recapture of earlier lost potentials; and Jenny Wade, who is one of the most competent developmentalists now writing, has presented an excellent overview of the unfolding of eight major waves of consciousness, spanning the entire spectrum.

Once again, although there are many important differences between these theories of the stages of self-development, one can't help but also notice the many profound similarities. The very names that these theorists have given to the self-stages tend to tell the story. Using only the terms from the theorists listed in charts 4a–c: Consciousness starts out largely autistic and undifferentiated from the material world. It then differentiates its bodily self from the material environment and emerges as an instinctive, impulsive self, but one that is still magically and animistically involved with the environment, and still struggling for egocentric power over the environment. As the conceptual mind begins to emerge, it differentiates from the body, and thus the self adds increasingly mental capacities to its sensory ones, and hence begins to move out of the narcissistic, first-person, safety/security/power orbit and into more widely intersubjective, communal, and social circles.

As rule thinking and the capacity to take the role of others emerge, *egocentric* gives way to *sociocentric*, with its initially conformist and conventional roles, mythic-absolutist beliefs, and often authoritarian ways. A further growth of consciousness differentiates the self from its embeddedness in sociocentric and ethnocentric modes, and opens it to formal, universal, worldcentric, postconventional awareness, which is an extraordinary expansion of consciousness into modes that are beginning to become truly global.

This postconventional stance is deepened with postformal development, which, most researchers agree, moves through *relativistic individualism* (where a belief in pluralism tends to lead to isolated, hyperindividualism) to *global holism* (which moves beyond pluralism to universal integration), so that the personal self becomes a more truly integrated, autonomous self. (Which I call the *centaur.* "Centaur" is a term used by Erikson to denote a mature mind-and-body integration, where "human mind" and "animal body" are harmoniously one. We might say that it is the highest of the personal realms, beyond which lie more transpersonal developments).

If consciousness continues its evolutionary spiral beyond the centaur, it can stably move into transpersonal, post-postconventional realms (psychic, subtle, causal, and nondual). A few of the modern Western pioneers studying these higher realms include Johann Fichte, Friedrich Schelling, Georg Hegel, Arthur Schopenhauer, Henri Bergson, Friedrich Nietzsche, Carl Jung, Martin Heidegger, Karl Jaspers, Edmund Husserl, Gustav Fechner, Henry James Sr., Ralph Waldo Emerson, Rudolf Steiner, Vladimir Solovyov, Josiah Royce, Annie Besant, Frederic Myers, Nikolai Berdyaev, Aldous Huxley, Erich Fromm, Roberto Assagioli, James Mark Baldwin, William James, and Abraham Maslow.[12]

Morals and Perspectives (Charts 5a-c)

Each time the self's center of gravity identifies with a new and higher basic wave in the unfolding Great Nest, it doesn't just have a new sense of *identity*, it has a new and higher *view* of the world, with a wider and more encompassing set of *morals* and *perspectives*, many of which are listed in charts 5a–c.

The pivotal figure here is Lawrence Kohlberg (chart 5a), whose work, building on that of Baldwin, Dewey, and Piaget, demonstrated that moral development goes through six or seven stages (spanning preconventional to conventional to postconventional to post-postconventional). The individual starts out amoral and egocentric ("whatever I want" is what is right), moves to sociocentric ("what the group, tribe, country wants" is what is right), to postconventional (what is fair for all peoples, regardless of race, color, creed). Kohlberg's highest stage—what he called stage seven—is "universal-spiritual" (post-postconventional).

Deirdre Kramer (chart 5a) has given a powerful overview of worldview development (preformal to formal to pluralistic to integral). Kitchener and King have done important and influential work on reflective judgment (from representation to relativism to synthesis; chart 5a). William Perry's work on social perspectives, which develop from rigidly dualistic to relativistic/pluralistic to synthetic committed (chart 5a), has been widely hailed by other researchers and is especially appreciated by college students, since it outlines their typical angst-ridden developments with great care. Robert Selman's studies on role-taking have elucidated crucial aspects of the development of the self and its intersubjective capacities (chart 5c). Carol Gilligan (chart 5c) outlined a hierarchy of female moral development ("selfish" to "care" to "universal care," yet another version of egocentric to sociocentric to worldcentric), which had an enormous influence on the popular culture to precisely the degree it was widely misinterpreted (as implying that only males go through hierarchical stages; the idea that women do not go through hierarchical development became one of the most influential cultural myths of the last two decades). Torbert's levels of action-inquiry have proven especially useful in business (chart 5a). Blanchard-Fields's work offers a significant overview of the evolution of perspectives, from egocentric to multiple to integrative (chart 5a). John Rawls's moral positions line up in a hierarchy (chart 5c), as do Cheryl Armon's stages of the Good (chart 5b) and Howe's important work on moral character structures (chart 5c).[13]

In other words, what all of these theories have in common is a general view of morals and perspectives evolving from preconventional to conventional to postconventional (to post-postconventional)—yet more general evidence for the Great Nest and its often universal currents.[14] Nonetheless, it should be emphasized that these different self-related developmental streams still retain a relatively independent character. For example, research continues to suggest that cognitive development is necessary but not sufficient for interpersonal development, which is necessary but not sufficient for moral development, which is necessary but not sufficient for ideas of the Good.[15] That underscores the fact that, once again, even though most of the individual developmental lines undergo a sequential holarchical unfolding, overall development itself does not.

OBJECTIONS

One criticism that has constantly been raised by advocates of pluralistic relativism is that any stage conception—such as Kohlberg's or Loevinger's—is inherently Eurocentric, marginalizing, and sexist. These are important concerns. However, over the last decade and a half these criticisms have been carefully investigated, and for the most part they have proven unfounded. Kohlberg's moral stages, for example, were claimed to be biased against women. "At this point there is little support for the claim that Kohlberg's theory is biased against females," reports the widely respected textbook *Social and Personality Development.* "Nor is there much evidence that females travel a different moral path and come to emphasize a morality of care more than males do. In fact, there is evidence to the contrary: when reasoning about real-life moral dilemmas that they have faced, *both* males and females raise issues of compassion and interpersonal responsibility about *as often as* or *more often than* issues of law, justice, and individual rights" (emphasis in original). In short, "Research has consistently failed to support the claim the Kohlberg's theory is biased against women."[16]

How about the claim that Kohlberg's research is eurocentric, with a Western bias that marginalizes other cultures? "Similar findings have emerged from studies in Mexico, the Bahamas, Taiwan, Indonesia, Turkey, Honduras, India, Nigeria, and Kenya. . . . So it seems that Kohlberg's levels and stages of moral reasoning are 'universal' structures . . . [and] Kohlberg's morals stages do seem to represent an invariant sequence."[17] As another researcher summarizes the evidence: "Comprehensive reviews of cross-cultural studies suggest that Kohlberg's theory and method are reasonably culture-fair and do reflect moral issues, norms, and values relevant in other cultural settings. Further, these data also support the developmental criteria implied by his stage model [giving] impressive support for his developmental theory and its nonrelativistic stance. . . ."[18]

Theories such as Kohlberg's have demonstrated their nonrelativistic stance precisely because, I would claim, those stages are surfing the waves of the nonrelativistic Great Holarchy, preconventional to conventional to postconventional to post-postconventional. These waves are flowing across a morphogenetic field and developmental space that spans insentient matter to superconscient spirit, while remaining, at every stage, fully grounded in that Spirit which is the suchness and isness of the entire display.

Spiral Dynamics: An Example of the Waves of Existence

We return now to Spiral Dynamics for a brief overview of one version of the self-streams and their waves of unfolding. Remember that this is simply one series of photos of the Great River; there are actually numerous different streams proceeding relatively independently through the basic waves; and individuals can simultaneously be at many different waves in their various streams (as shown in the integral psychograph, figs. 2 and 3). Spiral Dynamics does not include states of consciousness, nor does it cover the higher, transpersonal waves of consciousness.[19] But for the ground it covers, it gives one very useful and elegant model of the self and its journey through what Clare Graves called the "waves of existence."

Beck and Cowan (who have remained quite faithful to Graves's system) refer to these levels of self-existence as ^{V}MEMEs. A ^{V}MEME is at once a psychological structure, value system, and mode of adaptation, which can express itself in numerous different ways, from worldviews to clothing styles to governmental forms. The various ^{V}MEMEs are, in a sense, the "different worlds" available to the self as it develops along the great spiral of existence, driven by both its own internal dynamics and shifting life conditions. And each ^{V}MEME is a holon, which transcends and includes its predecessors—a development that is envelopment. I have included a "Graves Diagram" (fig. 4), which is a diagram Clare Graves himself used to indicate this nesting envelopment (what we would call a holarchy).

Beck and Cowan use various names and colors to refer to these different self-world levels, of which there are around eight or nine. But these are not just passing phases in the self's unfolding; they are permanently

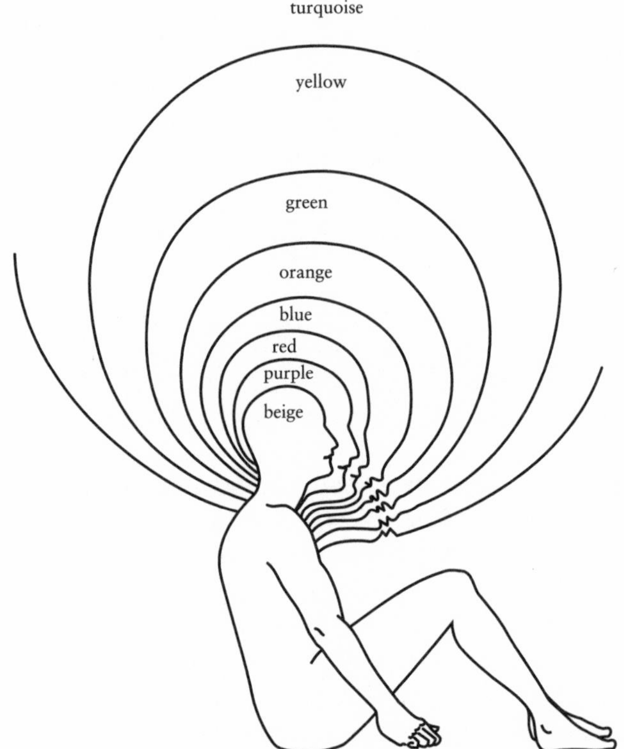

FIGURE 4. *Graves Diagram: Holons of Increasing Development*

available capacities and coping strategies that can, once they have emerged, be activated under the appropriate life conditions (e.g., survival instincts can be activated in emergency situations; bonding capacities are activated in close human relationships, and so on). Moreover, as Beck puts it, "The Spiral is messy, not symmetrical, with multiple admixtures rather than pure types. These are mosaics, meshes, and blends."[20]

The first six levels are "subsistence levels" marked by "first-tier thinking." Then there occurs a revolutionary shift in consciousness: the emergence of "being levels" and "second-tier thinking." Here is a brief description of all eight waves, the percentage of the world population at each wave, and the percentage of social power held by each.[21]

1. *Beige: Archaic-Instinctual.* The level of basic survival; food, water, warmth, sex, and safety have priority. Uses habits and instincts just to

survive. Distinct self is barely awakened or sustained. Forms into *survival bands* to perpetuate life.

Where seen: First human societies, newborn infants, senile elderly, late-stage Alzheimer's victims, mentally ill street people, starving masses, shell shock. 0.1 percent of the adult population, 0 percent power.

2. *Purple: Magical-Animistic.* Thinking is animistic; magical spirits, good and bad, swarm the earth leaving blessings, curses, and spells that determine events. Forms into *ethnic tribes.* The spirits exist in ancestors and bond the tribe. Kinship and lineage establish political links. Sounds "holistic" but is actually atomistic: "there is a name for each bend in the river but no name for the river."

Where seen: Belief in voodoo-like curses, blood oaths, ancient grudges, good luck charms, family rituals, magical ethnic beliefs and superstitions; strong in Third World settings, gangs, athletic teams, and corporate "tribes." 10 percent of the population, 1 percent of the power.

3. *Red: Power Gods.* First emergence of a self distinct from the tribe; powerful, impulsive, egocentric, heroic. Mythic spirits, dragons, beasts, and powerful people. Feudal lords protect underlings in exchange for obedience and labor. The basis of *feudal empires*—power and glory. The world is a jungle full of threats and predators. Conquers, outfoxes, and dominates; enjoys self to the fullest without regret or remorse.

Where seen: The "terrible twos," rebellious youth, frontier mentalities, feudal kingdoms, epic heroes, James Bond villains, soldiers of fortune, wild rock stars, Attila the Hun, *Lord of the Flies.* 20 percent of the population, 5 percent of the power.

4. *Blue: Conformist Rule.* Life has meaning, direction, and purpose, with outcomes determined by an all-powerful Other or Order. This righteous Order enforces a code of conduct based on absolutist and unvarying principles of "right" and "wrong." Violating the code or rules has severe, perhaps everlasting repercussions. Following the code yields rewards for the faithful. Basis of *ancient nations.* Rigid social hierarchies; paternalistic; one right way and only one right way to think about everything. Law and order; impulsivity controlled through guilt; concrete-literal and fundamentalist belief; obedience to the rule of Order. Often "religious" [in the mythic-membership sense; Graves and Beck refer to it as the "saintly/absolutistic" level], but can be secular or atheistic Order or Mission.

Where seen: Puritan America, Confucianist China, Dickensian England, Singapore discipline, codes of chivalry and honor, charitable good deeds, Islamic fundamentalism, Boy and Girl Scouts, "moral majority," patriotism. 40 percent of the population, 30 percent of the power.

5. *Orange: Scientific Achievement.* At this wave, the self "escapes" from the "herd mentality" of blue, and seeks truth and meaning in individualistic terms—hypothetico-deductive, experimental, objective, mechanistic, operational—"scientific" in the typical sense. The world is a rational and well-oiled machine with natural laws that can be learned, mastered, and manipulated for one's own purposes. Highly achievement-oriented, especially (in America) toward materialistic gains. The laws of science rule politics, the economy, and human events. The world is a chessboard on which games are played as winners gain preeminence and perks over losers. Marketplace alliances; manipulate earth's resources for one's strategic gains. Basis of *corporate states.*

Where seen: The Enlightenment, Ayn Rand's *Atlas Shrugged,* Wall Street, the Riviera, emerging middle classes around the world, cosmetics industry, trophy hunting, colonialism, the Cold War, fashion industry, materialism, liberal self-interest. 30 percent of the population, 50 percent of the power.

6. *Green: The Sensitive Self.* Communitarian, human bonding, ecological sensitivity, networking. The human spirit must be freed from greed, dogma, and divisiveness; feelings and caring supersede cold rationality; cherishing of the earth, Gaia, life. Against hierarchy; establishes lateral bonding and linking. Permeable self, relational self, group intermeshing. Emphasis on dialogue, relationships. Basis of *collective communities* (i.e., freely chosen affiliations based on shared sentiments). Reaches decisions through reconciliation and consensus (downside: interminable "processing" and incapacity to reach decisions). Refresh spirituality, bring harmony, enrich human potential. Strongly egalitarian, antihierarchy, pluralistic values, social construction of reality, diversity, multiculturalism, relativistic value systems; this worldview is often called *pluralistic relativism.* Subjective, nonlinear thinking; shows a greater degree of affective warmth, sensitivity, and caring, for earth and all its inhabitants.

Where seen: Deep ecology, postmodernism, Netherlands idealism, Rogerian counseling, Canadian health care, humanistic psychology, liberation theology, World Council of Churches, Greenpeace, animal rights, ecofeminism, postcolonialism, Foucault/Derrida, politically correct, diversity movements, human rights issues, ecopsychology. 10 percent of the population, 15 percent of the power.

With the completion of the green meme, human consciousness is poised for a quantum jump into "second-tier thinking." Clare Graves referred to this as a "momentous leap," where "a chasm of unbelievable depth of meaning is crossed." In essence, with second-tier consciousness, one can think both vertically and horizontally, using both hierarchies and heterarchies; one can, for the first time, *vividly grasp the entire spectrum of interior development*, and thus see that each level, each meme, each wave is crucially important for the health of the overall spiral.

As I would word it, since each wave is "transcend and include," each wave is a fundamental ingredient of all subsequent waves, and thus each is to be cherished and embraced. Moreover, each wave can itself be activated or reactivated as life circumstances warrant. In emergency situations, we can activate red power drives; in response to chaos, we might need to activate blue order; in looking for a new job, we might need orange achievement drives; in marriage and with friends, close green bonding.

But what none of those memes can do, on their own, is fully appreciate the existence of the other memes. Each of those first-tier memes thinks that its worldview is the correct or best perspective. It reacts negatively if challenged; it lashes out, using its own tools, whenever it is threatened. Blue order is very uncomfortable with both red impulsiveness and orange individualism. Orange achievement thinks blue order is for suckers and green bonding is weak and woo-woo. Green egalitarianism cannot easily abide excellence and value rankings, big pictures, or anything that appears authoritarian, and thus it reacts strongly to blue, orange, and anything post-green.

All of that begins to change with second-tier thinking. Because second-tier consciousness is fully aware of the interior stages of development—even if it cannot articulate them in a technical fashion—it steps back and grasps the big picture, and thus second-tier thinking appreciates the necessary role that all of the various memes play. Using what we would recognize as vision-logic, second-tier awareness thinks in terms of the overall spiral of existence, and not merely in the terms of any one level.

Where the green meme uses early or beginning vision-logic in order to grasp the numerous different systems and contexts that exist in different cultures, second-tier thinking goes one step further and begins to *inte-*

grate those pluralistic systems into integral and holistic spirals and holarchies (Beck and Cowan themselves refer to second-tier thinking as operating with "holons"). These holarchies include both interior and exterior levels of development, in both vertical and horizontal dimensions, resulting in a multileveled, multidimensional, richly holarchical view.

There are two major waves to this second-tier thinking (corresponding to what we would recognize as middle and late vision-logic):

7. *Yellow: Integrative.* Life is a kaleidoscope of natural hierarchies [holarchies], systems, and forms. Flexibility, spontaneity, and functionality have the highest priority. Differences and pluralities can be integrated into interdependent, natural flows. Egalitarianism is complemented with natural degrees of excellence where appropriate. Knowledge and competency should supersede rank, power, status, or group. The prevailing world order is the result of the existence of different levels of reality (memes) and the inevitable patterns of movement up and down the dynamic spiral. Good governance facilitates the emergence of entities through the levels of increasing complexity (nested hierarchy).

8. *Turquoise: Holistic.* Universal holistic system, holons/waves of integrative energies; unites feeling with knowledge [centaur]; multiple levels interwoven into one conscious system. Universal order, but in a living, conscious fashion, not based on external rules (blue) or group bonds (green). A "grand unification" is possible, in theory and in actuality. Sometimes involves the emergence of a new spirituality as a meshwork of all existence. Turquoise thinking uses the entire spiral; sees multiple levels of interaction; detects harmonics, the mystical forces, and the pervasive flow-states that permeate any organization.

Second-tier thinking: 1 percent of the population, 5 percent of the power.

With only 1 percent of the population at second-tier thinking (and only 0.1 percent at turquoise), second-tier consciousness is relatively rare because it is now the "leading-edge" of collective human evolution. As examples, Beck and Cowan mention items ranging from Teilhard de Chardin's noosphere to the growth of transpersonal psychology, with increases in frequency definitely on the way—and even higher vMEMEs still in the offing. . . .

At the same time, it might be noted that second-tier thinking has to emerge in the face of much resistance from first-tier thinking. In fact, as we will see in chapter 13, a version of the postmodern green meme, with its pluralism and relativism, has actively fought the emergence of more integrative and holarchical thinking. (It has also made developmental studies, which depend on second-tier thinking, virtually anathema at most universities, which is why the researchers presented throughout this book—and in the charts—are heroes and heroines by any definition, who have often pursued their studies in the most hostile of environments). And yet without second-tier thinking, as Graves, Beck, and Cowan point out, humanity is destined to remain victims of a global "auto-immune disease," where various memes turn on each other in an attempt to establish supremacy.

At the same time, it is from the large fund of green memes (and sometimes orange) that the second-tier emerges.[22] It is from the pluralistic perspectives freed by green that integrative and holistic networks are built. This book is therefore an invitation to those greens who find it appropriate to move on, not by abandoning green, but by enriching it.

Horizontal Typologies

Finally, a word about "horizontal" typologies, such as Jungian types, the Enneagram, Myers-Briggs, and so forth. For the most part, these are not vertical levels, stages, or waves of development, but rather different types of orientations *possible at each of the various levels.* Some individuals find these typologies to be very useful in understandings themselves and others. But it should be understood that these "horizontal" typologies are of a fundamentally different nature than the "vertical" levels—namely, the latter are universal stages through which individuals pass in a normal course of development, whereas the former are types of personalities that may—or may not—be found at any of the stages.

For example, we saw that cognitive development goes through the stages of sensorimotor, preoperational, and concrete operational, leading up to formal. According to the evidence to date, there are no major exceptions to those stages (see chapter 1). Thus, we can include those stages, and others like them, in any integral psychology with a fair amount of confidence. But we have no such confidence with the horizontal typologies. They simply outline some of the *possible* orientations that may, or may not, be found at any of the stages, and thus their inclusion is based more on personal taste and usefulness than on universal evidence: all individuals do not necessarily fit a particular typology, whereas all individuals do go through the basic waves of consciousness.

This doesn't mean that horizontal typologies are useless; on the contrary, they can be quite helpful for various purposes. The Enneagram, for example, is a sophisticated system that classifies people into nine basic personality types (the reformer, the helper, the motivator, the individualist, the investigator, the loyalist, the enthusiast, the leader, the peacemaker, the reformer).[23] The way to use such typologies is to realize that these nine different types can exist at each of the major levels of consciousness development.

Thus, to use the example of Spiral Dynamics for the vertical levels and the Enneagram for the horizontal, you can have Enneagram type 3 (the motivator) at the purple level, the red level, the blue level, the orange level, the green level, and so on. In this example, nine types at eight levels gives us a typology of seventy-two different personality types—and you can start to see what a truly multidimensional psychology might look like!

But that is simply one example of the multiple waves and streams—and types—that can be found in great River of Life. None of them have the final answer; all of them have something important to tell us.

CONCLUSION TO PART ONE

Waves, streams, and self. In Part One, we have briefly looked at the basic levels or waves of development (matter to body to mind to soul to spirit), the individual lines or streams of development (cognition, morals, identity, worldviews, values, etc.), and the self that navigates them both. We have seen the importance of "transcend and include," and thus the importance of honoring and embracing each and every wave and stream in the Great Nest of Being.

But as we look more carefully at the overall levels of consciousness, we can't help but notice that, with a few exceptions, the vast majority of modern researchers do not include, or even acknowledge, the higher, transpersonal, spiritual levels. Glancing through the charts, which span the entire spectrum, it is striking how many modern researchers stop somewhere around the centaur and vision-logic, and ignore or even deny the transpersonal and transcendental waves of superconscious development.

In premodern times, while it is true that much, or even most, of spirituality was magic, mythic, and prerational, nonetheless the most highly evolved yogis, saints, and sages had access to the transrational, transpersonal, transcendental realms—they embraced, in their own way and in their own terms, the entire Great Nest of Being, subconscious to self-conscious to superconscious. Those very rare souls evidenced not only a capacity for second-tier thinking (as evidenced in their extensive developmental models; see chapter 12), but they also transcended the thinking mind altogether in superconscious and supramental states. And by and large they were supported by the entire culture in their attempts to do so. This is why we say that the *wisdom of premodernity* was embodied in the Great Nest of Being. And even if the *average* individual did not awaken to the higher levels in the Nest, it was clearly understood that these higher potentials were available to any who wished to pursue a path of awakening, liberation, or enlightenment. Premodernity acknowledged these higher, transpersonal, spiritual realms, whereas modernity, for the most part, denies them altogether.

What's going on here? How could something universally widespread at one point in our collective history become resolutely erased at the next? It's a staggering scenario, fully comparable, in its own way, to the extinction of the dinosaurs. The most pervasive notion in human history and prehistory (namely, the existence of some sort of spiritual dimension) was simply pronounced, with the thundering authority of science, put with a zeal that was inversely proportional to its believability, to be a massive collective hallucination. The spiritual dimension, it was solemnly announced, was nothing but a wish-fulfillment of infantile needs (Freud), an opaque ideology for oppressing the masses (Marx), or a projection of human potentials (Feuerbach). Spirituality is thus a deep confusion that apparently plagued humanity for approximately a million years, until just recently, a mere few centuries ago, when modernity pledged allegiance to sensory science, and then promptly decided that the entire world contained nothing but matter, period.

The bleakness of the modern scientific proclamation is chilling. In that extraordinary journey from matter to body to mind to soul to spirit, scientific materialism halted the journey at the very first stage, and proclaimed all subsequent developments to be nothing but arrangements of frisky dirt. Why this dirt would get right up and eventually start writing poetry was not explained. Or rather, it was explained by dumb chance and dumb selection, as if two dumbs would make a Shakespeare. The sensorimotor realm was proclaimed the only real realm, and it soon came to pass that mental health would be defined as adaptation to that "reality." Any consciousness that saw something other than matter was obviously hallucinating.

The only word that can adequately define this cultural catastrophe is "horrifying." Still, if these higher spiritual and transpersonal dimensions are in fact *inherent potentials of the human bodymind*, then even this extensive cultural repression would not be strong enough to cure the soul of wonder or empty it of grace; not strong enough to hide the mystery of transcendence, ecstasy and liberation, radiant God and beloved Goddess.

If there is ever to be a truly integral psychology (or any sort of integral studies), this extraordinary rupture between premodernity and modernity—spiritual and material—needs to be confronted head on. Although there is a slow movement in the modern and postmodern world to reintroduce some sort of spirituality, nonetheless the "official" and most widespread worldview of the modern West is that of scientific materialism. And clearly, we cannot have an integral view of the levels of consciousness if modernity and modern science denies the existence of most of them. "Integral" means, if it means anything, the integration of all that is given to humanity; and if modernity insists instead on trashing everything that came before it, then the integral enterprise is derailed from the start. At the same time, it will do no good, as Romantics wish, to attempt a return to yesteryear, an attempt to "resurrect" the past with a "resurgence of the real," for modernity brought its own important truths and profound insights, which need to be harmonized as well; and yesteryear, full truth be told, just wasn't all that swell.

If we are to move forward to the bright promise of an integral approach, we need a way to honor *both* the strengths and the weaknesses of *both* premodernity and modernity. If we can find a coherent way to honor truths both ancient and modern, a truly integral approach might become more than a passing dream.

PART TWO

PATH

From Premodern to Modern

A TRULY INTEGRAL PSYCHOLOGY would surely wish to include the religious or spiritual dimensions of men and women. And yet, for the most part, the great systems of spirituality—Christianity, Judaism, Islam, Buddhism, Hinduism, Taoism, indigenous religions—are part of the legacy of premodernity. This is not to say that these religions don't exist or have influence in the modern world; only that their roots and foundations were largely laid in premodern times and their worldviews are deeply molded by premodern currents. Further, the actual historical epoch called "modernity" (especially the Enlightenment in the West) specifically defined itself as "antireligion." The scientific empiricism of the Enlightenment often set out to destroy the "superstitions" that, it felt, composed most of the tenets of organized religion.

If an integral psychology truly wishes to embrace the enduring insights of both "religious" premodernity and "scientific" modernity, there needs to be some way to reconcile, in a very general way, their antagonistic stances toward spirituality.

Therefore, in Part Two, we will take a very brief look at the great transition from the premodern to the modern worldviews, attempting to point out that they *both* possessed many strengths and many weaknesses, and that an integral approach might best proceed by taking the enduring insights from both, and jettisoning their limitations. I believe that there is no other way to generate a truly integral approach. Virtually every attempt at an integral model that I have seen suffers from either not appreciating the strengths of the ancient traditions, or not understanding the important contributions of modernity; I will try, as best I can, to outline both.

We will then return, in Part Three, and attempt to pull the pieces together—honoring both premodern and modern—and thus suggesting a constructive postmodern approach to an integral psychology.

5

What Is Modernity?

Something Unheard Of

What specifically did modernity bring into the world that the premodern cultures by and large lacked? What made modernity so substantially *different* from the cultures and epochs that preceded it? Whatever it was, it very likely will be an essential feature of any comprehensive or integral psychology.[1]

There have been many answers offered to the question, What is modernity? Most of them are decidedly negative. Modernity, it is said, marked the death of God, the death of the Goddess, the commodification of life, the leveling of qualitative distinctions, the brutalities of capitalism, the replacement of quality by quantity, the loss of value and meaning, the fragmentation of the lifeworld, existential dread, polluting industrialization, a rampant and vulgar materialism—all of which have often been summarized in the phrase made famous by Max Weber: "the disenchantment of the world."

No doubt there is some truth to all of those claims, and we need to give them sufficient consideration. But clearly there were some immensely positive aspects of modernity as well, for it also gave us the liberal democracies; the ideals of equality, freedom, and justice, regardless of race, class, creed, or gender; modern medicine, physics, biology, and chemistry; the end of slavery; the rise of feminism; and the universal rights of humankind. Those, surely, are a little more noble than the mere "disenchantment of the world."

No, we need a specific definition or description of modernity that allows for all of those factors, both good (such as liberal democracies) and bad (such as the widespread loss of meaning). Various scholars, from Max Weber to Jürgen Habermas, have suggested that what specifically defined modernity was something called "the differentiation of the cultural value spheres," which especially means the differentiation of art, morals, and science. Where previously these spheres tended to be fused, modernity differentiated them and let each proceed at its own pace, with its own dignity, using its own tools, following its own discoveries, unencumbered by intrusions from the other spheres.

This differentiation allowed each sphere to make profound discoveries that, if used wisely, could lead to such "good" results as democracy, the end of slavery, the rise of feminism, and the rapid advances in medical science; but discoveries that, if used unwisely, could just as easily be perverted into the "downsides" of modernity, such as scientific imperialism, the disenchantment of the world, and totalizing schemes of world domination.

The brilliance of this definition of modernity—namely, that it differentiated the value spheres of art, morals, and science—is that it allows us to see the underpinnings of *both* the good news and the bad news of modern times. It allows us to understand both the *dignity* and the *disaster* of modernity.

Premodern cultures certainly possessed art, morals, and science. The point, rather, is that these spheres tended to be relatively "undifferentiated." To give only one example, in the Middle Ages, Galileo could not freely look through his telescope and report the results because art and morals and science were all fused under the Church, and thus the morals of the Church defined what science could—or could not—do. The Bible said (or implied) that the sun went around the earth, and that was the end of the discussion.

But with the differentiation of the value spheres, a Galileo could look through his telescope without fear of being charged with heresy and treason. Science was free to pursue its own truths unencumbered by brutal domination from the other spheres. And likewise with art and morals. Artists could, without fear of punishment, paint nonreligious themes, or even sacrilegious themes, if they wished. And moral theory was likewise free to pursue an inquiry into the good life, whether it agreed with the Bible or not.

For all those reasons and more, these *differentiations* of modernity have also been referred to as the *dignity* of modernity, for these differentiations were in part responsible for the rise of liberal democracy, the end of slavery, the growth of feminism, and the staggering advances in the medical sciences, to name but a few of these many dignities.

The "bad news" of modernity was that these value spheres did not just peacefully separate, they often flew apart completely. The wonderful *differentiations* of modernity went too far into actual *dissociation*, fragmentation, alienation. The dignity became a disaster. The growth became a cancer. As the value spheres began to dissociate, this allowed a powerful and aggressive science to begin to invade and dominate the other spheres, crowding art and morals out of any serious consideration in approaching "reality." Science became *scientism*—scientific materialism and scientific imperialism—which soon became the dominant "official" worldview of modernity.

It was this scientific materialism that very soon pronounced the other value spheres to be worthless, "not scientific," illusory, or worse. And for precisely that reason, it was scientific materialism that *pronounced the Great Nest of Being to be nonexistent.*

According to scientific materialism, the Great Nest of matter, body, mind, soul, and spirit could be thoroughly reduced to *systems of matter alone*; and matter—or matter/energy—whether in the material brain or material process systems—would account for all of reality, without remainder. Gone was mind and gone was soul and gone was spirit—gone, in fact, was the entire Great Chain, except for its pitiful bottom rung—and in its place, as Whitehead famously lamented, there was reality as "a dull affair, soundless, scentless, colorless; merely the hurrying of material, endlessly, meaninglessly." (To which he added, "Thereby, modern philosophy has been ruined.")

And so it came about that the modern West was the first major civilization in the history of the human race to deny substantial reality to the Great Nest of Being. And it is into this massive denial that we wish to attempt to reintroduce consciousness, the within, the deep, the spiritual, and thus move gently toward a more integral embrace.

The Four Quadrants

There is, I believe, a simple way to understand this scientific reductionism—and a simple way to reverse it.

As I was comparing and contrasting the many systems listed in the charts, I noticed that, virtually without exception, they fell into four general classes. It eventually became apparent that these four classes represented the interior and the exterior of the individual and the collective, as can be seen in figure 5. The upper half of the diagram is individual, the lower half is communal or collective; the left half is interior (subjective, consciousness), and the right half is exterior (objective, material).

Thus, the Upper-Left quadrant represents the *interior of the individual*, the subjective aspect of consciousness, or individual awareness, which I have represented with the cognitive line, leading up to vision-logic. (Fig. 5 represents developments, starting with the Big Bang, up to today's average mode of consciousness; it does not cover transpersonal developments, which we will discuss in more detail later.) The full Upper-Left quadrant includes the entire spectrum of consciousness as it

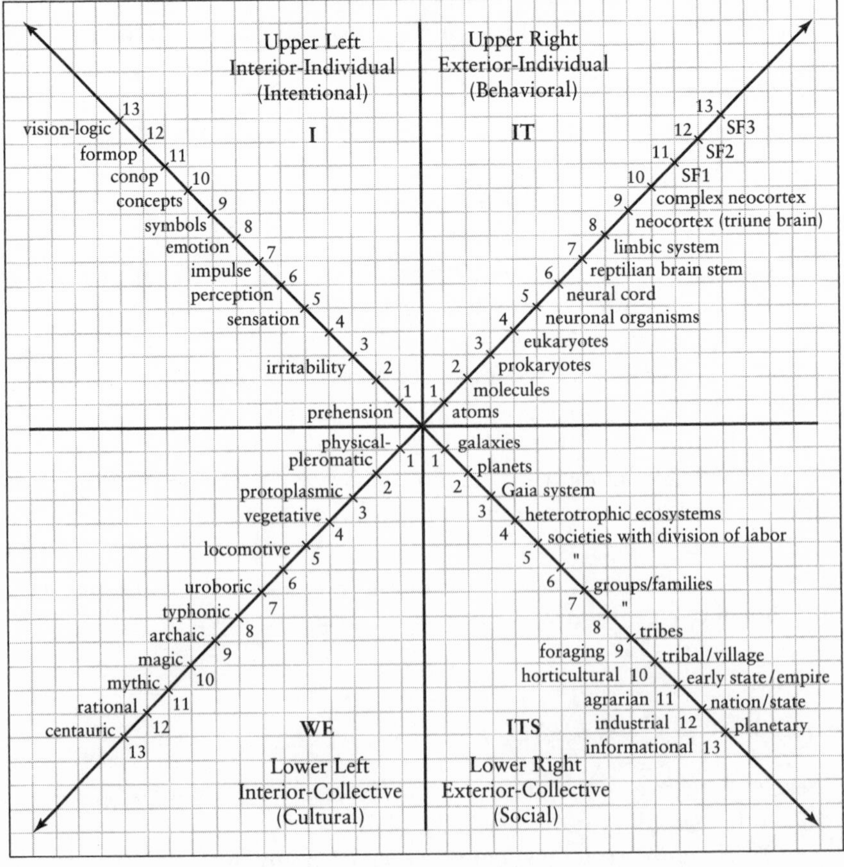

FIGURE 5. *The Four Quadrants*

appears in any individual, from bodily sensations to mental ideas to soul and spirit. The integral psychograph is a graph of this quadrant. *The language of this quadrant is I-language*: first-person accounts of the inner stream of consciousness. This is also the home of aesthetics, or the beauty that is in the "I" of the beholder.

The Upper-Right quadrant represents the *objective or exterior correlates* of those interior states of consciousness. Without worrying at the moment about the exact relation of interior mind and objective brain, we can simply note that the two are, at the least, intimately correlated. Thus, as you can see on figure 5, simple cells (prokaryotes and eukaryotes) already show "irritability," or an active response to stimuli. Neuronal organisms possess sensation and perception; a reptilian brain stem adds the capacity for impulses and instinctual behavior; a limbic system adds emotions and certain rudimentary but powerful feelings; a neocortex further adds the capacities to form symbols and concepts, and so on. (SF1, SF2, and SF3 represent higher structure-functions of the brain correlated with higher cognitions, as we will see). Researchers that study this quadrant focus on brain mechanisms, neurotransmitters, and organic computations that support consciousness (neurophysiology, cognitive science, biological psychiatry, etc.). *The language of this quadrant is it-language*: third-person or objective accounts of the scientific facts about the individual organism.

But individuals never exist alone; every being is a being-in-the-world. Individuals are always part of some collective, and there are the "insides" of a collective and the "outsides." These are indicated in the Lower-Left and Lower-Right quadrants, respectively. The Lower Left represents the *inside of the collective*, or the values, meanings, worldviews, and ethics that are shared by any group of individuals. In figure 5 I have represented all of these with *worldviews,* such as magic, mythic, and rational (which we will discuss later). *The language of this quadrant is we-language*: second-person or I-thou language, which involves mutual understanding, justness, and goodness—in short, how you and I will arrange to get along together. This is the *cultural* quadrant.

But culture does not hang disembodied in midair. Just as individual consciousness is anchored in objective, material forms (such as the brain), so all cultural components are anchored in exterior, material, institutional forms. These *social* systems include material institutions, geopolitical formations, and the forces of production (ranging from foraging to horticultural to agrarian to industrial to informational). Because these are objective phenomena, *the language of this quadrant, like that of the objective individual, is it-language.*

Since both the Upper-Right and Lower-Right quadrants are objective "its," they can be treated as one general domain, and this means that the four quadrants can be summarized as the "Big Three" of I, we, and it. Or the aesthetics of "I," the morals of "we," and the "its" of science. The Beautiful, the Good, and the True; first-person, second-person, and third-person accounts; self, culture, and nature; art, morals, and science.[2]

In other words, the four quadrants (or simply the Big Three) are actually *the underpinnings of the modern differentiation of the value spheres* of art, morals, and science. Where premodernity had tended to fuse, or not clearly differentiate, the Big Three, modernity clearly differentiated them and set each free to pursue its own path. This differentiation was part of the dignity of modernity, which, in allowing each domain to pursue its own truths, allowed each to make stunning and far-reaching discoveries, discoveries that, even the harshest critics agree, set modernity apart from premodernity.

But something else set modernity apart. The differentiation of the Big Three went too far into the dissociation of the Big Three: the dignity drifted into disaster, and this allowed an imperialistic science to dominate the other spheres and claim that they possessed no inherent reality of their own (scientism, scientific materialism, one-dimensional man, the disenchantment of the world). Gone was mind and soul and spirit, and in their place, as far as the eye could see, the unending dreariness of a world of its: "a dull affair, soundless, scentless, colorless; merely the hurrying of material, endlessly, meaninglessly."

And so it came about that virtually the entire spectrum of consciousness, and certainly its higher levels (soul and spirit), were reduced to permutations and combinations of matter and bodies. Put bluntly, all "I's" and "we's" were reduced to "its," to objects of the scientific gaze, which, no matter how long or hard it looked, could find nothing resembling the Great Nest of human possibilities, but saw only endless patterns of process its, scurrying here and there.

CONCLUSION: THE INTEGRAL TASK

Thus, it seems that premodernity had at least one great strength that modernity lacked: it recognized the entire Great Nest of Being, which is basically a general map of higher human potentials. But premodernity also had at least one great weakness: it did not fully differentiate the value spheres at any of the levels in the Great Nest. Thus, among other things, objective-scientific investigation of the spectrum was hampered; the specific and often local cultural expressions of the Great Nest were taken to be universally valid; and the moral injunctions recommended to all were tied to those limited cultural expressions. Giordano Bruno might have experienced many of the upper levels of the Great Nest, but because the value spheres were not fully differentiated at large and their individual freedoms were not protected by law and custom, the Inquisition cheerfully burned him at the stake.

Modernity, on the other hand, did manage to differentiate the Big Three of art, morals, and science, on a large scale, so that each began to make phenomenal discoveries. But as the Big Three dissociated, and scientific colonialism began its aggressive career, all "I's" and all "we's" were reduced to patterns of objective "its," and thus all the interior stages of consciousness—reaching from body to mind to soul to spirit—were summarily dismissed as so much superstitious nonsense. The Great Nest collapsed into scientific materialism—into what we will be calling "flatland"—and there the modern world, by and large, still remains.

Our job, it thus appears, is to take the strengths of both premodernity and modernity, and jettison their weaknesses.

6

To Integrate Premodern and Modern

ONE OF OUR AIMS is to integrate the enduring truths of premodern and modern approaches to psychology and consciousness. We have seen that the essence of the premodern worldview is the Great Nest of Being, and the essence of modernity is the differentiation of the value spheres of art, morals, and science. Thus, in order to integrate premodern and modern, we need to *integrate the Great Nest with the differentiations of modernity*. This means that each of the levels in the traditional Great Nest needs to be carefully differentiated according to the four quadrants. To do so would honor *both* the core claim of ancient spirituality—namely, the Great Nest—and the core claim of modernity—namely, the differentiation of the value spheres. And this would offer a foundation that might help us move toward a more integral psychology.

This can be represented, in a very simplistic fashion, as in figure 6, where I have differentiated each of the levels in the Great Nest according to the four quadrants. Modern science has already provided us with an impressive description of the evolution or development of the Right-Hand quadrants—atoms to molecules to cells to organisms, foraging to agrarian to industrial to informational. And in our own discussion we have seen numerous examples of the evolution or development in the interior quadrants—the waves, streams, worldviews, morals, and so forth.

But, *unlike modernity*, we wish to include *all* of the levels in the four quadrants, reaching from body to mind to soul to spirit (and not simply deny the higher levels). And, *unlike premodernity*, we wish to include *all*

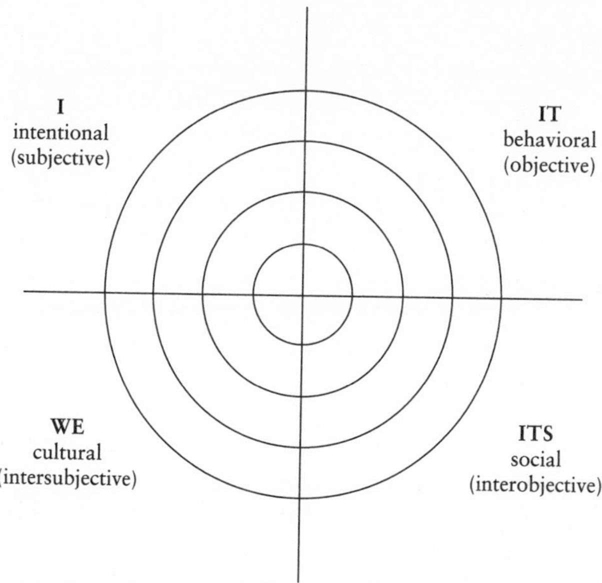

FIGURE 6. *The Great Nest with the Four Quadrants*

of the quadrants at each of those levels (and not fuse them indiscriminately).

Thus, the job of an integral psychology (as a subset of integral studies) is to *coordinate and integrate the research findings in all of the levels in all of the quadrants*. Integral psychology obviously focuses on the Upper-Left quadrant, but the whole point of the integral approach is that for a full understanding of this quadrant, it needs to be seen in the context of all the others. This "all-level, all-quadrant" integration was denied to premodernity (which was all-level but not all-quadrant) and denied to modernity (which was all-quadrant but not all-level). Those two grave inadequacies deserve a closer look.

Premodernity at Its Best: All-Level

The traditional Great Chain dealt almost exclusively with the Upper-Left quadrant, or the spectrum of consciousness as it appears in individual men and women (body to mind to soul to spirit). Although the Great Chain also referred to ontological spheres (or levels) of reality, those spheres were not clearly differentiated into the four quadrants, at least not on a wide scale. Thus, there was little or no understanding of the way in which consciousness is correlated with brain states, neurophysiology, and neurotransmitters (not reducible to brain states, but not purely "transcending" them, either). There was little or no understanding of how a person's view of the world—and a person's experience of the spectrum of consciousness—is profoundly colored and molded by the background cultural contexts in which the person lives. There was little or no understanding of how the material mode of production (foraging, horticultural, agrarian, industrial, informational) deeply affects the contours of an individual's consciousness and dramatically alters everything from gender roles to suicide rates to eating habits.

The traditional Great Chain, in short, focused mostly on the Upper-Left quadrant and almost totally ignored the differentiated details of the other quadrants, from objective brain states to intersubjective cultural contexts to interobjective social forces. It thus was a great, massive, *static* system, not yet clearly understood according to the differentiation of pluralistic cultural contexts, and their further integration into globally evolving systems—an understanding provided by modernity and postmodernity (as we will further see in chapter 12).[1] A Plotinus might personally develop and evolve all the way up the Great Chain, but the detailed correlations with the other quadrants were simply not well understood (precisely because they were not well differentiated at large).In particular, the Upper-Right quadrant (the material organism), because it is material, was placed by the perennial philosophers on the very lowest rung in the Great Chain (matter), thus failing to see that material forms are related to conscious states as exterior and interior, not merely lower and higher. Traditionally, every level above matter was usually viewed as "transcendent" to matter, *totally beyond it*, existing either in some sort of heaven or in some nonearthly estate, and this gave the Great Chain its largely "otherworldly" feel. Instead of seeing that the evolution of consciousness involves, on the *interior*, an increase in the *quality* of consciousness, and on the *exterior*, an increase in the *complexity* of matter (so that the human brain has more neural connections than there are stars in the universe: as the most complex piece of matter in existence, it is correlated with the highest degree of consciousness in the Kosmos)—instead of understanding that intimate correlation, with spirit being *interior* to nature, not perched on top of nature, the traditional Great Chain invited a rejection and devaluing of *this* world.

Moreover, when modern science discovered some of these intimate relations between "transcendent consciousness" and "material brain," the traditional Great Chain took a colossal hit from which it never recovered. If "otherworldly consciousness" is actually correlated with "this-worldly organism," might not all so-called metaphysical realities actually be aspects of *this* world? Do we even need any of those "spiritual" realities at all? Isn't everything given right here, to be seen with our senses, scientifically sharpened? In fact, isn't the belief in any sort of spiritual realities the way that men and women project their own potentials and thus remain alienated from themselves? Isn't religion nothing but the opiate of the masses?

In short, the strength of the traditional Great Chain was that it was admirably all-level, stretching from matter to body to mind to soul to spirit. But because it was not all-quadrant, it was ill-prepared to cope with modernity, and in fact was one of the first great casualties of the modern gaze.

Modernity at Its Best: All-Quadrant

The rise of modernity, I suggested, was marked by two profound events, one of which was wonderful and one of which was wretched. The good news: modernity managed, for the first time on a large scale, to fully differentiate the four quadrants (or simply the Big Three of art, morals, and science), which contributed to the many dignities of modernity.

And dignities they were. The differentiation of "I" and "we" meant that the individual I would no longer be merely subservient to the collective We (church, state, monarchy, herd mentality): the universal rights of man were everywhere proclaimed, which eventually led to the liberation movements from abolition to feminism. The differentiation of "I" and "it" meant that objective reality could no longer crush individual choice and taste, which, among other things, freed art from representation. The differentiation of "we" and "it" meant that science's investigation of objective truth was no longer subservient to dictates of church or state, which contributed to the stunning discoveries in physics, medicine, biology, and technology that, within the span of a mere few centuries, would, among other things, extend average lifespan around the world a staggering several decades. Truly, the differentiation of the value spheres allowed each to make colossal advancements previously undreamed of.

And thus we say that modernity at its best was all-quadrant. But it was not, alas, all-level, because, almost from the start, the major philosophers of the Enlightenment were committed to what we would recognize as an empirical-scientific outlook, in any of its many forms:

sensationalism, empiricism, naturalism, realism, materialism. And there was good reason for this empirical slant. If you look at figure 5, notice that all of the Left-Hand realities have Right-Hand correlates. Interior feelings, for examples, do have some sort of correlate in the objective limbic system. Formal operational thinking does seem to go with a neocortex, and so on. Thus, instead of trying to investigate the interior domains—which, after all, can be very slippery to pin down—let us focus our attention on the Right-Hand world of empirical, sensorimotor realities, from material objects to concrete social institutions to brain states. Those all have simple location; they can been seen with the senses or their extensions; they are all subject to quantification and measurement; they are therefore ideally suited to the scientific method, or some sort of controlled, objective, empirical investigation.

And that is exactly what the Enlightenment—and official modernity—set out to do. But the inherent downsides of this approach are perhaps obvious: it is all too easy to go from saying that all interior states have exterior, objective, material correlates, to saying that all interior states are nothing but material objects. In its understandable zeal to correlate all otherworldly "metaphysical" realities with this-worldly "empirical" realities (a legitimate agenda, since all Left-Hand events do indeed have Right-Hand correlates, as you can see in fig. 5), modernity inadvertently collapsed all interiors into exteriors (a disaster of the first magnitude). All subjective truths (from introspection to art to consciousness to beauty) and all intersubjective truths (from morals to justice to substantive values) were collapsed into exterior, empirical, sensorimotor occasions. Collapsed, that is, into dirt. Literally. The great nightmare of scientific materialism was upon us (Whitehead), the nightmare of one-dimensional man (Marcuse), the disqualified universe (Mumford), the colonization of art and morals by science (Habermas), the disenchantment of the world (Weber)—a nightmare I have also called flatland.

FLATLAND

Flatland is simply the belief that *only the Right-Hand world is real*—the world of matter/energy, empirically investigated by the human senses and their extensions (telescopes, microscopes, photographic plates, etc.). All of the interior worlds are reduced to, or explained by, objective/exterior terms.

There are two major forms of this flatland belief: subtle reductionism and gross reductionism. *Subtle reductionism* reduces all Left-Hand interiors to the Lower-Right quadrant; that is, reduces all "I's" and all "we's" to systems of interwoven "its" (systems theory is the classic example). *Gross reductionism* goes one step further and reduces all material systems to material atoms.

Contrary to what many popular Romantic writers have claimed, the thinkers of the Enlightenment were predominantly subtle reductionists, not gross reductionists. They believed, as scholars from Arthur Lovejoy to Charles Taylor have demonstrated, in "the great Universal System" of nature, a systems view of reality if ever there was one—but a systems view that allowed *only Right-Hand realities*.[2] The "crime of the Enlightenment" was not its gross reductionism (although there was plenty of that, as there has been ever since Democritus of Abdera), but rather its persuasive subtle reductionism, which gutted the interior dimensions and laid them out to dry in the blazing sun of scientific materialism and exterior holism: I's and we's were reduced to systems of its. As Foucault summarized the nightmare: men and women were seen as "objects of information, never subjects in communication." That subtle reductionism was applied to the interior dimensions of reality (such as soul and spirit), whereupon they promptly disappeared from view.

The many pop writers who claim that the major crime of the Enlightenment was gross reductionism and atomism, then claim that the cure for the Western flatland is *systems theory*, fail to see that systems theory is precisely part of the disease we are trying to overcome. Systems theory simply offers us holistic its instead of atomistic its, whereas both of those need to be integrated with the interior domains of the I and the we—the domains of consciousness and culture, aesthetics and morals, appreciated in their own terms. Dynamical systems theory, in all its many forms, is simply the Lower-Right quadrant, whereas we need all four quadrants without privileging any.

Thus, it is still quite common to hear statements such as: "Recently the ecologist C. S. Holling has discussed the conflict between 'two streams of science' and the confusion it creates for politicians and the public. One stream is experimental, reductionistic, and narrowly disciplinary. It is familiar to us as the scientific ideal. The less familiar stream is interdisciplinary, integrative, historical, analytical, comparative, and experimental at appropriate scales. Examples given of the first form are molecular biology and genetic engineering. The second form is found in evolutionary biology and systems approaches in populations, ecosystems, landscapes, and global systems. One stream is a science of parts, the other a science of the integration of parts."

And both are a science of flatland.

I am not saying systems theory is unimportant; I am saying it is true but partial, and being partial, it is not a genuine holism, but merely an exterior/objectivistic holism, which needs desperately a supplement of the soul to be fully complete—needs, that is, the entire interior dimensions as disclosed *in their own terms,* by their own methods, with their own truths, in their own way. So in our quest for an integral holism (which includes both the interior holism of I and we and the exterior holism of it and its), we want to *honor all four quadrants,* and not merely privilege one of them in a reductionism blatant or subtle.

In short, modernity heroically managed to differentiate the cultural value spheres (or the four quadrants)—so that, at its best, modernity was indeed all-quadrant, and that enduring contribution we can certainly honor. But then, instead of moving forward to integrate them, modernity all too often allowed that important and necessary *differentiation* to fall into unnecessary and pathological *dissociation*: art and morals and science fragmented, and this allowed an aggressive science to colonize and dominate the other spheres, so that, in "official reality," nothing was ultimately true except the truths of science, and the truths of science were all about frisky dirt. The entire interior and subjective realms—*including the entire Great Nest of Being and all of its levels, body to mind to soul to spirit*—were all rudely collapsed into their sensorimotor correlates, which is to say, they were murdered. Strained through the mesh of the monological gaze, shredded to fit the monochrome madness, all interior and subjective states—from feeling to intuition to states of consciousness to superconscious illumination—were pronounced epiphenomena at best, hallucinations at worst, and the modern world settled back, triumphant in its conquering stance, to fashion a life of dust and dirt, shadows and surfaces, scientific facts and valueless veneers.

Conclusion

What is required, then, if we can speak in extremely bold generalizations, is to take the enduring truths of the perennial traditions (namely, the Great Nest of Being), and combine that with the good news of modernity (namely, the differentiation of the value spheres), which means that each and every level of the Great Chain is differentiated into at least four dimensions: subjective or intentional, objective or behavioral, intersubjective or cultural, and interobjective or social—each with its own independent validity claims and equally honored forms of truth, from science to aesthetics to morals, as suggested in figure 6 (and simplified in fig. 7). This would take the best of ancient wisdom and integrate it with the best of modernity, while avoiding the downside of the ancient outlook (its lack of differentiation, pluralism, and contextualism) and the downside of modernity (its catastrophic collapse into flatland).[3]

And *that* marriage would allow us to move forward to the bright promise of a *constructive postmodernity*: the integration of art, morals, and science, at every level of the extraordinary spectrum of consciousness, body to mind to soul to spirit. That integration, I am suggesting, would involve the very best of premodernity (which was all-level), the best of modernity (which was all-quadrant), and the best of postmodernity (which, as we will see, involves their integration)—"all-level, all-quadrant."

It is toward just such an integral model that we can now turn.

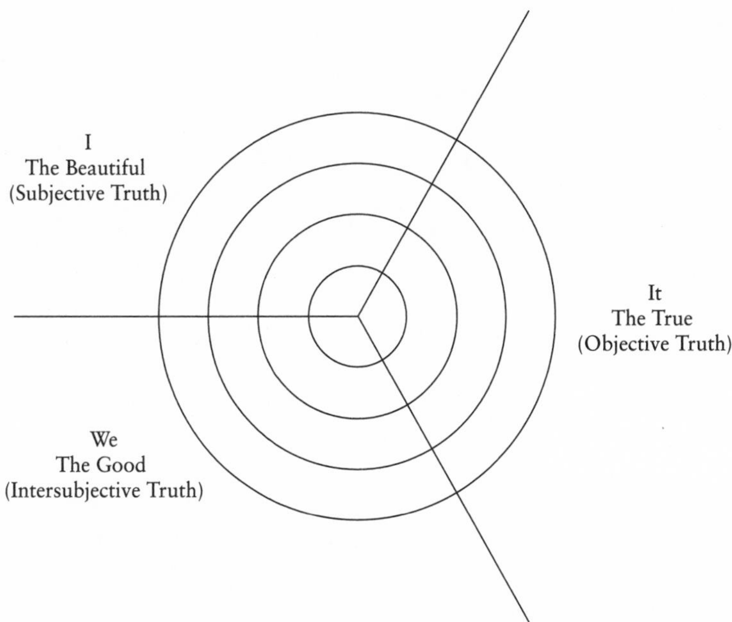

FIGURE 7. *Levels of the Good, the True, and the Beautiful*

7

Some Important Modern Pioneers

Introduction to an Integral Approach

An integral approach to the Kosmos would be free to investigate the many levels and lines in all of the quadrants, without attempting unwarrantedly to reduce any of them to the others.

If you look at figure 5, notice that all of the entities or holons in the Right-Hand quadrants possess *simple location*. You can see all of them with your senses (or their extensions). You can see rocks, villages, organisms, ecosystems, planets, and so on. But *none of the holons in the Left-Hand quadrants possess simple location*. You cannot see, running around in the exterior world, any feelings, concepts, states of consciousness, interior illuminations, cultural values, and so forth. None of those exist in physical or sensorimotor space. They exist in emotional space, conceptual space, spiritual space, the space of mutual understanding, the space of shared values and meanings, and so forth. Although those have correlates in the objective, physical world, they cannot be *reduced* to those correlates without completely destroying their own intrinsic contours.

When it comes to individual subjective consciousness (such as waves, streams, and states), their physical correlates (from brainwaves to neurotransmitters) all exist in sensorimotor space, and thus they can be arranged in hierarchies that emphasize *quantity* or size (organisms are bigger than cells, which are bigger than molecules, which are bigger than atoms). These Right-Hand hierarchies are not hierarchies of value—cells are not better than molecules, atoms are not better than quarks—but merely hierarchies of size and physical enclosure. But the subjective, interior, or Left-Hand correlates all exist in inner spaces that unfold in hierarchies of *quality* (compassion is *better* than murder; love is *better* than hate; postconventional is better than conventional which is better than preconventional, in terms of the moral depth and care extended to others).

Thus, an integral approach allows us to map the exterior correlates of interior states, without attempting to reduce one to the other. After all, compassion might be morally better than hatred, but serotonin is *not* better than dopamine; and thus if we reduce consciousness to neurotransmitters, we completely lose all value and meaning. In other words, we fall into flatland, where all Left-Hand meaning and significance are collapsed into valueless facts and meaningless surfaces—"a dull affair, soundless, scentless, colorless; merely the hurrying of material, endlessly, meaninglessly."

An integral approach, then, does not wish to reduce I and We to systems of interwoven Its. An integral approach does not wish to commit subtle reductionism; it does not wish to reduce interior holism to exterior holism (both rather includes them both). It does not reduce all art, beauty, morals, and consciousness to a flatland system of processes, data bits, neurotransmitters, a web of life, or any other system of holistic objects. It wishes to include, in a nonreductionistic fashion, the interior domains of subjective and intersubjective waves and streams and states, spanning body to mind to soul to spirit, even though the latter all have objective correlates of various sorts that can (and should) be approached in third-person, scientific, it-language terms.

You can see some of these important correlations in figure 8. The interior waves of the full spectrum of consciousness, as they appear in an individual—from body (feelings) to mind (ideas) to soul (luminosity) to spirit (all-pervading)—are listed in the Upper-Left quadrant. These cannot be reduced to material dimensions (because, unlike matter, they do not possess simple location). Nonetheless, feelings, mental ideas, and spiritual illuminations *all have physical correlates* that can be measured by various scientific means, from EEG machines to blood chemistry to PET scans to galvanic skin response. These physical correlates are represented by dotted lines on the Right-Hand quadrants.[1]

Thus, for example, certain archaic behavioral impulses have correlates in the reptilian brain stem. Various emotional states and feelings have correlates in states of limbic system arousal. Conceptual thinking

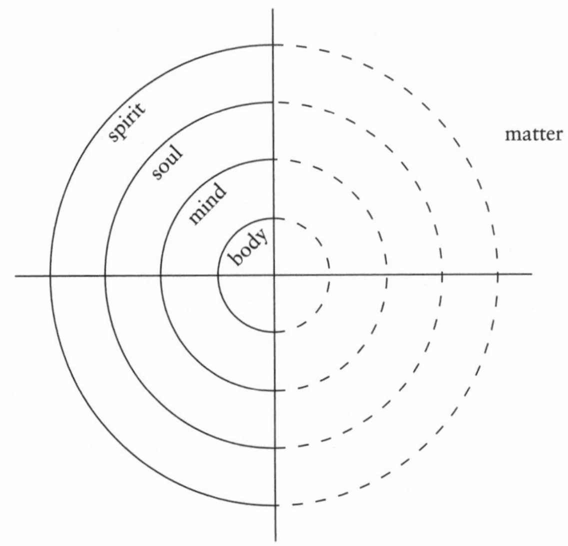

FIGURE 8. *Correlations of Interior (Consciousness) States with Exterior (Material) States*

shows activity particularly in the frontal cortex. Various meditative states show pronounced changes in brainwave patterns (e.g., high amplitude theta and delta waves, hemispheric synchronization, etc.).[2] From bodily feelings to mental ideas to spiritual illuminations (Left Hand), there are at least some physical correlates (Right Hand) for all of the states and stages of consciousness evolution.

And why don't we simply go all the way and say that consciousness is therefore nothing but a byproduct of complex brain structures, connectionist systems, digital processes, computational biocircuits, or some such? Because none of those Right-Hand correlates have any value gradations, which are the essence of the Left-Hand domains themselves.

For example, different brainwave patterns can be registered by an EEG machine; but nothing on the machine says that one pattern is *better* than another, only that they are *different*. Thus, ethnocentric prejudice and worldcentric fairness will both register brainwave patterns on the EEG machine; but nothing on the machine says, or can say, that one of those brainwaves is better, or more valuable, or more beautiful than another. None of those value gradations show up, or can show up, on the machine registering the Right-Hand correlates, because in the Right-Hand world you only have gradations of size and simple location, not gradations of value, depth, and meaning.

Thus, to the extent that we reduce states of consciousness to brain states, we lose all values. We end up in the disqualified universe. If we reduce joy to serotonin and morals to dopamine, if we reduce consciousness to neuronal pathways and awareness to connectionist systems, we completely erase value, meaning, depth, and Divinity from the face of the Kosmos itself: we fall into flatland, we fall into subtle reductionism.[3]

(You can see a schematic representation of flatland in fig. 13 on page 614. All the interior domains of the I and we have been reduced to their corresponding its, leaving the mind dangling in midair, with no understanding of how it is related to the external world and to its own organic roots—the infamous "mind-body" problem that we will investigate in chapter 14.)

The *realities* of the Left-Hand domains—from stages of consciousness development to degrees of moral growth—are all discovered, not by looking carefully at any exterior objects, but by investigating the interior domains themselves, whereupon it becomes obvious (as research into these domains shows) that some levels and stages of growth are better, higher, deeper, more encompassing, and more liberating—moving from egocentric to sociocentric to worldcentric—and although all of those interior waves have exterior correlates in organic brain functions (which can and should be studied), they cannot be reduced to those correlates without completely destroying the very factors that define them.

Thus, let us honor the differentiations (and dignity) of modernity, without falling into the dissociations (and disaster) of modernity. Thanks to the differentiations of modernity, we can investigate any structure or state of consciousness using first-person (Upper-Left), second-person (Lower-Left), *and* third-person (Right-Hand) approaches, honoring the Big Three on every level (body to mind to soul to spirit), as indicated in figure 8. We can, for example, investigate meditative states using first-person or phenomenal accounts (the accounts of those actually doing the meditating), while also investigating any effects meditation has on brainwave activity, blood chemistry, immune functions, and neurophysiology. We can examine the ways in which various cultural backgrounds, linguistic practices, and ethical systems affect meditative states; and the types of social institutions and practices that are most conducive to those states. We can, in short, adopt an "all-quadrant, all-level" approach.[4]

Exemplars

What I would like to do in this section is introduce several modern pioneers in an integral approach, an approach that, in important ways, attempts to be "all-quadrant, all-level." What all of these pioneers have in common is that they were fully cognizant of the important differentiations of modernity, and therefore they were increasingly aware of the ways in which science could supplement (not replace) religion, spirituality, and psychology. All of them, as we will see, used modern discoveries in the Big Three to elucidate the Great Nest. (All of them, in other words, were offering important elaborations of fig. 7.)

Early modern pioneers of an integral approach abound, such as Goethe, Schelling, Hegel, Fechner, and James. The early pioneers increasingly had access to scientific data on evolution, and thus increasingly understood something about the Great Nest that the premodern pioneers usually did not: it shows development not just in individuals, but in the species; not just ontogenetically, but phylogenetically. In this century, although pioneers also abound—from Steiner to Whitehead to Gebser—I would like particularly to mention James Mark Baldwin, Jürgen Habermas, Sri Aurobindo, and Abraham Maslow.

James Mark Baldwin

Of the four, James Mark Baldwin (1861–1934) is the most pivotal, and history might well find him to be America's greatest psychologist. A contemporary of James and Peirce, Baldwin forged an integral psychology and philosophy that is only now being recognized for its scope and profundity. He was the first great developmental psychologist in modern history; he was the first to clearly define a stage of development; he sought to integrate introspective phenomenology with scientific evolutionary epistemology; he believed that the three great modes of experience were aesthetic, moral, and scientific (the Big Three!), and he proposed *detailed developmental stages in each of those domains* (in other words, he was one of the first to trace development in all quadrants); he was also one of the first to outline stages of religious development. His cognitive developmental scheme was taken up by Piaget and Kohlberg; his studies on dialogical interaction were furthered by Dewey and Mead; his evolutionary epistemology was embraced by Karl Popper and Donald Campbell; his influence, in short, is almost impossible to overestimate. The only reason his name is a not a household word is that, shortly after his death, the positivist and behaviorist schools would raise flatland to a dogmatic belief, and integral studies of any sort were scrubbed from the curriculum.

Baldwin went through three main phases in his own development:

mental philosophy (of the Scottish school), evolutionary psychology, and developmental epistemology. In all of this, he was determined to include and equally honor the scientific, the moral, and the aesthetic, without trying to reduce any of them to the others or privilege any of them unwarrantedly. He included what he called "the metaphysic of intuition, the ontology of introspection" (i.e., the very real realities of the Left-Hand domains), along with a rigorous commitment to scientific experimentation. He at first found that the philosophy of Spinoza could best accommodate this integration, since Spinoza equally honored the interior/mental and the exterior/bodily; but it was the static nature of Spinoza's system that rendered it incapable of coming to grips with evolution. Baldwin came to the conclusion that "no consistent view of mental development in the individual could possibly be reached without a doctrine of the . . . development of consciousness."[5] Moreover, this developmental view had to be constructed without a retreat to mere empiricism, which badly misconstrues mental structures. Baldwin: "The older view of the soul was of a fixed substance, with fixed attributes. . . . The genetic [developmental] idea reverses all this. Instead of a fixed substance, we have the conception of a growing, developing activity. Functional psychology succeeds faculty psychology."[6] Baldwin made a deep study of the German Idealists, and found further evidence of the importance of a developmental approach.

Baldwin began this second phase (evolutionary psychology) with a reassessment of the research tools necessary: "How can the development of the mental order of phenomena be fruitfully investigated? The quantitative method, brought over into psychology from the exact sciences, must be discarded; for its ideal consisted in reducing the more complex to the more simple, the whole to its parts, the later-evolved to the earlier-existent, thus denying or eliminating just the factor which constituted or revealed what was truly genetic [developmental]."[7] Baldwin added to scientific investigation the tools of philosophical epistemology, or an analysis of the types of structures that could be empirically investigated, and this eventually lead to his third phase, developmental epistemology (represented in his acknowledged classic, *Thought and Things: A Study of the Development and Meaning of Thought, or Genetic Logic*).

Baldwin came to see consciousness as developing through a half-dozen qualitatively distinct stages or levels of consciousness (see chart 11), each of which hierarchically differentiates and reintegrates the lower elements on a higher level: the *prelogical* (similar to sensorimotor), the *quasilogical* (preop and early conop), the *logical* (formop), the *extralogical* (vision-logic), and finally, the *hyperlogical*, which we might call supralogical or translogical, for it represents a satori-like nondual awareness that transcends the subject and object dualism. This highest stage, as Baldwin put it, is "a form of contemplation . . . in which the immediacy of experience constantly seeks to reestablish itself. In the highest form of such contemplation, a form which comes to itself as genuine and profound aesthetic experience, we find a synthesis of motives, a mode in which the strands of the earlier and diverging dualisms are merged and fused . . . an experience whose essential character is just its unity of comprehension, [wherein] consciousness has its completest and most direct and final apprehension of what reality is and means."[8] This experience is of waking reality as a whole, immediately apprehended (what we would recognize as psychic-level cosmic consciousness, or union with the entire empirical world: "nature mysticism"). As Baldwin often pointed out, in this unity consciousness, all of the dualisms that were created during development (such as inner/outer, mind/body, subject/object, true/false, and good/bad) are transcended and united in an experience of completeness. And he stressed that this was hyperlogical, not prelogical. Through those half-dozen or so basic levels of consciousness, Baldwin traced the lines and stages of moral, aesthetic, religious, scientific, and self development.

In its general completeness, it was an integral psychology and philosophy the likes of which have rarely been equaled. Others, such as Aurobindo, would grasp the many stages of spiritual development with greater precision (what Baldwin called "hyperlogical" actually consists of at least four distinct levels of consciousness); others would display a more powerfully philosophical mind (Habermas, for example); still others would make more contributions to an experimental psychology. But few combined all of them with the rigor, depth, and breadth of Baldwin.

Baldwin's influence, as I said, was considerable. His stage-by-stage account of the dialectical development of self and other (in all three major domains—moral, aesthetic, scientific) had a major impact on the social sciences. Kohlberg's account is typical: "As I read more deeply into Baldwin, I realized that Piaget had derived all the basic ideas with which he started in the twenties from Baldwin: assimilation, accommodation, schema, and adualism, 'egocentricity,' or undifferentiated character of the child's mind. I saw, too, that Piaget's overall enterprise, the creation of a genetic epistemology and ethics which would use epistemology to pose problems for developmental psychology and use developmental observation to help answer epistemological questions, had also been Baldwin's."[9] But unlike Piaget, Baldwin's genius was his integral vision: he refused to reduce all development to cognitive development, which is why, as an overall system, Baldwin's is much more credible and enduring, as John Broughton and others have pointed out.

In moral development, psychologists and sociologists were generally agreed, by the early 1900s, that moralization proceeds through three broad stages. As McDougall put it in 1908: "The fundamental problem of social psychology is the moralization of the individual by society. This moralization proceeds through, first, the stage in which the operation of the instinctive impulses is modified by the influence of rewards and punishments; second, the stage in which conduct is controlled in the main by anticipation of social praise and blame; and third, the stage in which conduct is regulated by an ideal that enables man to act in a way that seems right to him, regardless of the praise or blame of his immediate environment."[10] These are, of course, the three broad stages now most often known as preconventional, conventional, and postconventional. As Kohlberg points out, "The Dewey-McDougall levels [just outlined] are described from the standpoint of the relation of the self to society. They do not clearly reflect the child's qualitative cognitive and epistemological growth. Our data suggested that Baldwin's three-level distinctions [adual, dualistic, and ethical] defined 'stages' (or sublevels) in the basic series, preconventional, conventional, and postconventional (autonomous-ethical)."[11] In other words, by also using Baldwin's developmental levels, Kohlberg was able to suggest a six-stage scheme of moral development, a scheme that research so far has found to be largely invariant and universal.[12]

Baldwin also presented one of the first, and still one of the most sophisticated, accounts of the stages of religious development. In order to do so, Baldwin had first to argue (successfully, I believe) that religious or spiritual interests were an independent domain, not reducible to economic, scientific, or moral interests. Rather, "Religious motivations stand alongside theoretical, moral, and aesthetic interests as one of the irreducible and, when properly understood, ubiquitous motivations of persons."[13] This pioneering line of research was later taken up most notably by James Fowler.

Perhaps most interesting of all is the fact that Baldwin saw consciousness development leading to, and culminating in, an experience of a type of profound unity consciousness, which was for Baldwin a supremely aesthetic experience that simultaneously united both the highest morals and the highest science.[14] This is, of course, a version of aesthetic idealism (derived from Kant, Schelling, Schiller), but which Baldwin reworked into his own system called *pancalism*, a word which meant that this cosmic consciousness is "all-comprehensive, with no reference outside of itself."

This unity experience is prefigured in the contemplation of a beautiful artwork. The artwork itself exists in the objective, exterior world, and *as an object* can be studied by scientific investigation. But the beauty and the value of the artwork is an interior and *subjective state*, brought to the art by the viewer (although anchored in objectively real features of the work). Thus, when you contemplate an artwork that you love and value, you are joining the subjective and objective worlds—the worlds of values and facts, morals and science, Left and Right—in a unified embrace.

Furthermore—and this is the crucial addition—according to Baldwin, "It is the nature of such synthetic experience to move beyond specific aesthetic objects of contemplation to reality itself as a whole. Such synthetic experience includes the idea of God, but now seen as referring to that organic or spiritual whole within which self and world can finally be known."[15] This aesthetic strand, too, undergoes stage by stage development, culminating in the consummate experience of cosmic consciousness.

Baldwin, in short, was one of the first great modern researchers who, in essence, took the Great Nest of Being and Knowing—prelogical body to logical mind to translogical spirit—and differentiated each of those levels into aesthetic, moral, and scientific modes of experience, and further, showed the development of each of those lines through each of those major levels. His accomplishment is not likely to be soon equaled.

Jürgen Habermas

Jürgen Habermas (born 1929) has, in the course of his distinguished career, applied his integral vision across a wide variety of domains—philosophy, psychology, anthropology, evolutionary theory, linguistics, politics (see chart 10). Habermas's overall model has three tiers. First is a theory of communication ("universal pragmatics"), which serves as the starting point for an account of the development of subjective (aesthetic), intersubjective (moral), and objective (scientific) consciousness (i.e., the Big Three; this developmental account of the individual is the second tier). The third tier, based on the first two, is an account of sociocultural evolution as a reconstruction of historical materialism, and a synthesis of systems theory, lifeworld, scientific, aesthetic, and moral domains.[16]

Habermas is the most comprehensive developmental philosopher now working. However, lamentably, he leaves out and totally ignores any of the stages of I, we, and it consciousness beyond vision-logic. As I would put it, Habermas is all-quadrant, but not quite all-level. Moreover, in placing his reliance on linguistically generated structures of understanding, Habermas places an unfortunate wedge between human and nonhuman nature, so that his approach to nature is essentially instrumental. In short, we might say that his integral view is inadequate to both the prerational and the transrational domains—inadequate to both nature and spirit (a major flaw, some would say). Nonetheless, for the ground it covers, his work has already assured him a place in history as being at least one of the half-dozen most important thinkers of this century, and it appears that no integral view can hope to succeed that ignores his profound contributions.

Sri Aurobindo

Aurobindo (1872–1950) was India's greatest modern philosopher-sage, and the magnitude of his achievements are hard to convey convincingly. His "integral yoga" is a concerted effort to unite and integrate the ascending (evolutionary) and descending (involutionary) currents in human beings, thus uniting otherworldly and this-worldly, transcendent and immanent, spirit and matter. He covered much of the scope of India's vast spiritual heritage and lineages, and brought many of them together into a powerful synthesis. He was also one of the first truly great sages to have access to the evolutionary record (disclosed by the differentiations of modernity), which allowed him to expand his system from a dynamic developmentalism of ontogeny (which all great perennial philosophers possessed) to one of phylogeny as well. Aurobindo's integral yoga, we might say, was India's first great synthesis of the truths of the premodern Great Nest with the truths brought by the differentiations of modernity.

Aurobindo's overall model of consciousness consists basically of three systems: (1) the surface/outer/frontal consciousness (typically gross state), consisting of physical, vital, and mental levels of consciousness; (2) a deeper/psychic/soul system "behind" the frontal in each of its levels (inner physical, inner vital, inner mental, and innermost psychic or soul; typically subtle state); and (3) the vertical ascending/descending systems stretching both above the mind (higher mind, illumined mind, intuitive mind, overmind, supermind; including causal/nondual) and below the mind (the subconscient and inconscient)—all nested in Sat-Chit-Ananda, or pure nondual Spirit.[17]

Aurobindo's greatest shortcoming is a shortcoming faced by all theorists, namely, the unavailability of the important discoveries made since his time. Aurobindo was most concerned with the transformations of consciousness (Upper Left) and the correlative changes in the material body (Upper Right). Although he had many important insights on the social and political system, he did not seem to grasp the actual interrelations of cultural, social, intentional, and behavioral, nor did his analysis at any point proceed on the level of intersubjectivity (Lower Left) and interobjectivity (Lower Right). He did not, that is, fully assimilate the differentiations of modernity. But the levels and modes that Aurobindo did cover make his formulations indispensable for any truly integral model.

Abraham Maslow

Abraham Maslow (1908–1970) is well known enough that I will only make a few passing comments. Like all truly great integral thinkers—from Aurobindo to Gebser to Whitehead to Baldwin to Habermas—he was a developmentalist. He was one of the first to gather substantial empirical and phenomenological evidence suggesting that each level in the Great Nest has a different need, that these needs emerge hierarchically and prepotently, and that each of us carries the potential for all of these levels-needs (see chart 7). Instrumental in founding both the Third Force (Humanistic-Existential Psychology) and the Fourth Force (Transpersonal), Maslow's ideas had an extraordinary impact on education, business, and values research.

Maslow's work fell into temporary disrepute during the eighties, when an extreme postmodernism, dominating both academia and the counterculture, made all forms of holarchy subservient to what certainly seemed to be a form of flatland dogmatism. But as the world awakens from that reductionism, Maslow's pioneering works are there to greet all who would genuinely embrace a more integral and holarchical view.

All of these integral thinkers are simply a few of the pioneering geniuses that can help guide us to even further integral visions. No matter how great any of them were, each new generation has a chance to move the integral vision forward in a substantial way, simply because new information, data, and discoveries are constantly being made. Hegel's towering brilliance was utterly bereft of exposure to Asian traditions. Schelling had no access to substantial anthropological data. Aurobindo missed the meticulous studies of modern cognitive science. Habermas is of a generation that never quite grasped the transpersonal revolution. Likewise, whatever contributions any of us might make will only be the shoulders, we can hope, upon which others will soon stand.

PART THREE

FRUITION

An Integral Model

A TRULY INTEGRAL PSYCHOLOGY, I have suggested, would involve the very best of premodernity (the Great Nest), modernity (the differentiation of the value spheres), and postmodernity (their integration across all levels in the Great Nest)—"all-level, all-quadrant." We can now begin to pull these strands together.

8

The Archeology of Spirit

Overview

The foregoing sections introduced us to a few of the many theorists and the many strands of research that need to be embraced, in a general way, for any current integral view.

They also introduced the major components, as I see them, of the evolution of consciousness: the *basic levels*, structures, or waves in the Great Nest (matter, body, mind, soul, spirit); the *developmental lines* or streams (moral, aesthetic, religious, cognitive, affective, etc.) that move relatively independently through the great waves; the *states*, or temporary states of consciousness (such as peak experiences, dream states, and altered states); the *self*, which is the seat of identity, will, and defenses, and which has to navigate, balance, and integrate all the various levels, lines, and states that it encounters; and the *self-related lines*, which are the developmental lines most intimately connected with the self (such as the self's central identity, its morals, and its needs). In short: waves, streams, states, self, and self-streams.

Altered states are very important, and certainly get much of the attention, but for them to contribute to *development* they must become structures/traits. Self-streams are crucial, but they are a subset of streams in general. Thus, in the simplest of terms, we can say that development comes down to waves, streams, and self.

THE BASIC WAVES

I have included, in charts 1a and 1b, a summary of some of the major components of an integral model.[1] We have already discussed some of these features, and I mean for all of that discussion to be included here. But I will simply make a few further comments about this model based on some of the items in the charts, and specifically with a view toward an "all-level, all-quadrant" approach.

On the left side, in each of the charts, are the basic structures, levels, or waves in the Great Nest of Being and Knowing.[2] What is worth keeping in mind is that, taken together, the basic levels in virtually every major system, ancient and modern, Eastern and Western, simply describe a vast *morphogenetic field*, or developmental space, and one that is *migratory*—it grades holarchically, transcending and including, nests within nests indefinitely, inviting a development that is envelopment.

Further, these different migratory conceptions listed on the charts show a remarkable harmony, not in specifics, but in the developmental space they portray. We have seen that scholars such as Huston Smith have made this argument for the perennial philosophy; what is not as often appreciated is that modern researchers (working on the stages from sensorimotor to formal to postformal) have reached quite similar conclusions. As Francis Richards and Michael Commons put it, after surveying the developmental research and data from Fischer, Sternberg, Kohlberg, Armon, Pascual-Leone, Powell, Labouvie-Vief, Arlin, Sinott, Basseches, Koplowitz, and Alexander (all of whom are represented on the charts): "The stage sequences [of all of these theorists] can be aligned across a common *developmental space*. The harmony of alignment shown suggests a possible reconciliation of [these] theories. . . ."[3]

What I have done is to take the results of that research, along with dozens of other modern theorists, and attempted to integrate it with the best of the perennial philosophers, to arrive at a master template of a *full-spectrum developmental space*, reaching from matter to body to mind to soul to spirit. (The holarchical nature of this unfolding is discussed in an endnote.)[4] As we have seen, these are the basic waves of being and knowing through which the various developmental streams will flow, all of which are balanced and (ideally) integrated by the self in its remarkable journey from subconscious to self-conscious to superconscious.

But, of course, this tortuous journey is not without its perils.

The Self and Its Pathologies

Column two in chart 1a gives the "general self-sense"—some of the general names I often use for the developmental stages of the proximate self (bodyego, persona, ego, centaur, soul). Notice that I have drawn a continuing arrow for each of them. There is a persistent confusion in the literature about whether, for example, the ego is retained or lost in higher development. Most transpersonal researchers refer to the higher stages as being "beyond ego" or "transegoic," which seems to imply the ego is lost. But this confusion is almost entirely semantic. If by ego you mean an *exclusive* identification with the personal self, then that *exclusiveness* is mostly lost or dissolved in higher development—that "ego" is largely destroyed (and the higher stages are correctly called transegoic). But if by ego you mean a functional self that relates to the conventional world, then that ego is definitely retained (and often strengthened). Likewise, if you mean—as psychoanalysis does—that an important part of the ego is its capacity for detached witnessing, then that ego is definitely retained (and almost always strengthened)—when Jack Engler says that "Meditation increases ego strength," he is absolutely right.[5] Also, if by ego you mean—as ego psychology does—the psyche's capacity for integrating, then that ego is also retained and strengthened.[6]

In short, the *exclusiveness* of an identity with a given self (bodyego, persona, ego, centaur, soul) is dissolved or released with each higher stage of self growth, but the important *functional capacities* of each are retained, incorporated (holarchically), and often strengthened in succeeding stages. The period of exclusive identification is what is indicated by the solid line in column two (a period that eventually comes to an end with higher growth). But the functional capacities of that stage remain as important subholons in subsequent stages, and that I have indicated with the continuing arrow. (In other words, the solid line indicates when each of those selves is the proximate self, or I; when its major dominant phase is over and consciousness moves on, that self becomes part of the distal self, or me.)

I'll briefly mention the following items in chart 1a, then we will look at them more closely in the next three sections. Column three ("specific aspects") indicates in more detail the nature of the proximate self at each of its stages and substages.[7] Column four ("defenses") gives some of the major defense mechanisms that can develop at each of the basic waves. "Possible pathology" refers in a very general way to the types and levels of pathology that can occur as the self navigates each of the basic waves. "Fulcrums" refers to the major milestones in the self's development—in other words, what happens to the proximate self when its center of gravity is at a particular level of consciousness.[8] And "treatment" is a summary of the types of psychological and spiritual therapies that appear to be most helpful for the different types of pathologies that beset the different levels of consciousness.

As we saw, each time *the center of gravity* of the self moves through a basic level of the Great Nest, it goes through a *fulcrum* (or a milestone) of its own development: it first identifies with a new level, then disidentifies with and transcends that level, then includes and integrates that level from the next higher level.[9] Throughout this discussion I have often summarized the Great Nest as possessing nine basic levels (as functional groupings: sensorimotor, phantasmic-emotional, rep-mind, rule/role mind, formal-reflexive, vision-logic, psychic, subtle, and causal/nondual—you can see these listed on the left column in each of the charts), and therefore I outline the *nine correlative fulcrums* that the self goes through in a complete evolution or development through the entire Great Nest. (Based on empirical research, such as Stan Grof's, I also include the birth fulcrum, F-0, which gives us ten or so major, qualitatively distinct milestones in the self's journey from conception to enlightenment.)

Each time the self (the proximate self) steps up to a new and higher sphere in the Great Nest, it can do so in a relatively healthy fashion—which means it smoothly differentiates and integrates the elements of that level—or in a relatively pathological fashion—which means it either *fails to differentiate* (and thus remains in fusion/fixation/arrest) or it *fails to integrate* (which results in repression, alienation, fragmentation). Each level of the Great Nest has a qualitatively different architecture, and thus each fulcrum (and pathology) likewise has a qualitatively different texture. We can now look more closely at these different pathologies faced by the self on its jostling journey through the great River.

LOWER PATHOLOGIES (F-0 TO F-3)

One of the major breakthroughs in depth psychology of the last several decades has been the realization that there are not just different *types* of psychopathology (e.g., obsessive-compulsive disorders, phobias, anxiety, depression) but also different *levels* of psychopathology (e.g., neurotic, borderline, and psychotic). These different levels of pathology are correlated, in part, with the three major stages of early self-development (particularly as disclosed by the pioneering research of Rene Spitz, Edith Jakobson, Margaret Mahler, and others). A developmental miscarriage at any of these stages can contribute to a corresponding level of pathology.[10] These are not, of course, rigid and discrete levels like the floors in a building, but overlapping waves of self-development and the many things that can go wrong at each of those general waves.[11]

These three early waves of self-development can be summarized fairly simply. The self starts out relatively undifferentiated from its environment.[12] That is, it cannot easily tell where its body stops and the physical environment begins (this is the start of fulcrum-1). Somewhere during the first year, the infant learns that if it bites a blanket, it does not hurt, but if it bites its thumb, it hurts: there is a difference between body and matter. The infant differentiates its body from the environment, and thus its identity switches from fusion with the material world to an identity with the emotional-feeling body (which begins fulcrum-2). As the conceptual mind begins to emerge and develop (especially around 3 to 6 years), the child eventually differentiates the conceptual mind and the emotional body (this is fulcrum-3). The proximate self's identity has thus gone from matter to body to early mind (and we can see that it is well on its way through the waves in the Great Nest).

Each of those self-stages (or fulcrums) ideally involves both *differentiation* and *integration* (transcendence and inclusion). The self differentiates from the lower level (e.g., body), identifies with the next higher level (e.g., mind), and then integrates the conceptual mind with the feelings of the body. A failure at any of those points results in a pathology—a malformation, crippling, or narrowing of the self in its otherwise ever-expanding journey. Thus, if the mind fails to differentiate from bodily feelings, it can be overwhelmed with painfully strong emotions (not simply feel strong emotions, but be capsized by them), histrionic mood swings are common, there is great difficulty with impulse control, and developmental arrest often occurs that that point. On the other hand, if mind and body differentiate but are not then integrated (so that *differentiation* goes too far into *dissociation*), the result is a classic neurosis, or the *repression* of bodily feelings by mental structures (ego, superego, harsh conscience).

Thus, the differentiation-and-integration process can go wrong at each and every self-stage (or fulcrum), and the *level* of the fulcrum helps determine the *level* of pathology. In fulcrum-1, if the self does not correctly differentiate from, and integrate its images of, the physical environment, the result can be psychosis (the individual cannot tell where his body stops and the environment begins, he hallucinates, and so on). In fulcrum-2, if the emotional bodyself has difficulty differentiating itself from others, the result can be narcissism (others are treated as extensions of the self) or borderline disorders (others are constantly invading and disrupting the self's fragile boundaries). In fulcrum-3, as we just saw, a failure to differentiate leaves a *fusion* with the labile emotional self, whereas a failure to integrate leads to a *repression* of the emotional self by the newly emerging mental-egoic self (classic psychoneurosis).

Another way to say the same thing is that each level of self development has different types of defenses. The self, at every level, will attempt to defend itself against pain, disruption, and ultimately death, and it will do so *using whatever tools are present at that level*. If the self has concepts, it will use concepts; if it has rules, it will use rules; if it has vision-logic, it will use vision-logic. At the first fulcrum (as you can see in chart 1a), the self only has sensations, perceptions, and exocepts (which are the early forms of sensorimotor cognition), along with the very earliest of impulses and images; thus the archaic self can defend itself in only the most rudimentary ways, such as fusing with the physical environment, hallucinatory wish fulfillment (in images), and perceptual distortion. At fulcrum-2, the self has the added tools of more intense feelings, emotions, and newly emerging symbols, and thus it can defend itself in more elaborate ways, such as splitting (dividing the self and the world into "all good" and "all bad" representations), projecting its feelings and emotions onto others, and fusing itself with the emotional world of others. By the time of fulcrum-3, the self has added elaborate concepts and beginning rules, and these very powerful mental tools can be used to forcefully repress the body and its feelings, displace its desires, create reaction formations, and so on. (Many of these defenses are listed in chart 1a, and the research behind them is discussed in the endnote.)[13] In short, the level of defenses, the level of self development, the level of pathology—all are facets of the same migratory unfolding across the qualitatively distinct waves in the Great Nest.

Likewise, in each of those cases, a somewhat different treatment has been found to be most helpful. Starting with fulcrum-3 and moving down the spectrum: With typical neurosis (F-3), the treatment involves relaxing and undoing the repression barrier, recontacting the repressed or shadow feelings, and reintegrating them into the psyche, so that the ongoing flow of consciousness unfolding can more smoothly continue.

These therapeutic approaches are generically called *uncovering techniques* because they attempt to uncover and reintegrate the shadow. This "regression in service of the ego" temporarily returns consciousness to the early trauma (or simply puts it back in touch with the alienated feelings, drives, or impulses), allows it to befriend and reintegrate the alienated feelings, and thus restores a relative harmony to the psyche. These approaches include classic psychoanalysis, aspects of Gestalt Therapy, the shadow facet of Jungian therapy, Gendlin's focusing, and aspects of ego psychology and self psychology, among others.[14]

(In therapies that acknowledge the higher or transpersonal domains, this healing regressive spiral is often used as a prelude to evolutionary and progressive transcendence to higher levels, as indicated in fig. 9. This curative spiral is not a regression to a higher ground, but to a lower one, which helps reset the foundations for a surer transcendence.)[15]

Moving down to the borderline level of pathology (F-2), the problem is not that a strong self represses the body, but that there isn't enough of a strong self to begin with. Techniques here are therefore called *structure building*: they attempt to build up the self's boundaries and fortify ego strength. There is little repressed material to "uncover," because the self has not been strong enough to repress much of anything. Rather, the aim of therapy here is to help complete the separation-individuation stage (F-2), so that the person emerges with a strong self and clearly differentiated-integrated emotional boundaries. These F-2 approaches

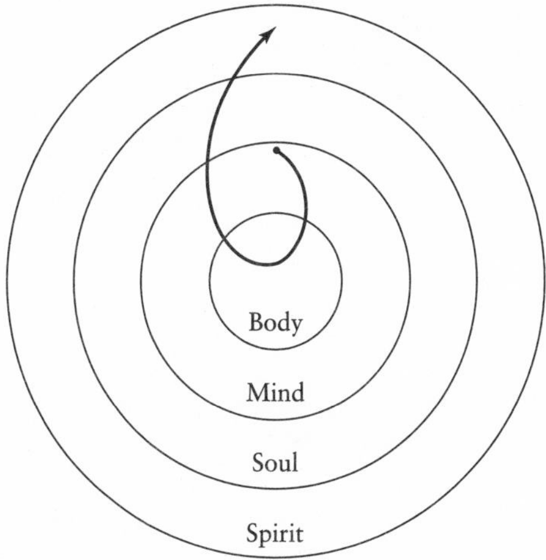

FIGURE 9. *The Curative Spiral*

include aspects of object relations therapy (Winnicott, Fairbairn, Guntrip), psychoanalytic ego psychology (Mahler, Blanck and Blanck, Kernberg), self psychology (Kohut), and numerous integrations of those approaches (such as those of John Gedo and James Masterson).

The earliest fulcrums (F-0 and F-1) have, until recently, resisted treatment (except for medication/pacification), precisely because they are so primitive and difficult to access. However, recent avant-garde (and highly controversial) treatments, ranging from Janov's primal scream to Grof's holotropic breathwork, have claimed various sorts of success, by again "temporarily regressing" to the deep wounds, reexperiencing them in full awareness, and thus allowing consciousness to move forward in a more integrated fashion.

INTERMEDIATE (F-4 TO F-6) AND HIGHER (F-7 TO F-9) PATHOLOGIES

As we move into the intermediate and higher fulcrums, we see the same overall process: because each of the basic waves in the Great Nest has a different architecture, each level of self development has a *qualitatively different* level of pathology, different types of defenses, and a correspondingly different type of treatment.[16] In fulcrum-4 (typically ages 6–12), the rule/role mind begins to emerge and the self's center of gravity starts to identify with that wave. The self begins to take the role of others, and therefore begins to shift from egocentric/preconventional to sociocentric/conventional. If something goes wrong at this general wave, we get a "script pathology"—all of the false, misleading, and sometimes crippling scripts, stories, and myths that the self learns. Therapy (such as cognitive therapy) helps the individual to uproot these false ideas about itself and replace them with more accurate, healthy scripts. In fulcrum-5, as the self-reflexive ego emerges, and the center of gravity begins to shift from conventional/conformist to postconventional/individualistic, the self is faced with "identity versus role confusion": how is the self to discover who or what it is, once it no longer depends on society (with its conventional ethics, rules, and roles) to make decisions for it? In fulcrum-6, the panoramic view of vision-logic brings existential issues and problems to the forefront, along with the possibility of a more fully integrated bodymind (or centauric self). In fulcrum-7, the transpersonal domains begin to come into focus, not simply as passing peak experiences, but as new and higher structures—with new and higher possible pathologies (as we will see below).

I have dealt with these nine or ten levels of pathology, defenses, and treatments in various books, and Rowan, among others, has given an extensive discussion of pathologies and treatments at each of these fulcrums.[17] For this simple overview, all we need note is that each level of the Great Nest has a qualitatively different architecture, and thus each wave of self-development, self-pathology, and treatment likewise has a qualitatively different tone. If you acknowledge any of the basic stages of development, you can probably also acknowledge that something can go wrong with any of them, thus producing qualitatively different pathologies and treatments.

The nine or ten general levels of therapy that I outlined are meant to be suggestive only; they are broad guidelines as to what we can expect, based on the extensive evidence compiled by numerous different schools of developmental psychology and contemplative spirituality. There is, needless to say, *a great deal of overlap between these therapies.* For example, I list "script pathology" and "cognitive therapy" as being especially relevant to fulcrum-4, which is where the self identifies, for the first time, with the rule/role mind and thus can begin to take the *role* of others and learn the *rules* of its society. As we saw, if something goes wrong during this general developmental period, the result is a "script pathology," a series of distorted, demeaning, unfair ideas and scripts about one's self and others. Cognitive therapy has excelled in rooting out these maladaptive scripts and replacing them with more accurate, benign, and therefore healthy ideas and self-concepts. But to say cognitive therapy focuses on this level of consciousness development is *not* to say it has no benefit at other levels, for clearly it does. The idea, rather, is that the farther away we get from this level, the less relevant (but never completely useless) cognitive therapy becomes. Developments in fulcrums 1 and 2 are mostly preverbal and preconceptual, so conceptual reprogramming does not directly address these levels; and developments beyond fulcrum-6 are mostly transmental and transrational, so mental reprogramming, in and of itself, is limited in its effectiveness.

So it is not that a given therapy applies only to one level of development, but that, in focusing on one or two levels, most forms of therapy increasingly lose their effectiveness when applied to more distant realms. All too often, one particular psychotherapeutic approach (psychoanalysis, Gestalt, neurolinguistic programming, holotropic breathwork, Transactional Analysis, biological psychiatry, yoga, etc.) is used for *all* types of psychopathologies, often with unfortunate results. Rather, the one thing we learn from the existence of the multiple levels of the spectrum of consciousness is just how many different dimensions of existence there are, and how a sensitivity to these multiple dimensions demands a multiplicity of treatment modalities.

Also, it is generally true, as I first suggested in *The Spectrum of Consciousness*, that the therapies of one level will acknowledge and often use the therapies from lower levels, but they are reluctant to recognize any level higher than their own. Thus, classical psychoanalysis will recognize the importance of instinctual and emotional drives, but downplay the importance of cognitive scripts themselves. Cognitive therapists emphasize the importance of those scripts but downplay or ignore the importance of the total psychophysical organism (or centaur), which humanistic and existential therapists emphasize. And many existential therapists vehemently deny the importance or even existence of the transpersonal and transrational levels. By assigning each therapy a general level on the overall spectrum of consciousness, I am also taking those particular facts into account—the therapy at one level will usually acknowledge and even use all of the therapies from lower levels, but rarely from any higher (whose existence, in fact, they often pathologize).

TYPICAL THERAPY

Not often will a therapist see a client so evolved as to present problems from all nine or ten fulcrums. Most adults' center of gravity is somewhere around mythic, rational, or centauric; and they have occasionally had psychic or subtle peak experiences (which they may or may not have trouble integrating). Typical individual therapy therefore tends to involve strengthening boundaries (F-2), contacting and befriending shadow feelings (F-3), cognitive rescripting (F-4), and Socratic dialogue (F-5 and F-6), with specific issues of getting in touch with one's feelings (F-3), dealing with belongingness needs (F-4), self-esteem (F-5), and self-actualization (F-6). Sometimes these are accompanied by issues of integrating peak experiences and spiritual illuminations (psychic, subtle, causal, or nondual), which need to be carefully differentiated from prerational magic and mythic structures. (See *Eye to Eye* for suggestions on differentiating between preformal magic and mythic and postformal psychic and subtle.)

As we have seen, intense regressive therapies (Grof, Janov) attempt to reexperience aspects of the earliest fulcrums (pre-, peri-, and neonatal; F-0 and F-1). Psychoanalytic ego psychology and self psychology tend to deal with the next but still rather early fulcrums (especially F-2 and F-3). Cognitive and interpersonal therapy tend to focus on beliefs and scripts (F-4 and F-5).[18] Humanistic-existential therapies tend to deal with all those issues *and* on actualizing an authentic self, existential being, bodymind integration, or centaur (F-6).[19] And transpersonal therapies, while addressing all of those personal fulcrums, also include various approaches to the higher spiritual domains (F-7, F-8, F-9; we will discuss these below; some good introductions to transpersonal psychology/therapy are listed in the endnote).[20]

Is there a common thread to all these levels of treatment? A common thread to psychoanalytic, cognitive, humanistic, transpersonal? In a very general sense, yes. It is this: *awareness in and of itself is curative.* Every therapeutic school we have mentioned attempts, in its own way, to allow consciousness to encounter (or reencounter) facets of experience that were previously alienated, malformed, distorted, or ignored.[21] This is *curative* for a basic reason: *by experiencing these facets fully,* consciousness can genuinely acknowledge these elements and thereby let go of them: see them as an object, and thus differentiate from them, de-embed from them, *transcend them*—and then integrate them into a more encompassing, compassionate embrace.

The curative catalyst, in every case, is bringing awareness or consciousness to bear on an area of experience that is (or has been) denied, distorted, falsified, or ignored. Once that area enters (or reenters) consciousness, then it can rejoin the ongoing flow of evolutionary unfolding, instead of remaining behind, stuck in a distorted or alienated loop and sending up painful symptoms (anxiety, depression, phobias) as the only indication of its imprisonment. Encountering (or reencountering) these disturbed or ignored facets allows them to be differentiated (transcended) and integrated (included) in the ongoing waves of ever-expanding consciousness.

In short, in the grand morphogenetic migration from matter through body through mind through soul through spirit, facets of consciousness can be split off, distorted, or neglected at any of those waves—facets of the body can be repressed, elements of the mind can be distorted, aspects of the soul can be denied, the call of spirit can be ignored. In each case, those alienated facets remain as "stick points" or lesions in awareness, split off or avoided—a fragmentation that produces pathology, with the type of pathology depending in large part on the level of the fragmentation. Contacting (or recontacting) those facets, meeting them with awareness, and thus experiencing them fully, allows consciousness to differentiate (transcend) and integrate (include) their important voices in the overall flow of evolutionary unfolding.

Subpersonalities

I mentioned that the self contains numerous *subpersonalities*, and nowhere does this become more obvious or significant than in pathology, diagnosis, and treatment. Authorities on subpersonalities point out that the average person often has around a dozen or more subpersonalities, variously known as parent ego state, child ego state, adult ego state, topdog, underdog, conscience, ego ideal, idealized ego, false self, authentic self, real self, harsh critic, superego, libidinous self, and so on.[22] Most of these are experienced, in part, as different vocal or subvocal voices in one's inner dialogue. Sometimes one or more subpersonalities become almost completely dissociated, which can result, in extremes, in multiple personality disorder. For most people, however, these various subpersonalities simply vie for attention and behavioral dominance, forming a type of subconscious society of selves that must be negotiated by the proximate self at any of its stages.

Each of these subpersonalities can be at a different level of development in any of its lines. In other words, subpersonalities can form at virtually any of the fulcrums: archaic subpersonalities (F-0, F-1), magical subpersonalities (F-2, F-3), mythic subpersonalities (F-3, F-4), rational subpersonalities (F-5, F-6), and even soul subpersonalities (F-7, F-8).[23]

Thus, considerable research suggests that not only can the various developmental lines unfold relatively independently, so can any of the various subpersonalities. For *both* of these reasons, *a person can therefore have facets of his or her consciousness at many different levels* of morals, worldviews, defenses, pathologies, needs, and so forth (which can be mapped on an integral psychograph, as in figs. 2 and 3). For example, the child ego state is usually generated at F-2 and F-3 (with preconventional morals, magic worldview, and safety needs), which becomes perfectly obvious when a person is gripped by a child ego state (e.g., explosive temper tantrum, with egocentric demands, narcissistic worldview, etc.), which can blow through the personality, commandeer it for minutes or hours, and then pass as quickly as it came, returning the person to his or her more typical, average self (which may be otherwise quite highly evolved).

Thus, when I outline nine or ten general levels of consciousness, worldviews, pathology, treatment, and so on, that does not in any way mean that a person is simply at one stage, with one type of defense, one type of pathology, one type of need, and one type of treatment. The dozen or more subpersonalities can each be at a different level, so that the individual has numerous types and levels of needs, defenses, and pathologies (e.g., from borderline to neurotic to existential to spiritual), and will therefore respond to a wide variety of therapeutic endeavors.

Subpersonalities, in their benign form, are simply functional self-presentations that navigate particular psychosocial situations (a father persona, a wife persona, a libidinal self, an achiever self, and so on). Subpersonalities become problematic only to the degree of their dissociation, which runs along a continuum from mild to moderate to severe. The difficulty comes when any of these functional personalities are strongly dissociated, or split from access to the conscious self, due to repeated trauma, developmental miscarriages, recurrent stress, or selective inattention. These submerged personae—with their now-dissociated and fixated set of morals, needs, worldviews, and so on—set up shop in the basement, where they sabotage further growth and development. They remain as "hidden subjects," facets of consciousness that the self can no longer *disidentify* with and transcend, because they are sealed off in unconscious pockets of the psyche, from which they send up symbolic derivatives in the form of painful symptoms.

The curative catalyst, again, is to bring awareness to bear on these subpersonalities, thus objectifying them, and thus including them in a more compassionate embrace. Generally speaking, individuals will present a symptomatology where one or two subpersonalities and their pathologies are dominant (a harsh inner critic, a prone-to-failure underdog, a low-self-esteem ego state, etc.), and thus therapy tends to focus on these more visible issues. As dominant pathologies are alleviated (and their subpersonalities integrated), less noticeable ones will often tend to emerge, sometimes forcefully, and therapeutic attention naturally gravitates to them. These subpersonalities can include both more primitive selves (archaic, magic) and any newly emerging transpersonal selves (soul, spirit).

Likewise, the various subpersonalities are often context-triggered: a person will do fine in one situation, only to have another situation trigger panic, depression, anxiety, and so on. Alleviating the dominant problem in one area will often allow less noticeable pathologies to surface, and they can then be worked through. The therapeutic ingredient—bring awareness to bear—helps the individual become more conscious of the subpersonalities, thus converting them from "hidden subjects" into "conscious objects," where they can be reintegrated in the self and thus join the ongoing flow of consciousness evolution, instead of remaining fixated at the lower levels where they were originally dissociated. For no matter how numerous the subpersonalities, it is the task of the proximate self to fashion some sort of integration or harmony in the chorus of voices, and thus more surely wend its way to the Source of them all.

THE ARCHEOLOGY OF THE SELF

We can give a simplified summary of the above discussion on the stages of self and pathology by using figure 10. This is again the Great Nest, but this time drawn to show *degrees of interior depth*. In other words, figures such as 1 and 6 show that the higher spheres transcend and include the lower; figure 10 shows that the higher spheres are *experienced* as being interior to, and deeper than, the lower, which are experienced, in comparison, as superficial, shallow, and exterior. Thus, the body is experienced as being inside the physical environment; the mind is experienced as being inside the body; the soul is experienced interior to the mind, and deep within the soul is pure spirit itself, which transcends all and embraces all (thus transcending inside and outside).

Figure 10 shows this archeology of Spirit, as the more superficial layers of the Self are peeled off to expose increasingly deeper and more profound waves of consciousness. This involves the *emergence* of ever-greater potentials, which therefore leads us forward, not backward, and shows us future evolution and growth, not past evolution and regression. This is an archeology of depth, to be sure, but a depth that plumbs the future, not the past; that reaches into a greater tomorrow, not a dusty yesterday; that unearths the hidden treasures of involution, not the fossils of evolution. We dig within in order to go beyond, not back.

A summary of this archeological expedition:

At the beginning of F-1, on the shallowest surface of Spirit, the self is still largely undifferentiated from the material world (as Piaget put it, "The self is here *material*, so to speak"); problems at this stage can therefore contribute to a disturbing lack of self-boundaries, infantile au-

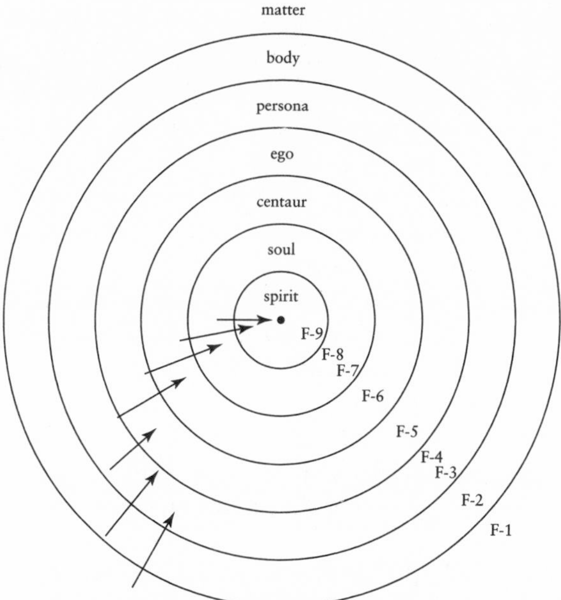

FIGURE 10. *Layers of the Self*

tism, and some forms of psychosis. The worldview of this stage is *archaic*, and this archaic consciousness, if not differentiated (transcended) and integrated (resolved), can lead to primitive pathologies. The trip to the Self is sabotaged at its first step, and the repercussions are severe.[24]

In F-2 (the separation-individuation stage), the emotional bodyself differentiates itself from the emotions and feelings of others. Problems at this stage can contribute to borderline and narcissistic conditions, where the self treats the world and others as mere extensions of itself (narcissism), or the world invades and painfully disrupts the self (borderline); both due to the fact that the world and the self are not stably differentiated. The worldview of this stage is *magical*—the self can magically order the world around in omnipotent fantasy, the environment is full of animistic displacements (not as a sophisticated form of panentheism, but as anthropomorphic impulse projections), and "word magic" reigns. Fixation at this magical level (and magical subpersonalities) is a large part of the cognitive repertoire of the borderline and narcissistic conditions.

With F-3, the early mental self (the early ego or persona) first begins to emerge and differentiate from the body and its impulses, feelings, and emotions, and attempts to integrate these feelings in its newly conceptual self. Failure at this crucial fulcrum (often summarized as Oedipal/Electra) can contribute to a classic neurosis: anxiety, depression, phobias, obsessive-compulsive disorders, and excessive guilt at the hands of the newly internalized superego. The conceptual self is frightened of, and overwhelmed by, the feelings of the body (especially sex and aggression), and in its misguided attempt to defend itself against these feelings, merely ends up sending them underground (as impulsive subpersonalities), where they cause even more pain and terror than when faced with awareness.

All of these early fulcrums (F-1 to F-3) remain heavily egocentric and preconventional (as for possible childhood spiritual experiences, see chapter 10). Fixation to their narcissistic modes keeps consciousness circling on the surface of the Self, and the journey to the Depths is derailed at some of the most superficial archeological layers.

This early mental self is at first a simple name self, then a rudimentary self-concept, but it soon expands into a full-fledged *role self* (or persona) with the emergence of the rule/role mind and the increasing capacity to take the role of other (F-4). The worldview of both late F-3 and early F-4 is *mythic*, which means that these early roles are often those found displayed in the mythological gods and goddesses, which represent the *archetypal roles* available to individuals. That is, these are simply some of the collective, concrete roles available to men and women—roles such as a strong father, a caring mother, a warrior, a trickster, the anima, animus, and so forth, which are often embodied in the concrete figures of the world's mythologies (Persephone, Demeter, Zeus, Apollo, Venus, Indra, etc.). Jungian research suggests that these archetypal mythic roles are *collectively* inherited; but, let us note, for the most part they are *not* transpersonal (a confusion common in Jungian and new-age circles).[25] These mythic roles are simply part of the many (sub)personalities that can exist at this preformal mythic level of consciousness development; they are preformal and collective, not postformal and transpersonal. A few "high archetypes," such as the Wise Old Man, the Crone, and the mandala, are sometimes *symbols* of the transpersonal domains, but do not necessarily carry direct experience of those domains.[26] In any event, we are here focusing on the concrete-literal mythic level itself.

These preformal, archetypal roles are bolstered by the specific cultural roles that the child begins to learn at this stage—the specific interactions with family, peers, and social others. As these cultural scripts are learned, various problems and distortions can arise, and these contribute to what we have generically been calling script pathology. Since the worldview of this level is *mythic* (mythic-membership), therapy at this level, by whatever name, often involves uprooting these myths and replacing them with more accurate, less self-damaging scripts and roles. Even the Jungian approach, which sometimes overvalues mythic displays, proceeds in a similar fashion, by differentiating-and-integrating mythic motifs and thus both honoring them and transcending them.[27]

But what is really happening here? In moving from preconventional and narcissistic to conventional and mythic-membership, consciousness has profoundly deepened from egocentric to sociocentric. It has expanded from *me* to *we*, and thus plumbed new depths on its archeological journey to the Self. It is slowly abandoning the pale and primitive surfaces, becoming less narcissistic, less of the shallows, less of the surface, and diving instead into the deep, where individual selves are increasingly united in that common Self which shines throughout the entire display, and in the move from egocentric-magic to sociocentric-mythic, the heart of the all-encompassing Self is increasingly intuited.

With the emergence of formal-reflexive capacities, the self can plunge yet deeper, moving from conventional/conformist roles and a mythic-membership self (the persona), to a postconventional, global, worldcentric self—namely, the mature ego (conscientious and individualistic, to use Loevinger's version). No longer just *us* (my tribe, my clan, my group, my nation), but *all of us* (all human beings without exception, regardless of race, religion, sex, or creed). Consciousness cuts loose from its parochial surfaces and dives into that which is shared by a global humanity, insisting on forms of compassion that are universal, impartial, just and fair for all.

Problems at this stage (F-5) often center around the incredibly difficult transition from conformist roles and prescriptive morality, to universal principles of conscience and postconventional identities: who am I, not according to mom or dad or society or the Bible, but according to my own deepest conscience? Erikson's "identity crisis" is a classic summary of many of the problems of this stage.[28]

As vision-logic begins to emerge, postconventional awareness deepens into fully universal, existential concerns: life and death, authenticity, full bodymind integration, self-actualization, global awareness, holistic embrace—all summarized as the emergence of the *centaur* (e.g., Loevinger's autonomous and integrated stages). In the archeological journey to the Self, the personal realm's exclusive reign is coming to an end, starting to be peeled off of a radiant Spirit, and that universal radiance begins increasingly to shine through, rendering the self more and more transparent.

As usual, the more we go within, the more we go beyond. In the extraordinary archeology of Spirit, the deeper the level, the wider the embrace—the within that takes you beyond. Within the world of matter is the body, but the vital body goes beyond matter in so many ways: its feelings respond while rocks do not; its perceptions recognize a world while insentience sleeps; its emotions move a body while dirt awaits in silence. Likewise, the mind exists within the vital body, but the mind goes beyond the body in so many ways: while the body feels its own feelings, the cognition of the mind takes the role of others, and thus expands consciousness from egocentric to sociocentric to worldcentric; the mind knits together past and future, and thus rises above the impulsiveness of the body's instincts; while the mind conceives the world of what might be and what should be, the body slumbers in its naive present.

Likewise, looking deep within the mind, in the very most interior part of the self, when the mind becomes very, very quiet, and one listens very carefully, in that infinite Silence, the soul begins to whisper, and its feather-soft voice takes one far beyond what the mind could ever imagine, beyond anything rationality could possibly tolerate, beyond anything logic can endure. In its gentle whisperings, there are the faintest hints of infinite love, glimmers of a life that time forgot, flashes of a bliss that must not be mentioned, an infinite intersection where the mysteries of eternity breathe life into mortal time, where suffering and pain have forgotten how to pronounce their own names, this secret quiet intersection of time and the very timeless, an intersection called the soul.

In the archeology of the Self, deep within the personal lies the transpersonal, which takes you far beyond the personal: always within and beyond. Experienced previously only in peak experiences, or as a background intuition of immortality, wonder, and grace, the soul begins now to emerge more permanently in consciousness. Not yet infinite and all-embracing, no longer merely personal and mortal, the soul is the great intermediate conveyor between pure Spirit and individual self. The soul can embrace the gross realm in nature mysticism, or it can plumb its own depths in deity mysticism. It can confer a postmortem meaning on all of life, and deliver grace to every corner of the psyche. It offers the beginning of an unshakable witnessing and equanimity in the midst of the slings and arrows of outrageous fortune, and breathes a tender mercy on all that it encounters. It is reached by a simple technique: turn left at mind, and go within.

A sickness of the soul is sickness indeed. The pathologies that beset psychic and subtle development are numerous and profound. The first and simplest are those that result from abrupt psychic and subtle peak experiences, before they have become permanent realizations and basic waves in one's own awareness. As we have seen, a person at the archaic, magic, mythic, rational, or centauric level can "peek"-experience any of the higher states (psychic, subtle, causal, nondual). In some cases these are so disruptive that, especially in a person with F-1 or F-2 deficiencies, they can trigger a psychotic break.[29] In others, the result is a spiritual emergency.[30] In yet others, the peak experience is a beneficial, life-altering occasion.[31] But in all of these cases, understanding the experience depends upon understanding both the level *from which* the experience originates (psychic, subtle, causal, nondual) and the level *at which* it is experienced and interpreted (archaic, magic, mythic, rational, centauric; or, more accurately, the level of development of the self and all of the self-related lines, including morals, needs, worldviews, and so on. As we saw, a transpersonal peak experience is experienced and interpreted very differently at, for example, different moral stages, and all of these various levels and lines need to be taken into account when assessing the nature and treatment of any spiritual emergency). In other words, an integral psychograph of the individual is the best guide in this—or any other—therapeutic endeavor.

Beyond nonordinary states and temporary peak experiences is permanent realization, and as adaptation to the soul realms begins, any number of pathologies can develop.[32] The self can be overwhelmed by the light, painfully lost in the love, inundated with a largess that its boundaries cannot contain. Alternatively, it can simply swell its ego to infinite proportions (especially if there are any F-2 or narcissistic-borderline residues). It can develop a split between its upper and lower realms (especially between the soul and the body). It can repress and dissociate aspects of the soul itself (producing F-7 and F-8 subpersonalities; not lower impulses trying to come up, but higher impulses trying to come down). It can remain fused with the soul when it should begin to let go of it. And the earliest, simplest pathology of all: denying the existence of one's very own soul.

A growing body of literature is increasingly attuned to the diseases of the soul, using the techniques of both traditional spiritual disciplines and modern psychotherapy (several such approaches are listed in the endnote).[33] For the more traditional techniques—which are also part of any integral therapy—I have listed in the charts the path of shamans/ yogis, the path of saints, the path of sages, and the path of siddhas (dealing with psychic, subtle, causal, and nondual, respectively), which I will also address in an endnote.[34]

In the archeology of the Self, we are at the point where the soul has emerged from the interior depths of the mind and pointed the way to a greater tomorrow. But, like Moses, the soul can see from afar, but never actually enter, the Promised Land. As Teresa would say, after the butterfly (soul) emerged from the death of the chrysalis (ego), so now the little butterfly must die. When the soul itself grows quiet, and rests from its own weariness; when the witness releases its final hold, and dissolves into its ever-present ground; when the last layer of the Self is peeled into the purest emptiness; when the final form of the self-contraction unfolds in the infinity of all space; then Spirit itself, as ever-present awareness, stands free of its own accord, never really lost, and therefore never really found. With a shock of the utterly obvious, the world continues to arise, just as it always has.

In the deepest within, the most infinite beyond. In ever-present awareness, your soul expands to embrace the entire Kosmos, so that Spirit alone remains, as the simple world of what is. The rain no longer falls on you, but within you; the sun shines from inside your heart and radiates out into the world, blessing it with grace; supernovas swirl in your consciousness, the thunder is the sound of your own exhilarated heart; the oceans and rivers are nothing but your blood pulsing to the rhythm of your soul. Infinitely ascended worlds of light dance in the interior of your brain; infinitely descended worlds of night cascade around your feet; the clouds crawl across the sky of your own unfettered mind, while the wind blows through the empty space where your self once used to be. The sound of the rain falling on the roof is the only self you can find, here in the obvious world of crystalline one taste, where inner and outer are silly fictions and self and other are obscene lies, and ever-present simplicity is the sound of one hand clapping madly for all eternity. In the greatest depth, the simplest what is, and the journey ends, as it always does, exactly where it began.

A Full-Spectrum Therapy

A few points might be emphasized in this archeology of the Self. As indicated in column two in chart 1a, these general waves of self development (material self, bodyself, persona, ego, centaur, soul) are not rigidly discrete rungs in a ladder, but overlapping streams of self unfolding, and they exist as functional subholons in subsequent development (barring pathology, such as being split off into dissociated subpersonalities). Although each fulcrum itself is fairly discrete, the functional capacities of each self remain in subsequent development, and this is indicated by the continuing arrows that are drawn in both chart 1a and figure 10. (Later, we will return to this idea and show yet another reason that these various "selves" can overlap and coexist to some degree; see *Different Lines of the Self* in chapter 9).

The point is simply that the average adult comes to therapy with, to use a simplified version, a physical body, a libidinal/emotional body, one or more body-images, one or more personae or conventional roles, one or more ego states—with dissociations at any of those levels producing dissociated complexes and subpersonalities at those levels—and a fledging soul and spirit awaiting a more genuine birth.[35] A full-spectrum therapist works with the body, the shadow, the persona, the ego, the existential self, the soul and spirit, attempting to bring awareness to all of them, so that all of them may join consciousness in the extraordinary return voyage to the Self and Spirit that grounds and moves the entire display.

In short, a full-spectrum therapist is an archeologist of the Self. But, as we saw, this is an archeology that unearths the future, not the past. This profound archeology digs into the within in order to find the beyond, the emergent, the newly arising, not the already buried. These ever-deeper sheaths pull us forward, not backward; they are layers of Eros, not Thanatos; they lead to tomorrow's births, not yesterday's graves.

(In this unfolding of higher potentials, should any aspect of the Self that has *already emerged* be repressed, lost, or alienated, then we need, therapeutically, to "regress in service of the self"—we need to return to the past, return to the more superficial and shallow layers—to the material self, the libidinal self, the early distorted scripts, and so on—and recontact those facets, release their distortions, reintegrate them in the ongoing stream of consciousness unfolding, and thus resume the voyage to the real depths undistracted by those surface commotions of much sound and fury, signifying, if not nothing, then nothing much. Most "depth psychology"—Freudian, for example—is really "superficial psychology," plumbing not the depths but the shallows of the Self.)

But to say that the deeper waves of the Self are archeologically uncovered is absolutely not to say they are simply pregiven, like a buried treasure chest fully existing and awaiting excavation. It simply means that these deeper waves are all basic potentials of the human (and sentient) condition. Each individual *discovers* the depths that are collectively given to all of us (we all have bodies and minds and souls and spirits, and none of us created those); but each individual discovers the depths by *creating* the surface features of each wave that will be *uniquely* his or hers (what you do with the body, mind, soul, and spirit: that is truly up to you). As always, we have to make the future that is given us; and the full-spectrum therapist is an assistant in this extraordinary voyage that is both discovery and creation.

Depth and Height

Finally, an important word about all these metaphors of "depth," "height," "ascent," "descent," and so on. In the first part of this presentation, I often used the metaphor of "higher" levels and waves, with an ascent of consciousness. Now I have switched to "depth," and a diving into the within. The fact is, all of these metaphors are useful, because they all emphasize different aspects of a consciousness that is greater than any conceptualizations. Yet time and again I have seen discussions come to a crashing halt because somebody didn't like "height" or "ascent," somebody else loathed "within," somebody else "depth." Surely we can appreciate the partial truths that all of these metaphors convey.

Huston Smith, in *Forgotten Truth*, points out that the traditions usually refer to greater levels of reality as *higher*, and greater levels of the self as *deeper*, so that the higher you go on the Great Nest of Being, the deeper you go into your own selfhood. I have just taken that approach in the Archeology of the Self. This is a completely valid approach, because, like all good metaphors, it takes something that we already know and applies it to something as yet unfamiliar, to help us better grasp the latter. In this case, we all know that the body is experienced as being within the physical environment, and we all know that the mind is experienced as being within the body. This metaphor of depth, of moving within, is thus a wonderful hint that the soul, too, is experienced as being within the mind, and yet also moves far beyond it, and that spirit is within and utterly beyond the soul, transcending all, embracing all. The metaphor of "layers of depth" or "sheaths of the Self" (as found in Vedanta, for example, or Teresa's seven interior castles) is a lovely metaphor, and it powerfully reminds us that what the vulgar world takes to be "deep" is often very shallow.

The metaphor of height is equally lovely. Although, as Huston reminds us, "height" is often used for levels of reality, in the final analysis levels of reality and levels of consciousness are two phrases for the same thing, and thus we can usefully speak of the ascent of consciousness, the heights of the soul and spirit, the moving beyond that is transpersonal and superconscious. This metaphor, too, is grounded in something that we know already: every time we move beyond a narrow concern to a broader perspective, we feel we have risen above the situation. There is a sense of being free, a sense of release, an increase in spaciousness, a transcendence. To move from egocentric to ethnocentric to worldcentric to theocentric is to ascend into greater and wider and higher spheres of release and embrace, transcendence and inclusion, freedom and compassion. Sometimes this ascent is also felt concretely, as when, for example, kundalini energy literally moves up the spinal line. The metaphor of vertical height also works well because in many spiritual experiences, we sense that Spirit is *descending* from above into us (a factor emphasized in many spiritual practices, from Aurobindo's descent of the supermind to the Gnostics' descent of the holy spirit). We reach up to Spirit with Eros; Spirit reaches down to us with Agape. These, too, are wonderful metaphors.

But we must be very careful to specify which metaphors we are using, because "depth" in each of them means something exactly opposite. With the depth or archeology metaphor, "depth" means a greater reality; with the ascent metaphor, depth means a lower reality. For example:

Working with the ascent metaphor, we can speak, as Assagioli did, of "height psychology" and "depth psychology." In this case, both "height" and "depth" are judged according to their relation to the average rational-ego. Anything *lower* than the ego (archaic impulses, vital emotions, magic-mythic fantasies) are part of "depth psychology" (which actually means lower, primitive psychology), and anything *higher* than the ego (soul and spirit) are part of "height psychology." In this metaphor, *evolution* is the ascent of consciousness from matter to body to mind to soul to spirit, and *involution* is the descent of consciousness through any of those vehicles. *Regression* is moving backward in the line of evolution, whereas *development* is moving forward in that line.[36] (In the depth metaphor, regression is moving toward the surfaces, and development is moving toward the depths: same thing, different metaphor.)[37]

I will continue to use all of those metaphors, and the context will make clear what is meant. (Figure 10 uses depth; figures 1 through 9 emphasize height.) The fact is, all of those metaphors are true in their own ways. Every within is a beyond, and a full-spectrum therapist is a guide to the ever-increasing depths that reveal ever-greater heights.

FOUR-QUADRANT OR INTEGRAL THERAPY

Notice that the above factors focused almost exclusively on interior developments in an individual (the Upper-Left quadrant). Those conclusions, while valid, need to be set in the context of the other quadrants, even when trying to understand individual development and pathology. All four quadrants mutually interact (they are embedded in each other), and thus *all* of them are required in order to understand pathologies in *any* of them.

We have seen that the subjective events in individual consciousness (UL) are intimately interrelated with objective events and mechanisms in the organism (UR), such as events in the brain stem, the limbic system, the neocortex, brainwave patterns (alpha, beta, theta, and delta states), hemispheric synchronization, neurotransmitter levels and imbalances, and so on.[38] All of those Upper-Right-quadrant factors need to be carefully included in any understanding of individual psychopathology. This includes the partial truths of biological psychiatry, which focuses on pharmacology and medicinal treatments of psychopathology (although we needn't reduce all consciousness to events in the Upper-Right quadrant).

Likewise, we need to look specifically at the larger cultural currents (Lower Left) and social structures (Lower Right) that are inseparable from individual consciousness development. What good does it do to adjust and integrate the self in a culture that is itself sick? What does it mean to be a well-adjusted Nazi? Is that mental health? Or is a maladjusted person in a Nazi society the only one who is sane?

All of those are crucial considerations. A malformation—a pathology, a "sickness"—in any quadrant will reverberate through all four quadrants, because every holon has these four facets to its being. So a society with an alienating mode of production (LR)—such as slave wages for dehumanizing labor—will reflect in low self-esteem for laborers (UL) and an out-of-whack brain chemistry (UR) that might, for example, institutionalize alcohol abuse as self-medication. Similarly, a cultural worldview that devalues women will result in a tendency to cripple individual female potential and a brain chemistry that could definitely use some Prozac.

And so on around the four-quadrant circle. Cripple one quadrant and all four tend to hemorrhage. We are fast approaching an understanding that sees individual "pathologies" as but the tip of an enormous iceberg that includes self-stages, cultural worldviews, social structures, and spiritual access to depth.[39] Individual therapy is by no means unimportant, but in many ways it is but a small slice of a dysfunctional (not yet integral) world. This is why a truly integral therapy is not only individual but cultural, social, spiritual, and political.

In the simplest terms, an integral therapy would therefore attempt to address as many facets of the quadrants as is pragmatically feasible in any given case. Mike Murphy's *Future of the Body* is an excellent compendium of an integral view, as is Tony Schwartz's *What Really Matters*. I outline aspects of an integral approach in *The Eye of Spirit*. Murphy and Leonard's *The Life We Are Given* is a practical guide to one type of integral practice, and is highly recommended.[40]

But anybody can put together his or her own integral practice. The idea is to simultaneously exercise all the major capacities and dimensions of the human bodymind—physical, emotional, mental, social, cultural, spiritual. In *One Taste*, I outline my own recommendations for one such integral ("all-level, all-quadrant") therapy; here are some examples, going around the quadrants, with some representative practices from each:

UPPER-RIGHT QUADRANT (INDIVIDUAL, OBJECTIVE, BEHAVIORAL)—

Physical

DIET—Atkins, Eades, Ornish; vitamins, hormones

STRUCTURAL—weightlifting, aerobics, hiking, Rolfing, etc.

Neurological

PHARMACOLOGICAL—various medications/drugs, where appropriate

BRAIN/MIND MACHINES—to help induce theta and delta states of consciousness

UPPER-LEFT QUADRANT (INDIVIDUAL, SUBJECTIVE, INTENTIONAL)—

Emotional

BREATH—t'ai chi, yoga, bioenergetics, circulation of prana or feeling-energy, qi gong

SEX—tantric sexual communion, self-transcending whole-bodied sexuality

Mental

THERAPY—psychotherapy, cognitive therapy, shadow work

VISION—adopting a conscious philosophy of life, visualization, affirmation

Spiritual

PSYCHIC (shaman/yogi)—shamanic, nature mysticism, beginning tantric

SUBTLE (saint)—deity mysticism, yidam, contemplative prayer, advanced tantric

CAUSAL (sage)—vipassana, self-inquiry, bare attention, centering prayer, Witnessing, formless mysticism

NONDUAL (siddha)—Dzogchen, Mahamudra, Shaivism, Zen, Eckhart, nondual mysticism, etc.

Lower-Right quadrant (social, interobjective)—

Systems—exercising responsibilities to Gaia, nature, biosphere, and geopolitical infrastructures at all levels

Institutional—exercising educational, political, and civic duties to family, town, state, nation, world

Lower-Left quadrant (cultural, intersubjective)—

Relationships—with family, friends, sentient beings in general; making relationships part of one's growth, decentering the self[41]

Community Service—volunteer work, homeless shelters, hospice, etc.

Morals—engaging the intersubjective world of the Good, practicing compassion in relation to all sentient beings

The general idea of integral practice is clear enough: *Exercise body, mind, soul, and spirit in self, culture, and nature.* (That is, try to exercise the full spectrum in the I, we, and it domains.) Pick a basic practice from each category, or from as many categories as pragmatically possible, and practice them concurrently. The more categories engaged, the more effective they all become (because they are all intimately related as aspects of your own being). Practice them diligently, and coordinate your integral efforts to unfold the various potentials of the bodymind—until the bodymind itself unfolds in Emptiness, and the entire journey is a misty memory from a trip that never even occurred.

9

Some Important Developmental Streams

WE HAVE LOOKED BRIEFLY at the basic levels or waves, the self navigating those waves, and some of the problems that the self can encounter when it does so. We turn our attention now to the developmental lines or streams.

It is, of course, up to the self to integrate all these various streams, and we have already followed the general story of the self and its overall development. Now we are simply taking a separate look at some of the more important lines that the self has to balance on its overall journey.[1] Each developmental stream—from morals to aesthetics to interpersonal relationship to cognition—represents an important facet of the great River of Life, and thus, in integrating these streams, the self is learning to be at home in the Kosmos. All of these developmental lines can be entered on an individual's psychograph (figs. 2 and 3), which is actually a graph of one's "at-home-ness" with the world. The deeper each stream, the more of the Kosmos it embraces, until it embraces the All, and is thus released into the Ground and Suchness of the entire display.

MORALS

In charts 1a and 5c, "Moral Span" refers to the stream of moral development, which in my scheme includes not only principles of moral judgment (Kohlberg) and care (Gilligan)—or how one reaches a moral decision—but also moral span, or those deemed worthy of being included in the decision in the first place. As with most streams, this runs from egocentric to ethnocentric to worldcentric to theocentric (or, more accurately, "pneumocentric," or spirit-centered, so as not to confuse the transpersonal realm with mythic theism). Each of those increasingly greater moral depths encompasses within itself a larger moral span (from "me" to "us" to "all of us" to "all sentient beings").[2]

Nowhere is the amazing expansion of consciousness more apparent than in the self's identity and its morals, an expansion that is mostly lost if we focus on flatland and describe psychology in nothing but Right-Hand terms, where there is simply the organism (UR) and its interaction with its environment (LR): the brain processes information through emergent connectionist systems, and driven by its self-organizing autopoietic mechanisms interwoven with its ecosystem, selects those responses that are more likely to get the brain and its genetic material passed forward in time.

All of which is true, and all of which misses the interior facts: What is it that you call *yourself*? With what do you identify this self of yours? For that *identity* expands from egocentric to ethnocentric to worldcentric to pneumocentric—you actually feel that you are *one with* each of those expanding worlds—and none of that is spotted by "organism-and-environment" schemes, which recognize only identities based on exterior quantitative entities (and not interior qualitative shifts).

This expanding identity is directly reflected in moral awareness (subjective identity is reflected in intersubjective morals: not just organism and environment, but self and culture). For you will treat as yourself those *with whom you identify*. If you identify only with you, you will treat others narcissistically. If you identify with your friends and family, you will treat them with care. If you identify with your nation, you will treat your countrymen as compatriots. If you identify with all human beings, you will strive to treat all people fairly and compassionately, regardless of race, sex, color, or creed. If your identity expands to embrace the Kosmos, you will treat all sentient beings with respect and kindness, for they are all perfect manifestations of the same radiant Self, which is your very own Self as well. This comes to you in a direct realization of the Supreme Identity, precisely because identity can span the entire spectrum of consciousness, matter to body to mind to soul to spirit, with each expansion bringing a greater moral embrace, until the All itself is embraced with passionate equanimity.

And where is the selfish gene in all of that? Only by focusing on the Upper-Right quadrant could so narrow a view of human reality gain credence. Since truth in any domain always carries certain types of advantages (wisdom has many rewards), it is fairly easy to find a few ways that these rewards translate into sexual payoffs (which they sometimes do), and thus it is easy to pretend that all these higher truths are nothing but elaborately clever ways to get laid.

And when the limited usefulness of that neoDarwinian game becomes apparent, it is easy enough to shift the entire concept of natural selection to that of "memes" (which are basically holons in any quadrant—intentional, behavioral, social, or cultural), and simply apply natural selection to anything that endures in time—a cultural trait, a social institution, a dress style, a philosophical idea, a music style, and so on. True as all that may be, it continues to ignore the central and crucial issue, which is not: How do holons or memes, once they have emerged, remain in existence? (yes, they are *selected* by evolutionary pressures of various sorts), but rather: Where do the *new* memes come from in the first place? Granted that successful memes are those that are selected once they have emerged; why and how do they emerge at all?

In other words, *creativity*, by any other name, is built into the very fabric of the Kosmos. This creativity—Eros is one of its many names—drives the emergence of ever higher and ever wider holons, a drive that shows up, in the interior domains, *as an expansion of identity* (and morals and consciousness) from matter to body to mind to soul to spirit. And the proof of *that* sequence is found, not by staring at the physical organism and its environment, but by looking into the subjective and intersubjective domains. But humanity has *already* done that very carefully for at least several thousand years, the general results of which are presented in charts 1 through 11.

In flatland, as we have seen, the Right-Hand world of objective entities and systems is thought to be the only "really real" world, and thus all *subjective* values are said to be merely personal, or idiosyncratic, or based on emotional preferences, but possess no grounding in reality itself. But if we reject the limitations of flatland, it becomes obvious that the subjective and intersubjective domains are simply the interiors of holons at every level in the Kosmos. Subjectivity is an *inherent* feature of the universe. Of course there are personal preferences within the subjective domains, but those domains themselves, and their general waves of unfolding, are as real as DNA, and even more significant. The expansion of moral identity is simply one of the more obvious manifestations of these profound waves of consciousness unfolding.

MOTIVATION: LEVELS OF FOOD

"Levels of Food" (chart 1b) refers to the levels of *need*, drive, or fundamental motivation (which may be conscious or unconscious). As I suggested in *Up from Eden* and *A Sociable God*, needs arise due to the fact that every structure (in both levels and lines) is a *system of relational exchange* with the same level of organization in the world at large, resulting in a holarchy of "food"—physical food, emotional food, mental food, soul food.[3]

Physical needs reflect our physical relationships and exchanges with the material universe: food, water, shelter, and so on. Emotional needs reflect our relationships with other emotional beings, and consist in an exchange of emotional warmth, sexual intimacy, and caring. Mental needs reflect our exchanges with other mental creatures: in every act of verbal communication, we exchange a set of symbols with others. (Monks who take vows of both celibacy and silence report that the lack of communication is much more painful than the lack of sex: these are genuine needs and drives, based on relational exchange.) And spiritual needs reflect our need to be in relationship with a Source and Ground that gives sanction, meaning, and deliverance to our separate selves (the unsatisfaction of those needs is described, one way or another, as hell).

In *Up from Eden* I discuss these levels of need and motivation in detail (giving eight general levels of motivation, not the simple four I am using here), and correlate them with similar conceptions, such as Maslow's, along with examples of how oppression and repression *distort relational exchanges*, resulting in pathology (physical illness, emotional illness, mental illness, spiritual illness; all of the pathologies that we discussed in chapter 8 are not just disruptions of the self, but disruptions of relational exchange with others). Although we may discern many different types and levels of needs, all genuine needs simply reflect the *interrelationships* necessary for the life of any holon (at any level).

WORLDVIEWS

"Worldview" (chart 1b) refers to the way the world looks at each of the basic waves in the Great Nest. When you only have sensations, perceptions, and impulses, the world is archaic. When you add the capacity for images and symbols, the world appears magical. When you add concepts, rules, and roles, the world becomes mythic. When formal-reflexive capacities emerge, the rational world comes into view. With vision-logic, the existential world stands forth. When the subtle emerges, the world becomes divine. When the causal emerges, the self becomes divine. When the nondual emerges, world and self are realized to be one Spirit.

But not in any sort of pregiven, fixed fashion. A worldview unfolds in a particular culture with its specific (and often local) surface features.[4] In general, "worldview" refers to the Lower-Left quadrant, or all of the intersubjective practices, linguistic signs, semantic structures, contexts, and communal meanings that are generated through shared perceptions and collective values—in short, "culture." This cultural dimension (Lower Left) is distinct from (but not separable from) the *social* dimension (Lower Right), which involves the exterior, concrete, material, institutional forms of collective life, including modes of techno-economic production, collective social practices, architectural structures, social systems, the written and spoken media of communication (print, television, internet), geopolitical infrastructures, family systems, and so on.

Worldviews are particularly important because all individual, subjective consciousness *arises within* the clearing created by cultural or intersubjective structures. For example, somebody at Kohlberg's moral stage 2 (morals are part of intersubjective structures), who faces a personal ethical dilemma, will have all of his thoughts governed, in the main, by the deep features of moral stage 2. He will *not* have a moral-stage-5 thought cross his mind. Thus, he is not "free" to think anything he wants. His subjective thoughts *arise in a space or clearing* that is created by, and largely controlled by, *the intersubjective structures of his cultural worldview* (including the moral stage of his individual self). As we saw, even if this person has a peak experience of a transpersonal realm, that experience will be largely interpreted and carried by the intersubjective structures which have developed in his own case. (Failing to see that subjective experiences *arise in the space created by intersubjective structures* is one of the main liabilities of many forms of spiritual and transpersonal psychology, and especially those that focus merely on altered or nonordinary states.)[5] Of course, individuals can, to some degree, transcend aspects of their own given culture; and when that happens, they seek out others with whom to share the new insights—thus creating a new culture. The point is that subjectivity and intersubjectivity—in fact, all four quadrants—are mutually arising and mutually interdependent.

Affect

"Affect" (chart 1b) refers to the developmental line of affects, or "emotions" and "feelings" in the broadest sense. There are two rather different meanings of the word "emotion" in the perennial philosophy, and I use both. One, emotion refers to a *specific level* of consciousness: the pranamayakosha, or the level-sheath of emotional-sexual energy (the basic structure of "impulse/emotion" on the charts). Two, it refers to the energetic *feeling tone* of any and all of the basic structures across the entire spectrum. (These are listed in "Affect" in chart 1b). I have often been accused of limiting "feeling" or "emotion" to the first definition and ignoring the second, but this is clearly incorrect. In *The Atman Project*, for example, I listed "affective tone" for each of the basic structures in the overall spectrum. Consciousness itself is more of a "feeling-awareness" than it is a "thinking-awareness," and there are levels of that feeling-awareness, or experiential vividness, across the Great Nest.

(One of the real problems in humanistic/transpersonal circles is that many people confuse the warmth and heart-expanse of postconventional awareness with the merely subjective feelings of the sensory body, and, caught in this pre/post fallacy, recommend merely bodywork for higher emotional expansion, when what is *also* required is postformal cognitive growth, not simply preformal cognitive immersion. Obviously bodywork has an important and foundational role to play in growth and therapy, but the elevation of preformal sensations to postformal love has caused endless problems in the human potential movement.)[6]

Gender

"Gender Identity" (chart 1b) follows the development of gender from its biological roots (which are biological givens, not cultural constructions), through conventional formations (which *are* cultural constructions, mostly), into transgender orientations (which are largely transdifferentiated and transconventional). Research continues to confirm that the *deep features* of the basic waves and most of the self-related streams (morals, needs, role capacities) are *gender-neutral* (i.e., they are essentially the same in men and women). However, men and women can negotiate these same structures and stages "in a different voice" (which is usually summarized by saying men tend to translate with an emphasis on agency, women on communion, although both use both).[7]

In *The Eye of Spirit* I argued that we need an "all-level, all-quadrant" approach to feminism and gender studies, or an "integral feminism." Many feminists unfortunately resist an integral approach because they often acknowledge only one quadrant (usually the Lower Left, or the cultural construction of gender), while denying the others (such as biological factors, since they suspect that of being another version of "biology is destiny," which it would be, if the Upper-Right quadrant were the only quadrant in existence. But biological factors are profoundly molded by cultural values, social institutions, and personal intentions; thus acknowledging some biological factors is not sexist but realistic). This narrow focus is unfortunate, but it needn't stop others from moving ahead with a more integral feminism, and many have, such as Joyce Nielsen, Kaisa Puhakka, and Elizabeth Debold.[8]

Aesthetics

"Art" (chart 8) refers to levels of aesthetic experience, and we can see here a very important phenomenon that applies to most forms of development. Namely, you can analyze a given activity (such as art) on the basis of both the level it *comes from* and the level it *aims at*—or the level producing the art and the level depicted in the art. (As with any mode of consciousness, you can analyze the level of the *subject* of consciousness—the level of selfhood—and level of reality of the *object* of consciousness, as explained in several endnotes.)[9] For example, art produced *by* the mental level can take as its object something in the material, mental, or spiritual realms, and you get a quite different art in each case. The resultant artwork is thus a combined product of the structures that are producing the art and the structures that are depicted in the art (i.e., the level of self producing the art, and level of reality depicted in the art). This gives us a grid of a very large number of different types of art, of which I have listed only a few representative samples on chart 8.[10]

To show what is involved in this dual analysis, notice that the earliest prehistoric artists (e.g., the cave painters of the Paleolithic), although presumably "closer" to nature and the sensorimotor realm, never painted nature in the way that moderns would. The Paleolithic artists do not use perspective, nor is their art empirical or "accurate" in any sense we moderns would accept (figures overlap each other with no concern for spatial separation, there is no depth perception, etc.). A plausible reason is that they were painting the sensorimotor realms *from* the magical structure, which lacks the capacity for spatial perspective. Likewise, in the mythic era, nature was never portrayed in perspective either, but always as part of a mythic-literal background. Only with the rise of modernity (starting in the Renaissance), and the widespread use of perspectival-reason, did perspective itself come to be seen and thus painted in art. We might say, only as consciousness gained some distance from nature, could it paint nature more realistically.

For the same reason, only with the (anti)modern reaction of Romanticism could emotional feelings become the object of expressive art. It was only with the widespread differentiation of mind and body that the body realms could be clearly perceived by the mind and thus portrayed. (And when the modern differentiation went too far into dissociation, that painful pathology could also become part of the existential expressivist themes of art.)

The same dual analysis (level of the subject producing the art and level of the object being portrayed) can be done with modes of knowing (and, in fact, with all modes of consciousness).[11] Rationality, for example, can take as its object the sensorimotor realms (producing empiric-analytic knowledge), the mental realms themselves (producing phenomenology and hermeneutics), or the spiritual realms (producing theology, mandalic reason, and so forth). This is important to realize because with modernity, some very high levels (e.g., reason) confined their attention to some very low realms (e.g., matter), with the result that modernity looked like nothing but regression, whereas it was only "half" regressive: a higher subject confining its attention to a lower object—a deeper self in a shallower world (the good news and bad news of modernity).[12]

Aesthetics is an extremely important developmental stream because it is one of the preeminent subjective streams (which doesn't mean "unreal" or merely idiosyncratic; it means very real as subjective ontology). We saw that Baldwin and Habermas, among others, recognized that development must be traced in at least three irreducible modes—aesthetic, moral, and scientific (i.e., the Big Three).[13] As I pointed out in *The Eye of Spirit*, all of the numerous developmental streams are basically variations of the Big Three. Some developmental lines emphasize the subjective components (e.g., self-identity, affects, needs, aesthetics); some emphasize the intersubjective components (worldviews, linguistics, ethics); and some the objective components (exterior cognition, scientific cognition, Piagetian cognitive line, etc.).[14] None of these can finally be separated from the others, but each developmental stream tends to be oriented toward a particular quadrant (e.g., aesthetics toward the subjective, morals toward the intersubjective, and cognition toward the objective). By emphasizing the importance of following developments in all four quadrants (or simply the Big Three), we can strive for a truly integral model. The holons in all four quadrants evolve, and a comprehensive model would attempt to honor all of those evolutionary streams.

Different Types of Cognitive Lines

Notice that in chart 3b ("Cognitive Development"), I have listed "overall cognitive lines." This refers to an alternative way to conceptualize cognitive development once we move from a monolithic one-axis model to an integral model of states, waves, and streams.[15] As indicated on the chart, we can picture not one uniform line of cognitive development, with each stage stacked on top of its predecessors like so many bricks, but several relatively independent lines of cognitive development, each developing alongside the others like columns in a beautiful mansion. Based primarily on the fact of *natural states of consciousness*—that is, on the undeniable existence and availability of gross/waking, subtle/dreaming, and deep sleep/causal states to individuals at almost every stage of their development—we can reasonably postulate that those states/realms might also have their own developmental lines. This would mean that we could trace the development of different types of cognition (gross, subtle, and causal) as they appear throughout a person's life. Instead of one appearing only after another, they would all develop simultaneously, at least in certain ways. Some examples:

The main characteristic of gross cognition is that it *takes as its object the sensorimotor realm*. This line of cognition would begin with sensorimotor development itself, move into concrete operational, and then both peak and begin to trail off at formal operational cognition. It tends to start trailing off at formal, and especially postformal, operations, because both of those increasingly take the world of thought as an object, and thus increasingly move into subtle cognition. We might say, then, that the gross (or more technically, the gross-reflecting) line of cognition runs from sensorimotor to preop to conop to formop and trails off at vision-logic. This cognitive line develops, as most lines do, from preconventional to conventional to postconventional, but it doesn't easily continue beyond that into postformal and post-postconventional waves, simply because in those higher stages the sensorimotor world, although not in any way abandoned, ceases to be the dominant object of awareness.

The main characteristic of subtle cognition is that it *takes as its object the world of thought*, or the mental and subtle realms altogether. This developmental line also begins in infancy (and probably in prenatal states; it is said to be the main cognitive mode in most of the bardos, as well as sleep with dreams and meditative states of savikalpa samadhi). This subtle line of cognition involves precisely all those perceptions whose study has been downplayed by western cognitive psychologists: first and foremost, states of imagination, reverie, daydreams, creative visions, hypnogogic states, etheric states, visionary revelations, hypnotic states, transcendental illuminations, and dozens of types of savikalpa samadhi (or meditation with form). What they all have in common, even in infancy and childhood, is that they take as their referents, not the material world of sensorimotor occasions, but the interior world of images, thoughts, visions, dreams. . . .[16]

We would generally expect the subtle-cognitive stream to have available to it the same basic waves as most other streams: preconventional, conventional, postconventional, and post-postconventional (or egocentric, sociocentric, worldcentric, and pneumocentric), but the point is that it is a developmental line reaching all the way back to infancy, and not simply jumping out at a higher, adult stage.

(In chart 3b I have shown subtle-cognition picking up importance at formal and beyond, but that is just an arbitrary indication. In fact, I suspect what we will find is that subtle-cognition shows a U-development, being more present in early childhood and then temporarily waning as conop and formop come to the fore, then picking up prominence again in the postformal stages, up to the causal. At the same time, we needn't get unduly Romantic over these implications, because the subtle cognition present in childhood is still a largely preconventional, egocentric cognition, no matter how otherwise vivid and imaginative [see chap. 11]. Still, the importance of looking at this as a developmental line is that childhood subtle-cognition could then be acknowledged and honored, which would also presumably have benefits at the postformal stages.)

The main characteristic of causal cognition is that *it is the root of attention* (and the capacity for Witnessing).[17] This line, too, can be traced to early childhood, although it comes increasingly to the fore in the postformal stages. (For the important reasons that the early infantile fusion states should not be confused with the higher enlightened states or Ground, see the endnote).[18] But this line, also, if recognized and honored, could be strengthened from its first appearances in childhood forward, presumably with multiple benefits then and later.[19]

DIFFERENT LINES OF THE SELF

We can apply the same type of modeling to the self and its development, suggesting that these three great realms—gross, subtle, and causal—are home to three different lines of self, which I generically call ego, soul, and Self (or frontal, deeper psychic, and Witness).[20] Just as we did with cognition, we can treat these three modes of self as relatively independent developmental lines, so that they do not develop one after the other, but alongside each other. That relationship is shown in column two in chart 4b and in figure 11.

Of course, most streams can and do develop relatively independently of each other—the various streams often progress at their own pace through the major waves—which is why overall development follows no linear sequence whatsoever. This section continues that theme, but more radically, for I am suggesting—just as with cognition—that what has traditionally been considered *one stream* (in this case, the self) might actually be *several different streams*, each developing relatively independently.

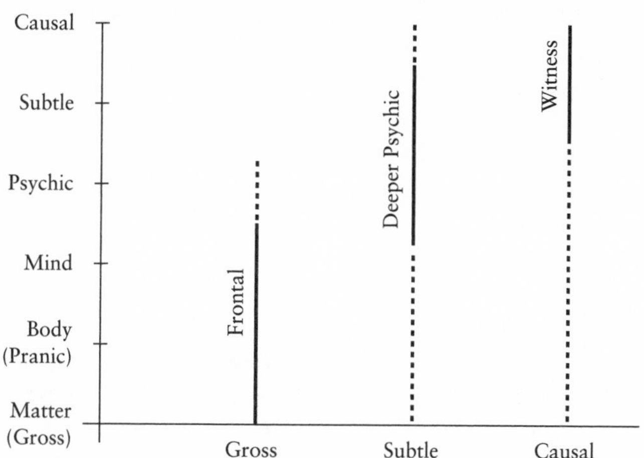

FIGURE 11. *The Development of the Frontal (or Ego), the Deeper Psychic (or Soul), and the Witness (or Self)*

We have already seen that the major stages of the self stream—such as bodyself, persona, ego, centaur—*depend* on the competences developed by the previous stages in that overall stream. Once those selves emerge, they overlap; but a great deal of research strongly confirms that they emerge in a generally hierarchical fashion (as indicated in column two in chart 1a and again in fig. 10).[21]

All of that is still true. The present conception does not replace that, but complements it: the realms of gross, subtle, and causal can develop, to some degree, independently of each other; and thus the frontal, the soul, and the Self can develop, to some degree, alongside each other. What researchers have been measuring as sequential self development is still accurate, but what they are measuring is the *frontal self* (bodyself to ego to centaur), and not the soul or spirit, which can develop, to some degree, *alongside* all of that, following their own holarchies and nests within nests, none of which is obvious in frontal terms.[22]

The ego (or frontal) is the self that adapts to the gross realm; the soul (or deeper psychic) is the self that adapts to the subtle realm; and the Self (or Witness) is the self that adapts to the causal realm. The frontal includes all of the self-stages that *orient consciousness to the gross realm* (the material self, the bodyself, the persona, the ego, and the centaur—all of which can be generically called "the ego"). The frontal is the self that depends on the line of gross cognition (sensorimotor to preop to conop to formop), and the frontal is therefore the self-stream responsible for orienting and integrating consciousness in the gross domain.

Alongside those developments, the soul (the psychic/subtle self) can follow its own trajectory, unfolding in its own holarchical stream. The soul or deeper-psychic line includes all the self-streams that *adapt consciousness to the many facets of the subtle sphere*. The soul is the self that depends on the subtle line of cognition (which includes, as we saw, imagination, reverie, daydreams, creative visions, hypnogogic states, etheric states, visionary revelations, hypnotic states, transcendental illuminations, and numerous types of savikalpa samadhi),[23] and thus the soul is the self-stream that orients and integrates consciousness in the subtle domain. In chart 4b, I have indicated the U-development that the subtle sometimes seems to go through: present early in development (as "trailing clouds"), then fading out as frontal (egoic) development starts to get underway, only to reassert itself in the postformal stages. (Since most theorists contest this U-development, I have left it out of fig. 11. We will return to this topic in chap. 11.)

Alongside both of those general-realm developments, the Self (or Witness) can follow its own unfolding stream.[24] The Witness is the self that depends upon the causal line of cognition (the capacity for attention, detached witnessing, equanimity in the face of gross and subtle fluctuations, etc.), and thus it is the self that orients and integrates consciousness in the causal domain. Just as important, this Self is responsible for the overall integration of all the other selves, waves, and streams. It is the Self that shines through the proximate self at any stage and in any domain, and thus it is the Self that drives the transcend-and-include Eros of every unfolding. And it is the Self supreme that prevents the three realms—gross, subtle, and causal—from flying apart in the first place. For, even though the three domains can show relatively independent development, they are still held together, and drawn together, by the radiant Self, the purest Emptiness that can impartially reflect, and therefore embrace, the entire manifest domain.

Although with higher development, the center of gravity of consciousness increasingly shifts from ego to soul to Self, nonetheless all of those are the necessary and important vehicles of Spirit as it shines in the gross, subtle, and causal realms. Thus, all three of them can be, and usually are, simultaneously present in various proportions throughout development, and the highest development itself simply involves their seamless integration as a chorus of equally valued voices of Spirit in the world.

Integral Psychology

Thus, the simplest generalization of an integral psychology is that it involves waves, streams, and states, ego, soul, and spirit.

When it comes to integral therapy, this means several things. First, although overall development still shows an unmistakable morphogenetic drift to deeper domains (ego to soul to spirit), the therapist can be alert to ways to recognize and strengthen the soul and spirit as they increasingly make their appearance, not simply after the ego, but within it and alongside it. Integral and transpersonal therapy works *concurrently* with the frontal, soul, and spirit, as they each unfold alongside each other, carrying their own truths, insights, and possible pathologies. Attunement to these different dimensions of consciousness can facilitate their more graceful unfolding.[25]

But this is not to suggest that gross-realm work (bodywork, ego strengthening) can be bypassed in favor of soul or spirit work, because without a strong ego as a foundation, the higher realms cannot be carried as a permanent, stable, integrated realization. Instead, the higher realms are relegated to transient peak experiences, temporary revelations, or even dissociated into spiritual emergencies. An individual who is at moral stage 2 in the frontal line of moral development can "holographically experience" all the transpersonal realms he desires, but he will *still* have to develop to moral stage 3, then 4, then 5, in order to begin to actualize those experiences in a *permanent,* nondistorted, postconventional, worldcentric, global, and bodhisattvic fashion. In fact, failure of the therapist to follow (and encourage) frontal line development, while merely encouraging altered states, can contribute to the client's failure to permanently integrate the higher and lower domains into a full-spectrum realization.

Thus, even though gross, subtle, and causal lines (and selves) can exist alongside each other in many ways, still, with continuing evolution and integral development, the *center of gravity* continues to shift holarchically toward the deeper layers of the Self (ego to soul to spirit), and around these deeper waves consciousness is increasingly organized. Concerns of the ego, while rarely disappearing, tend to fade from immediacy; the soul comes to the foreground more often. But then it, too, eventually tends to fade, becoming thinner and more transparent, as the center of gravity shifts more and more toward spirit. All of the lower selves, as functional capacities, continue to exist, holarchically enfolded in higher waves; they all continue to serve functional capacities, face their own problems, respond to their own treatments; but they increasingly lose their power to commandeer consciousness and claim it for their own.

Thus, for an overall integral development, the center of gravity of consciousness still moves through the nine fulcrums in the Great Nest, but it is a cacophony of many voices, many streams, often overlapping, always intertwining. But none of the major waves of consciousness can be totally bypassed on that account. The frontal cannot be bypassed,[26] vision-logic cannot be bypassed,[27] the subtle cannot be bypassed,[28]—not for permanent, enduring, integral development and awakening. All these waves and streams are headed toward the ocean of One Taste, pulled through that great morphogenetic field by the force of "gentle persuasion toward Love"—pulled, that is, by Eros, by Spirit-in-action, by the Love that moves the sun and other stars.

10

Spirituality: Stages or Not?

ONE OF THE THORNIEST of questions is whether spirituality itself necessarily unfolds in stages. This is an extremely touchy issue. Nonetheless, as I have often suggested, this question depends in large measure on how we define "spirituality." There are at least five very different definitions, two of which seem to involve stages, and three of which do not. All of them appear to be legitimate uses of the word "spirituality," but it is absolutely necessary to specify which you mean. In fact, I think these are five very important aspects of the broad phenomenon we call "spirituality," and all of them deserve to be included to some degree in any integral model.

Here are the common definitions: (1) Spirituality involves the highest levels of any of the developmental lines. (2) Spirituality is the sum total of the highest levels of the developmental lines. (3) Spirituality is itself a separate developmental line. (4) Spirituality is an attitude (such as openness or love) that you can have at whatever stage you are at. (5) Spirituality basically involves peak experiences, not stages.

1. *Spirituality involves the highest levels of any of the developmental lines.* In this definition, "spirituality" basically means the transpersonal, transrational, post-postconventional levels of *any* of the lines, such as our highest cognitive capacities (e.g., transrational intuition), our most developed affects (e.g., transpersonal love), our highest moral aspirations (transcendental compassion for all sentient beings), our most evolved self (the transpersonal Self or supraindividual Witness), and so

on.[1] In this usage, spirituality (or this particular aspect of spirituality) definitely follows a sequential or stage-like course, because it is, by definition, the post-postconventional stages in any of the developmental streams. This is a very common usage, reflecting those aspects of spirituality that embody the very highest capacities, the noblest motives, the best of aspirations; the farther reaches of human nature; the most highly evolved, the growing tip, the leading edge—all of which point to the highest levels in any of the lines.

2. *Spirituality is the sum total of the highest levels of the developmental lines.* This is similar to the previous definition, but with a slightly different (yet important) twist. This definition emphasizes the fact that, even though the individual lines unfold hierarchically, the *sum total* of the highest stages of those lines would show no such stage-like development. Like "overall development" and "overall self" development, "overall spiritual development" would *not* be stage-like. (Say there are ten developmental lines. Say that the post-postconventional stages of those lines are the ones we are calling "spiritual." One person might develop post-postcon capacities in lines 2 and 7. Another person, in lines 3, 5, 6, 8, and 9. Another person, in lines 1 and 5. Each of those lines is hierarchical, but the sum total obviously follows no set sequence at all.) Every person's spiritual path, in other words, is radically individual and unique, even though the particular competences themselves might follow a well-defined path. (Notice, however, that with this definition, precisely because the developmental lines *themselves* are still stage-like, the development in each of those lines could be tested for.) I believe that this definition, like all of them, points to some very real and important aspects of spirituality, aspects that any complete definition of spirituality would want to include.

3. *Spirituality is itself a separate developmental line.* Obviously in this case spiritual development would show some sort of stage-like unfolding, since a developmental line, by definition, shows development.[2] I have drawn together some two dozen theorists, East and West, in charts 6a–c, who present convincing and sometimes massive evidence that at least some aspects of spirituality undergo sequential or stage-like development. This includes most of the various meditative paths East and West. In all of these cases, these aspects of spirituality show holarchical sequential development (although again, that does not preclude regressions, spirals, temporary leaps forward, or peak experiences of any of the major states.)

Daniel P. Brown's extensive work on the crosscultural stages of meditative development deserves special mention as being the most meticulous and sophisticated research to date (chart 6b). What he and his coworker Jack Engler found is that "The major [spiritual] traditions we have studied *in their original languages* present an unfolding of meditation experiences in terms of a *stage model*: for example, the Mahamudra from the Tibetan Mahayana Buddhist tradition; the Visuddhimagga from the Pali Theravada Buddhist tradition; and the Yoga Sutras from the Sanskrit Hindu tradition [these were subsequently checked against Chinese and Christian sources]. The models are sufficiently similar to suggest an *underlying common invariant sequence of stages*, despite vast cultural and linguistic differences as well as styles of practice. . . . The results strongly suggest that the stages of meditation are in fact of cross-cultural and universal applicability (at a deep, not surface, analysis)."[3]

Their work is included in *Transformations of Consciousness*, along with an in-depth study by Harvard theologian John Chirban of the stages of spiritual development evidenced by saints in Eastern Orthodox Christianity (see chart 6c). Chirban's conclusion: "Although each saint describes his own experience (often in his own unique way), basic parallels emerge as one compares the stages of the saints with one another. This sameness confirms the catholicity of their experience . . ."—and the catholicity (or universal applicability) of the basic waves of consciousness themselves, which are similarly reflected in these numerous cross-cultural sources. Whether one is looking at Saint Teresa, Muhyiddin Ibn 'Arabi, Lady Tsogyal, Saint Dionysius, Patanjali, Hazrat Inayat Kahn, or Mahamudra (all listed in charts 6a–c), one is again struck by the broadly similar morphogenetic field or developmental space over which their stages migrate.

"Highest Yoga Tantra," which, next to Dzogchen, is said to be the highest of the Buddha's teachings, possesses an unsurpassed grasp of the extraordinary interrelation between conscious states and bodily energies (chart 6b). According to this teaching, in order to master the mind, one must concomitantly master the body's subtle energies—ch'i, prana, rLung, ki—and this yoga is an exquisite system of harnessing these subtle energies at every stage of development, right up to and including the enlightened state of Clear Light Emptiness. Highest Yoga Tantra outlines this overall consciousness evolution in terms of seven very clear-cut stages, each with a very striking phenomenological sign that accompanies the stage when it emerges. Thus, in meditation, when concentration reaches the point that the first basic structure (or skandha) is transcended, there arises in awareness a mirage-like appearance. When all five gross-realm basic structures are transcended, and subtle-realm consciousness emerges, there appears a vision like a "clear autumn moonlight." As subtle consciousness is transcended and one enters very subtle (or causal) consciousness, formless cessation appears as "the thick blackness of an autumn night," and so on (chart 6b).

Although these interior visions show a great deal of deep structural similarity with other meditative systems, several critics have, over the years, scolded me for implying that there are strong similarities between, for example, the Buddhist Dharmakaya (and Emptiness) and the Vedanta causal body (and nirguna Brahman). And yet—as only one example—according to Highest Yoga tantra, one type of the Dharmakaya is experienced in *deep dreamless sleep* (formlessness); the Sambhogakaya, in the *dream state*; and the Nirmanakaya, in the *waking state*. But notice: according to Vedanta, the causal body is experienced in deep dreamless sleep, the subtle body is experienced in the dream state, and the gross body in the waking state. Therefore, if you believe that there are similarities in deep dreamless sleep between individuals, it follows that there are some profound similarities between the Buddhist Dharmakaya and the Hindu causal body. (And likewise, similarities between the Buddhist Sambhogakaya and Hindu subtle body, and the Nirmanakaya and gross body.)

Of course there are many important differences between these Buddhist and Hindu notions, and those need to be rigorously honored. And yet—simultaneously—there seem to be important and profound similarities, and these cannot be cavalierly dismissed, as pluralists and relativists do. In all of my writings I have tried to emphasize both—certain similarities in deep features, important differences in surface features.

One of the major difficulties in coming to terms with a *stage conception* is that most people, even if they are in fact progressing through stages of competence, *rarely experience anything that feels or looks like a stage*. In their own direct experience, "stages" make no sense at all. With respect to cognitive development, for example, you can videotape children at a preop stage (where they will claim that when you pour an identical amount of water from a short glass into a tall glass, the tall glass has more water), and you can show them the videotape when they are at the conop stage (where it is "completely obvious" that the same amount of water is present in each glass), and they will accuse you of doctoring the videotape, because nobody could be that stupid, and certainly not them. In other words, they just went through a monumental stage in development, yet they actually experienced not the slightest thing that told them that an extraordinary milestone had just occurred.

So it is with stages in general. We spot them only by standing back from unreflective experience, comparing our experiences with others, and seeing if there are any common patterns. If these common patterns check out in numerous different settings, then we are justified in assuming that various stages are involved. But in all cases, these stages are the product of direct investigation and research, not abstract philosophizing. And when it comes to spiritual experience, all of the great wisdom traditions in charts 6a–c have found that some very important spiritual competences *follow a stage model*, not in a rigidly clunk-and-grind fashion, but as unfolding waves of subtler and subtler experiences, and that when you compare these experiences over a large number of people, certain similarities in unfolding occur. In other words, we have some stages.

My model has often been accused of being based solely on the Eastern meditative traditions. A quick glance at charts 6a–c is enough to dispel that misconception. I would in particular like to draw attention to the work of Evelyn Underhill. Her masterpiece, *Mysticism*, first published in 1911, is still in many ways an unsurpassed classic for the elucidation of the Western mystical and contemplative traditions. Underhill divides Western mysticism into three broad hierarchical stages (with numerous substages), which she calls *nature mysticism* (a lateral expansion of consciousness to embrace the stream of life), *metaphysical mysticism* (culminating in formless cessation), and *divine mysticism* (which she divides into dark night and union). These are in many ways quite similar to my own nature mysticism, deity mysticism, and formless/nondual mysticism. These *stages of spirituality* are deeply important, whether they appear East or West, North or South, and no account of spirituality is complete without them.

4. *Spirituality is an attitude (such as openness or love) that you can have at whatever stage you are at.* This is probably the most popular and common definition. Nonetheless, it has proven very difficult to define or even state in a coherent fashion. We can't easily say that the requisite attitude is love, because love, according to most research, tends (like other affects) to unfold from egocentric to sociocentric to worldcentric modes; and therefore this attitude is *not* fully present at all of the levels, but rather itself develops (do we really want to call egocentric love "spiritual"?). "Openness" might work, but again the question becomes: does

the capacity for openness itself simply show up fully formed, or does it develop? And just how "open" can a preconventional individual be, when he or she cannot even take the role of other? "Integration" would fit the bill—the degree to which whatever lines are present are integrated and balanced—but in my system that is just another name for what the self does, and thus is not anything specifically "spiritual." At any rate, I believe this is a legitimate definition, but thus far, coherent examples of it have been scarce.

5. *Spirituality basically involves peak experiences*. That is certainly true in many cases, and peak experiences (or altered states of consciousness) do not usually show development or stage-like unfolding. They are temporary, passing, transient. Moreover, states, unlike structures, are mostly *incompatible*. You cannot be drunk and sober at the same time. (This is quite unlike structures, which, because they transcend and include, can coexist: cells and molecules can both exist together, the one embracing the other—which is why growth and development occur by way of structures, not states, although the latter are significant in themselves and can have a direct impact on development). Therefore, if one's definition of spirituality is a peak experience, then that does not in itself involve a stage-like unfolding.

However, as I earlier suggested, you can examine peak experiences more closely and find that they generally involve psychic, subtle, causal, or nondual peak experiences interpreted through archaic, magic, mythic, or rational structures—and each of those show stage-like development. Still, this is an important definition of spirituality, and it goes to show that at virtually any stage of development, temporary peak experiences of the transpersonal realms are possible. However, to the extent these *temporary states* are converted to *enduring traits,* they become structures that show development. (I will include in the endnote a discussion of a plausible mechanism for this conversion: the self metabolizes temporary experience to produce holistic structure.)[4]

Those are five of the more common definitions of spirituality. The conclusion: not everything that we can legitimately call "spirituality" shows stage-like development. Nonetheless, many aspects of spirituality turn out, upon closer inspection, to involve one or more aspects that are developmental. This includes the higher reaches of the various developmental lines, as well as spirituality considered as a separate line itself. Peak experiences, however, do not show stage-like development, although both the structures that have the peak experiences, and the realms that are peaked into, show development if permanent realizations are acquired.

Does Psychological Development Have to Be Completed Before Spiritual Development Can Begin?

This depends, once again, almost entirely on how we define those terms. If spirituality is defined as a separate line of development, the answer is "No" (because it occurs alongside of, not on top of, psychological development). If spirituality is defined as peak experience, the answer is also "No" (because that can occur at any time). But beyond that it gets a little trickier.

First of all, what many theorists mean by "psychological development" is the *personal* stages of development (precon, con, and postcon), and what they mean by "spiritual" is the *transpersonal* stages (post-postcon). *Using those definitions*, and when looking at *any one developmental line*, the psychological must generally be completed before the spiritual can stably emerge (simply because, as much research indicates, you can't have postcon without first having con, and so on).

However—and this is what has confused many theorists—because the developmental lines themselves can unfold independently, an individual can be at a very high spiritual stage (transpersonal or post-postcon) in one line and still be at a very low personal or psychological stage (con or precon) in others. For example, a person might be at a transpersonal level of cognition (perhaps attained by meditative development), and yet still be at a personal or psychological (con or precon) stage of moral development. Thus, even though, with these definitions, the spiritual comes only after the psychological in any given line, nonetheless all sorts of spiritual developments can occur before, alongside of, or after, all sorts of psychological developments, precisely because the lines themselves are relatively independent. A person can be at a precon stage in one line, a postcon stage in another, and a post-postcon in three others, which, by these definitions, means two psychological levels and three spiritual levels, so obviously overall psychological development does *not* have to be completed before any sort of spiritual developments can occur.

If one's idea of spirituality is peak experiences, those can occur anytime, any place, so overall psychological development does not have to be completed for those, either. But to the extent those states become traits, they, too, will of necessity enter the stream of development and swim in its morphogenetic currents, flowing through the waves in the great River of Life.

THE IMPORTANCE OF SPIRITUAL PRACTICE

Finally, let us note an item of great importance. Whether, in the end, you believe spiritual practice involves stages or not, authentic spirituality does involve *practice*. This is not to deny that for many people beliefs are important, faith is important, religious mythology is important. It is simply to add that, as the testimony of the world's great yogis, saints, and sages has made quite clear, authentic spirituality can also involve direct *experience* of a living Reality, disclosed immediately and intimately in the heart and consciousness of individuals, and fostered by diligent, sincere, prolonged spiritual practice. Even if you relate to spirituality as a peak experience, those peak experiences can often be specifically induced, or at least invited, by various forms of spiritual practice, such as active ritual, contemplative prayer, shamanic voyage, intensive meditation, and so forth. All of those open one to a direct experience of Spirit, and not merely beliefs or ideas about Spirit.

Therefore, don't just think differently, practice diligently. My own recommendation is for any type of "integral transformative practice" (as outlined in chapter 8); but any sort of authentic spiritual practice will do. A qualified teacher, with whom you feel comfortable, is a must. One might start by consulting the works of Father Thomas Keating, Rabbi Zalman Schachter-Shalomi, the Dalai Lama, Sri Ramana Maharshi, Bawa Muhaiyadeen, or any of the many widely acknowledged teachers in any of the great lineages.

At the same time, be wary of those spiritual paths that involve simply changing your beliefs or ideas. Authentic spirituality is not about translating the world differently, but about transforming your consciousness. Yet many of the "new-paradigm" approaches to spirituality would simply have you change the way you think about the world: you are supposed to think holistically instead of analytically; you are supposed to believe, not in the Newtonian-Cartesian billiard-ball world, but in the world of systems theory and the great "web of life"; you are supposed to think in terms, not of patriarchal divisiveness, but of the holistic Goddess and Gaia.

All of those are important ideas, but they are merely ways to think about the Right-Hand world, not ways to transform the Left-Hand world. Most of these new-paradigm approaches recommend that we use vision-logic (or holistic thinking) in order to overcome our fragmented world. But, as we have repeatedly seen, cognitive development (such as vision-logic or network-thinking) is necessary, *but not sufficient*, for moral development, self-development, spiritual development, and so on. You can have full access to vision-logic and still be at moral stage one, with safety needs, egocentric drives, and narcissistic inclinations. You can totally master systems theory and completely learn the new physics, and still be very poorly developed in emotional, moral, and spiritual streams.

Thus, simply learning systems theory, or the new physics, or learning about Gaia, or thinking holistically, will not necessarily do anything to transform your interior consciousness, because none of those address the interior stages of growth and development. Open any book on systems theory, the new paradigm, the new physics, and so on, and you will learn about how all things are part of a great interconnected Web of Life, and that by accepting this belief, the world can be healed. But rarely will you find a discussion of the many *interior stages of the growth of consciousness* that alone can lead to an actual embrace of global consciousness. You will find little on preconventional, conventional, postconventional, and post-postconventional stages; nothing on what an enormous amount of research has taught us on the growth of consciousness from egocentric to sociocentric to worldcentric (or more specifically, the nine or so fulcrums of self unfolding); no hints about how these interior transformations occur, and what you can do to foster them in your own case—thus truly contributing to a worldcentric, global, spiritual consciousness in yourself and others. All you find is: modern science and matriarchal religions all agree that we are parts of the great Web of Life.

The ecological crisis—or Gaia's main problem—is not pollution, toxic dumping, ozone depletion, or any such. Gaia's main problem is that not enough human beings have developed to the postconventional, worldcentric, global levels of consciousness, wherein they will automatically be moved to care for the global commons. And human beings develop to those postconventional levels, not by learning systems theories, but by going through at least a half-dozen major interior transformations, ranging from egocentric to ethnocentric to worldcentric, at which point, and not before, they can awaken to a deep and authentic concern for Gaia. The primary cure for the ecological crisis is not learning that Gaia is a Web of Life, however true that may be, but learning ways to foster these many arduous waves of interior growth, none of which are addressed by most of the new-paradigm approaches.

In short, systems theory and the Web-of-Life theories do not generally transform consciousness because, hobbled with their subtle reductionism, they do not adequately address the interior stages of consciousness development—where the real growth occurs. They might be a fine place for one to start on the spiritual path—they are helpful in suggesting a more unified life—but they themselves do not appear to be an effective path to that life. They do not offer, in short, any sort of sustained interior practice that can actualize the higher and more global stages of consciousness. And, sadly, in claiming to offer a completely "holistic" view of the world, they often prevent or discourage people from taking up a genuine path of interior growth and development, and thus they hamper the evolution of just that global consciousness that they otherwise so nobly espouse.

11

Is There a Childhood Spirituality?

IS THERE A CHILDHOOD SPIRITUALITY?
By definitions 1 and 2, no. By definitions 3, 4, and 5, yes. Sort of.

Early Stages

Definition 1 (spirituality is the highest level in any line) and definition 2 (spirituality is the sum total of the highest levels in all the lines) rule out almost any sort of childhood spirituality, simply because during infancy and childhood most developmental lines are preconventional and conventional. This does not preclude other types of spirituality; it simply says that *to the extent* you define spirituality as transrational, supramental, postformal, superconscious, and post-postconventional, then those are not significantly present in childhood.

Definition 3 (spirituality is a separate line of development) maintains that infancy and childhood definitely have a spirituality . . . but only the lowest stages of spirituality, which by most definitions do not look very spiritual at all. Even according to the theorists who propose this definition, the love is egocentric, the beliefs are narcissistic, the outlook is self-absorbed, the capacity to take the role of others (and thus genuinely care for others) is rudimentary or missing altogether. Nonetheless, this definition considers those to be the *early stages* of lines that can be called "spiritual" because they will, with further development, unfold into capacities that most people would clearly recognize as spiritual. James

Fowler's "stages of faith" is exactly this type of model. By this definition, then, we should not conclude that infants are saints or sages, or permanently in touch with authentic spiritual realities, but rather are on a long road to authentic spirituality via higher development (and here this reverts to definition 1 or 2: "real" or "authentic" spirituality involves the post-postconventional stages of development).

Definition 4, on the other hand, strongly maintains that infants and children are directly in touch with spiritual realities, or at least can be, because they can be in touch with the attitude that defines spirituality (openness, love, fluidity, etc.). Moreover, most people using this definition claim that children are *more* in touch with this quality of, say, openness or fluidity, than are adults, and that a genuine spirituality involves the *recapture* of this openness.

The problem with that definition, as we saw, is that it has had difficulty producing credible and coherent examples. Does the "openness" just show up fully formed, or does it develop? If it can't take the role of other, how "open" can it really be? If the openness is egocentric, no matter how spontaneous and fluid, is that really what we mean by "spiritual"? Is a joyful narcissist "spiritual"?

It appears that what most people have in mind with this definition is that children often have a more open contact with a certain feeling-dimension of being (the prana-maya-kosha, élan vital, emotional-etheric sheath, second chakra, etc.), and that is very likely true. Moreover, it is definitely true that aspects of that dimension can be repressed by the higher structures of the mind (ego, superego, conscience), which can result in various types of painful pathology. And that, finally, a *recapture* (in the form of regression in service of the ego) of that lost potential is required in order to heal the damage and regain a more fluid, flowing, feeling-ful outlook on life.

I agree with all of those points. The question is, why call the preconventional feeling-dimension by the term "spiritual," when, as research has repeatedly demonstrated, it is egocentric in relation to others? For the mind to be in touch with the feelings of the body is extremely important, but spirituality *also* involves being in touch with the feelings of *others*, and a positively massive amount of research has consistently demonstrated that such role-taking and perspectivism steadily *increases* from preop to conop to formop to postformal.

If your idea of spirituality is feeling good, then childhood might be Eden;[1] but if your idea *also* involves doing good, by taking the role of others, and projecting your consciousness through multiple perspectives and pluralistic outlooks so as to include compassion, caring, and altruism, then childhood is a realm of diminished expectations, no matter how wonderfully fluid and flowing its egocentrism. What is regrettable about the repression of childhood capacities is not that, for the most part, it involves the repression of higher, spiritual dimensions (e.g., the vijnanamaya-kosha), but that it involves the repression of lower but invaluable foundations (e.g., pranamaya-kosha), whose dissociation can cripple further development. Moreover, the *repression barrier* erected by the ego to prevent lower, prerational impulses from coming up, can also act, in later development, to prevent higher, transrational impulses from coming down. The defenses against id can defend against God, simply because a wall is a wall. But what the childhood ego essentially represses is the preconventional id, not the postconventional God.

Altered States and Trailing Clouds

Definition 5 (peak experiences), however, offers a credible definition and a modest amount of evidence that at least some children have some types of spiritual experiences. I believe that is true, and I have offered a grid of such experiences—namely, peak experiences of the psychic, subtle, causal, or nondual realm interpreted through an archaic, magic, mythic, or rational outlook—for most children, that means magic or mythic. I realize that many theorists strongly object to calling that "spiritual," and research such as Fowler's would deny any higher or authentic spirituality to those structures; but I think we can refer to them as spiritual peak experiences, as long as we are careful to specify the exact contours.[2]

The one aspect of infancy and childhood that, if it exists, might be genuinely spiritual is that aspect I call the "trailing clouds of glory" (from Wordsworth: "Not in entire forgetfulness, but trailing clouds of glory do we come. . . ."), namely, the deeper psychic (or soul) dimension that, some evidence tentatively suggests, is present from prenatal through the early years, but then fades as frontal (egoic) development gets under way.[3] The "trailing clouds of glory" refers in general to all the deeper psychic (or soul) awareness that the individual brings to this life and which is therefore present in some sense from conception forward (however you wish to construe that—as reincarnation, or simply as deeper potentials present from the start). Hazrat Inayat Khan probably put it best, representing the traditional view: "The crying of an infant is very often the expression of its longing for the angelic heavens [through which it has just passed on its way to earthly birth—what the Tibetans call the rebirth bardo]; the smiles of an infant are a narrative of its memories of heaven and of the spheres above."[4]

This deeper psychic awareness is, according to various theories, either (1) the soul descending from the bardo realms (the realms between death and rebirth), or (2) a deeper ground or potential that is necessarily lost and buried as the analytic ego develops (but can be regained in enlightenment or full spiritual realization).

The second option, although it initially sounds feasible, seems to fall apart in the details. This ground is said to be the same ground one regains in enlightenment, but if so, why would anybody ever abandon it? If this ground is regained, why does development do something it does in no other system, namely, start running backwards? Would a chicken regress to an egg in order to find itself? If this ground is reunited with the ego, so that *both together* constitute full development, that means that the ground itself *is not complete*, and how could something inherently not complete be the ground of full enlightenment? Could a part ever be the ground of the whole? This view—which, incidentally, I once embraced—seems to be largely inadequate in both theory and data.[5]

That leaves option number one, the bardo realms, as the major contender, even though it sounds quite far-fetched to the conventional mind. Nonetheless, there is a modest amount of evidence that is suggestive.[6] It appears that this deeper psychic being is increasingly submerged and forgotten as frontal or egoic development gets under way (see chart 4b), although if development continues into the actual psychic level (F-7), this deeper psychic being emerges (which often brings flashbacks of childhood, when this deeper psychic was "watching" from afar).[7] But whatever this deeper psychic capacity is, it is *not* the resurrection of a prerational infantile structure, but the discovery of a transrational structure.

We can say, then, that infants and children at the very least seem to have access to some types of spiritual experiences (as peak experiences), even though these are interpreted through frontal structures that are preconventional and egocentric (and not, as it were, very spiritual themselves). But in possibly being in touch with the deeper psychic (or soul) realm, infancy and childhood might evidence a connection with one type of spiritual dimension, even though, once again, it is of necessity interpreted and expressed through preconventional and egocentric channels, and thus is not spiritual in any pure sense.

12

Sociocultural Evolution

Spirit-in-Action

It now seems apparent that there are at least four major inadequacies to the Great Chain as it was traditionally conceived, and in order to bring it into the modern and postmodern world—and develop a truly integral approach—these shortcomings need to be carefully addressed.[1]

The first, as we saw, is that the four quadrants were very seldom differentiated on an adequate scale. Thus, the great traditions rarely understood that states of consciousness (UL) have correlates in the organic brain (UR), a fact that has revolutionized our understanding of psychopharmacology, psychiatry, and consciousness studies. Likewise, the traditions evidenced little understanding that individual awareness (UL) is profoundly molded by both its background cultural worldviews (LL) and the modes of techno-economic production (LR) in which it finds itself. This left the Great Chain open to devastating critiques from the Enlightenment, from modern cognitive science, from neuropsychiatry, and from postmodern cultural and historical studies, among others, all of which demonstrated that consciousness is not merely a disembodied, transcendental noumenon, but is deeply embedded in contexts of objective facts, cultural backgrounds, and social structures. The Great Chain theorists had no believable response to these charges (precisely because they were deficient in these areas).

As we saw, each of the *vertical levels* of the Great Chain needs to be differentiated into at least four *horizontal dimensions* (intentional, behavioral, cultural, social). The Great Nest desperately needs to be modernized and postmodernized: it needs to recognize the importance of cultural background, relativistic surface structures and contexts, correlations with modern scientific discoveries, sensitivity to minorities that the mythic-agrarian structure often marginalized, the importance of pluralistic voices, and so on. Only as body, mind, soul, and spirit are differentiated into the Big Three can these objections be handled.

The second inadequacy is that the level of mind itself needs to be subdivided in the light of its *early development*. Here the contributions of Western psychology are decisive. To put it in a nutshell, the mind itself has at least four major stages of growth: *magic* (2–5 years), *mythic* (6–11 years), *rational* (11 onward), and integral-aperspectival or *vision-logic* (adulthood, if then). Precisely because the infantile and childish origins of the *preformal* levels of magic and mythic were not clearly understood, the traditions often confused them with the *postformal* states of psychic and subtle, and this pre/post fallacy haunts most of the perennial philosophy, injecting it not only with truly enlightened wisdom, but substantial stretches of superstition.

The third inadequacy: Because the traditional Great Chain theorists had a poor understanding of the early, infantile, prerational stages of human development, they likewise failed to grasp the types of *psychopathologies* that often stem from complications at these early stages. In particular, psychosis, borderline, and neurotic diseases often stem from problems at the early fulcrums of self-development, and can best be approached with an understanding of their developmental dimensions. Meditation—which is a way to carry development forward into the transpersonal—will not, as a rule, cure these prepersonal lesions (as hosts of American practitioners found out the hard way).

The fourth inadequacy in the traditional Great Chain is its lack of understanding of evolution, an understanding that is also a rather exclusive contribution of the modern West. This is easily remedied, because, as many theorists have pointed out, if you tilt the Great Chain on its side and let it unfold in time—instead of being statically given all at once, as traditionally thought—you have the outlines of evolution itself. Plotinus temporalized = evolution.

In other words, evolution to date—starting with the Big Bang—has unfolded approximately three-fifths of the Great Chain—matter, sensation, perception, impulse, image, symbol, concept, rule, and formal, in essentially the order suggested by the Great Nest. All that is required is to see that the Great Chain does not exist fully given and statically unchanging, but rather evolves or develops over great periods of time. And the fact is, despite the bluff of western biologists, nobody really understands how higher stages emerge in evolution—unless we assume it is via Eros, or Spirit-in-action.

This also means, as I have often pointed out, that what the perennial philosophy took to be eternally unchanging archetypes can better be understood as formative habits of evolution, "Kosmic memories," as it were, and not pregiven molds into which the world is poured.[2] This dynamic orientation can bring the Great Nest of Being more into accord with evolutionary thinkers from Peirce to Sheldrake to Kaufmann, and it is a view that is definitely implicit in Great Nest theorists from Plotinus to Asanga and Vasubandhu.[3]

The point is that, once the Great Nest is plugged into an *evolutionary* and *developmental* view, it can happily coexist with much of the God of the modern West, namely, evolution.[4] Moreover, it raises the stunning possibility: if evolution has thus far unfolded the first three-fifths of the Great Nest, isn't it likely that it will continue in the coming years and unfold the higher two-fifths? If that is so, God lies down the road, not up it; Spirit is found by going forward, not backward; the Garden of Eden lies in our future, not our past.[5]

Be that as it may, when one moves from pluralistic relativism to universal integralism (e.g., when one moves from green to yellow/turquoise and begins to take advantage of second-tier constructions), one is open to such meta-systemic theories as presented in charts 9a and 9b—namely, overviews of social and cultural evolution.

Collective Evolution

In my definitions, "social" refers to the Lower-Right quadrant (the interobjective dimension, including forms of the techno-economic base, social systems, institutions, and physical structures), and "cultural" refers to the Lower-Left quadrant (the intersubjective dimension, including collective worldviews, ethics, values, and meaning). The preponderance of evidence clearly suggests that evolution occurs in both of these quadrants, as it certainly does in the others. But this needs to be qualified in several respects.

For example, to say that a given society is at a magical level of development does not mean that everybody in that society is at that level. It only means that the *average* level of consciousness is generally magical, and that, more specifically, the defining laws, principles of cultural organization, and mores of everyday reality stem predominantly from the magical worldview. But any number of people can be above or below that average in their own case. For example, some individuals in a magical culture (unlike a child at the magical structure—and here is one of the many places that strict onto/phylo parallels break down) can be at a mythic, mental, or higher level of development. Habermas believes, for instance, that even in hunting and gathering societies, a few people developed the capacities for formal operational thinking, and I have suggested that a few went even further and developed postformal and *psychic capacities* (and these were, of course, the shamans).[6] Thus, unlike a child at the magical level, a truly developed shaman in a magical culture, having evolved various postconventional capacities, would be able to authentically experience the transpersonal realms (mostly the psychic, but also, on occasion, subtle and perhaps causal) and interpret them through non-narcissistic and postconventional structures: in other words, an authentic spirituality by any definition.

That, of course, is speculation, and would represent a highly developed shamanic vision. As for the more typical or common shamanic journey, the available evidence suggests that it was a magic-level peak experience of the psychic domains, and thus it retained preformal imprints and interpretations, heavily involved, as magic often is, with power drives and needs. "Power" or "strong medicine" remains the dominant tone of many shamanic drives, reflecting, perhaps, the fact that in the typical hunting and gathering society, the major scare resource, as Habermas pointed out, was power over nature, or simple safety needs, as Maslow might say.

Nonetheless, the profound importance of the shamanic voyage, in any of its versions, was that it was the first great discovery of, and exploration of, the transpersonal domains, and thus many shamanic insights, especially into the psychic realms, remained unsurpassed.[7] In particular, we may note that the shaman, as the first "psychotherapist," was the first to discover the extraordinary importance of transpersonal altered states of consciousness for ordinary healing, both physical healing and psychological healing—an insight that, disastrously, was one of the casualties of the modern flatland.

Still, the preponderance of evidence, when not subjected to an interpretation that is biased toward pluralistic relativism, suggests that, for the most part, both the average and the most advanced modes of development continued to deepen with subsequent evolution, and charts 9a and 9b outline some of the major contours of this evolutionary migration.

Social Evolution

Lenski has laid out the forms of social evolution in a way that is now uncontested by most scholars: foraging, horticultural, maritime, agrarian, industrial, and informational. Systems theorists (and structural-functionalists, including Parsons, Merton, Luhmann, Alexander, Bellah) have shed an enormous light on social action systems, their maintenance and self-reproduction.[8] Marxists and Neomarxists, despite the obvious failings of a system that attempts to reduce all quadrants to the Lower Right, have nonetheless outlined the many ways in which the techno-economic base profoundly influences the consciousness of men and women, and no integral theory can afford to overlook these important findings.[9]

The major drawback of systems theory (and Lower-Right theories in general) is their subtle reductionism: the attempt to reduce all interior domains (of the I and we) to objective it-domains—to information processing circuits, neuronal systems, social behavior, autopoietic self-maintenance systems, and "web-of-life" theories—all of which, to the extent they claim to be "holistic" and "all-encompassing," actually deny the lifeworld of the interior dimensions. Systems theory claims to offer a unified theory of everything, but in reducing all quadrants to the Lower Right, it actually leaves out "half" of the world, namely, the Left-Hand domains. As such, systems theory is actually part of the flatland project of modernity. It is part of the disease for which it claims to be the cure.

A genuine or integral holism would include both the exterior holism of systems theory and the interior holism of phenomenal consciousness, morals, values, waves, streams, and states, all embraced in their own terms, not forced into the molds of the others.

Cultural Evolution

Evolution in the cultural domain is a sensitive topic, with potential for abuse when not handled with care. Still, the evidence for it continues to mount, and numerous theorists have embraced it in qualified forms. (As we saw in chapter 4, for several decades the green meme successfully fought any evolutionary thinking in academia, understandably concerned over its potential for abuse. But post-green developments have managed to combine green sensitivity to multiple perspectives with second-tier constructions.) In recent times, cultural evolution has been championed, in various ways, by Gerald Heard, Michael Murphy, W. G. Runciman, Sisirkumar Ghose, Alastair Taylor, Jean Houston, Duane Elgin, Jay Earley, Daniel Dennett, Jürgen Habermas, Robert Bellah, Ervin Laszlo, Kishore Gandhi, and Jean Gebser, to name a few.[10]

The pioneering work of Jean Gebser is paradigmatic: he sees cultural worldviews evolving—to use his words—from archaic to magic to mythic to mental to integral (see chart 9b). Gebser's masterpiece, *Ursprung und Gegenwart* (*The Ever-Present Origin*), is certainly one of the most brilliant surveys of cultural evolution ever written, and no integral theory, in my opinion, can hope to succeed without taking its meticulous formulations into account. It should be noted, however, that Gebser's "integral structure" refers basically to the overall vision-logic wave, and does not adequately cover the higher, truly transpersonal stages (psychic, subtle, causal, and nondual). Gebser's foremost American interpreter, Georg Feuerstein, agrees. "I must side with Wilber on this point. I think there is sufficient evidence to usefully group a wide range of what would be considered spiritual experiences into three main categories: those that are basically *psychic* (I propose *psychosomatic*), *causal* (I propose *psychospiritual*), and *nondual* (I propose *spiritual*)."[11] Thus Feuerstein's overall spectrum includes archaic, magic, mythic, mental, integral, psychic, causal, and nondual—a much more accurate full-spectrum view than Gebser's. Nonetheless, in the domain of average collective development—archaic to magic to mythic to rational to integral—Gebser is unsurpassed.

Habermas's attempt to reconstruct historical materialism on the basis of universal pragmatics and communicative action remains the most sophisticated of modern attempts to trace sociocultural evolution. The great advantage of Habermas's formulations is their attempt at a comprehensive scope: a truly all-quadrant, almost all-level, view (see chart 10). We saw that the major drawbacks in his approach include an inadequate coverage of both the prerational and the transrational domains, which unfortunately renders his scheme unstable with respect to both nature and spirit (a major liability). Still, in the intermediate realm of mind, Habermas is indispensable.

Fortunately, several theorists, who are equally familiar with the higher levels of consciousness, have used their expertise to trace consciousness evolution on the whole. Of these, particular mention might be made of the work of Jean Houston (especially *Life-Force*, a superb book based in part on the important work of Gerald Heard; see chart 9a), Duane Elgin (whose *Awakening Earth* is a masterful overview of consciousness evolution; see chart 9b), and Allan Combs (the only reason I have not listed Combs on the chart is that his wonderful book, *The Radiance of Being*, is a summary and overview of Gebser/Aurobindo/Wilber, with many original insights, but without a radically new series of proposed stages, although he does offer his own model).[12]

Although the above scholars have made vital contributions to our understanding of sociocultural evolution, the entire topic itself remains deeply problematic to many theorists—especially to liberals (who suspect it of marginalizing tendencies), traditionalists (who do not understand why so much of religion was left behind by modern "evolution"), and Romantics (who often believe in devolution). Since evolution is one of the crucial ingredients—some would say *the* crucial ingredient—of the modern scientific worldview, and if we truly wish an integral embrace of premodern, modern, and postmodern, then we need a way to put the theory of evolution in a context that both honors its truths and curtails its abuses.

Five Important Hints

The crucial issue is this: In order for cultural evolution and morphogenesis to be embraced as an explanatory principle in human history, it faces exactly the profound objections that have led traditionalists, Romantics, and liberal social theorists to reject it. In other words, if evolution is operating in the human domain, how can we account for Auschwitz? And how dare we make judgments about some cultural productions being more evolved than others? How dare we make such value rankings? What kind of arrogance is that?

The traditionalists and today's perennial philosophers, for example, cannot believe in cultural evolution because of such modern horrors as Auschwitz, Hiroshima, Chernobyl. How can we say evolution is at work in humans when it produces such monsters? Better to deny evolution altogether, than to get caught up in having to explain those obscenities.

The Romantic critics of evolution, on the other hand, are responding to what seems to be a universal human sympathy for a time prior to today's turmoils. Primal men and women, on the whole, did not suffer the disasters of modernity—no industrial pollution, little slavery, few property disputes, and so on. By any scale of quality, haven't we in fact gone downhill? Isn't it time to get back to nature, back to the noble savage, and thus find a truer self, a fairer community, a richer life?

The liberal social theorists likewise have every reason to recoil in horror from the notion of cultural evolution. Its unbelievably crude forms, such as Social Darwinism, are not just lacking in compassion; much more sinister, this type of crass "evolutionism," pressed into the hands of moral tyrants, would produce exactly the type of ruinous and barbaric notions of the superman, the master race, the coming human demigods, who would chillingly goose-step their way into history, who would in fact inscribe their beliefs on the tortured flesh of millions, would press their ideology into the gas chambers and let it all be settled there. Liberal social theorists, reacting to such horrors, naturally tend to look upon any sort of "social hierarchy" as a prelude to Auschwitz.

Obviously, if consciousness evolution is to be used as any sort of explanatory principle, it faces several stern difficulties. What is therefore required is a set of tenets that can explain *both* advance and regression, good news and bad news, the ups and downs of a evolutionary thrust that is nonetheless as active in humans as it is in the rest of the Kosmos. Otherwise, we face the extremely bizarre situation of driving a virulent wedge right through the middle of the Kosmos: everything nonhuman operates by evolution; everything human does not.

What are the principles that can rehabilitate cultural evolution in a sophisticated form, and thus re-unite humanity with the rest of the Kosmos, and yet also account for the ups and downs of consciousness unfolding? Here are some of the central explanatory principles that I believe we need:

1. *The dialectic of progress.* As consciousness evolves and unfolds, each stage solves or diffuses certain problems of the previous stage, but then adds new and recalcitrant—and sometimes more complex and more difficult—problems of its own. Precisely because evolution in all domains (human and otherwise) operates by a process of differentiation and integration, then each new and more complex level necessarily faces problems not present in its predecessors. Dogs get cancer; atoms don't. But this doesn't damn evolution altogether! It means evolution is good news, bad news, this dialectic of progress. And the more stages of evolu-

tion there are—the greater the depth of the Kosmos—the more things that *can* go wrong. Modernity can get sick in ways that foragers could not even imagine, literally.

So evolution inherently means that new potentials and new wonders and new glories are introduced with each new stage, but they are invariably accompanied by new horrors, new fears, new problems, new disasters. And any truly balanced account of history is a chronicle of the new wonders and the new diseases that unfolded in the unrelenting winds of the evolution of consciousness.

2. *The distinction between differentiation and dissociation.* Precisely because evolution proceeds by differentiation and integration, something can go wrong at each and every stage—the greater the depth of the Kosmos, the more diseases there can be. And, as we saw, one of the most prevalent forms of evolutionary pathology occurs when *differentiation* goes too far into *dissociation*, whether ontogenetically or phylogenetically. In human evolution, for example, it is one thing to differentiate the mind and body, quite another to dissociate them. It is one thing to differentiate culture and nature, quite another to dissociate them. Differentiation is the prelude to integration; dissociation is the prelude to disaster.

Human evolution (like evolution everywhere else) is marked by a series of important differentiations, which are absolutely normal and altogether crucial for the evolution and integration of consciousness (it is only by differentiation that an acorn grows into an oak). But at each stage, these differentiations can go too far into dissociation, which converts depth into disease, growth into cancer, culture into nightmare, consciousness into agony. And any balanced account of history is a chronicle not only of the necessary differentiations of consciousness evolution, but also of the pathological dissociations and distortions that all too often followed in their wake.

3. *The difference between transcendence and repression.* To say that evolution proceeds by differentiation and integration is to say that it proceeds by transcendence and inclusion. Each stage includes its predecessors, then adds its own defining and emergent qualities: it transcends and includes.

But for just that reason, with *pathology*, the senior dimension doesn't transcend and include; it transcends and represses, denies, distorts, disrupts. Each new and higher stage has exactly this choice: transcend and include, befriend, integrate, honor; or transcend and repress, deny, alienate, oppress. And any balanced account of history is a chronicle of the great transcendent occasions of human evolution, as well as of the grotesque repressions, oppressions, brutalities.

4. *The difference between natural hierarchy and pathological hierarchy.* During the evolutionary process, that which is whole at one stage becomes a part of the whole of the next: whole atoms become parts of molecules, whole molecules become parts of cells, whole cells become parts of organisms. . . . Each and every thing in the Kosmos is a whole/part, a holon, existing in a nested hierarchy or holarchy, an order of increasing wholeness and holism.

But that which transcends can repress. And thus normal and natural hierarchies can degenerate into pathological hierarchies, into dominator hierarchies. In these cases, an arrogant holon doesn't want to be *both* a whole and a part; it wants to be a whole, period. It does not want to be a part of something larger than itself; it does not want to share in the communions of its fellow holons; its wants to dominate them with its own agency. Power replaces communion; domination replaces communication; oppression replaces reciprocity. And any balanced account of history is a chronicle of the extraordinary growth and evolution of normal hierarchies, a growth that ironically allowed a degeneration into pathological hierarchies, which left their marks burned into the tortured flesh of untold millions, a trail of terror that accompanied the animal who not only can transcend but repress.

5. *Higher structures can be hijacked by lower impulses.* Tribalism, when left to its own devices, is relatively benign, simply because its means and its technologies are relatively harmless. You can only inflict so much damage on the biosphere, and on other humans, with a bow and arrow (and this lack of means does not necessarily mean presence of wisdom). The problem is that the advanced technologies of rationality, when hijacked by tribalism and its ethnocentric drives, can be devastating.

Auschwitz is not the result of rationality. Auschwitz is the result of the many products of rationality being used in irrational ways. Auschwitz is rationality hijacked by tribalism, by an ethnocentric mythology of blood and soil and race, rooted in the land, romantic in its dispositions, barbaric in its ethnic cleansing. You cannot seriously attempt genocide with a bow and arrow; but you can attempt it with steel and coal, combustion engines and gas chambers, machine guns and atomic bombs. These are not rational desires by any definition of rational; these are ethnocentric tribalisms commandeering the tools of an advanced consciousness and using them precisely for the lowest of the lowest motives. Auschwitz is the endgame, not of reason, but of tribalism.

Those are a handful of the distinctions that, I believe, are necessary to reconstruct the evolution of human consciousness in a much more satisfactory and compelling fashion, a fashion that can clearly account for the undeniable advances as well as the undeniable disasters of human history.[13] With this approach, and with these five or so distinctions, I believe we can begin to re-unite humanity with the rest of the Kosmos, and not be saddled with a truly bizarre and rigid dualism: humanity over here, everything else over there.

No, it seems that we are part and parcel of a single and all-encompassing evolutionary current that is itself Spirit-in-action, the mode and manner of Spirit's creation. The same currents that run through our human blood run through swirling galaxies and colossal solar systems, crash through the great oceans and course throughout the cosmos, move the mightiest of mountains as well as our own moral aspirations—one and same current moves throughout the All, and drives the entire Kosmos in its every lasting gesture, an extraordinary morphogenetic field that exerts a pull and pressure which refuses to surrender until you remember who and what you are, and that you were carried to this realization by that single current of an all-pervading Love, and here "there came fulfillment in a flash of light, and vigor failed the lofty fantasy, but now my will and my desires were moved like a wheel revolving evenly, by the Love that moves the sun and other stars."

Spiritual Revelations: The Growing Tip of Evolution

With those five tenets, I believe we can more humanely approach the topic of evolution and draw upon its liberating insights. If, as we have seen, certain aspects of spirituality become more available in the higher stages of development, then an understanding of development—what it is, how to foster it—is part of the truly liberal agenda of liberty, freedom, equality. We have already examined the stages of individual ontogenetic development, and we are now surveying the correlative stages of phylogenetic/cultural development. In both cases, we need to be alert not only to the major emergents and positive advances, but also to the new pathologies, repressions, oppressions, and brutalities that each new evolutionary advance makes possible.

Up from Eden traces these cultural developments in both the *average mode* and the *most advanced mode* that typically defined a given era (see chart 9a). The general idea is simple: when the average level of consciousness of a given culture is, say, magical, what is the highest level of consciousness generally available?[14] We just saw that in magical times, the most highly evolved mode was generally shamanic. The shaman was *the growing tip of consciousness evolution* (reaching at least to the psychic domain, either as a permanent structural achievement, or, at the very least, as a series of altered states and shamanic voyages).[15] The magical/shamanic mode was the dominant form of consciousness for the largest period of humanity's stay on earth thus far, reigning from perhaps as early as 500,000 years BCE to around 10,000 BCE, with its peak period probably from around 50,000 to 7000 BCE[16]

As the average mode evolved from magic into mythic (beginning roughly around 10,000 BCE), and nature elementals and polytheistic figments increasingly gave way to a conception of one God/dess underlying the manifold world, the figure of the *saint* eventually became the dominant spiritual realizer. Often portrayed with haloes of light around the crown chakra (signifying the vivid awakening of the subtle realms of light and sound at and beyond the sahasrara), the saint was the great conveyor of growing-tip consciousness as it moved within and beyond nature mysticism to deity mysticism. These interior transcendental journeys—portrayed in brilliant manner by such exemplars as Saint John of the Cross, Ramanuja, Saint Teresa, Shinran, Saint Hildegard—disclosed depths of the soul, and heights of reality, that altered the very nature of consciousness at large, and left the world profoundly altered in its very structure.

As the average, collective mode of consciousness evolved from mythic to mental (beginning around the sixth century BCE), the most advanced mode evolved from subtle to causal, and the *sage*, more than the saint, embodied this growing tip of consciousness. Whereas the saint experienced divine interior luminosity, grace, love, and ecstasy, the sage experienced nothing. The sage, rather, was the first to push into the purely formless realm of sheer Emptiness, the causal of unmanifest absorption—nirvana, the cloud of unknowing, apophatic, nirvikalpa samadhi, nirodh, cessation. But far from being a literal "nothing" or stark blankness, Emptiness is the creative ground of all that is (hence "causal")—a vast Freedom and infinite Openness whose very discovery means Liberation from the world of form, suffering, sin, and samsara. Whereas, in the subtle, the soul and God find a communion or even union, in the causal, the soul and God both disappear into Godhead—the Atman that is Brahman, the Supreme Identity of the Sufi, "I and the Father are One," the separate self dissolves in Emptiness—and deity mysticism gives way to formless mysticism, the mysticism of the Abyss, the great Cloud of Unknowing, the Consciousness that is infinitely within and beyond the manifest world altogether.

But consciousness evolution is always "transcend and include," and having completely *transcended* the world of Form, consciousness awakens to a radical *embrace* of all Form: "That which is Form is not other than Emptiness, that which is Emptiness is not other than Form," says the *Heart Sutra*, in what is perhaps the most famous formula for this eternal, sacred equation. For pure Spirit (Emptiness) and the entire manifest world (Form) have become one eternal embrace. Shankara, one of India's great realizers, put this ultimate "transcend and include" as follows:

> The world is illusory,
> Brahman alone is real,
> Brahman is the world.

The World is illusory (transient, ephemeral, passing, finite, mortal), and it must be completely transcended in every way in order to find the sole reality of Spirit (Brahman). But once having completely let go of the world, and having plunged into the infinite Release of purest Spirit (unbounded, unlimited, timeless, formless reality), the finite world is then embraced and completely included in infinite Spirit, or the perfect union of manifest and unmanifest: Brahman *is* the world, and nondual mysticism takes it start with just that realization of One Taste.

The great Nondual traditions began around 200 CE, especially with such figures as Nagarjuna and Plotinus; but these traditions, particularly in their advanced forms as Tantra, began to flower in India around the eighth to the fourteenth century (coincident with the first collective or average-mode glimmers of vision-logic, exemplified in the West with Florence and the rise of Humanism, circa fourteenth century). It was during this time that Ch'an Buddhism saw its extraordinary rise in Tang and Song China (the seventh through the thirteenth centuries), and Padmasambhava brought Tantra to Tibet, which began its unparalleled flowering (especially the eighth through the eighteenth centuries).

These, too, are the most general of generalizations, but they are not without their usefulness. Among other things, distinguishing between average and most advanced allows us to avoid assuming that all the products of one era were generated by the same wave of consciousness. Scholars all too often look at a period in history and simply assume that everybody in that society was at the same level of consciousness (rather like looking back at our modern era and assuming Reagan and Krishnamurti were at the same level), and then proceed, on the basis of that assumption, to reach the most dubious conclusions. Deep ecologists often assume that in foraging cultures, everybody shared a shamanic consciousness, whereas the genuine shaman was a very rare bird—one shaman to a tribe, usually, and only one shaman in ten a true master (if that). Romantic theorists look back to ancient Egypt, notice that some adepts were clearly alive to the serpent power (kundalini), and then assume that the whole culture was awash in enlightened beings, whereas the number of kundalini adepts in any town could probably be counted on one hand (at most). It is then all too easy to assume that evolution has gone steadily downhill from these wonderful ancient days of rampant spirituality, whereas—if we actually follow the growing tip itself—spirituality has in many ways continued to deepen profoundly over the ages. Valentinus was amazing, but compare him to Eckhart. Magdelene was profound, but compare her to Saint Teresa of Ávila. Boethius was extraordinary, but compare him to Saint John of the Cross. And right up to Hakuin and Dogen, perhaps the most influential Japanese Zen adepts of all time; Sri Ramana Maharshi, one of India's greatest realizers (who died a mere few decades ago); and Aurobindo, her greatest philosopher-sage (also a mere few decades ago).

Further, by making that distinction (average and advanced), we can immediately see that, whereas some past epochs might look "very spiritual," their most common or *average mode* (such as magic or mythic) was actually *preformal,* not postformal. Only the fairly rare shaman, saint, or sage actually evolved into higher levels of psychic, subtle, or causal adaptation; and therefore the profoundly spiritual stages (psychic, subtle, causal)—*as a common, average mode of consciousness*—exist, if at all, in our collective future, not our past. Of course, any individual during any period—past, present, or future—can develop into the higher realms under his or her own power. But whole epochs of postformal spirituality, as a common attainment, were almost certainly never present at any point in past history. Scholars who mistake magic and mythic for authentic spirituality, and who therefore look at the past and think all forms of spirituality are behind us, are, I believe, in for a pleasant surprise. The *most advanced* figures of the past were plumbing the depths of the transpersonal levels, and those lie in our collective future, not our collective past.

In the extraordinary archeology of Spirit, those spiritual pioneers were ahead of their time, and they are still ahead of ours. They are thus voices, not of our past, but of our future; they point to emergents, not exhumations; they urge us forward, not backward. As the growing tip of humanity, they forged a future telos through which the trunk of humanity is now slowing heading, not as a rigid pregiven, but as a gentle persuasion. They are figures of the deepest layers of our own true Self, layers that whisper to us from the radiant depths of a greater tomorrow.

13

From Modernity to Postmodernity

No epoch is without its geniuses, its wisdom, its enduring truths. Moreover, to ignore past truths seems to be the very definition of pathology. Therefore, an integral approach—a sane approach—would surely attempt to honor, acknowledge, and incorporate these enduring truths in the ongoing sweep of consciousness evolution.

From the premodern heritage, we have learned of the Great Nest of Being and Knowing, and found that it is a roadmap to Spirit, not in a pregiven way, but as a morphogenetic field of gentle persuasion. From the modern heritage, we have learned of the need to recognize and honor art, morals, and science, and let each pursue its own truths without violence from the others (a respect that contributed to the rise of the modern democracies, feminism, ecology, and the postconventional ideals of liberty, freedom, and equality).[1] We also learned of the modern discoveries of *evolution* in the quadrants (a notion that is at least compatible with the Great Chain tipped on its side and set loose across geological, biological, and cultural time). And we have mentioned the "bright promise" of a constructive postmodernity, which involves the integration the best of premodernity (the Great Nest) and modernity (the differentiation and evolution of the Big Three), resulting in a more integral "all-level, all-quadrant" approach.

It is time now to finish this integral overview by looking, very briefly, at postmodernism itself—which is, after all, the leading edge of today's cultural evolution—and suggest exactly how it fits into an all-level, all-quadrant view.

Many people moan when "postmodern" anything is mentioned, so convoluted and indecipherable has postmodernese become. But these are important points, and I ask the reader to stick with me through this chapter, which I will try to make as painless as possible. We can then return, in the closing chapters, to a summary of what we have seen, and the implications for psychology, therapy, spirituality, and consciousness studies.

The Bright Promise

In trying to understand modernity, we asked the simple question: what made modernity different from the premodern era? We found many items (from industrialization to the liberation movements), but they could all be very generally summarized as the differentiation of the Big Three.

In attempting to understand postmodernity, let us ask again: what is it about postmodernity that makes it so different from modernity? We will see that there are also many items, but they can all be very generally summarized as an *attempt to be inclusive*—to avoid "marginalizing" the many voices and viewpoints that a powerful modernity often overlooked; to avoid a "hegemony" of formal rationality that often represses the nonrational and the irrational; to invite all races, all colors, all people, all genders into a rainbow coalition of mutual respect and mutual recognition. This inclusiveness is often simply called "diversity" (or "multiculturalism" or "pluralism"), and it is at the heart of the constructive postmodern agenda, in ways that we will explore throughout this chapter.

This attempt to be inclusive—holistic and embracing in the best sense—was in part a reaction to modernity's unfortunate slide into flatland, where the *dissociation* of the Big Three allowed a powerful science to colonize and dominate (and marginalize) all other forms of knowing and being. Postmodernity was a counterattempt to include the Big Three instead of merely differentiate and dissociate them. *Thus, where modernity differentiated the Big Three, postmodernity would embrace them*—the many I's and the many We's and the many Its—thus arriving at a more inclusive, integral, and nonexclusionary stance. And there, in a sentence, is the enduring truth, the integral truth, of the general postmodern movements.

But we will also see that, just as modernity has its downside, so too does postmodernity. The dignity of modernity slid into the disaster of modernity when the differentiation of the Big Three slid into their dissociation. Just so, the bright promise of a constructive postmodernity slid into a nihilistic deconstructive postmodernity when the pluralistic embrace turned into a rancid leveling of all qualitative distinctions. Postmodernity, attempting to escape flatland, often became its most vulgar champion.

In other words, postmodernity, just like modernity, has its good news and its bad news.

Good News

The entry to postmodernism begins with an understanding of the intrinsic role that *interpretation* plays in human awareness. Postmodernism, in fact, may be credited with making interpretation central to both epistemology and ontology, to both knowing and being. Interpretation, the postmodernists all maintained in their own ways, is not only crucial for understanding the Kosmos, it is an aspect of its very structure. *Interpretation is an intrinsic feature of the fabric of the universe*: there is the crucial insight at the heart of the great postmodern movements.[2]

Interpretation: The Heart of the Postmodern

Many people are initially confused as to why, and how, interpretation is intrinsic to the universe. Interpretation is for things like language and literature, right? Yes, but language and literature are just the tip of the iceberg, an iceberg that extends to the very depths of the Kosmos itself. We might explain it like this:

As we have seen, all Right-Hand events—all sensorimotor objects and empirical processes and "its"—can be seen with the senses or their extensions. They all have simple location; you can actually point to most of them (rocks, towns, trees, lakes, stars, roads, rivers . . .).

But Left-Hand or interior events cannot be seen in that fashion. You cannot see love, envy, wonder, compassion, insight, intentionality, spiritual illumination, states of consciousness, value, or meaning running around out there in the empirical world. Interior events are not seen in an *exterior* or *objective* manner, they are seen by *introspection* and *interpretation*.

Thus, if you want to study *Macbeth* empirically, you can get a copy of the play and subject it to various scientific tests: it weighs so many grams, it has so many molecules of ink, it has this number of pages composed of these organic compounds, and so on. That's all you can know about *Macbeth* empirically. Those are its Right-Hand, objective, exterior aspects.

But if you want to know the *meaning* of the play, you will have to read it and enter into its interiority, its meaning, its intentions, its depths. And the only way you can do that is by *interpretation*: what does this sentence *mean*? Here, empirical science is largely worthless, because we are entering interior domains and symbolic depths, which cannot be accessed by exterior empiricism but only by introspection and interpretation. Not just objective, but subjective and intersubjective. Not just monological, but dialogical.

Thus, you might see me coming down the street, a frown on my face. You can see that. But what does that exterior frown actually mean? How will you find out? You will ask me. You will talk to me. You can see my surfaces, but in order to understand my interior, my depths, you will have to enter into the interpretive circle (the hermeneutic circle). You, as a subject, will not merely stare at me as an *object*, but rather you, as a subject, will attempt to understand me *as a subject*—as a person, as a self, as a bearer of intentionality and meaning. You will talk to me, and interpret what I say; and I will do the same with you. We are not subjects staring at objects; we are subjects trying to understand subjects—we are in the intersubjective circle, the dialogical dance.

This is true not only for humans, but for all sentient beings as such. If you want to understand your dog—is he happy, or perhaps hungry, or wanting to go for a walk?—you will have to *interpret* the signals he is giving you. And your dog, to the extent that he can, does the same with you. In other words, the *interior* of a holon can *only* be accessed by interpretation.

Thus, to put it bluntly, exterior surfaces can be *seen*, but interior depth must be *interpreted*. And precisely because this interior depth is an intrinsic part of the Kosmos—it is the Left-Hand dimension of every holon—then interpretation itself is an intrinsic feature of the Kosmos. Interpretation is not something added on to the Kosmos as an afterthought; it is the very opening of the interiors themselves. And since the depth of the Kosmos goes "all the way down," then, as Heidegger famously put it, "Interpretation goes all the way down."

Perhaps we can now see why one of the great aims of postmodernism was to *introduce interpretation as an intrinsic aspect of the Kosmos*. As

I would put it, every holon has a Left- and a Right-Hand dimension (as you can see in fig. 5), and therefore every holon has an objective (Right) and an interpretive (Left) component.

(How far "down" you wish to push interiors or consciousness is, of course, up to you. Some people push it down to mammals, others to reptiles, others to plants, others all the way down to atoms. I find this a completely relative issue: however much consciousness one holon has—say, an amoeba—a senior holon has a little more—say, a deer—and its senior has even more—say, a gorilla. The lower on the Great Nest, the less sentience a holon has, until it fades into the shades that we cannot detect. We will return to this topic in chapter 14; for now, the simple point is that, at least by the time we get to humans, interiors definitely exist, and they can only be accessed by introspection and interpretation.)[3]

The disaster of modernity was that it reduced all introspective and interpretive knowledge to exterior and empirical flatland: it attempted to erase the richness of interpretation from the script of the world. The attempt by postmodernism to reintroduce interpretation into the very structure and fabric of the Kosmos was in part a noble attempt to escape flatland, to resurrect the gutted interiors and interpretive modes of knowing. The postmodern emphasis on interpretation—starting most notably with Nietzsche, and running through Dilthey's *Geist* sciences to Heidegger's hermeneutic ontology to Derrida's "there is nothing outside the text [interpretation]"—is at bottom nothing but the Left-Hand domains screaming to be released from the crushing oblivion of the monological gaze of scientific monism and flatland holism. It was the bold reassertion of the I and the We in the face of faceless Its.

Moments of Truth in Postmodernism

Precisely because postmodernism is in many ways attempting to jettison flatland and its demeaning legacy, postmodern philosophy is a complex cluster of notions that are often defined almost entirely by what its proponents *reject*. They reject foundationalism, essentialism, and transcendentalism. They reject rationality, truth as correspondence, and representational knowledge. They reject grand narratives, metanarratives, and big pictures of any variety. They reject realism, final vocabularies, and canonical description.

Incoherent as the postmodern theories often sound (and often are), nonetheless most postmodern approaches share three important core assumptions:

1. Reality is not in all ways pregiven, but in some significant ways is a construction, an interpretation (this view is often called *constructivism*); the belief that reality is simply given, and not also partly constructed, is referred to as "the myth of the given."
2. Meaning is context-dependent, and contexts are boundless (this is often called *contextualism*).
3. Cognition must therefore unduly privilege no single perspective (this is called *integral-aperspectivism*).

I believe all three of those postmodern assumptions are quite accurate, and need to be honored and incorporated in any integral view.

But, as we will see in the bad news section, each of those assumptions has also been blown radically out of proportion by the extremist wing of postmodernism, with very unfortunate results. The extreme postmodernists do not just stress the importance of interpretation, they claim reality is *nothing but an interpretation*. They don't just emphasize the Left-Hand (or interpretive) aspects of all holons, *they attempt to completely deny reality to the Right-Hand (or objective) facets*. This, of course, is precisely the reverse disaster of modernity—not reducing all Left to Right, but reducing all Right to Left—and we can see, as is frequently the case, that extreme reactions are often the mirror images of what they loathe. The important features of the Kosmos that are interpretive are made the *only* features in existence. Objective truth itself disappears into arbitrary interpretations, said to be imposed by power, gender, race, ideology, anthropocentrism, androcentrism, speciesism, imperialism, logocentrism, phallocentrism, phallologocentrism, or one variety or another of utter unpleasantness.

But the fact that all holons have an interpretive as well as objective component does *not* deny the objective component, it merely situates it. Thus, all Right-Hand exteriors, even if we superimpose conceptions upon them, nonetheless have various intrinsic features that are registered by the senses or their extensions, and in that general sense, all Right-Hand holons have some sort of objective reality. Even Wilfrid Sellars, generally regarded as the most persuasive opponent of "the myth of the given"—the myth of direct realism and naive empiricism, the myth that reality is simply given to us—maintains that, even though the manifest image of an object is in part a mental construction, it is *guided* in important ways by *intrinsic features* of sense experience, which is exactly why, as Thomas Kuhn said, science can make *real* progress.[4] A diamond will cut a piece of glass, no matter what words we use for "diamond," "cut," and "glass," and no amount of cultural constructivism will change that simple fact.

But that is the bad news. The point for now is that the postmodernists, in attempting to make room for those aspects of the Big Three that were excluded and marginalized by flatland, pointed out the *intrinsic* importance of interpretation, contextualism, and integralism, and in this regard, they were surely correct.

From Modern to Postmodern: The Linguistic Turn

The importance of constructivism, contextualism, and integral-aperspectivism came to the fore historically with has been called *the linguistic turn* in philosophy—the general realization that language is not a simple representation of a pregiven world, but has a hand in the creation and construction of that world. With the linguistic turn, which began roughly in the nineteenth century, philosophers stopped using language to describe the world, and instead started looking at language itself.

Suddenly, language was no longer a simple and trusted tool. *Metaphysics* in general was replaced with *linguistic analysis*, because it was becoming increasingly obvious that language is not a clear window through which we innocently look at a given world; it is more like a slide projector throwing images against the screen of what we finally see. Language helps to create my world, and, as Wittgenstein would put it, the limits of my language are the limits of my world.

In many ways, "the linguistic turn" is just another name for the great transition from modernity to postmodernity. Where both premodern and modern cultures simply and naively used their language to approach the world, the postmodern mind spun on its heels and began to look at language itself. In the entire history of human beings, this, more or less, had never happened before.

In the wake of this extraordinary linguistic turn, philosophers would never again look at language in a simple and trusting way. Language did not merely report the world, represent the world, describe the world. Rather, language creates worlds, and in that creation is power. Language creates, distorts, carries, discloses, hides, allows, oppresses, enriches, enthralls. For good or ill, language itself is something of a demi-god, and philosophy henceforth would focus much of its attention on that powerful force. From linguistic analysis to language games, from structuralism to poststructuralism, from semiology to semiotics, from linguistic intentionality to speech act theory—postmodern philosophy has been in large measure *the philosophy of language*, and it pointed out—quite rightly—that if we are to use language as a tool to understand reality, we had better start by looking very closely at that tool.[5]

And in this strange new world, most roads lead, sooner or later, to Ferdinand de Saussure.

Language Speaks

Most forms of postmodern poststructuralism trace their lineage to the work of the brilliant and pioneering linguist Ferdinand de Saussure. Saussure's work, and especially his *Course in General Linguistics* (1916), was the basis of much of modern linguistics, semiology (semiotics), structuralism, and hence poststructuralism, and his essential insights are as cogent today as they were when he first advanced them almost a century ago.

According to Saussure, a linguistic *sign* is composed of a material *signifier* (the written word, the spoken word, the marks on this page) and a conceptual *signified* (what comes to mind when you see the signifier), both of which are different from the actual *referent*. For example, if you see a tree, the actual tree is the referent; the written word "tree" is the signifier; and what comes to mind (the image, the thought, the mental picture or concept) when you read the word "tree" is the signified. The signifier and the signified together constitute the overall sign.

But what is it, Saussure asked, that allows a sign to mean something, to actually *carry meaning*? It can't be the word itself, because, for example, the word "bark" has a different meaning in the phrases "the bark of a dog" and "the bark of a tree." The word "bark" has meaning, in each case, because of its place in the entire phrase (a different phrase gives the same word a totally different meaning). Each phrase likewise has meaning because of its place in the larger sentence, and eventually, in the total linguistic structure. Any given word in itself is basically *meaningless* because the same word can have completely different meanings depending on the context or the structure in which it is placed.

Thus, Saussure pointed out, it is the *relationship between all of the words themselves* that stabilizes meaning. So—and this was Saussure's great insight—*a meaningless element becomes meaningful only by virtue of the total structure*. (This is the beginning of *structuralism*, virtually all schools of which trace their lineage in whole or part to Saussure. Present-day descendants include aspects of the work of Lévi-Strauss,

Jakobson, Piaget, Lacan, Barthes, Foucault, Derrida, Habermas, Loevinger, Kohlberg, Gilligan . . . it was a truly stunning discovery.)

In other words—and no surprise—every sign is a holon, a context within contexts within contexts in the overall network. And this means, said Saussure, that the entire language is instrumental in conferring meaning on an individual word.[6]

Meaning Is Context-Dependent

Accordingly—and here we begin to see the importance of *background cultural contexts* so stressed by postmodernists (especially starting with Heidegger)—meaning is created for me by vast networks of background contexts about which I consciously know very little. I do not fashion this meaning; this meaning fashions me. I am a part of this vast cultural background, and in many cases I haven't a clue as to where it all came from.

In other words—as we have often seen—every subjective intentionality (Upper Left) is *situated* in networks of intersubjective and cultural contexts (Lower Left) that are instrumental in the creation and interpretation of meaning itself. This is precisely why meaning is indeed context-dependent, and why the bark of a dog is different from the bark of a tree. This is also why individual states of consciousness must to some degree be interpreted within a cultural context, and why any truly postmodern view should attempt to move toward an *all-context sensitivity* (by stressing, for example, the endlessly holonic nature of consciousness).[7]

Not only is meaning in many important ways dependent upon the context in which it finds itself, these contexts are in principle *endless* or *boundless*. Thus there is no way finally to master and control meaning once and for all (because I can always imagine a further context that would alter the present meaning). Jonathan Culler has, in fact, summarized all of deconstruction (one of the most influential of the postmodern movements) in this way: "One could therefore identify deconstruction with the twin principles of the *contextual determination of meaning* and the *infinite extendability of context*."[8]

As I would put it, contexts are indeed endless precisely because reality is composed of holons within holons within holons *indefinitely*, with no discernible bottom or top. Even the entire universe right now is simply a part of the next moment's universe. Every whole is always a part, endlessly. And therefore every conceivable context is boundless. To say that the Kosmos is holonic is to say it is contextual, all the way up, all the way down.

Integral-Aperspectival

The fact that meaning is context-dependent—the second important truth of postmodernism, also called *contextualism*—means that a *multi-perspective* approach to reality is called for. Any single perspective is likely to be partial, limited, perhaps even distorted, and only by honoring multiple perspectives and multiple contexts can the knowledge quest be fruitfully advanced. And that "diversity" is the third important truth of general postmodernism.

Jean Gebser, whom we have seen in connection with worldviews, coined the term *integral-aperspectival* to refer to this pluralistic or multiple-perspectives view, which I also refer to as *vision-logic* or *network-logic*. "Aperspectival" means that no single perspective is privileged, and thus, in order to gain a more holistic or *integral* view, we need an *aperspectival* approach, which is exactly why Gebser usually hyphenated them: integral-aperspectival.

Gebser contrasted integral-aperspectival cognition with formal rationality (formop), or what he called "perspectival reason," which tends to take a single, monological perspective and view all of reality through that narrow lens. Where perspectival reason privileges the exclusive perspective of the particular subject, vision-logic *adds up all the perspectives*, privileging none, and thus attempts to grasp the integral, the whole, the multiple contexts within contexts that endlessly disclose the Kosmos, not in a rigid or absolutist fashion, but in a fluidly holonic and multidimensional tapestry.

This parallels almost exactly the Idealists' great emphasis on the difference between a reason that is merely formal, representational, or empiric-analytic, and a reason that is dialogical, dialectical, and network-oriented (vision-logic). They called the former *Verstand* and the latter *Vernunft*. And they saw Vernunft or vision-logic as being a higher evolutionary development than mere Verstand or formal rationality.[9]

Gebser, too, believed that vision-logic was an evolutionary development beyond formal rationality. Nor are Gebser and the Idealists alone. As we have repeatedly seen, many important theorists, from Jürgen Habermas to Carol Gilligan, view postformal, dialectical cognition as a higher and more embracing mode of reason than formop (as indicated on many of the charts). *To say cognitive development evolves from for-*

mal to postformal is to say that cultural evolution moves from modern to postmodern. This is, of course, a complex, four-quadrant affair, involving such important developments as industrial to informational; but the mode of cognition is a crucial element, and the postmodern world is, at its best, the postformal world.

This vision-logic not only can spot massive interrelationships, it is itself an intrinsic part of the interrelated Kosmos, which is why vision-logic does not just *represent* the Kosmos, but is a *performance* of the Kosmos. Of course, all modes of genuine knowing are such performances; but vision-logic is the first that can self-consciously realize this and articulate it. Hegel did so in one of the first and pioneering elaborations—vision-logic evolutionarily became conscious of itself in Hegel—and Saussure did exactly the same thing with linguistics.[10] Saussure took vision-logic and applied it to language, thus disclosing, for the first time in history, its network structure. The linguistic turn is, at bottom, vision-logic looking at language itself.

This same vision-logic would give rise to the extensively elaborated versions of systems theory in the natural sciences, and it would stand as well behind the postmodernists' recognition that meaning is context-dependent and contexts are boundless. In all of these movements and more, we see the radiant hand of vision-logic announcing the endless networks of holonic interconnection that constitute the very fabric of the Kosmos itself.

This is why I believe that the recognition of the importance of integral-aperspectival awareness is the third great (and valid) message of postmodernism in general.

Bad News

All of which is well and good. But it is not enough, we have seen, to be "holistic" instead of "atomistic," or to be network-oriented instead of analytic and divisive. Because the alarming fact is that *any mode of knowing can be collapsed* and confined merely to surfaces, to exteriors, to Right-Hand occasions. And, in fact, almost as soon as vision-logic had heroically emerged in evolution, it was crushed by the flatland madness sweeping the modern world.

Language Collapses

Indeed, as we have repeatedly seen, the systems sciences themselves did exactly that. The systems sciences denied any substantial reality to the

"I" and the "we" domains (in their own terms), and reduced all of them to nothing but interwoven "its" in a dynamical system of network processes. This was vision-logic at work, but a crippled vision-logic, hobbled and chained to the bed of exterior processes and empirical its. This was a holism, but merely an exterior holism that perfectly gutted the interiors and denied any sort of validity to the extensive realms of Left-Hand holism (of the "I" and the "we"). The third-person shackles were no longer atomistic; the third-person shackles were now holistically interwoven.

Precisely the same fate awaited so much of the general postmodern agenda. Starting from the admirable reliance on vision-logic and integral-aperspectival awareness—and yet still unable to escape the intense gravity of flatland—these postmodern movements often ended up subtly embodying and even extending the reductionistic agenda. They were a new and higher form of reason, yes, but *reason still trapped in flatland.* They became simply another twist on flatland holism, material monism, monological madness. They still succumbed to the disaster of modernity even as they loudly announced they had overcome it, subverted it, deconstructed it, exploded it.

Depth Takes a Vacation

In fact, most postmodernism would eventually go to extraordinary lengths to *deny depth* in general. It is as if, suffering under the onslaught of flatland aggression, it identified with the aggressor. Postmodernism came to embrace surfaces, champion surfaces, glorify surfaces, and surfaces alone. There are only sliding chains of signifiers, everything is a material text, there is nothing under the surface, there is only the surface. As Bret Easton Ellis put it in the *Informers*: "Nothing was affirmative, the term 'generosity of spirit' applied to nothing, was a cliché, was some kind of bad joke. . . . Reflection is useless, the world is senseless. Surface, surface, surface was all that anyone found meaningful . . . this was civilization as I saw it, colossal and jagged."

Robert Alter, reviewing William H. Gass's *The Tunnel*—a book claimed by many to be the ultimate postmodern novel—points out that the defining strategy of this postmodern masterpiece is that "*everything is deliberately reduced to the flattest surface.*" It does so by "denying the possibility of making consequential distinctions between, or meaningful rankings of, moral or aesthetic values. There is no within: murderer and victim, lover and onanist, altruist and bigot, dissolve into the same ineluctable slime"—the same sliding chains of equally flatland terms.

"Everything reduced to the flattest surface. . . . *There is no within*"—a perfect description of flatland, a flatland that, beginning with modernity, was actually amplified and glorified with extreme postmodernity: "Surface, surface, surface was all that anyone found . . . ."

And Alter is exactly right that behind it all is the inability or refusal to make "consequential distinctions between, or meaningful rankings of, moral or aesthetic values." As we have often seen, in the Right-Hand world there are no values and no interiors and no qualitative distinctions—no states of consciousness, no realms of transpersonal awareness, no superconscious revelations, no spiritual illuminations—for those exist only in the Left-Hand domains. To collapse the Kosmos to Right-Hand surfaces is thus to step out of the real world and into the Twilight Zone known as the disqualified universe. Here there are no interior holarchies, no meaningful rankings of the I and the We, no qualitative distinctions of any sort—no depth, no divinity, no consciousness, no soul, and no spirit: "Surface, surface, surface is all that anyone found."[11]

Extreme postmodernism thus went from the noble insight that all perspectives need to be given a fair hearing, to the self-contradictory belief that no perspective is better than any other (self-contradictory because their own belief is held to be much better than the alternatives). Thus, under the intense gravity of flatland, integral-aperspectival awareness became simply *aperspectival madness*—the contradictory belief that no belief is better than any other—a total paralysis of thought, will, and action in the face of a million perspectives all given exactly the same depth, namely, zero.

At one point in *The Tunnel*, Gass himself, the author of this postmodern masterpiece, describes the *perfect postmodern form*, which serves "to raunchify, to suburp [sic] everything, to pollute the pollutants, explode the exploded, trash the trash. . . . It is all surface. . . . There's no inside however long or far you travel on it, no within, no deep."

No within, no deep. That may serve as a perfect credo for extreme postmodernism. Just as modernity often slid into dissociation, postmodernity often slid into surfaces.

Conclusion

The enduring contributions of the postmodern era—the world is in part a construction and interpretation; all meaning is context-dependent; contexts are endlessly holonic—are truths that any comprehensive view would surely wish to embrace. All of these can be summarized, in the most general fashion, by saying that where modernity differentiated the Big Three, postmodernity would integrate them, thus arriving an inclusive, integral, and nonexclusionary embrace. This integral agenda is the heart of a constructive postmodernity, and the heart of any truly integral psychology and spirituality.

But just as modernity's differentiations often slid into dissociation, so postmodernity's integral embrace often slid into aperspectival madness—into the *denial* of qualitative distinctions of any sort, the denial of holarchies altogether. And since the only way you get holism is via holarchies, in denying the latter, postmodernity effectively denied the former, and thus offered the world not holism but heapism: diversity run amok, with no way to integrate and harmonize the pluralistic voices. No stance is inherently better than any other; all hierarchies are marginalizing and should be rejected; all voices should be treated equally, with no marginalizing and no judging.

The inherent contradiction in that agenda is simply this: the very stance of postmodern pluralism—relying as it does on postformal vision-logic and integral-aperspectival cognition—is itself the product of at least five major stages of hierarchical development (sensorimotor to preop to conop to formop to postformal). From the very high developmental stance of postconventional, postformal, pluralistic awareness—which nobly wishes to treat all peoples fairly and justly—postmodernism then denied the importance of development altogether, denied that any stance is higher or deeper than another, denied in effect the claim that worldcentric is better than ethnocentric—in short, it completely denied its own stance. And yet it is only from the high developmental level of postformal and postconventional awareness that pluralism can be grasped in the first place! To deny development and evolution is to deny pluralism altogether and slide into nothing but a world of equivalent surfaces, where qualitative distinctions and holarchies have disappeared altogether. This is why postmodern pluralists have always had difficulty explaining why we should reject the Nazis and the KKK—if all stances are equal, why not embrace them? Aperspectival madness.

Thus, under the important truths of relativism, pluralism, and cultural diversity, postmodernism opened up the world to a richness of multiple voices, but then stood back to watch the multiple voices degenerate into a Tower of Babel, each voice claiming to be its own validity, yet few of them actually honoring the values of the others. Each was free to go its own way, whereupon everybody went in vigorously different ways. This did not ultimately liberate the many pluralistic voices, as was claimed, but merely sent them scurrying off, isolated and alienated, to the far corners of a fragmented world, there to suckle themselves in solitude, lost in the shuffle of equivalent surfaces. Attempting to escape flatland, deconstructive postmodernism became its most vocal champion.

Constructive postmodernism, on the other hand, takes up the multiple contexts freed by pluralism, and then goes one step further and weaves them together into mutually interrelated networks. (You can see this on virtually all of the charts. By whatever name, pluralistic relativism gives way to integral holism. See especially Deirdre Kramer, Gisela Labouvie-Vief, Jan Sinnott, Don Beck, Clare Graves, Susanne Cook-Greuter, Kitchener and King, Blanchard-Fields, William Perry, and Cheryl Armon, among others.) This integral-aperspectivism—this unity-in-diversity, this universal integralism—discloses global interconnections, nests within nests within nests, and vast holarchies of mutually enriching embrace, thus converting pluralistic heapism into integral holism.

(In the terms of Spiral Dynamics, the great strength of postmodernism is that it moved from orange scientific materialism to green pluralism, in a noble attempt to be more inclusive and sensitive to the marginalized others of rationality. But the downside of green pluralism is its subjectivism and relativism, which leaves the world splintered and fragmented. As Clare Graves himself put it, "This system sees the world relativistically. Thinking shows an almost radical, almost compulsive emphasis on seeing everything from a relativistic, subjective frame of reference." And however important these multiple contexts are for moving beyond scientific materialism, if they become an end in themselves, they simply prevent the emergence of second-tier constructions, which will actually reweave the fragments in a global-holistic embrace. It is the emergence of this second-tier thinking upon which any truly integral model will depend—and this is the path of constructive postmodernism.)

For an integral psychology, postmodernism means many things. First and foremost, it is a reaffirmation of what psychology is all about: the *constructing* and *creating* capacity of consciousness itself: the world is not merely reflected by consciousness, it is co-created by consciousness—the world is not merely a *perception* but an *interpretation*.[12] Interpretation is an intrinsic aspect of the Kosmos, "all the way down," because consciousness and interiors are an intrinsic aspect of the Kosmos, *all the way down*, and the only way you can get at interiors is via introspection and interpretation. That consciousness is endlessly holonic is the final message of postmodernism.

Therefore, any integral theory would be wise to include constructive, contextual, and integral-aperspectival dimensions in its own makeup. It is to this integral conclusion that we may now turn.

14

The 1-2-3 of Consciousness Studies

The Mind-Body Problem

The first major problem that a truly integral (all-level, all-quadrant) approach helps to unravel is what Schopenhauer called "the world-knot," namely, the mind-body problem.

So let us start with a bold suggestion: a good deal of the mind-body problem is a product of flatland. Not the differentiation of mind and body, which is at least as old as civilization and never bothered anybody before; but the dissociation of mind and body, which is a peculiar lesion in the modern and postmodern consciousness, concomitant with the collapse of the Kosmos into flatland. For in flatland, we are faced with a truly unyielding dilemma as to the relation of mind and body: the mind (consciousness, feeling, thought, awareness)—in short, the Left-Hand domains—can find absolutely no room in the world described merely in Right-Hand terms (the material body and brain): the mind becomes the "ghost in the machine." We are then faced with two apparently absolute but contradictory truths: the truth of immediate experience, which tells me unmistakably that consciousness exists, and the truth of science, which tells me unmistakably that the world consists only of arrangements of fundamental units (quarks, atoms, strings, etc.) that possess no consciousness whatsoever, and no amount of rearranging those mindless units will result in mind.

Contrary to popular writers on the subject, the influential philosophers addressing the mind-body problem are more convinced than ever of its unyielding nature. There is simply no agreed-upon solution to this world-knot.[1] Much of the influential writing of the last several decades, in fact, has focused on the absolutely insuperable difficulties with the proposed solutions. As Keith Campbell summarized a vague and uneasy consensus, "I suspect we will never know how the trick is worked [the relation of mind and body]. This part of the Mind-Body problem seems insoluble. This aspect of humanity seems destined to remain forever beyond our understanding."[2]

Nonetheless, there have been many solutions offered, the two most influential being the *dualist* (interactionism) and the *physicalist* (scientific materialism). The dualist position was the most influential in the early part of the modern era (from Descartes to Leibniz), but the physicalist has been in the ascendancy ever since, and is now by far the dominant position.[3]

The physicalist (or materialist) approach claims that there is only the physical universe described best by physics and other natural sciences, and nowhere in that physical universe do we find consciousness, mind, experience, or awareness, and therefore those "interiors" are simply illusions (or, at best, byproducts without any genuine reality). Some versions of the physicalist approach allow for higher-level emergence of various complex systems (such as the brain, neocortex, autopoietic neuronal systems, etc.). But they point out that these higher-level systems are still objective realities with nothing that could be called consciousness or mind or experience, because experience has "qualia" or qualities, such as pain and pleasure, and those qualities are *not* properties of objective systems. Therefore there is no way that objective systems could give rise to those "mental" properties, and therefore those properties are simply illusory byproducts of complex systems, with no causal reality of their own.

(Using my terms, this argument says: objective systems are all described in it-language, whereas experience, consciousness, and qualia are all described in I-language, and thus if you believe that the world described by science is the "really real" world—and, after all, there are many good reasons to believe that science is our best hope of finding truth—then you naturally believe that qualia, experience, and consciousness are *not* "really real"—they are illusions or byproducts or secondary features of the real world disclosed by science.)

Although variations on physicalism are by far the most commonly accepted views, this is not so much because physicalism works well, but because the alternatives seem much worse. Even materialists acknowledge the massive problems with their own stance: Galen Strawson: "As an acting materialist, I . . . assume that experiential phenomena are realized in the brain. . . . [But] when we consider the brain as current physics and neurophysiology presents it to us, we are obliged to admit that we do not know how experience . . . is or even could be realized in the brain."[4] John Searle: "Criticisms of the materialist theory usually take a more or less technical form, but in fact, underlying the technical objections is a much deeper objection. . . . The theory in question has left out . . . some essential feature of the mind, such as consciousness or 'qualia' or semantic content. . . ."[5] Jaegwon Kim, whose "supervenience" theory is a very sophisticated emergent physicalism, concludes that the approach seems "to be up against a dead end."[6] Thomas Nagel concludes that "physicalism is a position that we cannot understand because we do not at present have any conception of how it might be true."[7] Colin McGinn states simply that we will *never* be able to resolve the issue of how consciousness emerges from a brain.[8] And that is the conclusion of the physicalists themselves!

The dualist therefore jumps on these insuperable difficulties in physicalism, and says to the materialists: We know that consciousness exists in some form, because it is one of the "hard-core" intuitions that humans possess, and therefore explaining it away will take some powerful explaining. We experience consciousness directly. But we do not directly experience quarks or atoms (or the fundamental units of the physical world). Therefore it is not necessary for me to proceed as you do, which is to start with quarks and then deduce that consciousness does not exist. It is necessary for you to start from consciousness and explain how you arrive at the ridiculous notion that it isn't there.

The dualist therefore maintains that, at the very least, there are two realities in the world: consciousness and matter. Neither can be reduced to the other; instead, they "interact" (hence the other common term for this position, interactionism). But then the dualist faces the age-old dilemma: how can two fundamentally different things influence each other? As everybody knows, ghosts walk through walls, they do not push walls around, so how can the ghostly mind actually have any real effect on the material body? The very move to show that mind cannot be reduced to matter leaves the dualist incapable of showing how mind can act on matter at all. And therefore the dualist has a very hard time explaining how, for example, I can even move my arm.

(The Idealists handled this by saying that mind and body are both forms of Spirit, and therefore they are not alien or ontologically different entities, but simply two different aspects of the same thing. This is an acceptable solution if one acknowledges Spirit, which most modern and postmodern philosophers do not, which is why this is not a commonly discussed option. We will return to this point shortly.)

Again, the dualists themselves point out the insuperable difficulties with their own position (which they hold mostly because the physicalist alternative is even worse). Geoffrey Madell notes that "interactionist dualism looks to be by far the only plausible framework in which the facts of our experience can be fitted" (because, we might say, interactionism at least acknowledges the undeniable realities of both I and it domains). Nonetheless, "the nature of the causal connection between the mental and the physical . . . is utterly mysterious" (how *does* the ghost move the wall?).[9] Sir Karl Popper states the central problem for dualism: "What we want is to understand how such nonphysical things as purposes, deliberations, plans, decisions, theories, tensions, and values can play a part in bringing about physical changes in the physical world."[10] The conclusion offered by dualist interactionism: that understanding, says Popper, "is unlikely to be achieved."[11]

What Do We Mean by "Mind" and "Body"?

Part of these difficulties, I am suggesting, is that both major positions have adopted the theoretical terms of flatland, and they attempt to juggle these terms to arrive at a solution, which has then been less than satisfactory, virtually all parties agree. If we instead use an "all-level, all-quadrant" approach, the first thing that we notice is that both "mind" and "body" have two very different meanings, showing that there are really four problems hidden in one. This can be followed fairly easily using figure 12.

To begin with, "body" can mean *the biological organism as a whole*, including the brain (the neocortex, the limbic system, reptilian stem, etc.)—in other words, "body" can mean the entire Upper-Right quadrant, which I will call "the organism." I will also refer to the organism as the "Body," capital *B*, as indicated in figure 12. Thus, the brain is in the Body, which is the commonly accepted scientific view (and an accurate description of the Upper-Right quadrant).

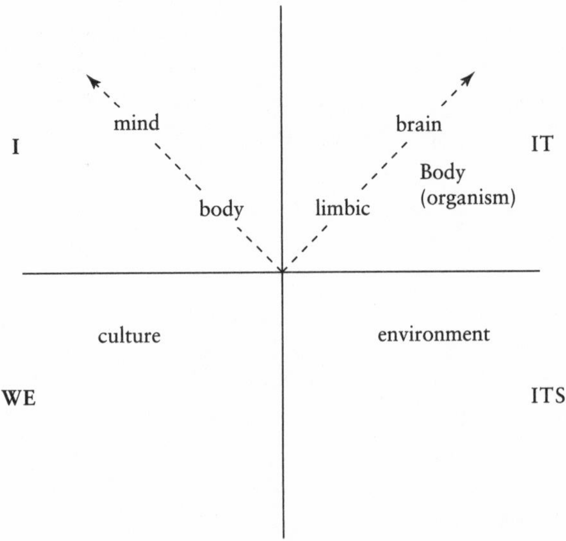

FIGURE 12. *Meanings of "Mind" and "Body"*

But "body" can also mean, and for the average person does mean, the subjective feelings, emotions, and sensations of the felt body. When the typical person says "My mind is fighting my body," he means his will is fighting some bodily desire or inclination (such as sex or food). In other words, in this common usage, "body" means the lower levels of one's own interior. In figure 12, I have labeled this as "body" in the Upper-Left quadrant, which simply means the feelings and emotions of the felt body (versus the Body, which means the entire objective organism).

Moving from body to mind, many scientific researchers simply identify "mind" with "brain," and they prefer to speak only of brain states, neurotransmitters, cognitive science, and so on. I will use the term "brain" to cover that meaning, which refers to the upper levels of the Upper-Right quadrant (e.g., the neocortex), as shown in figure 12.

On the other hand, when the average person says "My mind is fighting my body," he does not mean that his neocortex is fighting his limbic system. By "mind" he means the upper levels of his own interior, the upper levels of the Upper-Left quadrant (although he might not use exactly those terms)—in other words, his rational will is fighting his feelings or desires (formop is fighting the vital and sensorimotor dimensions). The mind is described in first-person phenomenal accounts and I-language, whereas the brain is described in third-person objective accounts and it-language. All of these are indicated in figure 12.

(There is a another general meaning for mind/body: "mind" can mean the interior dimension in general—or the Left Hand—and "body" the exterior dimension in general—or the Right Hand. I will specifically indicate that usage when it comes up.)

The Hard Problem

Here is the world-knot, the inherent paradox of flatland: the body is in the mind, but the brain is in the Body.

Both of those statements are true, but in flatland they appear contradictory, and those contradictions drive much of the world-knot.

The felt body is in the mind, as shown in figures 1, 3, and 8. That is, formop transcends and includes conop, which transcends and includes vital feelings and sensorimotor awareness: the mind transcends and includes the body (which is precisely why the mind can causally *operate on* the body, or why formop can operate on conop, which operates on sensorimotor, and so on, as every developmentalist knows). This "transcendent" part of the mind (e.g., my mind can move my arm) is what every physicalist *acknowledges* (and then tries to explain away by embracing only flatland), and what every dualist acknowledges and attempts to *incorporate* (but does so by turning it into a dualism that still accepts the flatland dissociation; see below).

With the collapse of the Kosmos into flatland (naturalism, physicalism, scientific materialism), the interior *realities* of the I-domain *are still felt* and *strongly intuited* (mind can control the body, a degree of free will is real, consciousness exists, there is a unity of experience), but these realities are faced with a world, thought to be ultimately real, in which there are only it-realities described by science. And in that world, the brain is simply part of the Body, part of the natural biological organism, and thus consciousness must somehow be a function of that brain. But there is absolutely nothing in that brain, as our authorities just told us, that even vaguely corresponds to the qualia or experiences or realities of the mind and consciousness. We must then either reduce consciousness to brain (and thus deny consciousness in its own terms), or accept the dualism as real, whereupon we can't even explain how I can move my arm (or how one reality affects the other).

I am suggesting that both those solutions occur within the flatland paradigm. The technical details I will reserve for an endnote.[12] In more general terms, we might simply note the following:

The materialist reduces the mind to the brain, and since the brain is indeed part of the organism, there is no dualism: the mind/body problem is solved! And that is correct—the brain is part of the organism, part of the physical world, so there is no dualism; nor are there any values, consciousness, depth, or divinity anywhere in the resultant universe. And that reductionism is exactly the "solution" that the physicalist imposes on reality, a solution still rampant in most forms of cognitive science, neuroscience, systems theory, and so on: reduce the Left to the Right and then claim you have solved the problem.

But the reason most people, even most scientists, are uneasy with that "solution"—and the reason the problem remains a problem—is that, even though materialism announces that there is no dualism, most people know otherwise, because they *feel* the difference between their mind and their body (between their thoughts and their feelings)—they feel it every time they consciously decide to move their arm, they feel it in every exercise of will—and they *also* feel the difference between their mind and their Body (or between the subject in here and the objective world out there). And the average person is right on both counts. To take them in that order:

There is a distinction between mind (formop) and felt body (vital and sensorimotor), and this can be experienced in the interior or Left-Hand domains. It is not a dualism, but is rather a case of "transcend and include," and almost every rational adult has a sense of the transcend part, in that the mind can, on a good day, control the body and its desires. All of that is phenomenologically true for the Left-Hand domains. But *none* of those *interior* stages of qualitative development (from body to mind to soul to spirit) are captured when "body" means Right-Hand organism and "mind" means Right-Hand brain—all of those qualitative distinctions are completely lost in material monism, which does not solve the problem but obliterates it.

The dualist, on the other hand, acknowledges as real both consciousness and matter, but generally despairs of finding any way to relate them. "Mind" in the general sense of "interiors" and "Body" in the general sense of "exteriors" seem to be separated by an unbridgeable gulf—a dualism between subject and object. And at the level of formal operational thinking (or reason in general), at which this discussion usually takes place, the dualists are right: inside and outside are a very real dualism, and attempts to deny that dualism can almost always be shown to be facile, a semantic sleight-of-hand that verbally claims that subject and object are one, but which still leaves the self looking at the world out there which seems as separate as ever.

This is where the *transrational stages of development* have so much to offer this discussion. In the disclosure known as satori, for example, it becomes clear that the subject and object are two sides of the same thing, that inside and outside are two aspects of One Taste. How to relate them is not the problem, according to the clear consensus of the many individuals who have tapped into this wave of development. The problem, rather, is that this genuinely nondual solution is not something that can be fully grasped at the rational level. In fact, simply stating, in a rational fashion, that subject and object are nondual leads to all sorts of intractable problems and paradoxes.[13] Besides, if this nondualism could be genuinely grasped in rational terms, then the great materialist and dualist philosophers (many of whom are acknowledged geniuses) would have figured this out long ago, and the mind-body problem would not be much of problem.

No, the reason that both sides of the argument have generally agreed that the mind-body problem is irresolvable, is not that they aren't smart enough to figure it out, but that it is only solved in postrational stages of development, stages which are generally suspect, ignored, or actively denied by most rational researchers. But in principle the problem is no different from this: A rationalist will maintain that there is a proof for the Pythagorean Theorem. A person at a prerational stage will not agree with, or even understand, that proof. Nonetheless, the rationalist is justified in making that claim, which is true enough to virtually anybody who develops to the rational level and studies geometry.

Just so with the nondual solution of the mind-body problem. Those who develop to the nondual stages of consciousness unfolding are virtually unanimous: consciousness and matter, interior and exterior, self and world, are of One Taste. Subject and object are *both* distinct realities *and* aspects of the same thing: a true unity-in-diversity. But that unity-in-diversity cannot be stated in rational terms in a way that makes sense to anybody who has not also had a transrational experience. Therefore the "proof" for this nondual solution can only be found in the further development of the consciousness of those who seek to know the solution. Although this solution ("you must further develop your own consciousness if you want to know its full dimensions") is not satisfactory to the rationalist (whether dualist or physicalist), nonetheless it is the only acceptable form of the solution according to a genuinely integral paradigm.[14] When we heard Campbell say that a solution to the mind-body problem is "forever beyond our understanding," we can amend that to: it is not beyond human understanding, it is simply beyond the rational stages of understanding. The solution is postrational, and fully available to all who wish to move in that direction.

TWO PHASES IN UNSNARLING THE KNOT

We can represent some of these dilemmas as in figure 13, which is a map of flatland. If you compare this map with that in figure 8, you will see that all of the interior domains (body, mind, soul, and spirit) have been collapsed to their exterior (physical) correlates, which alone are said to be ultimately real. This leaves the mind (or consciousness in general) hanging and dangling in midair. And that is exactly the problem.

More specifically, the insuperable problem (the world-knot) has been how to relate this mind to both the body (or the lower interior levels of feeling and desire) and to the Body (or the objective organism, brain, and material environment). As we saw, the physicalist reduces the mind to the brain or Body, and thus cannot account for the reality of the mind in its own terms, and the dualist leaves the mind dangling in midair, cut off from its own roots (in the body) and from the exterior world (of the Body)—hence the unacceptable dualism.

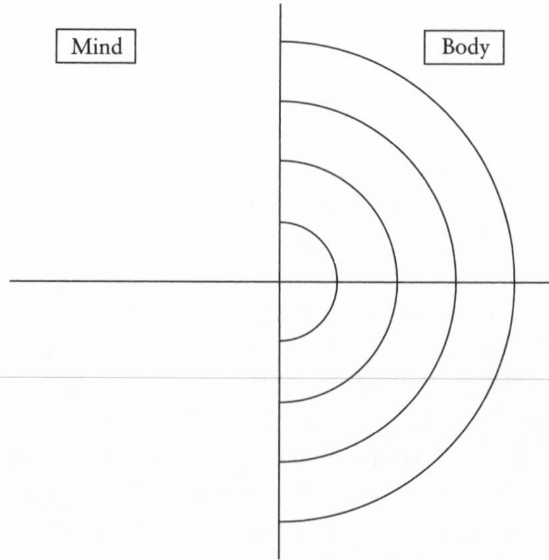

FIGURE 13. *Flatland*

Within the flatland paradigm depicted in figure 13, the problem is indeed unsolvable. The solution, I have suggested, involves an "all-level, all-quadrant" view, which plugs the mind back into its own body and intimately relates the mind to its own Body. And it does so, in the final analysis, through the disclosures of the postrational, nondual stages of consciousness development.

That means that part of this solution involves the existence of higher stages of development. But how do we proceed to unsnarl the world-knot if we have not yet reached these higher stages ourselves, and if we cannot expect that others will have done so? We can at least begin, I suggest, by acknowledging and incorporating *the realities of all four quadrants*. That is, if we cannot yet ourselves—in our own consciousness development—be "all-level" (matter to body to mind to soul to spirit), let us at least attempt to be "all-quadrant" (which means at least including the Big Three in our attempts to explain consciousness).

Thus, I am proposing two general phases for unsnarling the world-knot of the mind-body problem.[15] The first is a move from reductionistic accounts to all-quadrant accounts. This acknowledgment of the four quadrants (or simply the Big Three) allows an equal inclusion of *first-person* phenomenal accounts ("I"), *second-person* intersubjective backgrounds ("we"), and *third-person* physical systems ("it")—what we will call "the 1-2-3 of consciousness studies."

The second phase is then to move from "all-quadrant" to "all-level, all-quadrant." We will examine these two steps in that order.

Step One: All-Quadrant

It is not enough to say that organism and environment coevolve; it is not enough to say that culture and consciousness coevolve. All four of those "tetra-evolve" together.

That is, the objective organism (the Upper-Right quadrant), with its DNA, its neuronal pathways, its brain systems, and its behavioral patterns, mutually interacts with the objective environment, ecosystems, and social realities (the Lower Right), and all of those do indeed coevolve. Likewise, individual consciousness (Upper Left), with its intentionality, structures, and states, arises within, and mutually interacts with, the intersubjective culture (Lower Left) in which it finds itself, and which it in turn helps to create, so that these, too, coevolve. But just as important, subjective intentionality and objective behavior mutually interact (e.g., through will and response), and cultural worldviews mutually interact with social structures, as does individual consciousness and behavior. In other words, all four quadrants—organism, environment, consciousness, and culture—cause and are caused by the others: they "tetra-evolve."

(It does not matter "how" this happens; that "how," I am suggesting, is more fully disclosed at the postrational, nondual waves; at this point, it is only necessary to acknowledge that this interaction seems phenomenologically undeniable. Whether you think it is theoretically possible or not, your mind does interact with your body, your mind interacts with its culture, your mind interacts with the physical organism, and your organism interacts with your environment: they all "tetra-interact.")

As we have seen, the subjective features of consciousness (waves, streams, states) are intimately interrelated with the objective aspects of the organism (especially the brain, neurophysiology, and various organ systems in the individual), with the background cultural contexts that allow meaning and understanding to be generated in the first place, and with the social institutions that anchor them. As I suggested in *A Brief History of Everything*, even a single thought is inextricably embedded in all four quadrants—intentional, behavioral, cultural, and social—and cannot easily be understood without reference to them all.

Accordingly, in writings such as "An Integral Theory of Consciousness,"[16] I have stressed the need for an approach to consciousness that differentiates-and-integrates all four quadrants (or simply the Big Three of I, we, and it; or first-person, second-person, and third-person accounts: the 1-2-3 of consciousness studies).

That initially sounds like an impossibly tall order, but the fact is, for the first time in history we are actually at a point where we have enough of the pieces of the puzzle to at least begin such a project. Consider: in the Upper-Left quadrant of subjective consciousness, we have a body of research and evidence that includes the entire perennial philosophy (which offers three thousand years of meticulously gathered data on the interior domains) and a massive amount of modern research from developmental psychology. Much of that evidence is summarized in the charts, which are a startling testimony to the fact that, even if there are a million details yet to be worked out, the broad contours of the spectrum of consciousness have already been significantly outlined. The general similarities in all of those charts are most suggestive, and, from a bird's-eye view, hint that we are at least in the right ballpark.

The same can be said with a reasonable degree of confidence for the

Lower-Left quadrant (of intersubjective worldviews) and the Lower-Right quadrant (of the techno-economic base). A century or so of postmodernism has made the importance of pluralistic cultural worldviews and backgrounds abundantly clear (even rationally oriented theorists such as Habermas have agreed that all propositions are *always* in part culturally situated); moreover, scholars are in general agreement that cultural worldviews historically unfolded from archaic to magic to mythic to mental to global (although there is reasonable disagreement as to the respective values of those views). Likewise, in the Lower-Right quadrant, few scholars contest the evolutionary sequence of the social forces of production: foraging, horticultural, agrarian, industrial, informational. In both of those quadrants—cultural and social—although again a million details need to be worked out, the general contours are better understood today than at any other time in history.

Work in the Upper-Right quadrant—particularly in brain physiology and cognitive science—is yet in its infancy, and a fully integral view of consciousness will await more primary discoveries in this quadrant (which is one of the reasons I have written less about this quadrant than the others: cognitive science and neuroscience, despite the enthusiastic pronouncements of their proponents—the Churchlands, for example—is a babe in the woods). Still, our knowledge of this quadrant is growing as fast as babies usually do, and at this time we have enough knowledge to at least be able to situate neurophysiology in relation to the other dimensions of being, even as its contours continue to be elucidated.[17]

Thus, the time is certainly ripe for the beginning of an all-quadrant approach, or simply an approach that equally honors first-person phenomenal accounts, second-person intersubjective structures, and third-person scientific/objective systems: the 1-2-3 of consciousness studies.

There are many signs that this first phase is well under way. *The Journal of Consciousness Studies* regularly carries articles arguing for such balanced approaches, and several books have recently stated the case for such a balance in convincing terms. *The View from Within*, edited by Francisco Varela and Jonathan Shear, is a superb example. They defend a view that is predominantly a neurophenomenology, where first-person experience and third-person systems provide reciprocal constraints, often mediated through second-person positions. "It would be futile to stay with first-person descriptions in isolation. We need to harmonize and constrain them by building the appropriate *links* with third-person studies. (This often implies an intermediate mediation, a second-person position.) The overall results should be to move toward an integrated or global perspective on mind where neither experience [first-person, UL] nor external mechanisms [third-person, UR] have the final word. The global [integral] perspective requires therefore the explicit establishment of mutual constraints, a reciprocal influence and determination."[18] This is consonant with what I mean by saying that all quadrants are mutually determining (and "tetra-interacting").

Max Velmans's anthology *Investigating Phenomenal Consciousness* is another superb collection emphasizing an integral approach. It includes chapters by Alwyn Scott, Greg Simpson, Howard Shevrin, Richard Stevens, Jane Henry, Charles Tart, Francisco Varela, Wilber and Walsh, and Velmans. *Transpersonal Research Methods for the Social Sciences*, by William Braud and Rosemarie Anderson, is a fine collection of resources for what the authors call an "integral inquiry."

STEP TWO: ALL-LEVEL

I believe that the field needs to continue to flesh out that all-quadrant approach, and further, to move to the second phase, which is *all-level*.

Many of the all-quadrant approaches fully acknowledge the transpersonal domains of consciousness. Robert Forman, for example, points out that at least three transpersonal states need to be recognized: the pure consciousness event (or formless cessation), dual mystical consciousness (or permanent causal/witnessing awareness), and the nondual state (or permanent nondual realization).[19] Moreover, many of the all-quadrant approaches (including Jonathan Shear and Ron Jevning, Francisco Varela, James Austin, Robert Forman, Braud and Anderson, and others) have explicitly drawn much of their methodology from meditative and contemplative techniques.

Still, one is hard-pressed to find in many of those authors a full appreciation of the stage conceptions of consciousness development, such as the works of Baldwin, Habermas, Loevinger, Graves, Kohlberg, Wade, Cook-Greuter, Beck, Kegan, et al., even though, as we have seen, there is substantial evidence for their validity. It is not enough to simply note that first-person realities reciprocally influence and determine third-person mechanisms, and that both circulate through second-person intermediaries. It is also crucial to understand that *first-person consciousness develops*, and it does so through a variety of well-researched stages. Moreover, *second-person consciousness develops*, and this development, too, has been widely researched. Finally, *the capacity for third-person consciousness develops* (e.g., Piagetian cognition), and this has likewise been exhaustively studied.[20] Perhaps because many of the all-quadrant theorists have come from a phenomenological background, which in itself does not easily spot stages, they have tended to overlook the waves of consciousness unfolding in all four quadrants.[21] Be that as it may, a truly integral approach, in my opinion, will move from being merely all-quadrant to being all-level, all-quadrant. Or *1-2-3 across all levels.*

Obviously much work remains to be done. But a staggering amount of evidence—premodern, modern, and postmodern—points most strongly to an integral approach that is all-quadrant, all-level. The sheer amount of this evidence inexorably points to the fact that we stand today on the brink, not of fashioning a fully complete and integral view of consciousness, but of being able to settle, from now on, for nothing less.

15

The Integral Embrace

HOW THEN SHALL we see the world? An ancient era of resplendent wonder, a modernity gone merely mad? A postmodernity in pieces? Or perhaps evolution as unadulterated progress, today being the happiest days of all? Evolution, or devolution? The very fact that we recognize premodern, modern, and postmodern eras, means we implicitly recognize some sort of development. Even the theorists who label themselves "postmodern" imply some sort of improvements over their modern predecessors, yes? How shall we balance the undeniable improvements in history with the equally undeniable horrors that also followed? And how can this balance allow us, finally, to embrace the best of premodern, modern, and postmodern, an embrace that might allow a genuinely integral psychology to emerge?

From Premodernity

Each era has its enduring truths. Each has its pathological distortions.

Premodernity disclosed the Great Nest of Being in all of its radiant glory—and then often used that conception in a rigidly hierarchical fashion to justify the oppression of millions. Modernity differentiated the value spheres, ushering in everything from the liberal democracies to feminism—and then let those differentiations drift into dissociation, whereupon a rampant scientific materialism attempted to erase virtually every value originally freed by the differentiations: technical rationality nearly destroyed the humanity it had first made possible, and the modern disqualified universe settled like volcanic dust in a suffocating manner on all. And postmodernity, which set out nobly to deconstruct the nightmares of the modern flatland, ended up embracing and even amplifying them, so that not only was the integration offered by its own vision-logic not forthcoming, its integrative intent was set back decades.

While attempting to set aside the distortions of each epoch, we seek to honor the truths, for they are all truths of the human potential. To ignore past truths—in either phylogeny or ontogeny—is the very definition of pathology. Therefore, an integral approach—a sane approach—attempts to honor, acknowledge, and incorporate the enduring truths into the ongoing sweep of consciousness evolution, for they are the truths of our very own Self, even here and now.

From the premodern heritage, we have learned of the Great Nest of Being and Knowing, and found that it is a roadmap to Spirit, not in a rigid and predetermined fashion, but as a flowing morphogenetic field of gentle persuasion. The enduring truths of this ancient wisdom include the idea of levels or dimensions of reality and consciousness, reaching from matter to body to mind to soul to spirit, with Spirit fully and equally present at all of these levels as the Ground of the entire display. Each senior level transcends and includes its juniors, so that this Great Nest is a holarchy of extended love and compassionate embrace, reaching from dirt to Divinity, with no corner of the Kosmos left untouched by grace or care or luminosity.

The ancient sages taught us that, precisely because reality is multilayered—with physical, emotional, mental, and spiritual dimensions—reality is not simply a one-leveled affair lying around for all and sundry to see: you must be *adequate* to the level of reality you wish to understand. The soul is not running around out there in the physical world; it cannot be seen with microscopes or telescopes or photographic plates. If you want to see the soul, you must turn within. You must develop your consciousness. You must grow and evolve in your capacity to perceive the deeper layers of your Self, which disclose higher levels of reality: the great within that is beyond: the greater the depth, the higher the reality.

For an integral psychology, this means that we should attempt to honor the entire spectrum of consciousness, matter to body to mind to soul to spirit—by whatever names, in whatever guises, and in however many levels modern research can confirm (five, seven, twelve, twenty: the exact number matters less than the simple acknowledgment of the multidimensional richness involved). I have suggested around 16 major waves, which can be condensed into nine or ten functional groupings (all shown in the charts), but all such cartographies are simply different approaches to the many waves in the great River of Life, matter to mind to spirit, which is the most precious legacy of the ancient wisdom.

For an integral psychology, this also means that a person's deepest drive—the major drive of which all others are derivative—is the drive to actualize the entire Great Nest through the vehicle of one's own being, so that one becomes, in full realization, a vehicle of Spirit shining radiantly into the world, as the entire world. We are all the sons and daughters of a Godhead that is the Goal and Ground of every gesture in the Kosmos, and we will not rest until our own Original Face greets us with each dawn.

The ancient adepts would have this Great Liberation be a permanent realization, not a passing glimmer—a permanent trait, not merely an altered state—and thus they left us with an extraordinary battery of spiritual practices, all of which have one thing in common: they help us to unfold the higher levels of the Great Nest of our own Divinity—they accelerate our development to Godhood. The more complete spiritual practices emphasize the *ascending currents*—taking us from body to mind to soul to spirit—as well as the *descending currents*—taking spiritual insights and expressing them in and through the incarnated body and blessed earth, thus integrating both the transcendental and immanent faces of Emptiness.

Whenever we moderns pause for a moment, and enter the silence, and listen very carefully, the glimmer of our own deepest nature begins to shine forth, and we are introduced to the mysteries of the deep, the call of the within, the infinite radiance of a splendor that time and space forgot—we are introduced to the all-pervading Spiritual domain that the growing tip of our honored ancestors were the first to discover. And they were good enough to leave us a general map to that infinite domain, a map called the Great Nest of Being, a map of our own interiors, an archeology of our own Spirit.

FROM MODERNITY

From modernity we take the enduring truths of the *differentiation* and the *evolution* of the Big Three (the Good, the True, and the Beautiful).[1] As the average mode of consciousness continued historically to grow and evolve—and because evolution operates in part by differentiation-and-integration—the perception of the Great Nest became increasingly differentiated and integrated on a widespread, cultural scale (and not just in a few individual pioneers). Differentiations seen in the past only by the most highly evolved became ordinary, common perceptions.[2]

As the Big Three of art, morals, and science began to differentiate and clarify on a widespread scale—I, we, and it; first-person, second-person, and third-person; self, culture, and nature; the Beautiful, the Good, and the True—each was allowed to yield its own truths unburdened by invasion from others. That modernity let these differentiations collapse into dissociation (so that scientific materialism could and did colonize the other spheres), condemns the pathological dissociation, not the dignity of the differentiations themselves, for they ushered in everything from democracy to feminism to the abolition of slavery to the rise of the ecological sciences to the worldwide increase in lifespan of over three decades: great dignities, indeed.

And thus, from modernity, we learn that each of the levels in the Great Nest needs to be differentiated into the four quadrants (or simply the Big Three), and done so on a widespread scale. From modernity we also learn that *each of those quadrants evolves*, and thus an integral psychology follows those developments as they appear in any individual.

For an integral psychology, this means that the basic levels of consciousness available to men and women need to be carefully differentiated into their various developmental lines. Through the levels or waves of the Great Nest (body, mind, soul, spirit) run numerous different developmental lines or streams (cognitive, moral, aesthetic, affective, needs, identities, perspectives, etc.). *It is the job of an integral psychology to track all of these various waves and streams as they unfold in any given individual.*

We called this overall picture "an integral psychograph" (see figs. 2 and 3). This approach allows us to determine, in a very general way, the evolving streams of an individual's consciousness as those streams move into ever-deeper, ever-higher waves, body to mind to soul to spirit, precon to con to postcon to post-postcon. It also allows us to more easily spot any "stick points"—any pathologies, fractured fulcrums, developmental miscarriages, dissociated subpersonalities, alienated facets of consciousness—and, by better understanding their genesis and texture, treat them more effectively. Although the various types of pathology and treatment will have some important differences (due to the qualitatively different architecture of each basic wave), nonetheless they all attempt to *bring the problem into consciousness*, so that it can rejoin the ongoing sweep of holarchical embrace, the ever-deeper unfolding that is consciousness evolution, prepersonal to personal to transpersonal, subconscious to self-conscious to superconscious.

Evolution does not isolate us from the rest of the Kosmos, it unites us with the rest of the Kosmos: the same currents that produced birds from dust and poetry from rocks, produce egos from ids and sages from egos. Evolution in each quadrant is Spirit-in-action expressed in that mode, operating through gentle persuasion in the great morphogenetic field of increasing embrace. The evolutionary current of the Kosmos—this great River of Eros, binding human and nonhuman holons together in an ever-flowing caress—is indeed the Love that moves the sun and other stars. And modernity's enduring contributions—which disclosed the differentiation and evolution of the Big Three—simply allow us to track this evolving Love throughout its many waves and streams.

FROM POSTMODERNITY

Modernity's differentiation of the value spheres allowed postmodernity to see exactly how interrelated the four quadrants are. Every objective occasion has subjective and intersubjective components; every holon has four quadrants. The world is not merely an objective, Right-Hand occasion—it also has intrinsic depth, consciousness, the within, the interior, the Left-Hand worlds in all their glory. *Constructivism* means consciousness doesn't merely reflect the world, it helps construct it. *Contextualism* means that holons are nested, indefinitely. *Integral-aperspectivism* means that as many perspectives as humanly possible must be included in an integral embrace. That the Kosmos is endlessly holonic—there is the message of postmodernism.

For any integral studies, this means that we must take great care to insure that the important differentiations of modernity are in fact integrated, that the Big Three do not fly apart; that subtle reductionism does not creep into the picture, yielding a flatland holism; and that any approach to consciousness is indeed a 1-2-3 approach, including and equally honoring first-person, second-person, and third-person accounts of consciousness: first-person or phenomenal accounts of the stream of consciousness as it directly experienced by a person (Upper Left); second-person communication of those facts, set in particular linguistic structures, worldviews, and background contexts (Lower Left); and third-person scientific descriptions of the corresponding mechanisms, systems, and material networks, from brain structures to social systems (Right Hand).

That "all-quadrant" approach is the first step to a truly integral model. The second step adds an "all-level" approach, which investigates the *stages of development* of first-, second-, and third-person consciousness. In other words, it investigates the waves and streams, the levels and lines, in all of the quadrants.[3] The result is a "all-level, all-quadrant" approach to integral studies, across the spectrum of disciplines—science, history, religion, anthropology, philosophy, psychology, education, politics, business.

When it comes to the individual, the result is integral psychology, integral therapy, and integral transformative practice.

Spirit-in-Action Has Come to Awaken

Should this "all-level, all-quadrant" approach succeed, we will have embraced some of the more enduring truths of premodernity (all-level), modernity (all-quadrant), and the postmodern integration (all-level, all-quadrant).

My aim in this book, while focusing specifically on an integral psychology, has also been an integral approach in general, attempting to take, not just the best of today's schools, but the best of premodern, modern, and postmodern insights, while jettisoning their extremist distortions. Obviously, as I said in the Introduction, this type of approach can only begin with the most general of generalizations—outrageous generalizations, some would say—but if we are to start on this endeavor, we must start somewhere, and this type of approach is, I suppose, as good as any. But the major aim of this book is to act as just that: a beginning, not an end; the start of a discussion, not the finish.

If we really are living in an integral-aperspectival era, then these types of integral attempts will become increasingly common. Some will be better, some worse; some felicitous, some virulent; some truly integral, some angling. But there will be many, many such attempts, and all of them, I suspect, will contribute to the great integral rainbow now beginning to shine, however tentatively, all over the globe.

For the fact is, this is the dawning of the age of vision-logic, the rise of the network society, the postmodern, aperspectival, internetted global village. Evolution in all forms has started to become conscious of itself.

Evolution, as Spirit-in-action, is starting to awaken on a more collective scale. Kosmic evolution is now producing theories and performances of its own integral embrace. This Eros moves through you and me, urging us to include, to diversify, to honor, to enfold. The Love that moves the sun and other stars is moving theories such as this, and it will move many others, as Eros connects the previously unconnected, and pulls together the fragments of a world too weary to endure.

Some would call these integral endeavors "powerful glimmers of a true Descent of the all-pervading World Soul." Others would simply say the time is ripe for such. But this much seems certain: less comprehensive endeavors are starting to lose their appeal; the allure of flatland, the call of fragmentation, the regressive pull of reductionism, are becoming much less fascinating. Their power to enthrall the mind becomes weaker every day, as Eros works its subtle wonders in and through us all.

If we can believe the collective wisdom of the many the ages of humankind, we can perhaps say:

This Eros is the same Spirit-in-action that originally threw itself outward to create a vast morphogenetic field of wondrous possibilities (known as the Great Nest). Out of itself, as matter, it began; out of itself, as life, it continued; out of itself, as mind, it began to awaken. The same Spirit-in-action differentiated itself into modes of the good and the true and the beautiful, as it continued its evolutionary play. And it is now the same Spirit-in-action, starting to become collectively conscious of itself, that has initiated an era of integral embrace—global village to communications internet to integral theories to network society—as it slowly binds together the fragments of a world that has forgotten how to care.

Just so, the same Spirit-in-action has written this book, and it is the very same Spirit-in-action who is now reading it. From subconscious to self-conscious to superconscious, the great Play continues and the grand River flows, with all of its glorious streams rushing to the ocean of One Taste, never really lost, never really found, this sound of the rain on the temple roof, which only alone is.

Chart 1a. Wilber Correlations

	Correlative Basic Structures	General Self-Sense	Specific Aspects	Defenses	Possible Pathology	Fulcrum	Treatment	Moral Span (those deemed worthy of moral consideration)			
sensorimotor	-subatomic	material self				BPM: **F-0**	intense regressive therapies				
	matter-atomic		pleromatic								
	-molecular -polymer			distortion		**F-1**	pacification		autistic		
	sensation		uroboric	delusional proj. hallucination	psychosis	(physical	(Gedo: pacification)		symbolic		
	perception			wish fulfillment		self)			self-only		
phantasmic-emotional	**exocept**	bodyego	axial-body								
			pranic-body	selfobject fusion					impulsive		
	impulse/emotion		(typhonic)	projection	borderline	**F-2**	structure-building		magical		
	image		image-body	splitting		(emotional	(Gedo: unification, optimal disillusion)		narcissism		
	symbol		(magical)			self)		**preconventional**	hedonic		
rep-mind	**endocept**	persona	name-self	isolation repression	neurosis	**F-3**	uncovering				
	concept		concept-self	reaction form.		(self-	(Gedo: interpretation)	egocentric	safety-	**"me"**	locus of bodily self
			membership-self (mythic)	displacement		concept)			power		
conop	**rule/role** early		early	duplicitous transaction	script	**F-4**	script		mythic-		
	late		middle	covert		(role self)	analysis	**conventional**	membership		
	transition	ego	late	intentions				sociocentric	conformist	**"us"** family, group, tribe, nation	locus of mythic-membership
formop	**formal** early			suppression	ego	**F-5**	introspection		rational-		
	late		mature ego	anticipation sublimation		(mature	(Gedo: introspection)		reflexive		
	transition					ego)		**postconventional**			
postformal	**vision-** early	centaur	centaur	inauthenticity deadening	existential			worldcentric	universal-	**"all of us"** all humans without exception	locus of rational universal pluralism
	logic middle		(existential,	aborted self-actualization		**F-6**	existential		global		
	late		integrated self)	bad faith		(centaur)	therapy				
		soul						**post-postconventional** shamanic	panenhenic	**all earthly beings** without exception	locus of World-Soul
	psychic early			psychic inflation split-life goals	psychic	**F-7**	path of		all earthly beings		
	(vision) late		psychic self	pranic disorder yogic illness		(psychic)	yogis		(yogic)		
	subtle early		subtle self	failed integration	subtle	**F-8**	path of	bodhisattvic	panentheistic	**all sentient beings** in all realms without exception	locus of Brahma-lokas
	(archetype) late	spirit	(soul)	archetypal fragmentation		(subtle)	saints		all sentient		
									beings in all		
	causal early			failed differentiation		**F-9**	path of		realms (saintly)		
	(formless) late		Pure Self	Arhat's disease	causal	(causal)	sages				
			(Witness)					Buddhic	always	**all manifest and unmanifest** reality	self-liberation in primordial awareness
	nondual early					Ground			already		
	middle								(sage/siddha)		
	late		Nondual								

Chart 1b. Wilber Correlations

	Correlative Basic Structures	Affect	Levels of "Food" (relational exchange)	Gender Identity	Worldviews: name	Worldviews: general characteristics	
sensorimotor	-subatomic						
	matter-atomic			• morphological-			
	-molecular -polymer	• reactivity	**material exchange**	genetic givens			
	sensation	• sensations	-food		archaic	•undifferentiated, pleromatic	
	perception	• physiostates:	-labor	• undifferentiated			
phantasmic-emotional	**exocept**	touch, temperature,			archaic-	•hallucinatory wish fulfillment	egocentric
		pleasure, pain			magical	subject-object fusions	
	impulse/emotion	• protoemotions:	**emotional exchange**	• differentiated		"selfobject"	
	image	tension, fear, rage,	-sex	basic-gender	magical	•egocentric, word magic, narcissistic;	
	symbol	satisfaction	-safety,	identity		locus of magic power = ego	
rep-mind	**endocept**	• 2° emotions:	power		magic-	•omnipotence of ego challenged; security;	
	concept	anxiety, anger, wish-	-belongingness,		mythic	ego omnipotence transferred to gods	
		ing, liking, safety	care	• gender	mythic	•concrete-literal myths	ethnocentric
conop	**rule/role** early	• 3° emotions: love,	**mental exchange**	conventionality	(literal)	locus of magic power = deified Other	
	late	joy, depression, hate,	-membership	• gender	mythic-	•rationalization of mythic structures	
	transition	belongingness	discourse	consistency	rational	demythologizing, formalizing	
formop	**formal** early	• 4° emotions:	-self-reflective	(norms)	rational	•static universal formalism	worldcentric
	late	universal affect,	exchange		formalism	•static systems/contexts	
	transition	global justice, care,			pluralistic	•pluralistic systems, dynamic-	
postformal	**vision-** early	compassion, all-	-autonomous	• gender	relativism	multiple contexts/histories	
	logic middle	human love, world-	exchange	androgyny	holistic	•integrates multiple contexts, paradigmatic	
	late	centric altruism		(trans-	integralism	•cross-paradigmatic; dialectical	
				differentiated)		developmentalism as World Process	
	psychic early	• awe, rapture,	**soul exchange**		psychic	•union with World Process; nature	theocentric
	(vision) late	all-species love,	-psychic vision		(shamanic, yogic)	mysticism; gross realm unity	
		compassion	-God communion	• archetypal			
	subtle early	• ananda, ecstasy		gender union	subtle	•union with creatrix of gross realm;	
	(archetype) late	love-bliss, saintly	-God union	(tantra)	(archetypal,	deity mysticism; subtle realm unity	
		commitment			saintly)		
	causal early	• infinite freedom-	**spiritual exchange**	• beyond	causal	•union with source of manifest realms;	
	(formless) late	release,	-Godhead identity	gender	(formless, sage)	formless mysticism; causal unity	
		boddhisattvic-					
	nondual early	compassion	-sahaja		nondual	•union of form and formless,	
	middle	• one taste			(siddha)	Spirit and World Process	
	late					nondual mysticism	

Chart 2a. Basic Structures in Other Systems

	Basic Structures		Huston Smith levels (planes)	Plotinus	Buddhist Vijnanas	Stan Grof	John Battista	Chakras	General Great Chain	James Mark Baldwin
sensorimotor		-subatomic			(levels of	BPM: oceanic to birth				
	matter	-atomic		matter	csness)			1. material	matter	
		-molecular -polymer	body							
	sensation		(terrestrial)	sensation		somatic	sensation			prelogical
	perception			perception	1-5		perception			
phantasmic-emotional	exocept				five					
					senses	aesthetic			body	
	impulse/emotion			pleasure/pain			emotion	2. emotional-		
	image			images				sexual		
	symbol					psychodynamic				
rep-mind	endocept					Freudian				
	concept			concepts,		COEX systems		3. intentional-		quasi-
			mind	opinions				mind, power		logical
conop	rule/role	early	(intermediate)				cognition		mind	
		late								
	transition							4. community-		
formop	formal	early		logical	6. manovijnana			mind, love		logical
		late		faculty	(gross-reflecting		self-aware			
	transition				mind)			5. verbal-		
postformal	vision-	early		creative		existential		rational		extra-
	logic	middle		reason		death-rebirth		mind		logical
		late				(cf BPM)				
					7. manas			6. psychic-mind,		
	psychic	early		world	(higher mind)	astral-psychic		ajna (vision)		hyper-
	(vision)	late		soul		extra-human				logical
			soul			identifications		7. sahasrara,		
	subtle	early	(celestial)			archetypal	unition	transcendental	soul	
	(archetype)	late			8. tainted	deity, luminosity		↓ csness, light		
				nous	alayavijnana			(higher shabd		
	causal	early			(archetypal)	universal mind		chakras, to		
	(formless)	late				supracosmic		cessation)		
			spirit	absolute		void				
	nondual	early	(infinite)	one	9. nondual		absolute	(release of		
		middle			consciousness	ultimate		all chakras	spirit	
		late			as suchness			in the Real)		

Chart 2b. Basic Structures in Other Systems

	Basic Structures		General Great Chain	Aurobindo	Kabbalah	Vedanta: state	Vedanta: body	Vedanta: sheaths	William Tiller	Leadbetter (Theosophy)	Adi Da
sensorimotor	-subatomic					waking	gross	1. material			
	matter-atomic		matter	physical	Malkhut			(anna-	physical	physical	1. physical
	-molecular							mayakosha)			body
	-polymer										
	sensation			sensation					etheric	etheric	
										(fine	
	perception			perception							
										physical)	
	exocept										
phantasmic-emotional	**impulse/emotion**		body	vital-	Yesod			2. emotional-	astral	astral	2. emotional
	image			emotional				sexual		(emotional)	body
	symbol							(prana-			
rep-mind	**endocept**							mayakosha)	m-1		
	concept			lower mind					(lower mind)		
					Netzach/Hod						
conop	**rule/role**	early	mind	concrete mind							
		late						3. middle		mental	
	transition							mind			3. lower mind
formop	**formal**	early		logical mind		dreaming	subtle	(mano-	m-2		will-power
		late		(reasoning)				mayakosha)	(intellectual		gross-mind
	transition				Tiferet				mind)	causal	
postformal	**vision-**	early		higher mind						(higher	
	logic	middle		(systems)						mind)	
		late									4. higher mind
								4. higher			psychic
	psychic	early	soul (psychic and subtle)	illumined	Chesed/Gevurah			mind			opening
	(vision)	late		mind				(vijnana-	m-3		
								mayakosha)	(spiritual mind)	buddhic	
	subtle	early		intuitive	Chokhmah/Binah					(illumined mind)	5. supramental
	(archetype)	late		mind							psychic/subtle
								5. bliss		atmic	
	causal	early		overmind	Keter	deep sleep	causal	mind		(universal spirit)	6. formless
	(formless)	late			Ayn			(ananda-			cessation,
								mayakosha)	spirit	monad/logos	nirvikalpa
	nondual	early	spirit (causal and nondual)	supermind	Ein	turiya	turiya	Brahman-			
		middle			Sof			Atman			7. sahaja
		late		satchitananda				(turiyatita)			bhava

Chart 3A. Cognitive Development

Average age of emergence		Correlative Basic Structures	Piaget	Commons & Richards	Kurt Fischer level	Alexander (levels of mind)
		-subatomic				
		matter-atomic				
		-molecular -polymer				
0-18	sensorimotor	**sensation**			1. single sensorimotor set	
months		**perception**	sensorimotor	1a sensorimotor	(3-4 months)	1. sensorimotor
		exocept		actions	2. sensorimotor mapping	
				1b sentential	(7-8 months)	
1-3 yrs	phantasmic-emotional	**impulse/emotion**		actions	3. sensorimotor system	2. prana-
		image	preconceptual		(11-13 months)	emotion-
		symbol	preoperational	2a nominal actions	4. single representational set	desire
3-6 yrs	rep-mind	**endocept**	intuitive (conceptual)	2b preoperational	(20-24 months)	
		concept	preoperational	actions	5. representational mapping (4-5 yrs)	3. representa-
						tional mind
7-8	conop	**rule/role** early	concrete operational – substage 1	3a primary actions	6. representational system (6-7.5 yrs)	
9-10		late	" " – substage 2	3b concrete operations		
11-12		transition	transition [late conop/early formop (substage 1)]	4a abstract	7. abstract set (10-12)	
13-14	formop	**formal** early	formal operational – substage 2	4b formal	8. abstract mapping (11-15)	
15-19		late	" " – substage 3			4. abstract
19-21		transition	(transition – late formop/early polyvalent)	5a systematic	9. systems (19-21)	mind
open	postformal	**vision-** early	(polyvalent logic – systems of systems)	5b meta-systematic	10. systems of systems (24-26)	
↓		**logic** middle		6a paradigmatic		
[21-28]		late		6b cross-		
earliest expectable				paradigmatic		
[28-35]		**psychic** early				
		(vision) late				
						5. transcendental
[35-42]		**subtle** early				intuition
↓		(archetype) late				
[42-49]		**causal** early				6. root mind
		(formless) late				7. pure Self
[49-]		**nondual** early				8. Brahman-
		middle				Atman
		late				

CHART 3B. COGNITIVE DEVELOPMENT

	Correlative Basic Structures	overall cognitive lines	Pascual-Leone	Herb Koplowitz	Sri Aurobindo	Patricia Arlin	Gisela Labouvie-Vief	Jan Sinnott	Michael Basseches
sensorimotor	-subatomic								
	matter-atomic				physical				
	-molecular -polymer								
	sensation	gross							
	perception		sensorimotor			sensorimotor		sensorimotor	
	exocept								
phantasmic-emotional	**impulse/emotion**				vital-				
	image				emotional				
	symbol		preoperational			preoperational		preoperational	
rep-mind	**endocept**								
	concept				lower mind				
							symbolic		
conop	**rule/role** early	gross-reflecting			concrete mind	2a low concrete		concrete	1a preformal
	late		late concrete			2b high concrete			
	transition		early formal			3a low formal			
formop	**formal** early		formal	formal	logical mind	3b high formal	intra-systemic	formal	1b formal
	late		late formal		(reasoning)				2 intermediate postformal
	transition		pre-dialectical	systems		4a postformal	inter-systemic	relativistic	3 general advanced
postformal	**vision-** early		dialectical	general systems	higher mind	4b-e late	autonomous	unified-	4 advanced
	logic middle		transcendental-	unitary concepts	(systems)	postformal		theory	dialectical
	late		thinking	↓		(dialectical)			thinking
	psychic early				illumined				
	(vision) late				mind				
	subtle early	subtle			intuitive				
	(archetype) late				mind				
	causal early				overmind				
	(formless) late	causal							
	nondual early	nondual			supermind				
	middle								
	late				satchitananda				

Chart 4a. Self-Related Stages

	Correlative Basic Structures	Jane Loevinger (ego stages)	John Broughton (self epistemology)	Sullivan, Grant, and Grant (self-integration)	Fulcrums (Wilber)	Jenny Wade	Michael Washburn	Erik Erikson
sensorimotor	-subatomic				F-0 pre and perinatal; deeper psychic trail	pre, peri, neonatal		
	matter-atomic							
	-molecular -polymer				F-1	1. reactive (possible transcendental)	original	
	sensation	presocial,					embedment	trust vs.
	perception	autistic						mistrust
phantasmic-emotional	**exocept**						bodyego	
				1. differentiation				
	impulse/emotion	symbiotic		of self & nonself	F-2	2. naive	primal	autonomy vs.
	image						repression	shame and
	symbol	impulsive		2. manipulative-				doubt
rep-mind	**endocept**			demanding			mental	
	concept		0. self “inside,” reality “outside”	3. power:	F-3	3. egocentric	ego	initiative vs.
conop		self-protective	1. big-person mind, little-person body	a. rules-				guilt & anxiety
	rule/role early		2. naive subjectivism,	“cons”				
	late	conformist	mind and body differentiated	b. rules-	F-4	4. conformist		industry vs.
formop	transition		3. persona vs. inner self	conformist				inferiority
	formal early	conscientious-conformist	4. dualist or positivist	4. early				
	late	conscientious	cynical, mechanistic	individuation	F-5	5. achievement/		identity vs. role confusion
	transition	individualistic	5. inner observer	5. continuity		affiliative		intimacy/
postformal	**vision-** early	autonomous	differentiated from ego	6. self-consistency			regression	isolation
	logic middle	integrated	6. mind and body experiences	7. relativity-	F-6	6. authentic	in service of	generativity/stagnation
	late		of an integrated self	integration			transcendence	integrity/despair
	psychic early				F-7			
	(vision) late						regeneration	
							in spirit	
	subtle early				F-8			
	(archetype) late					7. transcendent		
	causal early				F-9			
	(formless) late							
						8. unitary	integration	
	nondual early							
	middle				nondual			
	late							

Chart 4b. Self-Related Stages

	Correlative Basic Structures		Major Self Line	Neumann: mythological stages	Neumann: psychological stages	Scheler (structural hardware)	Pascual-Leone (ego development)	Karl Jaspers	Rudolph Steiner	Don Beck (spiral dynamics)
	-subatomic									
	matter-atomic			pleroma	pleromatic				physical	
sensorimotor	-molecular -polymer				uroboric fusion				body	
	sensation			uroboros	alimentary uroboros	organismic				1. instinctive
	perception				uroboric Mother	survival			etheric	
	exocept				wish-fulfillment				body	
				the Great	magic	instinctual				
phantasmic-emotional	**impulse/emotion**			Mother	maternal incest	effects			astral (emotion)	2. magical-
	image				bodyself narcissism				body	animistic
	symbol			separation of the	Oedipus/Electra					
	endocept			World Parents	cs/uncs	associative			sensation-	3. power-
rep-mind	**concept**		frontal (or **ego**)	dragon fight	overcoming instincts	memory	stages of self development beyond phenomenological ego or ordinary adult ego = stages of transcendental ego (Kant, Husserl) or "ultraself"	level-types of existential-phenomenological reduction, or **meditative thinking**	soul	gods
				birth of the Hero	emergence of ego					
conop	**rule/role**	early		slaying of Mother	differentiation	practical				4. absolutist-
		late			of anima	intelligence				religious
	transition			slaying of Father	differentiation					
formop	**formal**	early			of animus				rational-	5. individualistic-
		late		captive and treasure	mature ego	creative-	1. existential self	1. empirical	soul	achiever
	transition					spiritual	2. duality self	2. conceptual		6. relativistic
	vision-	early		Transformation	ego/self	intelligence	3. dialectical self	3. temporal		7. systematic-
postformal	**logic**	middle		↓	integration		4. realized self	4. true	consciousness-	integrative
		late					(quaternity	meditative	soul	8. global-
			deeper psychic (or **soul**)				thinking)	thinking		holistic
	psychic	early							spirit-	9. coral
	(vision)	late							self	↓
	subtle	early							spirit-	
	(archetype)	late							life	
	causal	early	Witness (or **Self**)						spirit-	
	(formless)	late							man	
	nondual	early								
		middle								
		late								

CHART 4C. SELF-RELATED STAGES

	Correlative Basic Structures			Susanne Cook-Greuter: perspective	Susanne Cook-Greuter: self-sense	Susanne Cook-Greuter: characteristics	Clare Graves (ego types)	Robert Kegan	Fulcrums (Wilber)	
sensorimotor	-subatomic								F-0	
	matter-atomic									
	-molecular -polymer									
	sensation									
	perception			none	presocial	autistic,	1. autistic	0. incorporative	F-1	physical
	exocept					undifferentiated				
phantasmic-emotional										
	impulse/emotion			none	symbiotic	confused,	2. magical			
	image					confounded	animistic			
	symbol		preconventional	1st person	impulsive	rudimentary		1. impulsive	F-2	emotional
rep-mind	**endocept**					self-labeling	3. egocentric			
	concept				self-protective	basic dichotomies,				mental:
						concepts		2. imperial	F-3	self-concept
conop	**rule/role**	early		2nd person	rule-oriented	early roles	4. sociocentric			
		late	conventional		conformist	simple roles				role-self
formop	transition			3rd person	self-conscious	introspection		3. interpersonal	F-4	(persona)
	formal	early			goal-oriented	historical self,	5. multiplistic			
		late			conscientious	many roles	6. relativistic/	4. formal-	F-5	ego (rational
	transition		postconventional	4th person	individualistic	relativity of self	individualistic	institutional		reflexive)
postformal	**vision-**	early			autonomous	self as system	7. systemic			integrated:
	logic	middle		5th person	ego-witnessing	self as construct	(integrated)	5. postformal-	F-6	centaur
		late		6th person	construct-witnessing	self transparent		interindividual		
				global	universal	ego		↓		
	psychic	early		cosmic	cosmic	transcendence				soul:
	(vision)	late			↓	↓			F-7	psychic
	subtle	early								
	(archetype)	late							F-8	subtle
	causal	early								spirit:
	(formless)	late							F-9	causal
	nondual	early								
		middle							nondual	nondual
		late								

CHART 5A. THE SELF-RELATED STAGES OF MORALS AND PERSPECTIVES

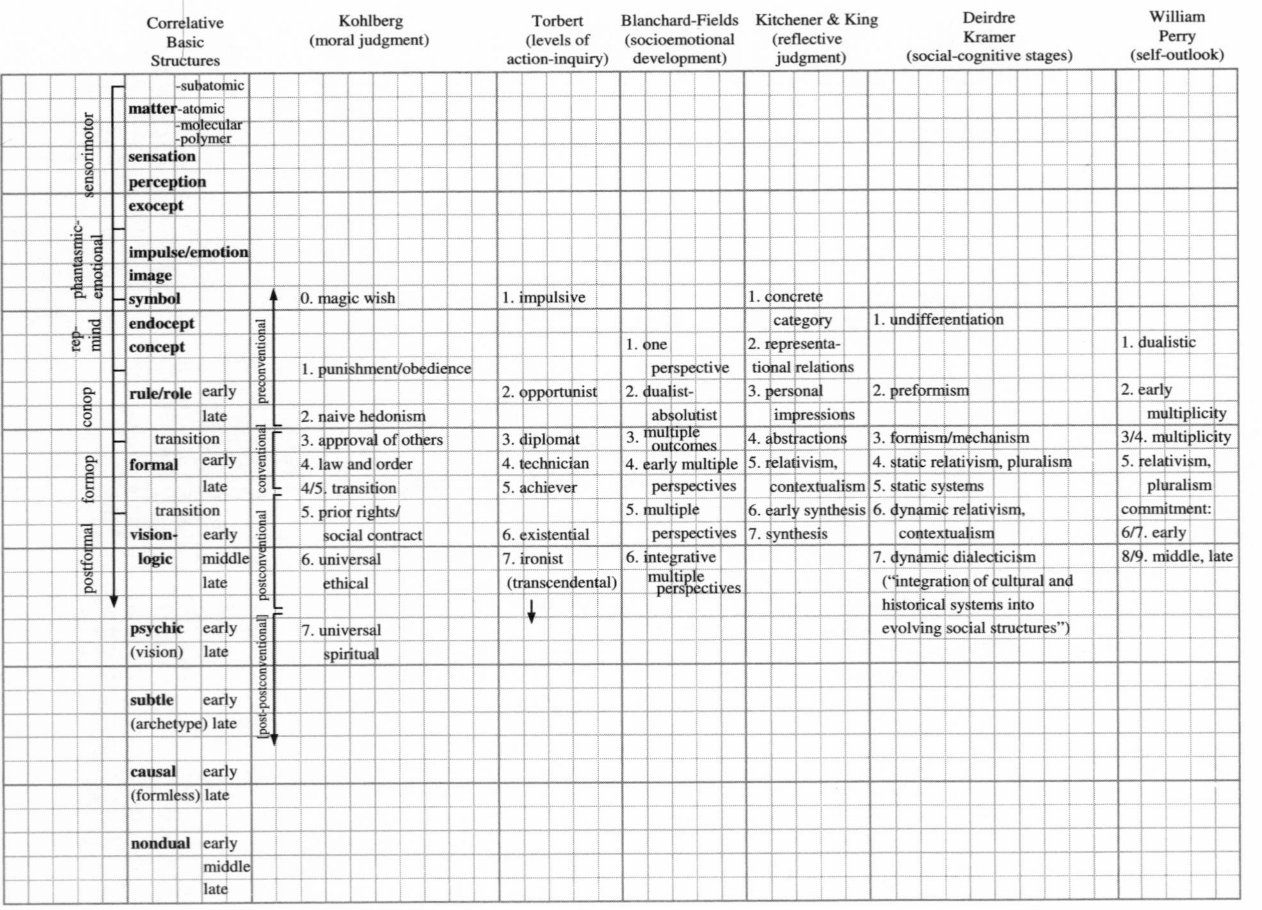

	Correlative Basic Structures			Kohlberg (moral judgment)	Torbert (levels of action-inquiry)	Blanchard-Fields (socioemotional development)	Kitchener & King (reflective judgment)	Deirdre Kramer (social-cognitive stages)	William Perry (self-outlook)
sensorimotor		-subatomic							
	matter	-atomic							
		-molecular -polymer							
	sensation								
	perception								
phantasmic-emotional	**exocept**								
	impulse/emotion								
	image								
	symbol		preconventional	0. magic wish	1. impulsive		1. concrete		
rep-mind	**endocept**						category	1. undifferentiation	
	concept					1. one	2. representa-		1. dualistic
				1. punishment/obedience		perspective	tional relations		
conop	**rule/role**	early			2. opportunist	2. dualist-	3. personal	2. preformism	2. early
		late		2. naive hedonism		absolutist	impressions		multiplicity
formop	transition		conventional	3. approval of others	3. diplomat	3. multiple outcomes	4. abstractions	3. formism/mechanism	3/4. multiplicity
	formal	early		4. law and order	4. technician	4. early multiple	5. relativism,	4. static relativism, pluralism	5. relativism,
		late		4/5. transition	5. achiever	perspectives	contextualism	5. static systems	pluralism
postformal	transition		postconventional	5. prior rights/		5. multiple	6. early synthesis	6. dynamic relativism,	commitment:
	vision-	early		social contract	6. existential	perspectives	7. synthesis	contextualism	6/7. early
	logic	middle		6. universal	7. ironist	6. integrative		7. dynamic dialecticism	8/9. middle, late
		late		ethical	(transcendental)	multiple perspectives		("integration of cultural and	
					↓			historical systems into	
	psychic	early	[post-postconventional]	7. universal				evolving social structures")	
	(vision)	late		spiritual					
	subtle	early							
	(archetype)	late							
	causal	early							
	(formless)	late							
	nondual	early							
		middle							
		late							

Chart 5b. The Self-Related Stages of Morals and Perspectives

	Correlative Basic Structures	Turner/Powell (social role-taking)		Cheryl Armon (Stages of the Good)	Peck (moral motivation)	Worldviews (Wilber): name	Worldviews (Wilber): general characteristics	
sensorimotor	-subatomic							
	matter-atomic							
	-molecular -polymer							
	sensation	level and type				archaic	•undifferentiated, pleromatic	
	perception	of role-taking:						
phantasmic-emotional	**exocept**					archaic-	•hallucinatory wish fulfillment	**egocentric**
						magical	subject-object fusions	
	impulse/emotion				amoral-		"selfobject"	
	image				impulsive	magical	•egocentric, word magic, narcissistic;	
	symbol	identificatory					locus of magic power = ego	
rep-mind	**endocept**	nonreflexive	preconventional			magic-	•omnipotence of ego challenged; security;	
	concept				expedient-	mythic	ego omnipotence transferred to gods	
conop		identificatory		1. radical egoism	self-protective	mythic	•concrete-literal myths	**ethnocentric**
	rule/role early	reflexive				(literal)	locus of magic power = deified Other	
	late	3rd party nonreflexive		2. instrumental egoism	conformist	mythic-	•rationalization of mythic structures	
formop	transition	3rd party reflexive	conventional	3. affective mutuality	(irrational-	rational	demythologizing, formalizing	
	formal early	interactive effect		4. individuality	conscientious)	rational	•static universal formalism	**worldcentric**
	late			4/5. subjective relativism		formalism	•static systems/contexts	
postformal	transition	interactive	postconventional		rational-	pluralistic	•pluralistic systems, dynamic-	
	vision- early	empathy		5. autonomy	altruistic	relativism	multiple contexts/histories	
	logic middle			6. universal holism		holistic	•integrates multiple contexts, paradigmatic	
	late	social genius				integralism	•cross-paradigmatic; dialectical	
							developmentalism as World Process	
	psychic early					psychic	•union with World Process; nature	**theocentric**
	(vision) late					(shamanic, yogic)	mysticism; gross realm unity	
	subtle early					subtle	•union with creatrix of gross realm;	
	(archetype) late					(archetypal,	deity mysticism; subtle realm unity	
						saintly)		
	causal early					causal	•union with source of manifest realms;	
	(formless) late					(formless, sage)	formless mysticism; causal unity	
	nondual early					nondual	•union of form and formless,	
	middle					(siddha)	Spirit and World Process	
	late						nondual mysticism	

Chart 5c. The Self-Related Stages of Morals and Perspectives

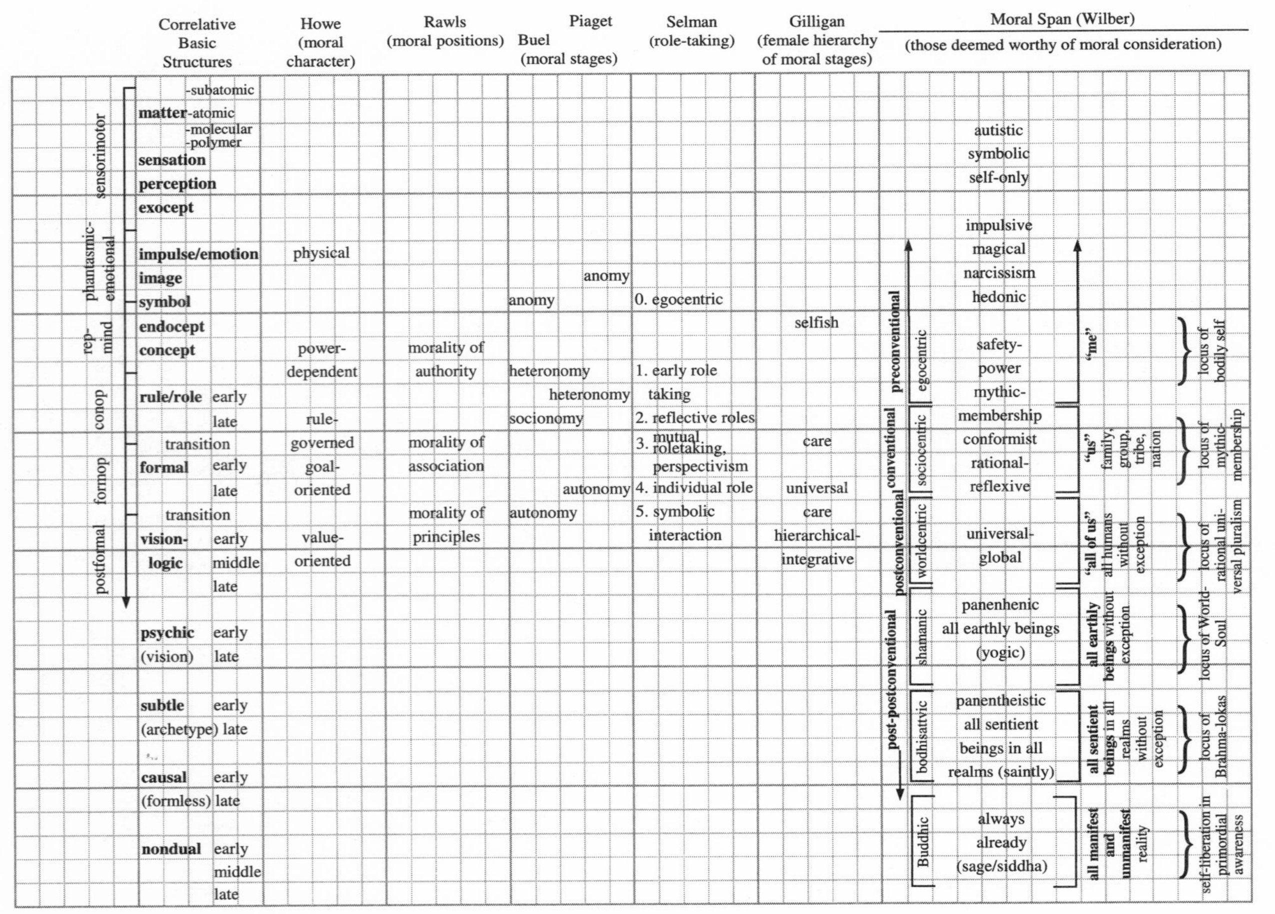

	Correlative Basic Structures	Howe (moral character)	Rawls (moral positions)	Buel (moral stages)	Piaget (moral stages)	Selman (role-taking)	Gilligan (female hierarchy of moral stages)	Moral Span (Wilber) (those deemed worthy of moral consideration)			
sensorimotor	-subatomic										
	matter-atomic										
	-molecular -polymer								autistic		
	sensation								symbolic		
	perception								self-only		
phantasmic-emotional	**exocept**										
									impulsive		
	impulse/emotion	physical							magical		
	image				anomy				narcissism		
	symbol			anomy		0. egocentric			hedonic		
rep-mind	**endocept**						selfish	**preconventional** egocentric		“me”	locus of bodily self
	concept	power-	morality of						safety-		
		dependent	authority	heteronomy		1. early role			power		
conop	**rule/role** early				heteronomy	taking			mythic-		
	late	rule-		socionomy		2. reflective roles		**conventional** sociocentric	membership	“us” family, group, tribe, nation	locus of mythic-membership
formop	transition	governed	morality of			3. mutual roletaking,	care		conformist		
	formal early	goal-	association			perspectivism			rational-		
	late	oriented			autonomy	4. individual role	universal		reflexive		
postformal	transition		morality of	autonomy		5. symbolic	care	**postconventional** worldcentric		**“all of us”** all humans without exception	locus of rational universal pluralism
	vision- early	value-	principles			interaction	hierarchical-		universal-		
	logic middle	oriented					integrative		global		
	late										
	psychic early							**post-postconventional** shamanic	panenhenic	**all earthly beings** without exception	locus of World-Soul
	(vision) late								all earthly beings (yogic)		
	subtle early							bodhisattvic	panentheistic	**all sentient beings** in all realms without exception	locus of Brahma-lokas
	(archetype) late								all sentient		
	causal early								beings in all realms (saintly)		
	(formless) late										
	nondual early							Buddhic	always	**all manifest and unmanifest** reality	self-liberation in primordial awareness
	middle								already		
	late								(sage/siddha)		

Chart 6A. Stages of Spirituality

	Correlative Basic Structures		Hazrat Inayat Khan (Sufism)	Mahamudra (stages of meditation)	Fowler (stages of faith)	Wilber	Underhill	Helminiak (spiritual development)	Funk (contact with Numinous)
sensorimotor	-subatomic								
	matter-atomic		matter						
	-molecular -polymer		(nasut)						
	sensation		vegetable		0. preverbal,	archaic			
	perception		animal		undifferentiated				
phantasmic-emotional	**exocept**					archaic-			
			mundane-			magical			
	impulse/emotion		person						libidinal,
	image		(bodily desires)			magical			prepersonal
	symbol			**concepts**	1. magical,				
rep-mind	**endocept**			and beliefs	projective	magic-			
	concept		material-	of gross mind		mythic			
			person			mythic-	conceptual		
conop	**rule/role**	early	(earthly gain)		2. mythic-	literal	faith and		personal
		late			literal	(mythic-	beliefs	conformist	
formop	transition			right	3. conventional	membership)			
	formal	early	artistic person	beliefs	4. individual-			conscientious-conformist	psychological
		late	(beyond		reflexive	rational-		conscientious	
	transition		conventions)	**foundations**	5. conjunctive	universal			creative
postformal	**vision-**	early		universal-	faith	integral-		compassionate	
	logic	middle	idealistic	ethical practices	6. universalizing	holistic	contemplative	cosmic	(global)
		late	(universal princi-		↓	(global)	illumination:		
			ples)	**meditation:**					
	psychic	early	djinn (genius)	access		**nature mysticism**	**1. nature mysticism**		nature
	(vision)	late	vision mind	**1. one-pointedness**		shamanic, yogic	union with stream of life		mysticism
			(malkut)	gross union		gross-realm unity	lateral expansion of csness		
	subtle	early	soul (angelic)	subtle perception		**deity mysticism**	**2. metaphysical mysticism**		archetypal,
	(archetype)	late	akasha-archetypal	luminosity		luminosity, saintly	recollection (archetypal)		theistic mysti-
			arwah- divine luminosity			subtle-realm unity	luminosity		cism
	causal	early	wahdat-witness	**2. simplicity**		**formless mysticism**	contemplation-divine love		
	(formless)	late	djabrut-cessation	cessation		cessation	divine ignorance (cessation)		
			formless	emptiness		causal unity	**3. divine mysticism** - dark night		spirit, union
	nondual	early	zat: absolute	**3. one taste**		**nondual mysticism**	- union		with absolute
		middle	consciousness	unity form/formless		constant			
		late	nondual	**4. non-meditation**		consciousness			

Chart 6b. Stages of Spirituality

	Correlative Basic Structures	Daniel Brown (cross-cultural stages of meditation)	Muhyiddin Ibn 'Arabi (stations of zikr)	St. Palamas	traditional samadhis (highest contemplative states)	Highest Yoga Tantra: seven stages of practice	Highest Yoga Tantra: levels of csness	Highest Yoga Tantra: phenomenological signs of appearance
	-subatomic							
sensorimotor	**matter**-atomic		mineral				form (1st	(1st dissolves
	-molecular -polymer		world				skandha)	into 2nd:)
	sensation		vegetal				sensation (2nd)	mirage
	perception		world					(2nd dissolves
	exocept						perception-	into 3rd:)
emotional							impulse (3rd)	smoke
	impulse/emotion		animal				emotion-	(3rd into 4th:)
	image		world				image (4th)	fireflies
	symbol							
mind	**endocept**							(4th into
	concept						gross mental	5th:)
							csness	flickering
conop	**rule/role** early						(5th)	butterlamp
	late		surface					
	transition		signs					
formop	**formal** early	• preliminary					80 gross mental	steady
	late	practices	universal				conceptions	butterlamp
	transition		order			① physical (gross) transcendence	(overall	
postformal	**vision-** early				supramental		**gross csness)**	
	logic middle		integral		meditative	② verbal (subtle) transcendence		
	late		ideas		consciousness:	in central channel		
		• concentration		vision			(dissolution of	
	psychic early	with support	intellect in				gross csness:)	
	(vision) late	• transcending	holy forms	recollection		④ (impure illusory body)	**subtle csness**	clear autumn
		gross perception	vision-wholeness			at heart	white appearance	moonlight
	subtle early	• subtle-	ascending sights	divine light	**savikalpa**	③ mental (causal) transcendence	(luminosity)	
	(archetype) late	perception	divine light	theosis	luminosity, deity form	winds dissolve:	red increase	clear autumn
		• luminosity	bliss		archetypal form		**very subtle**	sunlight
	causal early	• insight	witness-totality	formless	**nirvikalpa**-cessation		(causal) **csness**	
	(formless) late	• cessation	gnosis	illumination	**jnana**-nirodh, nirvana	at drop in heart	black near-attainment	thick blackness
		• advanced	a returned one		post-nirvana stages:		(cessation)	of autumn night
	nondual early	insight			**sahaja**-one taste	5. actual clear light	**clear-**	
	middle	• Enlightenment:			" -nonmeditation	6. learner's union	**light**	clear autumn
	late	a,b,c			post-Enlightenment: **bhava**	7. Buddhahood	**emptiness**	dawn

Chart 6c. Stages of Spirituality

	Correlative Basic Structures	General Great Chain	St. Teresa (seven stages of interior life)	Chirban (Eastern Orthodox Christianity)	St. Dionysius (pseudo)	Yoga Sutras of Patanjali	St. Gregory Nyssa	Alexander (TM)
	-subatomic							
sensorimotor	**matter**-atomic	matter						
	-molecular -polymer							
	sensation							
	perception							
	exocept							
phantasmic-emotional	**impulse/emotion**	body						
	image							
	symbol							
rep-mind	**endocept**							
	concept							
conop	**rule/role** early	mind						
	late				**prayer of**			
	transition		1. humility; 2. practice, prayer; 3. exemplary life		**simplicity**			
formop	**formal** early			image--	(vocal)	cleansing,	darkness	
	late			preliminary		restraint,	of sin	
	transition			orientation	**prayer of**	pranayana		
postformal	**vision-** early			metanoia--	**mind**			
	logic middle			turning toward	(subvocal)			
	late			spiritual		recollection		
					(purification)	dhyana	faith in God	
	psychic early		4. prayer of recollection	apatheia--	**prayer of**	one-		
	(vision) late		early visions	detachment	**recollection**	pointedness		
				purification	(illumination)	subtle perception		
	subtle early	soul	5. prayer of union	light-divine--	**prayer of quiet**	luminosity	light	
	(archetype) late		(ego dies, soul emerges)	luminosity	(unification)	shining forth		
			luminosity	theosis--	**prayer of union**	oneness of		
	causal early			oneness with	“glorious	buddhi	“not seeing”	transcendental
	(formless) late		6. cessation – formless	God	nothingness”	cessation	luminous	csness
			7. spiritual marriage		**(cloud of**	(nirodh)	darkness	Witness
	nondual early				**unknowing)**	raincloud		permanence
	middle	spirit						refined ”
	late							unity csness

Chart 7. Miscellaneous Developmental Lines

	Correlative Basic Structures		Erotic relationships (Fortune)	Needs (Maslow)	Levels of "Food" (relational exchange) (Wilber)	Modal Experience (Chinen)	Empathy (Benack)	Gender Identity (Wilber)	Affect (Wilber)
		-subatomic							
	matter	-atomic	physical					• morphological-	
sensorimotor		-molecular -polymer		physiological	**material exchange**			genetic givens	• reactivity
	sensation				-food				• sensations
	perception		instinctual		-labor			• undifferentiated	• physiostates:
	exocept								touch, temperature,
				beginning of					pleasure, pain
phantasmic-emotional	**impulse/emotion**		emotional	safety	**emotional exchange**			• differentiated	• protoemotions:
	image				-sex			basic-gender	tension, fear, rage,
	symbol				-safety,		**unwilling** to	identity	satisfaction
rep-mind	**endocept**			safety	power		assume others'		• 2° emotions:
	concept				-belongingness,	1. enactment	perspective		anxiety, anger, wish-
					care		**unable** to assume	• gender	ing, liking, safety
conop	**rule/role**	early	concrete		**mental exchange**		others'	conventionality	• 3° emotions: love,
		late	mental	belongingness	-membership		perspective	• gender	joy, depression, hate,
	transition				discourse	2. reflection	**willing** to assume	consistency	belongingness
formop	**formal**	early		self-esteem	-self-reflective		others' persp.	(norms)	• 4° emotions:
		late			exchange	3. representation	**able** to assume		universal affect,
	transition		abstract			4. pragmatic	others'		global justice, care,
postformal	**vision-**	early	mental	self-actualization	-autonomous	5. hermeneutic	perspective	• gender	compassion, all-
	logic	middle			exchange			androgyny	human love, world-
		late						(trans-	centric altruism
						6. attunement		differentiated)	
	psychic	early		self-	**soul exchange**				• awe, rapture,
	(vision)	late	concrete	transcendence	-psychic vision				all-species love,
			spirit	↓	-God communion	7. enlightenment		• archetypal	compassion
	subtle	early				↓		gender union	• ananda, ecstasy
	(archetype)	late			-God union			(tantra)	love-bliss, saintly
									commitment
	causal	early	pure		**spiritual exchange**			• beyond	• infinite freedom-
	(formless)	late	spirit		-Godhead identity			gender	release,
									boddhisattvic-
	nondual	early			-sahaja				compassion
		middle							• one taste
		late							

Chart 8. Miscellaneous

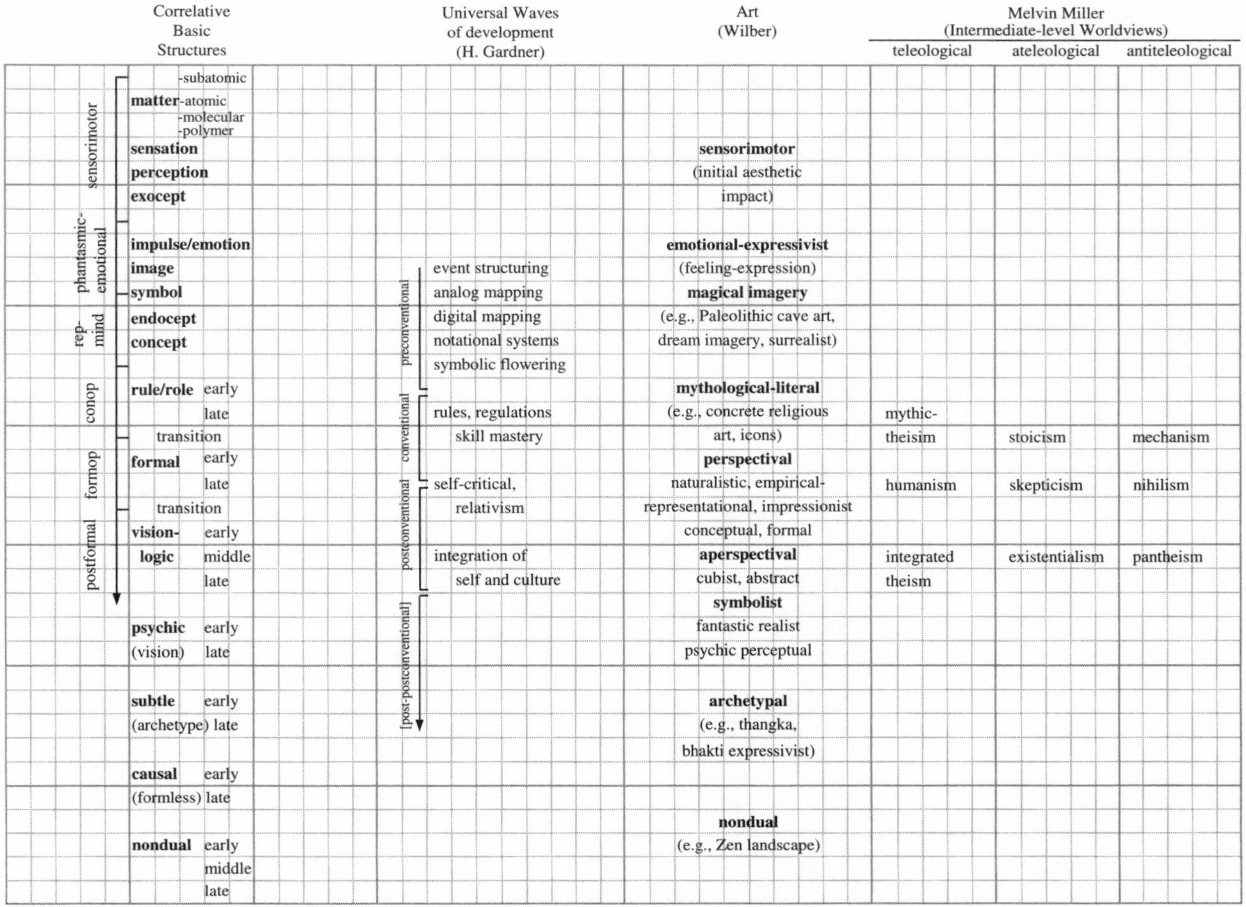

	Correlative Basic Structures			Universal Waves of development (H. Gardner)	Art (Wilber)	Melvin Miller (Intermediate-level Worldviews): teleological	ateleological	antiteleological
sensorimotor	-subatomic							
	matter-atomic							
	-molecular -polymer							
	sensation				**sensorimotor**			
	perception				(initial aesthetic			
	exocept				impact)			
phantasmic-emotional								
	impulse/emotion				**emotional-expressivist**			
	image		preconventional	event structuring	(feeling-expression)			
	symbol			analog mapping	**magical imagery**			
rep-mind	**endocept**			digital mapping	(e.g., Paleolithic cave art,			
	concept			notational systems	dream imagery, surrealist)			
				symbolic flowering				
conop	**rule/role**	early	conventional		**mythological-literal**			
		late		rules, regulations	(e.g., concrete religious	mythic-		
	transition			skill mastery	art, icons)	theism	stoicism	mechanism
formop	**formal**	early			**perspectival**			
		late	postconventional	self-critical,	naturalistic, empirical-	humanism	skepticism	nihilism
	transition			relativism	representational, impressionist			
postformal	**vision-**	early			conceptual, formal			
	logic	middle		integration of	**aperspectival**	integrated	existentialism	pantheism
		late		self and culture	cubist, abstract	theism		
			[post-postconventional]		**symbolist**			
	psychic	early			fantastic realist			
	(vision)	late			psychic perceptual			
	subtle	early			**archetypal**			
	(archetype)	late			(e.g., thangka,			
					bhakti expressivist)			
	causal	early						
	(formless)	late						
					nondual			
	nondual	early			(e.g., Zen landscape)			
		middle						
		late						

CHART 9A. SOCIOCULTURAL EVOLUTION

	Correlative Basic Structures		Major Epochs (Wilber): Cultural	Major Epochs (Wilber): Social	Habermas (epochs)	Jean Houston (G. Heard)	Habermas (scarce resource)	Age	Lenski (techno-economic base)
sensorimotor		-subatomic							
	matter	-atomic							
		-molecular -polymer							
	sensation								
	perception								
	exocept		archaic						
phantasmic-emotional								Paleolithic	simple hunting and gathering
	impulse/emotion			**foraging**	**archaic**				
	image			tribes	familiazation of male		power over		
	symbol		magic-typhonic	organized	**magical-animistic**	pre-individual constricted consciousness	nature	Mesolithic	advanced hunting and gathering
rep-mind	**endocept**			hunt	tribal kinship		(bodily		
	concept			**horticultural**	preconventional law		security)	Neolithic	simple horticultural
				village	**mythological**	proto-ind.			
conop	**rule/role**	early		**agrarian**	conventional law		legal security	Copper	advanced horticultural
		late	mythic-membership	early state	early state		(law and	Bronze	simple agrarian
	transition			**advanced ag.**	**mythic-rational**	mid-ind.	order)		
formop	**formal**	early		empire	empire			Iron	advanced agrarian
		late	rational-egoic	**industrial**	**rational-reflective**		value	Enlightenment	industrial
	transition			nation/state	nation-state	individual			
postformal	**vision-**	early		**informational**	postconventional law		meaning	Globalization	informational
	logic	middle	integral-centauric	planetary	**world citizens**				
		late	most advanced in each:	global	global				
						post-individual			
	psychic	early							
	(vision)	late	shaman						
	subtle	early							
	(archetype)	late	saint						
	causal	early							
	(formless)	late	sage						
	nondual	early							
		middle							
		late	siddha						

Chart 9b. Sociocultural Evolution

	Correlative Basic Structures			Sociocultural (Wilber)	Jean Gebser	A. Taylor (levels of social organization)	Jay Earley	Robert Bellah (evolution of religious systems)	Duane Elgin era (consciousness)
sensorimotor		-subatomic							
	matter	-atomic							
		-molecular -polymer							
	sensation								
	perception								
phantasmic-emotional	**exocept**		**archaic**						
					archaic			primitive	1. archaic humans
	impulse/emotion			foraging		S_1 – family,			(contracted
	image			tribes		clan, band	1. tribal		consciousness)
	symbol		**magic**		magic		hunting magic	archaic	2. hunter-
rep-mind	**endocept**								gatherer
	concept			horticultural		S_2 – tribe,	2. horticulture,		(surface
			mythic	village	mythic	territorial	villages,		consciousness)
conop	**rule/role**	early		agrarian			mythology	historic	3. agrarian
		late		early state		S_3 – theocratic	3. empires,		(depth)
formop	transition			advanced ag.	mental	empires	gods and heroes	early-	
	formal	early	**rational**	empire			4. medieval	modern	
		late		industrial		S_4 – national	5. modern,	modern	4. urban-industrial
	transition			nation	integral-	state	democracy,		(dynamic)
postformal	**vision-**	early	**centauric**	informational	aperspectival	S_5 – supra-	individualism		FUTURE:
	logic	middle		global		national	6. global		5. global
		late					consciousness		reconciliation
							↓		(reflective)
	psychic	early							
	(vision)	late							
	subtle	early							6. global bonding
	(archetype)	late							(oceanic)
	causal	early							7. global creativity
	(formless)	late							(flow)
	nondual	early							8. global wisdom
		middle							(integral)
		late							

CHART 10. JÜRGEN HABERMAS

	Correlative Basic Structures			Individual's identity	Level of communication	Idea of the good life	Domain of validity	Ethics
sensorimotor		-subatomic						
	matter	-atomic -molecular -polymer						
	sensation							
	perception							
phantasmic-emotional	**exocept**							
	impulse/emotion							
	image							
	symbol		(bodyego)	natural	actions and			
rep-mind	**endocept**			identity	consequences			
	concept				of actions			
						1. hedonism under obedience	nature and	naive
conop	**rule/role**	early					social environment	hedonism
		late	(persona)	role	roles	2. hedonism under exchange		
	transition			identity	systems of	3. concrete morality/ primary groups	group of primary reference persons	
formop	**formal**	early			norms	4. " " / secondary groups	members of the political community	specific order
		late				5. civil liberties,	all legal associates	rational
	transition		(ego)	ego	principles	legal freedom		natural law
postformal	**vision-**	early		identity		6. moral freedom	all humans as private persons	formalistic ethics
	logic	middle	(centaur)			7. political freedom	all humans as	universal ethics
		late					world citizens	of speech
	psychic	early						
	(vision)	late						
	subtle	early						
	(archetype)	late						
	causal	early						
	(formless)	late						
	nondual	early						
		middle						
		late						

from sixteen basic structures (in boldface) to thirty (counting sublevels); as functional groupings, I usually give nine or ten (i.e., sensorimotor, emotional-sexual, rep-mind, conop, formop, vision-logic, psychic, subtle, causal, nondual). What all this means—and why these different counts are all legitimate—will become more obvious as the descriptions unfold. I should say that what we count as a stage depends first and foremost on empirical and phenomenological evidence, and as that evidence becomes richer, our stage conceptions become clearer (see the Introduction to *Transformations of Consciousness* for a discussion of the meaning of, and evidence for, "stages"). The sixteen or so basic structures/stages presented in the charts are based on the textual reports of some three thousands years of meditative experience, coupled with recent psychological research; but they are always open to revision and clarification.

3. See *Sex, Ecology, Spirituality,* 2nd ed. (CW6), for an in-depth discussion of holons.

As Huston Smith points out in *Forgotten Truth* (see chart 2a), in the great traditions, the levels of consciousness (or levels of selfhood) are sometimes distinguished from the levels of reality (or planes of reality), and I also follow that distinction (see notes 1.5, 1.9, 1.10, 8.1, 8.2. 8.39, 12.12). However, for many purposes they can be treated together, as the being and knowing aspects of each of the levels in the Great Nest. In other words, the *basic structures of knowing* (the levels of consciousness/selfhood) and the *basic structures of being* (the planes/realms of reality) are intimately connected, and unless otherwise specified, both of these are indicated by the term *basic structures* or *basic levels* of the Great Nest. (Huston Smith indicates this by using the same figure of concentric circles to cover both levels of reality and levels of selfhood.) But the reason it is necessary to distinguish them is that a given level of selfhood can encounter a different level of reality, as we will see in subsequent discussions, and thus these need to be preserved as two independent variables. Nonetheless, there are advantages, in modern discourse, to emphasizing the epistemological component over the ontological, as I will point out in the following discussion. See notes 1.5, 1.9, 1.10, 8.1, 8.2. 8.39, 12.12.

4. See *Sex, Ecology, Spirituality,* 2nd ed. (CW6), and the Introduction to CW2 for a discussion of this topic.

5. This is similar to the Mahayana Buddhist notion of the alaya-vijnana, the "collective storehouse consciousness," which is present in every person, and which is said to be the repository of the memory traces (vasanas) of all past experiences, both of oneself and others (i.e., it is not just collective but transpersonal, embracing all sentient beings; in my system, it is the high-subtle to low-causal). It is said that, in higher stages of meditation, one can contact this transpersonal consciousness, which helps to release one from a narrow and restricted identity with the individual self. Thus, according to Mahayana Buddhism, the alaya-vijnana is: (1) a real transpersonal realm, an *actuality,* that exists in all people; (2) it is, however, rarely contacted in a conscious fashion, so for most people, that conscious contact is merely a *potential;* (3) as a collective storehouse, it is *evolving* and changing as more and more vasanas are collectively accumulated;

CHART 11. JAMES MARK BALDWIN

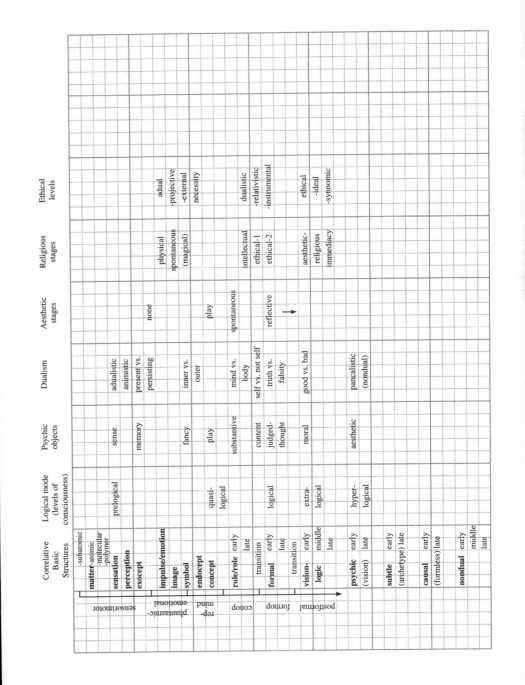

	Correlative Basic Structures		Logical mode (levels of consciousness)	Psychic objects	Dualism	Aesthetic stages	Religious stages	Ethical levels
sensorimotor		-subatomic						
	matter	-atomic -molecular -polymer						
	sensation		prelogical	sense	adualistic			
	perception				animistic			
	exocept			memory	present vs.			
					persisting	none		
phantasmic-emotional	**impulse/emotion**						physical	adual
	image						spontaneous	-projective
	symbol			fancy	inner vs.		(magical)	-external
rep-mind	**endocept**				outer			necessity
	concept		quasi-	play		play		
			logical					
conop	**rule/role**	early		substantive	mind vs.	spontaneous		
		late			body		intellectual	dualistic
formop	transition			content	self vs. not self		ethical-1	-relativistic
	formal	early	logical	judged-	truth vs.	reflective	ethical-2	-instrumental
		late		thought	falsity	↓		
	transition							
postformal	**vision-**	early	extra-	moral	good vs. bad		aesthetic-	ethical
	logic	middle	logical				religious	-ideal
		late					immediacy	-synnomic
	psychic	early	hyper-	aesthetic	pancalistic			
	(vision)	late	logical		(nondual)			
	subtle	early						
	(archetype)	late						
	causal	early						
	(formless)	late						
	nondual	early						
		middle						
		late						

Notes

Cross-references to notes in this section take the form (for example) "note 1.5," meaning note 5 for chapter 1. References to volumes in *The Collected Works of Ken Wilber* take the form "CW1," "CW2," and so on.

Note to the Reader

1. Quoted in translator's Preface, *Life after Death*, by G. Fechner, trans. H. Wernekke, written 1835, Chicago: Open Court Publishing, 1945. The book cover says *Life after Death*; the title page says *On Life after Death*; I am using the former, since that is what I first saw.
2. A. Zweig, "Gustav Theodor Fechner," in P. Edwards (ed.), *The Encyclopedia of Philosophy*, vol. 3.
3. Fechner, *Life after Death*, pp. 16–7.
4. Fechner, *Life after Death*, pp. 18.
5. A. Zweig, "Gustav Theodor Fechner," vol. 3.
6. This textbook has variously been called *System, Self, and Structure*; *Patterns and Process in Consciousness*; and *The 1-2-3 of Consciousness Studies*. The present book, *Integral Psychology*, is a highly condensed and edited version of the as yet unpublished two-volume work.

Part One

1. For a discussion of the importance of orienting generalizations and the way that I use them, see the Introduction to *Sex, Ecology, Spirituality*, 2nd ed. (CW6); and Jack Crittenden's Foreword to *The Eye of Spirit* (CW7).

Chapter 1. The Basic Levels or Waves

1. As we will see, I have numerous strong criticisms of the traditionalists, but their work is an indispensable starting point; see the works of F. Schuon, M. Pallis, A. Coomaraswamy, H. Corbin, S. Nasr. See also *The Eye of Spirit*; Huston Smith, *The World's Religions*; Roger Walsh, *The Spirit of Shamanism*.
2. Depending on how and what you count as a "level," I have listed anywhere

(4) thus its actual contours are constantly coevolving with people's experience—it is definitely *not* a pregiven, unchanging mold or eternal archetype; (5) *even though* it is constantly evolving, any individual, at any given time, by directly experiencing that realm, can be released from the constrictions of individuality; (6) thus, the fact that this subtle realm is evolving and changing does not mean that it cannot confer transpersonal liberation at any given time.

Of course, final liberation is said to be beyond even the subtle forms or vasanas, into the formless or causal (and then nondual). The causal is the only basic "level" that does not change and evolve, because it is purely formless. But even the nondual evolves in part, because it is a union of causal emptiness (which does not evolve) and the entire manifest world (which does).

To my mind, this conception (which is a reconstruction of the Buddhist view) is more adequate than that of eternally unchanging archetypal molds (see the Introduction to CW2 for a fuller discussion of this theme; some aspects of the Kosmos must still be assumed to be archetypal, but far fewer than the perennial philosophy generally imagined). In my opinion, all of the holons of existence (including the basic structures) are, in part, these types of evolutionary memories or habits. And, for the present discussion, it should be remembered that the higher levels are still evolving themselves, and thus they are great potentials, not pregiven absolutes, but this still does not prevent them from being able to release us from the constrictions of the lower realms.

6. See Eliot Deutsch, *Advaita Vedanta*. Incidentally, I use "the subtle realm" in two senses, broad and narrow. In the broad sense, I follow Vajrayana and Vedanta: matter is the gross realm, the unmanifest is the causal realm, and *everything in between* is the subtle realm (i.e., pranamayakosha, manomayakosha, and vijnanamayakosha, or vital, mental, and beginning transmental). In the narrow sense, I use "subtle" for just the *highest reaches* of the overall subtle realm. Context will determine which is meant.

7. Structures in the general sense are used by all schools of psychology and sociology, and not simply in the narrow sense given them by the various schools of structuralism. The *Oxford Dictionary of Sociology* defines structure as "a term loosely applied to any recurring pattern." The *Penguin Dictionary of Psychology* gives: "an organized, patterned, relatively stable configuration." I specifically define a structure as a holistic pattern, and it is roughly synonymous with "holon." For my tangential relation with the actual school of structuralism, see the Introduction to CW2.

   There are six types of structures that I have outlined: levels/lines, enduring/transitional, and deep/surface. The first set I have explained in the text (they are structures found in the basic levels and in the developmental lines). Enduring structures are ones that, once they emerge, remain in existence, fully functioning, but subsumed in higher structures (cognitive structures are mostly of this type). Transitional structures, on the other hand, tend to be *replaced* by their subsequent stages (e.g., ego stages and moral stages). The basic structures are *mostly* enduring structures; and the developmental lines consist *mostly* of transitional structures. All four of those types of structures have deep (universal) structures and surface (local) structures (although I now usually call these "deep features" and "surface features" to avoid confusion with Chomsky's formulations; also, deep and surface are a sliding scale: deep features can be those features shared by a group, a family, a tribe, a clan, a community, a nation, all humans, all species, all beings. Thus, "deep" doesn't necessarily mean "universal;" it means "shared with others," and research then determines how wide that group is—from a few people to genuine universals. The preponderance of research supports the claim that all of the basic structures, and most of the developmental lines, that I have presented in the charts, have some universal deep features). Commentators on my work have often confused deep structures with basic structures, and transitional structures with surface structures, no doubt due in part to lack of clarity in my exposition. But the six classes of structures (levels/lines, enduring/transitional, deep/surface) are distinct (yet overlapping) categories.

8. See in particular Charles Tart's exemplary work on states, *States of Consciousness*; B. Wolman, *Handbook of States of Consciousness*.
9. For the nature of the "nondual" state, see note 9.18. If we use around twenty basic structures, and four major states, we would have up to eighty different types of spiritual experience, and that is still very crude, since there are many different types (or subtypes) of states. Of course, the basic structures available to a person depend on his or her own developmental level (someone at the magic level can peak experience psychic, subtle, causal, or nondual, but will interpret them only in archaic or magical terms, *not* in mythic, rational, or centauric terms). As for the states, a person can peak experience any higher state that has not yet become a permanent structure—e.g., when individuals develop to the psychic level, they no longer have psychic peak experiences because the psychic is permanently available to them (but they can peak experience subtle, causal, and nondual). For further discussion of structures and states, see Wilber, "Paths beyond Ego in the Coming Decade" (in CW4 and in Walsh and Vaughan, *Paths beyond Ego*); numerous endnotes in *Sex, Ecology, Spirituality,* 2nd ed., such as chap. 14, note 17; *A Sociable God*; *The Eye of Spirit,* chap. 6, note 9; and notes 1.3, 1.5, 1.10, 8.1, 8.2. 8.39, 12.12.
10. A person at almost any stage of development can spontaneously in peak experiences (or naturally in the cycle of sleep) experience the psychic, subtle, causal, or nondual states; but those states/realms must be carried in, *and interpreted by*, the stage of development of the individual having the experience. Even if the peak experience itself is a "pure glimpse" of one of these transpersonal realms, it is either simultaneously or, soon thereafter, picked up and clothed in the subjective and intersubjective structures of the individual (i.e., it is carried in the preop, conop, formop, or vision-logic structure). As such, the full contours of the transpersonal realm are filtered, diluted, and sometimes distorted by the limitations of the lower structure (e.g., preop: its narcissism and egocentrism, its inability to take the role of others; conop: its concrete-literal mind, fundamentalistic and ethnocentric; formop: its tendency to rationally distance itself from nature and world).

It is only as a person *permanently* develops to the psychic level (i.e., has a permanent psychic basic structure) that the psychic realm is no longer of necessity distorted during its experience (and likewise with the subtle, causal, and nondual realms: only as they become basic structures, or realized patterns in consciousness, can they be experienced authentically). A person permanently awake to the psychic domain no longer has peak experiences of the psychic, just as we do not say of average adults, "They are having a verbal peak experience"—for they are permanently adapted to the verbal realm. Likewise, all the higher realms can become realizations that are *just as permanent.* Of course, a person at the psychic level could still have peak experiences of even higher realms—the subtle, causal, and nondual—but those will likewise be limited and distorted to some degree (until permanent growth to those higher levels occurs). A person at the subtle level (i.e., where the subtle realm has become not a passing peak experience but a permanent basic structure, or realized pattern in full consciousness) can have peak experiences of the causal and nondual. And so on—until "subject permanence," which is a continuous and permanent realization of that which witnesses the gross, subtle, and causal domains, at which point all of the higher realms—previously available to consciousness only as temporary peak experiences and nonordinary states—have become permanently available traits and structures. An enlightened being *still has access to subtle and causal levels* (since he or she still sleeps and dreams), which is why subtle and causal are also correctly referred to, at that point, as *enduring basic structures*, but they are constantly witnessed even as they continue to arise. See notes 1.3, 1.5, 1.9, 8.1, 8.2. 8.39, 12.12.

11. For further discussions of the idea that ontogenetic development up to formop is generally guaranteed (due to phylogenetic evolution to that point)—but beyond that you are on your own—see *Up from Eden, A Sociable God*, and *Transformations of Consciousness*. For a discussion of holons as Kosmic habits, see *Sex, Ecology, Spirituality*, 2nd ed.
12. The ages of emergence are generally true *only for the basic structures (and cognitive structures).* The ages of emergence of the self-related stages (e.g., identity, morals, needs, etc.) *vary considerably among individuals.* An adolescent with fully developed formop can be at moral stage 2, or 3, or 4, etc. The stages still occur in the same sequence, but their dates vary. The basic/cognitive structures are necessary, but not sufficient, for most other developments, and those other developments vary considerably as to their emergence, due to factors in all four quadrants (the four quadrants are introduced in Part Two).
13. The basic structures of each functional grouping are also shown in the charts (e.g., the "sensorimotor" functional grouping includes the basic structures of matter, sensation, perception, exocept; "phantasmic-emotional" includes impulse, protoemotion, image, symbol; "rep-mind" includes symbol, endocept, concept, early rule; and so on).

I have also subdivided many of the basic structures into early, middle, and late. Most researchers use "early" and "late," a few prefer the terms "low" and "high." I myself prefer "low" and "high" (as used in *The Atman Project*) because the evidence suggests that in most cases the substages are actually enduring structures that are taken up and incorporated into subsequent structures (they are enduring holons, not merely passing or transitional phases), and thus "low" and "high" are more appropriate terms. Nonetheless, almost everybody uses "early" and "late," and, although I will use both, I will generally follow suit, as long as this qualification is kept in mind.

14. I use "postformal" both ways (as the first major stage beyond formop—namely, vision-logic—and as *all* levels beyond formop), as context will tell; in this section, it means vision-logic.
15. Pp. 87–96.
16. See Commons et al., *Adult Development*, vols. 1 and 2; Commons et al., *Beyond Formal Operations*; Miller and Cook-Greuter, *Transcendence and Mature Thought in Adulthood*; Alexander and Langer, *Higher Stages of Human Development*; Sinnott and Cavanaugh, *Bridging Paradigms*; Sinnott, *Interdisciplinary Handbook of Adult Lifespan Learning*.
17. See the Introduction to CW4 and Wilber, *Boomeritis* (forthcoming).

CHAPTER 2. THE DEVELOPMENTAL LINES OR STREAMS

1. Howard Gardner's important research on multiple intelligences is an example of relatively independent developmental streams, and I am indebted to many of his significant conceptions. Gardner is also one of the first to use the terms "waves" and "streams," which I gratefully acknowledge. All of Gardner's books are highly recommended. Chart 8 contains a summary of Gardner's research on some of the universal waves of development (through which the various streams unfold). For a more extended discussion of his important contributions, see *The Eye of Spirit*.

   Perhaps the dominant theory in cognitive science at this moment is that of *modules*—the idea that the brain/mind is composed of numerous, independent, evolutionary modules, from linguistic to cognitive to moral. These modules are, in many ways, quite similar to what I mean by relatively independent developmental lines or streams, with two strong qualifications. Modules are all described in third-person it-language, thus overlooking (or even aggressively denying) first-person phenomenal realities (as will be explained in the text, modules are Upper-Right quadrant). Further, module theorists vehemently deny that there is any sort of transcendental self or unity of consciousness. And yet, according to their own theory and data, individuals are capable of being aware of these modules, and can in fact override them on occasion. If you can override a module, you are not just a module.
2. See Shaffer, *Social and Personality Development*; Commons et al., *Adult Development*, vols. 1 and 2; Commons et al., *Beyond Formal Operations*; Sinnott and Cavanaugh, *Bridging Paradigms*; Sinnott, *Interdisciplinary Handbook of Adult Lifespan Learning*; Loevinger, *Ego Development*; Kegan, *The Evolving Self* and *In Over Our Heads*; Beck, *Spiral Dynamics*; Wade, *Changes of Mind*; Miller and Cook-Greuter, *Transcendence and Mature Thought in Adulthood*; Alexander

and Langer, *Higher Stages of Human Development*; Broughton, *Critical Theories of Psychological Development*; and Sroufe et al., *Child Development*.

For various related aspects of development, see also Cicchetti and Beeghly, *The Self in Transition*; Mendelsohn, *The Synthesis of Self* (4 vols.); Parsons and Blocker, *Aesthetics and Education*; Clarkin and Lenzenweger, *Major Theories of Personality Disorder*; Dawson and Fischer, *Human Behavior and the Developing Brain*; Mitchell, *Relational Concepts in Psychoanalysis*; Cashdan, *Object Relations Therapy*; Kramer and Akhtar, *Mahler and Kohut*; Dana, *Multicultural Assessment Perspectives for Professional Psychology*; Segal et al., *Uniting Psychology and Biology*; Siegler, *Children's Thinking*; Ausubel, *Ego Development and Psychopathology*; Ribaupierre, *Transition Mechanisms in Child Development*; Csikszentmihalyi, *The Evolving Self*; Murphy et al., *The Physical and Psychological Effects of Meditation*; Hedaya, *Understanding Biological Psychiatry*; Ellenberger, *The Discovery of the Unconscious*; Reed, *From Soul to Mind*; Messer and Warren, *Models of Brief Psychodynamic Therapy*. Kagan and Lamb, *The Emergence of Morality in Young Children*; Nucci, *Moral Development and Character Education*; Wren, *The Moral Domain*; Haan et al., *On Moral Grounds*; Flavell et al., *Cognitive Development*. See also notes 8.11 and 8.20.

Kohlberg and Armon (in Commons et al., *Beyond Formal Operations*) have identified three different types of stage models: *epigenetic* (e.g., Erikson); *soft stages* (e.g., Loevinger, Kegan, Perry, Gilligan, Fowler); and *hard stages* (e.g., Piaget, Kohlberg). Most of the stage models in existence are soft-stage models. We might add *micro-stage* models, which present stages of development that can recur with the acquisition of any new skill or trait. Unless specified, "stages" as I use the term includes all four. All of the developmental levels and lines that I presented have evidence that they belong to one or another of those stage conceptions. At the same time, the general *developmental space* shown in the charts indicates that hard stages are in part responsible, and those hard stages are essentially the basic waves in the Great Nest.

3. See note 2.2 for some of this extensive research; see *The Eye of Spirit* for a summary.

Chapter 3. The Self

1. I describe the self in first-person as the *self-sense*, and in third-person as the *self-system*, both of which are anchored in second-person, dialectical, intersubjective occasions. See *The Eye of Spirit*.

   For an excellent anthology of approaches to the self, organized around Kohut's contributions (but not limited to them), see Detrick and Detrick, *Self Psychology: Comparisons and Contrasts*. See also the works of Edinger, Neumann, Blanck and Blanck, Kernberg, Winnicott, Masterson, Jung, Assagioli, Almaas, Baldwin, Mead, Erikson, Graves, Loevinger, Broughton, Lacan, Cook-Greuter, and Kegan, most of whom are discussed in this and the next chapter, and many of whom are represented on the charts.
2. See Shaffer, *Social and Personality Development*; Kegan, *The Evolving Self* and

In Over Our Heads; Beck, *Spiral Dynamics*; Loevinger, *Ego Development*; Wade, *Changes of Mind*; Miller and Cook-Greuter, *Transcendence and Mature Thought in Adulthood*; Alexander and Langer, *Higher Stages of Human Development*; Commons et al., *Beyond Formal Operations* and *Adult Development* vols. 1 & 2; Broughton, *Critical Theories of Psychological Development*; Sinnott and Cavanaugh, *Bridging Paradigms*; Sinnott, *Interdisciplinary Handbook of Adult Lifespan Learning*; and Sroufe et al., *Child Development*.

3. In the continuum I-I to I to me to mine, Loevinger's "ego"—which she defines generally as the conscious self-concept or self-idea—is right between the proximate I and the distal me, and might be called the "I/me": it is the individual self insofar as it can immediately become an object of knowledge and thus communicated to others. I generally include this "I/me" in the proximate self, but the whole point is that this scale is continuously sliding in development, as each I becomes a me until infinity (see *The Eye of Spirit*). For an expansion and clarification of Loevinger's ideas, see the important work of Susanne Cook-Greuter in, e.g., *Transcendence and Mature Thought in Adulthood* and Commons et al., *Adult Development* 2.
4. See *The Atman Project* (CW 2).
5. See *Transformations of Consciousness*.
6. See William James, *Principles of Psychology* and *The Will to Believe*; Rollo May, *Love and Will*; Assagioli, *The Act of Will*.
7. See, e.g., George Vaillant's wonderful *The Wisdom of the Ego* (1993). See also note 8.20.
8. For the mechanism of converting states to traits, see note 10.4.
9. More specifically, the self has numerous crucial functions: the (proximate) self is the locus of *identity* (an annexing of various elements to create a self-sense); the seat of *will* (the self is intrinsically involved in the good); a locus of *intersubjectivity* (the self is intrinsically a social, dialectical self, involved in justice and care); the seat of *aesthetic apprehension* (the self is intrinsically involved in the beautiful); the seat of *metabolism* (the self metabolizes experience to build structure); a locus of *cognition* (the self has an intrinsic capacity to orient to the objective world); the seat of *integration* (the self is responsible for integrating the functions, modes, states, waves, and streams of consciousness). These are largely functional invariants, and thus few of them are listed on the charts, which focus on diachronic elements; but the self and its functions seem to be absolutely crucial in any integral psychology.
10. Buddhists sometimes object that I am overlooking the Buddhist notion of anatta or "no-self," but I am actually using the Mahayana Buddhist doctrine of the relative reality of both the self and the dharmas; and I am here discussing the functions of the relatively real self-system. Along with Nagarjuna, I reject, as incomplete and incoherent, the Theravadin view of the self. See *Sex, Ecology, Spirituality,* 2nd ed. (CW6), chapter 14, note 1, for an extensive discussion of this topic. See also the discussion in the text, "The Self and Its Pathologies," in chap, 8 (page 523). See *Transformations of Consciousness* for a further discussion of the relative reality of the self and the pathologies that result when this self is not well formed.

CHAPTER 4. THE SELF-RELATED STREAMS

1. By "exclusive identification," I mean that the proximate self's center of gravity is predominantly at one general functional grouping (which generates a corresponding fulcrum of self-development, as explained in chap. 8). Since each basic wave, barring pathology, transcends and includes its predecessors, to say that the self is exclusively identified with, say, formop, means that the *overall self* includes all of the basic waves up to and including formop. Specifically, this usually means that the proximate self is organized around formop, and the distal self includes everything up to formop (from sensorimotor to conop). When the self's center of gravity shifts to vision-logic, formop becomes part of the distal self, and the proximate self is organized around vision-logic; and so on through the morphogenetic field of the Great Nest.
2. Three of the most important of the self-related lines of development are those of self-identity (e.g., Loevinger), morals (e.g., Kohlberg), and needs (e.g., Maslow). I have previously (as in *Transformations of Consciousness*) referred to all of them, in shorthand, as "self-stages," but I now reserve "self-stages" (or "stages of self") *exclusively* for the self-identity or proximate-self line of development (e.g., Loevinger, Erikson, Kegan), and I use "self-related stages," "self-related streams," or simply "self-streams" for *all* of the self-related lines of development (proximate-self, morals, needs, etc.).
3. Several stage conceptions, such as Levinson's, deal with the "seasons" of horizontal translation, not stages of vertical transformation. Erikson's higher stages are a murky combination of both; I have simply listed them on the charts in their approximate placement.
4. C. Graves, "Summary Statement: The Emergent, Cyclical, Double-Helix Model of the Adult Human Biopsychosocial Systems," Boston, May 20, 1981.
5. Don Beck, personal communication; this data is on computer file in the National Values Center, Denton, Texas, and is open to qualified researchers.
6. See Beck and Linscott, *The Crucible: Forging South Africa's Future* for an excellent discussion of the role of evolutionary thinking for defusing social tension.
7. Jane Loevinger, *Ego Development*. Cook-Greuter and Miller, *Transcendence and Mature Thought in Adulthood*; see also Cook-Greuter's excellent chapter in Commons et al., *Adult Development 2*.
8. Start with Pascual-Leone's contributions to Commons et al., *Beyond Formal Operations* and Alexander and Langer, *Higher Stages of Human Development*.
9. See, for example, chap. 19 in *Beyond Formal Operations*; and *Critical Theories of Psychological Development*. For a good summary of Broughton's work, see Loevinger, *Ego Development*.
10. Grof's research has used techniques from psychedelic drugs to holotropic breathwork. His book *The Cosmic Game* is a summary of this work; see also *The Adventure of Self-Discovery*. M. Washburn, *The Ego and the Dynamic Ground* and *Transpersonal Psychology in Psychoanalytic Perspective*; J. Wade, *Changes of Mind*.

Incidentally, many people have assumed that because I wrote a partially critical review of *Changes of Mind* in *The Eye of Spirit* that I somehow disagreed with most of its points, which is not so. I found some fault with Wade's embrace of Bohm's holonomic theories (although Jenny maintains that I read into that a stronger agreement than she intended), but those are minor points. My main criticism is that I found her model to be mostly a phase-2 type of model and not enough phase-3 (which in any event is easy to correct; she only has to specify that the different characteristics of each of her levels might in fact be relatively independent lines—not only in different contexts, but simultaneously in a single context [for the meaning of "phase-2" and "phase-3," see note 9.15]). Other than that (and a few misrepresentations of my work), her model is a good summary of the most recent research on a developmental view of consciousness, covering the eight or so basic levels of self and consciousness evolution, which I have included in the self-related stages chart (chart 4a). Those who have recently attacked a developmental view of consciousness would do well to study this book, since it suggests that they are perhaps out of touch with recent research, evidence, and theorizing. For an extended discussion of Grof, Washburn, and Wade, see *The Eye of Spirit.*

11. I am often asked about what I think of Steiner's writings. Although I have a great deal of respect for his pioneering contributions, I have not found the details of his presentations to be that useful. I believe recent orthodox research has offered better and more accurate maps of prepersonal to personal development, and I believe the meditative traditions offer more sophisticated maps of transpersonal development. Still, one can only marvel at the amount of visionary material he produced, and his overall vision is as moving as one could imagine. See *The Essential Steiner*, edited by Robert McDermott.

12. More recent transpersonal theorists include Charles Alexander, Hameed Ali, Rosemarie Anderson, Cheryl Armon, James Austin, John Battista, Michel Bauwens, Charles Birch, Harold Bloomfield, Seymour Boorstein, Sylvia Boorstein, William Braud, Crittenden Brookes, Haridas Chaudhuri, Allan Chinen, John Cobb, Allan Combs, Susanne Cook-Greuter, Jack Crittenden, A. S. Dalal, Olaf Deatherage, Elizabeth Debold, Han de Wit, Arthur Deikman, Steve Dinan, Norman Don, Duane Elgin, John Enright, Mark Epstein, Joseph Fabry, James Fadiman, Piero Ferucci, Jose Ferrer, John Firman, Robert Forman, Robert Frager, Joel Funk, Gordon Globus, Joseph Goguen, Tom Greening, David Ray Griffin, Christina Grof, Stanislav Grof, T George Harris, Arthur Hastings, Steve Hendlin, J. Heron, Edward Hoffman, Jean Houston, Russ Hudson, Leland Johnson, Dwight Judy, Sam Keen, Sean Kelly, Herb Koplowitz, Jack Kornfield, Joyce Kovelman, George Leonard, David Lukoff, Richard Mann, Robert McDermott, Michael Mahoney, Gerald May, Arnold Mindell, Donald Moss, Michael Murphy, John Nelson, Juan Pascual-Leone, Kaisa Puhakka, Kenneth Ring, Don Riso, Gillian Ross, Donald Rothberg, John Rowan, Peter Russell, Don Salmon, Andrew Samuels, Marilyn Schlitz, Stephen Schoen, Tony Schwartz, Bruce Scotton, Deane Shapiro, Jonathan Shear, Maureen Silos, Kathleen Singh, Jan Sinnott, Jacquelyn Small, Surya Das, Charles Tart, Eugene Tay-

lor, L. Eugene Thomas, Keith Thompson, Robert Thurman, William Torbert, Ronald Valle, Leland van den Daele, Brian van der Horst, Francisco Varela, James Vargiu, Frances Vaughan, Miles Vich, Frank Visser, Jenny Wade, Roger Walsh, Michael Washburn, John Welwood, Edward Whitmont, Auguste Wildschmidt, Bryan Wittine, Benjamin Wolman, Robert Wuthnow, and Michael Zimmerman, among many others.

13. For good short introductions to most of the theorists in this paragraph, see Jane Loevinger, *Ego Development*, and relevant contributions to Commons et al., *Adult Development*, volumes 1 and 2; Commons et al., *Beyond Formal Operations*; Miller and Cook-Greuter, *Transcendence and Mature Thought in Adulthood*; Alexander and Langer, *Higher Stages of Human Development*
14. See *The Eye of Spirit* for a discussion of this topic.
15. See Loevinger, *Ego Development*; Commons et al., *Adult Development*, volumes 1 and 2; Commons et al., *Beyond Formal Operations*; Miller and Cook-Greuter, *Transcendence and Mature Thought in Adulthood*; Alexander and Langer, *Higher Stages of Human Development*; Wilber, *The Eye of Spirit*.
16. D. Shaffer, *Social and Personality Developmen*, (1994), pp. 423–24, 435. This does not mean that men and women do not have characteristically "different voices" in certain life situations. The claim of research such as Deborah Tannen's, for example, is that men and women tend to speak in different voices in many circumstances. I have summarized that research as: men tend to translate with an emphasis on agency, women with an emphasis on communion; men tend to transform with an emphasis on Eros, women with an emphasis on Agape (see *Sex, Ecology, Spirituality, Second Edition*). But I have also emphasized the fact that the basic structures of the Great Nest, and the various self-stages, are in themselves *gender-neutral*—they are not biased toward either sex, and the research just mentioned supports that claim. The fact that men and women might navigate the basic waves in the Great Holarchy with a different voice, does not alter in the least the fact that they both face the same waves.
17. Shaffer, *Social and Personality Development*, pp. 417–18.
18. J. Vasudev, "Ahimsa, Justice, and the Unity of Life," in M. Miller and S. Cook-Greuter, *Transcendence and Mature Thought in Adulthood* (1994), p. 241. This does not mean that Kohlberg's model covers all the relevant morals issues in various cultures, only that it has proven to be universal in those stages that it does address. There is more to morals than moral reasoning—including moral affects and motivations—which are not covered well by Kohlberg's model (nor were they meant to be).
19. Although I know, from conversations with Don Beck, that he is very open to the ideas about transpersonal states and structures.
20. Don Beck, personal communication. See note 4.22.
21. Much of the following descriptions consist of direct quotes or paraphrasing from various publications of Graves, Beck, and Beck and Cowan. From C. Graves, "Human Nature Prepares for a Momentous Leap," *The Futurist*, April 1974; C. Graves, "Summary Statement"; Beck and Cowan, *Spiral Dynamics*; Don Beck, privately circulated papers and personal communication.

22. Jenny Wade, who has made a careful study of Graves, believes that orange (achievement) and green (affiliative) are not two different levels but two different choices offered to blue (conformist); so that both orange and green can advance directly to second-tier (authentic). In that conception, this book is an invitation to both orange and green to adopt second-tier perspectives.

At the same time, Spiral Dynamics—and developmental studies in general—indicate that many philosophical debates are not really a matter of the better objective argument, but of the subjective level of those debating. No amount of orange scientific evidence will convince blue mythic believers; no amount of green bonding will impress orange aggressiveness; no amount of turquoise holarchy will dislodge green hostility—unless the individual is ready to develop forward through the dynamic spiral of consciousness evolution. This is why "cross-level" debates are rarely resolved, and all parties usually feel unheard and unappreciated. It also alerts second-tier thinkers to look for ways to move the spiral, gently or by strategic rattling.

When I say, in the text, that green has often fought to prevent the emergence of second-tier thinking, I mean, of course, that all first-tier memes resist the emergence of second-tier consciousness. Scientific materialism (orange) is aggressively reductionistic toward second-tier constructs, attempting to reduce all interior stages to objectivistic neuronal fireworks. Mythic fundamentalism (blue) is often outraged at what it sees as attempts to unseat its given Order. Egocentrism (red) ignores second-tier altogether. Magic (purple) puts a hex on it.

Green accuses second-tier consciousness of being authoritarian, rigidly hierarchical, patriarchal, marginalizing, oppressive, racist, and sexist. In other words, it takes the pluralistic critique, which it developed and *correctly* aimed a pre-green positions (especially blue and orange, which are often guilty of all of the sins that green claims), and then incorrectly and inappropriately aims this pre-green critique at post-green developments, where it can be shown to be perhaps well-intentioned but misdirected (it generally distorts yellow and turquoise constructions, as second-tier researchers are quick to point out).

Green has been in charge of cultural studies for the past three decades. On the one hand, the pluralistic relativism of green has nobly enlarged the canon of cultural studies to include many previously marginalized peoples, ideas, and narratives. It has acted with sensitivity and care in attempting to redress social imbalances and avoid exclusionary practices. It has been responsible for basic initiatives in civil rights and environmental protection. It has developed strong and often convincing critiques of the philosophies, metaphysics, social practices, and sciences of the blue and orange memes, with their often exclusionary, patriarchal, sexist, and colonialistic agendas.

On the other hand, as effective as these critiques of pre-green stages have been, green has attempted to turn its guns on all post-green stages as well, with the most unfortunate results. In honorably fighting the rigid social hierarchies of blue, green has condemned all second-tier holarchies—which has made it very difficult, and often impossible, for green to move forward into more holistic, integral-aperspectival constructions.

On most of the self-related charts, you can see a movement from mythic absolutism and rational formalism (blue and orange), through stages of pluralism and relativism (green), to stages of integralism and holism (yellow and turquoise). The green meme, effectively challenging the absolutisms of blue and orange, then mistook all universals and all holarchies as being of the same order, and this often locked it tenaciously into first-tier thinking.

Still, it is from the *healthy* green ranks that second-tier emerges, as Spiral Dynamics points out, so most of my comments in my recent books have been directed toward green, as have my occasional polemical nudges, in an attempt to get green to look at its own premises more expansively. These jabs have not, in general, endeared me to greens, but it has jolted the conversation in ways that politeness consistently failed to do. (My first twelve books, over twenty years, were unfailingly polite, with not a single polemical sentence in any of them; my thirteenth book [SES] was polemical—as Miss Piggy put it, "I *tried* being nice.") Whether the polemical tone helped or hurt remains to be seen (see Introduction to CW7). But the message is simple enough: in order for green to make the jump into the hyperspace of second-tier, the following factors might be considered: (1) All systems are context-bound, according to green pluralism, so fully carry out that agenda: all relativities and all pluralities are therefore *also* context-bound: they themselves have wider and deeper contexts that bind them together into even larger systems—*therefore*, acknowledge these larger systems, and then begin to outline the universal-integral contexts binding them all together. (2) Systems evolve over space and time; therefore, trace this evolution and development. (3) The only way to do so is to include hierarchies with heterarchies (and thus arrive at holarchies). Once that happens, the important contributions of green can be taken up, embraced and included, in the ongoing unfolding of consciousness evolution. Green is not lost or denied, but included and enriched.

As for Spiral Dynamics, my only minor reservations are that it does not sufficiently include states of consciousness nor the higher, transpersonal structures of consciousness; and it is an example of a phase-2 model and not enough phase-3 (see note 9.15). That is, there is not enough sensitivity to the empirically demonstrated fact that different developmental lines can be at different levels in the same instance: not just that a person can be using a red meme in one circumstance and an orange meme in another, but that a person, in the *same* circumstance, can be cognitively orange and morally red. Finally, Spiral Dynamics does not sufficiently distinguish between enduring and transitional (see Introduction to CW7). From personal conversations, I believe Beck is open to all of these considerations.

Beck is also moving to incorporate the four quadrants into the Spiral Dynamics model, which he believes will help him more adequately distinguish between what he calls the healthy and unhealthy versions of the memes (the four quadrants are introduced in Part Two). Don writes that "The quadrants help differentiate the positive from negative versions of the ᵛMEMEs. They also show graphically why so many change initiatives are doomed to fail. Kids who are taken out of gang-infested neighborhoods and placed in an enrichment training program to enhance interior development, are often made worse when they are then dumped back into the same WE and ITS quadrants, which are toxic to the new level of development. Quadrants provide the missing element in the creation of healthy systems."

As another example of healthy/unhealthy vMEMEs, systems theory, which utilizes a yellow/turquoise meme, is often caught in flatland, where it recognizes only exterior systems described in it-language, and does not also acknowledge the interior stages described in I and We language (see chaps. 5, 6, and 7). Systems theory in itself is thus a partial, limited, flatland expression of second-tier thinking (and thus some of the examples of second-tier thinking given in *Spiral Dynamics* are actually unhealthy or not-fully-complete memes). I believe Beck is in substantial agreement with this view, and his new writings will reflect these minor adjustments. (As for the last three decades of cultural studies under green pluralism, see Wilber, *Boomeritis*, and Introduction to CW7.)

The point in all of this is that each meme—each level of consciousness and wave of existence—is, in its healthy form, *an absolutely necessary and desirable element* of the overall spiral, of the overall spectrum of consciousness. Even if every society on earth were established fully at the turquoise meme, every infant born in that society nonetheless starts at level 1, at beige, at sensorimotor instincts and perceptions, and must then grow and evolve through purple magic, red and blue myth, orange rationalism, green networking, and into yellow and turquoise vision-logic. All of those waves have important tasks and functions; all of them are taken up and included in subsequent waves; none of them can be bypassed; and none of them can be demeaned without grave consequences to self and society. *The health of the entire spiral is the prime directive, not preferential treatment for any one level.* No question about it: the higher the leading edge and the higher the governing body, the better—but only because second-tier consciousness can think of the health of the entire spiral.

23. See Riso and Hudson, *The Wisdom of the Enneagram*; and H. Palmer, *The Enneagram*. When we get to the discussion of subpersonalities, in chapter 8, this means that a subpersonality can be any *type* at any of the basic *levels*: a truly pluralistic society of selves!—nonetheless all navigated by the proximate self, which delivers a unity of experience to the ongoing flow of consciousness, however occasionally disrupted.

CHAPTER 5. WHAT IS MODERNITY?

1. See *The Marriage of Sense and Soul* for a fuller discussion of this theme.
2. Regarding the four quadrants, there is nothing magical about the number four; I am certainly not reifying it. The four quadrants are simply the results of the some of simplest distinctions that reality seems to make: inside/outside and singular/plural. But there are numerous, perhaps infinite, other dimensions that are also important. The only reason people have found the four quadrants so useful is that flatland doesn't even honor these simple distinctions, and thus, by compari-

son with the world of one-dimensional man, the four quadrants are positively complex.

The four quadrants (or simply the Big Three) are realities that are embedded even in ordinary language, which recognizes first-person (I), second-person (we), and third-person (it) perspectives, which is why, for example, individuals natively and easily understand the difference between art, morals, and science—and the need to include all three in any balanced approach to the world.

Chapter 6. To Integrate Premodern and Modern

1. See also the Introduction to CW 4 for a further discussion of this theme.
2. See Taylor's *Sources of the Self* for the concept of the great interlocking order; see Lovejoy's *The Great Chain of Being* for a discussion of the Enlightenment's belief in a systems view of reality; see *Sex, Ecology, Spirituality,* 2nd ed. (CW 6), for a discussion of systems theory, subtle reductionism, and their roots in the Enlightenment paradigm.
3. For premodernity's lack of pluralism and contextualism, see chapter 13; see also the Introduction to CW 4 and Wilber, *Boomeritis,* for a further discussion of this theme.

Chapter 7. Some Important Modern Pioneers

1. In figure 8, I have only indicated a few general waves in the Upper-Left quadrant, but the idea is that all of the levels, across all of the quadrants, can be investigated for their mutually constraining influences, thus arriving at a more integral, comprehensive model. See chap. 14.

   For very specific examples of levels of art, morals, and science—from body to mind to soul to spirit—see *The Marriage of Sense and Soul*, chap. 14.
2. For correlations of states/structures of consciousness and states/structures of organism-brain, see, e.g., Wade, *Changes of Mind*; Austin, *Zen and the Brain*; Alexander and Langer, *Higher Stages of Human Development*; Valerie Hunt, *Infinite Mind*; David Chalmers, *The Conscious Mind*; Laughlin et al., *Brain, Symbol, and Experience*. See also notes 14.1 and 14.17. Notice that, according to Ramana Maharshi, even complete spiritual Self-Realization has a *physical vibratory correlate* on the right side of the chest (i.e., every Left-Hand event, no matter how lofty, ascended, or transcendental, has a Right-Hand correlate).

   As for the traditional mind-body problem, it is given a fuller treatment in chap. 14. For the moment, a few points might be made with reference to figure 8. The Left-Hand domains refer loosely to "mind," and the Right-Hand domains to "body." These are ultimately nondual, but that nonduality can only be realized with causal-to-nondual development, at which point the mind-body problem is not solved, but dissolved: seen to be a product of nescience, ignorance, or nonawakening. Short of that, the mind-body problem cannot be satisfactorily solved (see *The Eye of Spirit*, chap. 3; and *A Brief History of Everything*). This nondual view is not a variety of philosophical monism, because the nonduality is realized only in the supramental, transphilosophical realms, and cannot be transposed downwardly into mental conceptions without generating antinomies and contradictions (see *Eye to Eye*, chaps. 1 and 2). There is an injunctive, but not descriptive, disclosure of nonduality (see chap. 3, *The Eye of Spirit*; and *Sex, Ecology, Spirituality,* 2nd ed.).

Short of nondual realization, what can be said, in a relative fashion, is that all four quadrants "tetra-interact"—they are mutually arising and mutually determining. It is not just that the individual mind and consciousness (UL) interacts with the individual body-brain-organism (UR), but that they both equally and mutually interact with the collective cultural mind (LL) and collective social body (LR).

Thus, this view is neither a monism nor a dualism. It is not a monism, because it does not maintain that mind and body are two aspects of an underlying reality, because that Reality, in its formlessness, does not have aspects (it is *shunya* of all conceptions). This is not pyschophysical identity, for those aspects nonetheless have relatively real and irreducible differences. Neither is it traditional interactionism, because the quadrants, while relatively real, are still of the world of maya, and thus interactionism is not the ultimate word.

The dominant forms of "solving" the mind-body problem today involve mostly types of emergent materialism, functionalism, connectionism, and autopoietic theories, all of which are subtle reductionisms (reducing Left-Hand events to Right-Hand dynamical systems). The fact that many of these are holistic, hierarchical, connectionist, and emergent, simply obscures the fact that they are still exterior holisms, not interior holisms (nor their integration). This is true even when they refer to themselves as "nonreductionist materialism"—they mean non-gross-reductionistic, not non-subtle-reductionistic. This tendency to subtle reductionism (a hangover from the project of flatland modernity) can best be countered by the simple reminder of "tetra-interactionism." See Wilber, "An Integral Theory of Consciousness," *Journal of Consciousness Studies*, vol. 4, no, 1, 1997 (CW7); *Sex, Ecology, Spirituality,* 2nd ed. (CW6), chap. 14, note 1; and chap. 14 of this book.

3. See *A Brief History of Everything* for a discussion of this topic.
4. See Wilber & Walsh in Velmans, *Investigating Phenomenal Consciousness.*
5. J. Broughton et al. (eds), *The Cognitive Developmental Psychology of James Mark Baldwin*, p. 31.
6. Ibid., p. 32.
7. Ibid., p. 36.
8. Ibid., p. 40.
9. Ibid., p. 280–1.
10. Ibid., p. 277.
11. Ibid., p. 296.
12. Kohlberg's stage six is an ideal limit, and not an actual stage. The evidence refers to his five stages, which to date have been found to be largely cross-cultural, universal, and nonrelativistic. See chap. 4 of this volume, the section "Objections."

13. Wallwork's summary of Baldwin's view, *The Cognitive Developmental Psychology of James Mark Baldwin*, p. 335.
14. Baldwin's "unity consciousness" is a gross-realm unity or nature mysticism (psychic level). It does not recognize archetypal mysticism, subtle consciousness, lucid dreaming, or savikalpa samadhi (all forms of deity or subtle-level mysticism); nor does it recognize formless consciousness (causal), and therefore it does not reach the pure nondual (which is a union of form and emptiness). Union with nature, when it does not recognize the formless state of cessation, is usually psychic-level, gross cosmic consciousness, or nature mysticism. Nonetheless, it is a genuine and profound transpersonal experience.

    One of the easiest ways to tell if a "unity experience" is gross realm (nature mysticism), subtle realm (deity mysticism), causal realm (formless mysticism), or genuine nondual consciousness (union of the form in all realms with the pure formless) is to note the nature of consciousness in dreaming and deep sleep. If the writer talks of a unity experience while awake, that is usually gross-realm nature mysticism. If that unity consciousness *continues into the dream state*—so that the writer talks of lucid dreaming, union with interior luminosities as well as gross exterior nature—that is usually subtle-realm deity mysticism. If that consciousness *continues into the deep sleep state*—so that the writer realizes a Self that is *fully present in all three states* of waking, dreaming, and deep sleep—that is usually causal-realm formless mysticism (turiya). If that formless Self is then discovered to be one with the form in all realms—gross to subtle to causal—that is pure nondual consciousness (turiyatita).

    Many nature mystics, ecopsychologists, and neopagans take the gross-realm, waking-state unity with nature to be the highest unity available, but that is basically the first of four major samadhis or mystical unions. The "deep self" of ecopsychology is thus not to be confused with the True Self of Zen, Ati of Dzogchen, Brahman-Atman of Vedanta, etc. These distinctions also help us situate philosophers like Heidegger and Foucault, both of whom talked of mystical-like unions with nature. Those were often profound and authentic experiences of gross-realm unity (Nirmanakaya), but again, those should not be confused with Zen or Vedanta, for the latter push through to causal formlessness (Dharmakaya, nirvikalpa samadhi, jnana samadhi, etc.), and then into pure nondual unity (Svabhavikakaya, turiyatita) with any and all realms, gross to subtle to causal. Many writers confuse Nirmanakaya with Svabhavikakaya, which ignores the major realms of interior development that lie between the two (e.g., Sambhogakaya and Dharmakaya).
15. This is Broughton and Freeman-Moir's felicitous summary of Baldwin's idea, *The Cognitive Developmental Psychology of James Mark Baldwin*, p. 331.
16. See Habermas, *The Theory of Communicative Action*; good overviews include Rehg, *Insight and Solidarity* and Outhwaite, *Habermas*. For Habermas's crucial corrections to the excesses of postmodernism, see *The Philosophical Discourse of Modernity*.
17. Aurobindo's yoga is referred to as "integral yoga"; thus his psychological system is properly referred to as "integral yoga psychology." See, for example,

Integral Yoga Psychology, by Dr. Reddy, and *The Concept of Personality in Sri Aurobindo's Integral Yoga Psychology and Maslow's Humanistic/Transpersonal Psychology*, by Dr. Vrinte.

CHAPTER 8. THE ARCHEOLOGY OF SPIRIT

1. As indicated in the text, states are very important, but for them to contribute to *development* they must become structures/traits. Planes or realms are important, but they cannot be conceived pre-critically as ontologically independent realities, but rather as coproductions of perceiving selves (see note 8.2). Thus, the simplest *generalization* is that individual development involves waves, streams, and self, without in any way denying the importance of all of those others factors, from states to planes to numerous heterarchical processes and patterns.
2. In my view, the basic structures in the Great Nest are simultaneously levels of both knowing and being, epistemology and ontology. For reasons discussed in the text (namely, modernity rejected most ontology and allowed only epistemology), I usually refer to the basic structures as "the basic structures of consciousness" (or "the basic levels of consciousness"); but their ontological status should not be overlooked. Generally, the perennial philosophy refers to the former as levels of consciousness (or *levels of selfhood*), and the latter as realms or planes of existence (or *levels of reality*), with the understanding that they are inextricably interwoven (see note 1.3). Thus, as Huston Smith pointed out (*Forgotten Truth*), the body level of consciousness corresponds with the terrestrial realm or plane of existence; the mind level of consciousness corresponds with the intermediate realm or plane of existence; the soul level of consciousness corresponds with the celestial plane of existence; and the spirit level of consciousness corresponds with the infinite plane of existence (see chart 2a). Since these are correlative structures (levels of consciousness and planes of existence), I include both of them in the idea of basic structures or basic levels of the Great Nest.

   However, on occasion it is useful to distinguish them, because *a given level of self can experience a different level or plane of reality*. I have often made this distinction when analyzing modes of knowing (see *Eye to Eye*, chapters 2 and 6; *A Sociable God*, chapter 8), and I will do the same in the text when we discuss modes of art. Moreover, in ontogeny, the structures develop but the planes do not (the self develops through the already-given planes or levels of reality); however, in both Kosmic involution and evolution/phylogeny, the planes/realms also develop, or unfold from Source and enfold to Source (so we cannot say that planes show no development at all: they involve and evolve from Spirit; see note 1.5 for the ways in which the planes themselves coevolve). But a given level of self, generally, can interact with different levels of reality, to various degrees, so that we need to keep these two (structures and realms) as independent variables.

   Thus, for example, as I pointed out in *Eye to Eye*, consciousness can turn its attention to the material plane (using its epistemological eye of flesh), the intermediate plane (using its epistemological eye of mind), or the celestial plane (using its epistemological eye of contemplation). The material, intermediate, and celestial *planes* are the *ontological* levels; in *Eye to Eye* I refer to them using the terms sensibilia, intelligibilia, and transcendelia (i.e., the objects in those planes or realms). The eyes of flesh, mind, and contemplation are the *epistemological* levels correlated with (and disclosing) those ontological planes of sensibilia, intelligibilia, and transcendelia. (Of course, this is just using a simple three-level version of the Great Nest; if we use five levels, there are then five planes of existence and five correlative levels of consciousness, and so on. In my scheme, since I often use seven to nine general levels of consciousness, there are likewise seven to nine general realms or planes of reality.)

But notice: you can make essentially the same points using only the levels of consciousness (since being and knowing are two sides of the same levels). You can say that the mind can investigate the intermediate realm, or you can simply say the mind can investigate other minds. You can say the mind can investigate the celestial realm, or you can simply say the mind can investigate the subtle level. They are essentially saying the same thing, as long as you realize that any given level of selfhood (or consciousness) can turn its attention to any level of existence (or plane of reality). These two independent scales, in other words, can be stated as "level of consciousness investigates planes of existence"; but they can also be stated as "level of consciousness investigates other levels of consciousness," as long as we understand the correlations involved.

I often use the latter formulation, simply because, as I said, it avoids the ontological speculations that modernity finds so questionable. Premodern philosophy was unabashedly *metaphysical* (i.e., it assumed the nonproblematic ontological existence of all the various planes, levels, and realms of transcendental reality); whereas modern philosophy was primarily *critical* (i.e., it investigated the structures of the subject of thinking, and called into question the ontological status of the objects of thought), and thus modernity brought a much needed critical attitude to bear on the topic (even if it went overboard in its critical zeal and sometimes erased all objects of knowledge except the sensorimotor).

A crippling problem with the perennial traditions (and the merely metaphysical approaches) is that they tend to discuss ontological levels (planes or axes) as if they were pregiven, independent of the perceiver of those domains, thus overlooking the substantial amount of modern and postmodern research showing that cultural backgrounds and social structures profoundly mold perceptions in all domains (i.e., the perennial philosophy did not sufficiently differentiate the four quadrants). For all these reasons, simply talking about "planes" as completely independent ontological realities is extremely problematic—yet another reason I have tended to emphasize the epistemological facets over the merely ontological ones.

This has led some critics to claim that I completely ignore planes of existence, but that is obviously incorrect. As we just saw, I often explicitly refer to the planes as "realms," "spheres," or "domains," and I have named the phenomena in the three major planes of terrestrial, intermediate, and celestial as sensibilia, intelligibilia, and transcendelia (I also refer to them as the physio/biosphere, noosphere, and theosphere; although, again, those realms can be subdivided into at least a dozen levels). It is true that I usually focus on the structures/levels of consciousness, but I *preserve these two independent scales* by saying that one level can interact with other levels. Thus, for example, in the charts in chapter 6 of *Eye to Eye* and chapter 8 of *A Sociable God* (which present five major modes of knowing: sensory, empiric-analytic, historic-hermeneutic, mandalic, and spiritual), the structures/levels of consciousness are on the left, and the structures/levels of existence (or planes/realms of reality) are on the right, so that these two scales are clearly differentiated. I will do the same thing in the text when we discuss modes of art.

Combined with an understanding of *states* of consciousness, the notions of *levels of consciousness* and *planes of reality* gives us a three-dimensional model (i.e., with three independent scales). I have been presenting this three-variable model since *A Sociable God* (1983). Recently, Allan Combs has offered a similar model, which has much to recommend it, but also has some fundamental problems, in my view. See note 12.12.

Most often, when it is not necessary to distinguish levels of consciousness and planes of existence, I try to use terms that can cover both (such as body, mind, soul, and spirit), and I implicitly use the basic structures or basic levels as referring to both, so as to avoid intricate discussions such as this. When it is important to distinguish them, I usually refer to the planes as "realms," "domains," or "spheres," although in each case the context will tell. See notes 1.3, 1.5, 1.9, 1.10, 8.1, 8.39, 12.12.

3. Alexander et al., *Higher Stages of Human Development*, p. 160, emphasis in original.
4. The question faced by any developmental model is, How much of a level in any line (moral, cognitive, affective, needs) do you have to satisfy before you can move on to the next higher level in that line? Research tends to suggest that a *general competence* needs to be established at each major wave in a stream in order for its successor to emerge. I have indicated this in figure 14. The nine basic waves are drawn as a cross-section of nine concentric circles. These are not "rungs in a ladder"—figure 14 is simply a cross-section of the concentric circles of the Great Nest (fig. 1), representing the holarchical waves through which the various developmental streams progress relatively independently (these holarchical waves or levels are the vertical axis on the psychograph, fig. 2). In other words, fig. 14 represents the basic levels in the various lines of development (morals, affects, cognition, needs, etc.), levels that span the entire spectrum from body to mind to soul to spirit. Since the various lines can develop relatively independently, overall development follows no linear sequence. But the question here is, *in any single developmental line*, how much of one stage/level in that line is necessary for the next stage/level in that line to stably emerge?

   Using vision-logic as an example, I have drawn four subphases—*a, b, c,* and *d.* I am using the subphases *a* and *b* represent a *basic competence* in vision-

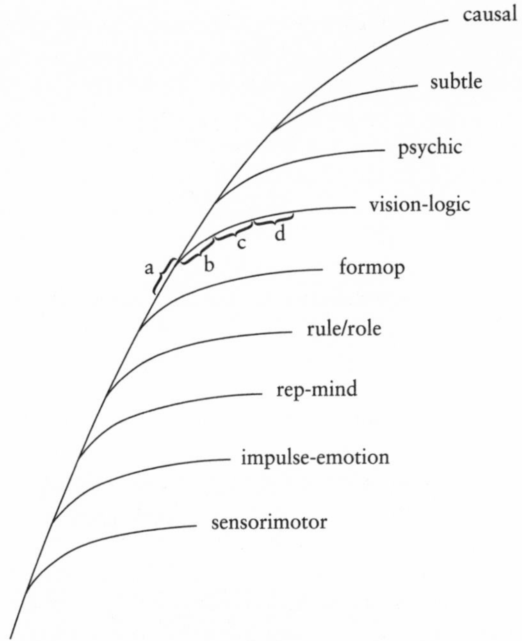

FIGURE 14. *The Basic Waves and Their Substages*

logic: a capacity to take multiple perspectives and to evidence some sort of postconventional, universal, panoramic awareness. This basic competence is necessary for higher, stable development. The subphases *c* and *d* are specialized, extreme developments of vision-logic, such as the capacity to think about systems of systems, and systems of systems of systems (what Commons and Richards all "paradigmatic" and "cross-paradigmatic" thinking; see chart 3a and notes 9.19, 9.27). These are *not* necessary for higher development. It is quite likely that Buddha and Christ would have passed tests for *a* and *b* (both the bodhisattva vow and the golden rule demand multiple perspectives), but they might have failed tests for *c* and *d* capacities; certainly many people have advanced into higher stages of development without mastering these intricate capacities for thinking about systems of systems of systems. In short, phases *a* and *b* represent postconventional awareness and multiple perspectives, which are necessary components (subholons) of higher development (transpersonal and spiritual) if the transpersonal is to become a stable adaptation and not merely a passing peak experience, but *c* and *d* are specialized, unnecessary developments.

The same conclusion would hold for each of the basic waves in any of the streams. The *a* and *b* subphases are the necessary prerequisites and/or ingredients of higher developments. A certain competence (*a* and *b*) is required in sensorimotor development, but one does not have to become an Olympic athlete (*c* and *d*), and so on. (Likewise, past saints and sages might not have mastered any of the extreme developments of vision-logic, but the people who gave the world the golden rule and the bodhisattva vow clearly mastered vision-logic to the degree necessary to transcend it.)

This diagram also indicates that, when figure 14 represents the basic structures themselves, which are mostly *enduring* structures, each wave remains in existence and can be exercised and developed on its own, indefinitely. One can extend and sharpen physical capacities, emotional intelligence, intellectual acuity, vision-logic capacities, and so on (i.e., one can even develop the *c* and *d* and even higher subphases in each of the basic waves).

Most of the *developmental lines*, on the other hand, are not enduring structures but transitional structures (see note 1.7). They still follow "transcend-and-include," in that each stage provides basic competences that are incorporated in the succeeding stages; but once a stage has served its purpose, it does not remain in existence as a *separate* function itself (e.g., a person at moral stage 5 does not simultaneously exercise moral stage 1, but a person at vision-logic can and does simultaneously exercise all of the lower basic structures, such as sensorimotor and emotional-sexual). But the same general developmental rule still applies: a general competence at each stage is required for the stable emergence of the next.

In many cases this competence is necessary but not sufficient for the emergence of the next stage; exactly why higher stages emerge, or conversely, why developmental arrest occurs in any line, is still not well understood, although theories abound. (The most likely candidate is a combination of numerous variables: individual constitutional factors, individual upbringing, individual interior dispositions, social institutions, life circumstances, possible past life history, cultural background, cultural values, and cultural encouragement/discouragement, to give a sampling from all four quadrants.) As for which aspects of a basic wave are *a, b, c,* etc., in most cases only empirical testing can tell.

5. See *Transformations of Consciousness*, chap. 1 (Jack Engler).
6. See M. Epstein, *Thoughts without a Thinker.*
7. In *The Atman Project*, I gave the following names and dates for the ego: early ego (ages 4–7), middle ego (7–12), and late ego (12–21). Those names and dates are still acceptable, but the problem is that the word "ego" is used in a thousand different ways by different theorists, which makes it very difficult to assign a definition. Psychological literature speaks of "early ego nuclei," "the bodyego," "the impulsive ego," "the mental ego," "the mature ego," "the synthesizing ego," "the analytic ego," and so on. I generally use the term "ego" in three different ways, reflecting common uses in the literature: (1) the ego is the sense of self or "I-ness" at any of the *personal* (or frontal) stages, from the material ego to the bodyego to the rational ego; (2) the ego is more narrowly the personal self that is based on formal-rational-reflexive capacities, which I also call "the mature ego"; (3) the ego is the separate-self sense or self-contraction in general, body to mind to soul. What *The Atman Project* called the early ego I now also call the self-concept (or the conceptual self; fulcrum-3); the middle ego (fulcrum-4) I often call the persona or the membership-self (in *The Atman Project*,

I used "membership self" to mean the *very beginning* of socialization, but since that socialization does not really become paramount until the rule/role mind, I now use "membership" and "mythic-membership" to refer to *the overall rule/role mind*, its worldview, and its fulcrum-4 self: a conformist role-self or persona); and the late ego (fulcrum-5), I generally call the mature ego. All of those terms as I now most often use them are indicated in chart 1a. Still, any of those terms are acceptable as long as we specify just what developmental period is meant, so in each case the context should tell.

8. One or two theorists have raised what they call a "devastating critique" of the centaur and vision-logic, namely: "We doubt the integrative capacity of the rational-egoic stage [fulcrum-5], at least as Wilber sees it. Either it does not fully integrate the mental with the physical, and then the developmental logic of transcend-and-include is violated, or it does fully integrate the mental with the physical, in which case the centaur [F-6] is redundant."

   This criticism comes from using philosophical abstractions instead of concrete psychological research. There is not simply "the" physical body and "the" mind, such that you have only two choices: integrate them or not. What these critics call "the" physical body actually consists of about a half-dozen levels (e.g., sensation, perception, exocept, impulse, emotion), and what they call "the mind" is also about a half-dozen levels (image, symbol, concept, rule, formal, vision-logic). Beyond those are the transrational, transpersonal levels (psychic, subtle, causal).

   If we use this more complete Great Nest, and not the simplistic "mind" and "body," the problem does not arise. Each of those levels accomplishes a great deal of integration at its own level—each follows "transcend-and-include." The formal-rational level (whose integrative power is questioned by these critics) transcends and includes (integrates) multiple concrete operations, numerous different perspectives, multiple roles, reversible operations, and mutual outlooks—it is an extraordinarily integrative structure! As integrative as the formal structure is, research shows that postformal cognition (i.e., vision-logic, whose existence is claimed to be redundant by these critics) is even more integrative. Postformal cognition transcends but includes (integrates) numerous formal operations, systems of thought, and meta-systemic perceptions (e.g., the work of Commons and Richards, Arlin, Fischer, Pascual-Leone, Sinnott, etc.). The evidence for both formal and postformal stages is quite substantial. But if your developmental stages include only body, mind, and their integration, you will miss all of that.

   Likewise with the self at each of those stages. The self identified with the role mind is the persona; the self identified with the formal mind is the mature ego; the self identified with vision-logic is the centaur. As can be seen in charts 3a–b and 4a–c, there is an extraordinary amount of evidence for all of those cognitive stages and for all of those self-stages. Again, if your developmental sequence is nothing but body, mind, and their integration, all of that is missed.

   Part of the difficulty these critics seem to be having is that, precisely because, barring pathology, each of those stages transcends and includes its predecessors, *each* of those stages shows a *relatively* greater capacity for integration. Thus "integration" is in fact a sliding scale whose potential capacity increases at every level. But researchers from Gebser to Neumann to Gilligan to Loevinger also call *specific stages* by the actual name "integrated"—usually, their very highest level is given that name, *not* because the lower levels lack all integration, but because this highest level has the greatest amount of it (and higher levels would have even more, since each is transcend-and-include, barring pathology).

Thus, I have often used Loevinger's summary of Broughton's highest stage (which correlates with the centaur): "Mind and body are both experiences of an integrated self." The critics have taken that to mean that the previous stage (the rational-egoic) has no integration of mind and body whatsoever—a strange notion—when all it actually means is that the ego has relatively less integrative capacity than the centaur, according to the research itself.

Each level, of course, has limits to its integrative power, which are the limits of that level itself. In the case of formal-rational, the limitations involve the inherently abstract nature of formal systems, which tend to close themselves off from other domains (even though those systems themselves have *already integrated* an enormous number of operations compared to the previous stage). These limitations, many researchers report, are themselves transcended with the development of vision-logic, which, because it begins to take a pluralistic, contextual, and relativistic stance (on the way to even higher integrations), can begin to include domains that formal rationality could not yet encompass. At each stage, once again, we see transcend-and-include. (The exception, of course, is pathology, which *is* pathology precisely because it does not transcend and include but denies and represses, fixates and arrests.)

Finally, a few critics have claimed that, according to the traditional Great Chain, there is nothing that would correspond with vision-logic and the centaur. On the contrary, as the charts show, almost every sophisticated Great Chain theorist had something that corresponded with vision-logic or higher reason (Plotinus's creative reason, Aurobindo's higher or integrative mind, Gebser's integral-aperspectival, and so on). Since the self can identify with any level in the Great Chain, I simply call the self at that level the centaur. If you use the complete Great Chain, and not simply a five-level or seven-level summary, once again this criticism does not arise.

9. For a discussion of the 1-2-3 process of each fulcrum (fusion/embeddedness, differentiation/disidentification/de-embedding/transcending, and integrating/including), see *Transformations of Consciousness*, *A Brief History of Everything*, and *The Eye of Spirit*.
10. See Mahler, Kernberg, Blanck and Blanck, Kohut, Gedo, Masterson, Stone, Neumann. See also notes 8.11 and 8.13.
11. As such, these three general levels of early self-development and self-pathology form only one part of a multifactorial etiology. It is an important part, but only a part, of a complex etiology that includes dispositions, constitutional factors, character types, predominant modes of functioning, independent defense mechanisms, interpersonal relations, environmental representations, among other

important factors (see, e.g., Stone's five-factor model in *Abnormalities of Personality*; Masterson and Klein, *Disorders of the Self*; Norcross and Goldfried, *Handbook of Psychotherapy Integration*). Moreover, not only are multifactorial approaches to the Upper-Left quadrant important, these need to be integrated with Upper-Right factors (neuromechanisms, neurotransmitters, brainwave states, psychopharmacology, etc.; e.g., Michel and Moore, *Developmental Neurobiology*; Harris, *Developmental Neuropsychiatry*; see note 14.17), as well as the Lower-Right and Lower-Left quadrants of social and cultural factors (e.g., Broughton, *Critical Theories of Psychological Development*, and the superb *Cultural Psychology* by Michael Cole).

As Lenzenweger and Haugaard put it in *Frontiers of Developmental Psychopathology* (1996), "Whereas many reports on developmental psychopathology focus on parent-child interactions, childrearing attitudes, dysfunctional parenting, and putatively related dysfunctional outcomes (e.g., maltreatment leading to impaired competence), few genuine attempts have been made to integrate genetic factors, neurotransmitter models, and neuroscientific processes, which as yet remain a relative rarity in the modal developmental psychopathology article or chapter. In the interest of not being misunderstood, we should like to emphasize that we are observing a relative imbalance in developmental psychopathology in favor of psychosocial models of pathological development over more biologically influenced models—quite frankly, however, we suggest that the best models will be those that *integrate across these levels* [my italics]. The importance of genetic factors in both normative and pathological development is indisputable (Rowe, 1994; Rutter, 1991) and the essential role of neurobiological factors in temperament (e.g., Kagan, 1994), emotion (Ekman & Davidson, 1994), personality development (e.g., Depue and Collins, in press), and the emergence of psychopathology (e.g., Breslin and Weinberger, 1990; Cocarro & Murphy, 1990; Grace, 1991) is axiomatic, some would even say confirmed. The meaningful integration of brain, emotion, behavior, and environmental influences currents represents an exceptionally active research area in various areas of psychological science, especially cognition and personality. In short, developmental psychopathology cannot afford not to heed these advances and emerging research strategies" (pp. vi-vii). Lenzenweger and Haugaard admirably stress at least some aspects in Upper Left, Upper Right, and Lower Right; but they are thin on Lower Left, and they ignore any of the higher levels in any of the quadrants. Still, this and other similar books show the steadily increasing interest in a more integral approach to psychology and therapy.

See also the superb *Handbook of Psychotherapy Integration*, edited by J. Norcross and M. Goldfried. Highly recommended, as working toward various types of psychology/therapy integrations over the past four decades, are the works of R. Woody, Jerome Frank, A. Ryle, Carl Rogers, S. Appelbaum, Aron Beck, L. Birk, A. Freeman, M. R. Goldfried, A. Lazarus, Deane Shapiro, J. Marmor, Stanley Messer (see his *Essential Psychotherapies*, coedited with A. Gurman), James Masterson, A. E. Bergin, J. Norcross, H. Arkowitz, John Gedo, V. Raimy, James Prochaska, J. Safran, H. H. Strupp, P. London, Paul Wachtel,

Abraham Maslow, and any of the brilliant works of Michael Mahoney (e.g., *Human Change Process*).

12. Daniel Stern, in such books as *The Interpersonal World of the Infant*, has argued that "undifferentiated" is an inappropriate term for early states, because even the earliest stages of an infant's awareness show certain discriminations and differentiations. Nonetheless, subsequent development shows even more of them; hence, the earliest stages, in comparison, are still properly referred to as relatively undifferentiated.
13. For a superb discussion of defenses in the first four fulcrums, see George Vaillant, *The Wisdom of the Ego* (1993).

    In chart 1a, the earlier defenses (F-1 to F-3) are based largely on psychoanalytic ego psychology, object relations, and self psychology (e.g., Anna Freud, Margaret Mahler, Otto Kernberg, D. Winnicott, W. Fairbairn, S. Arieti, Heinz Kohut, Blanck and Blanck, George Vaillant, M. H. Stone, J. Gedo, James Masterson). The intermediate defenses (F-4 to F-6), on transactional analysis, cognitive therapy, attribution theory, construct theory, role theory, and symbolic interactionism (e.g., E. Berne, A. Beck, George Kelly, Selman, Mead). The higher defenses (F-7 to F-9) are culled from the existential and contemplative traditions (e.g., Jaspers, Boss, Binswanger, May, Bugental, Yalom; kundalini yoga, Kashmir Shaivism, Sufism, St. John of the Cross, the Victorine mystics, the Rhineland mystics, Dzogchen, Highest Yoga Tantra, etc.). See *Transformations of Consciousness*. See also note 8.20.
14. Gendlin's "felt meaning"—a zone between bodily feelings and mental concepts—is what Arieti (*The Intrapsychic Self*) calls "endocept," which I have listed as one of the basic waves in the charts. Endocepts, as the link between felt-body and thought-mind, are the gateway to the emotional shadow. Gendlin's "felt meaning" has often been confused with centauric awareness, whereas it is basically typhonic (i.e., it is pre-body/mind differentiation, not trans-body/mind differentiation). This confusion, in my opinion, is based on an under-appreciation of the cognitive component of panoramic awareness offered by vision-logic. Endoceptual awareness is, by definition, part of centauric awareness (which transcends and includes all previous structures), but does not define it. For the place of endoceptual feeling in psychotherapy and meditation, see *One Taste*, Aug. 12 and Sept. 10 entries. See also notes 8.34, 8.35.
15. See *The Eye of Spirit* (especially chapter 6) for a full discussion of this theme and a critique of Washburn's retro-Romantic interpretation of this curative spiral. See also *One Taste*, Aug. 12 and Sept. 10 entries. See also notes 8.34, 8.35.
16. See notes 8.13, 8.17, 8.20.
17. See *Transformations of Consciousness*, *A Brief History of Everything*, and *The Eye of Spirit*. John Rowan's *The Transpersonal* is a good discussion of the pathologies and treatments at each of the nine fulcrums, marred only by an occasional confusion of mythic and subtle. This confusion is based on the pre/trans fallacy (which confuses prerational and transrational because both are nonrational—or any similar confusing of preformal and postformal, preconventional and postconventional, prepersonal and transpersonal, etc.; see *Eye to Eye*). This

confusion Rowan himself has spotted and redressed in subsequent publications, as well as a new afterword to the book, which Rowan sent me and from which I quote:

> When I finished writing this book in 1991 it was very much a pioneering effort. I was trying to put together a coherent story out of widely separated materials. And in doing so I did oversimplify one point.
>
> This is on the question of my definition of the transpersonal. In this book I consistently identified the transpersonal with the Subtle stage, the stage of the soul. The reason for this was that I wanted to make it very clear that this was the stage beyond the Centaur which was most relevant to therapy, and most used by therapists. . . .
>
> Well, this is perfectly OK and quite defensible. What is not defensible is to suggest that the Causal and Nondual stages are somehow not the transpersonal. Of course they are. They are just as much part of the transpersonal as the Subtle is, and much more studied and mentioned in the literature of transpersonal psychology. . . .
>
> On the other hand, I think I was right in emphasizing the importance of the Subtle. It is very much underrated and under-represented in the transpersonal literature. . . .
>
> One important reservation has to be made here, however. It is that people working in the subtle are typically rather careless about the Pre/Trans Fallacy. Because the prepersonal and the transpersonal are both rich in imagery, it is all too easy to slip from one to the other without awareness of the changeover.
>
> Joseph Campbell, one of the greatest proponents of the Subtle level and its importance, is also one of the great confusing people in the field, because he mixes up this [postformal Subtle] level with the [preformal] Mythic level quite habitually and as if thinking that they are the same thing. . . .
>
> What we can learn from all this is that if someone as well-read and capable as Joseph Campbell can make this sort of [pre/post] mistake, it must be even easier for those who are less experienced. In my own work I have done this, lumping together practitioners who are operating at the mythic level with those who are genuinely operating much of the time at the subtle level. This is something I intend to put right for the future, and what I have been trying to warn about here.

For further discussion, see notes 8.25, 8.27, 9.16.

18. See in particular the works of George Kelly, Aron Beck, and Albert Ellis. Transactional Analysis is still a fine approach to many of these scripts (see E. Berne, T. Harris).
19. See especially the pioneering works of Ludwig Binswanger, Medard Boss, Rollo May, Fritz Perls, Irvin Yalom, and Carl Rogers.
20. Good introductions to transpersonal psychology and therapy include Donald Moss (ed.), *Humanistic and Transpersonal Psychology*; Scotton et al., *Textbook of Transpersonal Psychiatry and Psychology*; Frances Vaughan, *The Inward*

Arc and *Shadows of the Sacred* (which are particularly recommended); Seymour Boorstein, *Clinical Studies in Transpersonal Psychotherapy* and *Transpersonal Psychotherapy*; Assagioli, *Psychosynthesis*; Grof, *Adventures in Self Discovery*; Tart, *Transpersonal Psychologies* and *States of Consciousness*; Washburn, *The Ego and the Dynamic Ground* and *Transpersonal Psychology in Psychoanalytic Perspective*; Zimmerman, *Eclipse of the Self*; Walsh and Shapiro, *Beyond Health and Normality*; Neumann, *The Origins and History of Consciousness* (see chart 4b); Chaudhuri, *Integral Yoga*; Epstein, *Thoughts Without a Thinker*; Deikman, *The Observing Self*; Kathleen Singh, *The Grace in Dying*; Duane Elgin, *Awakening Earth*; Ferucci, *What We May Be*; anthologies/books of John Welwood; Adi Da, *The Dawn Horse Testament*; Wade, *Changes of Mind*; Grof and Grof, *The Stormy Search for the Self*; Jean Houston, *The Possible Human*; N. Schwartz-Salant and M. Stein (eds.), *Archetypal Processes in Psychotherapy*; Aurobindo, *The Life Divine*; Maslow, *The Farther Reaches of Human Nature*; John Rowan, *The Transpersonal* (as Rowan himself has made clear in his subsequent writings, this book tends to confuse mythic and subtle domains—see note 8.17—but it is otherwise a fine overview); Tony Schwartz, *What Really Matters*; Walsh and Vaughan, *Paths beyond Ego*; Wilber et al., *Transformations of Consciousness*; Almaas, *Pearl beyond Price*; J. Firman and A. Gila, *The Primal Wound*; Murphy, *The Future of the Body*; Murphy and Leonard, *The Life We Are Given*; Cornett, *The Soul of Psychotherapy*; Doherty, *Soul Searching*; Browning, *Religious Thought and the Modern Psychologies*; Sovatsky, *Words from the Soul*; Shapiro and Astin, *Control Therapy*; Frager and Fadiman, *Personality and Personal Growth*.

21. Even behavior therapy reinforces responses that help people experience what they have avoided. Incidentally, as Arieti (*The Intrapsychic Self*) demonstrates, classical behaviorism deals predominantly with the exoceptual level of cognition. Modern cognitive behaviorism deals predominantly with F-4 and F-5 verbal behavior. In other words, there is ample room in an integral theory for the enduring insights of behaviorism, though not for its reductionism. Finally, when I say awareness is curative, this includes the working through; awareness needs to be stable and pervasive; it needs to permeate the problem.

22. See John Rowan's superb book *Subpersonalities*; see also *Ego States*, Watkins and Watkins. In my view, each subpersonality exists as a subconscious or unconscious "I," an aspect of the proximate self that was defensively split off, but with which consciousness remains fused, embedded, or identified (as a hidden "I"), with its own wants, desires, impulses, and so on. The nature of the subpersonality is largely determined by the level at which it was dissociated (archaic, imagic, mythic, etc.). These "little subjects" are all those hidden facets of self that have not been turned into objects, let go of, disidentified with, de-embedded, and transcended, and so they hold consciousness circling in their orbit.

    Each time the proximate self identifies with a basic wave, the self exists *embedded* as that wave: it is a material self, then a libidinal/emotional self, then a conceptual self, then a role self, then a reflexive self, then an integrated/authentic self, then a soul self, then a spirit self, each of which holarchically transcends and includes. As each "I" self is transcended, it becomes part of the "me" self (e.g., the feeling body, which was the proximate or "I" self of F-2, becomes simply "my body"—or part of the distal self or "me"—when the proximate self moves on).

A dissociated subpersonality results when facets of the "I" self are split off while consciousness *is still identified with them.* They thus become, not unconscious objects, but unconscious subjects, with their own morals, worldviews, needs, and so on (all determined by the level at which the subpersonality was split off). This is the key, in my opinion, *to distinguishing between repression and transcendence.* That is, dissociation (or repression) occurs when a proximate I is turned into a distal I; whereas transcendence occurs when a proximate I is turned into a distal me. In the former, the subjective identification/attachment (or I-ness) remains but is submerged (as an unconscious subject); in the later, the subjective identification is dissolved, turning the unconscious subject into a conscious object, which can then be integrated (transcend and include, not dissociate and repress). Therapy involves converting hidden subjects to conscious objects.

23. The lower-level subpersonalities are largely *preverbal* (archaic, uroboric, magical [UL]; reptilian/brain stem, paleomammalian/limbic system [UR]); the intermediate level subpersonalities are *verbal* (mythic, roles, formal, postformal [UL]; neocortex [UR]); the higher subpersonalities are *transverbal* (mostly subtle [UL], theta states [UR]). Each of those impinge on consciousness in a different manner: the preverbal, often as impulses and inarticulated urges; the verbal, as vocal or subvocal narratives; the transverbal, as luminosities, higher cognitions, and transcendental affects (from bliss to cosmic agony).

A dissociated component of any level of consciousness proceeds from a facet to a complex to a full-blown subpersonality, each layered with more complexity. This is similar to Grof's notion of COEX systems (systems of condensed experience). Any subpersonality includes one or more complexes, which themselves can be layered, going from the present level (say, F-5 or rational) back to earlier levels (mythic, magic, archaic), even back to perinatal matrices (F-0)—and further yet, some would claim, to past life experiences (however you wish to conceive that, from literally to phylogenetic residues; see *A Sociable God* for a further description of this layering of complexes). Likewise, some subpersonalities contain emergent qualities attempting to "come down" (from psychic, subtle, causal, or nondual domains).

24. For the highly controversial, possible role of F-0 in subsequent pathologies, see Grof, *The Adventure of Self-Discovery.*

25. "Archetype" has several different, very confusing meanings in the literature. I use it for both mythic forms and, occasionally, for subtle-realm forms. The original meaning, as with Plato and Plotinus, is of subtle-realm forms (the earliest forms in involution); but Jungians began using it to mean mythic forms (some of the earliest forms in evolution), a confusion that is impossible to uproot. See *Eye to Eye* and *The Eye of Spirit* for a full discussion.

In any event, most of the mythic archetypes—as identified, say, by Jean Bolen in *Goddesses in Everywoman* and *Gods in Everyman*—are simply *concrete operational role personae*; they are preformal, not postformal. There is nothing inherently transpersonal about them, which is why, despite the many claims to the contrary, working with these mythic roles is usually a fulcrum-4 therapy. I happen to believe it is a powerful form of F-4 therapy, and I often recommend it, but it does not directly or necessarily issue in transpersonal states or structures of consciousness, although, by clearing out pathologies at this level, it can (as can any good therapy) make higher, transpersonal development more likely. See notes 8.27, 9.16.

Jungian therapy of this sort can occasionally issue in transpersonal awareness, simply because the process of *objectifying* these mythic roles often engages the Witness, and the postformal Witness—not the preformal mythic roles—is indeed transpersonal. I personally believe that Assagioli's Psychosynthesis and Hameed Ali's Diamond Approach are more effective in this particular regard, as is awareness meditation in general (vipassana, Zen, etc.).

26. See *Eye to Eye*; *Sex, Ecology, Spirituality,* 2nd ed.; and *The Eye of Spirit* for extensive discussions of the meaning of archetypes, from Plato to Jung. See especially *The Eye of Spirit,* chap. 11, section "Points of Light," no. 4.
27. Joseph Campbell (*The Portable Jung*, p. xxii), has given a wonderful summary of the general Jungian approach: "Briefly summarized, the essential realizations of this pivotal work of Jung's career were, first, that since the archetypes or norms of myth are common to the human species, they are inherently expressive neither of local social circumstance nor of any individual's singular experience, but of common human needs, instincts, and potentials [again, "common" or "collective" does not necessarily mean transpersonal, any more than the fact that human beings collectively have ten toes means that if I experience my toes I am having a transpersonal experience; the mythic archetypes are simply some of the deep features of the late preop and early conop mind, and thus they are basic forms at those levels, which are devoid of content but fleshed out by particular cultures and individuals; in other words:]; second, that in the traditions of any specific folk, local circumstance will have provided the imagery through which the archetypal themes are displayed in the supporting myths of the culture; third, that if the manner of life and thought of an individual so departs from the norms of the species that a pathological state of imbalance ensues, of neurosis or psychosis, dreams and fantasies analogous to fragmented myths will appear; and fourth, that such dreams are best interpreted, not by reference backward to repressed infantile memories (reduction to autobiography), but by comparison outward with the analogous mythic forms (amplification by mythology), so that the person may see himself depersonalized in the mirror" of the collective human condition. In other words, the aim is to differentiate from (and integrate) these mythic forms and roles. Many Jungians directly equate these preformal mythic roles with postformal subtle structures, which is an unfortunate pre/post confusion, in my opinion (for a discussion of the meaning of "archetype" and its pre/trans confusions, see *Eye to Eye* and *The Eye of Spirit*). But the effects of mythic differentiation-and-integration remain essentially the

same however it is interpreted: consciousness befriends and transcends the grip of mythic archetypes and is thus allowed to continue its journey free of their unconscious spell, a differentiation-and-integration that Jung called individuation.

28. The psychoanalytic, objects relations, and self psychologists are increasingly recognizing a spectrum of treatment modalities up to and including F-5. As one example, on the charts I have included J. Gedo (e.g., *Beyond Interpretation, Advances in Clinical Psychoanalysis, Spleen and Nostalgia*), who admirably includes all of the first five fulcrums, their different pathologies and different treatments.

    Various horizontal typologies—such as the Enneagram—can also be used to elucidate the types of defenses used by individuals. Each type proceeds through the various fulcrums with its own typical defense mechanisms and coping strategies. These horizontal typologies can be fruitfully combined with the vertical fulcrums, as suggested in chap. 4.

29. See *The Atman Project* and *Transformations of Consciousness.*
30. Grof and Grof, *Spiritual Emergency.*
31. Maslow, *The Farther Reaches of Human Nature.*
32. See *Transformations of Consciousness*; also notes 8.13 and 8.20.
33. For approaches to "soul therapy," see note 8.20.
34. Again, there are many overlaps and numerous exceptions, but in very general terms, the path of shamans/yogis deals with the energy currents in the gross realm and gross bodymind (exemplified in *nature mysticism*), leading up to the sahasrara (i.e., the energy currents or shakti from to the first to the seventh chakra, at the crown of the head). The path of saints plumbs the interior depths of the psychic and subtle realm, often beginning at the fourth or fifth chakra, moving into the sahasrara, and then into numerous, more "within-and-beyond" spheres of audible illuminations and haloes of light and sound (exemplified in *deity mysticism*), occasionally culminating in pure formless absorption. The path of sages plumbs the pure emptiness of the causal domain (exemplified in *formless mysticism*), and often pushes through it to completely dissolve the subject-object dualism in any form (including that between self and God), to resurrect the nondual. The path of siddhas plays with *nondual mysticism*, which is always already accomplished in each and every gesture of this ever-present moment. See *Up from Eden*; *Sex, Ecology, Spirituality,* 2nd ed.; and *One Taste.*
35. A word on body therapy. In the sixties and early seventies, it seemed that body therapies, such as Rolfing, were aimed at the centaur, or a personal, postformal, bodymind integration; it has since become apparent that most of them, in themselves, deal with the preformal physical and emotional bodies. This does not mean that somatic therapy is useless; just the opposite, although it is less significant, it is more fundamental (see *Sex, Ecology, Spirituality,* 2nd ed.). Physical therapies of various sorts—from weight lifting to nutritional therapy to Rolfing, somatic therapy, and bodywork, insofar as they directly address the physical and feeling body (F-1 and F-2)—are all of great importance as the foundation, or first floor, of an integral therapy. But for postformal centauric

integration (e.g., achieving Loevinger's autonomous and integrated stages), vision-logic also has to be engaged and strengthened, and few body therapies actually do that.

Likewise, most of the therapies that call themselves "bodymind" therapies—such as bioenergetics and focusing—deal mostly with the predifferentiated aspects of the body/mind interface, not with the transdifferentiated or truly integrated aspects. That is, these "bodymind" therapies deal with the pranic dimension of vital emotional energy, endoceptual felt meanings, and visceral psychology, as they move from the bodily dimensions to the mental dimensions (from pranamayakosha to manomayakosha), the F-2 to F-3 range. The emphasis remains on what I am feeling, and how I can articulate these vague somatic gestalts. These therapies do not usually address the specific issues of worldcentric moral consciousness and/or transpersonal revelations (centauric and higher), although of course if these issues arise on their own most bodymind therapists will accommodate them. But the main focal point of somatic therapy remains endoceptual, not vision-logic (see chart 1a). Nonetheless, bodywork of various sorts, as a *foundation*, remains fundamental to all subsequent phases of integral therapy (mind to soul to spirit), in my opinion. See note 8.14.

36. In the stream of evolution, we can trace cosmogenetic, phylogenetic, ontogenetic, and microgenetic development. Cosmogenesis refers to the developments in the physiosphere, leading, via systems far from equilibrium, to the brink of life forms, whereupon phylogenetic evolution begins, within which ontogenetic evolution unfolds. It is not that any of these strictly recapitulates the others, only that the basic holons out of which each is built can only, after they have creatively emerged, be arranged in so many ways, and thus subsequent developments follow the grooves of previous selections—and hence, in broad outline, ontogeny recaps phylogeny recaps cosmogeny—each holon in each of the lines transcends and includes its predecessors.

Microgeny is the moment-to-moment unfolding of a developmental line. Generally speaking, microgeny recaps ontogeny. Thus, for example, a person at formop, who sees a tree and tells me about it, has this general microgenetic sequence: there is the sensation of the tree, which leads to perception, and an image of the tree forms; affective factors color this image (pleasant/unpleasant), and the person searches for a series of words (symbols and concepts) with which to label the tree; these concepts arise within the cognitive space of conop and formop, and the preconscious high-speed memory scan for appropriate words occurs within the given cultural background (the language is English, say, and not Italian), driven in part by a desire for intersubjective communication and mutual understanding. All of this summates the person saying to me, "I see a tree."

That microgenetic sequence recaps a person's own ontogenetic sequence (sensation to perception to impulse to image to symbol . . .). If I have only developed to conop, my microgenetic processes will stop at conop; if I have developed to the subtle, my microgenetic processes will continue into the subtle: the tree will be seen, *directly perceived*, not as a object out there in perspectival space, but as a radiant manifestation of spirit. Overall: microgeny recaps ontogeny recaps phylogeny recaps cosmogeny: matter to sensation to perception to impulse to image to symbol to concept to rule to formop to . . . whatever level in the Great Nest that I am presently adapted to. When the person turns to me and says, "I see a tree," the entire history of the Kosmos, up to that point, is enfolded in that simple utterance.

Not all processes in consciousness are "bottom up"; many are "top down"—that is, many start at my present level (or higher) and move down the great holarchy. When I have a creative vision (e.g., psychic level), I might translate that vision downward into vision-logic, or perhaps artistic expression, or even into simple images and symbols; I might execute my vision by beginning to convert it into overt behavior and thus materialize the vision: perhaps a new invention, a new piece of architecture, a new way to interact with others, writing a novel, and so on (e.g., will is a microgenetic involutionary imposing of the higher on the lower). In microgenetic evolution, processes move up to the highest that you are; in microgenetic involution, the highest you are moves down into lower processes. Both of these are very important; and they represent a sliding scale: the more you develop, the fuller the range through which both can move, until, with nondual awakening, they can literally move throughout the Kosmos.

37. Unfortunately, what many New Age new-paradigm thinkers mean by "depth" is actually something lower on the evolution line, not something deeper on that line.
38. See note 7.2.
39. Thus, to the standard three-variable (or "three-dimensional") model of individual subjective *structures*, *states*, and *realms*, we need to add different brain states (UR), types and levels of cultural values (LL), and modes of social institutions (LR). This gives us six independent variables, any one of which can be distorted or pathological, with concomitant reverberations throughout the others. The three-variable model marked phase-2 and phase-3; the six-variable model marked phase-4 (the four quadrants). See notes 1.3, 1.5, 1.9, 1.10, 8.1, 8.2., 12.12. For phases 2, 3, and 4, see note 9.15.
40. See also note 8.11.
41. The most prevalent and accessible forms of relationship therapy include family therapy and group therapy; classic approaches to each include those of Virginia Satir and Irvin Yalom, respectively. See also S. Gladding, *Family Therapy*, and Mikesell et al. (eds.), *Integrating Family Therapy*. "Relational therapy" in the broad sense also includes higher, spiritual relationships, for which the work of Robert Forman and the Forge Institute might be mentioned. See R. Forman in Crittenden et al., *Kindred Visions*.

Chapter 9. Some Important Developmental Streams

1. As we have seen, the proximate self is both a constant function and a developmental stream. It is a system of various functional invariants (the locus of identity, will, metabolism, navigation, defenses, tension regulation, integration,

etc.), which also undergoes its own development through the basic waves in the Great Nest (generally summarized as the nine fulcrums). As the locus of integration, the self is also responsible for balancing and integrating all of the levels, lines, and states in the individual. In this chapter, we are looking specifically at some of the more important developmental lines.

2. But the number of individuals reaching the greater depth becomes less and less (evolution produces greater depth, less span). The higher stages contain within themselves all of the lower stages, and thus the higher holons *themselves* become more and more significant and encompassing (cells embrace molecules which embrace atoms); but fewer individuals reach the higher stages (the span becomes less: there are fewer cells than molecules, fewer molecules than atoms). For human beings and the stages of consciousness development, this does *not* mean that only a few people can reach the higher stages; it only means they have to pass through the lower stages first (so that the total number of lower stages will always be greater than the higher, simply because growth starts at the lower; but growth can continue, and thus everybody at the lower can theoretically reach the higher). An atom cannot become a cell; but a precon individual *can* become con and then postcon.

   Although I sometimes use "theocentric" and "theosphere" for the general transpersonal realms, I prefer terms like "pneumocentric" and "pneumosphere," in order to avoid confusion with mythic theism, which is almost always, as we saw, ethnocentric. The mythic God/dess is said to be universal, and all can be saved—but *only* if you embrace that particular God/dess.

3. Technically, I distinguish between the basic-structure needs and the self-needs. *Basic-structure needs* (or simply basic needs) are those that involve the constant functioning of the basic structures (insofar as they have emerged in a person's development). Basic needs include physical exchange (food, water, warmth); biological exchange (especially breath, sex, élan vital); mental exchange (communication, exchange of symbols and units of meaning), and so forth. As explained in *Up from Eden* and *A Sociable God*, every basic structure (or basic wave in the Great Nest) is a *system of relational exchanges* with other holons in the world at a similar level of structural development, and its very life depends upon those exchanges (all agency is agency-in-communion): hence, that *dependence* is inwardly *felt as a need.*

   Likewise with the *self-needs*, except that, where the basic needs *remain in existence* (due to the enduring nature of the basic structures and their functional relationships), the self-needs are mostly transitional, phase-specific, and temporary, lasting only as long as the self is at a particular level of consciousness. Maslow's needs hierarchy (except for the physiological level) is a classic self-needs hierarchy, as are the motivational aspects of Loevinger's ego development. Thus, the self moves from impulsive needs to safety needs to conformist needs to autonomous needs, and each time it does so *the needs of the previous stage tend to be replaced by those of the higher stage.* At the autonomous stage, for example, one does not *simultaneously* have a huge set of impulsive needs—those have been transcended (barring fixation, dissociated subpersonalities, etc.); and yet the corresponding basic structures of those lower levels (images, symbols, and concepts) *remain perfectly present and fully functioning*, because they are basic rungs in the ladder of existence, and not a temporary by-product of the self's climb up those rungs. Thus those basic needs are still present and functioning (the need for food, breath, symbol exchange, and so on).

Overall, then, a person's *total motivations* include all of the basic-structure needs that have emerged to date (e.g., food, sex, symbolic communication, God communion), *plus* the major present self-need (e.g., safety, belongingness, self-esteem, self-transcendence), which is generated by the proximate self's exclusive identification with a particular basic structure or level of consciousness. I have included both of these two major types of needs in the "levels of food" chart; they are both the products of the demands of relational exchange at all levels.

In standard motivation theory, it is common to represent a "tendency to behavior" (T_B) as being the product of drive, expectation, and value ($T_B = D \times E \times V$). For example, my tendency to go to the refrigerator to get something to eat is a product of how hungry (D) I am (the more hungry, the more likely I will go); the expectation (E) that I can find something in the frig (perhaps I realize there isn't much food in the frig; the more I expect something to be there, the more likely I will go); and the value (V) of what's there (what if I know there are only sardines, and I hate sardines; the more I value what is there, the more likely I will go).

Thus, overall behavior, in my opinion, is a summation of all of the basic and self drives, the expectations of satisfying them, and the values placed on them at any given moment. The result is a fairly sophisticated calculus of motivations spanning the entire spectrum of consciousness.

The aim of a complete course of development is to divest the basic structures of any sense of exclusive self, and thus free the basic needs from their contamination by the needs of the separate-self sense. When the basic structures are freed from the immortality projects of the separate self, they are free to return to their natural functional relationships: one eats without making food a religion, one communicates without desire to dominate, one exchanges mutual recognition without angling for self-gain. The separate self, by climbing up and off the ladder of the Great Chain, disappears as an alienated and alienating entity, ends its self-needs altogether, and thus is left with the simple and spontaneous play of the basic needs and their relationships as they easily unfold: when hungry, we eat; when tired, we sleep. The self has been returned to the Self, all self-needs have been met and thus discarded, and the basic needs alone remain, not so much as needs, but as the networks of communions that are Spirit's relationships with and as this world.

4. I sometimes use "worldview" and "worldspace" synonymously, although technically the former refers more to the cognitive component of a worldspace; worldspace itself includes all manner of cultural contexts, backgrounds, and practices, some of which are nondiscursive and precognitive.
5. See *Sex, Ecology, Spirituality*, 2nd ed., chap. 14, note 17, for an extensive discussion of the fact that subjective intentionality arises within an intersubjective worldspace, and a critique of theories ignoring this.

6. See notes 8.14 and 8.35.
7. See note 4.15. For the gender-neutral status of the basic developmental stages, see, e.g., two widely respected textbooks, Shaffer, *Social and Personality Development,* and Sroufe et al., *Child Development*. See also *The Eye of Spirit.*
8. Joyce Nielsen gives an excellent overview of a feminism using all four quadrants ("Fusion or Fission?," in J. Crittenden et al., *Kindred Visions*, forthcoming). See also Kaisa Puhakka, "The Spiritual Liberation of Gender," and Elizabeth Debold, "Beyond Gender," both in *Kindred Visions*.
9. See notes 1.3, 1.5, 1.9, 1.10, 8.1, 8.2., 8.39, 12.12.
10. I have not differentiated the examples in chart 8 into level of the subject (producing the art) and level of the object (being depicted); both are simply included on the chart, though the reader is invited to make the appropriate distinctions. For example, the sensorimotor realm depicted by magic is Paleolithic art, by perspectival reason, is empirical Realism and Naturalism; the subtle depicted by mythic is literal religious iconic art, by the mental-ego, is Fantastic Realist, and so on.
11. See notes 1.3, 1.5, 1.9, 1.10, 8.1, 8.2., 8.39, 12.12.
12. See *The Marriage of Sense and Soul* and *A Brief History of Everything* for a full discussion of this theme.
13. "Aesthetics," as I use the term in the very broadest sense, means the direct apprehension of form, in any domain. In this broad sense, it is quite similar to empiricism in the broad sense: sensory empiricism, mental empiricism, spiritual empiricism. With the differentiations of modernity, Western philosophy, following Kant, decided for the most part to make *spirituality* a matter of intersubjective *morals* (Lower Left), instead of seeing that authentic spirituality is also a matter of direct personal experience, radical empiricism, immediate phenomenology, and—in all those senses—aesthetic apprehension (Upper Left). For the great contemplative traditions, spiritual experience is a direct "inner" apprehension of immediate forms in consciousness, unfolding from gross forms to subtle forms, which are finally released into causal formlessness, and forms that therefore become more and more sublime (aesthetic). Spirituality also involves the intersubjective sharing of these forms in morals, ethics, sangha, and discourse, but it cannot (contra Kant) be reduced to mere moral injunctions.

    More narrowly (and more traditionally), I also use "aesthetics" to mean the apprehension of forms judged to be pleasing, beautiful, sublime; the subjective judgments that are involved in judging forms to be beautiful; and the entire sphere of art, artistic production, and art criticism. Beauty is the depth of a holon, or its transparency to Spirit. Art is anything with a frame around it.

    See *Sex, Ecology, Spirituality,* 2nd ed. and *The Eye of Spirit* (especially chaps. 4 and 5) for extensive discussion of art, art theory, and aesthetics. For an interesting view of aesthetic apprehension as spiritual discipline in Aurobindo and Tagore, see W. Cenkner, "Art as Spiritual Discipline in the Lives and Thought of Rabindranath Tagore and Sri Aurobindo Ghose," in *Ultimate Reality and Spiritual Discipline*, edited by J. Duerlinger.
14. For an extended discussion of development in the Big Three, see note 14.20.

15. That is, from a phase-2 to a phase-3 model.

I have, for convenience, divided my overall work into four general phases. Phase-1 was Romantic (a "recaptured-goodness" model), which posited a spectrum of consciousness ranging from subconscious to self-conscious to superconscious (or id to ego to God), with the higher stages viewed as a return to, and recapture of, original but lost potentials. Phase-2 was more specifically evolutionary or developmental (a "growth-to-goodness" model), with the spectrum of consciousness unfolding in developmental stages or levels. Phase-3 added developmental lines to those developmental levels—that is, numerous different developmental lines (such as cognitive, conative, affective, moral, psychological, spiritual, etc.) proceeding in a relatively independent manner through the basic levels of the overall spectrum of consciousness. Phase-4 added the idea of the four quadrants—the subjective (intentional), objective (behavioral), intersubjective (cultural), and interobjective (social) dimensions—of each of those levels and lines, with the result being—or at least attempting to be—a comprehensive or integral philosophy. The present book is, of course, a phase-4 work. For a discussion of these phases, see *The Eye of Spirit* and *One Taste*, Nov. 16 entry.

16. In fact, as it develops, even the gross-cognitive line becomes more and more subtle: whereas sensorimotor cognition is the perception of the material environment, and concrete operational cognition is "thought operating on environment," formop is "thought operating on thought," and thus formop is already, to a significant degree, involved with subtle perception. However, this perception is still organized such that its ultimate referents are objects and operations in the gross realm, and thus I include formop in the gross-cognitive line. Vision-logic can partake of both gross and subtle realms, and can be included as an important component in both of those lines. In the gross line, vision-logic is generally the very highest and concluding stage; in the subtle, it is an intermediate stage, preceded by etheric, astral, fantasy and imagination, and superceded by psychic vision, subtle archetype, and intermediate-to-advanced meditative states.

Many psychological theorists who are investigating the subtle line of development—e.g., the Jungians, Jean Bolen, James Hillman—often confuse the lower, prepersonal levels in the subtle line with the higher, transpersonal levels in that line, with unfortunate results. James Hillman, for example, has carefully explored the preformal, imaginal levels of the subtle line, but constantly confuses them with the postformal levels of the subtle line. Just because theorists are working with dreams/images/visions does not mean they are necessarily working with the higher levels of that line (such as savikalpa samadhi or transcendental illumination); they are often working with the lower, prepersonal-to-personal levels in the subtle line (which they often mistakenly call the "soul," when what they are working with is more often the typhon, etheric/astral sheath, pranamayakosha, images/symbols, preformal mythic fantasies, and so on). All of the levels in the subtle line are important, but should not be confused or equated on that account. To do so is another type of "collapsing fallacy" (see note 9.18), where the various waves of a given stream of consciousness are collapsed and fused, simply because they are all in the same stream.

17. The causal sheath is viewed, by both Vedanta and Vajrayana, as the root source, and thus the "cause," of all the other levels of consciousness and reality. At the same time, it is itself one level among other levels (albeit the highest), and thus it is not ultimate. The ultimate or nondual state is not one level among others, but the ground, suchness, or emptiness of all levels and all states. That which obscures the realization of the nondual domain is precisely the subject/object dualism, and this dualism first arises in the causal domain as a constriction or contraction in consciousness (namely, as the dualism between subject and object, in this case, the unmanifest world of empty consciousness and the manifest world of objects). This dualistic contraction is the capacity for focused *attention*, which attends to this by *ignoring* that, and this *ignorance* (or attention forgetful of its nondual ground) is said to be the root cause of all suffering. The root of this attention is the causal realm, which is a constriction around the Heart, and appears in the form of the Witness, or the pure Subject split from the world of objects. This pure Witness or pure Subject then looses itself in the world of objects, which further fragments and splits consciousness, as it identifies with a soul, then an ego, then a body—all of which are actually objects, not the real Subject or Witness. In order to reverse this "fall," an individual has *first* to re-establish the capacity for Witnessing (by strengthening the capacity for attention, equanimity, and detachment—or disidentification from the objects of awareness, including the body, the ego, and the soul); and *second*, to then dissolve the causal Witness—and the root of attention—into pure nondual One Taste. In any event, the causal, as the root of attention, can be followed as a separate line of development in any of its forms of focused awareness, body to mind to soul to source.
18. To the gross, subtle, and causal lines, I have also added a "nondual line," for tracing the development of *states of subject-object union*, from prenatal to perinatal (e.g., cosmic fusion) to childhood (e.g., emotional bonding states) to adulthood (e.g., flow states) to states/traits of postformal samadhi to pure nondual One Taste. We are justified in including this nondual cognitive line because, just as with other cognitive lines, which were based on the existence of the *natural states* of waking, dreaming, and deep sleep (and thus available to all), so this nondual line is based on a *natural given*, namely, the natural mind or the primordial mind, the nondual mind that is ever-present in all sentient beings.

    Unfortunately, most Romantic writers confuse low levels of the nondual line with high levels in that line, and then assume that contacting the higher levels in that line is actually a recontacting (or recapturing) of the lower levels in that line. This confusion is based, not so much on a pre/trans fallacy (which the Romantics deny anyway; this present critique does not rely on it), but rather on a type of "collapsing fallacy." That is, simply because subject-object fusion states can give a sense of wholeness, *any and all unity states are equated*, and thus, higher and lower fusion states are all collapsed into a single "Ground." Then *anytime* a unity state occurs, it is assumed that it must be due to contacting or recontacting this *single* Ground, whereas, in fact, the nondual line itself unfolds across numerous quite different waves. But if these are collapsed, then anytime any subject and any object are fused, it is assumed to be the action of a this "single" Ground, so that this abstraction called "Ground" is reified and made the source of all nondual states. (Washburn typically exemplifies this collapsing fallacy, as do most of the Romantic theorists. I believe they also commit variations on the pre/trans fallacy, but that is an entirely separate issue and is not a part of this particular critique.) See note 9.16.

As with the other cognitive lines and states, the nondual itself only becomes a *permanent trait* with sustained postformal, post-postconventional development. Nonetheless, all four realms (psychic, subtle, causal, and nondual) can be traced as relatively independent cognitive lines all the way back to the earliest of stages.

19. Another benefit of this way of conceiving the relation between the cognitive lines is that it allows, for example, subtle cognition to begin *alongside* of gross cognition, not simply *after* it. In the gross-reflecting cognitive line, the very highest stages involve, as I suggested (see note 9.16), various types of vision-logic. To use Commons and Richards' version, the highest levels of the gross-cognitive line involve meta-systematic, paradigmatic, and cross-paradigmatic thinking (which work with systems, systems of systems, and systems of systems of systems). I believe that is true; but that does *not* mean that being able to think about systems of systems of systems is a necessary prerequisite for developing into the psychic, subtle, and causal realms (which it would be if these were all sequential stages in a monolithic line). A *basic competence* in vision-logic is certainly required in order for overall consciousness development to move permanently into the higher realms (see notes 8.4, 9.27), but cross-paradigmatic thinking is simply an extreme accomplishment in the gross-cognitive line, which may or may *not* be mastered by various individuals in their overall growth into the transpersonal realms. Seeing gross, subtle, and causal cognitive lines as in some ways parallel allows us to further accommodate that fact.

But that doesn't mean gross, subtle, or causal cognition can be bypassed in general development, or that sequential development looses its significance. First of all, there is no evidence that gross, subtle, or causal realms can be significantly bypassed, only that the extreme versions of some of their stages are not necessary for further development (see notes 8.4, 9.27, 9.28). Second, imbalances in, or between, any lines contribute to pathology. Schizophrenia is in some ways the classic example of what happens when people get lost in subtle-cognition without a grounding in gross-cognition. Third, the strongest drive of the self is to *integrate* all of the various developmental levels and lines in its own makeup, and an unbalanced growth—too much subtle, not enough gross—is felt as a major self-dissonance. Fourth, the highest developmental insight is nondual, or an integration of all three major realms in one embrace, which includes a *competent* gross, subtle, and causal consciousness—a major defect in one will obviously preclude balanced integration.

Thus, even though various streams can progress relatively independently through the waves in the Great Nest, a fully *integral development* still involves the holarchical unfolding of all of the major levels in a conscious fashion, with the self fully adapting to each. See notes 8.4, 9.27, 9.28.

20. *One Taste*, Nov. 16 and 17. The self and therefore *all of the self-related lines* can be modeled in this fashion, with gross, subtle, causal, and nondual streams (of morals, perspectives, drives, etc.) developing relatively independently. It must be strongly emphasized, however, that the number of these streams—if any—that actually develop independently *can only be determined by careful research guided by models of this type*. The lines (cognitive , self-related, etc.) are prevented from total independence by both the self's overriding drive for integration and the necessities of holarchical development in general. Many of these lines are necessary but not sufficient for others, and all of them are bound to some degree by the self-system (see *The Eye of Spirit*). Although a few of these relationships can be logically deduced, most of them can only be determined by careful research. Recently, several transpersonal theorists have proposed models of this type (i.e., phase-3 models), but they do so by simply proclaiming them to be true. I believe they are true to some degree; but to what degree, only research can tell.
21. See note 2.2 for some of the extensive research on developmental stages.
22. In this general scheme of three major self lines (ego, soul, and Self), what I am calling "frontal" or "ego" includes all of the self-stages in the gross and gross-reflecting realm (i.e., bodyself, persona, ego, and centaur); "soul" includes psychic and subtle; and "Self" includes causal and nondual. Since I am postulating that these particular independent lines are based on the *natural states* of consciousness of gross, subtle, causal, and nondual, those are the four independent lines of cognition and self-stages that I am proposing. (In the text I am treating causal and nondual as one.)

    Within the gross domain the various self-stages, although they overlap once they emerge, nonetheless still emerge in a generally holarchical fashion (bodyself to persona to ego to centaur), as research overwhelmingly continues to confirm. Alongside those developments, the soul and Self can unfold in often independent fashions, in ways that I will suggest in the text, and, to the extent they show *development* (and not just states), they also follow the holarchical contours of their own unfolding streams, with all of them nestled in the Great Holarchy of Being.
23. These are all of those items that are not measured by most developmental psychologists, which is why they tend only to see frontal self-development.
24. The pure transcendental Self or Witness does not itself develop, since it is sheer formlessness. However, access to this Self does develop, and that is what I mean by development in this line. For all three self lines, see *One Taste,* Nov. 17 entry.
25. See Vaughan, *The Inward Arc* and *Shadows of the Sacred*. See also note 8.20.
26. See notes 8.14 and 8.35.
27. Because vision-logic is listed as a general wave in the Great Nest, does that mean, *in overall consciousness evolution*, that a general (not extreme) competence in vision-logic is required for stable growth into higher levels? Yes, I very much believe so. Why? Because everything from the golden rule to the bodhisattva vow is impossible to comprehend without vision-logic. You cannot sincerely vow to liberate all beings if you cannot take the perspective of all beings

in the first place, and, researchers agree, that is a vision-logic capacity. We are not talking about an extreme development in vision-logic (such as cross-paradigmatic thinking; see notes 8.4, 9.19), but simply its general capacity for postconventional, worldcentric, multiple perspective taking. Without general vision-logic as a foundation, the higher levels (psychic, subtle, causal, and nondual) are experienced only as passing, altered states, without becoming permanent realizations, and for the simple reason that it is the nature of those higher states to be universal and global, and without a frontal development *capable of carrying that global perspective* (namely, vision-logic), those states cannot "fit" permanently, and without distortion, into the self. Only as vision-logic becomes a permanent capacity can the even-higher levels themselves become permanent.

Notice that, in the traditions, it is said that although all sentient beings contain Spirit, only human beings can *fully awaken* to that Spirit. In Buddhism, for example, not even the Gods and Goddesses (*devas*)—or any of the beings in the subtle realm—can become fully enlightened. Nor can those who are absorbed in the causal unmanifest (since they are seeking their own nirvanic salvation, neglecting others, and thus they are not bodhisattvas). In other words, even if we achieve extraordinary development in the subtle line (as do the Gods and Goddesses), and even if we achieve extraordinary development in the causal line (as do Pratyeka-buddhas or solitary causal realizers), we still cannot achieve full Enlightenment. Why? Because our development is not *integral*—it does not include gross and subtle and causal in an equal embrace. Only as consciousness awakens in all three realms—gross, subtle, and causal—can we hope to be of service to all sentient beings and thus fulfill the primordial bodhisattva vow ("no matter how limitless beings, I vow to liberate them all"). And only vision-logic in the gross realm can grasp all sentient beings in the gross realm. Thus, without vision-logic, there is no final Enlightenment. Of course individuals can achieve extraordinary development in the subtle and causal lines (as do the Gods and Pratyeka-buddhas), but without an integral embrace, including vision-logic, one cannot become samyak-sambuddha: a fully Realized One.

A few words about vision-logic itself. As a basic structure, it includes, as subholons in its own being, all of the previous basic structures, sensorimotor to emotive to fantasy to formal to its own postformal being, and, ideally, it integrates all of these components. It is not that vision-logic is without fantasy or emotion or rules, but that it simply holds all of them in its own wider space, so that all of them can flourish to an even greater degree. Commons and Richards, Fischer, and Sinnott tend to emphasize the cognitive component of vision-logic (and often its extreme developments), while Basseches, Pascual-Leone, Labouvie-Vief, and Deirdre Kramer highlight more of its dialectical, visionary, integrative capacities. Arieti stresses that vision-logic is an integration of primary and secondary processes—fantasy and logic—and thus it can be very creative (the "magic synthesis"), and Jean Gebser stresses the transparency, integrative capacity, and multiple perspectives of the "integral-aperspectival" structure. All of those, in my opinion, are important snapshots of vision-logic taken from different angles.

Vision-logic, like any cognitive capacity, can take as its *object* any of the *levels* in any of the *quadrants*, resulting in drastically different perceptions. To focus first on the quadrants. When vision-logic looks at the Lower-Right quadrant, the result is dynamical systems theory in any of many forms, from cybernetics to chaos to social autopoiesis to complexity theories. What they all focus on are the networks of *interobjective* processes and the dynamical patterns of existence and development. When applied to the human aspects of the Lower-Right quadrant, the result is a social systems science (e.g., Parsons, Merton) that highlights the importance and influence of the material modes of social interaction, forces of production, and relations of production (exemplars include Comte, Marx, Lenski, Luhmann).

When vision-logic looks at the Upper-Right quadrant, the result is a systems view of the individual organism, which depicts consciousness as an emergent of hierarchically integrated organic and neuronal networks. This emergent/connectionist view is perhaps the dominant model of cognitive science at this point, and is nicely summarized in Alwyn Scott's *Stairway to the Mind*, the "stairway" being the hierarchy of emergents said to result in consciousness. All of these emergents and networks—including all of the very influential models of autopoiesis—involve *objective systems* described in *third-person* it-language; a similar objectivistic view of consciousness can be found in Tart's systems approach to states of consciousness. I am not saying these accounts are wrong; I am saying they cover, at best, only one-fourth of the story. I myself use these approaches, as well as structuralism, which are all Right-Hand approaches to the phenomenon of consciousness; but I emphasize that consciousness itself must *also* be studied in first-person, Left-Hand, phenomenal approaches—direct experiential investigations of consciousness via introspection and meditation (see chap. 14). For convenience sake, I sometimes label a few of the levels in the Left-Hand quadrants with structural terms (e.g., conop, formop), but those are only markers for phenomenal events accurately seen and described only in first- and second-person terms. See *Sex, Ecology, Spirituality*, 2nd ed., CW 6 (especially chaps. 4 and 14) and "An Integral Theory of Consciousness," *Journal of Consciousness Studies* 4, no. 1 (1997), pp. 71–93 (CW 7).

When vision-logic looks at the Lower-Left quadrant, the result is an appreciation of the vast role of cultural contexts and backgrounds, a grasp of the role of mutual understanding, an intense focus on discourse, and a general understanding of hermeneutics. Exemplars in this approach include Heidegger, Hans-Georg Gadamer, Charles Taylor, Dilthey, and Kuhn, among others.

Incidentally, when these cultural or intersubjective *signifieds*, in their intersubjective semantic fields (LL), are viewed in terms of the exterior structure of their *material signifiers*—written word, spoken word, grammar and syntax (LR)—and especially when these signifiers are cut loose from any referents—the result is various forms of postmodern poststructuralism, from Foucault's archaeology (the grammar of discourse/archives) to Foucault's genealogy (the interobjective structures of power/knowledge) to Derrida's grammatology (the study of the chains of written signifiers)—all of which are LR approaches to LL phenomena, approaches that, used *exclusively*, destroy any genuinely intersubjective realms and, via performative contradiction, deny any existent referents. Again, I am not saying these approaches are wrong, but that they favor only one quadrant (in this case, they use LR techniques in an attempt to elucidate LL phenomena, and to the extent that these approaches go too far and deny the existence of the LL on its own terms, they end up committing subtle reductionism), and when they thus claim to have the final word, wind up in various untenable positions. (See *The Eye of Spirit*, chap, 5, note 12, for a discussion of an integral semiotics of signifier, signified, semantics, and syntax.)

When vision-logic is applied to the Upper-Left quadrant—when vision-logic looks within at its own domain—one of several things can result. First of all, as with any basic structure, the fact that a person has access to vision-logic does not mean that the person is *living from* vision-logic. Just as a person can have cognitive access to formop, and yet the self can still be at moral stage 1, so a person can have access to vision-logic and still remain at any of the lower levels of self and self-line development—moral stage 1, an impulsive self, safety needs, and so on (as we saw, basic structures are necessary, but not sufficient, for other developments). Thus, a person can be at a very low level of self, moral, and spiritual development, and yet still be a great systems theorist (they are applying vision-logic to the exterior world, but not to themselves). This is why simply learning the "new paradigm" does not necessarily transform a person, and why many "holistic" approaches often leave interior transformations untouched. (See *One Taste* and *Boomeritis*.)

It is only as the person's self—the center of gravity of the proximate self—moves from conop (where it is a conformist self or persona) to formop (where it is a postconventional self or mature ego) to postformal vision-logic (where it is a centaur, or relatively integrated, postconventional, global, autonomous, existential self)—only with that interior vertical transformation does vision-logic come to be directly applied to the person himself. His moral sense is thus postconventional and worldcentric; his needs are for self-actualization; his worldview is universal integral; and he stands on the brink of more permanent transformation into the transpersonal realms.

Likewise, vision-logic can be applied (as can most cognition) to any of the major *levels* (or realms) in any of the quadrants. As indicated in the text, I usually simplify these realms to body, mind, and spirit (or prepersonal, personal, and transpersonal). In its own quadrant (UL), vision-logic can look down to matter, across at mind, or up to spirit. Looking down to matter is the same as looking at any of the Right-Hand quadrants, since they are all material, and the result, we saw, is systems theory. Looking across at other minds is the same as looking at its own level in the Lower-Left quadrant, and the result, we saw, is hermeneutics. Looking up to spirit—or, alternatively, having a spiritual peak experience—results in the higher realms being interpreted according to the structures of vision-logic itself, and the result is what I have called mandalic reason (see *Eye to Eye*).

28. Can the subtle realm itself be completely bypassed in overall consciousness de-

velopment? Not in my opinion. Some theorists have suggested that various traditions—such as Zen—do not explore the subtle realm in their meditation practices and yet they achieve causal/nondual Enlightenment, so the subtle as a stage is not needed (or it can be completely skipped). Actually, all it means is that an extensive exploration of the subtle realm can to some degree be bypassed. But the subtle realm itself cannot.

The general subtle realm includes, for example, the dream state, and even fully enlightened beings continue to dream, but they do so *while remaining conscious* (e.g., lucid and pellucid dreaming; see *One Taste*). In other words, the subtle realm has become a *permanent conscious adaptation* in their own case. Intentionally and extensively exploring that realm as a means of awakening can to some degree be skipped, but not the realm itself, nor the fact that it becomes a *permanent basic structure* in the consciousness of the awakened one.

What can happen, particularly in the schools that emphasize causal and nondual techniques, is that extensive exploration of the subtle realm is largely set aside, and cognition in the causal and nondual lines is emphasized. Of course, the subtle realm is still present, since these individuals continue to dream. However, as causal witnessing becomes stronger and stronger, it tends to persist through the waking and into the dreaming state (pellucid dreaming—see *One Taste*); and thus, although the person is not *intentionally* investigating the subtle/dream realm, they are in fact *objectifying it* (thus transcending it, and thus including it in consciousness). The subtle as a *path* has to some degree been bypassed; but the subtle realm *itself* is transcended and included, as always, in permanent higher development. This *inclusion of the subtle* is also part of the self's inherent drive to integration. Thus, in overall consciousness development, the subtle realm is a permanent stage and structure in one's full development. See also *Sex, Ecology, Spirituality*, 2nd ed. (especially chap. 7) for a discussion of this theme. To say that somebody has "skipped" the subtle, even if it were possible (which it isn't), would only to be say that they had not completed integral development. See note 9.27.

CHAPTER 10. SPIRITUALITY

1. There is an important difference between the terms "postformal" and "postconventional," since the former usually refers to cognitive structures, the latter to the self-related stages (such as morals). Thus, in the cognitive line, development moves from preoperational to concrete operational to formal operational, and higher stages in that line are called *postformal*. The term *postformal* can technically apply to *all* cognitive developments higher than formal operational, and that would include both higher personal levels, such as vision-logic, and the more purely transpersonal cognitions (psychic, subtle, etc.). However, in the literature, postformal usually means just vision-logic (so that the more purely transpersonal cognitions we ought to call *post-postformal*; nonetheless, context will tell which I mean).

These cognitive developments (preop to conop to formop to postformal) are said to be necessary, but not sufficient, for the corresponding self-related stages (such as self-identity, morals, role-taking, and so on), which are generally said to develop from preconventional to conventional to postconventional, which covers development into the highest of the personal domains (the centauric). Several researchers (e.g., Kohlberg, Cook-Greuter, Wade, Alexander) have proposed that the self-related stages can also continue into genuinely *transpersonal* stages, in which case, to be consistent, we should refer to them as *post-postconventional* (which is what I do).

Nonetheless, you can see the semantic difficulties involved. There is no consistent agreement in the literature about how to use these "post" terms. I have tried to be consistent in my own usage, but the context in each case must be used for an accurate appraisal.

2. The difficulty with this definition is: how do you define a separate spiritual line in terms that do *not* use the other developmental lines, such as affect, cognition, or morals? In other words, if you say spirituality is one's capacity for love, love (or affect) is already itself a separate line, so you cannot use it to define spirituality if you want spirituality to be something different, to be its own separate line. Likewise, you cannot say spirituality involves awareness, cognition, morals, compassion, altruism, sense of self, or drives, for those are already separate lines themselves. In other words, coming up with a developmental line that is distinctively and purely "spiritual" is fairly difficult.

James Fowler, for example, has proposed that "faith" develops in five or six stages, but his test results are virtually indistinguishable from Kohlberg's, leading many theorists to suspect they are simply the same thing, and Fowler has added nothing new. However, I think Fowler's stages of faith are a legitimate, distinct line of development (because they are actually a useful amalgam, as I will discuss below), but it does point up the difficulty involved with this definition. I have also suggested (in *The Eye of Spirit*) that *concern* (Tillich's definition of spirituality as "ultimate concern") might also be considered a separate spiritual line of development, and there are others that seem to fit the bill (e.g., Baldwin). In any event, they would, by definition, show stage-like development.

However, what most people mean when they speak of spirituality as a separate line of development is actually *an amalgam of other developmental lines*, which is probably how people often experience "spirituality" in any event, and accordingly this is a very legitimate and important approach. Fowler's stages of faith, for example, are a mixture of morals, capacity for role taking, and worldviews. As I said, I believe that is a completely legitimate approach. Moreover, it is extremely common. Almost all of the theorists presented in charts 6a–c use this amalgam approach, even when they focus on more specific items (such as meditative experiences, contact with the numinous, and so on). These amalgams are important because in all of the cases presented in these charts, the amalgams have been shown to unfold in a developmental stage sequence as a functional grouping. The aspects of spirituality presented in charts 6a–c, in other words, definitely show holarchical stages.

3. The important research of Engler and Brown is presented in *Transformations of Consciousness*, chaps. 1, 6, 7, 8; my italics.

4. Blanck and Blanck, in a series of books (e.g., *Ego Psychology, Ego Psychology II, Beyond Ego Psychology*) have summarized a century of psychoanalytic theory and research on the development of the self by saying that the *self metabolizes experience to build structure*. This is also consonant with Piaget's work on constructivism (and thought as internalized action). The idea, as I would reconstruct it, is that the inchoate flux of experience—beginning with the early stages, dominated by impulsiveness, immediate gratification, and overwhelming emotional flooding—is slowly "metabolized" or processed by the self into more stable patterns (or holistic structures) of experience and awareness. These holistic structures allow the self to transcend its immersion and embeddedness in a lower wave by constructing more encompassing and holistic waves. Thus, temporary experiences are metabolized to produce enduring holistic adaptations. I believe the same process is at work in converting temporary peak experiences and altered states into enduring traits and structures of consciousness—which is why I have always included "metabolism" as one of the main characteristics of the self.

CHAPTER 11. IS THERE A CHILDHOOD SPIRITUALITY?

1. Roger Walsh, who is familiar with research on human happiness, denies even this version of a childhood Eden, and points out how little research supports it. "This is the childhood-is-bliss myth." As parents will attest, infants spend much of their time crying.
2. For an overview of childhood peak experiences, see E. Hoffman, "Peak experiences in childhood," *Journal of Humanistic Psychology* 1, 38 (1998), pp. 109–20.

   This does point up the difficulty of calling childhood peak experiences "spiritual" in an unalloyed sense. For example, as I started to say in the text, if a child at the early preconventional moral stage—which cannot take the role of other—has a peak experience, it will be captured in an egocentric, narcissistic orbit. *Unable to take the role of other* means unable to genuinely care for the other or possess authentic love for the other (as anything but a narcissistic extension of self). And just how authentically spiritual can a lack of care and lack of love be? No matter how authentic the spiritual realm might be that is "peaked," it is instantly snapped up and necessarily clothed in the psychological structures that are present at that time (cognitive, moral, ego, and so on), and the bulk of those, research confirms, are preconventional. This does not preclude other types of spiritual access (see the next paragraph in the text), but it does show how very careful we must be in these interpretations of childhood spirituality.

   It should also be noted that almost all of the evidence for infant and child spiritual experiences (including perinatal recollections) comes from *adults* who are "remembering" these early experiences. The grave (though I do not think fatal) difficulty with this evidence is that, except for massive regression to preverbal states (which cannot even be verbally communicated at the time), most of these "recollections" occur *through* the psychological structures that are irreversibly in place in the adult doing the recollecting, and thus the capacities and competences of these structures (such as the capacity to take the role of other) are *retrojected* (as Roger Walsh puts it) back into the childhood states, whereupon childhood incorrectly appears to be a time of wonderful fluidity *plus* the higher adult capacities, when it is no such thing at all. As Becker and Geer put it, "Changes in the social environment and in the self inevitably produce transformations of perspective, and it is characteristic of such transformations that the person finds it difficult or impossible to remember his former actions, outlook or feelings. Reinterpreting things from his new perspective, he cannot give an accurate account of the past, for the concepts in which he thinks about it have changed and with them his perceptions and memories."

Moreover, just as in the example of videotaping children who go through a profound developmental milestone—when they have no experience of doing so at all—these "retrojections" do not give the slightest warning that they are operative. The person "recalling" an early childhood peak experience will often describe it in terms of perspectivism, being sensitive to the role of others, taking their viewpoints, and so on—when a massive amount of research on actual children at that age *shows no evidence of any of those capacities at all.* Furthermore, on the occasions when an early childhood or even infantile recollection is shown to be veridical (e.g., when I was 8 months old, mother got very ill), those are often merely sensorimotor imprints that can be resurrected and then retrofitted with adult perspectives.

My point is simply that, no matter how authentic might be some of the realms "peeked" into with a childhood peak experience, the *interpretation* and *expression* of those realms can only occur through whatever structures (linguistic, cognitive, moral, etc.) *are actually present*, and this does not deny, but does considerably complicate, the existence of "childhood spirituality."

3. See *The Eye of Spirit.* For one version of this view, see T. Armstrong, "Transpersonal experience in childhood," *Journal of Transpersonal Psychology* 16, 2 (1984), pp. 207–31. Note that most of his examples are monological experiences (preconventional), pointing out again the difficulty in calling them "spiritual."
4. Notice that these "glory" potentials are not something that are part of the infantile stage itself—they are lingering impressions from other, *higher* spheres. And therefore, what is *recaptured* in enlightenment is *not* the infantile structure itself, but the actual higher spheres. The Romantic notion that the infantile self *is itself* a primordial paradise remains therefore deeply mistaken. See also the "collapsing fallacy" on which the Romantic agenda rests; note 9.18.
5. See *The Eye of Spirit*, chap. 6, for a full discussion of this topic and a critique of Washburn's Romantic view, which depends on the collapsing fallacy (see note 9.18).
6. For a summary of this data, see Jenny Wade's *Changes of Mind.*

   It should be emphasized that this deeper psychic self (or the subtle soul), which might be present in infancy, is *not* a causal or nondual self; it is not any sort of enlightened self or primal ground, but simply an intermediate level of the separate-self sense which migrates until Enlightenment. Romantic eulogizing of this separate-self sense is unwarranted.

7. None of this "watching from afar," however, is generally expressed by children at that time, possibly for the reasons I outlined in note 11.2 (they have not yet developed the frontal structures that could do the expressing). For this reason, none of this "deeper psychic" shows up on any of the tests developmentalists use. Nonetheless, a small amount of controversial evidence, summarized by Wade, suggest that this deeper psychic awareness undergoes a U-development, essentially the same U-development that tends to mark some of the subtle lines (as indicated, e.g., on chart 4b). As suggested in the text, however, this is not an unalloyed experience of the deeper psychic, because the structures that house it are still preconventional and egocentric. Only with the direct and permanent realization of the deeper psychic—which occurs at the psychic stage (or fulcrum-7)—does the soul itself begin to shine forth in its undiminished, unfiltered radiance.

Chapter 12. Sociocultural Evolution

1. For my numerous criticisms of the perennial philosophy, the classical Great Chain, and the traditionalists, see *One Taste*, June 5 entry; the Introductions to CW 2, 3, and 4; *The Eye of Spirit*, chaps. 1 and 2; and numerous entries in *Sex, Ecology, Spirituality*, 2nd ed. (CW 6).
2. See chap. 1 text ("The Great Nest Is a Potential, Not a Given") and notes 1.5, 8.2, and 12.1; see also the Introduction to CW 2, and *Sex, Ecology, Spirituality*, 2nd ed. (CW 6).
3. See *Sex, Ecology, Spirituality*, 2nd ed. (CW 6).
4. For an extensive discussion of this theme, see *The Marriage of Sense and Soul*.
5. See *Up from Eden*; and *Sex, Ecology, Spirituality*, 2nd ed. (CW 6); and *A Brief History of Everything* for a full discussion of this theme. I am talking here about collective evolution; individuals can advance on their own heroic efforts (usually in micro-communities).
6. Alternatively, the shaman might simply be at the magic level and have a temporary peak experience of the subtle realm. Should the shaman progress beyond random peak experiences, and begin to develop a competence in these temporary subtle journeys, even though his typical self remains at the magical structure, this indicates that, as per the discussion in Different Types of Cognitive Lines, the shaman is showing development in the subtle line, even while the gross line remains preformal and magical. In both of these cases, the subtle realm is distorted into preconventional and egocentric/power interpretations (as discussed in the text). But I also hold open the possibility, introduced in the text, that at least some shamans demonstrated frontal development into postconventional realms, which certainly seems possible, at least beginning with the late Paleolithic and Mesolithic (if there is evidence, as Habermas, Dobert, Nunner-Winkler et al. believe, that some individuals in foraging societies developed formop, I see no reason that a few could not have developed into postformal modes).
7. See Walsh, R. *The Spirit of Shamanism*.

8. Social systems theory remains indispensable for understanding the Lower-Right quadrant. The work of Talcott Parsons (and Robert Merton) is well-known, and still quite impressive. I would like especially to recommend the brilliant works of Jeffrey Alexander (*Theoretical Logic in Sociology*, four volumes; and *Twenty Lectures*) and Niklas Luhmann (especially *Social Systems*).
9. See, e.g., Thomas Sowell, *Marxism*; Leszek Kolakowski, *Main Currents of Marxism*, 3 vols.; A. Callari et al., *Marxism in the Postmodern Age*.
10. During the past several decades, it has been common for liberal scholars to assume that any sort of evolutionary theory of necessity marginalizes various peoples, and thus prevents their gaining the natural freedom that is every being's birthright. It has increasingly become obvious, however, that freedom is perhaps best defined as the freedom to have access to every level in the extraordinary spectrum of consciousness. The only way those levels become available is through growth and development and unfolding, and thus those liberal scholars who have shunned evolution have shunned an access to freedom for all of those whom they wished to protect. (See Afro-Caribbean specialist Maureen Silos's brilliant exposure of the standard liberal stance as being, in fact, highly reactionary, and evolutionary thinking as being the truly liberal stance, "The Politics of Consciousness," in J. Crittenden, *Kindred Visions*.)
11. G. Feuerstein, "Jean Gebser's Structures of Consciousness and Ken Wilber's Spectrum Model," *Kindred Visions*, edited by Crittenden et al. (forthcoming). For my critique of Gebser's archaic structure, see *Sex, Ecology, Spirituality*, 2nd ed. (CW6), note 17 for chap. 14.
12. Combs maintains that, in *Up from Eden*, I allow stages to be skipped, overlooking the fact that I presented each epoch as an average, not an absolute; and overlooking the fact that numerous altered states (or peak experiences) are available at all stages (both of those points are explained in the text and in note 12.14; see also the introduction to CW 2).

    Combs then presents a three-dimensional model of consciousness that is in many ways indistinguishable from my three-variable model of structures, states, and realms, which Combs calls "structures, states, and planes." He claims that his model takes these three variables into account, and that my model does not, and thus he offers his model to "correct the liabilities" in mine, whereas in many ways he has simply restated my model. I am not accusing Combs of borrowing my model; I believe he arrived at it in a largely independent fashion. What I find lamentable is that Combs strongly claims that I do not deal with structures, states, and realms; this is an egregious misrepresentation of my work.

    As for the particular version of this three-variable model that Combs presents, I believe it has some drawbacks, although I appreciate the care he has obviously given it; and I find it, on balance, to be a welcome addition to the field.

    To start with the liabilities, Combs presents his version of states and structures by, in my opinion, getting the definitions of states and structures backwards. Instead of seeing that a given state (such as drug, waking, dreaming) can contain many different structures (e.g., the waking state can contain magic, mythic, and rational structures), Combs says that a given structure supports many different states (which is rarely true: the rational structure, for example, does not usually support the drunken state, the dream state, the meditative state, etc.).

This confusion of states and structures leads him to likewise misrepresent both the Vedanta and Mahayana systems because it forces him to confuse sheaths/levels with body/states. For example, in his Table 1 in chapter 6, he presents the Vedanta as giving five levels and a corresponding five bodies, but the Vedanta actually gives five levels and only three bodies, because the subtle body (corresponding with the dream state) actually supports three of the levels (or structures), as I explained in the text (see chap. 1). In other words, because Combs believes that one structure can house many states (when it is mostly the other way around), he does not see that in Vedanta one state supports several levels/structures/sheaths, so he is forced to misread the Vedanta as giving five bodies instead of three. For instance, he says "Next is the subtle body, termed the *vijnanamaya kosha. . . .*" But in fact the subtle body is termed *sukshma-sharira*, and it *supports* the vijanamayakosha, the manomayakosha, and the pranamayakosha—in other words, *three* levels/structures supported by *one* state/body. The sukshma-sharira is the vehicle of, for example, the dream state and the bardo state. Thus the correct view is that one state can support several levels or structures or sheaths, and not the other way around, as Combs has it.

This confusion is confirmed when Combs compares the Vedanta with the Mahayana Buddhist system of the Trikaya (Dharmakaya, Sambhogakaya, and Nirmanakaya). He says, "The highest is the dharmakaya or the 'body of the great order.' This 'body' is identical with transcendental reality and seems to correspond to the level of the Self in Vedanta. The second is the sambhogakaya or 'body of delight' which seems analogous to the causal level, the sheath of bliss of Vedanta. The third body is the nirmanakaya or 'body of transformation,' which corresponds to the physical body itself. Comparing this three-part system to Vedanta discloses several of the levels or sheaths to be missing" (p. 125). Actually, nothing is missing. Combs has again confused body/states with levels/structures. As the discussion on Highest Yoga Tantra makes clear (see chap. 10), the Mahayana/Vajrayana system has 9 levels/structures of consciousness (the five senses, the manovijnana, the manas, the alayavijnana, and the pure alaya); treating the five senses as one level gives us five *levels*, just like the Vedanta. Further, the Three Bodies of Buddha are similar to the three bodies of Vedanta—gross, subtle, and causal, and they are all explicitly correlated with waking, dreaming, and deep sleep *states*, respectively. Again, by confusing levels/structures and states/bodies, Combs compares the three bodies of Mahayana with the five levels of Vedanta, and finds the Mahayana is "missing" levels; instead of comparing the five levels with the five levels, and the three bodies with the three bodies, and actually finding them in general agreement with each other as to *both* levels/structures and bodies/states.

Of course, one is free to define "state" and "structure" any way one wishes, as long as one is consistent, and Combs has given considerable care in doing so; and he is grappling with some very important issues in what I found a refreshing way. But I believe this general confusion haunts his model, and thus in my opinion his treatment, within his model, of my work, Gebser's, and Aurobindo's suffers. With my model, he ends up *equating* the basic structures with the separate developmental lines running through them (including worldviews). He thus collapses Gebser's structures (and their worldviews) with my basic structures, and he fails to differentiate the separate developmental lines involved with each. Combs thus talks as if by "structure" I mean only the narrow Gebserian structure, whereas for me "structure" is a term for any stable pattern in any level or line. When I then use the *worldviews* of the lower levels (such as archaic, magic, and mythic, which are not based merely on Gebser but on Piaget, Werner, Kernberg, Neumann, etc.), and I point out that development can *continue into higher levels* (such as psychic and subtle), Combs draws the erroneous conclusion that I am equating Gebserian structures with Vedanta planes, whereas there is simply a spectrum of consciousness (levels/structures of selfhood and levels/structures of reality)—and Gebser is addressing only some lines of a few of the lower-to-middle levels.

Tying "structures" to the narrow Gebserian version of structures (which Combs tends to do in his own model) means that, for Combs, his "structures" stop at Gebser's integral level, so that, as far as I can tell, *there are no genuinely transpersonal structures in Combs's model* (he only has *states* for the higher realms), making it impossible to account for permanent structural development into any of the transpersonal levels or sheaths.

Combs says he needs to do this, in part, because my "linear" model doesn't account for cross experiences (such as mythic level experience of subtle states), overlooking the extensive discussion I gave of just that phenomenon in *A Sociable God* (1983), where I outlined a grid (which is discussed in the text as: psychic, subtle, causal, or nondual *states* interpreted by archaic, magic, mythic, or mental *structures*) that is quite similar to the grid Combs presents in Table 4 of chapter 9. Those two dimensions or variables (structures and states), when combined with the fact that the subject of one level can take an object from another level (realm or plane)—as happens with different modes of knowing, art, etc. (see notes 1.3, 1.5, 1.9, 1.10, 8.1, 8.2., 8.39)—gives us *three largely independent variables* (structures, states, and realms) that have been part of my model starting with phase-2 in 1983 (those three variables have remained intrinsic in phase-3 and phase-4). I do not in least mind the fact that Combs is using a similar model with these three variables to account for the many facets of consciousness and its evolution; I regret the fact that he has to portray my model as lacking them.

In short, I believe that working with the basic structures, streams, states, self, and the realms/planes of the Great Nest of Being, gives us a multidimensional model that already accounts for all of the items that drove Combs to postulate his model, and it does so without his occasional misrepresentation of the Eastern systems and what seems to be confusions about states and structures. Moreover, my full model sets all of these variables in the context of the four quadrants (see note 8.39), which Combs seems to disregard completely, although he references *Sex, Ecology, Spirituality.*

Let me repeat, however, that Combs is grappling with some very important issues in his approach, and I believe we share much common ground. He does not, however, treat my work in a very comprehensive fashion, so his pronouncements on my material should be taken with caution. See notes 1.3, 1.5, 1.9, 1.10, 8.1, 8.2., 8.39.

13. For a fuller discussion of these themes, see *The Eye of Spirit*, chapter 2; *Sex, Ecology, Spirituality*, 2nd ed. (CW 6); and *A Brief History of Everything*. For various theories of macrohistory, see Galtung and Inayatullah, *Macrohistory and Macrohistorians*.

14. A few critics have claimed that this distinction (average and advanced) means stages are being skipped (i.e., if the overall general stages are archaic, magic, mythic, rational, psychic, subtle, causal, and nondual, how could somebody in a magic culture have a psychic experience without skipping stages?). Let me repeat the many reasons this is not a problem: (1) The average mode means just that, an *average*—any number of individuals can be above or below that average. We saw that Habermas believes that even in foraging societies, a few individuals had access to formal operational cognition; I have suggested that it is therefore completely plausible that a few individuals went even further and had access to postformal cognition, especially in its earliest transpersonal stages as psychic, and these individuals were, of course, the shamans (thus, stages are not being skipped). (2) Even if that type of higher structural development turns out not to be the case, there are two other intrinsic mechanisms that allowed the most advanced modes to reach considerably beyond the average, without violating stages where they apply. One is the existence of *peak experiences*. We have seen that virtually anybody, at virtually any stage of development, has access to various types of transpersonal peak experiences (psychic, subtle, causal, nondual). The contours of the shamanic voyage strongly suggest the presence of psychic/subtle level peak experiences, and these do not violate any stages. (3) If these peak experiences began to be mastered at will by a shaman—and there is evidence that this occasionally happened—this is evidence for, not just random or spontaneous peak experiences, but *development in the subtle line*, which can, we have hypothesized (see chap. 9), proceed *alongside* developments in the gross (even if the gross remains at the magical structure); and thus, again, no stages are being skipped.

Any or all of those three items explain why stages are not being skipped; they are either being followed (as in #1), or they are being followed while other, parallel events are also occurring (#2 and #3). Even a shaman (or an individual today) who is, say, at moral stage 3 in the frontal line, and who has repeated shamanic/psychic peak experiences (in the subtle line), will still, if he or she develops further morally, have to move to moral stage 4, then 5, and so on. There is no evidence whatsoever that any sorts of peak experiences, no matter how profound, allow those frontal stages to be skipped or bypassed (altered states might accelerate the rate at which the frontal stages unfold, but there is no evidence that those stages can be altered; see *The Eye of Spirit* for substantial research on this topic).

None of the three explanations given above violates any of those facts; and in no case are genuine stages *in any line* being skipped. There are either higher developments in one line, or parallel lines, and/or states occurring.

15. See note 12.14. The shamans were the earliest masters of bodily ecstatic energies—as with Mircea Eliade's classic definition of shamanism as "technique of ecstasy"—the earliest yogis, in that sense—and rode these energies and altered states to realms of the upper and underworlds (gross-to-psychic).

Joseph Campbell, in the *Historical Atlas of World Mythology*, gives what is probably one of the earliest, proto-kundalini experiences very likely common in even somc of the earliest shamanic voyages. "The supreme occasion for the activation of the ntum is the trance dance. The exertion of the ceaselessly circling dancers heats their medicine power, which . . . they experience as a physical substance in the pit of the stomach. The women's singing, the men say, 'awakens their hearts,' and the eventually their portion of ntum becomes so hot that it boils. 'The men say it boils up their spinal columns into their heads, and is so strong when it does this . . . , that it overcomes them and they lose their senses.' "

Those early yogic trances would be more extensively explored in subsequent yogic development and evolution. What we see with these "ntum experiences" is, I believe, an example of the early stages of the subtle line of development (especially psychic). This subtle line—the entire Sambhogakaya realm—would be explored in greater depth and detail by subsequent yogic paths; but these shamanic voyages are clearly in that lineage of early kundalini psychic-realm voyages. Eliade, *Shamanism*; Walsh, *The Spirit of Shamanism;* Harner, *The Way of the Shaman.*

16. See *Up from Eden*. Elements of shamanic trance mastery were taken up in subsequent yogic disciplines, refined, transcended and included (see note 12.15). Shamanic techniques, in themselves, are still powerful tools for accessing psychic domains, and a few modern explorers of consciousness have found them useful in that regard. See especially the works of Michael Harner.

Chapter 13. From Modernity to Postmodernity

1. To differentiate art, morals, and science is to differentiate I, we, and it. Differentiating I and we meant that individuals had rights and freedoms that could not be violated by the collective, the state, the monarchy—which was a strong contributor to the rise of democracy, abolition, and feminism. See *The Marriage of Sense and Soul* and *A Brief History of Everything* for a full discussion of this theme.
2. See chap. 9 of *The Marriage of Sense and Soul* for a fuller presentation. See also *Sex, Ecology, Spirituality*, 2nd ed. (CW 6), for critical discussions of postmodernists such as Heidegger, Foucault, and Derrida (consult index).

3. See also *Sex, Ecology, Spirituality,* 2nd ed. (CW 6), chaps. 4, 12, 13, 14.
4. See *The Marriage of Sense and Soul* for Kuhn's embrace of scientific progress. No wonder John Searle had to beat back this extreme constructivist approach in his wonderful *The Construction of Social Reality*—as opposed to "the social construction of reality"—the idea being that cultural realities are constructed on a base of correspondence truth which grounds the construction itself, without which no construction at all could get under way in the first place. Once again, we can accept the partial truths of postmodernism—interpretation and constructivism are crucial ingredients of the Kosmos, all the way down—without going overboard and attempting to reduce all other quadrants and all other truths to that partial glimpse.
5. Why is modern philosophy largely the philosophy of language? Because phylogenetic consciousness is starting to go transverbal in many important ways, and thus consciousness can look at the verbal realm, which it could not do when it was embedded in it. There is also an irony here: most postmodern philosophy therefore came out of literature and language departments in universities, not philosophy departments, which accounts for both its freshness and its naiveté.
6. The standard Enlightenment (and flatland) notion was that a word gains meaning simply because it *points to* or *represents* an object. It is a purely monological and empirical affair. The isolated subject looks at an equally isolated object (such as a tree), and then simply chooses a word to represent the sensory object. This, it was thought, is the basis of all genuine knowledge. Even with complex scientific theories, each theory is simply a *map* that *represents* the objective territory. If the correspondence is accurate, the map is true; if the correspondence is inaccurate, the map is false. Science—and all true knowledge, it was believed—was a straightforward case of *accurate representation*, accurate mapmaking. "We make pictures of the empirical world," as Wittgenstein would soon put it, and if the pictures match, we have the truth.

   This is the so-called *representation paradigm*, which is also known as *the fundamental Enlightenment paradigm*, because it was the general theory of knowledge shared by most of the influential philosophers of the Enlightenment, and thus modernity in general. Modern philosophy is usually "representational," which means trying to form a correct representation of the world. This representational view is also called "the mirror of nature," because it was commonly believed that the ultimate reality was sensory nature and philosophy's job was to picture or mirror this reality correctly.

   It was not the existence or the usefulness of representation that was the problem; representational knowledge is a perfectly appropriate form of knowing for many purposes. Rather, it was the aggressive and violent attempt to reduce all knowledge to empirical representation that constituted the disaster of modernity—the reduction of translogical spirit and dialogical mind to monological sensory knowing: the collapse of the Kosmos to nothing but representations of Right-Hand events.

   Saussure, with his early structuralism, gives one of the first, and still one of the most accurate and devastating, critiques of empirical theories of knowing, which, he points out, can't even account for the simple case of "the bark of a tree." The meaning doesn't come merely from *objective* pointing but from *intersubjective* structures that *cannot themselves be totally objectively pointed to.* And yet without them, there would be, and could be, no objective representation at all. All postmodern theories of knowledge are thus *post-representational.* Since they also draw more on vision-logic than on formop, they are also largely postformal. Thus: postmodern, post-representational, postformal.

7. Here, for convenience, is an edited version of the summary offered in *The Marriage of Sense and Soul* (chap. 9):

The postmodern poststructuralists took many of these profound and indispensable notions and, in carrying them to extremes, rendered them virtually useless. They didn't just *situate* individual intentionality in background cultural contexts, they tried to *erase* the individual subject altogether: "the death of man," "the death of the author," "the death of the subject"—all were naked attempts to reduce the subject (Upper Left) to nothing but intersubjective structures (Lower Left). "Language" replaced "man" as the *agent* of history. It is not I, the subject, who is now is speaking, it is nothing but impersonal language and linguistic structures speaking through me.

Thus, as only one of innumerable examples, Foucault would proclaim that "Lacan's importance comes from the fact that he showed how it is the structures, the very system of language, that speak through the patient's discourse and the symptoms of his neurosis—not the subject." In other words, Upper Left reduced to Lower Left, to what Foucault famously called "this anonymous system without a subject." And thus I, Michel Foucault, am not writing these words nor am I in any way primarily responsible for them; language is actually doing all the work (although this did not prevent I, Michel Foucault, from accepting the royalty checks written to the author that supposedly did not exist).

Put simply, the fact that each "I" is always situated in a background "We" was perverted into the notion that there is no "I" at all, only an all-pervading "We"—no individual subjects, only vast networks of intersubjective and linguistic structures. (Buddhists take note: this was in no way the notion of *anatta* or no-self, because the "I" was replaced, not with Emptiness, but with finite linguistic structures of the "We," thus multiplying, not transcending, the actual problem.)

Foucault eventually rejected the extremism of his early stance, a fact studiously ignored by extreme postmodernists. Among other spectacles, postmodernist biographers began trying to write biographies of subjects that supposedly did not exist in the first place, thus producing books that were about as interesting as having dinner without food.

For Saussure, the signifier and signified were an integrated unit (a holon); but the postmodern poststructuralists—and this was one of their most defining moves—shattered this unity by attempting to place almost exclusive emphasis on sliding chains of *signifiers* alone. The signifiers—the actual material or written marks—were given virtually exclusive priority. They were thus severed from both their signifieds and their referents, and these chains of sliding or "free-floating" signifiers were therefore said to be anchored in nothing but power, prejudice, or ideology. (We see again the extreme constructivism so characteristic of postmodernism: signifiers are not anchored in any truth or reality outside of themselves, but simply create or construct all realities, a fact that, if true, could not be true.)

Sliding chains of signifiers: this is the essential postmodern poststructuralist move. This is postSTRUCTURAL, because it starts with Saussure's insights into the network-like structure of linguistic signs, which partially construct as well as partially represent; but POSTstructural, because the signifiers are cut loose from any sort of anchoring at all. There is no objective truth (only interpretations), and thus, according to extreme postmodernists, signifiers are grounded in nothing but power, prejudice, ideology, gender, race, colonialism, speciesism, and so on (a performative contradiction that would mean that this theory itself must also be anchored in nothing but power, prejudice, etc., in which case it is just as vile as the theories it despises). Once again, important truths, taken to extremes, became self-deconstructing. We wish to include the truths of both the Upper-Left and Lower-Left quadrants, without attempting to reduce one to the other, which violates the rich fabric of those domains. We wish to stress the endlessly holonic nature of consciousness, and not only one version of it.

8. *On Deconstruction*, p. 215; my italics.
9. See Taylor, *Sources of the Self* and *Hegel*.
10. This is why one of the ways we can date the beginning of the general postmodern mood is with the great Idealists (note that Derrida does exactly that; Hegel, he says, is the last of the old or the first of the new).
11. To follow the genealogy of postmodernism is to follow an attempt to reintroduce the interiors and interpretation, through a series of reversals that ended up denying all of its original aims. We saw that postmodernism began as a way to reintroduce interpretation, depth, and interiors to the Kosmos—the world is not merely reflected by consciousness, it is co-created by consciousness; the world is not merely a perception but an interpretation. This emphasis on interpretation was eventually taken to extremes—there is nothing outside the text—and this removed objective truth from the postmodern script. Once truth was suspect, there was no way to finally judge anything, and the interior domains completely collapsed into nothing but subjective preferences. Depth collapsed entirely into equivalent surfaces and aperspectival madness—no within, no deep—and extreme postmodernism fell into the intense gravitational field of flatland. The genealogy of deconstructive postmodernism is a genealogy of despair, nihilism, and narcissism. The bright promise of a constructive postmodernism was largely derailed, for reasons explored in *Boomeritis* and the Introduction to CW 7. For examples of constructive postmodernism, see the excellent series of postmodern anthologies edited by David Ray Griffin (SUNY Press). The integral psychology that I am presenting is offered in the spirit of a constructive postmodernism.
12. See *Sex, Ecology, Spirituality*, 2nd ed. (CW 6), for a full discussion of this theme.

Chapter 14. The 1-2-3 of Consciousness Studies

1. See N. Humphrey, *Consciousness Regained*; K. Jaegwon, *Supervenience and the Mind*; M. Levin, *Metaphysics and the Mind-Body Problem*; G. Madell, *Mind and Materialism*; C. McGinn, *The Problem of Consciousness*; T. Nagel, *Mortal Questions* and *The View from Nowhere*; G. Strawson, *Mental Reality*; R. Swinburne, *The Evolution of the Soul*; A. Whitehead, *Process and Reality*; S. Braude, *First Person Plural*; C. Birch, *Feelings*; K. Campbell, *Body and Mind*; Paul Churchland, *Matter and Consciousness*; D. Dennett, *Consciousness Explained*; R. Penrose, *The Emperor's New Mind*; Popper and Eccles, *The Self and Its Brain*; D. Griffin, *Unsnarling the World-Knot*; W. Robinson, *Brains and People*; W. Seager, *Metaphysics of Consciousness*; R. Sperry, *Science and Moral Priority*; J. Searle, *The Rediscovery of the Mind* and *Mind, Language, and Society*; W. Hart, *The Engines of the Soul*; C. Hartshorne, *Whitehead's Philosophy*; O. Flannagan, *Consciousness Reconsidered*; R. Forman, *The Problem of Pure Consciousness*; G. Edelman, *Bright Air, Brilliant Fire* and *The Remembered Present*; J. Eccles, *How the Self Controls Its Brain*; Gazzaniga (ed.), *The Cognitive Neurosciences*; Patricia Churchland, *Neurophilosophy*; S. Pinker, *How the Mind Works*; Baars, *In the Theater of Consciousness*; Hunt, *On the Nature of Consciousness*; Scott, *Stairway to the Mind*; Deacon, *The Symbolic Species*; Finger, *Origins of Neuroscience*; Cytowic, *The Neurological Side of Neuropsychology*; Stillings et al., *Cognitive Science*; Carpenter, *Neurophysiology*; Varela et al.,*The Embodied Mind*; D. Chalmers, *The Conscious Mind*; Hameroff et al., *Toward a Science of Consciousness*; Wade, *Changes of Mind*; Block et al., *The Nature of Consciousness*; Laughlin et al., *Brain, Symbol, and Experience*; Wilber, "An Integral Theory of Consciousness," *Journal of Consciousness Studies* 4, 1 (1997), pp. 71–93 (also in CW7).
2. *Body and Mind*, p. 131.
3. See Griffin, *Unsnarling the World-Knot*, for an excellent summary of the present state of this argument. See *Sex, Ecology, Spirituality*, 2nd ed. (CW 6), for a discussion of the "major dilemma of the modern era," namely, the relation of the subjective self (consciousness) and the objective world (nature), especially chaps. 4, 12, and 13.
4. *Mental Reality*, p. 81.
5. *The Rediscovery of the Mind*, p. 30.
6. *Supervenience and Mind*, quoted in Griffin, *Unsnarling the World-Knot*, p. 4.
7. *Mortal Questions*, p. 176.
8. *The Problem of Consciousness*, pp. 1–7.
9. *Mind and Materialism*, quoted in Griffin, *Unsnarling the World-Knot*, p. 3.
10. *Of Clocks and Clouds*, quoted in Griffin, *Unsnarling the World-Knot*, p. 3.
11. *The Self and Its Brain*, p. 105.
12. See note 15.
13. To say that subject and object are two aspects of an underlying reality begs the question as to what this underlying reality is, since it cannot be stated in terms that are not merely combinations of "subjective" and "objective." Either this

third entity, the underlying reality, has subjective and objective properties, or it does not. If it does, is not really underlying; if it does not, it is not really unifying. Nagarjuna, and other nondual philosopher-sages, are adamant that the mind-body problem cannot be solved on a rational level. See *The Eye of Spirit*, chap. 3, for a full discussion of this topic.

14. See *The Eye of Spirit*, chap. 3.

15. More specifically, the mind-body problem involves three dilemmas: (1) how to relate Mind (interiors) and Body (exteriors, including brain); (2) how to relate mind (interior conceptual consciousness) and body (interior feelings); and (3) how to see the final relation of Mind and Body (subject and object).

In my opinion, those three items can be approached in this fashion, respectively: (1) acknowledge that every exterior has an interior (as shown in fig. 5), which binds Mind and Body; (2) acknowledge that there are interior stages of consciousness development (also shown in fig. 5), which binds mind and body; and (3) acknowledge that there are higher levels of consciousness development, which finally unites Mind and Body (thus preventing any form of dualism). To take them in order:

1. The problem of the relation of interiors (consciousness) and exteriors (matter) is usually stated as: the fundamental units of the universe (quarks, atoms, strings, etc.) consist of entities that possess no interiors; the mind possesses an interior; since the latter evolved from the former, how can you get interiors from exteriors? Since this seems to be impossible, we must either deny the causal reality of the interiors altogether (physicalism), or we must posit a miracle of existence (dualism), wherein an entirely new type of substance (interiors) jumps into being at some point. In the early part of the modern era, when God was still around, dualism was a popular solution, because God could be called on for this miracle. In today's world, this miracle—and its seeming impossibility—is one of the major reasons most philosophers flee to physicalism.

In my view, although the exact relation of interiors and exteriors is disclosed only in the postrational stages of development (the nondual wave), we can nonetheless understand rationally that every interior has an exterior, and vice versa, as indicated in figure 5. If interior and exterior really do arise correlatively, there is no miracle required; I will argue for this in a moment. (As for the nondual stage, when it is disclosed it does indeed involve spirit, but in the most ordinary and down-to-earth way: "How miraculous this! I draw water, I carry fuel." In no case is a supernatural miracle called for.)

This part of the solution (every exterior has an interior) would appear to involve some sort of panpsychism, except that, as explained in *Sex, Ecology, Spirituality,* 2nd ed. (notes 13 and 25 for chap. 4), every major form of panpsychism equates "interiors" with a *particular type of interior* (such as feelings, awareness, soul, etc.), and then attempts to push *that* type all the way down to the fundamental units of the universe (quarks, atoms, strings, or some such), which I believe is unworkable. For me, consciousness in the broad sense is ultimately unqualifiable (Emptiness), and thus, although interiors go all the way down, no *type* of interior does. I am a pan-interiorist, not a pan-experientialist, pan-mentalist, pan-feelingist, or pan-soulist. The *forms* of the interior show developmental unfolding: from a fuzzy something-or-other (see below) to prehension to sensation to perception to impulse to image to concept to rules to rationality and so forth, but none of those go all the way down in one specific form. Most schools of panpsychism take *one* of those interiors—such as feeling or soul—and maintain that *all* entities possess it (atoms have feelings, cells have a soul) and this I categorically reject. Cells have an interior, whose form is protoplasmic irritability (fig. 5), and electrons, according to quantum mechanics, possess a "propensity to existence," but none of those are "minds" or "feelings" or "souls," but rather are merely some very early forms of interiors.

I accept, in a very general sense, the notion of Whitehead (Hartshorne, Griffin) that we can picture "prehension" as perhaps the earliest form of interiors (every interior touches—prehends—an exterior at some point, since interior and exterior mutually arise), but when that prehension is explained in terms such as feeling or emotion, I believe that is overdoing it. This is also why, when I present the four quadrants, I usually say that readers are free to push interiors down as far—or as little—as they wish. Since interiors are *ultimately* unqualifiable (in my view, every interior is basically an opening or clearing in which correlative exteriors arise; see *Sex, Ecology, Spirituality,* 2nd ed. [notes 13 and 25 for chap. 4]), and since the relation between interiors and exteriors is finally disclosed only in postrational awareness (see item 3), I am not concerned to solve the mind-body problem by arguing that interiors go all the way down (although I believe they do); the final solution lies elsewhere (see item 3). Rather, for the average presentation, I am more interested in communicating to the reader why I believe that, at least by the time we reach human beings, there are four quadrants in existence, because it is the integration of the Big Three at the human level that is the most urgent requirement, in my opinion (and that integration will eventually help to solve the mind-body problem at all levels).

The major reservation I have about Whitehead's view of prehension is that it is largely monological. Each subject or I prehends its immediate ancestors as objects or its; each I then passes into the stream as an it for the new I: I becomes it as new I prehends old I. This stream of subjects/objects is partially true, I believe, and I think Whitehead's analysis of the phases of prehension is a brilliant addition to philosophy. But Whitehead, in *arguing from human experience to atoms of experience* (which I believe is justifiable), *has not started with the correct view of human experience*, and therefore he analogously injected the wrong types of actualities into the atoms of existence. Human experience is not a monological subject grasping monological objects, but is in fact a four-quadrant affair: every subject arises only in an intersubjective space (the essence of postmodernism). In other words, the atoms of experience are four-quadrant holons, not monological holons. Whitehead, as I argued in *The Eye of Spirit* (note 11 to chap. 10), has taken flatland and made it paradigmatic for all experience.

Most Whiteheadians strongly object to my characterization of their view as largely monological, pointing out that their real stance is *relational* and *ecologi-*

cal. But ecology is monological; and systems theory is a perfect example of a relational process view that is also monological. For it is not merely that a subject prehends its objects. Rather, *intersubjectivity* is the space in which the subject prehends its objects. The We is intrinsically part of the I, not as objective prehensions, but as subjective constitutive elements. The We space in which the I arises is not simply an object for the I, but rather is the background space *in which* the I arises to prehend its objects, and which therefore partly enters the I *for the first time* as subject component, not object prehension (this part of intersubjectivity is therefore not "an object that once was subject," which is the standard Whiteheadian reworking of causality as perception, and which is indeed relational, process, ecological, and monological, in my opinion. Partially true, it is not sensitive enough to the nonreducible realities in all four quadrants, all the way down).

David Ray Griffin's *Unsnarling the World-Knot* is a superb exposition of Whitehead's view, along with Griffin's proposed solution of panexperientialistic physicalism (based on Whitehead/Hartshorne). I am in a fair amount of agreement with his presentation, except for items 1 and 3 in this endnote (I do not identify interiors with feelings; and I believe the relation of interior to exterior is only finally disclosed in transrational nondual awareness; it cannot be "thought through" as Griffin and Whitehead propose). I believe I know what Griffin means by "feeling" (prehension in the most rudimentary sense), but the word "feeling" or "experience" is just "too much" to push all the way down. Also, as I just said, I do not believe the fundamental units of human experience or the universe are monological (Griffin tells me that he does not, either; see Introduction to CW8 for our exchange on this issue).

A minor point: Griffin's line of compound individuality does not quite seem complete, in my opinion. Griffin/Whitehead's view is, of course, "a hierarchy of emergent compound individuals" (a holarchy of holons). But Griffin seems to have an evolutionary lineage that moves from atoms to macromolecules to organelles to cells to neurons to mind. Neurons are the "highest-level enduring individuals" next to mind, and mind is the prehensive experience of billions of individual neurons. This is too great a jump, in my opinion, and a more accurate view is represented in figure 5. That is, the corresponding interior of neurons is sensation; the organism with a reptilian brain stem is a true compound individual (holon), whose interior is impulse; the organism with a limbic system is a true compound individual, whose interior is emotion; the organism with a complex neocortex is a true compound individual, whose interior is conceptual mind. At each of those levels, not only do interiors prehend their corresponding exteriors, they prehend their own past (Griffin would agree with that, I believe). This appears to account not only for Mind-Body (interior-exterior) interaction, but for interior causation, interior inheritance, and mind-body interaction.

Thus, Griffin jumps from neurons to mind too quickly, in my opinion. I believe he would say that neurons are the highest-level enduring individuals prior to mind because the reptilian stem and limbic system are simply organizational aggregates, not compound individuals, which is the point I would dispute. For example, the limbic system of a horse is a highly organized system that is converted from an aggregate to an individual by the skin boundary of the horse (which is analogous to the cell membrane of a eukaryote; if the latter is a compound individual, so is the former). The limbic-system compound individual is compounded again in the neocortex compound individual—these are distinct levels of both exteriors and interiors (fig. 5). Thus the jump from neurons to mind is not as large as Griffin presents it. Many philosophers have found it very hard to go straight from neurons to rational consciousness; but instead of one huge (and puzzling) jump, we have a series of mini-jumps: from neurons to neural cord to reptilian brain stem to paleomammalian limbic system to neocortex, which seems easier to see (as is the corresponding interior development from sensation to perception to impulse to emotion to image to concept to rule to rationality)—and each of those is a holon, a true compound individual.

The worldview of physics is often used to support the notion that the fundamental units (quarks, strings, atoms) do not have interiors. I do not argue, with the panexperientialists, that atoms must have feelings, but rather that exteriors have no meaning without interiors, and that if atoms have exteriors, they certainly have interiors. Wherever there is a boundary between physical objects—for example, between one atom and another atom—then those atoms have exteriors, and wherever there is an exterior there is an interior: you cannot have one without the other. Interior and exterior arise together with the first boundary of a universe—they are mutually arising and mutually determining—and thus, both interiors and exteriors go all the way down (as long as down has any meaning). To say that the physical universe is a universe of all exteriors and no interiors is like saying the world has all ups and no downs—it makes no sense at all. Inside and outside arise together whenever they arise; and interiors go as far down as down as has any meaning.

At the very lowest levels, insides don't have much meaning because outsides don't either: have you really looked at the reality described by quantum mechanics? At the lowest levels of existence, both inside and outside become meaningless; they dissolve in that primordial miasma in which there might not be any mind, but there isn't any matter either; and when the outside crystallizes, so does the inside: they arise together whenever they arise. Every Left has a Right, and vice versa.

I agree entirely with Leibniz/Whitehead/Hartshorne/Griffin that only the entities known as compound individuals (i.e., holons) possess a characteristic interior. Holons are different from mere heaps or aggregates, in that the former possess actual wholeness (identifiable pattern, agency, regime, etc.). Individual holons include quarks, electrons, atoms, cells, organisms, and so on (as shown in fig. 5), whose interiors include prehension, propensity, irritability, sensation, tropism, perception, impulse, image, and so on (fig. 5). Heaps, on the other hand, are holons that are accidentally thrown together (e.g., a pile of sand). Holons have agency and interiors (every whole is a part, and thus every holon has an interior and an exterior), whereas heaps do not. A *social holon* stands between the two: it is more than a heap, in that its individuals are united by patterns of relational exchange, but it is less than an individual holon in terms of the tightness of its regime: social holons do not possess a locus of self-awareness at any stage of their development (whereas higher-level individual holons have interiors that become increasingly conscious, so that at the level of human compound individuals, self-awareness is possible in individuals, but not in societies. The upper two quadrants are individual holons, the lower two quadrants are social holons. For extensive discussions of compound individuals, see *Up from Eden* and *Sex, Ecology, Spirituality,* 2nd ed.).

This simple distinction (holons have interiors, heaps do not [except for any holons that might be in the heaps]), along with the understanding that "interior" means only the correlative to any exterior (it does not mean feelings, soul, self-consciousness, etc.—which are all types of interiors) goes a long way to making pan-interiorism more palatable. The common panpsychism view (but not Whitehead/Griffin's) is that, for example, rocks have feelings or even souls, which is untenable (and is, in fact, a belief of the magical-animistic level of development, not the nondual). Rocks as heaps have no interiors (there is the inside of a rock, but that is just more exteriors); rocks, however, do contain atoms, which are holons, and those holons have one of the very lowest types of interiors (propensities and patterns that endure across time)—but in no case does a rock have "feelings," let alone a soul. (A rock is a manifestation of spirit, but does not itself contain a soul.)

Both interiors and exteriors develop or co-evolve; and in both lines, there is *emergence*, with the introduction of some degree of genuine *novelty* or *creativity* at each stage (which a physicalist calls "inexplicable" and an integralist calls "Eros"). Many physicalists (from Dennett to Alwyn Scott) agree with *emergent evolution*, but they try to derive *interior* consciousness by having it pop out at the top level of *exterior* development (because they believe only exteriors are real, and the "consciousness pops out at the top" is a concession to the hard-core intuition that consciousness exists—which is then explained as "nothing but" the functional fluke of complex exteriors; or more rarely, as a dualism). That is, as Eccles put it, "Just as in biology there are new emergent properties of matter, so at the extreme level of organized complexity of the cerebral cortex, there arises still further emergence, namely the property of being associated with a conscious experience." But the Left is not a higher level of the Right, it is the interior of the Right at every level, and both go all the way down (see *Sex, Ecology, Spirituality,* 2nd ed., chap. 4, and "An Integral Theory of Consciousness"). Nagel is quite right that a subject that has a point of view simply cannot arise out of exterior objects that do not. (Griffin calls this the "emergence category mistake," which I avoid by seeing that interiors and exteriors arise correlatively.)

On the other hand, says Nagel, "if one travels too far down the phylogenetic tree, people gradually shed their faith that there is experience there at all." Quite right, which is why I do not push experience (or feelings or souls or any specific *type* of interior) all the way down; I simply maintain that wherever there are exteriors, there are interiors, and when it comes the interiors of the lower levels, I don't think we are really able to say what is "in" them with any sort of assurance. I cannot prove what is in them for the same reason a physicalist cannot disprove them.

Dennett, incidentally, sees a type of sentience emerging with amoebas. I am willing to settle for that, not because I am being wishy-washy about levels lower than that, but because when we get to the atomic and subatomic realm, the mathematical formalisms of quantum mechanics become much weirder than can be imagined, and most physicists disagree strongly on what it all means anyway. I myself believe atoms have interiors, but I'm not going to argue the point to the death, simply because the universe gets too fuzzy at that level, and because the actual relation of interiors to exteriors is determined in the transrational, not prerational, realms. Human beings *can* know the transrational realms directly and immediately, whereas the subatomic realms are understood, if at all, only by abstruse mathematical formalisms, which are still in process of being formulated.

2. By acknowledging that the interiors develop (as do their exteriors), we can see that mind (interior mental consciousness) and body (interior feelings) are related as transcend and include (as shown in the Upper-Left quadrant of fig. 5, in figures such as 1 and 8, and in all of the charts showing interior development). The mind dangling in midair, as in figure 13, is plugged back into its roots in the felt body. This is explored in more detail in *Sex, Ecology, Spirituality*, 2nd ed., chaps. 12 and 13.

Interior development, precisely because it is composed of holons (as is exterior development), is composed of a series of wholes that become parts of subsequent wholes, indefinitely (as we saw, for example: sensorimotor is a whole cognition that becomes part of concrete operational, which is a whole cognition that becomes part of formop, which is a whole cognition that becomes part of vision-logic, and so on).

Nagel implies that perhaps the major problem with any sort of pan-interiorism is that we lack a conception of "a mental whole-part relation" that could explain the hard-core intuition of *the unity of experience* (i.e., how "a single self can be composed of many selves"). But we have seen innumerable examples of the fact that interior experience is composed of streams of holons, of whole/parts, of wholes that pass into parts of succeeding wholes in a cohesive and seamless fashion. This is true of the self-stream as well (the subject of one stage becomes an object of the next—the whole proximate self of one stage becomes part of the distal at the next, so that at *every* stage "a single self is composed of many selves"). In each case "the many become one, and are increased by one"—Whitehead's famous dictum. Whitehead is discussing micro prehension, but the dictum is true for macro stages as well, since the former is the basis of the latter, and both are simply yet another version of *transcend and include*. Nagel's major objection, in other words, seems to be handled by the consensus conclusions of developmental psychology.

3. By acknowledging higher levels of development, including the nondual stages, the final relation of Mind and Body (interior and exterior, subject and object) is disclosed in a clear and satisfactory fashion: Mind and Nature are

both movements of Spirit, which is why there is neither dualism nor reductionism. This is discussed in more detail in *Sex, Ecology, Spirituality,* 2nd ed., chaps. 12, 13, and 14.

The "hard problem"—the jump to qualia (i.e., how can exterior quantities give rise to interior qualities?)—is finally solved, not by seeing that every exterior has an interior (item 1), since that merely says they are correlative (and leaves the hard problem still pretty hard)—but by *developing* to the nondual realm, whereupon the problem is radically (dis)solved. The solution is what is seen in satori, not anything that can be stated in rational terms (unless one has had a satori, and then rational terms will work fine). The reason the hard problem cannot be solved—and has not yet been solved—in rational and empirical terms is that the solution does not exist at those levels. Philosophical geniuses trying to solve the mind-body problem at that level have failed (by their own accounts) not because they are stupid, but because it can't be solved at that level, period. See *The Eye of Spirit,* rev. ed. (CW 7), chap. 11.

16. *Journal of Consciousness Studies* 4, 1 (1997), pp. 71–93.
17. See Gazzaniga (ed.), *The Cognitive Neurosciences*; P. Churchland, *Neurophilosophy*; Edelman, *Bright Air, Brilliant Fire* and *The Remembered Present*; Pinker, *How the Mind Works*; Baars, *In the Theater of Consciousness*; Hunt, *On the Nature of Consciousness*; Scott, *Stairway to the Mind*; Deacon, *The Symbolic Species*; Finger, *Origins of Neuroscience*; Cytowic, *The Neurological Side of Neuropsychology*; Stillings et al., *Cognitive Science*; Carpenter, *Neurophysiology.*

    Not that all of those approaches are reductionistic; but for approaches to consciousness (mind and brain) that are avowedly nonreductionistic, see, e.g., Chalmers, *The Conscious Mind*; Hameroff et al., *Toward a Science of Consciousness*; Griffin, *Unsnarling the World-Knot*; Wade, *Changes of Mind*; Block et al., *The Nature of Consciousness*; Laughlin et al., *Brain, Symbol, and Experience*; Wilber, "An Integral Theory of Consciousness," *Journal of Consciousness Studies* 4, 1 (1997), pp. 71–93 (also in CW7). See especially Varela et al., *The Embodied Mind*, and my constructive criticism of it in *Sex, Ecology, Spirituality,* 2nd ed., chap. 14, note 1.
18. *The View from Within*, p. 2.
19. See Robert Forman's excellent, "What Does Mysticism Have to Teach Us About Consciousness?," in *Journal of Consciousness Studies.* 5, 2 (1998), pp. 185–202. Forman is one of the theorists mentioned who is also alive to the importance of stages of development. See also his *The Problem of Pure Consciousness, The Innate Capacity, Meister Eckhart*, and *Mysticism, Mind, Consciousness.*
20. In present-day ontogeny, there are two different senses in which we can speak of third-person (or Right-Hand) development. In individuals, there is the growth of the Upper-Right quadrant itself: the growth of the biological organism, neuronal pathways, brain structures, and so on. This growth and development is investigated by biology, neurophysiology, and organic systems theory, for example (see note 14.17). Holons in this quadrant grow, develop, and

evolve (as do holons in all quadrants), and that development can be investigated using empirical sciences. These objective holons and their behavior can be approached with the natural sciences, and hence are "third-person" in that sense—they are development *in* the Right-Hand domains.

But there is also the growth, in individual consciousness (Upper Left), of the capacity to cognitively grasp objective, Right-Hand domains, and this cognitive capacity (of the Upper Left to grasp Right-Hand objects) is the capacity studied by Piaget and by most cognitive psychologists. "Cognition," recall from the text, is defined by most Western researchers as the capacity to grasp objective phenomena, and this capacity (of the Upper Left to grasp Right-Hand objects) grows and evolves from sensorimotor to preop to conop to formop. This is the development, in the first-person individual subject, of the capacity to accurately grasp third-person objects, and thus this is the second sense in which we can speak of the growth of third-person consciousness.

When I say that in individuals, aesthetics, morals, and science all evolve (or that there is development in first-person, second-person, and third-person consciousness), "science" or "third-person" is meant in both senses—the growth of the objective organism (as disclosed by science, neurobiology, etc.), and the interior growth of the cognitive (scientific) capacity to grasp objects. (This is another example of the difference between levels of self and levels of reality, or structures and realms/planes—or again, growth in the epistemology of the subject, and growth in the objects that are known, ontology. Unless otherwise stated, I generally mean both, although context will tell.)

Of course, both first-person and third-person consciousness exist interrelated with networks of second-person, intersubjective structures, and these, too, grow and develop (i.e., the quadrants *themselves* develop, and the *subject's* capacity to grasp those quadrants develops). In other words, all of these quadrants are intimately interrelated (e.g., the growth in the other quadrants—such as biological neuronal pathways and intersubjective structures of discourse—are requisite for the subject to even be able grasp these other quadrants).

The integral psychology that I am presenting argues for an integrated approach to development in all of those quadrants—more precisely, an "all-level, all-quadrant" approach: following all of the levels and lines in all of the quadrants. This means following both the growth *in* each quadrant, and the growth in the capacity *of* the subject to grasp each quadrant (i.e., the growth in the subject's capacity to grasp its own subjective quadrant and the other quadrants as well). This means following the self's growth *in relation* to three environments or three worlds (the Big Three), namely, its relation to its own *subjective* world of inner drives, ideals, self-concepts, aesthetics, states of consciousness, etc.; its relation to the *intersubjective* world of symbolic interaction, dialectical discourse, mutual understanding, normative structures, etc.; and its relation to the *objective* world of material objects, states of affairs, scientific systems, cognitive objects, etc. Each of those evolves from prepersonal to personal to transpersonal waves (i.e., each of the quadrants evolves, or can evolve, through all of the levels in the Great Nest, body to mind to psychic to subtle to causal to nondual), and thus an all-level, all-quadrant approach follows the developments of all of the levels and lines in all of the quadrants.

(I am simplifying the lines of development to the three major ones: aesthetics/subjective, morals/intersubjective, and science/objective, but the actual number of lines in each of the quadrants is quite numerous: in the subjective or UL domain we have seen upwards of two dozen developmental lines, for example. All of those are implied in the simple formula, "all of the levels and lines in all of the quadrants," or even simpler, "all-level, all-quadrant.")

Dobert, Habermas, and Nunner-Winkler ("The Development of the Self," in Broughton, *Critical Theories of Psychological Development*), have presented a model that, although it is not all-level, is admirably and impressively all-quadrant in many ways. That is, it traces the development of the self in relation to the Big Three realms (subjective, intersubjective, and objective). They attempt an integration of the Big Three domains in self identity formation, pointing out that in doing so they are also integrating three of the most influential schools of developmental psychology (Freudian, or subjective; symbolic interactionist, or intersubjective; and Piagetian cognitive psychology, or objective). This identity formation involves the development of the self (as it does in integral psychology: in my view, identification is one of the functions of the self), and thus their formulations in some ways are quite consonant with the views presented here.

"The developmental problems linked with the concept of identity formation have been dealt with in three different theoretical traditions: (1) the cognitivist psychology of development founded by Jean Piaget, (2) the social psychology of symbolic interactionism that goes back to G. H. Mead, and (3) the analytic ego psychology derived from Sigmund Freud. In all of these theoretical formulations, the developmental trend is characterized by increasing autonomy vis à vis at least one of three particular environments [the Big Three]. In other words, development is characterized by the independence the self acquires insofar as it enhances its problem-solving capacities in dealing with: (1) the reality of external nature of both manipulable objects [UR] and strategically objectified social relations [LR]; (2) the symbolic reality of behavioral expectations, cultural values, and identities . . . [LL]; and (3) the inner nature of intentional experiences and one's own body [UL], in particular, those drives that are not amenable to communication. Piaget's theory of cognitive development tackles the first aspect, Mead's theory of interactive development the second, and Freud's theory of psychosexual development the third. Certainly, we must not overestimate the convergence of the three approaches. But there is no denying the fact that the theoretical perspectives they stress complement each other" (pp. 278–79).

Indeed they do. And these Big Three domains, according to the authors, are all tied together by the *self* (as we have seen; the self is the navigator, and integrator, of all the waves and streams in the individual being). Note that the authors point out that for these three major schools, development involves *increasing autonomy* (which is one of the twenty tenets of evolution; see *Sex, Ecology, Spirituality,* 2nd ed., chap. 2.) Increasing autonomy is one of twenty tenets shown by all evolving systems, including the self—and the final Autonomy is simply the pure Self, outside of which nothing exists, which is therefore a state of full autonomy: the pure Self is the entire Kosmos in all its radiant wonder, and is fully autonomous because there is nothing outside of it. The reason that development shows increasing autonomy is that development is headed toward the ultimate Autonomy of the pure and nondual Self.

In note 10.4, I hypothesized that the self metabolizes experience to build structure, and that this is the mechanism that converts temporary states into enduring traits. I noted the broad similarity of this concept to that proposed by psychoanalytic ego psychology and Piagetian constructivism. Dobert et al. also note these similarities. "For all three theories, the transposition of external structures [and nonstructured actions] into internal structures is an important learning mechanism. Piaget speaks of 'interiorization' when schemes of action—meaning rules for the manipulative mastery of objects—are internally transposed and transformed into schemes of comprehension and thinking. Psychoanalysis and symbolic interactionism propose a similar transposition of interaction patterns into intrapsychic patterns of relations, one which they call 'internalization.' This mechanism of internalization is connected with the further principle of achieving independence—whether from external objects, reference persons, or one's own impulses—by actively repeating what one has first passively experienced" (p. 279). (Note that increasing "interiorization" is also one of the twenty tenets.)

Furthermore, the authors maintain that each of those domains, according to the preponderance of evidence, "reflects a hierarchy of increasingly complex structures" (p. 280). (Increasing complexity/structuration is one of the twenty tenets.)

Central to the model of Dobert et al. is the notion of *interactive competence*, which is the major integrating factor of the self and its development. Moreover, according to the authors, this interactive competence develops *in three major stages* (or waves), which are preconventional, conventional, and postconventional, with each growth representing an expansion of consciousness and an increase in interiorization and autonomy. "For the preschool age child, still situated cognitively at the preoperational level, the action-related sector of the symbolic universe consists primarily of individual concrete behavioral expectations and actions as well as the consequences of actions that can be understood as gratifications or sanctions. As soon as the child has learned to play social roles, that is, to participate in interactions as a competent member [conventional, mythic-membership], its symbolic universe no longer consists of actions that express isolated intentions only, for instance, wishes or wish fulfillments. Rather, the child can now understand actions as fulfillments of generalized behavioral expectations or as offenses against them. When, finally, adolescents have learned to question the validity of social roles and action norms, their symbolic universe expands once again. There now appear [postconventional] principles according to which controversial norms can be judged" (p. 298).

Unfortunately, their all-quadrant model of self-development is not all-level, and thus it falls short of a truly integral psychology. It deals only with the gross line of personal development. Nonetheless, as far as it goes, it is much more comprehensive than most available developmental models, and its insights are important contributions to any truly integral psychology.

21. See *Sex, Ecology, Spirituality,* 2nd ed. (esp. notes for chaps. 4 and 14) for a discussion of the importance—and limitations—of phenomenology.

Dobert et al. (see note 14.20) criticize phenomenology, as I have, for its incapacity to comprehend intersubjective structures not given in the immediacy of felt bodily meaning, and thus its incapacity to deal effectively with the *development* of consciousness and the social world. "Indeed, phenomenological research has a similar intention, in that it aims to capture general structures of possible social life worlds. However, from the beginning, the execution of this program was weighed down by the weakness of a method copied from the introspective approach of the philosophy of consciousness"—namely, an immediate introspection that, as useful as it is, does not spot any of the *intersubjective* structures in which subjective introspection occurs (e.g., somebody at moral stage 5 can introspect all they want, and they will never see the structure of moral stage 5). "Only the points of departure taken by competence theory in linguistics and developmental psychology have created a paradigm that combines the formal analysis of known structures with the causal analysis of observable processes" (p. 298). See also *Sex, Ecology, Spirituality,* 2nd ed. chap. 14, note 1. This is also the major problem with Whitehead's prehension: he made paradigmatic this same weakness of the philosophy of consciousness (see note 14.15).

Chapter 15. The Integral Embrace

1. It is formop, not preop or conop, that has the capacity to differentiate the value spheres. As Cook-Greuter pointed out, preop possesses first-person, conop second-person, and formop third-person, and thus only formop can differentiate all three spheres of I, we, and it (aesthetics, morals, science). Thus, to say that modernity collectively differentiated the spheres is also to say that modernity was an evolution from mythic-membership (conop-based) to perspectival-ego (formop-based). The early Greeks, who precociously developed aspects of formop and vision-logic, also famously differentiated the Good, the True, and the Beautiful, which is why they are considered, in this regard, forerunners of modernity. They did not press this rationality (with its postconventional morals) into culture on a truly widespread scale, however (or they would have ended slavery, among other things). At the same time, the most highly evolved philosopher-sages—from Plato to Plotinus to Asanga—always differentiated the Big Three (because they had access to vision-logic and beyond); but there was little support for this in the *average level* of cultural consciousness: that awaited modernity and its dignities. We might say: a Christ could see the Golden Rule (and beyond), but it took modernity to make it a law and back it with full cultural sanction.
2. This is one of the many reasons that we cannot merely say that the ontological planes of reality are lying around waiting to be perceived. Those planes coevolve

with the growing tip of consciousness, for all of them are open to evolution, which is simply Spirit-in-action in all domains. Those models that have recourse to independent ontological planes are metaphysical in the "bad" or pre-critical sense, and have not come to terms with the modern and postmodern refinements necessary to accommodate the ongoing differentiation-and-integration of all realms of being and knowing. See note 1.5.

3. For a description of the methodology of "simultracking" levels and quadrants, see "An Integral Theory of Consciousness" (CW 7). Psychology traditionally focuses on the levels and lines in the Upper-Left quadrant. Integral studies in general focus on the levels and lines in all of the quadrants. For example, lines in the Lower-Right quadrant include forces of production (from foraging to horticultural to agrarian to industrial to informational), geopolitical structures (towns, states, countries), ecosystems, written legal codes, architectural styles, modes of transportation, forms of communication technologies, etc. Lines in the Upper-Right quadrant include organic structures, neuronal systems, neurotransmitters, brainwave patterns, nutritional intake, skeletal-muscular development, etc. Lines in the Lower-Left quadrant include worldviews, intersubjective linguistic semantics, cultural values and mores, background cultural contexts, etc. The point is that, even though psychology focuses on the Upper-Left quadrant, all four quadrants are required for psychological understanding, since all four quadrants determine the state of consciousness of the individual.

Sources

"Death, Rebirth, and Meditation." In Gary Doore (ed.), *What Survives?: Contemporary Explorations of Life after Death*. Los Angeles: Jeremy P. Tarcher, 1990. Copyright ©1990 by Ken Wilber.

Foreword to Alex Grey, *The Mission of Art*. Boston: Shambhala Publications, 1998. Copyright ©1998 by Alex Grey.

Foreword to Bruce W. Scotton, Allan B. Chinen, and John R. Battista (eds.), *Textbook of Transpersonal Psychiatry and Psychology*. New York: Basic Books, 1996. Copyright ©1996 by Ken Wilber.

Foreword to Chagdud Tulku, *Lord of the Dance: The Autobiography of a Tibetan Lama*. City: Padma Publishing, 1992. Copyright ©1992 by Chagdud Tulku. Reprinted with permission.

Foreword to M. J. Ryan (ed.), *The Fabric of the Future: Women Visionaries Illuminate the Path to Tomorrow* (Berkeley: Conari Press, 1998). Copyright ©1998 by Conari Press.

Foreword to Frances Vaughan, *Shadows of the Sacred: Seeing Through Spiritual Illusions* (Wheaton, Ill.: Quest Books, 1995). Copyright ©1995 by Frances Vaughan.

Foreword to Georg Feuerstein, *Yoga: The Technology of Ecstasy*. Los Angeles: Jeremy P. Tarcher, 1989. Copyright ©1989 by Georg Feuerstein.

Foreword to J. E. Nelson, *Healing the Split: Madness or Transcendence?: A New Understanding of the Crisis and Treatment of the Mentally Ill*. Los Angeles: Jeremy P. Tarcher, 1991. Copyright ©1990 by Ken Wilber.

Foreword to Lex Hixon, *Coming Home: The Experience of Enlightenment in Sacred Traditions*. Los Angeles: Jeremy P. Tarcher, 1989. Copyright ©1989 by Ken Wilber.

Foreword to Philip Rubinov-Jacobson, *Drinking Lightning*. Forthcoming. Copyright ©1999 by Ken Wilber.

Foreword to Seymour Boorstein, *Clinical Studies in Transpersonal Psychotherapy*. Albany: SUNY Press, 1997. Copyright ©1997 by SUNY Press.

"In the Eye of the Artist: Art and the Perennial Philosophy." Foreword to Alex Grey, Ken Wilber, and Carlo McCormick, *Sacred Mirrors: The Visionary Art of Alex Grey*. Rochester, Vt.: Inner Traditions International, 1990. Copyright ©1990 by Ken Wilber.

Transformations of Consciousness: Conventional and Contemplative Perspectives on Development, by Ken Wilber, Jack Engler, and Daniel P. Brown. Boston: Shambhala Publications, 1986. Copyright ©1986 by Ken Wilber.

"Introduction." *The Holographic Paradigm and Other Paradoxes: Exploring the Leading Edge of Science.* Boston: Shambhala Publications, 1982. Copyright ©1982 by Ken Wilber.

"Of Shadows and Symbols": Introduction to *Quantum Questions: Mystical Writings of the World's Great Physicists.* Boston: Shambhala Publications, 1984. Copyright ©1984 by Ken Wilber.

"Paradigm Wars: An Interview with Ken Wilber." *The Quest,* Spring 1989, pp. 6–12. Copyright ©1989 by Ken Wilber.

"Paths beyond Ego in the Coming Decades." In Roger Walsh and Frances Vaughan, *Paths beyond Ego: The Transpersonal Vision.* Los Angeles: Jeremy P. Tarcher, 1993. Copyright ©1992 by Ken Wilber.

"Sociocultural Evolution." Written in 1983. Copyright ©1999 by Ken Wilber.

"Sheldrake's Theory of Morphogenesis," *Journal of Humanistic Psychology* 24, no. 2 (1984), pp. 107–115. Copyright ©1984 by the Association for Humanistic Psychology. Reprinted by permission of Sage Publications, Inc.

"Stages of Meditation: An Interview with Ken Wilber." *The Quest,* Spring 1994, pp. 43–46. Copyright ©1994 by Ken Wilber.

"Integral Psychology." Copyright ©1999 by Ken Wilber.

"Two Humanistic Psychologies?: A Response," *Journal of Humanistic Psychology* 29, no. 2 (1989), pp. 230–43. Copyright ©1989 by Sage Publications, Inc. Reprinted by permission of Sage Publications, Inc.

"A Unified Theory of Development." Originally published as "Two Patterns of Transcendence: A Reply to Washburn." *Journal of Humanistic Psychology* 30, no. 3 (Summer 1990): 113–136. Copyright ©1990 by Sage Publications, Inc. Reprinted by permission of Sage Publications, Inc.

"What Is Transpersonal Psychology?" *The Laughing Man* 5, no. 2 (1984), p. 16. Copyright ©1984 by Ken Wilber.

"A Working Synthesis of Transactional Analysis and Gestalt Therapy," in *Psychotherapy: Theory, Research, and Practice* 15, no. 1 (1978), pp. 68–79. Copyright ©1978 by Ken Wilber.

Books by Ken Wilber

The Spectrum of Consciousness (1977)
No Boundary: Eastern and Western Approaches to Personal Growth (1979)
The Atman Project: A Transpersonal View of Human Development (1980)
Up from Eden: A Transpersonal View of Human Evolution (1981)
The Holographic Paradigm and Other Paradoxes: Exploring the Leading Edge of Science (1982)
A Sociable God: Toward a New Understanding of Religion (1983)
Eye to Eye: The Quest for the New Paradigm (1983)
Quantum Questions: Mystical Writings of the World's Great Physicists (1984)
Transformations of Consciousness: Conventional and Contemplative Perspectives on Development, by Ken Wilber, Jack Engler, and Daniel P. Brown (1986)
Spiritual Choices: The Problems of Recognizing Authentic Paths to Inner Transformation, edited by Dick Anthony, Bruce Ecker, and Ken Wilber (1987)
Grace and Grit: Spirituality and Healing in the Life and Death of Treya Killam Wilber (1991)
Sex, Ecology, Spirituality: The Spirit of Evolution (1995)
A Brief History of Everything (1996)
The Eye of Spirit: An Integral Vision for a World Gone Slightly Mad (1997)
The Marriage of Sense and Soul: Integrating Science and Religion (1998)
One Taste: The Journals of Ken Wilber (1999)
Integral Psychology (2000)

INDEX